The Atlantic Iron Age

'Jon Henderson's detailed scholarship makes a major contribution to our understanding of the Atlantic Seaways in Prehistory. It is essential reading'.

Sir Barry Cunliffe, Professor of European Archaeology,
University of Oxford

'A logical and scholarly sequel to Barry Cunliffe's overview *Facing the Ocean,* this authoritative survey of the Atlantic Late Bronze Age and Iron Age is a benchmark study of a regional interaction and archaeological identities along the Atlantic façade'.

Prof. Dennis Harding, Abercromby Professor of Archaeology,
University of Edinburgh

It may be surprising to learn that this book is the first ever survey of the Atlantic Iron Age: this tradition is cited in archaeology frequently enough to seem firmly established, yet has never been clearly defined. With this book, Jon C. Henderson provides an important and much-needed exploration of the archaeology of western areas of Britain, Ireland, France and Spain to consider how far Atlantic Iron Age communities were in contact with each other.

By examining the evidence for settlement and maritime trade, as well as aspects of the material culture of each area, Henderson identifies distinct Atlantic social identities through time. He also pinpoints areas of similarity: the possibility of cultural 'cross-pollination' caused by maritime links and to what extent these contacts influenced and altered the distinctive character of local communities. A major theme running through the book is the role of the Atlantic seaboard itself and what impact this unique environment had on the ways Atlantic communities perceived themselves and their place in the world.

As a history of these communities unfolds, a general archaeological Atlantic identity breaks down into a range of regional identities which compare interestingly with each other and with traditional models of Celtic identity.

Bringing together the Iron Age settlement evidence for the Atlantic regions in one place for the first time, this excellent and original book is certain to establish itself as the definitive study of the Atlantic Iron Age.

Jon C. Henderson is currently Lecturer in Archaeology at the University of Nottingham. His areas of research lie within the settlement archaeology of the European Iron Age, with a particular focus on the Atlantic regions of Scotland, Ireland, Wales, Cornwall and Brittany. He is also actively involved in underwater archaeology and in 2004 established the Underwater Archaeology Research Centre at Nottingham. He is a Fellow of the Society of Antiquaries of Scotland and a Member of the Institute of Field Archaeologists.

The Atlantic Iron Age

Settlement and identity in the first millennium BC

Jon C. Henderson

Routledge
Taylor & Francis Group

LONDON AND NEW YORK

First published 2007
by Routledge
2 Park Square, Milton Park, Abingdon, Oxon OX14 4RN

Simultaneously published in the USA and Canada
by Routledge
711 Third Avenue, New York, NY 10017

Routledge is an imprint of the Taylor & Francis Group, an informa business

First issued in paperback 2011

Typeset in Bembo by Keyword Group Ltd.

British Library Cataloguing in Publication Data
A catalogue record for this book is available from the British Library

Library of Congress Cataloging in Publication Data
Henderson, Jon C.
The Atlantic Iron Age: settlement and identity in the first millennium
BC/Jon C. Henderson.
p. cm.
Includes bibliographical references and index.
1. Iron age--British Isles. 2. Iron age--France--Armorica. 3. Land
settlement patterns, Prehistoric--British Isles. 4. Land settlement patterns,
Prehistoric--France--Armorica. 5. Trade routes--British Isles. 6. Trade
routes--France--Armorica. 7. Civilization, Celtic. 8. Excavations
(Archaeology)--British Isles. 9. Excavations (Archaeology)--France--
Armorica. 10. British Isles--Antiquities. 11. Armorica (France)--Antiquities.
I. Title.
GN780.22.G7H46 2007
936.1--dc22   2007017434

ISBN 13: 978-0-415-43642-7 (hbk)
ISBN 13: 978-0-415-68382-1 (pbk)
ISBN 13: 978-0-203-93846-1 (ebk)

Here on the old world's western edges,
The finistères, the ambivalent ends,
Where the grey Atlantic, ominous,
From the black rocks whose gull-whitened ledges,
Break the sheer plunge to the curdled foam,
Stretches away to the strange Americas,
(a world outside our known allegiance),
Here an ancient people find a home.

'*The Western Edges*' by Stuart Piggott 1946
The Piggott Archive, Institute of Archaeology, University of Oxford

Contents

Figures

Acknowledgements

While sea levels continue to rise through global warming, it is perhaps ironic that the impact of the sea on the collective imaginations of the West has been falling at a similarly dramatic rate. The sea is often called to our attention as a destructive force in the media, while at the same time its romantic connotations are never far away; but in this age of air travel the sea has, in many ways, lost its significance to our society.

As a truculent teenager growing up on the west coast of Scotland I always felt isolated from 'where it was all happening' and yet also strangely connected to the wider world. Gazing out at the Atlantic, at ships and boats island-hopping up and down the coast, I constantly felt the potential for travel – that I could leave at any time if I wanted to, that I was just a small part of a much, much larger world. At the time this was teenage wistfulness certainly but I think this general mind-set has stayed with me and indeed has helped to shape the kind of archaeological research I do today. As a result I would like to dedicate this book to my Atlantic family – a testament to the memory of my late mother, her brothers and her parents.

I would like to thank a number of friends and colleagues who have helped by reading and commenting on various parts of this book in draft from. In particular I would like to thank Simon Gilmour for his thorough reading of a full final draft and John Barber, Dennis Harding, Andrew Heald, Henrietta Quinnell and Julian Henderson for their helpful comments and advice on individual chapters. I am also indebted to Graeme Cavers for preparing a number of the final illustrations.

Many of the ideas explored in this book were formed during my time as a post-graduate student at the University of Oxford and I owe a huge debt to the wisdom and guidance of Barry Cunliffe and to the lively, and much missed, opinions of the late Andrew Sherratt. I would also like to thank a number of archaeologists who have shared their ideas with me, allowed me to use their illustrations or kindly sent me information: Ian Armit, Barry Raftery, Claire Cotter, Richard Harrison, Simon James, Philip de Jersey, Kristian Kristiansen, Euan MacKie, Stuart Needham, Connor Newman, the late Graham Ritchie, Marisa Ruíz-Gálvez, Aidan O'Sullivan, Etienne Rynne, John Waddell and the late Patrick Wormald.

Finally I would like to thank Annamaria who in agreeing to become my wife has become my new family.

1 Atlantic Europe

The lands of the continuity of tradition

Introduction

This book is an examination of the archaeological evidence for the existence of an Atlantic axis of contact and interaction along the north-western coasts of Europe in the first millennium BC. Throughout this period Atlantic Europe was composed of distinctive cultural zones which nonetheless shared, at various times, close links and common socio-cultural attributes. Aspects of settlement, society, and material culture in Atlantic facing areas are examined to provide insight into the existence, scale, and significance of maritime communication between them. The central concern of the book is how far potential maritime links between Atlantic communities could be said to form zones of similarity (zones in contact) and what effect such contact may have had on the distinctive character of local communities. At what points in the sequence can socio-cultural similarities be explained as the result of contact and, conversely, at what points are these apparent similarities over-exaggerated and more likely to be due to parallelism or development from a common background?

The aim is not to attempt the impossible task of reconstructing western Atlantic trade routes but rather to consider whether the shared experience of living along the Atlantic seaboard united communities at a broad level conceptually if not (at all times) physically. The settlement record will be examined in detail alongside the role of the Atlantic landscape in helping to create and maintain distinct cultural identities. It will be examined how far it is possible to recognise an archaeological Atlantic identity or, more likely, a range of regional identities which are distinct from traditional models of Celtic identity. This will involve a consideration of how far archaeological identities inferred from settlement evidence and material culture can be taken to reflect real group identities in the Iron Age.

In purely geographic terms Atlantic Europe may be seen as the western Atlantic facing coasts of Europe from Scandinavia to Iberia. However, as Bradley (1997: 17) has pointed out, in archaeological literature the term 'Atlantic Europe' usually pertains to the coastal region between the Shetland Islands in the north down to the Straits of Gibraltar in the south taking in northern and western Scotland, Ireland, Wales, south-west England, Armorica, western France, and Iberia (Figure 1.1).

For the past six thousand years or so the Atlantic sea routes have provided a corridor of communication for the communities of western Europe. At certain points in

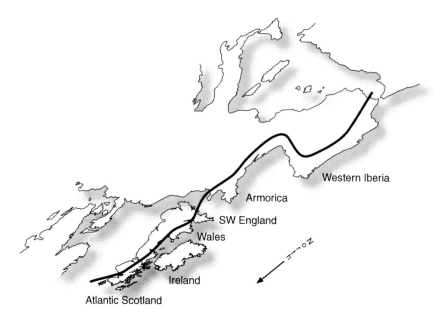

Figure 1.1 Atlantic Europe.

the archaeological record evidence for these contacts can be seen. From at least the fourth millennium BC there was coastal traffic along the Atlantic coasts which interconnected and ultimately linked Iberia to Ireland and north-western Scotland. The wide distribution of megalithic architecture, and specifically passage graves, at this time clearly suggests that 'different communities must have been developing their belief systems in the general knowledge of what was happening elsewhere' (Cunliffe 1997: 147). The Atlantic distribution of common ideas and concepts reflected in shared tomb morphologies and aspects of material culture implies that people and objects, even if in quite limited numbers, were also moving up and down the coasts. From at least 2300 BC symbolic objects such as stone battle axes, halberds, gold lunulae, bronze razors and faience beads were being traded along the Atlantic seaboard and placed in individual burials in pits and cists. By the Late Bronze Age (*c.* 1200 to 600 BC), the widespread distribution of related metalwork forms provides compelling evidence for the intensification and expansion of Atlantic maritime contacts. The occurrence of elites and the networks of exchange they used at this time can be viewed as very much the end result of the alliances and traditions created in earlier periods, compounded by a greater need and desire for metals both within the Atlantic zone itself and throughout west-central Europe. These networks of metalwork exchange came to an end around 600 BC and apart from some evidence of cross-Channel trade between southern Britain and Armorica in the first century BC, there is little evidence for the exchange of material goods between Atlantic communities throughout the Iron Age. After the Iron Age, contacts are clearly visible once again through the historic movement of Britons to Brittany in the fourth and fifth centuries AD and the importation of Mediterranean and western French pottery, along with presumably commodities to Cornwall, Ireland, Wales and Scotland (Wooding 1996).

A detailed consideration of what happened in the Iron Age, occupying the interlude between evidence for intense Late Bronze Age exchange and the beginning of the wine trade in the mid-first millennium AD, constitutes the main focus of this book. In other words, as Cunliffe (1990: 246) has stated the purpose is to 'explore what happens between the demise of one system and the inception of the other'. The study begins during the Late Bronze Age (*c.* 1200 to 600 BC) when evidence for contact and exchange along the Atlantic coastal zones is strong and archaeologically visible through the widespread distribution of common metalwork forms. The main focus, however, is on the pre-Roman Iron Age,[1] from the seventh century BC until the end of the first millennium BC, a period during which the depositional practice of the Late Bronze Age ceases and there is much less material evidence for Atlantic contact. The generally undiagnostic nature of Atlantic material assemblages at this time has led to the impression in general texts that Atlantic Iron Age societies were static and peripheral. Where identified, cultural change in the Iron Age is too often attributed to either factors established during the Bronze Age or to contacts developed during the Roman period. On this reading one would be forgiven for thinking that nothing actually happened to Atlantic societies during the Iron Age. Views which stress stability and conservatism do not explain the social and cultural transformations which did take place such as the appearance and development of dominant, often stone-built, architectural forms across many Atlantic areas. Archaeologists continually pay lip service to the concept of an Atlantic Iron Age tradition but there has been little work to define the exact nature of such a tradition beyond stressing its apparently passive and conservative nature.

The areas examined in depth in this study relate to the northern half of the Atlantic seaboard, namely: Armorica, south-west England, Wales, Ireland, and Atlantic Scotland (Figure 1.2). Only passing mention will be made of developments in south-western France and western Iberia. It would be impossible in a work of this length to do a detailed study of the whole area and through necessity this approach has to be selective. Although articulating with the northern Atlantic areas in a manner that demands further examination, the southern areas would have to be studied in relation to a different range of cultural stimuli to those seen in the north. In other words, they would have to be placed within their own unique cultural contexts – in the case of the development of western Iberian communities, for example, this would necessitate a detailed consideration of complex relationships with the Mediterranean world. The focus of this book is a detailed examination and re-working of settlement sequences to allow broad comparisons to be made. Iron Age research in the northern Atlantic areas is based on settlement archaeology and as a result there is a much richer published settlement record than that of the southern zone, where until recently research has tended to concentrate on the study of artefacts. In addition, there are traditional links between the northern areas and their peoples both historically through place names, church dedications and population movements

Figure 1.2 The north western Atlantic zone.

(Bowen 1977; Bradley 1997: 19), and in terms of the modern cultural perception of the nations of the 'Celtic fringe' (Sims-Williams 1998; James 1999).

The areas around the Irish Sea, often referred to as the Irish Sea Province (Fox 1947; Moore 1970; Thomas 1972), are also not considered in any detail here. The extremely limited number of excavated Iron Age sites from these areas makes it impossible to consider them at the same level of detail as the other areas studied in this book. As a result my approach becomes primarily concerned with areas facing the open Atlantic. The dynamic of Atlantic areas as seaward facing zones – the *Ultima Thule* of prehistoric Europe – may well have had an importance in the creation of shared cultural and social similarities over time. The concentration on contacts, first

but clearly, anything
bluded by Ireland is
NOT facing the Atlantic

between Atlantic Scotland and Ireland and then second between Armorica and south-west England, allows us to examine the case for distinct Atlantic identities in different contexts. The former representing outer areas geographically removed from continental European trends, and the latter Atlantic coastal areas influenced more directly by west-central European developments. A geographical coverage which concentrates on the evidence from the northern part of the Atlantic seaboard is in no way incomplete or partial because contacts along the Atlantic coasts should not be viewed as a single functioning system – there is no 'one-ness' or natural unity to the contacts as assumed in traditional hyper-diffusionist models. On saying this, the whole area will be discussed from time to time so that broad characteristics and changes within Atlantic Europe can be identified.

The argument develops in two distinct but complementary directions. The first, which forms the main core of the book, is an examination of the settlement sequences and associated material culture of each area in an attempt to identify distinct Atlantic social identities through time. The second considers the nature of the Atlantic seaboard itself and what impact this unique environment had on the ways Atlantic communities inhabited, understood and imagined their world.

Atlantic settlement

Due to the sparsity of material evidence a full consideration of the settlement record is seen as central to any examination of the development of Atlantic communities during the Iron Age. Atlantic material assemblages tend to be utilitarian in nature and are usually not distinctive or diagnostic enough to sustain close chronologies or cultural identities. Equally, contacts are not archaeologically visible through the traditional media of traded goods or exotica. The amount of excavation and survey work carried out in Atlantic areas has substantially increased in recent years and the re-consideration, and in some cases re-dating, of Atlantic settlement sequences is long overdue.

Substantial domestic settlements appear in the Atlantic west in great numbers from the Late Bronze Age onwards. In many areas these take the form of stone-built hut circles or roundhouses which develop in the Iron Age into more visible and impos-ing forms. Most are single but monumentally built homesteads, representing a single family or extended family group, which although they stand alone occur in large numbers in an apparently densely packed landscape. They were built to be seen and impress, and as such were clearly an important element in the construction and mediation of Atlantic social groups and identities. Despite this, most work on Atlantic settlement has come from a strong functionalist perspective with studies focusing on defining particular architectural devices or constructing arcane classificatory schemes (cf. Smith 1977; Johnson and Rose 1982; Harding 1984; Armit 1992; Arbousse-Bastide 1993; Maguer 1996; Stout 1997; MacKie 2002). The idea that settlements were more than simply passive domestic wrappers has been slow to take hold in Atlantic studies, with the result that their potential to define local group identities and reflect evidence of wider cultural continuities has not been fully realised.

In this book Atlantic settlements are considered as socially meaningful places in the landscape which reflect culturally specific ways of understanding the world.

Constructing distinctive settlement forms according to local conventions was a collective community practice reflecting the existence of shared ideas and values. As such the study of settlements can provide crucial information for studying group identities and the dynamic relationship between Atlantic communities and the land-scapes they inhabit.

Sea

Throughout the book, broader considerations of the ways in which Atlantic commu-nities may have perceived the world around them are carried out. How far is it pos-sible to identify distinctive world views, *mentalités*, or collective belief systems in Atlantic areas which can be seen to be separate from that of the rest of Europe? Evidence from a wide range of sources is touched upon at various points including the evidence for distinctive Atlantic ritual behaviour, the significance of Atlantic language developments, social aspects of the settlement record, and how communi-ties may have given meaning to the Atlantic landscape itself.

Central to this approach is an awareness of the role of the sea. No community living next to the sea could have failed to be conscious of its awe inspiring power, its poten-tial for contacts and its mystery. It is widely accepted that prehistoric communities often imbued natural places in the landscape with symbolic and ritual significance (Green 1986; Webster 1995). It seems highly likely that the dynamic environment of the Atlantic Ocean had a strong association with metaphysical phenomena in the eyes of the people who lived along the coasts – its unpredictable and unforgiving nature quite literally holding the power of life or death over those who chose to work and travel on it (Needham 1998). This power was undoubtedly acknowledged by Atlantic societies and perhaps needed to be placated and reconciled as part of indigenous belief systems. It will be examined to what extent the sea as a conceptual, as well as a physi-cal, entity played a role in what Cunliffe (2001: 565) has termed an 'oceanic mental-ity', and how far such an outlook, if indeed it exists, could be said to indicate related social identities along the Atlantic coasts in the Iron Age.

The socialisation and development of Atlantic communities within a particular landscape is not envisaged as a deterministic but rather a dynamic process where communities simultaneously create, and in turn are shaped by, the world in which they live (Gosden 1994: 15–22). The effects of this process can work at various levels within a society and can be seen to operate in both long- and short-term timescales. From a long-term perspective it will be argued that the Atlantic axis has a coherent *directedness*,[2] reflected in the similarities of its archaeological monuments and mate-rial culture, which can ultimately be viewed as the result of unconscious, long-term continuities which are beyond the experience of communities or individuals. From a shorter-term perspective shared concepts are maintained through the periodic linking up of communities through maritime contacts. The extent of such contacts along the Atlantic seaboard did not remain constant through space and time: contacts between individual societies increased and decreased as internal and external stimuli took effect. At times external contacts would wane or the trajectory of the develop-ment of an individual community would be so strong that it would over-ride outside influences and cause purely indigenous developments to occur. In addition to the changeable intensity of Atlantic contacts, there was a network of east–west contacts which linked Atlantic communities to the developments of the La Tène heartlands of west-central Europe. Such processes and contacts ensured that each Atlantic society evolved in a distinctive but yet undeniably related way.

Perceptions of Atlantic Europe

Classical and Early Medieval sources

The belief in the existence and cultural influence of maritime contacts along the Atlantic seaboard is much older than the discipline of archaeology itself. Nineteenth- and early twentieth-century historians had long been aware of Classical and Early Medieval references to the use of Atlantic sea routes for trade. The main impetus for prehistoric trade between Mediterranean and Atlantic areas was considered, from the classical sources, to have been the acquisition of metals rare or unobtainable in the Mediterranean and temperate European zones. Deposits of copper, silver, gold, and most importantly, tin are abundant amongst the old hard rocks of the Atlantic zone from western Iberia to Ireland (these mineral resources are discussed further in Chapter 2). Early Medieval Mediterranean written sources, and to a lesser extent Irish and Welsh sources, referring to the movements of Christian saints and the wine trade in the latter half of the first millennium AD linking Britain, Ireland, France, North Africa and the Mediterranean, were also known (Fulford 1989; Wooding 1996).

The classical references to prehistoric contacts were the most influential on antiquarian perceptions of Atlantic contacts. Cornish tin was the most well-known source at the time and there had been a long-held, but wholly erroneous, British myth about Phoenicians coming to Cornwall for tin, who then travelled on to supply all the ancient civilisations of the Mediterranean and the Near East (Penhallurick 1986: 123–31). The myth probably had its roots in *Ora Maritima* or 'The Maritime Shores', a poem written by Avenius in the fourth century AD. It was thought to have included quotations from an early sailing manual, the *Massilliot Periplus*, widely believed to date to the sixth century BC (Hawkes 1977: 19). The poem – and therefore one must assume the original manual – describes the routes used by Tartessan and, later, Carthaginian traders northwards along the western seaboard from southern Iberia to Britain (*Oestrymnis*) where tin and lead are reported to be found.[3]

Atlantic contacts in a fourth-century BC context are mentioned in reference to the journeys of Pytheas, a Greek sailor whose account of a voyage around 325-320 BC from the Mediterranean to Brittany and beyond survived in the Geography of Strabo (Pliny *Natural Histories* IV.30.16; Hawkes 1977, 1984; Cunliffe 2002; Figure 1.3). The reference to *Belerion* – the Land's End peninsula – suggests that Pytheas may have been following a by now established trade route, but unfortunately no further details are given (Cunliffe 1997: 150).

The later writings of Diodorus Sicilus (V.22) and Pliny (*Natural Histories* X. 166; IV.104), both quoting earlier sources,[4] tell of an organised trade in tin ingots with south-western British communities on an island just off the mainland,

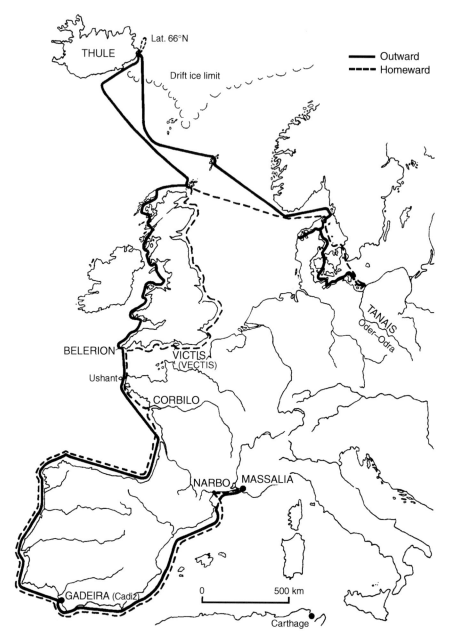

Figure 1.3 The actual routes and ports-of-call used by Pytheas are extremely contentious (cf. Hencken 1932: 158–88; Dion 1968; Maxwell 1972; Hawkes 1977, 1984; Cunliffe 1982a; Mitchell 1983) and the routes proposed here by Hawkes (1984: fig. 1), although certainly plausible, cannot be accepted as historical fact as they are wholly based on rather confused and anecdotal classical sources.

the identity of which has been the subject of much academic debate (Hencken 1932: 176–8; Bowen 1972: 58-60; Maxwell 1972; Cunliffe 1982a; 1983; Hawkes 1984; Penhallurick 1986: 139–47). A good case has been made for the promontory of Mount Batten on the Plymouth Sound as – if not the actual referenced island itself – at the very least a coastal site performing a similar function to that described in the sources (Cunliffe 1982a, 1983, 1988a).

Caesar provides us with eyewitness accounts of the maritime abilities of the Veneti of the Armorican peninsula from his confrontations with them between 55 and 54 BC: 'They have a great many ships and regularly sail to and from Britain. When it comes to knowledge and experience of navigation, they leave all the other tribes standing' (*Bellum Gallicum* III.8). Strabo later added some trading emphasis to the maritime activity of the Veneti: 'The Veneti are those who fought at sea against Caesar, for they were prepared to hinder his voyage to Britain as they were using the emporion there' (*Geog.* IV.4.1). Caesar also noted the general similarities of British coastal districts with those of Gaul, and recorded that Gauls had actually settled in Britain, mentioning the *Belgae* by name (*Bellum Gallicum* II.14-19). Also, interesting in terms of contacts between continental and British groups is the occurrence of identical tribal names in either zone such as the occurrence of *Atrebates* and *Parisi* in both England and northern France.

It must be remembered that the written sources reflect a classical Roman point of view and that, Caesar's comments aside, they were written many centuries after the period they describe, with authors often simply repeating details drawn from earlier sources.[5] It is widely thought that the growth of the Roman world, particularly the foundation of *Provincia Gallia Transalpina* in 124 BC, fundamentally altered the focus and axis of cross-channel and Atlantic contacts, and that this may have had an effect on the views expressed by contemporary classical authors (Cunliffe 1982a, 1984). What the classical sources do demonstrate is that maritime contacts undoubtedly existed along the Atlantic coasts prior to the Roman period, and that there was some level of organised maritime exchange between Atlantic communities and the Mediterranean world – particularly in relation to the procurement of south-west English tin (Cunliffe 1982a: 41, 1990: 247, 1997: 150–1). The importance of the Atlantic trade routes to the Mediterranean world is demonstrated by the mere fact that they are mentioned in the classical sources at all. Equally, as Cunliffe (1984: 247) points out, the fact that such accounts survive 'is a fair indication that trade may have been intensive'.

As well as the classical references, origin legends from far-off lands figure largely in myth and folklore throughout Europe. In Atlantic areas these legends usually refer to sunken islands of origin or population movements by sea (Johnson 1977). For example, there are numerous references in Irish history and folklore to overseas folk movements and contacts, such as the *Goidelic* Celts arriving in Ireland from Scythia via Spain (Waddell 1992: 29). Significantly, in the first century AD the classical historian Tacitus speculated on the connections between western British groups and peoples from Hispania.

Knowledge of the Classical and Early Medieval references very much coloured views of north-western European origins. A belief in Atlantic and Mediterranean contacts figured prominently in the broad, sweeping antiquarian studies of the eighteenth and nineteenth centuries, and it was commonly believed that Greeks, Egyptians and Phoenicians had all sailed the Atlantic at one time or another. From this background the discipline of archaeology began to develop in the late nineteenth and early twentieth centuries. The first interpretative frameworks for prehistory – the diffusionist models – viewed the development of northern European and Atlantic societies in relation to the arrival of cultural advances, beliefs, technologies and peoples directly from the Mediterranean and Near East. The development of the changing roles and perceptions of the Atlantic sea-lanes in archaeology is discussed below, but first we shall briefly examine some popular modern perceptions of the Atlantic areas studied in this book.

Modern perceptions

The Irish, Welsh, Scots, Manx and Bretons are widely considered in the public arena to be 'Celtic' peoples, in that they are related to each other and constitute the direct surviving descendants of the continental Iron Age Celts.[6] The concept of what constitutes 'Celtic' identity has been the subject of much discussion in archaeology (Chapman 1992; Collis 1994, 1996, 1997; Megaw and Megaw 1996, 1998; James 1997; Sims-Williams 1998; Ó Donnabháin 2000; Harding and Gillies 2005), the result of which has been that the majority of scholars now accept that to view any of the prehistoric peoples of Britain and Ireland as 'Celtic' is wholly erroneous (Collis 1997; James 1999). The concept of Irish and British 'Celts' is an entirely modern invention ultimately created by the naming of the indigenous languages of Scotland, Ireland, the Isle of Man, Wales, Cornwall and Brittany as 'Celtic' languages by the Welsh scholar Edward Lhuyd in 1707. This pronouncement coincided with rising feelings of nationalism and separate identity throughout these areas.[7] Prior to this no one in Britain or Ireland had ever considered themselves a Celt or Celtic and equally there are no written Irish, Welsh or Classical sources which refer to the people of these areas as 'Celts' (Cunliffe 1997: 146; James 1999: 16–25). In the current archaeological literature, the Iron Age peoples of Britain and Ireland are most commonly viewed as related indigenous communities which display varying shared cultural elements with each other and with the Iron Age communities of continental Europe (some of which *were* referred to by classical authors as 'Celts').

Despite the problems inherent in the use of the terms 'Celt' and 'Celtic', the close links, both linguistically, culturally, and historically, between the peoples of Scotland, Ireland, Wales, Cornwall and Brittany are very much a reality (Sims-Williams 1998). Modern language studies have confirmed that the indigenous tongues of the British and Irish are closely related to that of the Gauls (Macauley 1992). There was, and is, undoubtedly a considerable continuity of culture and language between the Atlantic areas. They were of course far less affected by the Roman conquest than the rest of western Europe. While other formerly Celtic speaking areas came to speak Latin Romance languages, native languages survived along the Atlantic fringes. Indigenous Iron Age traditions – in terms of culture and settlement – persisted the longest in Ireland and Scotland because they were never subjected to Roman occupation. Equally the effects of Romanisation in Wales, south-west England and Brittany were very much less pronounced compared to areas further east. The continuity of traditions persisted in these Atlantic areas long after the Roman period. From the latter stages of the first millennium AD onwards this was largely due to their peripheral position, both economically and politically, to the dominant centres of European power. Ways of life continued with little change for centuries, and in this sense the Atlantic areas do indeed have a claim to be closer to their direct Iron Age ancestors than other areas of Europe (although this of course does not necessarily make them Celtic). The continuity of language, art and literature in Wales and Ireland alongside the strong musical traditions of Ireland and Scotland formed the basis of the eighteenth-century Celtic revival.

The western Atlantic lands have thus rightly been termed 'The Lands of the Continuity of Tradition' (Bowen 1972: 9). The economy, traditions and way of life of the people of the Atlantic maritime fringes of Ireland and Scotland, for example, have changed little over the centuries. The only modernisation that has taken place has largely been the result of development funds from the European Community in the latter half of the twentieth century. Much of this development work has focused on the building of networks of roads, making, for the first time in these areas, local journeys over land quicker than by sea. As recently as the 1930s the Hebridean Islands were regarded as a 'cultural backwater' (Curwen 1938). The simple farming and fishing existence practised by the majority of the inhabitants of these areas in the first half of this century, many speaking Scots Gaelic or Irish languages directly related to Q-Celtic, ensured the survival of a way of life which had vanished from the rest of western Europe. The modern Atlantic communities of Wales, south-west England and Brittany are geographically less remote from modern centres of commerce and power and are thus more fully integrated into the contemporary social milieu; but even so the rural traditions and economic base of these communities have changed little over the centuries and in this respect they can be viewed as conservative. Perhaps most importantly of all, each of these areas has retained a deeply felt community level of identity that they feel makes them distinct from their mainland neighbours but less different to other Atlantic communities (Tanner 2004).

Development of the concept of Atlantic Europe in archaeology

1900–1970: the western seaways

While the Classical sources helped to create a general awareness of Atlantic maritime activity, the archaeological concept of the Atlantic seaboard as a zone of contact has its roots firmly in the diffusionist traditions of the first half of this century. Diffusionist theorists such as Crawford (1912, 1936); Fleure and Roberts (1915); Fox (1932); Daniel (1941); Childe (1946) and Bowen (1969, 1970, 1972) emphasised the role of long-distance links along the 'western seaways' of Atlantic Europe in the spread of culture.[8] The 'western seaways' concept was a direct attempt by diffusionist scholars to highlight the role of the sea as a highway of contact against the commonly held views of geographers at the time who viewed the sea as a natural barrier.

The most influential of these land orientated geographers was Sir Halford Mackinder who, in 1902, produced *Britain and the British Seas*, in which he argued that the main route of cultural influx into Britain was the lowland South-East, using the evidence of the Anglo Saxons and the Belgae to back up his argument. He devised the earliest classification of the British seas, dividing them into four main sections: the first, which he called the 'Narrow Seas and Ferry Towns', was seen as the main link to the continent; while the other three – the 'Channel Entries', the 'Inland Sea of Britain', and the 'Oceanic Border of Britain' – were seen as more peripheral areas which looked northwards and westwards to the Atlantic Ocean (Mackinder 1902: 17–25, figs. 11 to 14), Figure 1.4. The areas studied in depth in this book approximate to Mackinder's 'Oceanic Border of Britain' and 'Channel Entries' areas. For Mackinder the south-east/north-west division of Britain was paramount: 'The clue to many contrasts in British geography is to be found in the opposition of the south-eastern and north-western – the inner and outer faces of the land' (Mackinder 1902: 14).

Mackinder undoubtedly viewed the sea as a barrier that divided cultures while land routes served to unite cultures. For example, he refers to the North Channel, which separates south-west Scotland from northern Ireland, as completing the 'insulation of Ireland' (1902: 21). This stressing of land communication becomes more understandable when one considers the cultural context of the late nineteenth-century. At this time views of the past were heavily reliant on classical sources and were steeped in classical tradition – archaeology and the study of arte-facts was very much in its infancy. There was much admiration for the Roman Empire as 'the greatest land-based Empire the world had ever seen' (Bowen 1969: 1) and as a result nineteenth-century authors tended to concentrate on the land while rarely taking into account events at sea – just as the classical authors themselves had done before them. Equally, more contemporary trends may have had an effect, such as the beginnings of the break-up of the British Empire, which had of course been built on maritime power, and perhaps, as some have suggested (Wooding 1996: 3), a peculiarly widespread Victorian fear of the sea. In terms of the contemporary context, Mackinder was stressing the importance of land contacts as opposed to maritime ones at a time when communication in Britain was changing from the older sea routes (ships) to overland routes (railways). In a sense the end of the Victorian period was the end of the prime importance of Atlantic and maritime sea routes in general.

The first discussions of Atlantic maritime contacts in a historical context came from the scholars of the Early Medieval period around the turn of the century (cf. Krusch 1885; Plummer and Earle 1892; Bury 1905; Meyer 1909; Lindsay 1911; Vendryes 1920; Kenney 1929). As was briefly mentioned above, there were widely known written references dating from the period to maritime contacts between Britain, Ireland and the continent. Most notable amongst these early historians was the work of Heinrich Zimmer who in a succession of papers from 1902 to 1910 examined the external contacts of Early Christian Ireland (Zimmer 1901, 1902, 1909–10). Of particular resonance were his views on the maritime wine trade between Gaul, western Britain and Ireland, the substance of which later resurfaced in Crawford's (1936) and Bowen's (1969, 1970, 1972) 'western seaways' discussions.

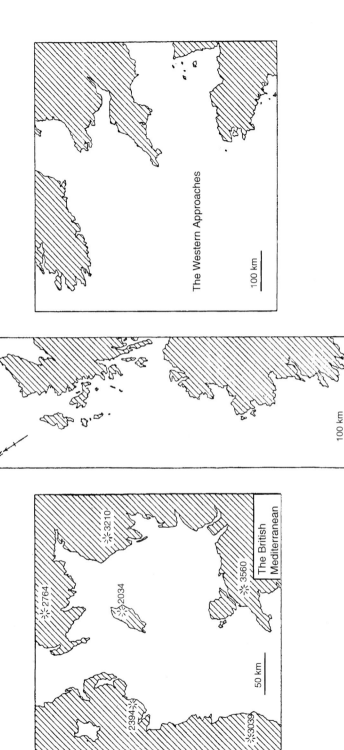

Figure 1.4 Mackinder's divisions of Atlantic Britain (after Bowen 1970: fig. 4; after Mackinder 1902: figs. 12–14).

The 1912 paper, 'The Distribution of Early Bronze Age Settlements in Britain', by O. G. S. Crawford, is generally regarded as one of the first archaeological papers to recognise the existence of western maritime routes in a prehistoric context (Bowen 1970: 14). In this seminal paper, Crawford discussed the distribution of Irish gold *lunulae* in Britain and further south in relation to Atlantic maritime and peninsula isthmus routes. Later papers, such as 'Archaeological Problems of the West Coast of Britain', by H. J. Fluere and J. E. Roberts in 1915, further investigated the importance of the western sea routes particularly in terms of the cultural relationship between Britain and Ireland.

In the 1927 report on his excavations at Chûn Castle in West Penwith, Cornwall, E. T. Leeds carried out one of the first detailed treatments of the development of Atlantic trade in the Bronze and Iron Ages (Leeds 1927: 223–55). His discussion focused on the evidence for trading links, alongside more general similarities in settlement and material culture, between Britain and Iberia in the Iron Age, ultimately comparing Chûn and related Cornish sites with the *castros* of north-west Spain and Portugal. He viewed metal exchange as the main impetus for contacts and his theories were very much influenced by invasionist precepts:

> the fortresses of Cornwall were constructed by a detachment from Iberia, who, as there, established themselves in strongholds from which they could command the copper and tin trade.
>
> (op. cit. 235)

His views were influential at the time and, invaders aside, he was one of the first to recognise the broad similarities shared by Atlantic circular drystone settlements in the Iron Age. The further examination of the significance of these similarities is a major objective of this book. Leeds also correctly identified Iberian influence in three Iron Age fibulae[9] recovered from south-west England (op. cit. 229–30). In 1930, C. D. Forde produced a paper entitled 'The Early Cultures of Atlantic Europe' which significantly treated the Atlantic zone as a cultural entity in its own right, tracing developments and similarities from the beginnings of Mesolithic flint industries to the end of the megalithic period.

However, the most important statement to appear since Crawford's first paper came in 1932 with the publication of *The Personality of Britain* by Sir Cyril Fox. In this hugely influential work, Fox considered the existence of western maritime contacts crucial to the development of archaeological distributions in his self-termed Highland Zone of Britain[10] and devised, for the first time, an actual map of the potential sea routes involved (Figure 1.5). In a display of geographic determinism typical of the period, Fox stated there were three main routes by which 'ideas, new cultures or invaders' could reach Ireland (1932: 42) and divided the Atlantic sea routes into three main sections based largely on Mackinder's 1902 divisions. The first, the southern section, extends from the Atlantic coast of Portugal up to the western ends of the English Channel and the entry into the Irish Sea zone. The second section, termed the Irish Sea zone, included the seas between south-west England, southern Ireland and the Severn estuary into and including St George's Channel and the Irish Sea itself. The third section comprises the seas between

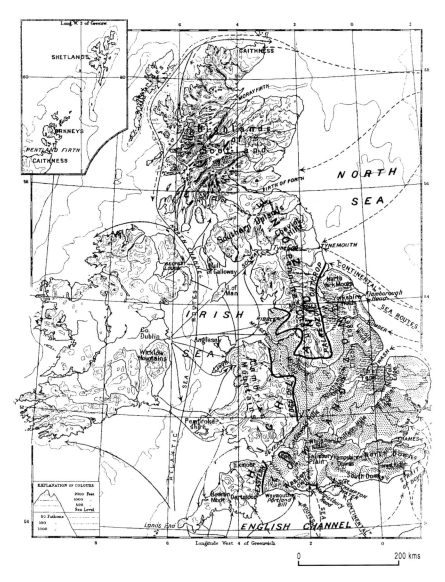

Figure 1.5 One of the first archaeological maps of the western sea routes of Britain (after Fox 1932: Map B).

northern Ireland and Scotland following on from the Irish Sea through the North Channel up to the Western Isles, with branches into the Clyde estuary and around the north-west mainland up to Orkney and Shetland. Although not necessarily 'natural' routes of contacts or culturally significant, Fox's and particularly Mackinder's divisions are useful in that they break the Atlantic up into convenient units for study. Mackinder's 'Oceanic Border of Britain' is basically the area of Scotland and Ireland studied in Chapter 5 while his 'Channel Entries' area is the unit covered in Chapter 6.

Up until this point the majority of studies had concentrated on the British part of the Atlantic sea routes. The first consideration and mapping of the southern section, considering connections across the English Channel to Brittany and beyond, was made by O. G. S. Crawford in 1936 (Figure 1.6). Discussion of Atlantic contacts in Iberia and France were carried out mainly in relation to the metalwork finds of the Bronze Age. The concept of an 'Atlantic Bronze Age' was introduced in Iberia in the late 1930s by J. M. Santa Olalla (1938–1941) and expanded upon by Almagro Basch (1940, 1952), Savory (1949) and MacWhite (1951) to encompass western Iberia, France, southern Britain and Ireland. The typological affinities seen throughout western Europe led authors to consider the Atlantic as a discrete cultural area, as Forde (1930) had done before them, rather than simply a network of sea routes (Savory 1949; Briard 1965; Burgess 1968). A view echoed in Glyn Daniel's 1941 paper, 'The Dual Nature of the Megalithic Colonisation of Prehistoric Europe', which argued the case for the use of Atlantic sea routes in the spread of megalithic architectural and cultural traditions in western Europe.

In 1938, and again in 1939, the enigmatic Sir Mortimer Wheeler led his famous field expeditions to Brittany and Normandy, attempting to shed light on his belief in the existence of extensive trading contacts between Armorica and southern Britain throughout the pre-Caesarian Iron Age (Wheeler and Richardson 1957). Wheeler's work was influential in terms of providing physical proof of the similarities in defensive structures between the two areas, particularly those between the cliff-castles of Brittany and south-west England, which worked to underline the archaeological reality of the up to then purely textual references to trade between the two areas.

After the publication of *The Personality of Britain* (Fox 1932), interest in Britain and Ireland on maritime sea routes focused on identifying connections across the Irish Sea. It was Fox who first described the Irish Sea as a cultural province: 'there is a definite tendency for the shores of the Irish Sea to form a cultural province' (1947: 44). A number of scholars agreed with the concept (Davies 1946; De Valera 1951: 180; MacWhite 1951; Radford 1956, 1966; Thomas 1959; Alcock 1963; Chitty 1965; Bowen 1969; Savory 1978) but the idea only became fully formed during the 'Irish Sea Province in Archaeology and History' conference held in Aberystwyth in 1968 (Moore 1970), and the conference held on the 'Problems of the Iron Age and the Irish Sea Province' in Cardiff in 1969 (Thomas 1972a). Irish Sea connections were seen as particularly important because it was thought that Ireland transformed influences from Britain via these routes 'into something new and characteristically its own and then re-diffused the modified cultures into Britain and beyond' (Bowen 1970: 16). Despite this initial interest in the area and some opposition to the concept of the Irish Sea as a distinct cultural province (Raftery, J. 1972: 8; Powell 1972), one paper by Waddell (1992) aside, there has been little follow-up work or re-examination of the significance of prehistoric Irish Sea contacts.

In his 1970 paper, 'Britain and the British Sea', Bowen extended Crawford's definition of the 'western seaways' to include the entire western coasts of Europe

Figure 1.6 Crawford's 1936 map of the western sea routes (after Crawford 1936: 183).

(Bowen 1970: 14–16); Figure 1.7. His books (Bowen 1969, 1972, 1977) further developed the concept, frequently drawing parallels between the Early Medieval period and prehistory. Although significant in stressing the importance of maritime communications along the Atlantic coasts, Bowen's work tended to greatly exaggerate the scale and frequency of maritime contact, and thus the 'spread of cultures by

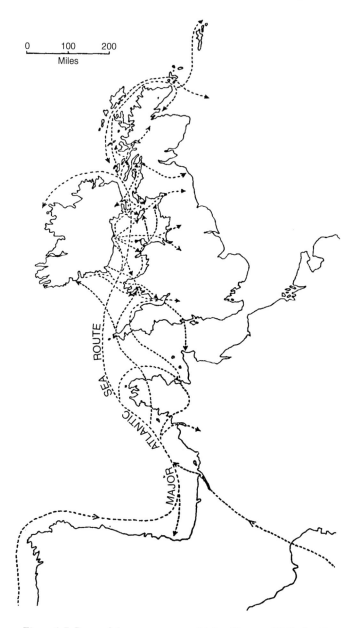

Figure 1.7 Bowen's 'western seaways' (after Bowen 1970: fig. 3).

sea from one territory to another' (1972: 8). His discussions of Iron Age Atlantic contacts were ultimately flawed by a strict adherence to Hawkes' A, B, and C invasion scenarios (Hawkes 1931: 60; 1959: 170) which were seen as the driving forces behind periods of contact along the western sea-lanes due to population displacements (Bowen 1970: 28–50; 1972: 61–70).

From the beginning of the century up until the early 1970s, then, there was an increasing academic awareness of the importance of the western sea routes – or as they were sometimes more militaristically termed: the 'western approaches'. Throughout this period long-distance maritime contacts up and down the Atlantic coasts – and the concept of an Atlantic Europe – featured in a number of general works (Childe 1935: 78; 1946; Hawkes J. 1938; Hawkes 1940; Lewis 1958; Alcock 1963). Many of these general works spoke boldly of major, sweeping sea-routes linking western Europe with the Mediterranean world, along which hundreds, if not thousands, of colonists were considered to have moved, amongst them 'megalithic missionaries' (Hawkes 1940: 211), foreign chiefs with 'magical attributes' (Childe 1935: 78), and practitioners of Mediterranean mother-goddess cults (Hawkes 1938: 172).

Diffusionist studies such as those of Crawford (1912, 1936) and Bowen (1969, 1970, 1972) made no analysis of maritime or socio-economic factors. They simply constructed maps of sea routes, or 'natural' routes of contact, by directly linking up find distributions. By doing so, uncritically, the image of a complex and constant range of maritime contacts was quickly created:

> We may picture these grey seas as bright with Neolithic Argonauts as the western Pacific is today.
>
> (Childe 1946: 36)

Such studies therefore typically tended to aggrandise the scale and role of maritime contacts in the spread of culture. The spirit of the diffusionist period – its reversal of contemporary geographers' views – can be summed up by the following quote from E. G. Bowen, one of the most outspoken supporters of the 'western seaways':

> For the student of early western cultures no longer does the sea divide and the land unite; on the contrary, the seas unite the lands around their shores, while the mountains and the boglands of inland territories divide one culture from another.
>
> (Bowen 1970: 14)

The use of terminology such as 'western seaways' and 'western sealanes' is avoided in this book because it implies a desire to re-construct the actual routes and paths of Atlantic contact. The evidence for actual objects traded along an Atlantic axis is extremely sparse and often poorly dated for the Iron Age period, making it impossible to identify particular routes of travel. Instead, the aim in this study is to consider how far perceived similarities between Atlantic areas – in terms of material culture, settlement sequences and society – can be attributed to those areas being in contact. As Hillgarth (1984: 13–14) states 'more crucial than the question of routes is that of reception'.

1970 – present: the Atlantic façade

It was P. R. Giot who first coined the term 'la façade atlantique' to refer to the western maritime fringes of the British Isles and continental Europe in the prehistoric period (Giot 1963: 3). However, the concept of an 'Atlantic façade' is probably now most usually associated with the Iron Age period largely as a result of the work of Barry Cunliffe and his adoption of the term (Cunliffe 1997: 145–67; James 1999: 19). More than simply being an elegant turn of phrase, the concept of a 'façade' along the Atlantic coasts comprehensively encompasses the contrasting opinions of modern archaeologists as to the existence and importance of Atlantic maritime contacts in a prehistoric context: to some the Atlantic façade is the exterior edge of Europe with clear limits to what can be discerned further inside (inland), while others feel that façade is equally apt as a label because it implies something that is merely window dressing and that ultimately lacks any substantive meaning as a concept.

As Wooding (1996: 1) notes, the diffusionist 'seaways' concept has entered and influenced archaeological thought up until the present. The 'western approaches' or Atlantic routes of Europe are constantly referred to in general works, often with little re-examination of the concept (cf. Cunliffe 1997: 145–67; Kristiansen 1998: 144–60; Waddell 1998: 257–8). It is either accepted by some as a valid argument in at least stressing the importance of maritime contacts, or dismissed by others as a throwback to outmoded diffusionist theory. In this respect the debate has progressed little since Crawford's first mention of western sea routes in 1912.

The rise of processual methodology in the 1960s and 70s by its very nature did little to further the 'western seaways' debate. Processual or 'New' Archaeology was born out of the radiocarbon revolution which clearly demonstrated that a number of discoveries and practices previously thought to have developed in the eastern Mediterranean were in fact dated earlier in parts of western Europe (Renfrew 1973). As a result, processual approaches stressed indigenous developments within regional contexts in a direct reaction against the large-scale, but admittedly over-simple, movements and contacts envisaged in the diffusionist period. Instead of looking for outside influence as the major factor in the development of communities, processual methodology emphasised local factors such as environmental change, population pressure, site catchment constraints, and local technological capacity.

The more recent post-processual or 'interpretative' studies of the last decade have, although many can be said to deal with wide-ranging concepts such as social identities, memory, symbolism and meaning, also tended to emphasise the importance of specific cultural contexts and the role of the individual in society. Some studies have successfully examined long-term social transformations over large areas incorporating regional studies within a broader chronological and geographical framework (Bradley 1990, 1997; Barrett 1994; Cunliffe 2001; Gerritsen 2003). On the whole though, modern archaeological studies tend to shun large-scale overviews, regarding them as superficial, and prefer instead to construct detailed regional sequences. This is not to say that no progress has been made on the nature of Atlantic contacts, merely that the majority of more recent discussions have been carried out within the context of localised, regional or national studies.

One notable exception to this is Barry Cunliffe's *Facing the Ocean: the Atlantic and Its Peoples* (2001) which provides a synthesis of the evidence for Atlantic connections over ten thousand years from the Mesolithic, around 8000 BC, right through to the voyages of discovery in AD 1500. Cunliffe's approach, like the western seaways diffusionists before him, leans towards the environmentally deterministic side as he places geography at the centre of his interpretation, arguing that it is the essential framework which constrains and empowers human action (Cunliffe 2001: 19). From this standpoint he argues that the Atlantic was a natural route of communication for thousands of years. An undeniable point, certainly, but from this observation he reaches the conclusion that the existence of this Atlantic route resulted in the formation of common values and beliefs amongst the peoples who lived along its coasts (op. cit. 364). While this may be true, there is little examination of the connections between geography and the creation of widespread social values in his book, and as a result his interpretation remains speculative and difficult to test, particularly when applied to specific areas and periods. In viewing the developments along the Atlantic from an almost immobile geohistorical perspective Cunliffe's approach owes more to the work of Fernand Braudel (1972) than to recent advances in social archaeological theory, a fact he openly embraces in his many references to the *longue durée*. It is not my intention to underestimate the massive contribution *Facing the Ocean* makes to Atlantic studies, or that Cunliffe's overall conclusion that the cultural similarities throughout the area are the result of the long-term spread of knowledge and beliefs across the seaboard is necessarily incorrect. Rather my purpose here is to point out that Cunliffe's study leaves a serious need to examine the evidence for specific periods in detail and, more importantly, to look beyond the superficial integrity of the region in order to identify local and regional Atlantic identities. My research represents a long-overdue attempt to do this for the Iron Age, a period when there is less evidence for contacts in the traditional archaeologically visible form of traded goods, but in which a number of Atlantic communities take on a distinctive cultural character which forces us to question whether or not they were in maritime contact with each other.

In terms of period-based studies the most progress has probably been in the examination of Atlantic Bronze Age contacts. Although the majority of studies have concentrated upon the occurrence of regionalised metalwork forms (Savory 1968; Almagro-Gorbea 1977; Monteagudo 1977; Coffyn 1983, 1985; Ruíz-Gálvez 1984, 1987: 251–3), or the wider connection of particular forms such as shields (Coles 1962) or cauldrons (Briggs 1987; Gerloff 1987), more work is now being carried out on the broader implications of Atlantic contacts, especially the effects of such contacts on the development of local communities (Coffyn *et al.* 1981; Brun 1991; Ruíz-Gálvez 1991) and the use of 'Atlantic' as a cultural term to describe them (papers in Chevillot and Coffyn 1991 and especially Jorge 1998). Most scholars would now view the Atlantic zone in the Bronze Age not as a uniform cultural area but as being composed of a range of distinct communities which develop according to their own regional traditions within a wider Atlantic milieu. The nature of Atlantic contacts in the Late Bronze Age is the subject of Chapter 3.

As regards identifying specifically Atlantic Iron Age contacts, the work of Barry Cunliffe over the past couple of decades on maritime links between southern Britain and north-western France has perhaps been the most influential (Cunliffe 1978, 1982a, 1984, 1987, 1988a, 1990, 1992, 1997: 145–67, 2000; Cunliffe and Galliou 1995, 2000, 2004, 2005; Burns *et al.* 1996; Cunliffe and de Jersey 1997). There are a few papers which consider the wider Atlantic Iron Age contacts of Atlantic Scotland and Ireland (Raftery 1991a, 1992, 2005; Gilmour 2000a; Henderson 2000; MacKie 2000; Harding 2005a, 2005b), while in the 1990s the Western Stone Forts Project was set up as part of the Irish Discovery Programme with the remit to examine the wider Atlantic affinities of a group of impressive stone forts located along the western seaboard of Ireland (Cotter 1993, 1995, 1996, 2000). There has also been a recent interest in the existence of Atlantic cultural traits in Galicia and western Iberia (Gibson 2000; González-Ruibal 2004). Apart from the above projects, however, work concentrating on Atlantic contacts in an Iron Age context remains thin on the ground and there has as yet been no detailed study of the zone as a whole.

Conceptualising the Atlantic Iron Age

This book attempts to bridge the gap between the macro-diffusionist scale and more geographically limited processual studies by taking a combined approach to the data, such as that proposed by Sherratt (1993a: 1), where detailed regional sequences are examined within a broader conceptual and geographical context. The view that large-scale contact (interventionist) and regional (autonomist) approaches are diametrically opposed has worked to the detriment of studies concerned with large-scale processes over a broad geographical area (Sherratt 1995). Although it widely recognised that large-scale and long-lasting processes were more extensive in scope than can be covered by period specific regional projects, the current theoretical concerns with agency, gender and the body have tended to explore small-scale social changes from the perspective of the individual or local group.

Interpretative frameworks have been put forward in recent years which attempt to incorporate regional data-sets within broader research perspectives – most significantly in 'core-periphery' and 'world systems' approaches. However, due mainly to its geographical location, the Atlantic has consistently been given a peripheral role in these models of later prehistoric Europe (cf. Sherratt 1993a; Frankenstein 1994; Kristiansen 1994; Cunliffe 1995b; Ruíz-Gálvez 1995; Mederos Martín 1996: 111–12). In its purest form 'world systems' analysis is an economic examination of the exchange of bulk food products for manufactured goods taking place between independent political entities at different levels of social organisation and development in what has been termed a classic 'core-periphery' relationship (Wallerstein 1974). However, while the role of exchange has remained central to the 'world systems' model, the concept has been expanded and adapted by archaeologists to include all forms of exchange allowing an analysis of social, cultural and political developmental impact between separate systems or areas of interaction as well as purely economic aspects.

There are problems with the application of 'core-periphery' models to the Atlantic. Generally, cores are defined as regions that supplied finished goods or luxury products to peripheral regions which in turn equipped the cores with raw materials – such a transaction is usually taken to imply the existence of a 'technology gap' (Frankenstein and Rowlands 1978; Sherratt 1993a: 3–4, 1993b, 1994a). It is doubtful whether such a scenario can be applied to the Atlantic zone in a later prehistoric context. For example, in the Late Bronze Age it was metalworking and other technologies that were communicated to the Atlantic not actual objects themselves. In addition, there is now mounting evidence that many objects of Atlantic origin found their way into continental Europe and the Mediterranean (Briard 1979: 202; Lo Schavio 1991: 214–19; Gibson 2000).

Although he does not consider the Atlantic zone in any detail, Kristiansen (1994) recognises the need for a more balanced view of the relationships between the broad cultural systems of later prehistoric Europe (Figure 1.8). He argues (op. cit. 7) that one can trace the formation of common traditions of metal production/technology and socio-religious belief systems accompanying the exchange of bronze from at least the Late Bronze Age. These common exchange and ideological practices served to unite the large-scale systems of Europe into a background of common interdependence (i.e. Nordic, Atlantic, West-Central European, Mediterranean). These areas retained their identities through the re-contextualisation of new information, gained from trading contacts, into their existing cultural traditions. The recognition of

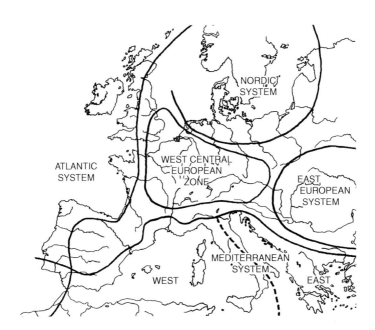

Figure 1.8 The main cultural systems of Europe in the first millennium BC.

the ways the Atlantic area re-contextualised influences from western-central Europe to fit its own cultural dialect, and how far these influences could be said to affect the course of Atlantic (maritime axis) development, is another key element of this book.

Moving down a scale to the separate areas themselves, a similar kind of 'systems' analysis can be applied at a regional scale. Within the Atlantic system various communities were united to some extent by common technological know-how and similar systems of social and ritual development, which served to create the existence of Atlantic shared experiences or traditions. The diversity within the Atlantic system occurs for the same reasons that Europe, at a much broader level of abstraction, can be broken up into Atlantic, Nordic and Mediterranean systems, in that each local area, within a given system, while sharing common traditions, re-contextualised these shared traits to fit their own local dialects. It is perhaps more constructive, then, to view the relationships between Atlantic areas and the continent or the Mediterranean as 'symbiotic' in an effort to avoid the developmental implications of terminology such as 'periphery' and 'core'. Finished goods, technologies and ideas were moving in both directions throughout the prehistoric period.

Bradley (1997: 17–18) has discussed the fact that 'Atlantic Europe' is used by some writers to refer to the geographical areas united by contacts themselves, and by others as an analytical concept which 'sees the Atlantic as a barrier to developments which began much further to the east'. These views are not diametrically opposed and have much in common. As we shall examine in the following chapters, there are elements which occur within a distinctly Atlantic axis and at times Atlantic cultural influences would appear to act as a barrier – conceptual rather than physical – to influences and trends that emanate from continental Europe. However, we shall also see that the Atlantic areas are in no way isolated but instead respond to, and in some cases depend upon, a number of east–west contacts and influences.[11] The views described by Bradley have in common the widely accepted archaeological notion of Atlantic Europe as a periphery which has little role to play in the mainstream of European prehistory and development. Such a notion is untenable, and is a result more of the development of archaeological sequences and archaeology itself in continental areas, than a true reflection of the potential importance of Atlantic areas.

On saying this, the concept of 'periphery' may have a more constructive connotation. The Atlantic seaboard was peripheral in the sense that it can be considered as the *Ultima Thule* of prehistoric Europe – unique in that it represented, at the time, the edge of the known world. Nowhere else during the first millennium BC was it possible to stand on the edge of the European peninsula and gaze over a vast and seemingly infinite ocean, unsure what, if anything, lay beyond the horizon. The sea would have played a major role in the daily lives of Atlantic coastal communities and must have had a considerable effect on the way these communities perceived and understood the world around them. The Atlantic was not peripheral then in terms of the opportunities it offered for transport and communication, but it did form a very real physical and conceptual boundary for communities between the known world and the unknown, between the everyday and the exotic.

Contact in the Atlantic Iron Age

In the majority of publications to date the occurrence of long-distance contacts is seen as being the result of the linking up of a number of shorter journeys:

> Certainly short coastal journeys between communities must have been common and could have formed an interconnecting chain of contacts extending considerable distances along the Atlantic coasts of Europe.
>
> (Waddell 1992: 29)

Cunliffe (1994: 354) envisages the movement of ideas and commodities along the Atlantic seaboard as taking place within a 'series of interlocking systems of trade and exchange based on easy access to the sea'. The explanation of long-distance contacts as being the result of a system of small-scale interlocking regional exchange networks could be viewed as a rather blatant attempt to use processual concepts (e.g. Ellison 1980) to allow the discussion of the effects of long-distance contact. This is perhaps done to deflect the possibility of being branded a diffusionist – to view foreign contacts as having significant and visible effects on the indigenous development of communities has been unfashionable since the inception of processual archaeology. In any case this may be a moot point as it is often impossible to distinguish between concepts and ideas communicated through interlocking regional systems and those delivered directly: the important thing then is perhaps to assess the effects of contacts rather than obsess on the details of their execution.

It is not the purpose of this study to point out that ideas and commodities moved along the Atlantic seaboard in the first millennium BC, because it is clear that they did and it would be asinine to claim anything to the contrary. Rather the aim is to provide insight into the scale and organisation of this contact and how far it was due to and, conversely, affected the social organisation of Atlantic communities. One of the key questions to be asked is which meanings did settlements and material culture have in the later prehistory of Atlantic regions, and how did these meanings change over time? To answer this question we have to analyse available regional data-sets, both at the synchronic scale to determine the conscious actions of individuals and communities at given points in time and at the diachronic scale to identify longer-term trends that occur both within and beyond the conscious awareness of human groups. It is widely accepted that people effect change through agency – that the actions and decisions of individuals and communities are culturally mediated and are capable of not just replicating social norms but also of reinterpreting them (Barrett 1997, 2001). What is less clear is how far individual and community level agency can cause subtle yet fundamental social and cultural transformations over time. Such insight can only be gained in a study with a long chronological depth carried out over a large geographical area.

The examination of Atlantic settlement trends and material culture are considered here within such a broad perspective approach. The aim is to provide a context for the explanation of *similarity*, which may or may not be related to maritime contact, and *divergence*, which may be related to local or regional trends, independence and/or periods of isolation. In other words, a key issue is the identification, as far as is possible, of the role of *external* versus *internal* factors in promoting changes and similarities – it is fully appreciated that this depends on the level of abstraction employed and that ultimately 'internal dynamics both affect and are affected by external factors' (Kristiansen 1998: 6), thus making the separation and recognition of such factors fraught with difficulties. It is recognised, for example, that by taking the geographically wide, diachronic approach proposed here more emphasis will be placed upon collective community level ideas and values than those of the individual. Attempts will be made to overcome this by focusing in on the detail of particular sites from time to time, but it would obviously be impossible to attempt to do this for every site and structure within this vast study area. In any case, the creation of community level identities are the direct result of the decisions and actions of individuals in possession of agency which creates a structure we can recognise at a broad level even if it is not always possible to identify particular individual actions. Ultimately, then the focus in the book will remain on identifying regional and cultural diversity along the Atlantic seaboard, and then consider whether or not we can talk of an Atlantic axis of social interaction and cultural contact in the Iron Age.

2 Atlantic land and sea

Introduction

Over the past two decades, there has been a movement away from considering past landscapes simply as economic resources that were exploited by human groups and which worked to shape and constrain their development. Such limited functionalist approaches have been replaced by an increasing concern with attempting to identify wider social, ideological and symbolic aspects of landscape and how particular landscapes may have been viewed by past communities. Although there has been no consensus on what landscape is, or at least what the archaeological definition of landscape should be, most approaches view landscape as something that is culturally constructed by the people who lived and worked in it. The acknowledgement of an ideational aspect to landscape forms an important underlying principle in this book which is concerned with the impact of the Atlantic landscape in the formation and expression of community identities.

The existence of broad similarities between Atlantic cultures have been viewed as being due more to the determining effects of the geography of the zone than shared cultural contact or traditions between communities (cf. Warner 1981: 47). Certainly, the occurrence of stone-built settlements may have more to do with the availability of stone throughout the western seaboard and the paucity of other building materials than cultural contact. However, it must be remembered that 'geographical determinism' as a philosophical concept can 'cause' nothing in itself; similarities in the constructional style, layout and use of sites along the Atlantic seaboard cannot all be explained by environmental factors. Settlements and social systems are inevitably shaped in some degree by their environment, but this does not make resulting similarities any less meaningful – if anything it further serves to unite areas during periods of contact and allows them to distinguish themselves as a unit, or at least a series of related entities, from inland communities with contrasting environmental and economic backgrounds. Building settlements in stone across the Atlantic zone meant they were often inhabited for several generations and, unlike wooden structures, formed permanent markers in the landscape. This permanence must have had an impact on the social meaning and value of sites to Atlantic communities over time and it is likely that individual sites were associated with particular family groups and ancestors as they were occupied over the centuries (Gerritsen 2003: 36). As the site was modified by successive generations they were not only updating their living space but also updating their social identities and their place in the wider community. Viewing settlement form as an aspect of identity construction it is easy see how the similarities in architectural forms and devices are likely to reflect more than just the use of stone as a building material and its existence as a resource. As John Barrett (1994: 64) points out, 'human responses to given material conditions must ... be regarded as culturally mediated'.

The appearance and use of settlements is just one aspect of identity construction, as it was also present in the full range of interactions that human groups had with the landscape. 'People-land' relationships which appear to be ecologically driven were negotiated by communities within a culturally mediated ideological and symbolic understanding of the landscape making it quite wrong to view such activities in purely functionalist terms. While it is accepted that the Atlantic landscape was 'constructed' by past communities that construction was imposed upon a very real landform. The physical and ecological components of the Atlantic zone set parameters which although they may or may not have featured in the cosmological landscapes of past societies nonetheless impacted upon their social and cultural practices. The physical environment has a dynamic of its own that has to be taken into account, albeit without viewing it as the sole determining factor shaping and driving the development of human groups. This chapter is concerned with the physical dynamic of the Atlantic landscape. First, the geographical characteristics and environmental conditions of the Atlantic regions studied in this book are discussed. Then a consideration of the food producing strategies employed is carried out in an effort to determine the economic base of the Atlantic zone. Attention then turns to the sea and, after a brief discussion of the Atlantic maritime environment, finishes with a comment on the potential level of maritime technology in the area.

The Atlantic landscape

The coastline of the Atlantic seaboard is extremely long owing to its heavily indented nature and extends lineally some 2,500 kilometres from the Straits of Gibraltar to the Shetlands (Wooding 1996: 6). Bradley (1997: 19–20), following McGrail (1993), has argued that it is perhaps most useful for the archaeologist to view Atlantic Europe as a series of projecting promontories of land linked by areas of sea: Cabo de São Vicente in southern Portugal; Cape Finisterre in north-west Spain; Finistère itself and the Point du Raz on the western tip of Brittany; Land's End in south-west England; and Carnsorre Point in south-east Ireland (Figure 2.1). In other words the Atlantic zone can be conceptualised as interdigitating land-masses and sea inlets.

The land

The European land masses which edge the Atlantic Ocean are usually considered as 'uplands' by archaeologists. Much of the Atlantic area is indeed mountainous although there is often a corridor of relatively flat coastal land backing on to mountains further inland such as in Argyll, southern Wales, parts of south-west England and Galicia.

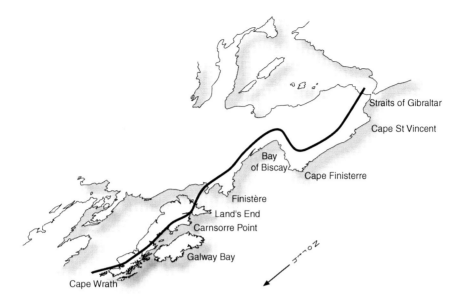

Figure 2.1 Atlantic Europe as a series of projecting promontories of land linked by areas of sea: Cape St Vincent in southern Portugal; Cape Finisterre in north-west Spain; Finistère itself on the western tip of Brittany; Land's End in south-west England; Carnsorre Point in south-east Ireland; Galway Bay in western Ireland and Cape Wrath in north-west Scotland (after Bradley 1997, fig. 2.1).

Atlantic areas of Scotland, situated on the northern and western edges of the Highlands, northern Wales, and northern Ireland share high hills and mountains, many of which approach the sea creating distinctive undulating and cliff-lined coastlines dotted with numerous bays and promontories. The other mainland areas under study – southern Ireland, south-west Wales, south-west England and Brittany – feature less abrupt altitude changes than the north but are still very much upland zones. As a result these areas are subjected to very high rainfall and have mostly acidic soils of low agricultural value.

The uplands of the western Atlantic zone are composed of the two great mountain systems of Europe north of the Alps, the Caledonian and Armorican systems, which converge westwards to meet and mingle in southern Ireland and Wales (Embleton 1984; Joly and Embleton 1984). The older Caledonian system, composed of mainly granites and other crystalline rocks, extends in a north-east to south-west direction from Scandinavia through to Scotland, Wales and Ireland creating characteristically rugged and mountainous landscapes. The younger Armorican mountain ranges, which consist of predominantly hard sandstones, extend in an east to west direction from central Europe through to Brittany and south-west England where they form distinctive but less dramatic plateaus, uplands and rolling valleys. The Armorican mountain ranges are part of a range of

Hercynian massifs which form a series of detached uplands and plateaus of varied relief and complex geology extending in the Atlantic from the Cork peninsula in southern Ireland through to the peninsula at Cabo de São Vicente in south-west Iberia. As a result of the trends of the Caledonian and Hercynian systems, valleys and coastal features in the north tend to be aligned along a north-east/south-west axis while those in the south follow a general east to west trend (i.e. compare the Armorican and south-west English peninsulas with the Highlands of Scotland).

The northern Atlantic zone has a larger proportion of peninsulas than any other sea (Cotter 1974: 4). The coastline has been shaped by the enormous erosive forces of the sea etching out the younger, softer rocks over the millennia while leaving the older, more resilient rocks projecting out into the sea as jagged headlands. While erosion is a major factor in the current appearance of the Atlantic seaboard, the impact of rising sea levels (eustatic change) coupled with the localised warping and sinking of the coastline (isostatic change) over the last ten thousand years is responsible for the drowning of the lower reaches of river valleys throughout the zone, forming distinctive *ria* type coastlines with long winding indentations. Such coastlines can be most clearly seen along Atlantic Scotland, western Ireland, south-western England, Armorica and Galicia where they offer opportunities for the influence of seaborne contacts to penetrate far inland via numerous bays, estuaries and inlets, but also danger in the form of hazardous rocky shoals and strong, unpredictable maritime currents.

As well has providing an ideal building resource, the old hard rocks of the Atlantic zone are extremely rich in minerals (Figure 2.2). Extensive tin, copper and silver deposits occur in western Iberia and gold is known from the Cantabrian Mountains (Tylecote 1987; Shepherd 1993). Although relatively little mineralised for its size, the Armorican massif of north-west France contains significant lodes of tin, lead and iron, small and scattered amounts of silver and gold, along with very small quantities of copper (Galliou 1982: fig. 3; Halbout *et al.* 1987: fig. 2). Up to fifty possible sites of prehistoric tin extraction have been identified but it is not certain whether any of these were used in the first millennium BC (Briard 1965: 15; de Jersey 1994: 4). Cornish tin is especially well known for its quality and extensive deposits are present amongst the rocks of the granite uplands which are eroded over time and deposited as tin bearing gravels in the valley bottoms (Fox 1973: 21–4, fig. 2). Smaller quantities of copper, silver and gold can also be found on the moors of Devon and Cornwall. Iron ores are present in south-west England but there is little evidence they were utilised in the later prehistoric period (op. cit. 22). Significant quantities of copper and gold can be found in Wales and Ireland – the latter area in particular becoming one of the biggest gold producing centres in Europe from the second millennium BC onwards (Eogan 1994). The rich iron ore deposits of Skye notwithstanding, there are few mineral resources of any value in Atlantic Scotland. The rarity of these mineral resources elsewhere in western Europe ensured the importance of contacts with Atlantic areas throughout the prehistoric period and undoubtedly stimulated the early development of maritime contacts between coastal communities.

The opportunities offered by the heavily indented Atlantic coastline contrast strongly with the difficult prospect of overland travel over the uneven and predominantly upland

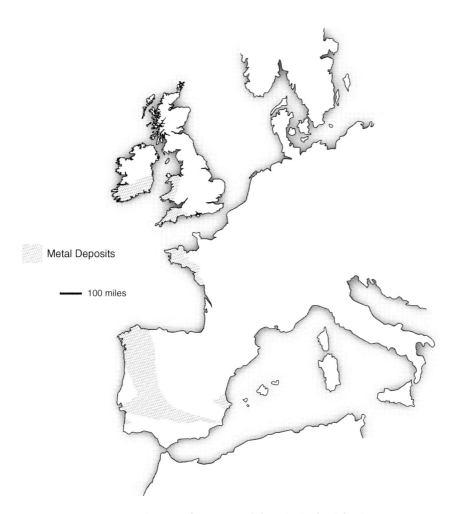

Figure 2.2 Distribution of major metal deposits in the Atlantic zone.

topography of the interior zone (Ruíz-Gálvez 1989: 103). For the most part, later prehistoric settlement was located along the coasts due to the fact that the lower lying coastal zones offered a milder climate along with the best, and in some cases the only, workable agricultural land. In northern and western Scotland, for example, the pattern is one of settlement along the coasts as often only a narrow coastal platform exists before the land begins rise steeply into the Highlands (Geikie 1901). In the Outer Hebrides the contrast between coast and interior is even more distinct. Later prehistoric settlement is focused along the congenial western machair coastlands, known locally today as 'whitelands', which back on to the unproductive and largely uninhabited peat encroached uplands of the interior, locally termed 'blacklands'.

Ireland is remote from the European mainland but the high ratio of coast to interior, the existence of penetrative river systems and the evidence for the construction of extensive trackways during the Iron Age (Raftery 1990) ensured the interior was open to Atlantic orientated contacts. In Wales the Cambrian range effectively splits the country in two, creating an outward looking coastal zone backing onto mountains on one side and a separate zone of valleys – the Welsh Marches – on the eastern interior side. The south-west English peninsula stretching some 257 kilometres into the Atlantic is surrounded on all sides save the east by the sea (Pearce 1981: 17). With a coastline of over 800 kilometres and a land width of only around 50 kilometres, the peninsula could be said to be, for the most part, geographically remote from the rest of southern Britain. Certainly it is dominated by the sea: 'at no point in Devon is the sea more than 40 km away; for Cornwall the figure is scarcely more than 25' (Todd 1987: 1). The term Armorica is derived from the Celtic words *Ar–mor*, 'the country of the sea', and refers to the long indented coastline and hinterland of a roughly triangular peninsula projecting westwards into the Atlantic Ocean. In common with the south-west English peninsula it is dominated by the sea, which borders around two-thirds of its perimeter (Giot 1960a: 15). Sea ward projecting promontories are common, the most dramatic being the granitic ridges of Cornouaille which end in the Pointe du Raz.[1]

While the sea made contact between Atlantic communities along a north–south axis inevitable, the existence of major west-flowing river systems throughout the zone ensured that these communities were not completely isolated from the wider European world. Large navigable rivers such as the Seine, the Loire and the Garonne provided direct access to continental European communities and through these links ultimately opened the Atlantic to Mediterranean influences (albeit indirectly). The Seine and the Loire penetrated deep into continental Europe and by overland portage both could link to the Rhône and thence to the Mediterranean. The Garonne offered a shorter and more direct westerly route by linking, via the Carcassonne Gap, with the Aude. Cunliffe and other scholars have clearly demonstrated that these riverine routes, linking the Mediterreanean with the Atlantic west, were in use by the first century BC through the distribution of Roman wine amphorae (Cunliffe 1982a, 1984, 2000; McGrail 1983). These amphorae are archaeologically visible markers of local systems of exchange that most likely have a greater antiquity. As will be seen at various points in this book, pulses of influence from continental Europe can be recognised amongst Atlantic Iron Age societies but often these influences were re-contextualised to fit a more specifically Atlantic cultural milieu.

As explained in Chapter 1 the areas south of the Armorican peninsula are not considered in any detail in this book. There is little evidence that the coastal communities of western France, south of the Loire, and northern Spain from the Pyrenees to Cape Finisterre were actively involved in Atlantic contacts during the Iron Age. These coasts offer few natural anchorages and are largely uncongenial to mariners. Indeed the rough seas of the south of the Bay of Biscay and the strong north-westerly winds provide major problems to modern day sailors. The Bay of Biscay is a lee shore and straying to the east of a direct route between Brittany and north-west Iberia could easily have led to embayment. It is likely that Iron Age sailors gave this area a wide berth, keeping well out to sea to avoid the lee shore.

The Gironde estuary and the River Garonne certainly had an importance as a major point of access between the Atlantic and the Mediterranean, as noted above, but there is little evidence for Atlantic coastal communities in this zone in the first millennium BC. Articulation with Atlantic trade took place further inland, most likely at what is now modern Bordeaux (Roman *Burdigala*). From the Loire to the Pyrenees the sea has eroded the soft shoreline and through longshore currents has built long sinuous bars of sand and shingle. Behind these barriers, with the land still sinking due to isostatic warping, extensive marshlands have developed fed by silts brought down by rivers. As well as being unsuitable for substantial permanent coastal occupation, these sand dunes and marshlands would have served to isolate communities further inland to the east from Atlantic influences and communications by sea.

One area that does deserve further consideration in this study is Galicia in north-western Iberia. Similar to the other areas examined in detail here, the coastal lands of Galicia form a narrow strip backing on to mountains and for the most part look only to the sea. The coastline is characterised by wide *ria* inlets which offer an abundance of safe sheltered anchorages but it suffers from isolation and remoteness as much of it is rocky, steep and inaccessible from the landward side. Due to the effects of warping and folding the main valleys and rivers in Galicia run in a south-westerly direction and some penetrate as far as 30 kilometres inland. However, Galicia has remained geographically remote from the rest of Spain as the numerous mountain chains of the north-west (such as the Trasos Montes, Sierra Cabrera, Montañas de León and Cordillera Cantabrica) effectively cut the region off from the more fertile central tableland of the interior – the Meseta. As a result Galicia has maintained a strong regional identity throughout history and its prehistoric communities have often been thought to possess a distinct Atlantic identity (Cunliffe 1997: 165–6). Certainly the area, along with the rest of western Iberia, was involved in the widespread metalwork exchanges of the Atlantic Bronze Age discussed further in Chapter 3. It is less clear what happens during the Iron Age, and after we have examined the communities of the northern zone in detail we shall return to Galicia and consider how far the region was influenced by northern Atlantic contacts.

The Iberian coastline south of Galicia is smooth and consists of long, low sandy dunes sometimes over 4 miles wide culminating in the projecting hard rock promontories flanking either side of the Tagus. Certainly these areas demand further examination as regards the influence of Atlantic contacts in the Iron Age, but as stated in Chapter 1 this would require a detailed consideration of the effects of strong Mediterranean cultural influences. Such a study is beyond the scope of this book which is essentially about the archaeology and identity of Atlantic communities in insular coastal areas and projecting peninsulas. It is easy to see how such geography could foster strong regional identities in the first millennium BC with coastal areas linked to each other by the sea and separated from communications and influences inland by inhospitable topography or mountain ranges (Bowen 1957). Societies living along the coast would have likely been more aware of each other than populations further inland and this may have helped create a broad level of shared Atlantic coastal identity and belonging between regional community-level traditions. The existence of an Atlantic identity, or more likely identities, amongst coastal communities is discussed in more detail later in the book; but first we shall turn our attention to the environmental and climatic conditions of the Atlantic zone.

Atlantic climate and environment in the first millennium BC

Although much environmental work has been carried out across the Atlantic seaboard (Lamb 1977; Robinson 1990; Housley and Coles 2004), the climatic conditions of the first millennium BC remain only very generally understood. This is mainly because very few studies have been designed to specifically investigate Iron Age questions. Where such studies have taken place – on Dartmoor, south-west England (Simmons 1970; Silvester 1979), the Lairg Project in Sutherland (McCullagh and Tipping 1998), or the palynological study in Co. Louth, Ireland (Weir 1995) – the results have allowed the correlation of environmental and archaeological data to produce, in many areas for the first time, detailed models of human interaction with the landscape. In general, however, the vast majority of environmental analyses are focused on earlier periods of time with little regard being given to the later prehistoric period.

Along the Atlantic coasts of Europe, the climatic conditions can be summed up in two words: warm and wet. The Atlantic European environment is defined by its relationship with the ocean, the warm North Atlantic Drift, the cyclonic and often very strong winds, and the large percentage of days with rainfall. The North Atlantic Drift or 'Gulf Stream' is a warm current originating in the Caribbean which hits the Atlantic coasts at the Armorica peninsula and splits into a northern course running up to the Shetlands and a southern flow running down the coasts of western Iberia to North Africa (Cotter 1974: 50). Its main effect is to exert a moderating influence on the temperature along western coastal areas which in particular ameliorates the effects of winter at the coasts compared to areas further inland – a phenomenon sometimes referred to as the Oceanic or Maritime Climate (Minshull 1984: 18). The prevailing westerly air currents ensure that the Atlantic coasts have a much higher rate of rainfall than inland areas to the east. For example, at present some areas in the western part of Britain have rainfall of over 250 cm (100 in.) per year, while the eastern extremity of East Anglia has under 150 cm (60 in.) (Cunliffe 1995a: 14). The sea winds are often quite severe, stunting vegetation growth and exacerbating soil erosion in exposed areas. However, the climate is generally warmer than areas inland, there are very few days with significant snowfall, and heavy frosts are rare. Of course on exposed, high ground and mountainous areas the beneficial effects of the marginally higher Atlantic temperatures are negated – high ground in Atlantic areas is very marginal land where viability can be affected by very small fluctuations in environmental conditions. Therefore such fluctuations could have a disproportionately large effect on Atlantic societies and could cause major dislocations in settlement patterns. However, the evidence suggests that this was not the case. At a number of Atlantic settlements in potentially marginal environments, the evidence indicates domestic stability with continuous occupation apparently lasting over very long periods of time with no visible breaks.

The extreme and variable environmental conditions of the Atlantic coastal areas helped to create highly specialised communities in terms of economy (predominantly pastoral) and undoubtedly played a role in the occurrence of distinctly regional patterns of settlement. In a modern context these same conditions can have a detrimental effect on the ease of collection and the reliability of the environmental data recovered. For example, much of the pollen evidence from Atlantic areas appears at first glance to be conflicting. It must be kept in mind, however, that pollen cores only reflect local conditions, meaning that patterns of pollen dispersal and taphonomy must be carefully considered at each core or soil profile site. For example, analysis of the surface pine pollen in current conditions on Barra in Atlantic Scotland has shown that the pollen rain is very localised, with a reduction from 98 per cent within a plantation to 2 per cent or less only 20 m downwind (Gearey 1992). With problems such as this and an assumed tendency to favour only specific locations within such a windswept landscape, the recovery of generalised vegetation data for Atlantic Iron Age remains extremely difficult (Gilmour 2000b: 7). There are further problems, as Hirons (1983) has shown, depending upon what basis pollen diagrams are prepared. For example, traditional pollen percentage diagrams from Killymaddy Lough, Co. Tyrone, Ireland, show a major reduction in tree cover in the Iron Age, whereas a pollen influx diagram from the same site indicates that the more drastic change took place in the Early Bronze Age (Bell 1996: 12). Such factors must always be fully considered when discussing the evidence for the Atlantic Europe.

The palynological work undertaken to date has been primarily focused on the question of tree cover. Although an important question, it has meant that factors such as changes in landscape management and agricultural strategies have rarely been examined in detail, and even more rarely examined in relation to the Iron Age. On the whole, Atlantic areas are considered to have been cleared later than the lowland fertile areas of Britain – much of the clearance is assumed to have taken place in the mid to late Iron Age (Turner 1981: 277; Bell 1995: 151). In the Outer Hebrides and in northern and western Scotland, however, the development of heathland, moorland and blanket bog occurred well before the first millennium BC. By the Iron Age it is widely believed that virtually no woodland remained. This appears to be supported by the contemporary Iron Age settlement patterns – Atlantic roundhouses and related structures discussed in Chapter 5 – which reflect an open landscape with mainly pastoral but some limited arable activity (MacKie 1974; Dickson and Dickson 1984). However, the occurrence of fossilised tree stumps in the peatlands of the Western Isles (Wilkins 1984) and the undoubted need for timber in the construction of Atlantic roundhouses may indicate that the assumed lack of woodland in Atlantic Scottish areas has been over-emphasised. At the other end of the scale and our study area, it has only recently been suggested that the traditional view of Iron Age Armorica as being heavily forested with only a few areas of cleared, cultivated ground needs to be seriously modified to one of an agricultural landscape already much denuded of trees where cleared ground was dominant (Marguerie 1990: 117; Giot *et al.* 2005: 35–8). Peat bog stratigraphy also appears to be heavily influenced by localised climatic factors as there can be considerable disagreement in the evidence obtained between adjacent areas (Turner 1981: 251–6). Obviously this can make generalisations about climatic conditions extremely difficult to construct.

General environmental trends

Prior to the period under study the environment along the Atlantic coasts was significantly warmer and drier than it is today. Favourable conditions from the Late Neolithic onwards allowed farming to expand into marginal, upland areas. The general trend then is one of continuous agricultural expansion in most areas up until the end of the Late Bronze Age. In Dartmoor, for example, there is evidence of widespread clearance at the time when the reaves (stone field boundaries) were constructed *c.* 1300 BC (Maguire *et al.* 1983).

Late Bronze Age

During the Late Bronze Age there were significant environmental changes. Evidence for colder and wetter conditions is seen through the expansion of peat bogs in Atlantic areas. It is widely accepted that there was a 2°C drop in overall mean temperature in the first quarter of the first millennium BC (Cunliffe 1995a: 16). This would have substantially shortened the growing season and thus have a drastic effect on marginal, upland Atlantic communities. Many upland settlements had to be abandoned and open upland moors became waterlogged, resulting in widespread peat formation – in part due to over-exploitation (leading to soil changes) but mainly due to the climatic downturn (increased rainfall). This set of circumstances is dramatically seen in the abandoned field systems and farmsteads, dating to the second and early first millennia BC, in Dartmoor. Evidence from sites throughout the Atlantic area suggests the onset of wetter climatic conditions in the first half of the first millennium BC. On the Somerset Levels in south-western England, for example, the renewed construction of wooden trackways, sometimes prompted by particular episodes of flooding, is seen (Coles and Coles 1986). It perhaps comes as little surprise that the Late Bronze Age sees a major period of lakeside settlement and artificial islet construction in both Ireland and Scotland (O'Sullivan 1997; Henderson 1998).

Late Bronze Age climatic deterioration

The majority of environmental studies confirm a very general picture of climatic deterioration from the Late Bronze Age into the Early Iron Age (Lynch 1981; Turner 1981; Bell 1996) but opinions have varied over the years on the scale and consequences of this downturn. At the more extreme end of the scale, the end of Late Bronze Age is viewed as a period of intense and relatively rapid economic decline leading to population contraction, a decrease in agricultural activity accompanied by a regeneration of woodland and expansion of blanket bog. A number of authors have considered these conditions to have had a limiting, and in extreme cases an almost catastrophic, effect on the development of Atlantic communities (Burgess 1974, 1985, 1989; Raftery 1994).

With waterlogged and ruined crops, with rivers bursting their banks and weeks of leaden skies and unceasing rain, Ireland's Late Bronze Age farmers – soaked, cold and hungry – could have felt themselves on the brink of Armageddon.

(Raftery 1994: 37)

The view of climatic change as cataclysmic and a major cause of cultural change is, however, somewhat outdated. Most authors now view the climatic deterioration at the end of the Late Bronze Age as a slower process, at its wettest and declining most rapidly between *c.* 850 BC and 650 BC. Conditions are seen to have varied from area to area, as seen in the peat bog stratigraphies (Turner 1981: 256–61), and change may have been slow and imperceptible in some areas and to some societies while being more dramatic in others as yields began to drop below the needs of populations which were less able to adapt to change. The broad view of gradual upland abandonment, peat bog expansion and decreasing agricultural activity is undoubtedly correct – it is the perceived effects of this on societies, and especially their ability to quickly adapt, that has changed. The effects of short-term climatic events – which may have been the most significant to communities living in marginal environments – are extremely difficult to determine as the required chronological resolution is virtually impossible to achieve.

Fluctuations in prehistoric climatic conditions are notoriously difficult to determine and their social and economic consequences even more difficult to assess. Short-term climatic problems might not be recognizable in coarse pollen records, yet a quick succession of poor harvests might be disastrous for a community dependent on arable agriculture. If there was significant and widespread climatic deterioration, societies with a predominantly pastoral economy may have been able to accommodate its consequences to a greater degree.

(Waddell 1998: 218)

In Ireland in particular there is a widely held view of a decline in agriculture and an increase in woodland across the second half of the first millennium BC. This is usually interpreted as evidence for climatic deterioration and/or soil erosion through over-exploitation leading to the expansion of blanket peat in many areas (Mitchell 1976; Aalen 1978; Lynch 1981; Edwards 1990: 60; Kelly 1997: 4; Mitchell and Ryan 1997: 237–8).

However, there is growing evidence that the picture may be more complex than once thought. It is worth bearing in mind some of the problems associated with pollen profiles and the fact that the majority of the Irish evidence comes from areas of low agricultural potential featuring equally poor palynological resolution such as raised bogs or large lakes. In areas of better land we may expect quite a different picture. Turner (1981: 247–75) has identified a number of Irish sites which indicate forest *clearance* during the Iron Age. Equally, a recent palynological study from an area of good agricultural land in Co. Louth revealed evidence of agricultural activity throughout the Late Bronze Age and Iron Age (Weir 1995). Several sites included in the study, such as Essexford Lough and Redbog, demonstrated that agricultural activity was maintained across the Late Bronze Age transition period. At one site,

Whiterath Bog, the most extensive clearance activity actually occurred *during* the Iron Age, from *c.* 400 to 200 BC, with total arboreal pollen falling to 30 per cent suggesting the existence of a very open landscape (Weir 1995: 98–100, fig. 43). This is similar to the situation recorded at Loughnashade, Co. Armagh where extensive clearances also occurred during the Iron Age (op. cit. 105; Cooney and Grogan 1994: 181).

The evidence suggests that the commonly held view of wholesale agricultural decline and abandonment throughout Ireland is simplistic. There is little doubt that there was a contraction in cleared land in many areas of the country at the end of the Late Bronze Age. This is apparent from the number of pollen profiles in which the indicators of cleared land can be seen to decrease around 800 BC[2] and easily fits in with more widespread evidence for climatic deterioration seen elsewhere in Atlantic Europe (Lamb 1981). However, such a realisation does not support traditional views of Ireland being massively depopulated and undergoing a 'Dark Age' from 600 to 300 BC (*contra* Raftery 1994). From the evidence recorded to date, although admittedly still piecemeal, agricultural decline seems more likely to have been a highly regional issue dependent on localised circumstances. Some areas will have experienced decline while in others agriculture would have continued or even intensified.

There is some evidence of settlement continuity throughout this period from, for example, the series of circular structures built at Emain Macha Site B (Lynn 1986) from 800 to 100 BC without any apparent upheaval or the evidence of activity at site 26 at Carrowmore (Cooney and Grogan 1994) to accompany the evidence of continued agricultural activity from some of the pollen sites. As will be argued later in the book, the lack of recognition of Iron Age sites in Ireland has much more to do with problems of the current classification schemes used than archaeological reality.

The effects of climatic deterioration at the end of the Late Bronze Age are traditionally believed to have a drastic effect on the communities of south-west England causing a settlement shift from the high moorland locations to lower altitudes (Simmons 1970; Pearce 1981; Todd 1987; Bell 1996). However, recent research has confirmed that although this is true as a general trend, it was in reality a long-drawn-out process with localised factors playing an extremely important role (Caseldine and Hatton 1996).

Iron Age

Climatic deterioration persisted well into the Iron Age. There was continued abandonment of upland areas leading, one may presume, to increased competition for land in lowland areas – this is likely to have been a factor in the development of defended settlement throughout the period. Periods of climatic downturn at this time may also have had an impact on the stormy nature of the Atlantic, making maritime communication even more difficult or, in extreme cases, quite impossible.[3] Stormy conditions may have been a contributing factor, but certainly not a cause, of the lack of continental influences or contacts in Atlantic Scotland, Ireland, and south-west England from *c.* 600 to 200 BC.

From *c.* 400 BC the climate began to improve, becoming drier and warmer, and by the end of the Iron Age was probably similar to today with temperatures *c.* 0.5°C below current levels (Lamb 1982: 144–7; Barber 1985: 52; Armit 1992: 4; Astill and Davies 1997: 35). The warm period lasted until at least the fifth century AD (Turner 1981: 261). From *c.* 400 BC then there was once again an expansion of agricultural activities, this time, however, with the introduction of iron, onto previously unworkable heavy, damp soils rather than forest or marginal land (Haselgrove 1989). This may partly explain why several Atlantic areas show a notable increase in woodland at the close of the first millennium BC and into the first few centuries AD (Edwards and Whittington 1997). From the Late Iron Age onwards there was a considerable increase in settlement and therefore presumably population levels – both trends being very much pan-European phenomena.

Atlantic food-producing strategies

The view of the Atlantic as unproductive and peripheral has much do to with Fox's (1932: 29, 40–2) classic division of Britain into Lowland and Highland zones. Highland areas were seen to suffer from more extreme environmental conditions and poorer soils and were therefore considered to have been sparsely occupied by inward looking pastoral communities, conservative in nature and slow to respond to change (Childe 1946; Piggott 1958). The better studied Lowland zone of Britain was, in contrast, seen as a veritable paradise, densely populated by settled cereal growing communities.

This view was of course over-simplistic but the mindset it created amongst British archaeologists has stuck and we are still not fully free from it. Prior to the widespread practice of systematic archaeobotanical sampling, interpretations of Atlantic economies were based almost entirely on animal bone data and artefactual evidence such as quernstones, spindle whorls and stone ards. Using such limited data, it is easy to see why pastoralist pursuits were emphasised and the importance of other aspects of Atlantic economies not fully considered (Bond 2002: 178). The establishment of sieving as standard practice over the last two decades has provided more substantial evidence for cereal cultivation at Atlantic sites being carried out alongside stock rearing. Atlantic food-producing strategies seem to have involved the use of a diverse range of resources including the exploitation of wild animals and plants which were carried out to support core mixed farming activities. Communities in marginal environments are well used to employing a broad spectrum approach in acquiring food and it is likely that such strategies were well established and, more importantly, would have been reliable. The success and stability of Atlantic economies is clearly demonstrated by the existence of long-term and continuous settlement throughout the Iron Age and beyond, with occupations commonly enduring over centuries. Such evidence challenges the traditional view of struggling and environmentally fragile communities in so-called marginal areas.

Three main problems are encountered when trying to reconstruct Atlantic food-producing strategies. First, floatation was a much neglected practice until recently while, second, and more irreversibly, the existence of predominantly acidic soils in Atlantic regions rarely leads to the preservation of significant amounts of bone material (Cunliffe 1991: 393). Floatation techniques are now widely practised on modern excavations but the samples recovered from Atlantic sites tend to be small, making estimations about the relative importance of cereal types extremely difficult. Finally, the lack of any clearly defined sampling of on-site data, both faunal and floral, often makes it difficult to compare assemblages between sites.

The bone assemblages recovered from the majority of Atlantic sites indicate the predominance of pastoralist economies. Although cereal cultivation has been attested at many Atlantic sites (Marguerie 1990: 118; Cunliffe 1991: 393–403; Raftery 1994: 121–5; Tipping 1994: 36), the actual volume of material present on individual sites suggests that during the first millennium BC arable agriculture in most Atlantic areas was generally restricted to self-sufficiency. Certainly it seems unlikely that Atlantic households would have been able to create a significant surplus of cereals for trade. The creation of any surplus would most likely come in the form of livestock from pastoralist pursuits. On saying this, it is worth bearing in mind that cereal trade leaves no archaeological footprint and bulk transport is easy by sea and all but impossible over land.[4]

Atlantic Scotland and Ireland

Atlantic Scottish and Irish food-producing strategies appear to have been quite similar as both areas provide evidence of stock-rearing economies dominated by cattle with some subsistence level farming supplemented by the exploitation of wild resources. Cereals in small amounts have been recovered from all the recent excavations carried out across Atlantic Scotland and have confirmed six-row barley as the staple cereal crop of the region (Boyd 1988; Dickson and Dickson 2000; Bond 2002; Church 2002; Bond et al. 2005; Cerón-Carrasco et al. 2005). The practice of a barley monoculture throughout Atlantic Scotland and its apparent dominance in the admittedly limited Iron Age evidence from Ireland contrasts with other Atlantic areas which, in common with the rest of Britain, were cultivating spelt wheat from as early as the Late Bronze Age (Harding 2004: 11). Rather than reflecting environmental limitations or a lack of trading contacts it is possible that this difference represents cultural choice coupled with a reluctance to fundamentally change successful food procurement strategies with a proven pedigree.

Cattle dominate the majority of Atlantic Scottish bone assemblages, closely followed by sheep/goat and then pig (Gilmour and Cook 1998: 333). There is some variation from site to site – at Dun Mor Vaul and Dun Vulan, for example, sheep/goat numerically dominated assemblages (MacKie 1974: 187–98; Parker Pearson et al. 1999: 234–74). Meat production was undoubtedly the major economic mainstay of Atlantic communities, with dairy products perhaps similarly or more important at some sites. Debate has focused on the identification of primarily dairy economies as opposed to those focused on meat production. However, the identification of such patterns from cattle bone assemblages alone are ultimately not provable either way and often simply end up a matter of opinion (compare Gilmour and Cook 1998 with Parker Peason et al. 1999 for differing views on the Dun Vulan, South Uist assemblage or in Ireland, Crabtree 1990 with McCormick 1992 on the Dún Ailinne, Co. Kildare assemblage). Some assert that calves are killed early due to a lack of winter fodder, thus precluding dairying, while others see neonatal and calf mortality as patterns *indicative* of a milking regime. On balance either scenario is possible within a dairy or meat production regime and therefore such factors cannot be taken to prove conclusively the dominance of one strategy over the other. It is equally possible that the predominance of such regimes varied both temporally and from site to site and thus, for our present purposes, it is only of interest that livestock were reared and managed in the first place.

The generally warm and wet Atlantic climate allows year-round growth of grass, and the keeping of animals outdoors throughout the winter is commonplace today, even in the most exposed and western areas. In general, much of the economic evidence, such as the early culling of young animals, is interpreted as evidence of a harsh climate coupled with a lack of winter fodder and poor husbandry practices (Gilmour and Cook 1998: 333–4). The lack of winter fodder is generally assumed on the basis of a lack of evidence for hay. However, it is rare for the probable locations for storing hay – most likely outside or in external buildings – to be carefully sampled or even excavated. An alternative view would suggest that the Atlantic Iron Age landscape was full of resources, both wild and domestic, and that there is no reason to suspect that a lack of winter fodder was a problem (Cerón-Carrasco *et al.* 2005). The suggested mechanism of harvesting cereals in Atlantic Scotland by uprooting the entire plant would in fact be conducive to the production of hay (Smith 1999: 332). Equally, other fodder alternatives are possible. The occurrence of animal dung with straw at the Howe on Orkney might suggest the use of straw as fodder, while other macrofossil remains such as spiral tassleweed (*Ruppia cirrhosa*) could serve a similar role (Dickson 1994: 127).

Collecting and gathering wild resources was very much a part of Atlantic Scottish economies. Wild edible plants are a regular feature of Iron Age assemblages, as are marine resources. Shellfish, especially limpets, winkles and whelks, were commonly collected and there appears to have been opportunistic exploitation of whales, breeding seals and nesting sea birds (Smith and Mulville 2004; Cerón-Carrasco *et al.* 2005). In contrast to the intensive levels of cod fishing seen in the Norse period, Iron Age fishing is thought to have been undertaken at a much smaller scale (Barrett *et al.* 1999). Small, inshore species (predominantly saithe) dominate fish assemblages recovered from Iron Age contexts in the Western Isles (Parker Pearson *et al.* 1999: 274–81; Smith and Mulville 2004: 54, 59–60; Cerón-Carrasco *et al.* 2005: 227–8) and the Northern Isles (Nicholson and Dockrill 1998; Sharples 1998; Nicholson 2004; Bond *et al.* 2005: 213–14) suggesting low-risk shore based or shallow water coastal fishing practices. This evidence, coupled with the apparent absence of fish middens and the general scarcity of Iron Age fishing artefacts, suggest that fishing was only ever a secondary activity at this time carried out primarily to complement the main food staples (livestock and cereals). Claims for deep sea fishing practices have come from Bu on the Orkney Islands where bones of plaice and cod were identified, but the contextual integrity of these finds remains open to question (Colley 1987: 126–34; Nicholson 2004: 155). Certainly elsewhere in Atlantic Scotland the occurrence of deeper sea species and evidence for the intensification of fishing practices is not seen until the mid-first millennium AD at the earliest and does not reach its full expression until the Norse period.

The high proportions of red deer recovered from bone assemblages throughout Atlantic Scotland demonstrate the significant role this particular wild resource played in local economies (cf. Gilmour and Cook 1998: tables 1 and 2; Cerón-Carrasco *et al.* 2005: fig. 67; Mulville and Thoms 2005: table 17). This has led some to suggest that red deer populations were actively managed by Atlantic groups though the mechanisms of this 'management' remain elusive but conceivably would have involved some form of selective culling (McCormick 1991; Cerón-Carrasco *et al.* 2005: 228–9; Mulville and Thoms 2005: 241). Gilmour and Cook (1998: 334) have suggested that there may have been some level of exchange of livestock between the Scottish islands. This seems likely as a number of the smaller Scottish islands, such as Iona, Mingulay and Pabbay, which produce bone assemblages with deer and cattle, would have been too small to support breeding populations. The creation of a livestock surplus, including the management of deer herds as well as domestic forms, to produce animals for trade may have been a major concern of local communities with trade in livestock forming a significant element of exchanges between Atlantic Scottish communities. With this in mind it is interesting to note the occurrence of purging blackthorn wood alongside roe deer, pine martin and badger remains at Dun Vulan, South Uist, none of which are thought to have been native to Atlantic Scotland, meaning that their presence can only be explained through the existence of wider maritime contacts with Ireland and Britain (Smith and Mulville 2004: 54–5).

Mulville and Thoms (2005: 241–2) have argued that deer as wild animals that had to be hunted are likely to have had a symbolic importance to communities in the Western Isles. They argue that they were being treated differently to other animals, citing the fact that deer bones appear to be absent from structured deposits of animals in pits in domestic contexts, the occurrence of an arc of deer jawbones deliberately laid around a hearth at A'Cheardach Bheag on South Uist (Fairhurst 1971), and that artistic representations of deer exist on pottery from Kilphaeder wheelhouse, South Uist (Lethbridge 1952), and on a carved wooden handle from Dun Bharabhat, Lewis (Harding and Dixon 2000: fig. 34). More work is needed to define the role of deer in Atlantic Iron Age society but it is clear that the hunting of these animals was a major component of local ways of life and that this practice represents a significant regional difference with the rest of Britain.

Bone assemblages from Irish sites are very much a rarity given the lack of sites confidently dated to the Iron Age – especially in the west. The documentary sources for the succeeding Early Christian period make it clear that cattle were, at that time, the most important element of the rural economy and there seems little reason to assume that this marks a drastic break with Irish Iron Age economies (Edwards 1990: 56; Raftery 1994: 125). Around 80 per cent of the bones recovered from the Late Bronze Age/Early Iron Age lake-side settlement of Ballinderry 2, Co. Offaly, were those of cattle (Hencken 1942).

The most detailed Iron Age faunal study comes from Dún Ailinne, Co. Kildare, where around 55 per cent of the 19,000 identified bones were those of cattle, with around 36 per cent pig, while only 7.3 per cent were sheep/goat (Crabtree 1990). Only 13 barley grains were identified despite a large area of the site being excavated, perhaps lending some support to the theory of agricultural decline in the Irish Iron

Age compared to the preceding periods discussed above (Raftery 1994: 122). Dún Ailinne did produce a sizable amount of hazelnut shells and wild plant seeds, indicating that the gathering of wild resources was used to supplement the diet (Wailes 1990). Interestingly, deer bones were also present but only in very small quantities.

The only other Iron Age site which has produced a large bone assemblage is Emain Macha, Co. Armagh (Lynn 1986), where pig was found to be the dominant species with twice as many pigs recovered as cattle and nine times as many as sheep or goat. The significance of this is difficult to assess not least because, as Raftery (1994: 126) points out, it is not possible to differentiate clearly between Bronze and Iron Age levels at the site. The presumed ritual character of Emain Macha, coupled with the ritual connotations of the pig in Celtic mythology, have led to the suggestion that the bones may represent a ritual rather than domestic assemblage (Raftery 1994: 126; Waddell 1998: 340). Worthy of a mention is the discovery of the skull and jawbones of a Barbary ape found in a context dating between 390 and 20 BC. The ape, a native of North Africa, could only have come to the Irish site by ship and can be considered a vivid example of the extent of Atlantic contacts (Raftery 1994: 79; Waddell 1998: 340; Figure 2.3).

In comparison to the Atlantic Scottish evidence it is worth looking at the assemblage from Leacanabuaile, Co. Kerry (Ó Ríordáin and Foy 1941), situated in the Atlantic zone but traditionally dated to the mid or latter part of the first millennium AD. Cattle bones made up 90 per cent of the assemblage alongside a significant amount of sheep/goat remains and lesser amounts of pig. This is of course similar to Iron Age assemblages in Atlantic areas of Scotland, but what is more interesting is the analogous evidence for the collection of wild and maritime resources. Red deer remains are present alongside evidence of grey seal, small horse, dog, badger, birds and marine molluscs. The latter comprised predominantly of periwinkle and limpet but also included oyster, cockle and mussels (op. cit. 95–6).

South-west England and south-west Wales

Field systems in the upland moorland massifs of south-western England, thought to date to the Late Bronze Age, indicate perhaps initially a greater emphasis on cereal cultivation here in comparison to other Atlantic areas. However, the fields are quite small and it is possible they were simply a supporting element to pastoral pursuits rather than the focus of the economy, as larger enclosures which could have been used for stock, although unexamined, are also known on the moors (Johnson and Rose 1994; Gearey and Charman 1996).

Whatever the case, there was a definite, though not perhaps sudden, move to lower altitudes in the mid-millennium BC, and pastoralism became the focus of Iron Age economies in these areas, as indeed it remained up until the Medieval period (Gearey and Charman 1996: 118). This is perhaps most evident through the widespread occurrence of large enclosures, widely thought to have been for the keeping of livestock, connected to or surrounding settlements (Fox, 1953: 18–20; Thomas 1966; Silvester 1979; Pearce 1981: 104–7; Quinnell 1986: 114; Todd 1987: 166). A number of these sites, known as multiple enclosure forts, featured stock enclosures with massively

Figure 2.3 The skull and jawbones of a Barbary Ape were discovered at Navan Fort, Co. Armagh. The hatched area of the map indicates the approximate distribution of the ape in antiquity (after Raftery 1994: fig. 45).

built ramparts, larger than would be needed for a strictly utilitarian function. Such sites may therefore reflect the importance of pastoralism in south-western society, implying a correlation between the keeping of animals, social standing, and the display of status.

Evidence for crops and herds from excavations in south-west England is extremely lacking. The few available Iron Age bone assemblages, such as that from Mount Batten (Grant 1988), show that cattle were the dominant species represented, with smaller amounts of sheep/goat. Cereal grains are known from a few sites, including the multiple enclosure fort of Killibury which produced emmer, spelt and oats, and the univallate enclosure at Goldherring where barley, oats and rye were recovered. However, the samples obtained to date have always been very small and it has thus proven impossible to assess the importance of cereal growing to south-western economies. It seems most likely, given the lack of storage pits, four-poster granaries, and Iron Age field systems in the area, that cereal production was again providing a supporting role to pastoralist pursuits. Souterrains appear to have been the only potential source of storage and it is possible these were connected to the storage of dairy products, a view which would add further support to the existence of a pastoral focused economy (Tangye 1973; Armit 1997).

The evidence for south-west Wales is similarly fragmentary. Cunliffe (1991: 394–8, fig. 15.9) divides Wales into two main zones: a mountainous central zone suited to pastoralism and lower lying northern and south-western Atlantic coastal pasture zones where conditions were capable of supporting mixed farming. It is possible that cereal production formed a larger part of Iron Age economies in south-west Wales compared to other northern Atlantic areas. There is much evidence for arable agriculture in the zone: field systems are recorded in association with Iron Age sites at Stackpole Warren and Pembrey Mountain, the latter site producing emmer and spelt from dated Iron Age contexts (Williams 1981); pre-rampart plough marks were seen at Woodborn Rath and Drim while iron plough tips were recovered from Walesland Rath; cereal grains have been recovered from several settlements including Merryborough, Woodside and Caer Cadwgan, Dyfed (Austin 1984,1985). In contrast to other Atlantic areas evidence for four-poster granaries are a much more common feature of Iron Age enclosures, perhaps implying that more grain was being produced. Wales also is the only northern Atlantic area to lack souterrains.

Despite the evidence for increased arable activity, in common with the other Atlantic areas, pastoralism is likely to have formed the backbone of south-western Welsh economic strategies. Bone assemblages generally suggest a preference for the keeping of cattle.[5] At Coygan Camp, Dyfed, for example, cattle made up 64 per cent of the recovered bone assemblage, sheep/goat 16 per cent, and pig 15 per cent (Wainwright 1967). Interestingly, evidence was also recovered for the collection of shellfish. At Pen y Coed, where four-poster structures and querns were found, environmental evidence from the site suggested that it had been surrounded by an essentially pastoral landscape. This is a general environmental picture backed up by the evidence from Tregaron Bog for pastoral clearances (Turner 1964).

On balance the limited evidence from sites in south-west England and south-west Wales suggest predominantly pastoral economies with cereal growing carried out in areas where conditions were favourable. There is some evidence to suggest that arable agriculture was more widely carried out in south-west Wales.

Armorica

Mixed farming appeared to have been more firmly established in Armorica – at least by the close of the first millennium BC. Deforestation began much earlier here, most probably in the Neolithic, and by the Iron Age pollen profiles indicate a predominantly open meadow landscape alongside evidence for cereal pollen (Marguerie 1990).

Some profiles indicate the survival of areas of forest cover and it seems likely that Iron Age populations were actively managing woodland areas within a landscape densely filled with farming enclosures (Le Bihan 1984: 172).

Despite the high occurrence of cereals in general pollen profiles, stock production appears to have been the primary concern of the Armorican economy, with cattle again the dominant species at most sites (Buchsenschutz 1994). Armorican farmsteads are well known from the excavation of sites such as Le Boisanne, Côtes d'Armor (Menez 1996) and Le Braden I, Finistère (Le Bihan 1984, 1988, 1990), and consist of a number of linked enclosures, delimited by low ramparts, palisades, and/or hedges, which are devoid of occupational evidence and interpreted as compounds for livestock (Le Bihan 1990; Menez 1996: 206). This interpretation is supported by the occurrence of simple entrances and antennae trenches which appear to have been designed to facilitate the movement of animals. Excavations within suspected animal folds at La Hattaie in Brittany revealed high phosphate levels (site H80, Astill and Davies 1997: 65) as did a building interpreted as a cowshed or stable at Paule, Saint-Symphorien, Côtes d'Armor (Arramond and Menez 1992: 265).

Cattle were predominant in the bone assemblage recovered from Le Boissane, Côtes d'Armor (Menez 1996: 191), the most intensively excavated site of the region. Interestingly there is also evidence for the exploitation of wild resources with 6.9 per cent of the bone assemblage found to comprise wild deer. This was interpreted by the excavator as evidence for hunting for sport (op. cit. 192) but is more likely to represent evidence for the exploitation of a wide range of resources comparable to the evidence recovered from sites in Atlantic Scotland.

Pollen evidence recovered from the banks and ditches of the enclosures at Le Boissane suggested that although the surrounding landscape was composed predominantly of open meadow and moor there was some evidence, from the recovery of cereal pollen, of cultivated fields within 100 m of the farm (op. cit. 191). The majority of the surrounding enclosures were considered to be too large for cultivation (Menez 1996: 206); smaller plots, perhaps defined by more ephemeral means such as wattling, may have existed. Certainly there was some cereal production at the site, but taken together the faunal evidence, the layout of the enclosures, the occurrence of a purpose built 'pond' (op. cit. 185), and the form of the entrance constructions indicate that stock rearing was the primary function (op. cit. 206).

In the last few centuries BC there is evidence for an expansion in the number of farmsteads and an accompanying intensification in cereal production (Menez 1996; Leroux *et al.* 1999). Souterrains were commonly associated with farmsteads prior to this period but after 100 BC they appear to fall out of use and four-poster granary structures and silos begin to be widely used. It is argued later in the book that this expansion may be related to an increase in the intensity of contacts with west-central Europe owing to the development of Roman markets in Gaul.

Discussion

In the Late Bronze Age subsistence strategies appear to become more mixed with animals and crops exploited in more complex ways than before. This was possibly due to necessity, as a response to worsening climatic conditions, but it may reflect changes in people's attitudes to food production and a move towards exploiting a wider range of resources. Where possible mixed farming was carried out at Atlantic sites but obviously local factors such as altitude and soil type dictated the kind of subsistence strategies pursued and the balance between crops grown and livestock reared. Evidence from a number of Atlantic assemblages from Atlantic Scotland – and potentially Ireland – provide evidence for the exploitation of an even wider range of resources. A strategy that includes, alongside cereal cultivation and pastoral pursuits, the exploitation of coastal resources such as shellfish, the gathering of wild plants and the hunting of wild animals is usually considered to be inferior and more unreliable than one based upon mixed farming. However, if anything such a strategy could be considered more flexible and less likely to completely collapse.

Such a view is supported by the permanent and substantial nature of much of the stone-built architecture in the Atlantic Scottish and Irish zone which, taken with the evidence of occupation periods lasting over hundreds of years, suggests more success- ful and stable societies than are usually assumed for so-called peripheral Atlantic communities. This permanence and continuity, as we shall see paralleled in many of the Atlantic communities, implies a stronger sense of social stability than that reflected by the less substantial timber roundhouses seen in the rest of Iron Age Britain and Europe.

Significantly, Kristiansen (1998: 246) has recently argued that Atlantic Late Bronze Age economies were actually *more* able to adapt to the climatic deterioration at the end of the period rather than less so precisely because they were more reliant on animal husbandry as opposed to cereal production. He states that a deteriorating climate would have had more of an impact on the primarily agricultural communi- ties in west-central Europe, lowering the holding capacity of the land and creating conditions of population pressure. At the end of the Urnfield period west-central Europe was more densely settled than ever before and therefore highly vulnerable to changes in climate and ecology, which might lead to a decline in lowland agricul- tural productivity. Such a scenario offers a context for the development of the decen- tralised western Hallstatt C, chiefly elites in these areas *c.* 750 BC and their apparent shift back to predominantly pastoralist practices. Changes in society and material culture are therefore more drastic in west-central Europe and more visible through the breakdown of late Urnfield ways of life to the more warring and pastoral pursuits of Hallstatt C chiefdoms (Härke 1979, 1989).

Whatever the case, by the La Tène period *c.* 450 BC, the apparent dominance of pastoralism in the Atlantic is a marked contrast to the food producing strategies prac- tised in southern England and central France where meat production was only a secondary consideration. In northern Atlantic areas the focus was on self-contained farming establishments many of which were stable and extremely long lived. There is little evidence for the centralised creation of surpluses. Pastoral dominated economies are generally considered to prevent the development of centralised populations and complex hierarchical social structures. This may be one reason why organisational devel- opment in Atlantic areas followed a different evolutionary trajectory than other parts of Europe. Atlantic economies were very much synchronised with their environments and, given the long continuities of occupation seen throughout the zone, they were undoubtedly successful. This specialisation could create a stronger sense of continuity of traditions within local areas and, in turn, a stronger sense of identity between Atlantic communities. The continuity of tradition is a recurrent theme in Atlantic areas – if the exploitation of a wide range of resources was a successful subsistence practice there would have been little need to change, perhaps even a marked reluctance to do so.

The evidence at present is sparse and localised and there was undoubtedly more variety within and between Atlantic areas. Unfortunately there are insufficient samples from across the zone to identify whether there are significant intra-regional differences or similarities related to landscape and environment (Hambleton 1999: 90). In highlighting pastoralist pursuits only the broadest element of Atlantic food-producing strategies have been identified. The most palaeobotanical and environmental work has taken place in Atlantic Scotland and here elements of cultural and symbolic choice are beginning to be recognised in food-producing strategies (Smith and Mulville 2004; Bond *et al.* 2005). This work suggests that continuity and stability is less due to environmental factors (and the effects they can have) and more to do with the flexibility and adaptability of local agricultural systems with communities building economic buffers into their strategies involving the use of alternative resources (wild, marine, stored) and traded produce (including livestock) alongside cereal cultivation.

The Atlantic sea-lanes

The Atlantic maritime approaches are notoriously difficult to navigate, even for modern mariners, as they are stormy, unpredictable, affected by strong, quickly shifting winds and very wide tidal ranges. Atlantic weather patterns produce strong south-westerly winds that make the traditionally assumed method of prehistoric sea travel – coast hugging – particularly hazardous. In addition, many of the western-facing peninsulas of the Atlantic seaboard are, or at least appear, completely unapproachable by sea. Caesar himself noted during his campaigns against the Veneti of south-west Brittany in 56 BC and his passage to Britain that navigation was made extremely difficult for the Romans due to the lack of safe harbours and open sea conditions:

> … because the difficulty of navigation on a vast and open sea, with strong tides and few – nay, scarcely any – harbours was extreme.
>
> (*Bellum Gallicum* III.12)

> … they [the Romans] could see that navigation on a land-locked sea was quite different from navigation on an Ocean very vast and open.
>
> (*Bellum Gallicum* III.9)

Maximum tidal ranges of less than 50 centimetres in the Mediterranean contrast with ranges of 4 to 6 m in Britain and Ireland and up to 12 m of the French Atlantic coast. Despite proving difficult for the Romans, we can have little doubt that these conditions were seen as 'normal' to Atlantic societies and that they had adapted their sailing techniques accordingly. While Atlantic sea conditions were challenging and treacherous, undoubtedly commanding respect amongst indigenous communities, they were not so terrifying as to coerce travellers to go overland in preference or to deny the possibility of long-distance voyaging. Although very little is known about Atlantic prehistoric maritime technology there can be little doubt that by the Iron Age, sea-going craft were sufficiently advanced to serve community needs. On more than one occasion Caesar compliments the vessels and seamanship of the Veneti (*Bellum Gallicum* III.7–11, 16–18; Weatherhill 1985b: 163–9). The realisation that Atlantic societies were well adapted to their maritime environment and capable of carrying out long-distance crossings does not of course automatically support a model of constant seaborne contact between coastal communities. However, it must be remembered that sailing is a pragmatic skill and one that has to be practised to be maintained, making some level of coastal contact in areas where sailing traditions existed more or less inevitable.

Tidal streams are virtually absent from the Mediterranean; the very existence of tides in the Atlantic warranted a mention from classical geographers (Strabo, *Geographica* III.3.3). Knowledge about the times of tides and locations of currents would be essential to planning journeys. For example, a number of dangerous offshore shoals and rocks exist off the western end of Brittany such as at Les Platresses or the submerged rocks of La Plate la Vielle, Île d'Ouessant and Île de Beniquet. Strong tidal streams and rocks are also a factor off Land's End, south-west England, and to this day sailors struggle with strong tides and winds in the south of Biscay and the mouth of the English Channel (Wooding 1996: 7–8). Tidal patterns, landing places, low and high water times, and detailed knowledge of the locations of shoals, winds and weather are all factors that would have been learned at an early age by mariners sailing the Atlantic (McGrail 1998: 258).

It is not impossible that a body of relatively precise astronomical knowledge underpinned Iron Age navigation. As Ruíz-Gálvez (1991: 286) has stated, the orientation and association of many megalithic structures indicate the existence of astronomical expertise from the Neolithic onwards which would also have facilitated navigation. Later prehistoric communities inherited this knowledge and no doubt extended it: Caesar mentions the Gauls' knowledge of astronomy (*Bellum Gallicum* VI.14) while Piggott (1974: 104–5) has outlined the emphasis on the moon – of obvious importance in terms of understanding tides – apparent in Iron Age ritual. All in all, there can be little doubt that an intimate knowledge of winds, tides and currents existed and that alongside a utility in measuring time and facilitating maritime travel, this knowledge probably held a ritual significance which may have enhanced the cosmological importance of the sea to Atlantic communities.

Knowledge of navigational techniques is virtually impossible to document archaeologically. However, given the prevailing winds and rugged, rocky coasts of the Atlantic we can be sure that indigenous mariners, unlike their Mediterranean counterparts, must have been well used to sailing out of sight of land (Marcus 1980; McGrail 1983; Wooding 1996: 16–21). For example, McGrail (1983: 300) has argued that to cross from north-western France to Cornwall along one of the shortest routes a sail-propelled vessel travelling around 2.5 knots would be out of site of land for around 20 hours. When visible coastal features such as headlands and mountains would have made excellent navigational aids[6] but once obscured or out of site mariners must have turned to other means of navigation.

Although we lack Atlantic prehistoric examples of sounding leads we can be reasonably confident that Atlantic mariners were taking depth measurements using them and probably also sampling sea-floor sediments to help determine location (Cunliffe 2001: 79–80). As mentioned above, we can also assume that Iron Age sailors used their knowledge of celestial bodies for navigation. In addition to the use of stars at night, the position of the sun could be used to determine direction (its rising and setting provided a rough orientation of east and west, while its zenith indicates due south every day of the year). It's also possible that there was an appreciation of the flight patterns of migratory birds and which particular birds indicated proximity to land (Hornell 1946; Marcus 1980: 114–15). However, the prevalence of fog and heavy rain in the Atlantic would have often rendered such knowledge obsolete. It is most likely that navigation out of sight of land was achieved by close observation of the performance of the boat (taking note of variables such as average speed and leeway slippage) and through detailed knowledge of tidal patterns and winds. 'Steering by run of the sea' is a common practice in northern navigation: the ship is orientated in relation to a well-known coastal landmark and its position is maintained by steering a consistent angle across a prevailing swell pattern (Wooding 1996: 16–17). Fishermen in Shetland were successfully navigating routes using this method as late as the nineteenth century AD (Walton 1974: 10). As such the timing of voyages would be important as they would have to coincide with beneficial tidal flows, with vessels either anchored or beached during unfavourable tides.

McGrail (1998: 259–60; 2001: 171) has argued that, as in the Mediterranean, there may have been a summer sailing season in place in Atlantic areas to avoid the extremes of the weather. Certainly the best time of the year to navigate Atlantic waters is between April and September, at which time the weather is at its most predictable and gales are at their lowest frequency. However, it seems unlikely that contacts would cease altogether in the winter interlude. Areas united only by sea are much more likely to accept the need to navigate dangerous waters, changing their strategies accordingly.

Atlantic maritime technology

From at least 1300 BC onwards, the diplomatic and economic archives of Egyptian, Assyrian and Levantine cities clearly show that maritime technology was sufficiently developed in the eastern Mediterranean to enable reliable and regular long sea voyages (Harding 1984). It is probable that Atlantic shipping evolved roughly in step with Mediterranean technology. There was certainly contact between the two zones throughout the later prehistoric period (Almagro-Gorbea 1977; Coffyn 1983, 1985; Ruíz-Gálvez 1992) and there is no reason to assume that advances in maritime technology were not communicated between them. Phoenician contacts with western Iberia began in the Late Bronze Age and were fully established through the foundation of the Phoenician port-of-trade at Gadir (Cádiz) by the eighth century BC (Cunliffe 1997: 134). It is worth bearing in mind that 'ships are by definition mobile, so technical innovations may move from one region to another in the fabric of maritime architecture' (Wooding 1996: 8).

The recognition of potential Mediterranean influences in western Europe has been unpopular over recent decades and instead the emphasis has been on stressing the indigenous development and autonomy of western European communities (Renfrew 1968; Watkins 1976; Harding 1984). However, there is a plethora of evidence to support pre-colonial contacts between the Mediterranean and western Iberia from around 1200 BC onwards (Ruíz-Gálvez 1986; Martín de la Cruz 1987; Burgess 1991; Lo Schiavo 1991). It seems extremely unlikely that Atlantic Iberian coastal peoples in contact with Mediterranean maritime peoples would not have developed or enhanced their own maritime technology if their own was indeed inferior. This goes against the commonly held view that Iberian Bronze Age communities had poorly developed nautical skills in comparison to their central Mediterranean counterparts (Frankenstein 1979; Alvar 1981: 190; Ruíz-Gálvez 1988: 6, 1984: 521; Coffyn 1985: 159).

The boat depictions in Iberian rock-art that have been dated to the Late Bronze Age (Almagro-Gorbea 1988: 389) support the view that maritime technology was well developed and considered important at this time. Over 20 boat representations are known from the rock shelters of Laja Alta in Cádiz, Pilas in Castlliejo, Puerto de los Ladroñes, in Malaga, Las Zorrilos in Cádiz (ibid. 390–1) while more recently one rock carving was found as far north as Oia, Pontevedra in Galicia (Peña Santos and Rey 2001: 56-7; Figure 2.4). Although they are only iconographic representations, these carvings depict boats with large sails, prominent bows, and oars. Such vessels would be suitable for long-distance sailing, and they can be paralleled with central Mediterranean Bronze Age representations of sea-going ships such as those from Skyros in the Cyclades and Enkomi in Cyprus (Harding 1990: 141–2).

In the Nordic zone, at the opposite end of the Atlantic seaboard, Late Bronze Age ships, some apparently in large fleets, are also a common motif on rock carvings, whilst many Baltic islands have elite boat-shaped stone slab graves (Thrane 1995; Kristiansen 2004). The Scandinavian motifs depict high prowed, shallow draught vessels propelled by oars (Figure 2.4). It has been suggested that the Scandinavian vessels may be ornate ritual vessels used for short journeys rather than those used for longer sea voyages. They may not appear to be particularly seaworthy vessels (despite their passing resemblance to later Viking ships), especially due to the lack of evidence for sails, but at the very least they do illustrate that the technology to produce complex boats was in place at this time.

The ship representations in the Nordic zone and south-western Iberia are a testament to the importance of ships, and presumably the contacts they imply, to indigenous communities in the Late Bronze Age. The well-documented Bronze Age contacts between the Mediterranean world and the Nordic zone (Sørensen 1987; Sherratt 1993a) physically links the areas of the two shipping traditions and from this we can perhaps assume that knowledge of the sail made to Atlantic areas from either here or more directly via south-western Iberia by the Late Bronze Age. The clear increase in the amount of material moving along the Atlantic seaboard in the Late Bronze Age, discussed in Chapter 3, suggests that there had been sufficient advances in maritime technology during this period (perhaps indirectly learned from the Mediterranean where there is a similar increase in maritime trading activity slightly earlier) to allow more efficient and reliable voyages over longer distances.

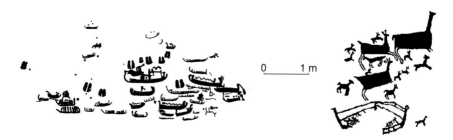

Figure 2.4 Representations of ships on Late Bronze Age rock carvings from either end of the Atlantic: on the left Lökeberg, Sweden (after Thrane 1995: fig. 53) and on the right Oia, Pontevedra in Galicia (after Peña Santos and Rey 2001).

Documentary evidence suggesting an early date for the sail in Atlantic waters comes from the fourth-century AD *Ora Maritima* poem by Avenius which is thought to have been embedded with extracts from a now lost *periplus* – the so-called *Massilliot periplus* – dating to the sixth century BC (Hawkes 1977: 19). McGrail (1995: 256) points out that this *periplus* describes two-day voyages by hide boats from western Brittany to Ireland which, if accepted, must have been made under sail. This does not of course prove that indigenous populations were also using the sail at this point. Apart from the *Ora Maritima* poem, the earliest documentary and iconographic evidence for the use of the sail in the north-western Atlantic are Caesar's observations on the sea-going plank built ships of the Veneti of Brittany in *Bellum Gallicum* (Book III.13) and the mast on the Broighter gold model boat from the north of Ireland, both of which date to the first century BC (Farrell and Penney 1975; Figure 2.5). Significantly the Broighter model also features oars – nine on each side – which might indicate that oars remained a common feature of Atlantic vessels as they would be invaluable in times of unfavourable wind and current to help steer vessels clear of reefs and other hazards, especially at landfall or when entering harbours.

The existence of Middle to Late Bronze Age shipwrecks on either side of the Channel has been inferred from finds of metalwork in maritime contexts interpreted as the surviving cargo of sunken vessels (Coombs 1975; Muckleroy 1980, 1981). It comes as no surprise that the first evidence for prehistoric shipwrecks in Atlantic waters date to the Middle to Late Bronze Age period as prior to this contacts are likely to have been less frequent and on a smaller, more symbolic, scale (Ruíz-Gálvez 1991: 287). The discovery of these cargoes, however, also suggests that networks of contact were already in existence, and to some extent formalised, permitting the exchange of commodities from region to region, most probably from the establishment of alliances during earlier periods of contact (Rowlands 1980).

Discoveries throughout north-west Europe of inland water vessels (ferries and boats including plank-built boats) demonstrate that a knowledge of sophisticated and complex boat construction techniques existed from at least the early second millennium BC onwards (Arnold 1985; McGrail 1995, 1998, 2001). The technical specifications of the boats recovered at North Ferriby on the Humber estuary (Wright 1990)

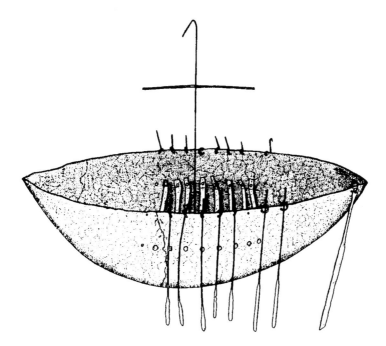

Figure 2.5 Model gold boat from Broighter dated to the first century BC (after Raftery 1994: 111; after Farrell and Penney 1975).

and from the River Dour at Dover (Wright *et al.* 2001) clearly demonstrate that there was a well-developed boat-building tradition going back centuries in existence by the first millennium BC. Although these examples were river craft and not therefore seaworthy, it is not unreasonable to assume that this highly developed boat-building expertise was also used in the construction of sea-going vessels (Ruíz-Gálvez 1991: 286).

Certainly Atlantic woodworking technology was advanced enough by the Late Bronze Age to have been able to produce complex sea-going vessels. A range of specialist tools appear during the period, including adzes, saws, chisels and gouges and various types of specialised axe, all presumably used in woodworking and carpentry. We can assume that woodworking skills were sufficiently advanced to require such specialised tool kits. The impact of advanced woodworking technology in the Late Bronze Age can perhaps be seen in, amongst other things, the widespread occurrence of permanent houses from this time. The development and increasing sophistication of carpentry skills must also have had an impact on boat-building techniques, improving them and leading to the production of more seaworthy vessels.

The lack of discovery of prehistoric shipwrecks in the Atlantic is likely to be a question of preservation and survival. Wooden shipwrecks are unlikely to survive in an Atlantic context as the rocky and turbulent seabed conditions of the zone are not conducive to their preservation. Wooden vessels are likely to break up during, or soon after, wrecking and ship timbers will only be preserved where they have been quickly covered by seabed material such as sand or silt as this protects them from the ravages of shipworm (*Teredo navalis*). Unfortunately, as wooden material in an Atlantic maritime context needs to be sealed with seabed material to survive, it becomes virtually impossible to locate unless bottom penetrating sonar techniques are used. To use such techniques effectively the general location of the site needs to be known. It is revealing that the oldest shipwreck to be excavated in Atlantic waters, the *Mary Rose* which sank in 1545, was totally buried in seabed sediments and was located only after six years of intensive survey even though the area where the wreck went down was tolerably well known (Marsden 2003). As a result the discovery of a wooden ship of any period is extremely rare in Atlantic waters and we know little of developments in ship architecture in this area up until the post-Medieval period.[7]

Types of vessel used in Atlantic waters

The most common type of sea-going vessel used by Atlantic communities is thought to have been the hide boat or *currach* which was essentially 'a hide or leather water-proof covering fastened to a framework of light timbers' (McGrail 1995: 264–5). Literary evidence for the use of such vessels in the Atlantic comes from the previously mentioned *Ora Maritima* (101–6) and more generally from a number of Roman authors of the first century BC to the third century AD: Pliny (*Nat. Hist.* IV.104; VII.205–6), Caesar (*Bellum Gallicum* I.54), Strabo (*Geographica* III.3), Lucan (*Pharsalia* IV.130–8), Dio Cassus (*Epitome*, 48 19–19) and Salinus (*Polyhistor* II.3). The fact that such boats were deemed worthy of special comment, coupled with the comparatively large number of references that actually survive, suggests that hide boats were a common but distinctive trait of Atlantic waters in the later first millennium BC (Cunliffe 2001: 66–8).

Hide boats are often too readily dismissed as flimsy and unseaworthy. However, they could be strongly constructed yet light and flexible vessels, ideally adapted to the unpredictable Atlantic seas where the ability to ride the crest of a high wave or land on almost any cove was a distinct advantage. Strabo (*Geographica* III.3.7) specifically states that the Iberians 'used boats of tanned leather on account of the flood tides and shoal waters'. The usual mental image of a hide boat is of a flimsy, circular one-man *currach* propelled by a paddle meandering along a river. While such vessels undoubtedly existed one must not forget that there would potentially have been a wide diversity of *currach* types in existence from small one-man paddle vessels to large sea-going vessels up to 17 m long capable of carrying large cargoes measured in terms of tonnes and powered primarily by sail. A vessel similar to that represented in the Broighter boat model would have performed well at sea and would have been capable of carrying a considerable cargo. In addition to the steering oar, mast and yard depicted in the Broighter model, it is likely that sea-going Iron Age *currachs* had keels – Caesar makes mention of keels when he orders hide boats to be built during the Civil War in Spain based on the type he had seen in Britain a few years earlier (*Bello Civili* 1.54). *Currachs* with keels and sails are described in the sixth/seventh century AD text *Vita St. Columba* (Adomnán II.45; Anderson and Anderson 1961: 452) while large keeled *currachs* displaying all the technical sophistication of wooden built vessels and capable of carrying considerable cargoes were still in use in Irish waters in the late seventeenth century AD (Marcus 1980: 12–13; Cunliffe 2001: 67, fig. 3.2). The modern day tarred canvas currachs of the Atlantic seaboard of Ireland are primarily smaller-scale oared craft – the small sail where present merely acting as an auxiliary – but they remain ideally suited to Atlantic sailing conditions and are capable of taking loads of around 2 tonnes. Stories abound about the dexterity and skill of modern currach crews and the performance of their resilient craft in sea conditions considered far too rough for other types of vessel (Synge 1907: 97–8; Marcus 1980: 3–4, 12–15).

The existence of plank-built boats is attested to from freshwater river finds in north-western Europe (McGrail 1995: 265–6, 2001: 184–91). In England and Wales sections of some 11 sewn-plank boats are known from the Humber estuary (Ferriby, Brigg and Kilnsea); the Severn estuary (Caldicot and Goldcliff); the Test estuary (Testwood); and from the River Dour at Dover (McGrail 2006: 35–9). Taken as a group these technically sophisticated vessels date from *c.* 1900 BC to *c.* 400 BC. In common with Atlantic prehistoric logboat finds, however, all of the freshwater plank boats discovered to date lack evidence for sail attachments and feature insufficient freeboard (height of sides above waterline) and transverse stability to have been used safely at sea except under extremely calm conditions (McGrail 1995: 261–4, 2004: 57–60). However, the technical competence and expertise needed to construct these craft coupled with advanced features such as the plank-keel on the Ferriby 1 boat (Wright 1990) suggests that the capacity to produce vessels capable of sailing in open water existed during the Iron Age. The lack of evidence for maritime examples, as discussed above, is necessarily a problem of survival in turbulent Atlantic environments, as from Caesar's description of the ships of the Veneti in his *Bellum Gallicum* we can be sure that there were plank-built boats with sails in Atlantic waters by the late Iron Age. The fact that the Venetic ships described by Caesar, with their leather sails, flush-laid oak planking and 'seaweed' caulking (*Bellum Gallicum* III.11-16), appear to have been better equipped to deal with Atlantic sea conditions than the Roman vessels, and that Caesar goes on to compliment the seamanship of the Venetic sailors, implies that there had been a strong maritime tradition in existence in this area for a considerable period of time (Weatherhill 1985b). A further indication of the existence of substantial sea-going Iron Age vessels can be inferred from a large iron anchor with 6.5 m of attached chain found in a Late Iron Age context at the hillfort of Bulbury, not far from Poole Harbour in Dorset (Cunliffe 1972).

In addition, there are representations of ships on coins from the late Iron Age. A first-century BC Atrebates gold coin features a representation of an indigenous sailing ship which, although very stylistic, portrays a vessel with a relatively deep hull and a bow projection (McGrail 1990: 43; Figure 2.6). Other ships known from later AD issues such as those on two bronze coins issued in the first century AD by Cunobelin of the Catuvellauni of south-eastern Britain which depict deep hulled merchant ships propelled by square sails capable of carrying large cargoes (Muckelroy *et al.* 1978; McGrail 1995: 267; Figure 2.6).

The technical features of a dozen or so boats dating to the first to third centuries AD from the Severn and Thames estuaries, Guernsey, the lower reaches of the Rhine, and from the Swiss lakes appear to echo elements of Caesar's description of the Venetic ships (McGrail 2001: 196–7). This has led McGrail (1981: 23–4) to claim that these vessels can

  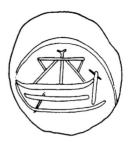

Figure 2.6 Drawings of the ships represented on the first century BC Atrebates gold coin (left), and the first century AD Cunobelin coins from Canterbury (middle) and Sheepen (right) (after McGrail 1990: figs. 4.9 and 4.12)

be differentiated as a group from the contemporary Mediterranean and northern European traditions and that as such they reflect the existence of what he terms a distinct 'Romano-Celtic' boat-building tradition. In particular these boats differ from other styles in being constructed frame first, and although the use of sawn planking probably reflects Roman influence, all the other technical features, such as the use of plank-keels, appear to be indigenous (McGrail 2004: 62–3). The fully realised technical features of these boats suggest that this north-western European boat-building tradition had evolved over a long period of time beginning well before the arrival of the Romans. Further support for the existence of a separate maritime tradition comes from recent discussions about the derivations of the word for 'sail' used in Celtic languages having an indigenous and possible pre-Roman conquest origin (Thier 2003; Sayers 2004).

Atlantic maritime capability

The current corpus of evidence suggests that long-distance maritime communications were possible and well within the technological capabilities of indigenous Atlantic societies; this does not, however, lead automatically to a hyper-diffusionist conclusion that there was constant sea travel in the area. Present arguments focus on the potential existence of sophisticated sea-going vessels in Atlantic waters, but there is no solid evidence in the form of a surviving wooden hull and, given the turbulent conditions of the Atlantic mentioned above, such evidence is unlikely to be forthcoming in the near future. Our knowledge of first millennium AD northern European maritime technology, where vessels and written sources actually exist, is still extremely limited, making discussions about the actual features of potential Iron Age vessels nothing more than speculation (Wooding 1996: 21). On saying this, the evidence that does exist, though largely circumstantial, strongly indicates that indigenous Atlantic groups were capable of long-distance maritime travel from the Late Bronze Age and certainly had a developed boat-building technology in place by the close of the first millennium BC.

In the following chapters, we shall consider the evidence for similarities between Atlantic communities and what these similarities indicate in terms of the existence and scale of maritime contacts between Atlantic areas.

3 The Atlantic Late Bronze Age (1200–600 BC)

Introduction

From *c.* 1200 BC onwards there was a major increase in the scale of contacts along the Atlantic seaboard, archaeologically visible through the widespread deposition of related bronze metalwork forms. Prior to this time long-distance contacts between Atlantic communities were symbolic, involved relatively small amounts of material, and were presumably negotiated at an elite gift exchange level. By the Late Bronze Age, and especially from 900 BC, this contact appears to have intensified to something approaching a mercantile trade level. Accompanying the exchange in metalwork we can detect important changes in the activities and concerns of Atlantic communities which laid the foundations for the development of the Iron Age societies and ways of life discussed later in the book.

The chronological and regional phases of the Atlantic Late Bronze Age are identified almost exclusively through industrial metalwork traditions. These have been well defined elsewhere (Briard 1965; Burgess 1968; Coffyn 1985; Brun 1991) and are only briefly discussed below. The ins-and-outs of metal typology do not concern us here, as whether it was the actual objects themselves or the idea of the objects that was communicated is unimportant for our present purpose – each infers that cultural contact and a level of common development was in place. I shall begin by sketching the broad networks of exchange and the resulting similarities in metalwork styles. It would be impossible to examine the full complexity of the Atlantic Late Bronze Age in just one chapter so here my emphasis will be on the northern part of the zone concentrating on the areas discussed later in the book. This chapter is intended as nothing more than a broad outline, and to consider two major points: the recognition of the Atlantic as an interaction zone that can be clearly distinguished from the continental zones to the east; and perhaps more importantly, insight into how these contacts created similarities between Atlantic communities which resulted in them sharing, at a broad level, collective identities and modes of behaviour discrete from those in existence elsewhere in Europe.

There was not, of course, cultural uniformity between Atlantic communities, and similarities between them waxed and waned at various times throughout the period. However, during the Late Bronze Age it is possible to define regional traditions occurring within a broader Atlantic continuum. This is clearly seen in the development of Late Bronze Age regional centres of bronze production. These centres are recognisable from the distribution and form of metalwork types and are inter-connected through regular maritime contacts to form a functioning trade network. One of the problems in trying to define a generalised Atlantic metalwork tradition, or set of criteria applicable to all the Atlantic coastal areas, is that each regional area, each localised system, has its own indigenous character and is subject to its own internal stimuli creating considerable diversity along the seaboard. For example, most areas produce their own range of metalwork which are distinctive enough to be easily recognisable as indigenous forms and representative of particular areas and traditions. Nevertheless, at a broader level, they are executed within general Atlantic conventions and, taken as part of a whole, can be differentiated from west-central European Urnfield forms.

Essentially the Atlantic can be defined archaeologically on the basis of metalwork finds as a large-scale cultural complex created through the interconnection of regional spheres of interaction, themselves created through the exchange and depositional activities of local groupings. As Brun (1993: 172) states, 'a cultural complex is a zone of relative stylistic uniformity, made up of nested sub-sets. In the current state of research we can distinguish within a complex groups of cultures, cultures and cultural groups'. In other words, different identities can be defined through the association of metalwork types depending on the level of abstraction used. Following Brun (1991) and Kristiansen (1998: 66–7) one can define, for example, the overall cultural complex as western Europe; the cultural tradition, based on metalwork styles, as Atlantic; a regional tradition as, for example, Atlantic Scotland; and a local tradition reflecting the output of perhaps one or more workshops as, in this case, the Western Isles (Caledonian or Minch tradition) (Figure 3.1). The stylistic regularity of the metalwork produced throughout the Atlantic zone suggests that at least some cultural and social values may have been common to all Atlantic communities. Metalwork was produced and exchanged according to accepted conventions on how things should look and ultimately be used in the ritual and social spheres. Material forms of Atlantic origin can be quite clearly differentiated from Urnfield material providing clear evidence for the existence of separate cultural complexes (Figure 3.2).

The formation of regional identities with defined boundaries and interaction across them are a characteristic feature of Late Bronze and Early Iron Age Europe (Kristiansen 1998: 85–94). At boundaries between separate cultural traditions differences are often more forcefully displayed than elsewhere. Brun (1993) has identified the existence of a boundary between Urnfield and Atlantic traditions in north-west France[1] (Figure 3.3). He defines a buffer zone, some 60 kilometres wide, visible through the high concentration of metalwork (single finds, hoards and river deposits) which crucially consists of central European Urnfield and Atlantic forms (Brun 1993: fig. 17.3). The zone also contains hillforts which, taken with the increase in metalwork deposition of both traditions, have led Brun to consider the zone as an area of political instability where differences between cultural groups are clearly marked. In such areas relations can become conflictual and may result in reciprocal exclusion. Equally, however, boundaries may be 'a neutral zone between two regional traditions where exchange took place at specialised settlements (e.g. hillforts).

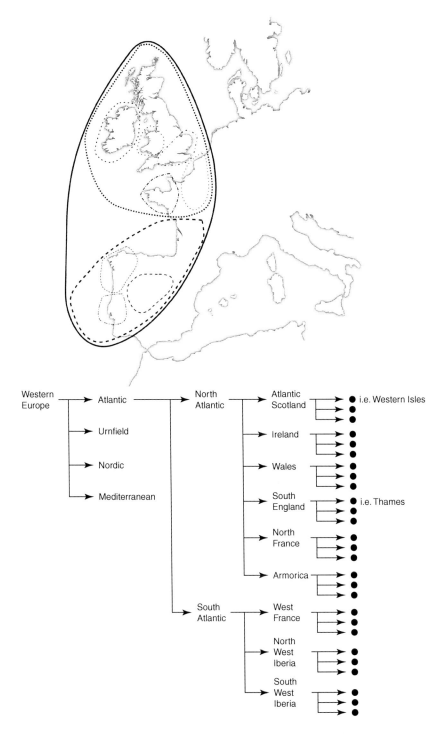

Figure 3.1 Regional traditions and sub-sets of the Atlantic Late Bronze Age as suggested by Patrice Brun (after Brun 1991: figs. 3 and 4).

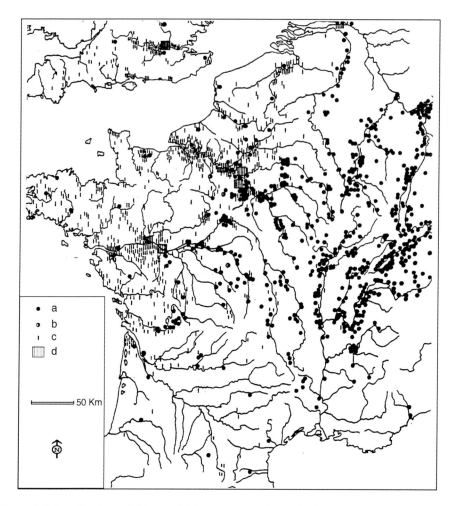

Figure 3.2 Distribution of objects of Atlantic type and Urnfield type (north-Alpine) at the beginning of the Late Bronze Age (after Brun 1998: fig. 3.): (a) objects of north-Alpine type; (b) mixed hoards with objects from both traditions; (c) objects of Atlantic type; (d) refers to zones with concentrations of hoards in or near rivers (the majority of which are of Atlantic type).

Local (mixed) boundary cultures may develop over time, just as the boundaries may shift in a process of political expansion' (Kristiansen 1998: 87).

Chronology

The chronology of the Late Bronze Age is entirely dependent on the typological divisions of metalwork within a given region. Metalwork is usually dated by

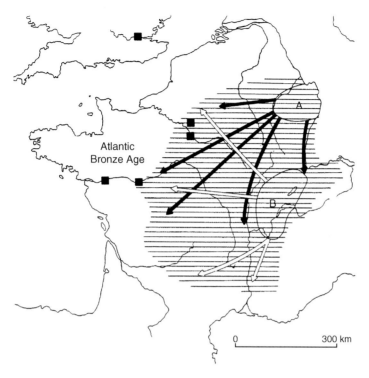

Figure 3.3 Two phases (A and B) of later Urnfield expansion into France from the western Rhine-Swiss group, followed by boundary formation between the Urnfield tradition (hatched) and the Atlantic tradition (unhatched), characterised by concentrations of hoards (squares) (after Kristiansen 1998: fig. 41; after Brun 1988: figs. 3, 4 and 6).

association with forms from the few reliably dated hoards (see Brun 1991 for a list of these; Burgess 1968; Megaw 1979: 242–343; Needham 1996; Champion 1999: 96) or through association with types, or styles, of central European or Mediterranean origin whose dating is considered more secure. Recently a number of British Bronze Age metalwork forms with attached organics were subject to a programme of radiocarbon dating which, although it generally confirmed the accepted chronological divisions, extended the use of some types back by as much as one and a half centuries (Needham *et al.* 1997). Similar systematic dating programmes have yet to be applied to Irish, French and Spanish material. As a result the absolute dating of chronological phases is somewhat uncertain and they are best considered as roughly dated stages in the general development of metalworking. Equally the lack of archaeological associations accompanying the vast majority of metalwork finds makes a chronological system dependent on them of limited use. In terms of dating domestic settlements to the Late Bronze Age radiocarbon remains the most useful technique.

This chapter deals with the northern half of the Atlantic coastal zone from Armorica to Scotland during the period from *c.* 1250 to the beginning of the Iron Age in the Atlantic – generally considered to be around the seventh century BC. The chronological phases in each regional area, named after characteristic metalwork assemblages (which in turn are named after the findspots of actual hoards), are roughly contemporary with some overlap. They are arranged chronologically in Figure 3.4. The chronology of the Atlantic Iron Age is discussed in Chapter 4.

Atlantic Late Bronze Age exchange

Atlantic Late Bronze Age contacts appear to form two main networks of exchange (Brun 1991; Figure 3.1): one in the north centred on southern England and north-west France but including Wales, Ireland and, to a much lesser extent, Atlantic Scotland (Burgess 1968); and a southern zone centred on north-western Iberia tied mainly into northern Atlantic networks but also with some contacts to the

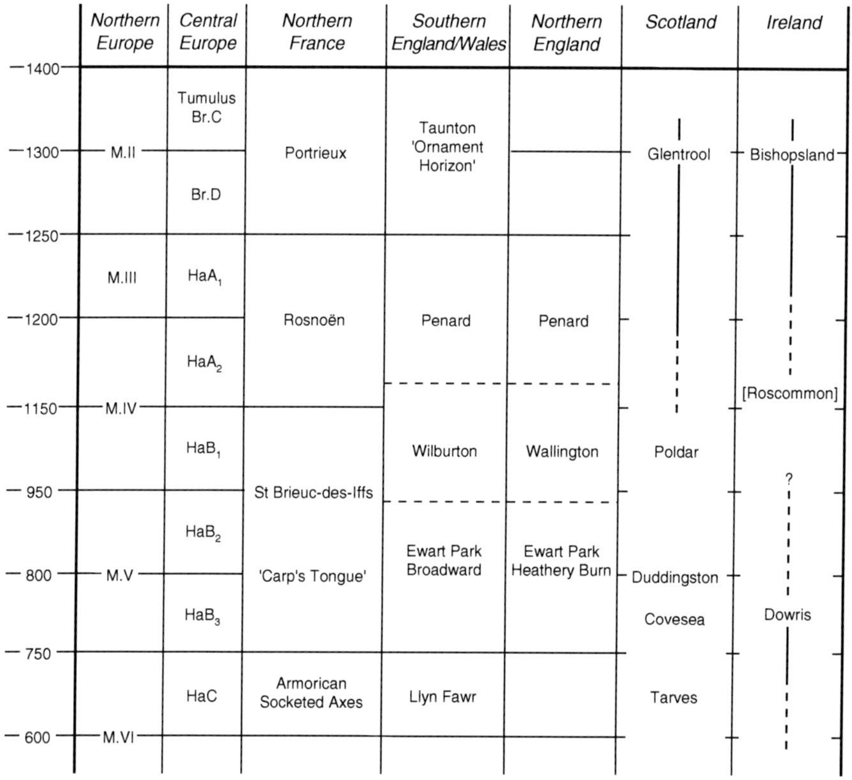

	Northern Europe	Central Europe	Northern France	Southern England/Wales	Northern England	Scotland	Ireland
−1400							
		Tumulus Br.C		Taunton 'Ornament Horizon'			
−1300	M.II		Portrieux			Glentrool	Bishopsland
		Br.D					
−1250							
	M.III	HaA₁					
−1200			Rosnoën	Penard	Penard		
		HaA₂					
−1150	M.IV						[Roscommon]
		HaB₁		Wilburton	Wallington	Poldar	
− 950			St Brieuc-des-Iffs				?
		HaB₂		Ewart Park Broadward	Ewart Park Heathery Burn		
− 800	M.V		'Carp's Tongue'			Duddingston	
		HaB₃				Covesea	Dowris
− 750							
		HaC	Armorican Socketed Axes	Llyn Fawr		Tarves	
− 600	M.VI						

Figure 3.4 Chronology of the Atlantic Late Bronze Age.

Mediterranean world (Burgess 1991; Chevillot and Coffyn 1991; Ruíz-Gálvez 1997; Gibson 2000). It is the northern areas, centred on north-west France and south-east England, at the end of the second millennium BC (*c.* 1200–900 BC) which first provide evidence of Atlantic exchange through related metal forms and ceramics (O'Connor 1980). From this initial centre of metalworking, networks of exchange expanded from the ninth century BC to include almost the whole Atlantic seaboard from Scotland to western Iberia.

Late Bronze Age cultural areas are generally defined by the regional styles and variants of common utilitarian items such as tools (axes, knives, sickles, gouges, etc.). Superimposed upon these it is possible to recognise a wider circulation of elite metalwork (weapons and feasting items). The distribution of these high status items reveals the existence of long-distance contacts between regional groups along the Atlantic coasts (Figures 3.5 and 3.6). Underlying these long-distance contacts we can envisage multiple small-scale networks of interlocking regional exchange at work up and down the Atlantic coastline. The basic form of exchange, and indeed the basis of similarities along the Atlantic, would have been down-the-line neighbour-to-neighbour interaction, but we cannot underestimate the possible regularity of direct long-distance contacts between particular areas.[2] The regional stylistic traditions and concentrations of deposited elite goods reveal centres in Ireland, south-east England, Armorica and north-west Iberia. Outside these centres we encounter generalised Atlantic metalwork distributions.

Atlantic contacts c. 1200–950 BC: northern beginnings

From the beginning of the Late Bronze Age *c.* 1200 BC to 1000 BC there are close connections between the regional metalwork traditions known as Rosnoën (north-western France), Saint-Just-en-Chausée (northern France), Taunton/Penard (southern England and Wales) and late Bishopsland/Roscommon (Ireland), each of which has a range of types in common. Concentrations of shared Penard types such as Ballintober swords, cylinder-socketed sickles and basal looped spearheads imply that areas in Ireland and south-east England (centred on the Thames) were in direct contact, with intermediate finds suggesting the traffic went through south Wales (Figure 3.7). Equally, the southern English Penard group has strong associations with the north-western French Rosnoën group such as the common occurrence of straight-bladed and leaf-shaped swords with hilt tangs. Sword finds from the Thames demonstrate the strong links south-east England had with both Ireland and northern France. For example, Chelsea style swords resemble Irish Ballintober forms while the Lambeth form has close parallels with French straight-bladed Rosnoën swords[3] further seen in their shared shoulder styles (Figure 3.8).

These connections continue through *c.* 1000 BC to 800 BC with strong similarities visible between the Saint-Brieuc-des-Iffs (northern France), Wilburton (southern England) and Roscommon/Dowris (Ireland) traditions. V-shouldered leaf-shaped swords with a more emphasised leaf than those of the continental Hemigkofen and Erbenheim types are found in all three groups including examples from the Thames and the Seine with curved ricassos (Figure 3.9). Spears with lunate openings, long tongue chapes and tubular spear ferrules are characteristic of the

Figure 3.5 Distribution of Irish cauldrons (▼), Breton sickles (■) and double looped axes (●) (after Coffyn *et al.* 1981: carte 25).

Wilburton and Saint-Brieuc-des-Iffs groups but are found earlier in the Irish Roscommon hoard which is usually dated to between 1100 and 1000 BC but favouring a date towards the latter end of the range (Eogan 1964: 288–93, 1965). Developed palstaves are another important feature of this period, while socketed axes appear in Atlantic areas for the first time (later these develop into the ubiquitous Armorican socketed axe form).

Although Wilburton material is more common in Ireland than in northern England, Wales or Scotland, demonstrating the existence of connections with south-east

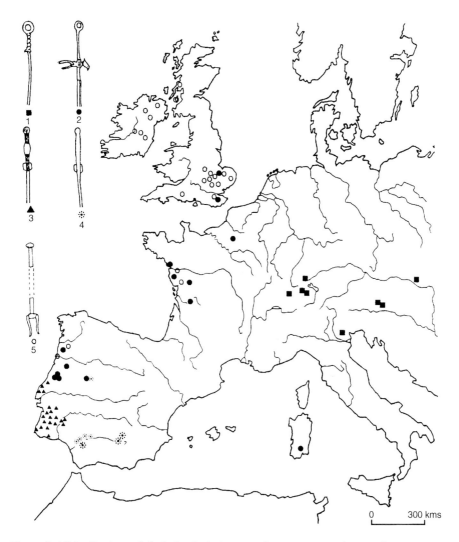

Figure 3.6 Distribution of flesh hooks/spits according to type (after Coffyn *et al.* 1981: carte 28): (1) Continental; (2) Atlantic; (3) south-west Iberian; (4) south-east Iberian.

England and north-western France (Coombs 1989), it certainly seems that Irish links with the latter areas declined during this period compared to the proceeding Bishopsland/Penard phase. Eogan (1964) has termed this period in Ireland the Roscommon phase, but his term has not gained wide acceptance because it is based on a limited body of evidence consisting of only two hoards,[4] a couple of dozen Wilburton swords, and a small number of stray spearheads, ferrules and tongue chapes. Despite the dominance of Wilberton forms, the occurrence of Wallington

Figure 3.7 Distribution of Ballintober swords and related weapons (after Burgess 1968: fig. 7).

material in Ireland, particularly transitional palstaves and square-mouthed socketed axes, illustrate the existence of links with northern England (Burgess 1968: 14).

Other areas of Britain were not as fully involved with the metalwork innovations and exchange visible between southern England, north-western France, and to a lesser extent Ireland. If anything Ireland, northern England, and Scotland form something of an outer Atlantic exchange zone at this time. North of the Humber, Wilburton types become rare and bronze technology appears to be of a more archaic form.

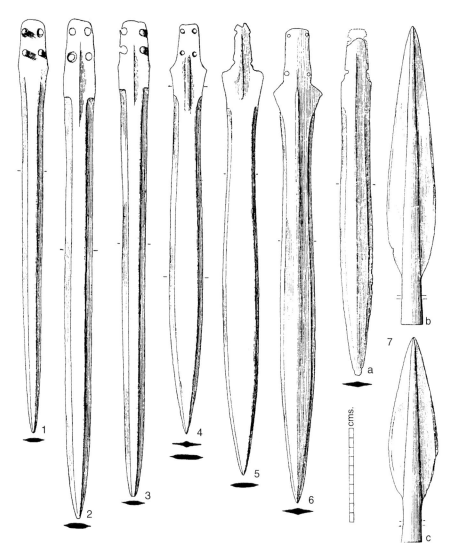

Figure 3.8 Penard-Rosnoën groups (after Burgess 1968: fig. 3). Findspots: (1) Thames at Lambeth; (2) Thames at Kingston; (3) Seine at Rouen; (4) Thames at Chelsea; (5) Pont de Primel, Nantes; (6) Ballintober, Co. Mayo; (7a, b, c) Worth hoard, Devon.

The Wallington complex consists of earlier Penard style items, and significantly, even some pre-Penard style items are still in use. Interestingly, while southern England and northern France switch to lead-bronze in the tenth century BC, the areas in the outer Atlantic zone continue to use tin-bronze, further illustrating their conservative and comparatively indigenous nature[5] (Burgess 1968: 13). Compared to northern England, Wilburton types are more common in Scotland, where the metalwork traditions are termed the Poldar phase (Coles 1960). However, once again older

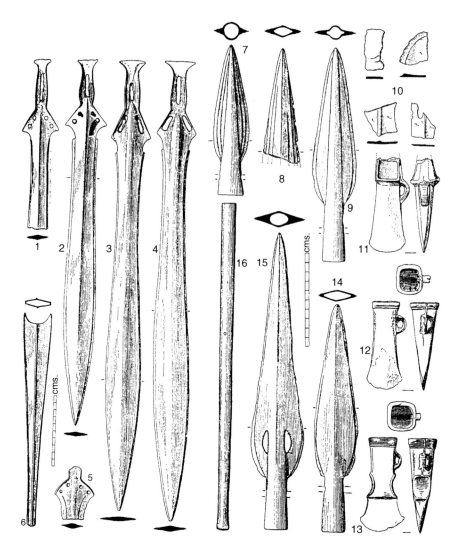

Figure 3.9 Wilberton-St Brieuc des Iffs groups (after Burgess 1968: fig. 9). Findspots: (1) St Anne de Campbon Brivet, Loire Atlantique; (2) Thames at Sion Reach; (3) Thames at Battersea; (4) Seine at Paris; (5) Kerguerou hoard, Finistère; (6, 9, 10, 11, 14, 15, 16) Guilsfield hoard, Wales; (7) Walthamstow, Essex; (8) Unprovenanced; (12, 13) Wilburton hoard, Cambridgeshire.

traditions are dominant and it is possible that some of the Wilburton finds actually post-date the Wilburton phase (Burgess 1968: 14).

Atlantic contacts c. 950–600 BC: intensification

By the middle of the ninth century BC there is an increase in the amounts of metal moving through exchange networks and in the amounts of metalwork being produced in all areas. This increase is pan-European occurring not only in the Atlantic zone but also in the Mediterranean, Urnfield and Nordic zones. There appears to be a general opening up of contacts at this time and certain objects are exchanged over larger areas than in earlier phases. Previously, for example, Wilburton swords were mainly concentrated in south-eastern England but from the middle of the ninth century BC the Wilburton's successor, the Ewart Park sword (Cowen 1967), a similarly indigenous, British leaf-shaped sword, and its related types are the standard form throughout the whole of the British Isles and Ireland (Figure 3.10). The distribution of this sword demonstrates that there were links between all the metalworking traditions throughout Britain. By the end of the eighth century BC a wide variety of weapons, tools, prestige goods and ornaments were being 'manufactured and traded on an unprecedented scale, vigorous local production centres maintained high standards of inventiveness, and a common market existed between Britain and Atlantic Europe' (Cunliffe 1991, 56).

From *c.* 950 to 650 BC the Wilburton group in south-east England and the St Brieuc-des-Iffs group in north-western France are replaced by the Atlantic Carp's Tongue sword industry (Savory 1948). The term is used to designate a parallel sided sword strengthened by a marked central rib which narrows sharply towards the point, similar, one is led to believe, to a carp's tongue – the metaphor is further extended by the fact that these swords often had pommels in the shape of fish tails. Unlike the leaf-shaped swords which could be quite varied, the Carp's Tongue swords were made to a set design and had few variants. The distribution of these swords is the most vivid example of Atlantic exchange and can be considered the climax in Atlantic metalwork and its ritual deposition (Figure 3.11). Hundreds of complete examples exist and if we include the fragments found in hoards we can estimate that thousands were made (Briard 1979: 201). The main centres of production appear again to have been initially north-western France, where the style most likely originated (Megaw 1979: 315), and south-east England, but the Carp's Tongue sword marks the opening up of Atlantic contacts to the south and important production centres flourish along the French Atlantic seaboard and in north-western Iberia. In fact, Carp's Tongue swords have a vast distribution and are found from south-east England, through northern Germany, to the south-east Iberian peninsula. Some were even exported to the Mediterranean with variations of these swords recorded in Italy and in the Nuraghic culture of Sardinia, testifying to the extensive nature of the bronze trade by the eighth century BC (Briard 1979: 202).

One of the most striking developments at this time is the expansion of trade networks southwards (Savory 1949). Although there is evidence for Atlantic exchange prior to this in southern areas, they became involved more slowly and the amounts of material traded were relatively small meaning that for the most part southern communities developed independently. The distribution of Carp's Tongue swords and their related forms clearly demonstrate that from at least 950 BC Atlantic exchange networks involving significant amounts of material extended as far as western Iberia. Equally, the uniformity of the Carp's Tongue style throughout Atlantic facing areas supports the existence of shared concepts between Atlantic communities which contrast with those of west-central Europe.

Figure 3.10 Ewart Park and related swords (after Burgess 1968: fig. 12).

Carp's Tongue sword styles in south-east England develop in tandem with those in western France and are often accompanied by a new assemblage of objects known collectively as the Carp's Tongue Complex.[6] This new assemblage includes a number of new and innovatory forms such as bag shaped chapes, knives (hog's back and triangular), socketed axes, socketed knives, pegged and socketed spearheads, end-winged axes, chisels and gouges, and a number of decorative attachments such as 'bugle-shaped' objects and other unidentified objects, some of which may be horse gear (Figure 3.12).

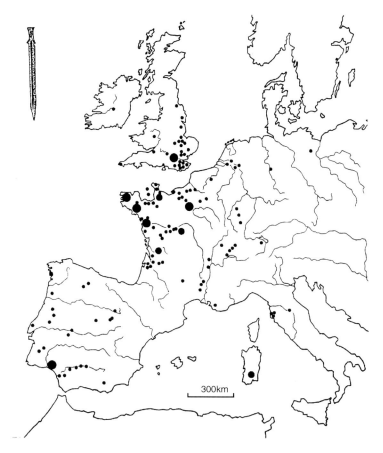

Figure 3.11 The distribution of Carp's Tongue Swords. Larger symbols indicate hoards where several swords where found (after Kristiansen 1998: fig. 74; after Coffyn 1985: carte 18).

Carp's Tongue swords and other Atlantic forms are found along the coastal regions of northern France and Belgium which formed an exchange zone with south-central and south-eastern England throughout the period, essentially linking the Seine and the Rhine with the Thames (Cunliffe 1997: 149). The exchange seems to be centred on bronze as a raw material, tantalising evidence of which comes from the Dover and Saltcombe wrecks (Muckleroy 1980, 1981), as further inland these continental areas become fully Urnfield in character.

On the western coasts of France, from the Vendée to the Gironde, communities display strong cultural affinities with the central French Urnfield Rhine-Swiss-French Group (Briard 1974; Brun 1988) especially in terms of ceramic styles. The metalwork in these areas, however, is firmly orientated towards the Atlantic.

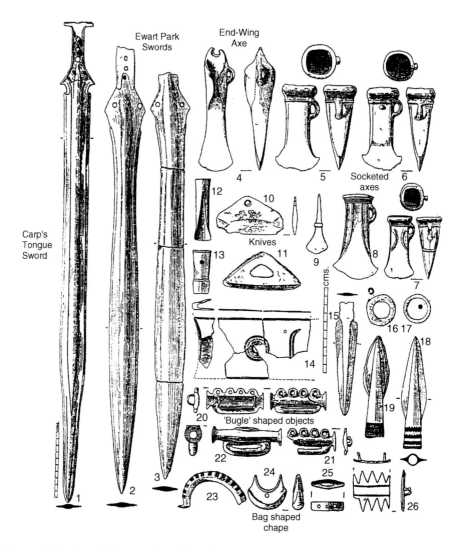

Figure 3.12   Carp's Tongue Complex (after Burgess 1968: fig. 13). Findspots: (1) River Thames; (2) Unprovenanced; (3, 12, 14, 22, 25, 26) Watford hoard, Hertfordshire; (4) Thames at Brentford; (5) Thames at Battersea; (6) Unprovenanced; (7) Thames at Old England; (8, 13, 23) Menez Tosta hoard, Finistère; (9) La Torche, Plomeur, Finistère; (10) Leigh-on-Sea hoard II, Essex; (11) Eaton hoard, Norwich; (15) Unprovenanced; (16, 17) Plessé hoard, Loire Atlantique; (18) Chingford Reservoir, Essex; (19) Vern en Moëlan hoard, Finistère; (20) Prairie de Mauves hoard, Nantes; (21) Thames at Sion Reach; (24) Levington hoard, Suffolk.

The situation is perhaps best summed up by the most famous hoard from this area, the Vénat hoard, which dates to the Late Bronze Age/Early Iron Age transition. The hoard displays a wide range of influences from all over Europe but is ultimately dominated by Atlantic items, most notably the Vénat forms of Carp's Tongue swords (Figure 3.13).

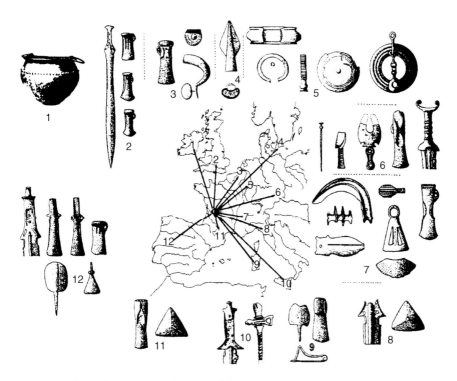

Figure 3.13 The wide European relations of the Vénat hoard (after Kristiansen 1998: fig. 77).

The cultural affinities of coastal communities further to the south-west of France and in the Basque region of Spain are much less clear owing to a lack of archaeological evidence. This is partly due to the lack of fieldwork in these areas, but it may also indicate that these areas were not fully part of Atlantic trading routes. The sea in the southern part of the Bay of Biscay has a formidable reputation today for being rough, and we can assume that conditions in the Late Bronze Age were similar or even slightly worse (especially towards the end of the period and on into the Iron Age). The projected peninsula to peninsula movement of ships put forward in Chapter 2 may have meant that a route from Ushant to Galicia and vice versa would have made more sense, thus isolating north-eastern Spain and south-western France from main Atlantic routes. Equally, the areas south of the Gironde may have had very little to offer trading groups because they were isolated not only from maritime routes of communication through rough seas but also from those on land due the Cantabrian and Pyrenees mountain ranges on their landward side. This geographical predicament was undoubtedly a factor in the continued cultural isolation of these areas well into the historical period.

There is evidence of wider Atlantic contacts during the earlier megalithic and Argaric periods in western Iberia but by the Middle Bronze Age these seem to have dislocated and coastal communities appear more introverted and isolated. By the beginning of the Late Bronze Age, however, Atlantic bronze forms are once again seen along Atlantic Iberian coasts, with the largest concentrations of types seen in the north-west where palstaves, socketed axes and spears, and variable Rosnoën type leaf-shaped swords are recorded whose closest parallels are with the north-western French Saint-Denis-de-Pile Group (Coffyn 1985; Brun 1991). It is widely accepted that Atlantic relations in western Iberia began on a small scale around 1250 BC (Almagro-Gorbea 1977, 1986; Kalb 1980; Ruíz-Gálvez 1984, 1995) but that the area was not fully incorporated into Atlantic exchange networks until after 1000 BC – again most spectacularly seen through the distribution of Carp's Tongue sword forms (Almagro-Gorbea 1977: 345; Coffyn and Sion 1993).

Carp's Tongue swords are found throughout the Iberian region and are representative of how established contacts between Iberian and north-western Atlantic metalworkers were from the ninth century BC onwards (Ruíz-Gálvez 1987, 1995). The most prolific variations are those discovered from the hoards of south-western Spain (Huelva), from Charente (Vénat) and from the island of Sardinia (Monte Sa Idda), providing some indication of the range of the Carp's Tongue form (Fernández-Castro 1995: 145–7, fig. 10.1). From 950 BC until *c.* 650 BC there is a steady increase in the production of metal objects in western Iberia along with considerable evidence for the use of Iberian metal sources (Northover 1982; Bradley 1988; Ruíz-Gálvez 1989a).

The evidence for Atlantic contacts in Iberia corresponds with evidence for contacts between Iberia and the central Mediterranean (Almagro-Gorbea 1977; Coffyn 1983, 1985; Ruíz-Gálvez 1992) and with the establishment of larger and more complex settlement forms in many parts of northern and central Portugal and south-western Spain. There can be little doubt that the Mediterranean world was fully aware of the Atlantic sea-lanes through contacts with western Iberia either directly or, more likely, through Phoenician traders who had a trading centre based at Gadir (Cádiz). It was most likely via these contacts that a number of Atlantic products reached the communities of the Mediterranean.

Atlantic Iberia can be split into two main zones (Cunliffe 1997: 149): north-western Iberia (including Galicia, Asturia and Cantabria) looking to the northern Atlantic zone; and south-western Iberia (a zone from the Tagus to the lower Guadalquivir) with strong links to the Mediterranean. North-western Iberia is defined by gold and tin resources, distinctive stone-built roundhouse settlements or *castros*, and in terms of access to metalwork forms, appears to have been fully linked to the Atlantic trading network from at least 900 BC. Conversely the ceramics of the area most closely resemble those of the inland Meseta (Las Cogotas) cultures, but no metal products correspond between the two areas. The communities of south-western Iberia have access to copper and silver deposits and sit precariously between the Atlantic and Mediterranean worlds (Gibson 2000). By the time of the Huelva hoard in the ninth century BC contacts are in existence from Ireland to

Sardinia and central Italy. Interestingly, despite the existence of Mediterranean colonists, the area retains cultural, ethnic and linguistic links with the Atlantic Bronze Age world (Bradley 1997; Kristiansen 1998), perhaps most visible through the occurrence of warrior stelae and distinctive burnished ceramic styles (Galán Domingo 1993).

Despite their wide Atlantic coastal distribution, Carp's Tongue swords in the British Isles were restricted almost exclusively to south-east England. It is the associated Carp's Tongue objects, not the swords themselves, that illustrate the existence of links between the southern English industries and the rest of the British and Irish industries. South-east England looked more fully towards the wider Atlantic European world, while the picture in the rest of Britain was one of increasing regionalism in metalwork styles superimposed upon which there is some limited evidence of forms travelling significant distances between different industrial zones and along Atlantic routes. For example, objects from outside the south-eastern Carp's Tongue area, such as Ewart Park swords and 'South Welsh' socketed axes, are found in French hoards (Burgess 1968: 19).

From 750 to 650 BC then, various different regional industries can be identified throughout Atlantic Britain and Ireland with different metalwork types apparently dominant in each area. Weapon hoards and horse gear become common throughout Britain, suggesting a widespread adherence to warrior values at this time (see later discussion). In southern England, outside the Carp's Tongue area, barbed spears of the Broadward type are dominant; throughout the Midlands the majority of hoards also contain Broadward spears or similar forms; while in northern England, hoards are dominated by swords especially of the Ewart Park type; in Ireland spears were fashionable during the Dowris phase and leaf-shaped forms with lunate openings in the blade are an undoubted Atlantic type with related examples known in Scotland, England, France and Spain (Waddell 1998: 239). It is perhaps worth mentioning that the further one travels away from the Carp's Tongue Complex area in the south-east, the rarer weaponry becomes, perhaps reflecting a weakening in the impact of warrior values and ideology. In Ireland and Scotland domestic hoards are more common[7] than weapon hoards (Coles 1960; Eogan 1983).

Throughout the Late Bronze Age Ireland is the major Atlantic centre of gold production and was perhaps more gold-producing than bronze-receiving (Waddell 1998). High quality gold objects, found singly and in hoards, are known from the Bishopsland phase onwards, but it is during the Dowris phase (Eogan 1964: 293), from *c.* 800 BC to 600 BC, that we see a dramatic increase in the production and sheer workmanship of Irish goldwork. The uniquely Irish style of many of the objects, which include personal ornaments, torcs, bracelets, earrings and dress rings, along with the spectacular sheet gold metalwork, reveal contacts with Britain and north-west Europe. Indeed, a good many of the objects produced in Ireland can be found exchanged along a northern Atlantic axis (Figure 3.14).

Moving away from the goldwork, Ireland is also an important bronzeworking centre during the Dowris phase, displaying advanced casting and sheet metalworking techniques through the production of prestige objects such as the Dowris Bucket,

Figure 3.14 Distribution of Gold Bar Torcs (after Waddell 1998: 74).

complex horns and a series of Atlantic cauldrons (see later discussion); 80 per cent of all Irish hoards belong to the Dowris period.[8] A number of less exotic bronze objects from the Dowris phase display direct parallels with industries in Britain such as the occurrence of Irish Ewart Park sword variations, short chapes comparable to those found in the Broadward tradition, bag shaped chapes of Carp's Tongue Complex affinity and various forms of Irish socketed axe directly comparable to types in northern England and Scotland.

Scotland is not generally considered in general overviews of the Atlantic Bronze Age. Whilst it is true that it was not directly connected to the main Atlantic networks, there is an increase in bronze metalwork in areas of Scotland in keeping with developments elsewhere. The regional traditions of the Scottish mainland have been studied (Coles 1960) but the potential of Atlantic maritime contacts have not really been considered in any detail. Instead, Scotland is generally regarded as obtaining its metalwork through mainland routes via the northern English traditions. Much bronzework did undoubtedly arrive from this direction, but the evidence for Atlantic influences arriving via Ireland is also impressive. A consideration of the production of sunflower pins of Irish type at Jarlshof, possibly by an Irish bronzesmith, along with the mould for a Ewart Park sword (Hamilton 1956: 26), quickly puts the possible extent of Atlantic Scottish maritime contacts into context. Evidence for contacts between Ireland and Scotland occur throughout the Late Bronze Age from 1300 BC, during the heavily Irish influenced Glentrool phase, to the appearance of Irish axe forms and Irish gold, including dress fasteners and gold bracelets during the Ewart Park/Duddingston phase (Figure 3.15). The longevity of Atlantic connections between Ireland and Scotland are important to consider given the similarities visible in the Iron Age between areas of Atlantic Scotland and Ireland discussed in Chapter 5.

The Adabrock hoard, found at the northern tip of Lewis, is one of the finest Late Bronze Age hoards in Scotland and includes Irish bronze implements, beads of Irish gold, some Baltic amber, a piece of possibly Mediterranean glass, and a broken bronze cup of most probably central European origin (Coles 1960: 50). Also present were fragments of a beaten bronze vessel, most likely a Class B Atlantic cauldron, which features horizontal grooving patterns under the rim which perhaps echo motifs from earlier Hebridean pottery styles (Armit 1992: 101). There are many finds of hoards or more especially of single bronze objects found mainly deposited in peat bogs throughout the Hebridean island chain and north-western Scottish coastal area. There are enough distinctive bronze swords to define a regional tradition, the 'Minch' or Caledonian tradition (Colquhon and Burgess 1988), which produces swords larger than the other Ewart Park related swords found in Scotland.

Comprehensive metalwork assemblages are known from other Atlantic Scottish coastal areas such as those from Gurness, Orkney Islands and Dunagoil, Isle of Bute (Marshall 1964; Harding 2004: 141–4). Also, numerous metalwork finds have been made in western Scotland (see Coles and Livens 1958) including sword fragments from sandy beach deposits from south-west Scotland to the machair of Lewis.

Figure 3.15 Distribution of Irish gold and bronze 'dress-fasteners' and related bracelets (after Hawkes and Clarke 1963).

Patterns of contact

The study of the distribution of Late Bronze Age metalwork forms allows us to build up a general picture of the main axes of contact between Atlantic regions. Such a picture is, of course, biased by archaeological recovery and there are always a few objects that can indicate direct linkages between specific areas that do not follow the generalised patterns. For example, Savory (1976) discusses metalwork affinities that he argues may indicate direct contacts between the Loire–Gironde estuary region of western France and Welsh coastal areas as far north as Anglesey. Such finds indicate that the networks of relationships taking place are more complex than we can possibly hope to completely reconstruct. It would be possible to call upon a vast amount of typological evidence to indicate specific local interactions and regional exchange systems, the re-contextualisation of certain objects and the rejection of others, but sufficient has been said at this point to indicate that the overall conventions and style of metalwork types are shared between Atlantic areas.

The mineral wealth of Ireland, Wales, Armorica and western Iberia can be cited as being responsible in some part for their status as areas rich enough to acquire significant amounts of metalwork. However, it is clear that south-west England, although rich in tin, does not become an important centre of Atlantic metalwork production or deposition (Pearce 1979, 1983; Christie 1986). South-eastern England, on the other hand, despite not being rich in minerals, does become an important area of metalworking and innovation. It is certain that the Thames area was a major centre of production at this time given the wide range of metalwork deposited there and the fact that the wear and damage of objects appears to increase with distance from the area (Needham and Burgess 1980; Taylor 1982, 1993; Needham 1990). It seems likely that groups in south-east England and Armorica acted as middlemen, exploiting their position between the metal rich Atlantic world and the metal-consuming communities of west-central Europe. Under such a scenario it is plausible that groups in south-central and south-eastern England may have simply used south-west England as a procurement zone for tin. However, it is equally possible that, contrary to expectations created by the later classical references to Cornish tin, the mineral wealth of the area may not have been exploited on any significant scale during the Late Bronze Age.

Armorica maintains a distinctive metalworking identity throughout the Bronze Age (Briard 1979: 17) partly due to its rich mineral resources, particularly tin, and partly to its unique location at the mouth of the Loire, a major route into and out of the continental Urnfield areas of west-central France. Via this confluence Armorica could receive influences and innovations from west-central Europe while remaining firmly anchored in the midst of Atlantic exchange networks, in a very real sense enjoying the best of both worlds. There can be little doubt that groups living on the Armorican peninsula exploited their position and used it to their advantage; new metalwork types and techniques could be obtained from continental Europe and then adapted to suit Atlantic tastes. Indeed, initial metalwork types in Armorica were based on central European types which were then developed into a range of distinctive Atlantic types. This is particularly true of sword styles which were imitated and quickly transformed into Atlantic types.[9]

Armorican metalwork traditions are very much orientated towards the Atlantic façade and it produces a number of objects that become widely popular including the Tréboul group, palstaves of Breton type, arguably Carp's Tongue swords and, as we shall consider later, Armorican socketed axes (Briard 1965). There is little evidence for Urnfield types in Armorica,[10] and it is likely that Urnfield objects were melted down and re-cast into Atlantic types. Groups in Armorica may have been keen to see the conceptual Atlantic/Urnfield boundary remain intact not simply for reason of attached ritual symbolism, but also so that they could continue to exploit both markets. Armorica retains its sense of separateness within an Atlantic tradition in the Iron Age (actively resisting the cultural implications of the material it comes into contact with) and continues to function as a gateway to the Atlantic for continental communities.

As the evidence from Armorica and south-east England suggests, Atlantic metalwork traditions have their roots, and one may perhaps assume gained their attached ritual meaning, in the Urnfield traditions of continental Europe. Central European metalwork types initially inspired Atlantic bronzes which then evolved and developed a distinct character of their own. Both the Atlantic and Nordic areas accepted elements of Urnfield society and ideology in the Late Bronze Age but they were each influenced by strong continuity with earlier indigenous traditions and, as a result, although they accepted some outside influences retained their own identity. The combination of indigenous culture and Urnfield influences created an entirely distinctive cultural zone. At various points evidence of general European influence or actual central European types are found in an Atlantic context. However, the bulk of types are Atlantic and indicate that the main focus of contact was along that axis – in many cases European forms are re-contextualised to fit into Atlantic modes of behaviour. This is a testament to the strength of Atlantic cultural traditions and their sense of separateness from Urnfield and to a lesser extent Nordic traditions. The dynamic between east and west, continental and Atlantic, in Europe is apparent throughout the prehistoric period. However, it is important to keep in mind that these two areas were in constant contact and despite representing different cultural traditions influenced and stimulated each other in what could be termed an ongoing symbiotic relationship.

Trace element analysis of copper has revealed that although sources from western Atlantic areas were used, much of the bronze metalwork of the Wilburton phase in south-eastern England can be traced to distinctive copper deposits in the Alpine area of continental Europe (Northover 1982; Champion 1999: 106). The types produced with the raw material, however, were still distinctively Atlantic in expression with close north-west French and Irish correlates. The bronzes from the Dover wreck cargo (Muckleroy 1980) further demonstrate that north-Alpine material was exported directly towards Atlantic areas, in this case again to southern England (Northover 1982). However, the fact that a number of the forms from the find, such as the median winged axes, are virtually unknown in England reinforces the strength of the existing stylistic traditions, the implication being that they were to have been melted down on arrival and then re-cast into Atlantic types. In other words, it would seem that it was the raw material that was important and desirable, especially in a system where the supply of bronze was presumably unpredictable.[11] Melting down outside types maintained the stylistic boundaries, and in turn the separate social structures, between the Atlantic and continental European worlds.

A number of connections, ideas and concepts were spread throughout Europe suggesting that there was a basic degree of social and ritual correspondence (Coles and Harding 1979: 459–532). In terms of metalwork, the development, use and significance of certain objects including swords, fibulae, razors, beaten bronze drinking buckets and cups crossed cultural tradition barriers within the wider

European cultural complex. For example, rapiers of the eastern European Rixheim type were exported as far west as Brittany and northern France (Briard 1979: 198). However, in most cases Atlantic communities preferred to transform types and technical innovations from the east in their own foundries and workshops to create something new. To follow our example of the Rixheim rapier, similar rapiers were produced in north-west France and southern Britain, called the Rosnoën and Lambeth types respectively, each of which featured similar notches or rivet holes to the eastern examples but crucially the tang of the Atlantic rapiers was rectangular – a detail that allows us to distinguish them from those made in the east. Therefore types can display clear similarities between cultural traditions and were often traded between them, but ultimately the resulting style and decoration of objects produced within a cultural tradition were sufficiently diagnostic to distinguish cultural and, further, regional identity. In other words, 'copying took place, but with a distinctive style' (Briard 1979: 198).

The development of the distinctive Atlantic leaf-shaped bronze sword demonstrates the ability of the Atlantic zone to produce a distinct and widely used Atlantic type in conjunction with frequent and diverse contacts with forms produced in the continent. Imported continental leaf-shaped swords appear in the Thames Valley in the Penard phase *c.* 1200 BC. The earliest Atlantic leaf-shaped swords, as we have seen, are the Irish Ballintober swords which are traditionally seen as a hybridisation between Atlantic rapiers and the early Erbenheim and Hemigkofen continental leaf-shaped swords as they combine the hilt from the Rosnoën parallel bladed rapiers with the leaf-shaped blade of the continental swords (Cowen 1951; Rowlands 1976; Brun 1993: 173).[12] From this early development leaf-shaped swords become a major type in the Atlantic throughout the Late Bronze Age, with workshops from Ireland to Iberia producing analogous but slightly differing indigenous forms. In southern Britain, for example, the early Ballintober swords develop into locally produced Wilburton swords by the end of the second millennium, which are subsequently replaced by Ewart Park swords in the middle of the ninth century BC.

Warrior values in the Atlantic zone

The growing importance of weaponry throughout the Late Bronze Age suggests that the symbolic repertoire of the warrior and its associated ideology were being communicated from Urnfield areas to the Atlantic. From *c.* 1200 BC onwards evidence for the warrior in Atlantic society is seen through the increasing amounts of weaponry produced and deposited (swords, daggers, spearheads, armour, shields and axes – many of which are non-functional and clearly symbolic), the appearance of defended hilltop settlements in many Atlantic areas (see Chapter 4) and evidence for feasting and elite drinking (animal bones and metalwork finds).[13] The dominance of warrior iconography on Iberian stone stele, in the form of schematic drawings of a range of objects including shields, swords, spears, the occasional human figure and what appear to be wheeled vehicles, has been used to confirm the existence of an elite warrior ideology in south-west Iberia (Almagro Basch 1962, 1963, 1966, 1974; Bendala Gálan 1977, 1987; Varela Gomes and Pinho Monteiro 1977; Barceló 1989;

Celestino Pérez 1990; Ruíz-Gálvez and Gálan Domingo 1991; Gálan Domingo 1993; Jorge 1996; Harrison 2004). Throughout the Late Bronze Age there is evidence for increasing competition within society and an apparent emphasis on the individual rather than the collective group in life and death; a growing population; a food production increase; and a concern for territory seen through the development of enclosures and field systems.

Taken as a whole this evidence suggests that becoming a warrior, or rather obtaining the symbolic repertoire of a warrior, was an important way of acquiring and displaying status in Atlantic areas. In west-central Europe the control of the production and exchange of prestige metal objects symbolically related to warfare has been interpreted by various authors as representing the rise of a male warrior elite (Bradley 1981: 235; Kristiansen 1984, 1987; Shennan 1993; Treherne 1995). The existence of similar elites has been claimed for Atlantic areas (Brun 1991, 1998; Sherratt 1994b) but there is still some evidence for differentiation between east and west implying a degree of re-contextualisation of ideas. For example, cauldrons and flesh hooks are confined to Atlantic areas, while buckets and cups are more common in central Europe (Coffyn 1985); swords and sheet armour are found throughout Europe but Atlantic areas tend to feature only swords, shields and helmets and not the fuller range of material such as breast plates and grieves that have been found elsewhere (Champion 1999: 110).

The widespread occurrence of a restricted range of warrior paraphernalia throughout the Atlantic zone in the Late Bronze Age further supports the existence of shared concepts between Atlantic communities. Traditionally two pieces of warrior/prestige equipment, Atlantic Class A and B sheet bronze cauldrons[14] and U- and V-notched shields, have been seen as indicative of contact across the Atlantic seaways. Turning to the cauldrons first, it was initially thought that Class A cauldrons were based on eighth-century BC Mediterranean prototypes and then distributed along the Atlantic seaboard (Hawkes and Smith 1957). However, further research has suggested they may be based on earlier northern and central European types (Coombs 1971: 318; Eogan 1974: 322; O'Connor 1980: 148; Briggs 1987: 163). Gerloff (1987) has carried out the most detailed study of the cauldrons and dates the earliest Class A British examples, the Colchester and Shipton types, to the end of the second millennium BC, and also suggests that they were originally inspired from central European types. Gerloff relates the spread of the idea from the Danube and across France to the distribution of 'pan-European' weaponry (i.e. the spread of warrior paraphernalia such as swords and armour through Europe). After this initial communication of the idea, the production and development of specifically Atlantic cauldrons is confined to Ireland (Briggs 1987; Figure 3.5), from where Atlantic examples were traded to Britain, Armorica, western France, Denmark and the Iberian peninsula. This tradition apparently continued with the later Class B cauldrons which date to the seventh and sixth centuries BC. Whether a result of central European inspiration or indigenous invention, there can be little doubt that the later distribution of the distinctive Irish cauldrons was restricted to Atlantic areas.

The distribution of so-called U- and V-notched shields is often considered to be another traditional indicator of Atlantic maritime contacts (Raftery 1992). The name stems from the presence of a V-shaped or U-shaped indentations or notches on concentric ribs which decorate the front of some Late Bronze Age European shields (Coles 1962). Bronze U-notched examples, termed Herzsprung shields, have a distinctively northern European distribution centred around Denmark (Figure 3.16). V-notched shields are only recorded in Ireland, where they are made of leather or wood, and in south-western Iberia, where they are inscribed on stone stele such as the

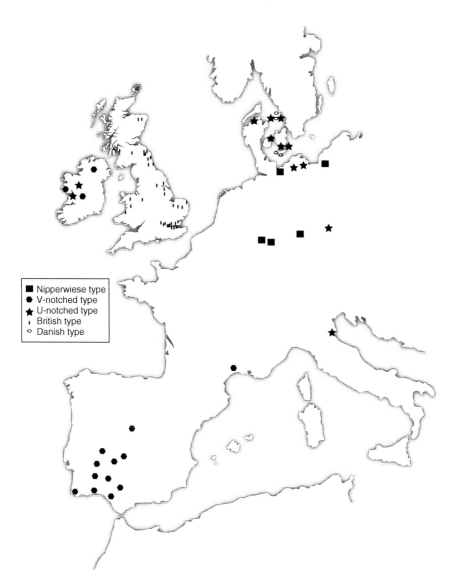

Figure 3.16 Distribution of Atlantic Late Bronze Age shields (after Coles 1962: fig. 1).

shield depicted on the Brozas stele, Cáceres (Figure 3.17). V-notched shields are represented in Ireland by just one leather example and two wooden moulds while two wooden shields account for the U-notched examples. There are no surviving bronze examples known, indeed it is unknown whether bronze examples ever existed.

This distribution of V-notched shields has invited speculation about direct Iberian and Irish contacts. There are at least similarities in terms of the overall design between the Irish shields and those featured on the Iberian stele. However, no actual Iberian shields are known, only the representations on stele, and the number of Irish examples is small; additionally, although widely believed to date to the Late Bronze Age, both the Iberian stelae and the Irish shields lack contextual associations, meaning their dating lacks clarity.[15] Too much can be made of the similarities between the two Irish U-notched shields and the continental European Herzsprung bronze

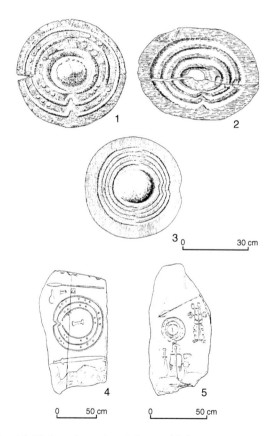

Figure 3.17 Shields with V-shaped notches (after Waddell 1998: fig. 103). (1) Leather shield from Cloonbrin, Co. Longford; (2) Wooden mould for a shield from Churchfield, Co. Mayo; (3) Wooden shield from Cloonlara, Co. Mayo; (4) Engraved slab of eighth to seventh century BC date from Brozas, Cáceres, Spain, depicting a shield with V-notched ribs and bosses, a sword, spear, fibula, comb and mirror; (5) Engraved slab with V-notched shield, a two-wheeled chariot and helmeted warrior with equipment from Cabeza de Buey, Spain.

shields although it remains a possibility that the occurrence of the feature is a decorative echo of the European shields. It seems that the U- and V-notch design of these shields has been emphasised at the expense of other features and purely utilitarian explanations have been offered for the existence of both U- and V-notches. For example, it has been suggested that V-notches were cut into early leather shield prototypes in order to achieve a slight convexity and that its occurrence in two different areas may be totally unconnected or reflect unrelated images of a once more widespread prototype (Waddell 1998: 240). Equally the U-notch mark may have been a purely functional development to allow the attachment of a rivet for a handle such as that seen on the handle attachments of fifth century BC situlae from Italy.

There are a number of bronze shields from Ireland which find their closest parallels with bronze shields in Britain (Waddell 1998: 242). Neither British nor Irish bronze shields feature U- or V-notches but are decorated with concentric ribs and bosses, and as such find a number of parallels with examples in northern and central Europe (Coles 1962). It is perhaps more useful to view the development and use of shields in Atlantic areas as related to the communication of warrior values from continental Europe in much the same way as the development of other forms of weaponry in the Atlantic are viewed. The Irish and British bronze examples are distinctive and resemble each other most closely but are executed in the knowledge of the technology and forms of northern and central Europe. The spread of the use of shields as a concept is more important than trying to match typological and stylistic details from what is largely an undated corpus of finds. Let us not forget that round shields are also known dating to the eighth century BC from Etruscan contexts, clearly indicating the concept was widespread.

The development of Atlantic cauldrons and shields highlight the duality of trading contacts between Britain, Ireland and the continent (Cunliffe 1991: 55–6). Each type was initially based upon forms created in central Europe which made their way to Britain via the Rhine, Seine and possibly Loire routes. Irish and British smiths then developed their own indigenous versions which took on their own distinctive appearance and were subsequently exchanged within the Atlantic system.

1200–600 BC: a time of transformation in the Atlantic zone

Before discussing some of the wider changes that occurred in Atlantic areas we should briefly consider why contacts intensified at this time, ultimately creating a massive bronze exchange network on a scale previously unseen. As Ruíz-Gálvez (1991: 287–92) has stated, by the Late Bronze Age the 'means, motives and opportunity' for frequent and reliable long-distance contacts were in place. These can be quickly summarised as the rise in demand from central Europe for metal ores; the fact that, as was briefly mentioned in Chapter 1, a tradition and network of early contacts along the Atlantic seaboard was in place since at least the late Neolithic; this desire for links with far-away lands continued into the Late Bronze Age – there can be little doubt that the ability to obtain fine metalwork of exotic origin was seen as a desirable and prestigious activity; and that ship technology, perhaps courtesy of the

Phoenicians, had suitably advanced to make long-distance maritime contacts easier and, more importantly, reliable.

The Atlantic was an important source for copper and tin at a time when bronze was indispensable throughout Europe. The existence of such extensive deposits along the Atlantic seaboard obviously promoted the development of contacts both within the region itself and with the metal hungry central European markets which had no tin and very few copper deposits of their own (Barrett and Bradley 1980; Rowlands 1980; Sørensen 1989; Kristiansen 1994). However, as Kristiansen (1998: 144) points out, it cannot be simply taken that the existence of these deposits results in the formation of a large-scale Atlantic interaction zone because, as we have seen, the archaeological record reveals a much more complex pattern of certain areas becoming widely involved in bronze exchange, or at least the deposition of bronze objects, while other areas, despite boasting extensive metal ores, appear to be less involved.

It is widely appreciated that the Late Bronze Age represents a time of major transformation in Europe (Bradley 1978, 1984, 1990, 1998: 97; Coles and Harding 1979; Burgess 1980; Collis 1984; Wells 1984; Koch 1991; Waddell 1995; Champion 1999: 95). There can be little doubt that accompanying the exchange of bronze we can envisage a spread in knowledge, people, technology (metalworking, agricultural and maritime), beliefs, codes of conduct and, of course, the development of common means of communication (Helms 1988; Brun 1991; Ruíz-Gálvez 1991: 277). It is these forms of exchange which ultimately draw communities together, form alliances and create similarities over large areas. Individuals are drawn to discern and interpret their environment in similar ways through face-to-face contact, and therefore express themselves ritually, symbolically and artistically in comparable ways. As Brun (1993: 172) states 'when exchange of marriage partners or goods occurs, symbolic representations are also transferred between the participants and this leads to a unification of world views'. Brun (1991, 1993, 1998) cites exchange, and its ability to create similarities within and between communities, to explain the formation and maintenance of cultural entities such as the Atlantic interaction zone without the need or influence of large-scale political control or centralisation.

Basic similarities in beliefs and behaviour would be widespread but the fact that smaller groups, at the village or farmstead level, would exchange with each other more regularly ensured the creation and maintenance of local identities within the system. Although the Atlantic Bronze Age is defined in terms of metalwork typology, meaning that smaller community level groupings prove harder to recognise, Brun (1991) points to evidence of community level identity through the recognition of production areas or workshops and the recognition of collective identity through the existence of the wider Atlantic techno-economic complex itself.

Accompanying the evidence for metal exchange we can detect contemporary changes in the concerns which drove Atlantic communities (Figure 3.18). The Late Bronze Age is a period of important changes in social and settlement organisation. It is initially a dry, stable period during which population increases and agriculture intensifies. From 1000 BC onwards, however, the climate begins to get colder and wetter and deteriorates up to c. 600 BC. In central Europe c. 900–750 BC these factors led to settlement centralisation and a degree of stratification in settlement generally.

FEATURES OF THE ATLANTIC LATE BRONZE AGE
1. Large increase in the circulation and production of bronze
2. Deposition of prestige metalwork in watery locations
3. Absence of burial traditions
4. Appearance of permanent settlement
5. Evidence for a common *lingua franca*
6. Period of environmental stability/decline and demographic increase
7. Agricultural intensification – new production methods and technology (pan-European)
8. Evidence for the organisation of landscape through field boundaries and systems (pan-European)

Figure 3.18 Features of the Atlantic Late Bronze Age.

In Atlantic areas, however, although there may be some limited evidence, through the appearance of hilltop enclosures, for a degree of centralisation and possibly hierarchy, the effects of climatic deterioration were ultimately pressure on communities in marginal environments visible through evidence for a gradual abandonment of upland areas by the end of the period.

Permanent settlement and field systems

Prior to the Late Bronze Age there is very little evidence for permanent domestic settlement along the western Atlantic seaboard. The expansion and appearance of permanent settlement at this time, accompanying evidence for demographic increase, is a pan-European phenomenon related to improvements in agricultural technology (Thomas 1997; Kristiansen 1998: 98–103). However, it is possible that the occurrence of more visible and substantial domestic settlements in the Atlantic zone is directly related to the development of contacts along a maritime axis bringing new technologies, knowledge and perhaps even crops accompanying the metal exchange which would encourage the formation of permanent settlement (Ruíz-Gálvez 1991).

Late Bronze Age domestic settlements take on a similar form in most Atlantic areas and comprise small, generally stone-built, circular settlements often with some evidence of stone wall boundaries. The occurrence of circular settlements along the western fringes of Europe, and their widespread and exclusive use in the British Isles, have led a number of authors to suggest that the circular form may represent one visible aspect of a cultural tradition distinctive from the rest of the European continent (Hodson 1964; Harding 1972; Bradley 1997). It may well be that the construction of circular dwellings was a specifically Atlantic trait, further representing the existence of a level of shared beliefs or shared views of the world.

Accompanying the appearance of permanent settlement and agricultural intensification we can detect clear evidence for the extensive re-organisation, division and exploitation of the agricultural landscape. For example, divisions of land have been studied in the English chalk downs at Salisbury Plain (Bradley *et al.* 1994), where long bank and ditch earthworks divide the landscape into clearly defined territories, each containing settlements and arable and pastoral land. Such field divisions and boundaries are widespread throughout Europe but are best documented in Atlantic areas due to the use of stone. The most highly organised and complex stone bound-aries and divisions survive in the high moorlands of Dartmoor and Bodmin Moor in south-west England. The best evidence comes from Dartmoor as it has been the subject of intense archaeological study and survey (Fleming 1978, 1983, 1984, 1985). After *c.* 1400 BC the Dartmoor landscape was divided into territories by stone banks called reaves, with each territory including valley land, upland pasture and access to open moorland. These territories had well-defined field systems and stone-built circular settlements. The creation of such boundaries represents changing attitudes to land, in particular the emergence of new strategies of tenure or ownership, and as such are important to the interpretation of the social life and outlook of the period (cf. Fleming 1985; Barrett *et al.* 1991; Barrett 1994; Bradley *et al.* 1994; Hingh 1998; Theuws and Roymans 1999).

The increasing concern for organisation, enclosure and dividing of land at this time is often thought to be directly related to the circulation of prestige goods and militaristic metalwork (cf. Thomas 1989: 276), and considered to be a pan-European phenomenon. It remains a fact that the earliest dated Bronze Age field systems belong to the Atlantic zone[16] (Johnston 2000), but efforts to make them part of a distinctive Atlantic practice are flawed because they do not represent any unified tradition, and numerous field system forms occur widely throughout continental Europe from the Late Bronze Age onwards (cf. Müller Wille 1965; Fries 1995; Waterbolk 1995; Huth and Stäuble 1998). However, it remains a possibility that the widespread occurrence of field systems throughout continental Europe, coupled with their increasing numbers throughout the Atlantic zone during the Late Bronze Age, may be related to Atlantic contacts communicating advances in agricultural technology between the two zones (field systems could have been part of the inno-vations that were spread through Atlantic areas via maritime routes). At the very least, the creation of boundaries and field systems represents a fundamental change in the way Atlantic communities lived in and perceived their landscape. Permanently mark-ing and more prominently inhabiting the landscape would have promoted a sense of belonging in individual family groups and a general growing awareness of family and community held territories. In this it is tempting to see the early beginnings of Atlantic ways of expressing local identities through the domestic arena that ulti-mately reached its culmination in the construction of highly visible and long-lasting settlement forms in the Iron Age.

Atlantic ritual practice and ideology

Ideological changes are apparent through the absence of burials from this period coinciding with the widespread and undoubtedly highly symbolic and ritually signif-icant behaviour of depositing elaborate metalwork in watery locations. Although it does occur elsewhere in Europe, the deposition of prestige metalwork in rivers is most common in western Europe. In general metalwork is found in grave contexts elsewhere. Riverine deposition is therefore 'a common feature of the Atlantic world and one which must be regarded as forming part of the stock of ideas and beliefs, which arrived with the Atlantic networks' (Ruíz-Gálvez 1991: 286). In addition, the practice of hoarding, although it is intensely varied throughout the zone, can be regarded as another linking factor in the chain of contacts (Coombs 1998: 153).

The lack of burials is of particular interest since earlier phases of the Bronze Age had been characterised by burial evidence, often under barrows, and by the erection and the construction of major ceremonial monuments. By the Late Bronze Age the traditions of formal burial all but disappear for more than a millennium in most Atlantic areas while there is little or no evidence for activity at the previously important ritual complexes of the Late Neolithic and Early Bronze Age. The practice of metal deposition in rivers may have been part of a new rite that replaced the burial to some extent combining ritual, perhaps funerary, purpose with displays of personal prestige (Cooney and Grogan 1994). As such, metalwork in rivers has been described as reflecting 'graveless grave goods' (Eogan 1964: 285). It is of course difficult to prove such a view but it is at least consistent with the evidence. Bradley (1990: 110–11; 1998) has clearly described the long-lived tradition of votive offerings in Europe and views the prominence of high status weaponry in rivers by the Late Bronze Age as representing a significant change in depositional behaviour from the Early Bronze Age when the focus of deposition occurred in burial contexts.

Cremation may have been the preferred funerary rite throughout Europe in the Late Bronze Age with the practice of depositing ashes in Urnfields carried out only in central Europe. It is possible that in the Atlantic zone metalwork was deposited in rivers alongside a cremation which would leave no lasting trace in the archaeological record. The metalwork deposited could have been the belongings of the deceased or an opportunity for a display of personal prestige by the survivors/mourners – the idea of giving funerary gifts and enhancing one's own personal prestige need not be mutually exclusive (cf. Bradley 1998: 135–42). As an alternative or addition to cremation there is some evidence to suggest that there may have been a practice of excarnation carried out, at least in Britain, based upon the amount of unburnt human bone found on British sites and the possible correlation between bronze metalwork and human skulls in the Thames[17] (Bradley and Gordon 1988). As Bradley (1998: 136) has suggested, it is possible that 'the declining emphasis on monuments is associated with the destruction of the body by cremation, and possibly with a rite of excarnation in which the individual's remains might be dispersed' (Bradley 1998: 136).

Whatever the real meaning of the practice of riverine metalwork deposition it is likely to have been complex and never fully revealed through archaeological methods. We can at least say that there appears to be a general correlation between the appearance of this behaviour and the disappearance of recognisable burials in Atlantic areas. The lack of visible burial traditions represents a break with earlier traditions where links with the dead, and indeed the building of permanent monuments to the dead, seem to have had a major importance. The links between the living and the dead were less visible by the Late Bronze Age, and the preoccupation with warrior symbolism and display may indicate that was instead a greater focus on what could be achieved by individuals in the land of the living. Individual expressions of warrior values in Atlantic areas had a related character, reflected in the distinctively Atlantic styles and metalwork types produced and the deposition of these forms in common watery locations throughout the zone.

An Atlantic lingua franca?

Many authors have claimed that a common lingua franca developed during the Late Bronze Age accompanying the contacts revealed by the metalwork trade (Piggott 1979, 1983; Koch 1986, 1991; Ruíz-Gálvez 1991; Waddell 1995; Cunliffe 2001). Archaeologists have in the past attempted to crudely associate language change with technological or cultural events such as Harbison (1975) equating Indo-European with the Beaker people or MacEoin (1986) associating Q Celtic with the appearance of Hallstatt C swords in Ireland. It is now recognised that language change is a process that takes place over considerable time and cannot therefore be linked to, or wholly explained by, any one event. This means that although individual events may have had some effect[18] we have to look for other long-term processes to account for language changes. The development of regular exchange networks in the Late Bronze Age from 1250 to 600 BC may have been one such long-term process, a process that was extensive and important enough to facilitate language change amongst participating societies. In socio-linguistic fields there is abundant evidence to support the importance of economic contacts and trade in developing and causing language changes (Waddell 1995: 161). As Coulmas (1992: 154) stresses, in the development and evolution of language the role of the economic environment is crucial.

Some level of common trade language, or lingua franca, would have been vital to facilitate not only the exchange of bronze but also the communication of the ideas and innovations discussed above. How far such a language or languages would have impacted upon the everyday lives of Atlantic communities to influence or become their main form of communication is open to debate. In terms of reinforcing similarities with others or creating identity, a common language is often seen as central. Language is also immensely important on an ideological level because it can fundamentally alter a person's view of the world, or at least how to express that view. Thus in terms of creating an awareness of an Atlantic axis of interaction and similarity the development and use of a common language in the Late Bronze Age may have been one of the most important developments.

Ruíz-Gálvez (1991), following Sherratt and Sherratt (1988), has outlined the importance of Atlantic contacts to the western Iberian peninsula in helping to establish permanent settlements, technological and agricultural improvements and long-distance exchange networks occurring in much the same way as we have examined. Interestingly, though without any real evidence to back up her assertion, she views Luisitanian as a pre-Celtic trade language which was established by Atlantic traders.

Atlantic Late Bronze Age society

There can be little doubt that the increase in exchange, and in turn maritime activity, during the Late Bronze Age had a major impact on the organisation and outlook of Atlantic Bronze Age societies. Access to exotic items through long-distance contacts was no longer in the hands of a restricted few as wealth and prestige could now be attained, stored and displayed by enterprising groups or individuals. At this point the role and significance of metal changed from being a socially restricted item of prestige to a more attainable symbol of competition (Ruíz-Gálvez 1991: 287). This shift in attitudes and developing focus on the role of the individual is echoed in the wider trends that occur during the Late Bronze Age which seem to emphasise competition and the division and control of land.

From the beginnings of prehistoric exchange in Europe it seems that distance was of major importance in adding ritual status to goods (Helms 1988). Along the Atlantic seaboard from at least the Neolithic period there seems to have been an importance attached to objects and symbols obtained or negotiated through long-distance contacts (Bradley 1997: 21–31). Owing to the fact that there is a large increase in the number of objects exchanged during the Late Bronze Age it is common for archaeologists to talk of organised trade with clear economic aims and motivations. There is perhaps a tendency to over-emphasise the mercantile nature of Late Bronze Age contacts at the expense of its potential ritual significance. Conversely, as exchange was on a much smaller scale prior to this period, there is a greater willingness to invest earlier exchange with stronger ritual meaning. The association of trading and ritual activities is a common aspect of prehistoric trade and the two must be seen as inextricably linked and considered together (Thrane 1988; Bradley 1998). Therefore, the vast increase in objects exchanged during the Late Bronze Age may indicate an increase in the commonality of ritual beliefs between Atlantic communities. Metal objects would not have travelled in a silent vacuum; they came with attached stories and symbolic meaning (biographies). Whilst it is possible that the meanings of objects were recontextualised within different societies, some common interpretative ground must have existed between groups to account for the exchange in the first place. The fact that the types exchanged and produced are highly stylised and made according to commonly held models, which we can assume reflect widely recognised social conventions, supports this view. And the fact that distinctive Atlantic types are not that regularly updated, with archaic forms being produced over centuries, suggests that metalwork is likely to have strong ritual connections. Ritual meaning tends to be long-lasting in prehistoric contexts and less open to negotiation with ritual objects less likely to reflect current technological advances or stylistic changes than purely functional objects. It is perhaps significant then that the evidence for Late Bronze Age exchange networks comes not from potential trading sites such as hilltop enclosures but from objects that have been deliberately deposited. The ritual connotations of the practice of watery deposition and the concurrent lack of evidence for burials suggests that the deliberate deposition and consumption of prestige bronzes, whether as part of a funeral ritual or as a gift to the gods, would make a strong and, more importantly, highly public statement about an individuals status.

The existence of elites in the Atlantic Bronze Age is usually postulated in order to explain the patterns of preferential metalwork exchange (Childe 1954; Rowlands 1976; Gilman 1988; Brun 1991, 1993, 1998). Certainly there would have been a need for people within societies who, being aware of the social and political conventions required, were able to conduct exchanges between different groups. These people must have been able to sustain their positions over time in order to account for the regular and long-lasting systems of exchange seen throughout the Late Bronze Age, perhaps indicating that a system of hereditary succession – typical of hierarchical elites or chiefdoms – would have been in place. The fact that our view of Atlantic Late Bronze Age societies is based almost entirely on metalwork makes it virtually impossible to specify the composition of these proposed elites or indeed how they operated. However, given its restricted nature and presumed attached social and symbolic value, the very existence of the metalwork suggests that there was at least the potential for social differences to develop within communities. The production, distribution and deposition of this material must have been co-ordinated and controlled at some level. However, it is far from clear whether this was done by restricted groups who monopolised access to metalwork, or if much larger elements of society were involved in the process. The small-scale nature of Atlantic farmsteads, coupled with the lack of any obvious settlement hierarchy, would perhaps support the latter view. However, it is also possible that elites grew out of controlling the land and its resources and that this power base enabled Atlantic maritime exchanges to intensify. This could be seen to partly account for the filling up of the landscape, the appearance of permanent settlements, field divisions and agricultural intensification – all hallmarks of areas subject to wider control.

Whatever the case, the nature of the material suggests that the emerging social groups ascribed to what can be loosely termed a warrior ethos, and it is easy to build up an impression of Atlantic Late Bronze Age society as a competitive, and at times violent, quest for metalwork, prestige and power (both ritual and economic). The deposition of single weapons and smaller hoards may indicate the existence of lesser, local chiefs or warriors who owe allegiance to the more powerful elites. The growing bronze markets offered new opportunities to individuals and presumably created new social divisions within Atlantic communities. For example, elite groups, however they were organised, must have been able to support a class of specialised metalworkers and – if they were not carrying out exchanges themselves – merchants and traders. The range of tools and specialised objects present in a number of bronze hoards suggest that all levels of craftworking could have progressed at this time perhaps allowing the creation of full-time specialists. Equally, the increase in maritime contacts would require groups of specialist seamen who may themselves have formed elite groupings through not only their specialist skills but also their knowledge of, and association with, exotic items and far-off lands (Coombs 1998: 151). Ruíz-Gálvez (1991), following Harding (1984), points out that the ship is likely to have become a valuable item and an indicator of wealth and prestige in the Late Bronze Age: the owner of a ship would be able to control access to wealth and would also presumably support a crew and other dependants (such as shipbuilders and sea-going merchants). The rise of the importance of bronze to the maintenance and development of Late Bronze Age societies created new ways in which wealth and prestige could be attained and necessarily implies important changes in social organisation. Farming communities, living for the most part in single isolated farmsteads, formed the economic base of Atlantic societies that ultimately made these changes possible.

The material evidence for prestige activities means that archaeologists tend to concentrate on the hierarchical nature of Late Bronze Age societies, often imposing their own modern western views of society and class structure on the evidence.[19] It is simply not known how clear-cut such inequalities actually were in Bronze Age daily life, particularly as our view of Atlantic societies is almost solely dependent on the male symbolism of prestige bronze weaponry.[20] Age, gender, belief and ethnic affiliation may have been equally important in defining a person's place in society but such aspects remain difficult to detect. In any case there was likely to have been a much more complex relationship between status, prestige metalwork, control of materials, resources and technological know-how in operation than we can reconstruct archaeologically. There can be little doubt, however, that the acquisition, deposition and control of metalwork played a major role in Bronze Age societies.

The general picture is one of independent communities with organised elites forming a wide network of interacting local production centres and exchange systems, linked together within an overall Atlantic network of metalwork exchange. Other less detectable items may also have been exchanged, including salt, livestock, hides and forms of artistic work such as wooden objects and textiles. The production and deposition of metalwork must be interpreted in social terms as an expression of status within Atlantic societies – a status which likely had strong ritual connotations with metalwork forms communicating strong cosmological messages as well as being a means of value accumulation. For over half a millennium a core of shared symbols and meaning was communicated along the Atlantic seaboard. This meaning would have been recontextualised to some extent in different local Atlantic contexts, but a common core meaning would have remained similar throughout the zone. Through depositing metalwork in watery locations, creating field boundaries and constructing permanent settlements, Atlantic communities were investing their landscapes with new meaning. In this way, we can begin to move beyond metalwork typology and see the Atlantic Late Bronze Age as a culturally constructed, deeply cosmological landscape brought into being by conscious and related human agency.

The end of the Atlantic Late Bronze Age, 700–600 BC

The mass production of small rectangular socketed axes from *c.* 700 BC to 600 BC is widely considered to mark the end of the Atlantic Bronze Age. Produced in Brittany and Normandy, and therefore not surprisingly known as Armorican axes, traded examples reached southern England, Ireland, the Netherlands and north Germany, although none appear to have penetrated Iberia (Figures 3.19 and 3.20). Little is known about the background or context of Armorican socketed axes but they were manufactured on a massive scale, measured in tens of thousands (*c.* 32,000 examples currently known). Most have such high lead contents (from 30 to 60 per cent), especially those produced towards the end of the period, as to have

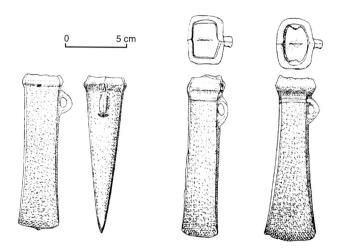

Figure 3.19 Armorican socketed axes (after Briard 1995: 183).

Figure 3.20 Distribution of Armorican axes (after Briard 1995: 192).

rendered them functionally useless and they have therefore been considered by some to represent an attempt to provide measured amounts of metal for supply, a form of ingots or even proto-currency (Briard 1965, 1979: 207; Megaw 1979: 337; Cunliffe 1991: 420). They are most commonly found as hoards placed in cylindrical cavities in the ground or jars. The axes are placed in layers, their wedge shape allowing them to be arranged in circles with the cutting edge pointing towards the centre. Such hoards can include massive numbers of axes, for example, the 800 axes found at both Loundéac, Côtes-d'Armor and Le Trehou in Finistère (Briard 1979: 207). At one site, Maure-de-Bretagne, Ille-et-Villaine, over 4,000 axes were recovered. They are rarely associated with other objects[21] and their deposition in such large quantities does resemble a monetary treasure hoard. In north-west France alone it is estimated that there are about 315 recorded hoards which have provided some 25,000 axes (op. cit. 164).

The production of Armorican axes in huge numbers may represent the end of an initial period of wealth, overlapping with the latter stages of the massive trade networks and activity visible in the Carp's-Tongue sword distributions, followed by over-production at a time when the rest of the European markets were turning to iron but Atlantic areas stubbornly continued to produce bronze. Many axes may have been hoarded because they no longer held a marketable enough value and due to the collapse of the bronze networks remained in the ground. Such a situation would also go some way in explaining the apparent poverty of material culture and traded exotica in the early Iron Age societies examined in the following chapters.

Armorican axes were still being produced possibly as late as the sixth century BC[22] and the end of their production effectively marks the beginning of the Iron Age in Atlantic areas. Armorican axes were the last visible manifestation of the Atlantic bronze trade and the period of their production and deposition runs parallel with growing evidence for continental Hallstatt C (720–600 BC) influences in Irish, British and north-western French metalwork (Cunliffe 1991: 405-19). Evidence for actual continental types is sparse and concentrated in Britain to eastern and especially south-eastern parts of the country. The general picture, particularly in western areas, is of generally unchanged regional metalworking traditions featuring some Hallstatt C influenced, but indigenously produced, prestige items such as swords, horse gear, feasting paraphernalia, razors, swans neck pins and brooches. The Llyn Fawr hoard, Glamorganshire, which lends its name to final phase of the Late Bronze Age in southern Britain, and dates to the late seventh century BC, amply demonstrates the wide range of influences acting upon communities at this time. The hoard contains a range of indigenous types, including an iron socketed axe, alongside North European Hallstatt C forms and two bronze cauldrons of Atlantic type.

The division between increasingly continental influenced south-eastern and eastern Britain and a more conservative western Atlantic Britain occurs at this time and is a dynamic that persists throughout the second half of the first millennium BC. Southern and eastern British communities absorb La Tène influences and ways of life while La Tène material is either taken up more slowly or is virtually non-existent in western Atlantic facing areas. There can be little doubt, however, that maritime contacts continued between Atlantic communities that were organised and substantial enough to warrant a mention by classical authors in the fourth century BC and then by Caesar in the first century BC.

By around 600 BC in Europe, Late Bronze Age ways of life and axes of contacts had shifted. Iron was now the dominant metal throughout the European mainland although, significantly, bronze was still used for high quality art and may thus have retained its ritual importance, while the new sharper, harder but less malleable iron was used for more utilitarian objects such as weaponry and tools. The elites of west-central Europe now looked to the south, to the expanding and evolving Greek and Italian state societies, for exotic objects and trade: metal ores could now be supplied from southern Iberia (Tartessus and the south-east), which was now fully articulated with the Mediterranean world. There was thus a major drop in the demand for Atlantic tin, which ultimately made the Atlantic less involved with developments in the rest of Europe.

It has already been suggested that the deposition of metalwork may be linked to ritual activities as well as enhancing prestige. Of course it may also have served a more practical function. While the deposition of metalwork enhanced status (either in death or in life) it also controlled the circulation and therefore the value of metalwork. Such activity consolidated the existing social order but only in the short term, as increasing pressure to satisfy demand led to escalating competition between elites and ultimately, one may assume, conflict. Such a system would either have to change, as was the case in central Europe with the coming of iron, or collapse, as was the case in the Atlantic zone. Here we witness the over-production of bronze while the adoption of iron and its associated ideology seems to have been actively resisted.

Contacts between Atlantic Europe and central Europe were strong enough for iron and its associated technology to be quickly adopted in the west. However, there is a real lack of iron-working throughout Atlantic areas, suggesting that its use and associated ideological context had little relevance to Atlantic communities. Very little is known about the beginnings of iron-working in the Atlantic zone and it is difficult to determine how long bronze-working traditions, with origins in the Late Bronze Age, persisted into the mid and later first millennium BC. Atlantic communities are described as 'Iron Age' because they date from 700/600 BC. It seems that although iron technology was known in the west, and there are early examples of items produced in iron (examined in Chapter 4), it was very little used throughout the zone as a whole.[23] Perhaps significantly, the adoption of iron-working was most retarded in those areas in which river metalwork deposition was important (Pleiner 1980, 1981).

Bradley (1998: 150–4) has argued that the change from bronze to iron represented a change in ritual practice and was not therefore a purely economic change. Bronze objects were deposited in very different ways to iron objects. Iron was adopted in central Europe but was rejected in the west due to the change in ritual behaviour it represented. For whatever reasons, Atlantic elites continued to prize bronze and its associated depositional practice in watery contexts over the new iron metalwork which, in continental Europe, appeared in grave contexts. For example, Mindleheim swords, a central European type, were produced in both iron and bronze, but river finds of this type were found to be made almost exclusively of bronze and concentrated largely in the west, while iron examples were found in central European grave contexts (Torbrügge 1971; Bradley 1998: 152; Figure 3.21). This division in depositional practice can also be seen through the distribution of Gundlingen bronze swords which are found deposited mainly in graves in central Europe and in rivers in the Atlantic (Cowen 1967; Schauer 1972).

Cooney and Grogan (1994) have recently argued that Dowris bronzeworking traditions could have persisted in Ireland until the third century BC.[24] Although it seems unlikely that Irish bronze smiths would produce metalwork for close to five centuries without any appreciable change in form, it is just possible that a number of bronze forms which we would automatically date to the Late Bronze Age remained in use throughout the Iron Age. Some ceremonial objects could have remained in use for centuries. A number of cauldrons, for example, display evidence for frequent repairs, some of which are in iron[25] (Gerloff 1987: 86–7). It is possible that because Ireland, and perhaps other Atlantic communities, had little contact with the continent between the sixth and the third centuries BC, that they followed a rather insular path. Cooney and Grogan (1991, 1994) argue convincingly that there

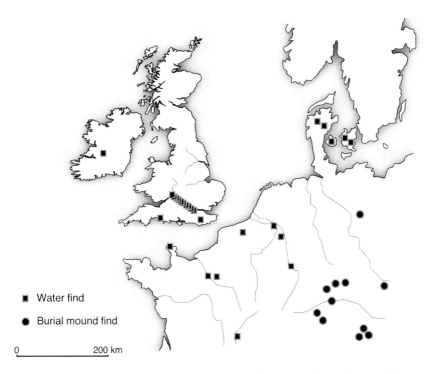

Figure 3.21 Distribution of bronze Mindelheim and Thames swords, emphasising the contrast between water finds and those from burial mounds (after Bradley 1998: fig. 35).

is considerable continuity in other spheres in Ireland from *c.* 600 BC to 300 BC. If there was any hiatus in Ireland it was a temporary one given the whole series of La Tène artefacts from beehive querns to decorated bronzes which are exchanged in the last few centuries BC and into the first millennium AD (Raftery 1984: 337). They prefer to view the gap as a gap in depositional behaviour and not necessarily in settlement, burial and everyday material culture. Around 300 BC the practice of metalwork deposition re-emerges – or at least is more easily datable given the occurrence of La Tène forms.

There was, at least initially, a more active rejection of La Tène influences in Atlantic areas and from this point onwards Atlantic communities appear to be, to a greater or lesser extent, isolated from direct continental influences. The demise of the Atlantic bronze networks often encourages catastrophic interpretations of system collapse due to the introduction of ironworking which is seen to challenge the very core of Atlantic societies, turning once prosperous communities into isolated, impoverished peripheries. Although the collapse of the bronze trade – or at least the practice of deposition – is very real, it seems unlikely that the contacts it made archaeologically visible would have ceased altogether in the Iron Age, especially given the rather long prehistoric pedigree of Atlantic contacts (Cunliffe 2001). If we accept, as seems likely, that bronze played an important role in the maintenance and creation of elite group-ings in the Atlantic then the introduction of iron would certainly have disrupted this process, resulting in bronze over-production within the Atlantic zone and eventually the demise of the practice of bronze deposition. As bronze was just one element of society it does not follow that there was a wider socio-economic collapse after it ceased to be such a sought-after commodity (Waddell 1992: 38). If anything, as we shall examine, there is evidence for stability, continuity and permanence in the settle-ment record of the Atlantic Iron Age rather than crisis.

The unified tradition of metalwork production and deposition which charac-terised the Atlantic Late Bronze Age reached its climax around the eighth to seventh centuries BC. The complex network of trading contacts and inter-changes established at this time do not equate a cohesive cultural identity for the entire zone, but they do result in a level of commonality shared between Atlantic areas: a commonality visible not only in the metalwork finds but also through the similar practices of ritual deposition, domestic life and, potentially, language which, taken as a whole, allow us to culturally contrast the Atlantic zone with west-central European and Mediterranean communities. The events of the Atlantic Late Bronze Age are extremely important in terms of setting the stage for subsequent Iron Age develop-ments. While the scale and intensity of contacts may have declined along the Atlantic seaboard during the Iron Age, Atlantic ways of life created through previous Late Bronze Age contacts may have continued and developed in related ways.

4 Atlantic settlement in the first millennium BC

Introduction

In the Late Bronze Age it is metalwork that defines the period and the inter-action between Atlantic areas. In the Iron Age, however, there are significant changes in the nature of the archaeological data available. The evidence for material culture as a whole, let alone prestige items such as metalwork, becomes extremely sparse throughout the Atlantic zone and it is not possible to assess the existence of cultural contacts through the comparison and distribution of archaeological finds. Instead, the focus of discussion will switch to the better documented part of the Atlantic Iron Age, the settlement record.

Late Bronze Age settlement development along the Atlantic seaboard

Living in the round

> It may well have been during the Later Bronze Age that a specifically Atlantic tradition of circular houses became widely established.
>
> (Bradley 1997: 30)

Late Bronze Age domestic settlements take on a similar form in most Atlantic areas and comprise small, usually stone-built, circular structures often associated with evidence of stone wall boundaries. The occurrence of circular settlements along the western fringes of Europe, and their widespread and exclusive use in the British Isles, have led a number of authors to suggest that the circular form may represent one visible aspect of a cultural tradition distinctive from the rest of the European continent (Hodson 1964; Harding 1972; Bradley 1997). It is perhaps more than a coincidence then that it is during the period when we have evidence for widespread contacts throughout the Atlantic zone that we also have, for the first time in many areas, evidence for substantial permanent settlements.[1] The western Atlantic distribution of circular dwellings is such that the possibility of these reflecting shared cultural elements, shared ways of viewing the outside world, cannot be ignored.

The practice of building circular structures in western Europe has an impressive pedigree, the roots of which can be traced back thousands of years to the circular tent settings of Mesolithic gatherer-hunter groups through to the ritual monuments and megalithic tombs of the Neolithic and Early Bronze Ages. The development of megaliths is viewed by some as an expression of the indigenous identities of western coastland populations in the face of incoming central European groups using recti-linear long houses and cult houses (Shee Twohig 1993; Sherratt 1996, 1998; Lodewijckx and Bakels 2000).

Sherratt (1998) views the development of rectilinear long mounds in Atlantic France from the middle of the fifth millennium BC as being ultimately inspired from contacts, including population movements, with agricultural societies surrounding the fertile loess-lands of the Paris Basin and the Rhineland to the east, themselves in close contact with the villages of rectilinear timber houses and cult-houses of the central European Neolithic and Copper Age. The development of circular, passage grave traditions, on the other hand, are viewed as being the handiwork of indigenous Atlantic coastal populations. Sherratt argues that a 'typological tension' had been created in the organisation of space, one circular and the other rectilinear, which continues between western and central Europe through the prehistoric period:

> It would be simplistic to take these tombs and ceremonial settings too literally as reflections or echoes respectively of the loess-land long-house and the Atlantic hunter's tent, continued in the round-house; yet this opposition, however subse-quently transformed, accurately epitomises the dialectic between centre and west in Europe, and the contrasting houseplans themselves no doubt encapsulate further dimensions of cosmic ordering, whether of calendrical cyclicality or of appropriate orientation and rectitude.
>
> (Sherratt 1998: 120)

The occurrence of roundhouses from the Middle and Late Bronze Ages onwards in Atlantic areas as opposed to the rectilinear house forms found elsewhere in west-ern Europe at the time may indicate the survival of long-held ideological concep-tions and expressions of structure. Atlantic groups may have been stressing their continuity with previous Atlantic traditions and social conventions that had been in existence prior to the expansion of long-distance contacts seen by the Late Bronze Age.

This is not to claim that the building of circular settlements is exclusive to the Atlantic zone: it would be quite wrong to simply claim that the building of circular as opposed to rectangular or square dwellings is significant in itself. Building dwellings 'in the round' is widespread throughout the hunter-gatherer and mobile human populations of the world, and is a practice that represents no link between societies other than a common way of enclosing space around a central hearth. If anything, the construction of circular buildings is the most logical development from the simple campfire arrangement or tent.

On saying this, it would be equally reckless to under-estimate the significance of the appearance and style of dwellings to their respective societies. Recently in archaeology it has become clear that domestic settings, living spaces, and the deposition of material within these spaces, are often arranged in highly structured ways. This realisation has had a particular impact on the study of roundhouses, as it appears clear that in the later prehistoric period such settlements were used not simply as domestic structures by their inhabitants, but also as the main setting for ritual activities. As a result, roundhouses have been the subject of many recent studies into the structure of domestic space, its potential ideological significance, and the interweaving of domestic and ritual activities within that space (Hill 1989; Ried 1989; Hingley 1990; Fitzpatrick 1994; Parker Pearson and Richards 1994a,b; McOmish 1996; Parker Pearson 1996; Parker Pearson *et al.* 1996; Oswald 1997). Parker Pearson *et al.* (1999: 16) view the domestic dwelling as 'a central arena of social relationships, a repository of traditional knowledge and values, and the principle artefacts of integrated and symbolic action'. The significance of the circularity of Atlantic settlements, and of their layouts, then, may indeed reflect something deeper than simple functionality.

The attached ritual and symbolic importance of dwellings, especially in terms of representing collective identity, is amply demonstrated by an example from the recent history of North America. When, in 1931, Native Americans were forced to live in the rectangular homes built on government reservations by invading Europeans, Black Elk, a holy man of the Oglala Sioux, was recorded as saying:

> You have noticed that everything an Indian does is in a circle, and that is because the Power of the World always works in circles, and everything tries to be round ... the *Wasichus* [Europeans] have put us in these square boxes. Our power is gone and we are dying ... there can be no power in a square.
>
> (Neihardt 1974: 194–6)

Atlantic Scotland

As is the case in most other Atlantic areas there is a tradition of open, circular dry-stone settlement throughout most of Atlantic Scotland during the Late Bronze Age and the beginning of the Iron Age (*c.* 1000–500 BC). These sites are very much understudied but hut circles incorporating stone-built walls are known from mainland northern and western Scotland, the Inner Isles and potentially the Western Isles (Armit 1996: 103–5). There are thousands of such sites in Caithness and Sutherland (RCAHMS 1911; Fairhurst 1971; Mercer 1980, 1981, 1985; McIntyre 1999) with similar numbers reported in Argyll (RCAHMS 1971–1988).

Many hut circles, along with associated field systems, have been identified on Skye and a recent excavation at Coile a Ghasgain (Wildgoose *et al.* 1993) has revealed a structure with features foreshadowing that of the later Atlantic Iron Age roundhouses (Figure 4.1). Of particular interest is the evidence for an expanded, emphasised entrance which implies continuity from the earlier chambered tomb tradition and, significantly, the plan reveals a circle of postholes, which may hint at the presence of radial divisions – a form that is repeated time and time again later in the Atlantic Scottish settlement record. A number of similar hut circles have been identified in the Western Isles, but they have not yet been examined in any detail (Armit 1996: 104).

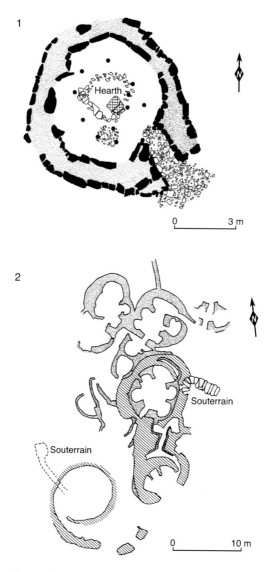

Figure 4.1 Late Bronze Age settlements in Scotland: (1) Coile a Ghasgain, Skye (after Armit 1996: fig. 6.7); (2) Jarlshof, Shetland (after Cunliffe 1991: fig. 3.15).

Throughout Atlantic Scotland stone-built hut circles can be regarded as a precursor to the development of more substantial and architecturally elaborate roundhouse forms in the Iron Age.

The Late Bronze Age settlement of Orkney and Shetland contrasts with that of the rest of Atlantic Scotland because there is a long-established tradition of dry-stone, cellular settlement which was established in the Neolithic and lasts until the

Late Bronze Age. These forms are best illustrated at Jarlshof on Shetland (Hamilton 1956) where several drystone houses are internally divided into cells in a radial arrangement around an open central area containing a hearth (Figure 4.1). This domestic arrangement is extremely important as it demonstrates continuity with previous house forms in the Northern Isles, and survives alongside the monumental developments seen in the Iron Age. These radial spatial divisions are a recurrent theme throughout the period up to the construction of wheelhouses and into the re-establishment of cellular settlement which are arranged in an almost identical form in the first half of the first millennium AD.

Recent evidence from Cladh Hallan on South Uist suggests that the Late Bronze Age settlement record in Atlantic Scotland may be more varied and complex than previously thought (Parker Pearson *et al.* 2000). Here six co-joined roundhouses dating from the eighth to the third centuries BC have been uncovered, confirming the use of stone-built roundhouses (albeit not thick walled examples) in the Early Iron Age developing from earlier Late Bronze Age forms. Significantly the agglomeration of structures in one place at Cladh Hallan and the cellular nature of some of the units are reminiscent of Late Bronze Age forms in the Northern Isles. The site has also produced evidence for bronze metalworking, indicating the existence of wider contacts since the items produced adhere to established Late Bronze Age styles and technology. Most interestingly, this metalworking appears to continue into the earlier Iron Age as indicated by the recovery of a disc of a wheel-headed pin which corresponds stylistically with a pin found at Garton Slack in east Yorkshire dated to the fourth century BC (op. cit. 27). Further work on settlement forms which date to the Late Bronze Age in Atlantic Scotland remains an important research priority.

Ireland

Evidence for Late Bronze Age settlement forms in Ireland consists of a handful of hilltop enclosures alongside smaller open and enclosed settlements. In each of these settlement types where evidence of domestic units can be discerned they are predominantly circular in form (Eogan 1995: 129; Doody 2000: 139). Small, scattered open settlements are thought to have been the norm in the Late Bronze Age (Raftery 1994: 18) but owing to their very nature they are extremely difficult to detect archaeologically. For example, two sites in Co. Tipperary, Curraghatoor and Ballyveelish, were revealed only owing to work on the Cork to Dublin pipeline; there were no surface indications of either site. Ballyveelish took the form of a sub-rectangular enclosure while Curraghatoor provided evidence of at least eight small circular houses, all around 4 to 6.5 m in diameter. Both sites were radiocarbon dated to the late second/early first millennium BC (Doody 1987a; 1987b).

The site of Carrigillihy, Co. Cork (O'Kelly 1951, 1989: 221) is particularly interesting in terms of the later development of circular stone-built settlement in Atlantic areas in the first millennium BC (examined in Chapter 5). The site is an oval stone-built enclosure, with 2.7 m thick walls and measuring 24 by 21 m internally, which surrounds a strongly built oval house, measuring about 11 by 8 m (Figure 4.2). A black habitation layer, that included charcoal and pottery (over 166 coarse

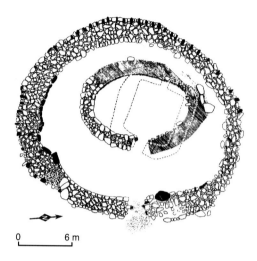

Figure 4.2 Carrigillihy, Co. Cork (after Waddell 1998: fig. 86).

flat-bottomed pottery sherds similar to sherds recovered at Lough Gur), provided two radiocarbon samples which, when calibrated, provided a wide dating range between 1510 and 850 BC.[2] Activity late in the Late Bronze Age was suggested by the discovery of an uncontexted bronze socketed axe. This site is morphologically similar to stone-built forms, termed *cashels*, which are dated in Ireland to the first millennium AD. A square house with opposing doors was later built on the site most probably in the first millennium AD (Waddell 1998: 210) making the resemblance to later forms even closer. However, the dating of the main period of activity at this site to the Middle to Late Bronze Age should serve as a warning against the common practice of using morphology as a chronological indicator. This site, along with the others discussed below, suggests that there may be a significant number of sites in the large and varied Irish drystone record built prior to the first millennium AD.

Two stone-built circular enclosures very similar to Carrigillihy and also of Late Bronze Age date have been recorded at Aughinish, Co. Limerick (Kelly 1974; Lynn 1983). The first enclosure contained shell-filled pits featuring coarse pottery, saddle querns, a bronze tanged chisel, a bronze knob headed pin, and a corroded iron object (possibly a bridle bit). It had no postholes but did have a circular central area of levelled ground, presumably for a building. The second enclosure also featured pits with shells and coarse pottery but, more significantly, provided evidence of a circular house plan, *c*. 8 m in diameter, and an unpublished radiocarbon date calibrating between 1000 and 500 BC (Limbert 1996: 282). Limited excavations at Carrownaglogh, Co. Mayo, revealed a circular stone hut with a central hearth set within an irregular stone walled enclosure covering *c*. 2.2 hectares. The site is thought to represent a ninth-century BC farmstead with associated field systems and cultivation ridges (Herity 1981).

The majority of the evidence for enclosed and unenclosed Late Bronze Age settlements in Ireland comes from the wetland environment. There are a large number of lakeside dwellings and crannogs that date to the Late Bronze Age, several of which have been excavated: Knocknalappa, Co. Clare; Sroove, Lough Gara; Ballinderry No. 2, Co. Offaly; Rathtinaun, Co. Sligo; Ballinderry; Moynagh, Co. Meath; Lough Eskragh, Co. Tyrone; and Island McHugh, Co. Tyrone (O'Sullivan 1998: 69–95). These sites usually consist of oval mounds of brushwood and timber and rarely provide information on house structure. However, where house plans do survive they are invariably circular. Lake dwellings and lakeside dwellings should be viewed very much within the same cultural context as their counterparts on land. For example, the settlement at Lough Gur, Co. Limerick, features several timber roundhouses dating from *c.* 1200 to 800 BC on what was probably once an island and can be broadly paralleled with the hut clusters at Curraghatoor. In Lough Eskragh, Co. Tyrone, roughly circular brushwood and timber platforms were found to date to the beginning of the first millennium BC (Williams 1978).

A Late Bronze Age oval enclosure with three circular wickerwork walled houses was discovered in a raised bog at Clofinlough, Co. Offaly (Moloney 1993). Although the site was tentatively interpreted by the excavators as a crannog, it features a layout more closely comparable with later ringfort settlements (see Chapter 5). Dendrochronology indicated the site was in use between 908 BC and 886 BC. The site was only preserved owing to the onset of waterlogged conditions and provides a salutary reminder of what may have been lost from the dryland archaeological record.

Excavations at Dún Aonghasa on the Aran Islands, Co. Galway, revealed Late Bronze Age occupation considered by the excavator to pre-date the imposing monumental drystone walls present at the site (Cotter 1993, 1995, 1996). Structural evidence came in the form of a series of small revetted circular buildings within and, at least partly, underlying the multi-faced inner enclosure wall (Figure 4.3). Artefactual evidence in the form of clay moulds for swords, spears, rings and pins, indicate an Atlantic island community in touch with the latest metalwork fashions and technology of the day. Cotter (1996: 14) claims that 'the settlement could be described as approaching village status' – equally, in terms of importance, the site's strategic location at the mouth of Galway Bay may be significant.

The Late Bronze Age structural remains consist of four certain hut foundations (numbered 1, 2, 5 and 8 on the plan), two possible examples (numbers 4 and 6) and traces of walling (number 3). Hut 1 survived as several lines of edge set stones, *c.* 4.8 m in diameter, associated with a paved floor, a stone-lined hearth and a clear occupation layer. This layer produced coarse pottery, fragments of clay moulds and two crucibles, along with a series of radiocarbon dates indicating activity in the tenth to the eighth centuries BC. Although *all* the excavated structural evidence is considered by the excavator to belong exclusively to the period 1000–800 BC, the range of radiocarbon dates obtained suggest a much longer period of occupation and use (Henderson 2000: 131–3). An earlier horizon of activity, from 1500 BC to

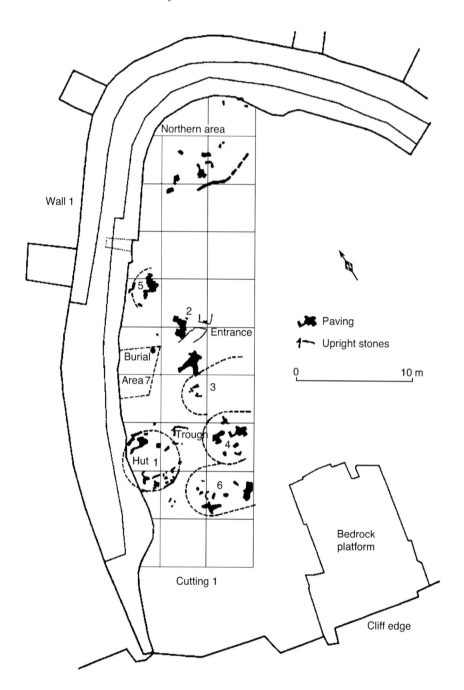

Figure 4.3 Dún Aonghasa, Aran Islands, Co. Galway: Late Bronze Age occupation (after Cotter 1995: fig. 2).

1000 BC, is clear from a range of dates recovered from the inner enclosure.[3] Equally, as will be discussed in more detail in Chapter 5, later dates indicate that occupation continued well into the Iron Age.

Late Bronze Age occupation material was also found outside the inner enclosure extending to the east, within the middle enclosure (Figure 5.16). A 2 m wide stone wall, surviving to a height of 50 cm, was uncovered running for a distance of 9 m in a north-east to south-west direction in this area. Occupational material including pottery, part of a bronze ring, bone pins, animal bone, limpet shells and stone artefacts abutted this wall. The upper levels of this material dated to between 900 and 540 BC and thus provided a *terminus ante quem* for the actual construction of the wall.

This wall remains the only securely dated wall on the site, but some form of enclosure for the Late Bronze Age structures would have been a necessity given the very open and exposed conditions at the site (Cotter 1996: 13). Given that there are a number of wall alignments visible in all the drystone ramparts at Dún Aonghasa there can be little doubt that they were added to and remodelled over time and do not therefore date to any one particular period. The inner enclosure wall, for example, is composed of at least three distinct vertical walls built up against each other (Cotter 1993: 8–9). Stratigraphically the Late Bronze Age deposits can be seen to run under the inner and outer sections of this wall (Wall 1) thus providing a *terminus post quem* for these structures.[4] However, this does not mean that the whole of the wall was built after the Late Bronze Age as excavations have not yet revealed whether the deposits run under the double-faced core 'middle' wall – this part of the wall could have been in existence before the outer and inner skins of masonry were added.

It is possible that an original Late Bronze Age enclosure existed consisting of a stone wall which ran, on the west, along the line of Wall 1 to join with the wall uncovered in the middle enclosure and then joining an earlier element of the middle enclosure wall (Wall 2a). It is probable that the enclosing wall also once extended along the Atlantic side of the settlement to provide protection from the elements (for possible models of the layout of the Late Bronze Age ramparts see Cotter 1996: fig. 4).

The closest parallel for the projected Late Bronze Age drystone ramparts envisaged for Dún Aonghasa are the trivallate ramparts at Mooghaun South, Co. Clare (Raftery 1972: 45; Bennet and Grogan 1993; Grogan 1995, 1996). Located prominently with views of the Shannon estuary on a low hill about 80 m above sea level, three concentric stone banks enclose a total area of 12 ha (Figure 4.4). Unlike the well finished walls at Dún Aonghasa they are roughly built dump stone ramparts with no significant stone facing, revetments or architectural features, but in common with the Aran Island site they are very massive; the inner enclosure rampart, for example, is 4 to 6.5 m wide and survives up to 1.5 m in height.

Mooghaun is dated to the Late Bronze Age on the basis of a single radiocarbon date of 1260–930 BC obtained from burnt soil *underneath* the outer rampart (Bennet and Grogan 1993: 60). Grogan (1995: 56) suggests this dates construction of the rampart because there is a lack of deposits between the pre-rampart material and the rampart itself. He goes on to apply this date to the entire site on the grounds that there are no great gaps before any of the walls were built and that other pre-rampart deposits produced 'typical' Late Bronze Age material – coarse, bucket shaped pottery

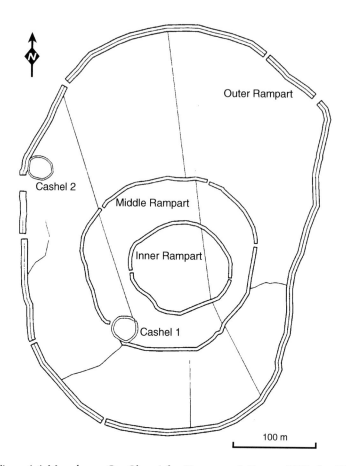

Figure 4.4 Mooghaun, Co. Clare (after Bennet and Grogan 1993: fig. 22).

and animal bone – implying that all three ramparts are likely to be contemporary. His argument is not entirely convincing because the preparation of any new rampart would involve the digging of foundations which would be likely to remove existing earlier deposits and in the absence of any more radiocarbon dates the dating of this site must be considered insecure. The later evidence from this site and its possible Iron Age connotations are examined in Chapter 5.

Evidence for large circular houses first constructed in the Late Bronze Age comes from the hilltop enclosures of Rathgall and Emain Macha, both in Co. Armagh. Rathgall (Raftery 1976) consists of four concentric ramparts situated on a low ridge enclosing an area of 7.3 ha and is very similar in plan to sites such as Dún Aonghasa and Cahercommaun (see Chapter 5). The inner enclosure is a polygonal stone rampart, *c.* 45 m in diameter, which is usually considered to be medieval but is not

securely dated – as at Dún Aonghasa it was only demonstrated that the late prehistoric levels *partly* underlay the walling. It remains a possibility that the remaining
three ramparts, which are more denuded, may belong to the first millennium BC.
Excavations within the central enclosure revealed an annular ditched enclosure,
c. 35 m in diameter, surrounding a large 15 m diameter timber-built circular house.
The entrance, which was orientated to the east, was flanked by two large posts and
the walls turned inwards to form a porch with a second inner doorway (evidence of
entrance elaboration). In the pre-mound features at Emain Macha Site B (Mallory
1995), a circular ditch, *c.* 45 m in diameter, encloses a sequence of circular houses,
c. 12–13 m diameter, with paddocks and pens dating from *c.* 800 to 100 BC. A
Hallstatt C chape was found on the site but otherwise it seemed to be little more
than a farmstead during this period. Evidence for a Late Bronze Age circular hut,
16.3 m in diameter, was also found at Site A.

South-west England

The south-west of England has an existing tradition of simple drystone roundhouse
settlement dating to the Middle and Late Bronze Ages. Settlements, in the form of
single, unenclosed, stone-walled huts, along with open and enclosed hut groups, are
predominantly found on higher ground centred on the moors of Dartmoor, Exmoor,
Bodmin, Penwith, and to a lesser extent, Wendron and Hensbarrow (Figure 4.5).
    From at least 1300 BC onwards hundreds of small round stone huts were being
constructed on the moors, their doorways sometimes shielded from the elements by
a curved porch. At Dean Moor (Fox 1957) the huts featured various internal fittings
such as hearths, central posts, or rings of posts presumably to support a conical roof of
wood or thatch. Some huts were clustered together and enclosed by stone walls,
locally known as 'pounds'. Grimspound on Dartmoor (Pattison and Fletcher 1996;
Figure 4.6), for example, consists of a stone enclosure wall surrounding an ovoid area
of *c.* 1.45 ha in which there are twenty-four round stone-built huts. Another example, Shaugh Moor (Enclosure 15), was stone built and oval in shape, some 75 m in
diameter, and strangely did not appear to have any entrances to access the five stone
walled circular huts within. Excavation determined that it was occupied from the mid-
second millennium BC to *c.* 850 BC (Wainwright *et al.* 1979; Wainwright and Smith
1980; Balaam, Smith, and Wainwright 1982). Finds were predictably sparse but
included quernstones, flint scrapers and some crude pottery – the virtual absence of
grain despite an intensive sieving campaign supports a pastoral function.
    Bronze Age huts and hut groups are associated with field systems while saddle
querns and corn rubbers are common finds suggesting that cereal growing was an
aspect of the economy, but owing to the small size of the fields pastoralism is considered the dominant activity (Pattison and Fletcher 1996: 32). Fieldwork has demonstrated that Dartmoor is broken up into a series of well-defined territories, each of
which divides into a smaller system of allotments, marked out by linear stone banks
called 'reaves'[5] (Fleming 1978: fig. 2; Pearce 1981: 96). Similar drystone boundaries
with associated huts have been recorded on Bodmin Moor (Johnson and Rose
1994: 73–4).

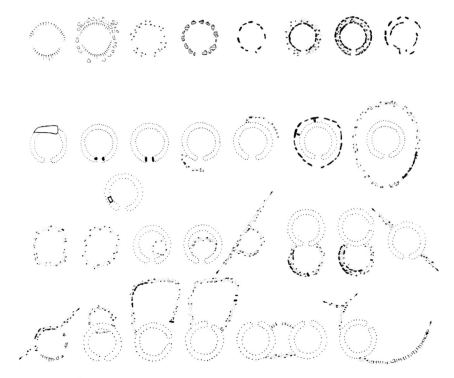

Figure 4.5 Prehistoric hut types on Bodmin Moor (after Johnson and Rose 1994: fig. 34).

The increasing concern for territorial boundaries is of course a common trend during the Late Bronze Age throughout western European communities. For the south-west, the division of the landscape implies a society organised and stable enough to create an effective system of land management and establish rights without any indication or evidence of tension in the form of defensive works.

The full range of south-western Late Bronze Age settlement types can be found on Dartmoor where there has also been a large amount of environmental work, making it possible to map ecological variations in relation to the contemporary settlement patterns (Simmons 1970; Cunliffe 1991, fig. 3.8). From 1300 BC blanket bog seems to have been well developed in areas above 427 m; below this there was open grass or heathland down to 160 m, where the settlements were constructed (ibid.). Land below 160 m seems to have been densely forested. The areas of clearing are thought to have been made during the third millennium BC and used right up until the mid-first millennium BC, implying a continuity and stability in terms of settlement location and, presumably, function.

Different types of settlement appear to have been built to exploit different climatic environments (Simmons 1970; Silvester 1979; Cunliffe 1991: 41–9). Substantial stone enclosures surrounding a number of stone-built circular huts, such as at Rider's

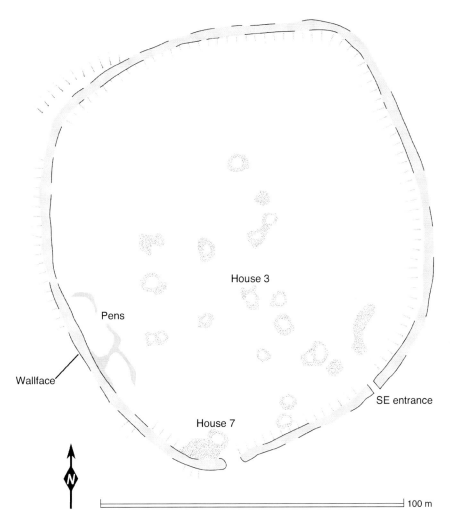

Figure 4.6 Grimspound, Dartmoor (after Pattison and Fletcher 1996: fig. 4).

Rings, Legis Tor and Yes Tor (Figure 4.7), are concentrated on the southern part of the moor, often near water supplies, and are interpreted as serving a pastoral role although small-scale cultivation within the enclosures may have taken place (Cunliffe 1991: 41). Unenclosed circular hut clusters are found on the wetter western fringes of Dartmoor. Some of these are quite large, for example, up to sixty-eight huts have been recorded at Stanton Down, and feature huts linked together by low stone walls creating small enclosures that could have been used for cultivation or stock. Unenclosed huts, often associated with stone-walled fields, make up the other major group and cluster to the drier eastern side of the moor which features fertile 'brown soils'. These huts

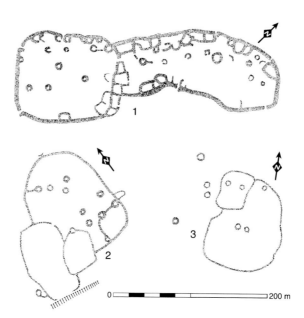

Figure 4.7 Late Bronze Age settlements on Dartmoor (after Cunliffe 1991: fig. 3.9): (1) Rider's Rings; (2) Legis Tor; (3) Yes Tor Bottom.

are thought to represent arable farms although it has been noted from the surviving complete examples that the area under cultivation would have been inadequate to support the associated huts assuming that they all served a contemporary domestic function (Cunliffe 1991: 45). These sites may represent different responses, both in space and time, to different environmental conditions. However, as no single settlement appears to be wholly self sufficient it is possible that they are part of a contemporary transhumance pattern with communities wintering in the arable farms and then spending the summer on the wetter western and southern pastures with their livestock (Denford 1975; Cunliffe 1991: 45–6).

These sites on Dartmoor are difficult to date owing to their sparse material culture, but the pottery has been used to suggest a Middle Bronze Age date (Read 1970), while some clearly survive into the early first millennia. Whatever their exact dating these Middle–Late Bronze Age settlements provide a clear indigenous background to the settlement developments throughout the first millennium BC in the south-west.

Armorica

There is very little settlement evidence for the Bronze Age as a whole in Armorica, making a discussion that focuses purely on Late Bronze Age forms virtually impossible. Structural evidence is extremely thin on the ground and the vast majority of

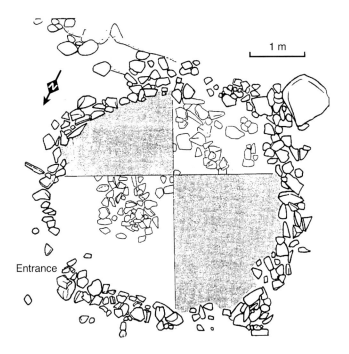

Figure 4.8 La Grosse-Roche, Saint-Jacut-de-la-Mer, Côtes d'Armor (after Briard and Nicolardot 1985).

occupational sites that can be ascribed to the Bronze Age are usually only ceramic and/or flint scatters – termed '*habitat diffus*' by Briard *et al.* (1988: 17). Some traces of Bronze Age occupation are known from sites where the actual structural evidence is dated to different periods, such as at a number of promontory forts (i.e. at La Torche á Plomeur, Finistère; Briard 1995: 153) and other coastal sites (i.e. Landéda, Ille de Guennoc, Finistère).

The only securely dated Late Bronze Age structural evidence comes from la Grosse-Roche, Saint-Jacut-de-la-Mer, Côtes d'Armor (Briard and Nicolardot 1985). The site consists of a small circle of stones, about 6 m in diameter, interpreted as a domestic dwelling and dated to the Late Bronze Age on the basis of the ceramics recovered (Figure 4.8). The site is very similar to the Bronze Age hut circles known in Britain, especially those with similar stone footings found in Atlantic areas.

As Late Bronze Age sites such as la Grosse-Roche were presumably open settlements they would be very difficult to find in the heavily cultivated Armorican countryside. The detection of Iron Age sites has been aided by the existence of large enclosing ditches which can be recognised easily from the air. There are some structural parallels to la Gross-Roche but they remain undated. A very similar circular stone construction has been recorded at Lanmodez, Côtes-d'Armor, but as the site is situated in the inter-tidal zone there are no surviving associated deposits to provide a date (Briard *et al.* 1988: 17). Another broadly similar circular stone structure which seems to be associated with other Bronze Age features (a fossil field system and a tumulus) has been recorded at Brennilis, Finistère. The remains of a broadly comparable circular structure measuring 8–10 m in diameter are known from Le Vivier, Quiberon, but it was dated to the Middle Bronze Age on the evidence of the pottery recovered (Briard *et al.* 1988, 1995: 159). More recently, a potentially Late Bronze Age dating has been proposed for a circular post-built structure unearthed near Caen in Calavados, Caen (San Juan *et al.* 1996). The structure, which has a diameter of *c.* 7 m, was dated through its association with a large rubbish pit containing the remains of Late Bronze Age and Early Iron Age ceramics. Large-scale excavations at Cahagnes, also in Calvados, produced evidence for at least twenty circular post-built structures ranging from 6 to 8 m in diameter, and apparently accompanied by several smaller rectangular structures dating to between 900 and 700 BC (Jahier 1997).

The settlement record for the Armorican Bronze Age is extremely poor and is surprising given the large amounts of metalwork produced in the area. The evidence that has been recovered to date indicates there was, in common with other Atlantic areas, a tradition of circular hut building. It is perhaps worth mentioning that the earliest dated Iron Age settlement in Armorica, Mez-Notariou on the I'île de Ouessant (Le Bihan and Villard 2001), dating to *c.* 650–450 BC, featured evidence for a number of timber built roundhouses (see Chapter 6).

Circular settlement in Britain in the first millennium BC

Circular domestic forms are found throughout Britain from the Late Bronze Age and are not geographically restricted to Atlantic coastal areas. Small clusters or lone examples of insubstantial circular structures, such as the cluster of five circular post-hole structures at Black Patch, East Sussex (Drewett 1982), were the norm throughout Britain. Simple circular structures such as this remained in use in many areas into the mid-first millennium BC.

There is some evidence for regionality in settlement forms, broadly following the areas of metalwork traditions discussed in Chapter 3, but in each the circular roundhouse is the main domestic form. For example, roundhouses with ploughed terraces are found in the Anglo-Scottish borders similar in many respects to those found in Atlantic areas but constructed in wood rather than stone (Jobey 1980). Late Bronze Age settlement forms in north-west England and Wales are not well known at all, but hut-circles are presumed to be the norm in the former area (Cunliffe 1991: 50), while a similar horizon of stone roundhouses to those seen in the Atlantic areas may exist amongst the diverse and largely unstudied drystone structures of north Wales (Smith 1977). The house forms associated with hilltop sites in the northern Welsh Marches, such as at Dinorben (Savory 1971a,b), Moel-y-Gaer (Guilbert 1973, 1975), and the Breiddin (Musson *et al.* 1991), which begin in the Late Bronze Age are predominantly circular. Distinctive defended enclosures with large circular houses are seen after *c.* 900 BC in the south-east at, for example, Mucking North Ring in Essex (Bond 1988) and Springfield Lyons, Essex (Buckley and Hedges 1987). A circular building within a square enclosure is known at Lofts Farm, Essex (Brown 1988), perhaps indicating some direct west-central European influences and foreshadowing the future axis of contacts of the south-east.

Hilltop enclosures in the northern Atlantic zone

Following trends seen elsewhere in north-western Europe, there is some evidence for the construction of enclosures on hilltops in Atlantic areas from the Late Bronze Age. In Scotland, hilltop enclosures are not well dated, especially in the Atlantic zone, but the large quantities of Late Bronze Age metalwork from Dunagoil on the Isle of Bute and Traprain Law in East Lothian, and the excavations of sites such as Brown Caterthun, Angus, and Eildon Hill North, Roxburghshire, suggest beginnings for such sites around 1000 BC (Armit 1997: 46–54). More work has been done in Ireland where a number of hilltop and larger enclosures have provided evidence of Late Bronze Age activity at Cathedral Hill, Co. Down, Clogher, Co. Tyrone, Freestone Hill, Co. Kilkenny, Haughey's Fort and Navan Fort, Co. Armagh, Rathgall, Co. Wicklow, and Mooghaun, Co. Clare (Raftery 1994: 18–22, 58–62). Late Bronze Age dates have been obtained for the construction of palisade defences at the Welsh hilltop sites of Moel y Gaer, Dinorben and the Breiddin (Cunliffe 1991: 313–16). There is no firm evidence from south-west England but this may simply be due to a lack of work because, as Todd (1987: 157) points out, 'a number of sites later occupied by hillforts have produced chance finds of later Bronze Age metalwork, but the original context of this material is not known'.[6] Radiocarbon dates in the tenth and ninth centuries were obtained for the hilltop site of Killibury, Cornwall, but it is unclear whether these relate to the earliest phases of occupation at the site (Miles 1977: 100–1). In addition some of the ceramics from the hillfort at Hembury could well belong to the Late Bronze Age (Miles 1977: 111) and may correlate with an early palisaded phase at the site described by Cunliffe (1991: 313–14). There is even less evidence from Armorica, but again little work has been carried out. The identification of some ceramics from Kercaradec, Finistère, as final Hallstatt suggests that the dating of hilltop enclosures in Armorica may be in line with developments elsewhere in western Europe (Le Bihan 1984). In contrast, a good number of western Iberian hilltop enclosures have been assigned Late Bronze Age construction dates including Sao Juliao and Torroso in Galicia (Ruíz-Gálvez 1991: 280–1) and Alto do Castelo, Alvaiázere, Castelo de São Bras, Corõa do Frade, Castelo do Giraldo, Azougada, Monte de São Martinho, and Outeiro do Circo in central and southern Portugal (Gibson 2000).

Despite the evidence for early origins, and indeed their continued construction and use throughout the first millennium BC, hilltop enclosures were by no means a major Atlantic type. There are very few hillforts in the Atlantic zone compared to areas further east and certainly nothing to compare to the densely packed hillfort zones which develop in Wessex, the Welsh Marches and eastern Scotland. Little is known about the interiors of northern Atlantic hilltop enclosures; roundhouses appear to be the norm but there is little evidence that any were densely occupied. It seems that rather than serving as permanently populated tribal centres, hilltop enclosures in Atlantic areas more likely served as seasonal meeting places or assembly points perhaps in some way related to the pastoral cycle and the gathering of herds. Sites such as Dunagoil on the Isle of Bute also indicate some involvement in the articulation of trade – in this case, given the site's coastal location, potentially maritime trade which may have also been carried out at the far more numerous defended promontory locations (see later discussion). By serving a range of specialised communal needs, such as trading locations and meeting places, hilltop enclosures may also have had a ritual significance to Atlantic communities.

The Atlantic Iron Age 700 BC–AD 100

Chronology

There is no clear archaeological horizon between the end of the Late Bronze Age and the beginning of the Iron Age throughout most of western Europe and this is especially true of the Atlantic areas. Although, as we have seen, the Atlantic bronze networks had gone out of use by *c.* 600 BC there was not an automatic transition to iron technology. In fact, throughout the Iron Age iron was never a major part of Atlantic society, and it is far from clear whether iron objects were produced on any significant scale at all in an Atlantic context prior to the end of the first millennium BC. If anything, the trend is one of strong continuity in social practices and settlement in western coastal areas from the Late Bronze Age to the Iron Age. For the Atlantic at least, then, the division between the two periods is an arbitrary one and is set here as seventh century BC, corresponding to Iron Age dating elsewhere and the beginning of the decline of the bronze exchange networks which were out of use by *c.* 600 BC.

When discussing Iron Age Armorica the French chronological divisions are employed: Premier Age du Fer (Hallstatt C and D) 750–450 BC; Early and Middle La Tène 450–120 BC; Late La Tène 120–56 BC; and the Gallo-Roman period from 54 BC. In south-west England the chronological divisions of the Iron Age are variable from study to study. In Cornwall the period is usually seen as beginning *c.* 600 BC and is divided into an Early Iron Age 600–400 BC, a Late Iron Age after 400 BC with the Romano-British period beginning in AD 43 (Quinnell 1986: 112). In contrast, Thomas (1958: 15) uses the term Early Iron Age for the whole of the pre-Roman Iron Age while Haselgrove (1999: 114) suggests a division of 800 to 300 BC for the Early Iron Age and *c.* 300 BC–AD 43/44 for the later period. In this study the south-western Early Iron Age will be defined as the period 700 to 100 BC to correlate with Hallstatt and Early/Middle La Tène in Armorica, while the Late Iron Age will be seen as 100 BC to AD 43/44. This is done not only to fit with divisions elsewhere but also because it roughly correlates with the horizons of recognised ceramic phases in the south-west (i.e. South-Western Decorated ware from the fourth to the first century BC and Cordoned ware from the first century BC to third/fourth centuries AD).

The Roman conquest had a limited effect on developments in Atlantic Scotland and Ireland and this is reflected in the longer temporal definitions of the Iron Age in these areas. In Atlantic Scotland the Early Iron Age has been viewed as being from *c.* 800 BC to the end of the first millennium BC and the Later Iron Age as from the beginning of the first millennium BC to the arrival of Norse settlement in the area around AD 800 (Armit 1990; Harding 1990). Others have divided it into Early (*c.* 800 to 100 BC), Middle (100 BC to AD 300 or 400) and Late (up to AD 800) periods based on the clustering of radiocarbon dates from settlement sites (Foster 1990: Ill. 9.3; MacKie 1995); the latter division is preferred here.

In Ireland the Iron Age is thought to have begun somewhere around 700 BC, but it is by no means a clear horizon and is rarely perceived as a definitive cultural change. Between 700 BC and 500 BC is often called the Late Bronze Age/Early Iron Age owing to the perceived continuity in Ireland of earlier Dowris traditions (Waddell 1998). The appearance of La Tène forms in north-eastern Ireland is usually simply referred to as the Irish La Tène Iron Age (Raftery 1994). The next major horizon then is the Early Christian period beginning around AD 400 (Mytum 1992). The same chronological divisions as those applied to Atlantic Scotland will be applied to Atlantic Ireland with an Early phase (*c.* 800 BC to 100 BC) and a Later period (*c.* 100 BC to AD 400), with the Early Christian or Early Historic period from AD 400.

The beginning of the Iron Age in Atlantic areas

Interest from west-central Europe in the Atlantic zone began to wane as Urnfield ways of life gave way to the development of decentralised warrior elites from the Hallstatt C period onwards (*c.* 750 BC) with their emphasis on the control and use of iron technology (Kossack 1959; Kristiansen 1998: 240–8). The rise of these groups had major effects on the trading relationships which were the key to the success of Late Bronze Age prestige economies as trade to the north and west emanating from the Mediterranean[7] or west-central Europe itself declines steadily throughout the period (Kristiansen 1998: 211–22). Iron producing areas were understandably less interested in obtaining tin and copper from the Atlantic zone and instead western Hallstatt C groups focused to the east and to the south on the developing city states of the Mediterranean zone for their import needs (Figure 4.9). Iron could be mined locally while silver, gold and copper could be obtained from the developing Tartessian groups in south-west Iberia and northern Italy (ibid. 210). At the same time the production of bronze objects declined in west-central Europe and instead Hallstatt C chiefdoms began to import complex bronze objects from the Etruscans and Greek colonies.

Iron technology was in use in west-central Europe from *c.* 750 BC and is visible in the amounts of imported and indigenous iron objects in west Hallstatt grave contexts. Evidence for the adoption of iron in the Atlantic, on the other hand, is extremely patchy and very difficult to plot. After an initial surge of early evidence around the seventh century BC[8] there is basically very little evidence of iron-working in the Atlantic zone until the end of the millennium. If anything the lack of iron-working and iron technology could be seen as a feature of Atlantic areas in the Iron Age[9] and

Figure 4.9 The initial distributions of Hallstatt C groupings formed around the Adriatic city state zone. The western Hallstatt C groups are defined by the occurrence of the Hallstatt iron sword: solid circle = bronze sword; cross = iron sword. Note the predominance of bronze forms in the west and lack of material in Atlantic zones (after Kristiansen 1998: fig. 111; after Kimmig 1983: Abb. 43).

defines the region as a separate zone as strongly through its absence as bronze objects did through their ubiquity in the previous period.

Kristiansen has suggested that iron producing areas – which were more likely to be areas which lacked tin because 'iron was produced in situations where bronze was lacking' (1998: 211) – deliberately attempted to monopolise iron technology and that the wider dissemination of this knowledge ultimately caused the collapse of Hallstatt C chiefdoms at the end of the seventh century BC (op. cit. 217). The well-documented problems of working iron and the complex processes involved[10] compared to bronze working may be another reason why iron was not widely adopted in the Atlantic west (Geselowitz 1988). However, the reasons for the lack of iron in the Atlantic through-out almost the whole of the first millennium BC, even after the technology was mastered elsewhere, are less easily explained and may be much more deeply rooted.

As well as the ritual aspects discussed at the end of Chapter 3, iron and its associated technology may have been actively resisted in the Atlantic zone precisely because of the destabilising effects it had already had on west-central European communities.[11] The early occurrences of iron demonstrate that its existence was definitely known in Atlantic areas – it simply was not widely adopted. The Late Bronze Age social and ritual system relied on the fact that tin was difficult to obtain and could thus only be accessed by a controlling elite. The fact that iron was much more widely available would work to undermine such a system just as it appears to have done in west-central Europe.

The Hallstatt C period in the Atlantic was essentially a period of the continuation of the contacts and bronze metalworking traditions established in previous centuries and which witnessed the last large Carp's Tongue hoards and the small hoards of the Llyn Fawr phase (Savory 1976; Burgess 1979; Thomas 1989). The final flourish of the Armorican socketed axe hoards, as we saw in Chapter 3, marked the end of the system; metalwork and its deposition had lost its role in Atlantic society. Influences were adopted from the Hallstatt world but significantly these were re-contextualised to fit Atlantic cultural traditions. As well as the development of distinctive British and Irish types from Hallstatt forms,[12] objects made in iron and deposited in burials in continental Europe were produced in bronze and deposited in watery contexts in Atlantic areas (i.e. swords of Hallstatt derivation; Figure 3.23).

By the subsequent Hallstatt D period (*c.* 625–450 BC) there was a significant drop in the occurrence of imported and continentally influenced material reaching Atlantic areas – a lack of exchange activity which coincided with the demise of the Atlantic bronze networks. This adds weight to the argument that it was a lack of continental interest in Atlantic metal resources which ultimately brought an end to the Atlantic Bronze Age. As has been argued above, south-eastern Britain now broke off from the Atlantic exchange systems and looked towards Belgium and northern France via the Thames, the Seine, and the Rhine routes.

The shift of emphasis in south-eastern England from Atlantic axes of influence to those of continental Europe can be seen in the distributions of iron bars thought to correspond exactly with elite Hallstatt D centres (Kristiansen 1998: 216; Figure 4.10). A clear area of production can be seen in south-eastern England linking the zone directly into west-central European traditions. In south-east England, weaponry now followed continental Hallstatt D fashions with daggers replacing the sword, and bow brooches used for fastening clothes instead of ring headed pins. There were no such Hallstatt D influences in Atlantic Scotland, Ireland, Wales or south-west England – no fine dagger series such as those seen in the Thames area and south-east England.

In Armorica the picture is slightly different. Cunliffe (1997: 152–4) has convincingly argued that from the late sixth century BC west-central European influences are visible in Armorican pottery styles and from a few pieces of imported metalwork.[13] He claims the highly distinctive style of Armorican stamp decorated pottery belongs 'in general, to a broad category of stamped pottery found throughout central Europe in the fifth and fourth centuries' (Cunliffe 1997: 152). He uses this evidence to suggest that Armorica provided west-central Europe with access to the Atlantic maritime routes from the Hallstatt D period onwards: 'it would be easy to transport

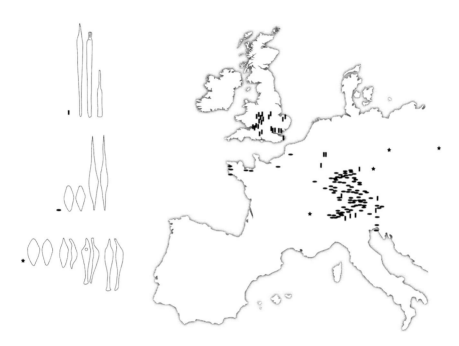

Figure 4.10 Distribution of iron 'currency' bars and iron smelting centres in Early Iron Age western Europe. Note the occurrence of bars in south-east England and Armorica (after Kristiansen 1998: fig. 108; after Pliener 1980: fig. II.2).

metals along the Loire to the western extension of the late Hallstatt chiefdom zone in Burgundy' (op. cit. 152).

Hallstatt C forms were extremely rare throughout the peninsula, suggesting that west-central European groups were still gaining access to Atlantic networks via the south-east and the Thames at this time. By the Hallstatt D period the route into the Atlantic may have shifted to Armorica and, although we can still assume that the demand for bronze had considerably lessened, there may still have been a need for access to Atlantic networks albeit on a much diminished scale (Figure 4.11). Armorica, as we shall see, maintains a unique balance between the two different systems throughout the Iron Age in that it remains primarily part of the Atlantic sphere of interaction but is responsive to certain west-central European influences.

The reasons for this shift are likely to have been complex. It may have been more difficult for south-eastern groups to continue exploiting Atlantic networks while they were becoming more and more continentally influenced themselves. The Loire may simply have been a more convenient route for continental Hallstatt D chiefdoms. It may also be significant that the hillfort zone of central southern England which had been developing since 700 BC was densely packed with hillforts from 600 to 400 BC (Cunliffe 1982b: fig. 3) and this area may have acted as a buffer zone between

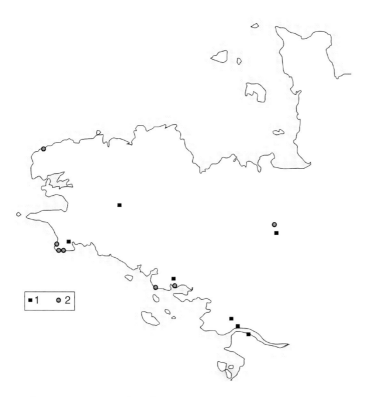

Figure 4.11 Hallstatt D imports and Early La Tène imports in Armorica. ■ = Ha D ● = ELT (after Galliou 1990: fig. 1). Note concentration at the mouth of the Loire and along the south coast suggesting use of the Loire route.

long-lived Atlantic traditions to the west and the fledgling Hallstatt system in the south-east (Cunliffe 1997: 164). Indeed, the central southern hillfort zone may owe its initial formation to the unstable social conditions created by being caught between these two systems of interaction[14] (ibid.), and may have blocked trading links during the Iron Age between the south-east and Atlantic areas. Certainly from this point onwards there is a clear and well recognised zonation in British Iron Age settlement, the broadest differences being between a zone of largely non-defensive settlement in the east, the hillfort dominated landscape of the Marches and central southern England, and a western Atlantic zone composed of small strongly defended settlements (Cunliffe 1991).

As we shall examine in the following chapters, within the Atlantic zone there are further, perhaps equally significant, sub-divisions. From 600 to *c.* 200 BC there is a general decline in contact between the Irish and British Atlantic zones and west-central Europe. The outer fringes of the Atlantic zone, Atlantic Scotland and western Ireland, appear most isolated, while south-western England and Wales have their closest parallels not within the rest of Britain, but with the developments across the English Channel in Armorica.

Atlantic material contacts in the Iron Age

What little evidence there is for the exchange of goods along the northern Atlantic coasts in the Iron Age has been fully discussed by Cunliffe (1982a, 1990, 1997: 150–4). Despite the classical references briefly mentioned in Chapter 1 there is not strong evidence for a Mediterranean presence on the Atlantic seas.

The occurrence of small bronze figurines of generalised 'Mediterranean' type in Armorica and south-western Britain however, may be the result of fourth to first century BC cross-Channel contacts. Two figurines, one from Aust in the Severn estuary, the other from Sligo in Ireland, are thought to be of Iberian origin (Smith 1905: 136; Jacobstahl 1938). To these eight from Blandford, Dorset (Jacobstahl 1938: 53–4), one from Maiden Castle, Dorset, one from Dartmoor, and two from Mount Batten have been added (Cunliffe 1990: 247). Henig (1988: 70-2) has dated all of these figurines to the third century BC and considers them to be of Etrusco-Itallic manufacture. Although the contexts of these objects are either unknown or undated, Cunliffe (1987, 1990: 247) states that it remains a possibility that some, if not all, of these western British finds were imported along Atlantic trade routes soon after they were made.

Cunliffe has also pointed out that at least some of the relatively large number of un-contexted Greek and Carthaginian coins discovered in Armorica, western France and southern Britain are likely to have been contemporary imports (1990: 247; 1997: 150).

Further evidence comes from the finds of Iberian type fibulae. Three fibulae from the cemetery at Harlyn Bay, Cornwall (Whimster 1977: 77–8), two from the settlement site at Mount Batten, Devon (Boudet 1988), and one each from two sites in Finistère: Kerancoat, Ergué-Armel and Roz-an-Tremen, Plomeur (Giot 1958), have been compared with types which occur in Iberia and Aquitania and date to the Early La Tène period (Leeds 1927: 229–30; Mohen 1980; Cunliffe 1990: 247). Boudet (1988) has argued that the two brooches from Mount Batten are of local British manufacture, implying that they were simply made in a style that is known to occur throughout Atlantic Europe and not directly traded from Iberia or western France. However, even if all the examples are of indigenous manufacture the existence of a common stylistic Atlantic tradition is implicit.

These small numbers of finds provide insufficient evidence in themselves for the existence of Atlantic contacts in the Iron Age. In general, the utilitarian character of domestic material assemblages found at sites throughout the northern Atlantic are not considered to be sufficiently distinctive or diagnostic to sustain close chronologies or exclusive cultural identities within their own areas, let alone providing evidence of wider maritime contacts. It is considered by many that the lack of evidence for material exchange indicates that Atlantic communities had become isolated and peripheral after the collapse of the Atlantic bronze networks by the end of the seventh century BC.

However, it is important not to underestimate the role of even utilitarian assemblages because, at the very least, they can provide evidence of similar levels of organisation in the domestic sphere as well as allow inferences as to the concerns and beliefs of societies (e.g. at a very basic level, such as whether pottery is decorated or not indicating elaboration in the domestic sphere). Other commonly found objects, such as amber beads and ring headed pins, although not diagnostic or closely datable, do provide evidence of some level of long-distance contact.

Contacts between Atlantic areas in the Iron Age are simply not visible through the exchange of exotica or items of prestige. The similarity of Atlantic domestic assemblages and resources may have negated the impetus for the exchange of forms, but ideas and information may still have been communicated. Contacts may be inferred from the general similarities between Atlantic areas in other spheres, for example, through their settlement forms and level of social organisation. In other words, within the context of shared traditions: traditions that are sufficiently similar across the seaboard, and equally distinct from other European events, to imply that some form of cultural exchange along a maritime axis was taking place. The use of the sea as a medium of contact or uniting entity provides a context for the continuity of shared Atlantic traditions that can be contrasted with more La Tène influenced populations further inland.

A case for the existence of shared traditions in Atlantic areas has been convincingly argued by Cunliffe through the close stylistic similarities seen between Armorican ceramics and western British and Irish bronzework, dating from the fifth century to the second century BC (Wheeler 1943: 216; Fox 1961: 196; Cunliffe 1990: 248–50; Cunliffe and de Jersey 1997: 38–40; Figure 4.12). The shape of Armorican Early and Middle La Tène bowls, with widely outflaring rims *(jattes basses)*, their internally grooved rims *(bords à cannelure interne)* and curvilinear decoration, have many aspects in common with the La Tène bronze bowls of western Britain, such as with the designs on the Cerrig-y-Drudion 'hanging bowl', north Wales[15] (Smith 1926); the Rose Ash bowl, north Devon (Fox 1961); the bowl from Youlton, Cornwall (Smith 1926: 280–81; Fox 1961: 192–3); the Birdlip bowl, Gloucestershire (Staelens 1983); and the similar though undecorated bowl from Bulbery, Dorset (Cunliffe 1972). Cunliffe (with de Jersey 1997: 39) has also drawn attention to the striking similarities between the pottery bowl from Hennebont (Côtes-d'Armor), which features a recurved animal head looped to the rim of the shoulder (Menez 1986: fig. 65), and the bronze bowl with animal head attachment from Keshcarrigan, Co. Leitrim in Ireland (Jope 1954: fig. 2).

These finds imply the existence of a shared tradition created, articulated and communicated through the movement of high status metal vessels. The curvilinear designs on Armorican Iron Age ceramics were undoubtedly influenced by motifs used by metalworking craftsmen in the Marne and Moselle regions (Cunliffe 1990: 249; with de Jersey 1997: 38). The connection between Armorica and west-central Europe, recognised in the preceding Hallstatt D period through stamped pottery decorations, persisted then into the Early and Middle La Tène. Further evidence of this relationship is seen in the occurrence of about half a dozen double pyramidal iron ingots of supposedly central European type in Armorica (Giot 1964). Two similar ingots are

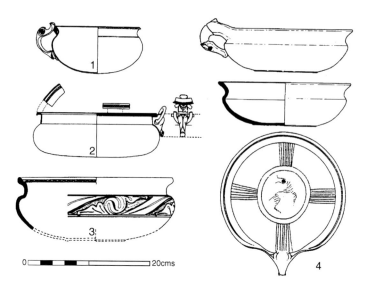

Figure 4.12 Similarities between Armorican ceramics and western British and Irish bronzework fifth to second centuries AD (after Cunliffe and de Jersey 1997: fig. 29). (1) Bronze bowl from Keshcarrigan, Co. Leitrim, Ireland; (2) Bronze bowl from Rose Ash, Devon, England; (3) Pot from Blavet, Hénon, Côtes d'Armor, Brittany; (4) Pot from Hennebont, Côtes d'Armor, Brittany.

known from Portland Bill overlooking Weymouth harbour (Grinsell 1958: 137) and are thought to have been imported from Armorica (Cunliffe 1990: 247).

Discussion will now turn to the settlement record, the best documented part of the Atlantic Iron Age, in an effort to consider the evidence for Atlantic cultural contacts and similarities. The choice of settlements as a unit of study is the most useful way forward as Atlantic Iron Age archaeology is essentially a settlement archaeology, it is currently impossible to construct detailed ceramic typologies for Atlantic areas, or to identify clear regional traditions in material assemblages.

Atlantic Iron Age settlement

When considering the settlements of the Atlantic seaboard we are faced with two main problems. First, the dating of the majority of Atlantic sites lack chronological clarity: often all that can be said is that a certain site dates to somewhere in the earlier or later part of the first millennium BC. In particular, it is often very difficult to date sites to the conventional date range of the Early Iron Age (700/600–400 BC) due to the well documented problems with the accuracy of radiocarbon calibration curve over the period *c.* 800–400 BC (Stuvier and Pearson 1993). Throughout the Atlantic areas, but especially in Scotland and Ireland, the dating of Atlantic stone-built settlements has been further blurred by a refusal to recognise that the latest (i.e. surviving) occupation may not be chronologically indicative of construction and initial occupation (Harding 1984, 2005a). Monumental stone-built structures, if regularly maintained, could have lasted in use for hundreds of years, leaving in many cases minimal traces of their primary occupation. In fact, the continuity of occupation, lasting over a number of centuries, is a common feature of Atlantic settlement and reflects a stable social environment.

The second problem is that there are dangers in assuming that technical similarities between settlement types implies cultural continuity. Many authors, such as Warner (1981: 47), claim that 'apparent similarities need mean no more than that similar problems, within similar societies and technologies are extremely likely to invite similar responses'. Shared elements of architectural detail such as intra-mural cells, door rebates or stone corbelling between Scottish Atlantic roundhouses and the stone forts of Ireland are not usually taken to be convincing evidence of a community of culture contacts along the Atlantic sea-lanes. Similar arguments for a strong Iberian element in Ireland based on the architectural similarities of stone forts and *chevaux-de-frise* defences remain equally unconvincing (Harbison 1971, 1979; Raftery 1991b, 1994: 61–2: fig. 33).

However, it is also possible to underestimate the significance of such architectural similarities – the reasons why Atlantic areas already possessed similar societies and technologies demands explanation rather than being an explanation in itself. Forms may have been developing in an awareness of what was happening elsewhere and while this does not indicate the existence of a maritime exchange network on the scale of Late Bronze Age trading contacts, it would similarly establish and re-confirm social continuities along an Atlantic maritime axis. The themes of *similarity* and *divergence* are relevant to the study of Atlantic settlement trends; distinctive local or regional characteristics (divergence) occur within a much broader background of shared cultural elements (similarity). These themes will be well demonstrated in the following chapters by the reconsideration, and in some cases re-dating, of Atlantic settlement trends.

Although enclosed farmsteads occupied by single households are the dominant Iron Age settlement type throughout north-western Europe and Britain, the single domestic unit defended homestead can be viewed as a distinctively Atlantic type in that they are most usually circular and occur in isolation in the landscape. As Cunliffe (1997: 160) has stated, the one essential characteristic binding Atlantic 'communities together was a similar social structure based on the family unit or lineage group'. Evidence for population centralisation beyond the family or lineage group is very rare in first millennium BC Atlantic settlement sequences. As has been suggested above, the few larger hilltop enclosures that do occur in Atlantic areas do not appear to have been settlements supporting large, permanent populations but were most likely meeting places for pastoral communities during annual festivals or those times of the year when flocks and herds needed to be gathered in.

Atlantic Iron Age roundhouses and curvilinear enclosures

Circular enclosure and house forms continue to be the dominant types in most Atlantic areas throughout the Iron Age, implying the survival in the west of long-held ideological conceptions and expressions of structure. While the beginnings of circular house forms can be traced back in some areas into the second millennium BC, circular settlement traditions only become widespread throughout northern Atlantic areas during the Late Bronze Age around the same time as communities were participating in extensive bronze exchange networks. It is possible that the two phenomena are related, certainly new technologies and ideas, including commodities such as hardier cereals, would have been communicated between groups as a result of the increased contacts in the Late Bronze Age (Ruíz-Gálvez 1991). This may have helped the development of long-lived permanent settlements, creating in areas such as the Atlantic – perhaps for the first time in many places – the necessary conditions to make permanent settlement a viable option.[16] It is interesting in this context that the most substantial, and some of the earliest, examples of domestic forms are first seen in Atlantic areas – in many cases beginning settlement sequences and traditions that continue unbroken for hundreds of years. Equally the development of the most elaborate and monumental roundhouse forms in Iron Age Europe are seen, as we shall examine later in the next chapter, in the furthest fringes of the Atlantic west (Hingley 1995).

It is perhaps significant that circular domestic settlements appear in the west after the use of communal circular ritual monuments comes to an end. The evidence for the deposition of animal and human bones, and household and prestige objects in an organised and structured fashion at roundhouse sites, suggests that the ritual significance of the earlier circular form and its associated beliefs have been transferred to a domestic setting. In other words, in the later prehistoric period the house may have become the focus of ritual life, rather than the ceremonial complex or burial. The occurrence of formalised votive deposits within roundhouses alongside other aspects such as the orientation of entrances and the radial patterning of internal space suggest the existence of complex and long-lived patterns of belief occurring within broadly related traditions (Foster 1989a, b; Hill 1989; Ried 1989; Hingley 1990; Fitzpatrick 1994; Parker Pearson and Richards 1994a, 1994b; McOmish 1996; Parker Pearson 1996; Parker Pearson *et al.* 1996; Oswald 1997). Communities in north-western Europe may have been stressing their continuity with the earlier Atlantic orientated traditions and social conventions that were in existence prior to the expansion of contacts with groups based in central Europe during the first millennium BC: 'rectangularity becomes an aspect of the movement and influence out from central Europe, associated mainly, though not exclusively, with the "Urnfield culture" before and after 1000 BC' (Harding 1972: 54).

Although southern and eastern parts of Britain began to look more towards west-central Europe from the Iron Age onwards, circular house forms remained the dominant tradition of house construction throughout the majority of the country up until the Roman invasion in the first century AD.[17] The general tendency towards building 'in the round' is very much a western Atlantic phenomenon (including the whole of the British Isles) and as such offers a contrast to the rectangular building traditions associated with central European communities.

The occurrence of roundhouses throughout Britain in the Iron Age indicate at one level widespread continuities in the construction and expression of domestic forms.

However, there is a marked regionality in the roundhouse and enclosure forms encountered throughout Britain and those in Atlantic areas, as small isolated defended circular homesteads tend to resemble each other more closely than types found further east. Stone roundhouse forms in northern and western Scotland form a cohesive regional zone in the Iron Age, and as a group have much in common with drystone forms in Ireland. The domestic enclosure forms of south-west Wales and south-west England are closely related to each other and have close parallels with the earthen *rath* enclosures of Ireland and with settlements in Armorica.

In contrast, the rest of Britain from *c*. 600 to 100 BC is a more socially varied area. Ring-ditch and ring-groove houses, alongside more substantial timber post-built roundhouses, are the dominant forms and can be found throughout the hillfort dominated zone of the centre south, northern England and southern and eastern Scotland. In northern England small sub-rectangular or D-shaped enclosures, such as at West Brandon, Co. Durham, predominate, whereas the extremely diverse range of oval and curvilinear enclosures and roundhouse forms found in southern and eastern Scotland imply the existence of a distinctly complex society here from the middle of the first millennium BC. In general, the eastern coasts of Britain feature communities with access to a wide range of elite goods and styles that are very similar to, and undoubtedly influenced by, those on the continent. Direct cultural contacts can be inferred from the appearance of the Arras culture in the Yorkshire area, practising elite burial rites with two-wheeled wagons and associated goods very similar to those seen in the Lower Seine, the Haine, and the Ardennes (Stead 1979; Dent 1982, 1985). The contrast with Atlantic social systems is most clearly seen in southern and eastern parts of the country, however, where open village size settlements and enclosures, often featuring rectilinear or irregular plans, are found that have their closest parallels with forms in west-central Europe especially northern France and Belgium (Cunliffe 1997: 161).

The situation in Armorica is more complex: the peninsula develops closer links with west-central Europe throughout the Iron Age and particularly in the centuries prior to the Roman invasion in 56 BC. Curvilinear enclosure forms are common, particularly in western areas, but rectilinear forms also develop resembling types found in west-central Europe. In terms of house construction, sub-rectangular forms appear to be the most common type, but it must be kept in mind that the vast majority of building forms known in Armorica date to the late La Tène or Gallo-Roman period[18] (cf. Menez *et al.* 1990). Circular house forms resembling those in other Atlantic areas do occur, perhaps demonstrating, as Duval (1990: 282) has stated, at least a partial adhesion by Armorican communities to '*un monde celtique atlantique*'. Significantly, roundhouse forms appear to be more common in western Armorica and areas facing the ocean (Duval 1990). It would be over-simplistic to consider all round forms as Atlantic types and rectangular forms as purely Continental – it is not as if the right-angle was unknown in the west and both forms can be found in either area.[19] However, as a generalisation the distinction remains valid and epitomises the dialectic between centre and west in Europe, apparent throughout the later prehistoric period in other spheres such as material culture. The construction of roundhouse forms throughout the Atlantic zone could therefore represent the maintenance of deep cultural continuities and long-lived patterns of belief.

Atlantic promontory forts

Before embarking on a detailed examination of Atlantic Iron Age settlement sequences, consideration will be given to the occurrence of coastal promontory forts and souterrains throughout the northern Atlantic zone. In common with circular forms, the restricted Atlantic distributions of these sites have long been considered to be visible expressions of Atlantic cultural distinctiveness.

Promontory forts are found in numbers all along the Atlantic seaboard (Figure 4.13). There are well-defined groups on the Iberian peninsula (Harbison 1971), a great number in north-western France (Wheeler and Richardson 1957; Bender and Cailland 1986; Maguer 1996), south-west England (Sharpe 1992; Herring 1994), Wales (Hogg 1972; Crane 1999), Ireland (Raftery 1994; Redmond 1995; Cotter 2000), northern Scotland (Lamb 1980; Mercer 1981: 71–8), eastern Scotland (Ralston 1980), and Argyll and the Inner Hebrides (RCAHMS 1971–1988) while modern field survey has significantly increased the number of sites known in the Outer Hebrides (Armit 1992: 94–6; Burgess 1999).

Some authors have used their Atlantic distribution as evidence for a distinct promontory fort tradition (Gordon 1940: 111; Wheeler and Richardson 1957: 5; Hogg 1972: 22; Lamb 1980: 6) or invasion (Hogg 1972: 15; Thomas 1972: 78). However, the concept of enclosing a seaward promontory through the construction of one or more ramparts is a basic one and does not require an introduction from any particular area. Promontories are everywhere taken advantage of for defence and the practice cannot be used in isolation to sustain specific cultural identities. On saying this, promontory forts are undoubtedly found in their highest concentrations within the Atlantic zone. Although the indented nature of the Atlantic coastline is undoubtedly a factor, the widespread construction and use of promontory enclosures during the Iron Age may go beyond deterministic interpretations and reflect commonalties in behaviour between Atlantic communities. With this in mind, the potential significance of promontory forts to Atlantic communities demands further investigation.

The most usual definition of a promontory fort is a site 'formed by erection of defences across the landward end of a promontory' (RCAHMS 1928: xxxix; 1988: 30). Unsurprisingly, such a loose definition lumps together a wide diversity of sites of varying size, structure, date and presumably function. Univallate, bivallate and multivallate forms are known, but the vast majority of sites remain unsurveyed while very few have been subject to excavation on any scale and even fewer properly published. The locations and appearance of promontory sites vary: some examples are located high above the sea on remote rocky outcrops offering no immediately obvious domestic or defensive functions; others in less elevated locations and more approachable by sea may have had a more obvious maritime role; some appear to be unfinished; some as only slight and apparently short-lived earthworks, whilst others are quite complex sites featuring multiple rampart arrangements sometimes

Figure 4.13 Distribution of promontory forts (after Lamb 1980: fig. 1).

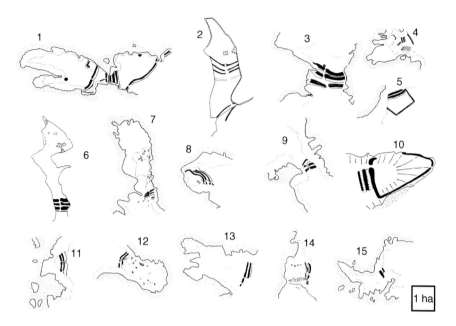

Figure 4.14 Multivallate promontory forts in Armorica and south-west England:
(1) Trevelgue, Cornwall; (2) Castel-Coz, Finistère; (3) The Rumps, Cornwall; (4) Carn Les
Boel, Cornwall; (5) Castel-Meur, Finistère; (6) Treyarnon, Cornwall; (7) Gunard's Head,
Cornwall; (8) Griffin Point, Cornwall; (9) Black Head, Cornwall; (10) Kergastel, Finistère;
(11) Redcliff Castle, Cornwall; (12) Chynhalls, Cornwall; (13) Penhale, Cornwall; (14) Maen
Castle, Cornwall; (15) Park Head, Cornwall (after Johnson and Rose 1982: fig. 10; Maguer
1996: 3).

incorporating drystone architectural elements. Contrary to usual reports, however,
small univallate types, most usually enclosing less than one hectare and featuring a
single low earthen rampart, appear to be the most dominant form along the Atlantic
seaboard.[20] Very little is known about these simple sites because attention has tended
to focus on the more imposing multivallate examples (Figure 4.14).

The promontory forts of Armorica, or *la presqu'îles* as they are sometimes termed
in French publications, and those from south-west England, locally known as cliff-
castles, are better documented than the rest (Wheeler and Richardson 1957: 103–12;
Cotton 1959, 1961; Maguer 1996). This is largely due to the early interest taken in
them based upon the now discredited belief that the occurrence of promontory forts
in western Brittany and south-west England was the result of the direct diffusion of
the form from Brittany to Cornwall by the maritime Veneti tribe of Caesar's Gallic
War commentaries (*Bellum Gallicum* III: 8; Cotton 1959: 116; Hawkes 1966; Fox, A.
1973: 141). The use of promontory forts, and souterrains, in south-west England
and Armorica undoubtedly reflects the existence of shared cultural traditions
between the two peninsulas, but there is no longer any need to think in terms of the
introduction of one type from one area to the next.

Activity on promontory locations throughout the Atlantic seaboard spans the Neolithic to the first millennium AD (Sharpe 1992), but the construction of ramparts to demarcate these promontories, and therefore the concept of a promontory fort or cliff-castle, is usually dated, from the current limited excavation evidence, stray ceramic finds, and analogies with other enclosures, to the Iron Age period (Wheeler and Richardson 1957: 102–32; Herity and Eogan 1977: 227; Lamb 1980: 62–4; Armit 1992: 96; Giot 1995: 276–83; Maguer 1996: 110–20). The vast majority of excavated sites throughout western Britain, Ireland and Brittany have provided evidence of activity during the Iron Age and it would appear that their use, certainly in terms of use associated with the construction of their defences, focused on this period. Due to the lack of concerted fieldwork on promontory sites, however, their precise dating range remains obscure.

Promontory forts are the largest group of forts in Atlantic Scotland.[21] In many cases there are obvious architectural relationships, and therefore one may assume chronological relationships, between promontory forts and complex Atlantic round-house architecture either in terms of the promontory fortification itself or the location of Atlantic roundhouses on promontories (Lamb 1980). The 5 m thick wall built across the neck of an exposed coastal promontory at Barra Head on Berneray in the Western Isles, for example, featured superimposed intra-mural galleries and a distinctive low entrance with bar holes (Armit 1992: 94; 1997: 59; Figure 4.15). The rich Late Bronze Age metalwork assemblage from the coastal hill-fort of Dunagoil on the Isle of Bute, located right next to the sea and featuring at least three rock-cut boat nausts, can perhaps be taken to suggest an early date for other coastal fortifications in the area. Recently, a univallate promontory fort

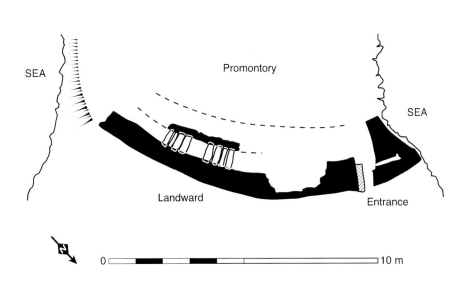

Figure 4.15 Barra Head, Western Isles (after Armit 1992: Ill.9.2; after RCAHMS 1928).

enclosing less than half a hectare at Gob Eirer on the Isle of Lewis was radiocarbon dated to *c.* 600–500 BC (Burgess 1999; Harding 2004: 146).

Around 250 promontory forts are known from Ireland, mainly located along the west coast, (Raftery 1994: 48; Cotter 2000: 176) but so far dating evidence comes from only two examples. The drystone defences at Dunbeg in Co. Kerry were shown from radiocarbon determinations to have been built sometime prior to the eighth century AD and sometime after the construction of a ditch that also cut off the promontory dating to around the eighth century BC (Barry 1981: 308; Figure 5.19). Gallo-Roman potsherds dating to the first century AD were recovered from disturbed occupation soil at the triple-ditched promontory fort at Drumanagh, Co. Dublin, suggesting that at least some promontory sites may date to the turn of the millennium (Raftery 1994: 48).

The Cornish cliff-castles of Maen Castle and Trevelgue have produced some of the earliest Iron Age pottery in the south-west, each producing sherds assigned to the Late Bronze Age/Early Iron Age transition (Nowakowski 2004). The large assemblage of South Western Decorated ware from Trevelgue indicates that occupation continued there throughout the Iron Age while the small amount of cordoned ware recovered suggests that, in common with multiple enclosure forts and hillforts in the south-west, the site was out of use by the Roman period. Excavations at the bivallate site at Penhale, Cornwall, produced South Western Decorated pottery and two radiocarbon dates centred in the middle of the first century BC (Smith 1984).

Herring (1994) has suggested that simple univallate sites such as Maen Castle may be earlier than the more complex multivallate examples like Treryn Dinas, which he dates from *c.* 200 BC onwards. There really has not been enough work done to assess whether such an assumption is true, but on present evidence – restricted mainly to surface finds – it does seem that the simpler sites tend to produce unequivocally earlier Iron Age pottery than the multivallate examples. Significantly, simple univallate promontory sites have also been dated to early periods in Iron Age settlement development in south-west Wales (Williams 1988: 33–40). Bearing in mind that many sites probably represent multiple phasing and the creation of multiple ramparts may have more to do with individual site circumstances than chronology, a general move towards more complex forms sometime *c.* 200 BC onwards in the south-west would compare well with the trends seen in other settlement types in the western Atlantic zone examined later.

Many of the multivallate examples undoubtedly represent works of more than one period. At the Rumps, St Miniver, Cornwall, for example, three ramparts involving at least three phases of construction were built (Brooks 1974). Finds of datable ceramics – South Western Decorated ware and cordoned ware – suggest occupation from fourth century BC to the first century AD. Gunard's Head ramparts are similarly complex (Gordon 1940), particularly the massive stone inner defences, but in this case the site produced exclusively South Western Decorated ware (Gordon 1940: fig. 8). In Armorica, the promontory fort of Kervédan, île de Groix, Morbihan, features a main rampart with at least three outer defences, all of which appear to have gone through several modifications (Thriepland 1945; Giot 1995: 282; Figure 4.16).

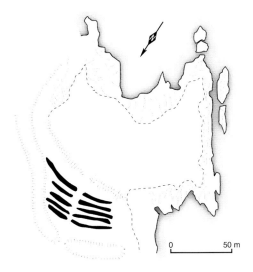

Figure 4.16 Kervédan, île de Groix, Morbihan (after Giot 1995: 281).

As in the south-west, the majority of the Armorican sites are associated with evidence of earlier activity – pottery, burial monuments, and other finds – but there is good evidence to date the actual construction of ramparts in promontory locations to the first millennium BC. The clearest evidence comes from the Catuélan and Pleine-Garenne ditches at Cap d'Erquy, Côtes-d'Armor, which have been radiocarbon dated to between 820 and 390 BC, and 800 and 50 BC[22] respectively (Bender and Cailland 1986: 64; Giot 1995: 277; Figure 4.17). Primel, Plougasnou, a 4 hectare multivallate site with four earth and stone ramparts situated on the north coast of Finistère at the Bay of Morlaix, provides further Iron Age dating evidence; Giot (1995: 287) reports the finding of Iron Age ceramics and Dressel 1 sherds alongside evidence of hearths and shell middens (Maguer 1996: 113).

The function of promontory sites is a matter of debate and given the considerable diversity of types included within the class, a range of different functions and uses for different sites seems likely. Interpretations from site to site vary from being simply places of refuge, coastal expressions of enclosure forms found inland, ritual centres, or trading sites involved in maritime trade (cf. Johnson and Rose 1982: 155; Quinnell 1986: 115; Cunliffe 1991: 259; Sharpe 1992: 65–8).

Domestic use

The idea of promontory forts performing the same function as inland hillforts but in a coastal situation owes much to interpretations of Caesar's comments on the coastal sites of the Veneti. Caesar's references to what he terms the *oppida*[23] of the Veneti makes it clear that some promontory locations were used as

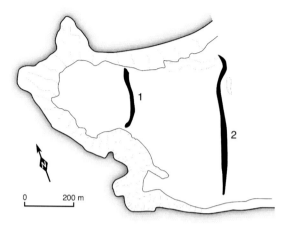

Figure 4.17 Cap d'Erquy, Côtes d'Armor (after Giot 1995, 277). A headland of *c.* 15 hectares is delimited by the Catuélan ditch (1) sometime in the Late Bronze Age/Early Iron Age. At the end of the Early La Tène the enclosed area extends to *c.* 35 hectares with the construction of the Pleine-Garenne ditch (2).

defensive strongholds in Armorica during the Gallic Wars in the middle of the first century BC:

> The positions of the strongholds were generally of one kind. They were set at the end of tongues and promontories, so as to allow no approach on foot, when the tide rushed in from the sea – which happens every twelve hours – nor in ships, because when the tide ebbed again the ships would be damaged in shoal water. Both circumstances, therefore, hindered the assault of the strongholds; and, whenever the natives were in fact overcome by huge siege-works ..., they would bring close inshore a number of ships, of which they possessed an unlimited supply, and take off all their stuff and retire to the nearest strongholds, there to defend themselves again with the same advantage of position.
>
> (*Bellum Gallicum* III.12)

Caesar's comments do not automatically imply that promontory forts performed a similar range of activities as inland enclosures. It must be kept in mind that while his description may suit some sites it cannot be applied to all promontory enclosures – many would not have been protected by the tide, feature defensively insubstantial ramparts overlooked by higher land, are extremely small, and are totally unapproachable by ship (Lamb 1980: 6; Hogg 1972: 22; Herring 1994: 53). Although not a feature of Caesar's description, it is implicit when viewing promontory forts as simply coastal expressions of inland enclosures (Johnson and Rose 1982: 155) that they performed some form of domestic role – if one goes further and compares them to hillforts then this domestic role should be for a relatively large population.

It seems unlikely that many promontory forts represented permanent domestic residences in the Iron Age, based on the evidence of the poorly built and unimposing size of the domestic structures that have been recovered to date. The exception in terms of numbers is Castel Meur, Finistère, where around ninety-five rectangular and oval hut platforms, varying in size from 3 by 2.5 m to 10 by 3.6 m, were recognised, but it remains unclear whether these all relate to an Iron Age occupation, as evidence for Neolithic and later medieval activity was also recovered from the site (du Chatellier 1890; Wheeler and Richardson 1957: 109; Maguer 1996: 116). Evidence for domestic activity at other sites is usually restricted to a few hut platforms, most often situated immediately behind the inner rampart. There are hut platforms behind the walls as at Tower Point and St Davids Head, both Pembrokeshire (Wainwright 1971), Caeran Henllan, Cardiganshire (Savory 1976: 455), The Rumps, Kenidjack Castle, Gunard's Head and Treryn Dinas, Cornwall (Gordon 1940, 100–6; Herring 1994: 54), Castel Coz, Finistère (Wheeler and Richardson 1957: 109), Kervédan, île de Groix, Morbihan (Giot 1995: 282), and stone-built cellular structures at Dúcathair, Aran Islands, and Dunbeg, Co. Kerry, both in Ireland. Often no clear structural evidence is found; investigations at Penhale cliff-castle in Cornwall (Smith 1984), for example, despite opening up an area of 700 square m, revealed evidence for only one small roundhouse. It is inescapable that the majority of promontory locations are very exposed and were therefore not conducive to permanent occupation, and it is often difficult to imagine anyone – let alone an elite grouping – choosing to live on them.

A permanent or seasonal pastoral role, for some promontory sites at least, remains a possibility: there are many modern and recent historical examples of promontories used as stock enclosures. Certainly some examples in the south-west, such as the Rumps and the Dodman, Cornwall or Bolt Tail, Devon (Sharpe 1992: 65), enclose large areas of fairly level ground and could therefore have performed a similar function to that of enclosures inland, offering shelter to people and livestock (Johnson and Rose 1982: 155; Quinnell 1986: 115). Excavation of the Rumps produced, alongside evidence of timber roundhouses with hearths and querns, sheep bones and spindle whorls indicating a pastoral function similar to that envisaged for multiple enclosure forts in the south-west. The site of Embury Beacon, Devon (Jeffries 1974) revealed similar evidence but on closer examination actually appears to be a heavily eroded multiple enclosure fort rather than a true cliff-castle.

Trading sites

Another common function ascribed to promontory sites is their involvement in the articulation of maritime trade. Sites are 'explained as enclosed trading centres – used on an intermittent or seasonal basis by local traders and coasting merchantmen – far from being for defence against violent assault, the ramparts were to protect high value goods and to symbolise the status of the traders within' (Sharpe 1992: 65). Once again, however, this is an interpretation that is not suited to all promontory sites. The precipitous surroundings of many promontory forts make them wholly unsuitable as trading sites because they would have been totally unapproachable by sea. Some, however, do occur near natural harbours or contain areas which could have served as boat nausts.[24] The recognition of such features has been much neglected, and as a result the occurrence of mooring points has never been quantified. There are few descriptions of sites which include whether there was easy access to the sea, either directly or via nearby beaches.

In general, it has been the imposing multivallate forms which have received the most attention. These are often impressively sited on rocky promontories and as a result tend to be the examples that are unapproachable by sea. Such sites are unlikely to reveal evidence of trading activity. Simple univallate forms are far more common and many are situated in lower-lying locations more suited to a trading role. Equally, while the construction of a single, low earthen rampart would not provide adequate security for a permanent settlement, it would do so for people and goods involved in short seasonal or one-off trading transactions (Herring 1994: 53).

The few assemblages so far recovered from promontory forts in Atlantic Europe tend to be rather poor and fragmentary, often consisting of only a few flints, spindle whorls and pottery sherds. Rather than negating a trading role, this paucity of finds may in fact support such a use. If some promontory sites were performing an intermittent, perhaps even seasonal, trading role, evidence for such activity would be very difficult to find, particularly if the materials being traded were high-status because they would be unlikely to be lost and deposited in the archaeological record. Recent work on determining the location of coastal trading sites and anchorages in Denmark (Ulriksen 1994) has highlighted how difficult such sites are to find and, more importantly, what can be achieved when they are actively sought out through intensive field survey. Significantly, a number of the Danish examples were archaeologically unremarkable promontory locations, sometimes demarcated by a slight bank, which only after intrusive investigation revealed small scatters of flints, ceramics, or more rarely items of metalwork (op. cit. 805). In Atlantic areas such locations have not yet been subject to intensive investigation.

There simply has not been enough work done to ascertain whether promontory sites were involved in maritime trade in the pre-Roman Iron Age. It is self-evident that there was maritime activity moving metalwork along the Atlantic seaboard during the Late Bronze Age, but it is unknown if there were specialised coastal sites with accessible anchorages where goods were unloaded to carry on, whether by navigable rivers or land routes, to sites further inland.[25] Occasional finds of high-status items, such as bronze metalwork, polished axes and ornaments, on promontory locations, along with finds such as the Late Bronze Age metalwork assemblage from the coastal enclosure of Dunagoil[26] on the Isle of Bute (Marshall 1964), provide some indication that there may have been. Despite a lack of structural or occupational evidence, excavations on the promontory of Mount Batten overlooking the Plymouth Sound (Cunliffe 1988) recovered a significant range of imported artefacts, including two Iberian fibulae and two Italo-Etruscan bronzes, suggesting that the site had been involved in 'interregional systems of exchange from the late Bronze Age to the end of the middle La Tène period' (Cunliffe 1990: 250). There is certainly some later, though it must be said not overwhelming, evidence for trading activity on promontory locations such as the ceramic finds from Alet and Le Yaudet in northwestern Armorica (Cunliffe 1982a; de Jersey 1993; Cunliffe and Galliou 1995) and the as yet unpublished evidence of trade in Roman items at Drumanagh, Co. Dublin (Raftery 1994: 207).

All that can be said at this stage is that some form of trading role for some promontory forts remains a distinct possibility. The possible role of at least some of these sites in controlling maritime routes of traffic is an interesting one that needs to be developed further. For example, the promontory site of Penchâteau au Pouliguen, Loire-Atlantique, overlooks the mouth of the Loire and has long thought to have been in some way involved with the articulation of trade and with the referenced *emporium* of Corbilo, described by Strabo, quoting Polybius (Strabo IV, 2.1), as an important commercial centre in the area during the second century BC (Wheeler and Richardson 1957: 102–3; Giot 1995: 282). The actual site of Corbilo remains unknown but recent excavations at Penchâteau produced quantities of Middle and Late La Tène pottery and, on account of the complex sequence of ditches and at least four lines of rampart which enclose the promontory, the site was considered to have had a strategic function controlling maritime trading routes to and from the Loire river (Gaiffe *et al.* 1995). A more complete landscape knowledge of contemporary sites linked to promontory forts as part of trading routes, perhaps via riverine routes, may cast new light on the execution and control of Atlantic trade and exchange.

Ritual foci: the lure of extremities

In his study of promontory forts in northern Scotland, Lamb (1980) noted that the majority of sites could not be simply explained as defensive or domestic locations and therefore considered them to have a social significance beyond the humdrum activities of everyday life. Recently it has been more conspicuously suggested that some promontory forts may have primarily functioned as places of ritual observance and worship (Sharpe 1992: 65–8; Herring 1994; Cunliffe 2001: 364).

Sharpe (1992) has pointed out that a number of promontory forts in south-west England, including Treryn Dinas, Kenidjack Head, Gunard's Head, Tubby's Head in Cornwall and Giant's Castle, Scilly Isles, demarcate uninhabitable, jagged outcrops of rock which seem to offer nothing more than dramatic locations overlooking the sea. Many of these sites are strategically indefensible as they are overlooked by higher ground and are unsuitable as trading centres owing to their inaccessibility and lack of flat ground. Sharpe suggests that these sites fit into a long-lived prehistoric tradition of anthropogenically demarcating prominent natural features in the landscape in an effort to enhance their symbolic and ritual significance. This tradition is seen as having its roots in the construction of kerbed cairns and defined boulder features in the Neolithic, developing into the construction of tor cairns and tor enclosures in the Bronze Age, and finally, by the Iron Age, expressed through the demarcation of rocky headlands looking out to sea:

> In each case the constructional vocabulary is similar – a prominent natural feature whose special significance is indicated by the addition of a constructed encircling ring of stone.
>
> (Sharpe 1992: 67)

It is impossible to test such an interpretation but the spectacular locations of a number of promontory forts, on elevated positions overlooking the interface between land and sea, may well have had strong ritual meaning to prehistoric communities; certainly it is difficult to assign such sites with any clear secular function. The classical records suggest that Iron Age ritual was practised in natural places, such as groves, forest clearings, pools, lakes and islands (cf. Cunliffe 1991: 510–22; Webster 1995; Bradley 2000). Those sites apparently most favoured for 'communion with the super-natural world were liminal places, such as hills between earth and sky, caves between the living world and the natural world, settlement boundaries between the domestic and the wild, and rivers between land and sea' (Armit 1997: 90). It is not a major leap of faith therefore to consider the possible ritual ramifications of promontory forts given their dramatic liminal locations between land and sea. The imposing nature, spectacular views and beauty of a great number of promontory sites across the Atlantic seaboard would, and still do, promote a sense of awe at the elements.

Further aspects may hint at a ritual usage, namely the *longue durée* of non-secular activity at a number of promontory sites and the use of multivallation as a symbol of display to mark sites above the level of normal enclosures. The use of promontory locations can be seen to have an extremely wide chronological range from beginnings at some sites in the Neolithic, through to the re-use and establishment of new promontory sites in the first millennium AD. The evidence for early prehistoric activity at promontory locations is predominantly non-secular. Neolithic and Bronze Age megalithic monuments, cairns, tumuli and burials are often associated with promontory sites, while finds of prestige items such as polished stone axes, flints, bronze weaponry and ornaments are known. For example, there is evidence from the promontory fort of Camp du Lizo á Carnac, Morbihan, of activity from the Neolithic through to the Gallo-Roman period including at some point the construction of a Bronze Age tumulus (Giot 1995: 278). At the *presqu'ile* at Pointe du Blair en Baden, Morbihan, an earthwork encloses *c.* 14 hectares from which querns and early Iron Age (Hallstatt C and D) ceramics have been recovered alongside several small Bronze Age burials and a Neolithic dolmen which produced polished axes and flints (ibid.). The site of le Torche en Plomeur, Morbihan, produced Iron Age ceramics and glass beads within a promontory rampart which also enclosed a megalithic tomb (ibid.). The relationship between promontories and non-secular activities continues into the first millennium AD and the Middle Ages, with many sites used or re-used as locations for Christian worship, sometimes as cemeteries such as at Cladh, South Uist, Rubha Cladh Eòin, Argyll and, until relatively recently, Annait on Skye, or are closely associated with religious settlements such as at Downpatrick Head, County Mayo through to the construction of a Templar site on the promontory of Arzon, Morbihan, north-west France (Wheeler and Richardson 1957: 103). The attraction of remote locations overlooking the sea for Early Christian monks may reflect the re-contextualisation and continuation of earlier pagan traditions; promontories are common locations for churches and monasteries throughout the first millennium AD and beyond.

The occurrence of multiple ramparts most often occurs in association with a site delimiting a dramatic rocky outcrop, rather than anything that could be considered a settlement. It seems unlikely, therefore, that in these cases the ramparts were intended to perform a defensive function. Indeed, the majority of examples are quite insubstantial when compared to the defensive outworks of hillfort settlements; there are few multivallate promontory forts that feature suitably massive or closely spaced enough ramparts to suggest the use of sling warfare. In terms of defensive capacity, the only use Lamb (1980: 59) could muster for multivallate promontory forts in northern Scotland was not sling warfare but simply throwing stones at the enemy. There is also little evidence of heavily defended entrances. At the majority of sites access is central and runs straight through the defences, and where there are obstacles such as *chevaux-de-frise* they seem to be placed to guide and impress rather than to impede.

Examples of rocky outcrops delimited by multiple ramparts are seen throughout the Atlantic zone. At Castle Kenidjack in Cornwall a jagged rock headland is delimited by five separate ramparts (Figure 4.18), at Beg Monom in north Finistère, bivallate defences cut-off a rocky area of just under one hectare featuring breathtaking views and, perhaps significantly, a prominent extremity of rock which stands *c.* 6 m high (Maguer 1996: 114). Ceramics have been recovered from both sites dating to the Late Bronze Age/Early Iron Age (ibid.). At Doon Esk in Co. Kerry (Westropp 1910: 281; Lamb 1980: 54), three ramparts separated by rock-cut ditches featuring an entrance straight through their centre and an inner stone-faced bank delimit a spectacularly high rocky headland (Figure 4.19).

Recognising a ritual aspect to promontory sites is a step forward in their interpretation and does not negate the possibility of different activities taking place at other

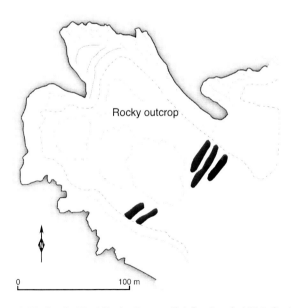

Figure 4.18 Castle Kenidjack, Cornwall (after Lamb 1980: fig. 23).

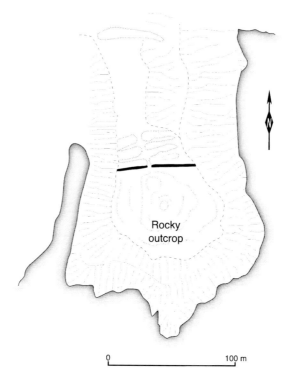

Rocky
outcrop

0   100 m

Figure 4.19 Doon Esk, Co. Kerry (after Lamb 1980: fig. 21).

promontory sites, or a range of activities occurring on the same site. It is now widely accepted by archaeologists that prehistoric sites do not have to conform to single functional or ritual activities (Bradley 2005). Places of specialised function, such as hillforts or trading sites, normally indicate the power and status of one or more groups and therefore also become symbolically important places. Although ritual and trading activity may have been taking place at different promontory sites we should not view these activities as mutually exclusive.

Treryn Dinas, Cornwall (Sharpe 1992: 66; Herring 1994), for example, with at least four phases of rampart construction, has a complex layout which may reflect the co-existence of both ritual and trading/utilitarian activity. The outermost rampart consisting of a massive bank and ditch bears comparison with the defensive earthworks of many hillforts and encloses an area of moderately level ground within which there is evidence for a series of slighter banks and ditches (Figure 4.20). Iron Age activity is attested to in this area through the discovery of South Western Decorated pottery sherds. The rocky end of the promontory, known as Castle Treen, is defined by its own earthen and stone rampart. This craggy rock area features a very prominent upstanding rock, the Logan Rock, which has been ascribed supernatural

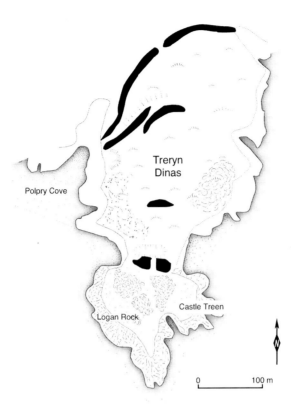

Figure 4.20 Treryn Dinas (after Herring 1994: fig. 6).

powers in local legend. Herring (1994: 52) reported the discovery of large sherds of a
Bronze Age cremation urn together with pieces of charcoal and bone eroding out of
crevices in the exposed rock near Logan Rock suggesting the existence of a burial –
providing prehistoric evidence of ritual in what recent local traditions already held
was an area with sacred properties (Nowakowski 1986; Sharpe 1992; Herring 1994);
this area has also produced some Iron Age ceramics (Sharpe 1992: 66). The function
of the flatter area may have been any of the possibilities discussed above. Interestingly
though, while the rocky area is completely unapproachable by sea, the main enclosure sits next to a navigable sandy beach (Polpry Cove on Figure 4.20), a rarity in
this stretch of coastline otherwise composed of craggy cliffs. The surface evidence for
slight ditches in this area appear to be aligned towards the beach area and could have
once formed part of a direct route to the beach.

Modern divisions between secular and ritual activity are now widely regarded as
inappropriate to the study of prehistoric societies (Bradley 2005). What may appear
as common, utilitarian activities in the modern world could have, and probably
were, bound up in sophisticated spiritual beliefs in prehistory, with many important

functional tasks communicated through ritual. Some promontory sites may have gained an importance to communities as trading sites where new goods, ideas and influences were received. Ritual and symbolic importance could also have been attached to promontory sites for similar reasons, their connection with the sea as an entity which brought new opportunities and contacts as well as a natural force to be respected in its own right.

Souterrains

A further link in social practice and potentially belief between Atlantic communities is suggested by the occurrence of souterrains throughout the northern Atlantic area.[27] Souterrains are subterranean or semi-subterranean passages associated with later prehistoric settlements and have been recognised in Atlantic and eastern Scotland (Wainwright 1953; 1963), Ireland (Warner 1979; 1980; Edwards 1990; Clinton 2001), and most famously in Cornwall (Clarke 1961; Maclean 1992; Cooke 1993) and western Armorica (Giot 1960a, b, 1976, 1990, 1995). There are no examples currently known from Wales.

Differences in construction and dating exist across the zone but similarities in conception, situation, and associated assemblages imply that a link may have existed in terms of the function and the behaviour represented by such sites. Irish, Scottish and Cornish examples are usually, though not exclusively, excavated trenches lined with drystone walling, roofed with either stone lintels or timber. Armorican sites differ in that they are simply tunnels and chambers cut into the ground (Figure 4.21). There are also differences across the zone in the complexity and number of chambers present at individual sites, but it is possible to define some basic regularities: sites consist of a main chamber, longer than it is wide, which usually has a slight curve; many sites have subsidiary chambers off this – in Ireland and Cornwall these can be circular with corbelled ceilings; many sites have more than one entrance but there is usually only one main entrance, larger and more easily accessible than the others; and most importantly of all, they are always, where appropriate examination has taken place, associated with ground level settlements.[28]

Souterrains are perhaps one of the most distinctive monument types in Armorica and are found exclusively in the western part of the peninsula – an area bounded by the Rance and the Vilaine[29] (Figure 6.6). The distribution of souterrains along with the similar distribution of stone stelae and to a lesser extent promontory forts are usually seen as proof of the Atlantic character of western Armorica (Duval 1990: 282). Giot (1995: 286–94) has clearly defined the Armorican type of souterrain: they were underground structures cut into the ground with at least one, and as many as ten chambers connected by passageways or ventilation shafts. Surface access was provided through one or more vertical shafts or a tilted passage. The chambers themselves can be a variety of shapes from oblong through to ovoid and elliptical forms and were usually 3 to 5 m wide with 2 m standing space. The ceilings were usually no less than 1 m thick and chambers at extreme depths of up to 4 m are known. Connecting passageways and shafts were often very narrow and could connect groups of chambers into a horizontal network from 3 m to 40 m in

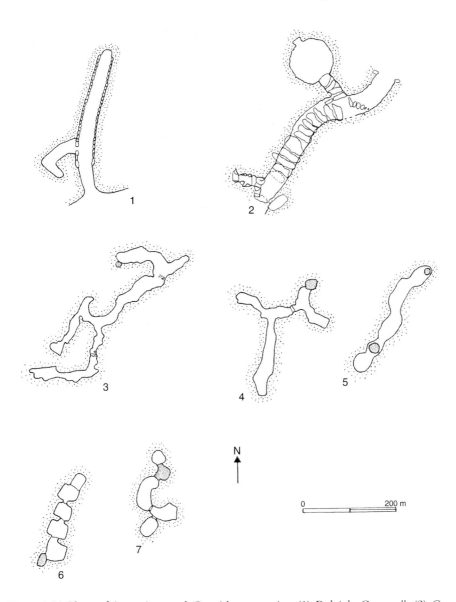

Figure 4.21 Plans of Armorican and Cornish souterrains: (1) Boleigh, Cornwall; (2) Carn Euny, Cornwall; (3) La Motte à Sizun, Finistère: (4) Kervéo en Plomelin, Finistère; (5) Pendreff en Commana, Finistère; (6) Stang–Vihan en Concarneau, Finistère; (7) Lamphily en Concarneau, Finistère (after Christie 1978: fig. 3; Pearce 1981: fig. 3.12; Giot 1995: 285).

overall size. In Armorica, the use of souterrains spans the late Hallstatt period to the end of the Middle La Tène from *c.* 600 to 100 BC; in contrast to the other areas there is no evidence for the construction or use of souterrains here during the late La Tène (Giot 1973: 57).

The distribution of souterrains, or fogous as they are locally known, in south-west England is constrained to western Cornwall with the majority of examples occurring on the Land's End peninsula (Clarke 1961; Maclean 1992; Cooke 1993). None are currently known from Devon or the granite upland of central and eastern Cornwall and only one uncertain example has been recorded from Scilly (Ashbee 1990). The Cornish sites consist of a principal, long, slightly curved, stone-built, lintelled passage averaging around 1.8 to 2.1 m high, 1.5 to 1.8 m wide and 9 to 12 m long (Cooke 1993). Associated features include very low and constricted side passages, called 'creeps', door checks and sometimes a side chamber off the long passage. Significantly, many Cornish fogous appear to have been quite visible, sometimes incorporating upstanding portions, often covered with a mound. Others were built up from ground level and incorporated into massive stone walls (op. cit. 35), as seen at Porthmeor (Hirst 1936), and invite comparison with intra-mural passages in the drystone sites of Atlantic Scotland and Ireland (see Chapter 5).

Of the 62 referenced souterrain sites in Cornwall (Cooke 1993: 45) only three, Halligye (Startin 1982; Cooke 1993), Carn Euny (Borlase 1868; Christie 1978) and Porthmeor (Hirst 1936), have been excavated and published to a standard that allows detailed analysis. The evidence from these three sites and general finds from other examples suggest a broadly similar starting date range to the Armorican sites, in the mid-first millennium BC, but in contrast to the French examples, souterrains in Cornwall appear to have continued in use well into the first millennium AD and sometimes later.

Excavations at Halligye indicated the primary fogou chamber was built contemporary with the earthwork around the fourth or fifth centuries BC. At a later unspecified date a subsidiary chamber was added along with a creep passage. Then between 75 BC and AD 50 the main chamber was extended and the original entrance to the ditch modified; the extension to the main chamber may well have included an entrance to the interior of the earthwork site. Sometime later the ditch entrance was blocked and the ditch re-cut on a larger scale. This second ditch was slighted, though only partially, around the second century AD and there may have been a break in occupation. Finally, the main chamber extension was backfilled in the seventeenth century AD or later when it was used as a smugglers' hideaway (Cooke 1993: 60–1).

At Carn Euny a similar sequence of development was recognised by the excavator with the primary construction of a large circular corbelled 'beehive' sometime in the fifth century BC followed by the construction of a curving souterrain passage and creep in the fourth to third centuries BC (Christie 1978, 325–7). The passage was then modified during the first century AD to provide immediate access from a courtyard house. Further evidence for the later use of a souterrain comes from the courtyard house settlement of Porthmeor which is dated to the second century AD (Hirst 1937). Limited excavations in the area surrounding Boleigh fogou identified traces of settlement and at least two enclosure banks dated on the basis of ceramic finds from the sixth to fifth centuries BC, with some sherds suggesting activity continued into the first millennium AD (Young 2001: 138–9). Unfortunately, however, the excavations did not establish whether any of this activity was contemporary with the fogou, but the suggested date range can be paralleled with Carn Euny.

There are thousands of souterrains known in Ireland, mainly located in the north-eastern and western parts of the country (Clark 1961: 73; Thomas 1972: 75; Warner 1979, 1980; Clinton 2001). Although the Irish sites can be broadly compared with those found in Scotland, Cornwall and Brittany in terms of construction, layout and associated finds, they are thought to have an exclusively first millennium AD dating, usually placed *after* the sixth century (Edwards 1990: 29). Certainly the more complex Irish forms featuring multi-level passages, multiple 'beehive' chambers, shelves, benches, hearths and chimneys do represent later activity but it remains a possibility that some of the simpler sites associated with ringforts and promontory forts may have an Iron Age origin (see Chapter 5). Evidence for a souterrain associated with a ringfort type enclosure dating to the Iron Age comes from Cush, Co. Limerick (Ó Ríordáin 1940), and with a promontory fort at Porth, Co. Mayo (Westropp 1911: 22). Interestingly, both stone-revetted forms similar to Scottish and Cornish examples and simple excavated tunnel forms comparable to the Breton sites are found in Ireland, while examples constructed entirely from wood have been revealed at Ballycatteen, Co. Cork and Coolcran, Co. Fermanagh (Clinton 2001: 10–12). We may be witnessing in Ireland the continuing development and elaboration of long-established traditions which not only have earlier origins elsewhere along the Atlantic seaboard, but have actually developed and died out in these areas by the time they come to flourish in Irish societies.

There are about two hundred recorded souterrains in Scotland and, similar to promontory forts, their distribution is not restricted to the Atlantic zone, with examples also known along the east coast in Angus, Perthshire, Aberdeenshire and Midlothian (Wainwright 1953, 1963; Ritchie and Ritchie 1991: 115–16). The mainland east coast examples have been better studied, dating evidence coming from a group of timber-walled souterrains from Dalladies in Kincardineshire which date to the third century BC, while the stone-walled example at Newmill in Perthshire was built in the first century BC (Barclay 1981; Watkins 1981). Souterrains then appear to have remained in use throughout the first three centuries AD (Wainwright 1963). One at Crichton in Midlothian, however, was certainly built no earlier than AD 150, since Roman dressed stones were used in its construction (Armit 1997: 72–3). Although dating evidence is sparse, a similar range can be envisaged for Atlantic examples. A drystone lintelled souterrain associated with a settlement at Tungadale on the Isle of Skye was recently radiocarbon dated to the third century BC (Armit 1996: 132, fig. 7.12) while a similar example at Underhoul on Shetland was certainly built sometime in the earlier Iron Age, if not before, on account of the 'broch period' pottery found within it (Small 1966: 229). The use of souterrain structures appears to continue into the first half of the first millennium AD and occur in post-complex Atlantic roundhouse phases associated with cellular settlement, as at Loch na Beirgh on Lewis (Harding and Gilmour 2000: 24–5), while the final post-wheelhouse phase at Cnip, also on Lewis, featured a possible souterrain structure interpreted by the excavator as a linear house (Harding and Armit 1990: 84–94, Illus. 6.13).

None of the current theories on the use of souterrains are entirely satisfactory. They were once thought to be refuges or bolt-holes (Hencken 1932: 139), but their visibility above ground make this highly unlikely not to mention foolhardy (contra Maclean 1992; Clinton 2001). Equally, they could not have been used as byres (contra Wainwright 1963), since their entrances often seem purpose-built to make access difficult for people, let alone animals. Although they were entered from houses, there is no evidence for domestic occupation, while the lack of light and air would have prevented their use as industrialised workshops. However, finds of charcoal and slag are common in the later fill of souterrains, suggesting that many were perhaps used for this purpose after they had fallen into disrepair and were perhaps no longer roofed.

One of the most important aspects of souterrains is their close association with domestic settlements and it is for this reason that a storage function seems most likely possibly linked, given their subterranean nature, to 'a belief in the power of chthonic deities to preserve and protect stored commodities' (Cunliffe 1997: 156). The majority of examples, offering cool, dry conditions and easily controlled access, would have made secure cellars for the storage of agricultural products such as grain, milk, and cheese.[30] The storage interpretation has been challenged (Maclean 1992: 41–7) as some sites appear today to be quite damp but such conditions do not have a particularly adverse effect on the preservation of dairy products while grain could still have been stored in sealed containers.[31]

There is no definite evidence that souterrains were used as places of ritual practice but there are certainly ritual aspects to their use. At Kerellen in Tréglonou, Finistère, thirteen gold beads belonging to a necklace dated to c. 650–450 BC were found, but usually finds of any nature are rare (over half of the recorded examples have nothing in them) and where present are seen to consist of a few animal bones, sherds, and quern fragments. There is evidence that sites were deliberately sealed with sterile fill after use rather than being allowed to deteriorate naturally (Barclay 1985; Giot 1995: 292). This may have been done in many cases due to the continued use of a settlement on the surface but, significantly, also seems to occur at sites where there was no later surface occupation. In many cases the drystone masonry could have been re-used and there is evidence of burning near the entrance, further supporting the occurrence of some ritual observance. Christie (1978: 332; 1979) favoured a ritual function for the souterrain at Carn Euny owing to the impracticality of access, the narrow side passages or 'creeps', and discovery of fragments of cremated human bone associated with its construction. Fragments of human bone are also common at Armorican sites, such as at the souterrain of Rugéré in Plouvorn, Finistère, where two pieces of human cranium were found (Giot 1990). The occurrence of a relief figure of a man holding a spear or serpent on the entrance jamb at Boleigh fogou on the Land's End peninsula is frequently quoted as an example of ritual use (Clark 1961: 61–2; Thomas 1972: 77; Cooke 1993) but it remains undated and without parallel (Todd 1987: 174). At Trézéan in Pédernec, Côtes d'Armor, three Armorican stele were found stored in one of the chambers of a souterrain, but this is probably more indicative of a functional storage use than an ideological one. Cooke (1993: 210–12) has demonstrated that the majority of Cornish souterrains have a general east/north-east to west/south-west orientation and suggests that this may have ritual connotations; specifically the southern ends of the main passages align roughly on the midwinter sunrise and sunset while the northern ends align towards midsummer sunrise and sunset. These alignments are not exactly diametrically opposed and could therefore account for the curvature seen in all Cornish souterrains; the vast majority of Cornish sites always bend towards the right (east-north-east) from the south.

On balance it seems likely that there was a non-secular aspect to the construction and use of souterrains. There is no reason why a structure associated with food storage could not also be linked to ritual practice and belief. This is unsurprising if one considers, as has been argued for the construction of roundhouses and some promontory enclosures above, that everyday life in the Iron Age was impregnated with ritual and symbols.

The main Iron Age methods of storage – 'four-poster' granaries and large storage pits – are rare in Atlantic areas. Four-posters are absent from Atlantic Scotland and Ireland and not well known in other Atlantic areas until the last few centuries BC. Significantly, four-posters are found in Wales, perhaps offering an explanation for the lack of occurrence of souterrains in this area. Equally, large storage pits are also not as common in Atlantic areas as they are elsewhere in Iron Age Britain (Champion 1979: 354; Gent 1983: 251). The dating of Armorican souterrains is of considerable interest as they appear to go out of use in the late La Tène at the same time as four-poster granary structures and pits interpreted as grain silos begin to be used (Le Bihan *et al.* 1990; Menez 1994, 1996). As will be examined in Chapter 6, there is evidence for the growing influence of west-central European traditions in Armorica during the late La Tène accompanying an expansion in agricultural production. The apparent change in indigenous storage practices from souterrains to four-poster granaries may be a further reflection of the impact of these influences (a move to store more of the harvest to supply the growing Roman markets). Whatever the case, elsewhere in the western Atlantic zone dates of abandonment vary, but certainly use of souterrains continued into the first millennium AD during which time they were eventually phased out in favour of above ground barns, and perhaps centralised stores controlled by elites in the emergent post-Roman kingdoms in Britain, and conversely become more widespread and elaborate in Ireland.

Atlantic praxis

Despite dating and structural differences throughout the Atlantic zone, the use of souterrains represents a comparable way of storing food that contrasts with areas further inland and, in this respect, suggests the existence of shared modes of behaviour and traditions between Atlantic communities. In a similar way the use and enclosure of promontories may also be a reflection of shared Atlantic social and ritual practices. The existence of related behaviour occurring over long periods of time is more easily explained if one accepts that both souterrains and promontories had attached ritual meaning and significance to the communities using them. Ritual belief tended to be long-lasting in prehistoric contexts and was not open to the same day-to-day negotiation we experience in modern societies. As a result, ritual beliefs and versions of the same beliefs could persist over generations across the Atlantic seaboard, creating continuities when viewed from a diachronic perspective even though there is considerable synchronic variation in their expression. This could partly explain why souterrains appear to be used in different areas at different times.

The use of promontory locations has very early origins and continues throughout the prehistoric period and into the first millennium AD. The use and re-use of such locations may hint at the continuity of social practices and belief throughout the Atlantic zone. Promontory sites may have performed an important role in the Neolithic and Early Bronze Age simply as territorial markers or points of identification (i.e. re-affirming local or group identity) as Sharpe (1992: 65-8) has suggested, or perhaps as ritual locations linked to the importance of the sea and the spread and exchange of ideas with other communities (Cunliffe 2001: 364). It is surely of some significance that the visible Neolithic and Bronze Age use of promontories relates to burial and, through this, to ancestors. The fact that promontories were already recognised as important symbolic places may have influenced their enclosure in the first millennium BC. Certainly the use of promontories intensifies and changes sometime in the Late Bronze Age, as ramparts are constructed to delimit them, and it is possible that some sites took on a more pronounced trading role, or at least were related to the widespread maritime exchange in metalwork. Atlantic communities may have stayed in touch with their past lifeways by continuing to use promontory sites in a ritual sense, albeit re-contextualised and perhaps at some sites linked to trading activity.

The act of enclosure itself would have formalised the relationship between Atlantic groups and promontories, allowing them to make a direct association with past communities, both physically and symbolically. It would also have reinforced community level identities as the digging of ramparts and their continued upkeep would have been carried out by organised groups over generations. This communal activity coupled with the past associations of particular promontories would have allowed groups to situate themselves within a wider mythological and historical landscape. In this way promontories may have ultimately reinforced, for Atlantic communities, concepts of belonging and the connections between symbolic locales and community level identity.

Interpretations related to trading and ritual activity have been considered for promontory sites and it has been suggested that these activities are not mutually exclusive. Certain sites, particularly univallate ones, are approachable by sea and may well have been used for sailing and trading activities. Other sites instead occur on dramatic rocky outcrops surrounded by rough seas which could never have been approached by sea. These sites are more likely to be multivallate and would have provided impressive settings for ritual activities and it is not hard to imagine that rituals related to the sea would have been performed at such sites. There may have been a need to placate the unforgiving power of the sea to ensure safe passages over water through rites carried out on these sites with the rocks, precipitous cliffs and stormy waters of the promontory actually symbolising the dangers faced by sailors.

As we saw in the Late Bronze Age, trading activity is likely to have been carried out within a strong ritual and symbolic context; as a result sites used for trading and/or ritual activity would have been cosmologically linked and part of the same cultural tradition. Promontories, whether used for trade or ceremony, would have been symbolically charged locations for maritime communities where they could consider their own place in the landscape, and their wider connections with more distant communities.

To date, research on promontory forts and souterrains has lacked a systematic approach, useful classifications, and, not least, thorough excavation programmes. Without more problem orientated investigation it is difficult to describe the significance and role of these sites in specific Atlantic cultural contexts. Instead, I have offered a general reading of these sites as reflecting the existence of shared behaviour between Atlantic communities. While promontory forts may indicate the existence of common ritual beliefs at the community level, souterrains are associated with settlements and tend to occur within the domestic living space. As a result the use of souterrains may reflect commonalities in belief expressed at the household level. If one accepts that the ideational dimensions of human existence are just as likely to be found in the remains of everyday life as in sacred places, then both souterrains and promontory forts can be viewed as archaeologically visible expressions of related symbolic beliefs prevalent along the Atlantic seaboard. In the following chapters we will develop this view of shared Atlantic ways of life and consider in more detail the role settlements play in the construction of Atlantic social groups and identities in the first millennium BC.

5 The *Ultima Thule*

Atlantic Scotland and Ireland 700 BC–AD 200

Introduction

The romantic notion of *'Ultima Thule'* conjures up images of remote and uncharted lands, but it is a concept that has a particular resonance when applied to the Iron Age communities of Atlantic Scotland and Ireland. In a very real sense these coastal communities sat on the edge of the then known world and marked the north-western limits of European Iron Age culture: beyond them lay the seemingly infinite Ocean and the unknown. Academic studies have in turn tended to regard Atlantic Scotland and Ireland as rather mysterious lands that were peripheral to the main developments of the European Iron Age. The communities of these regions are often considered, at best, conservative and, at worst, culturally retarded when compared to their continental European counterparts. However, the settlement evidence, when studied on its own merits, reveals the existence of highly distinctive and lively communities capable of producing the most sophisticated and complex architectural structures known in Iron Age Europe. Strong regional identities are reflected through traditions of monumental drystone architecture that have more to do with the exis-tence and cultural importance of maritime connections along the Atlantic seaboard than with developments in La Tène Europe.

Atlantic Scotland

Atlantic Scotland, as usually defined, comprises the northern and western mainland of Scotland along with the Western and Northern Island chains. This area was first described as the Atlantic Province by Piggott in 1966 and his definition remains a useful means of orientation although regional diversity in settlement types and development have led to a further breakdown, followed here (after Armit 1990: 194–210), into the Northern Settlement Sequence (including Shetland, Orkney, Caithness and Sutherland), the Western Isles Settlement Sequence, and the Argyll and Inner Isles Settlement Sequence. The western coasts of south-west Scotland are often left out of wider Atlantic discussions because studies have tended to consider the whole of the south-west region as a discrete cultural unit, following Piggott's defini-tion of a 'Solway-Clyde' province (1966: fig. 1). However, such an approach ignores the fact that there are a number of settlement forms in the west of the region that have their closest parallels with Atlantic Scottish types. As a result the western Atlantic coasts of south-west Scotland are considered here as a fourth regional tradition comparable to the better known traditions in the north (Figure 5.1).

The Atlantic settlement record of Scotland is characterised by its own variety: there is a diverse range of forms including roundhouses, promontory forts, hillforts, island *duns* and crannogs almost all of which are constructed in stone. Strongly built circular drystone roundhouses, collectively known as Atlantic roundhouses, form the

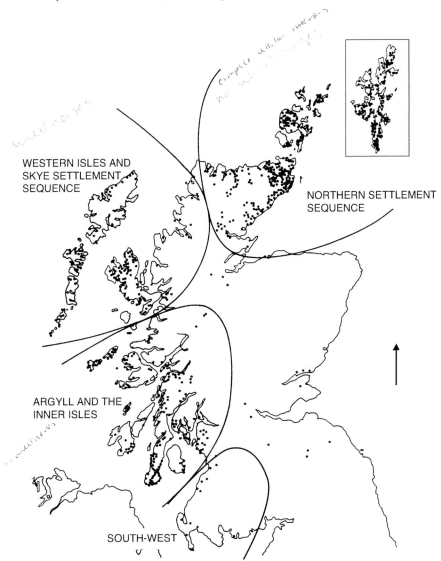

Figure 5.1 Distribution of Atlantic roundhouses in Atlantic Scotland (after Cunliffe 1991: fig. 13.32).

main domestic unit across the zone (Armit 1990, 1992, 1997, 2003). The term 'Atlantic roundhouse' includes the range of structures referred to by some authors as *brochs*, semi-*brochs*, *duns*, island *duns*, galleried *duns*, and other associated variants (cf. MacKie 1995, 1997, 1998, 2002; Parker Pearson *et al.* 1996; Parker Pearson and Sharples 1999; Sharples 1998; Sharples and Parker Pearson 1997). Armit's terminology is ultimately successful because, unlike the current definition of a *broch* (MacKie 1991: 150–1), it makes no pre-conceived assumptions about the origin or function of sites based on the visibility of a strict range of architectural traits. Instead, it allows a consideration of the full range of drystone roundhouses in Atlantic Scotland and recognises that not all such sites have to feature a list of complex *broch* architectural devices to be considered as part of a wider related Atlantic drystone tradition.

Armit identifies two main groupings within the Atlantic roundhouse class: simple roundhouses and complex roundhouses which feature the range of architectural devices such as galleries, wall chambers and scarcements previously ascribed to the

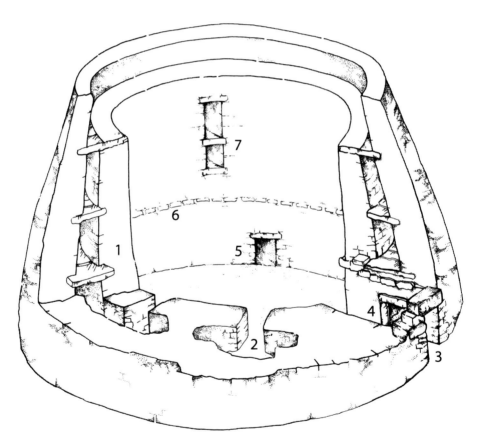

Figure 5.2 Typical features of complex Atlantic roundhouse architecture: (1) circular, hollow, drystone wall built of two concentric walls of masonry bonded together with horizontal rows of flat lintels; (2) intramural cell; (3) low lintelled entrance passage; (4) guard cell; (5) entrance to stairs; (6) scarcement; (7) stress relieving gaps (Drawing by Elizabeth Timney).

broch tradition. Within this complex grouping Armit identifies a further sub-group which he terms *broch* towers, here referred to as complex towers, which incorporate complex architectural features within a tall tower-like building. This grouping forms the most striking class and includes the well-preserved site of Mousa on Shetland, where the tower walls survive to just over 9 m in height incorporating two floor levels and an upper parapet, and Dun Carloway on Lewis which survives to around 8 m in height (Figure 5.2). Armit insists his classification of simple and complex forms is a distinction that merely recognises the limitations of recognition in the field (Armit 1996: 115). However, as he admits, the chronology beginning to emerge from Atlantic Scotland, particularly as we shall see from the northern sequence, tends to support an evolution from basic simple examples to forms of increasing complexity apparently culminating in the complex tower form.

The appearance of complex architectural features is not restricted exclusively to drystone roundhouses, and a few structures exist which are clearly not roundhouse sites but which have intra-mural galleries, wall chambers and scarcements. The promontory fortifications on Barra Head, Lewis (Armit 1992: 94) and Clickhimin, Ness of Burghi and Loch of Huxter on Shetland (Lamb 1980), for example, feature intra-mural galleries and low lintelled entrances. It is perhaps most useful to view these sites as prototypes to fully complex architecture in some way, but comments can only be speculative at present because promontory sites have proven to be noto-riously difficult to date. Many complex Atlantic roundhouses are associated with promontory fortifications in Orkney, Shetland and Caithness: at Crosskirk in Caithness these defences can be seen to be earlier than the roundhouse (Fairhurst 1984; Cunliffe 1991: 300). The sequence at Clickhimin also seems to suggest the blockhouse there, which features complex architectural elements, was earlier than the roundhouse structure (Hamilton 1968).

Much of the early work on Atlantic roundhouses was concerned with a search for their origins. Previously, the influence for the construction of Atlantic roundhouses was seen to come from southern Britain – particularly south-west England and Wessex (Childe 1935; Hamilton 1956; MacKie 1965). Most of these views are now discredited and it is accepted that due to the traditions of drystone construction that already existed in the area no external catalyst is required. The search for a single origin within the Atlantic province itself has proven equally fruitless. Some authors claim that the occurrence of blockhouses or, more convincingly, the earliest yet known datable dry-stone roundhouses, point towards a northern origin, which then spreads to the west (e.g. Hamilton 1968; Hedges 1987). The opposite view claims that the simplest forms exist in the west and spread to the north becoming increasingly more complex (MacKie 1965). Although the earliest dated examples do support a northern origin this may have more to do with the fieldwork carried out to date. The development of the distinctive drystone roundhouse continuum throughout Atlantic Scotland is the result of a number of contacts which occurred for over half a millennium, making it unlikely that any one source can be identified or indeed could be solely responsible.

The development of the roundhouse form of settlement was a feature of the Bronze Age in western Europe. In Chapter 4 it was briefly discussed how this devel-opment may be seen as an Atlantic phenomenon defining an area that can be contrasted with the predominantly rectangular forms of central Europe and the

Urnfield culture. It has been argued by some authors that the Atlantic roundhouse form, rather than demonstrating the existence of a distinct cultural zone, is merely a reflection of the timber substantial roundhouse form, but built in stone, and therefore demonstrates continuity with other areas of Scotland and England (Hingley 1992: 28). This is undoubtedly true to a point but should not be used to deny that Atlantic Scotland is a discrete cultural zone. Examples of continuity in Atlantic areas with areas further east are often used to argue against the existence of an Atlantic axis of contact and interaction. However, the existence of Atlantic contacts should not be viewed as an all-or-nothing dialectic; an acceptance of the fact that coastal areas were in contact with each other does not rule out the possibility of contact with other areas. During the first half of the first millennium BC the traditions of building substantial roundhouses in wood are a recurrent if discontinuous feature of the archaeological record from southern England to Scotland. In most areas of Scotland these traditions were abandoned by the middle of the millennium with a movement towards much smaller domestic units. Only in Atlantic Scotland did substantial roundhouses continue to be built until at least the end of the millennium, with a visible horizon of complexity towards the last few centuries BC. It must also be kept in mind that the architectural traditions of building in stone were culturally mediated and thus indicate that a different social materiality was in existence in Atlantic areas whether geographically determined or not.

Regional traditions in Atlantic Scotland

Northern settlement sequence

The earliest evidence for the construction of thick-walled drystone roundhouses comes from Orkney at sites such as Bu (Hedges and Bell 1980; Hedges 1987); Pierowall (Sharples 1984); Quanterness (Renfrew 1979: 194); St Boniface (Lowe 1998) and Tofts Ness (Dockrill 1988) and from Caithness at Cnoc Stanger (Mercer 1996). Dating from *c.* 800 to 400 BC these sites represent a clear departure in terms of scale and external appearance from the stone-built forms of the Late Bronze Age while they foreshadow the development of more complex stone roundhouses incorporating galleries and cells within their walls. The massively built roundhouse at Bu on Orkney is usually taken to be the type site of this simple form of Atlantic roundhouse (Hedges 1987; Figure 5.3). Despite featuring a wall some 5 m thick, there was no evidence of intramural cells, galleries or stairs constructed within it. Instead the wall was found to have been a composite construction where an inner wall, 3 m thick, had been refaced both internally and externally to produce a progressively thicker wall. The surviving height of the wall was just 1.5 m and there was little surviving rubble, leading to the suggestion that it was built as a single-storey structure (Armit 2003: 42). It seems clear that it was the overall thickness of the wall and outwardly the impression that this construction created that was of prime importance to the builders.

The construction of these first Atlantic roundhouses as imposing structures which stood alone in the landscape represents an important break from the non-monumental

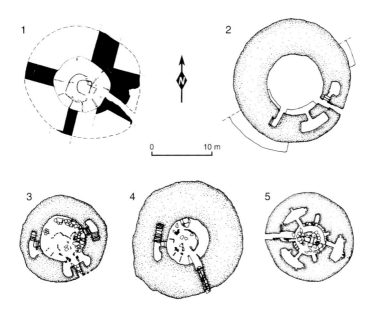

Figure 5.3 Atlantic roundhouses in Northern Scotland: (1) Bu, Orkney; (2) Crosskirk, Caithness; (3) Howe, Orkney (*c.* 400–200 BC); (4) Howe, Orkney (*c.* 200 BC–AD 100); (5) Mousa, Shetland.

cellular building styles of the Neolithic and Bronze Ages. They offered communities the opportunity to outwardly express status and identity, and as such they have been interpreted by many authors as monumental markers communicating territorial claims or the consolidation of power (Childe 1935; Barrett 1981; Macinnes 1984; Sharples 1984; Armit 1990; Nieke 1990). In terms of their internal layout, however, there is little evidence of a major cultural break because these new roundhouse forms feature the same kind of cellular radial divisions seen on preceding domestic sites. The stone slabbed interior at Bu, for example, creates an internal domestic space which is almost identical to previous Bronze Age interiors. In many ways this makes the widespread adoption of the roundhouse form all the more significant and remarkable as it was actively incorporated into existing domestic structural traditions. As such the inclusion of roundhouse forms and the construction of massively thick walls clearly reflect indigenous social concerns and expression: a desire to communicate something through monumental architecture coupled with unchanged levels of social organisation within the domestic sphere. The construction of roundhouse forms may have developed independently in the Northern Isles or may have been related to the construction of substantial roundhouses, albeit in timber, seen elsewhere in Britain during the Iron Age (Hingley 1995).

The construction of more complex Atlantic roundhouse forms appears to have begun in the north from *c.* 400 BC onwards (Gilmour 2002; Armit 2003). A date in the fourth century BC was obtained from a vitrified, galleried roundhouse at Langwell in Sutherland (Nisbet 1994) while excavations at Old Scatness, Shetland

(Dockrill 1998, 2003) have dated a roundhouse, featuring a staircase and at least one cell in its wall, to the mid-first millennium BC. Significantly the complex roundhouse at Scatness appears to have been out of use and superseded by an aisled roundhouse in the later centuries of the first millennium BC (Dockrill *et al.* 2005: 60). Radiocarbon dates from the complex Atlantic roundhouse at Crosskirk in Caithness suggest it was built by at least 200 BC if not well before (Fairhurst 1984), while the important sequence from the Howe on Orkney features a simple roundhouse built prior to 400 BC being replaced by a complex roundhouse featuring two intramural stairs and cells sometime after this but before 200 BC (Ballin Smith 1994: 37). This complex roundhouse was itself remodelled between 200 BC and AD 100 to create a massively constructed complex roundhouse featuring walls up to 6 m thick and which could therefore have originally been built to tower-like proportions.

The appearance of fully formed complex roundhouse towers, exemplified by well-preserved sites such as Mousa in Shetland, cannot be dated to before 200 BC in the Northern Isles or indeed anywhere else in Atlantic Scotland. For example, complex roundhouses built sometime prior to the second century BC at Crosskirk and the Howe do not appear to have been built substantially enough to support tower constructions higher than 4.5 m, which is around half the height of later complex towers (Armit 2003). The construction of such towers by the closing centuries of the first millennium BC is best regarded as the culmination of the monumentality and visibility of the roundhouse form which began *c.* 800 BC (Armit 2003: 51).

Around certain complex Atlantic roundhouses such as the Howe, Gurness, Lingro and Midhowe on Orkney, and Crosskirk, Nybster and Keiss Road in Caithness, are a range of external buildings usually interpreted as contemporary villages (Figure 5.4). This is a feature unique to northern Scotland and is not seen in any other part of Atlantic Scotland. The structures are most numerous and developed in Orkney where the culmination of roundhouse monumentality, the final complex tower, is traditionally thought to have occurred within a context of ancillary drystone structures, with the roundhouse serving to dominate the settlement (Hedges 1987, 1990; Foster 1989b; Barrett and Foster 1990; Ballin Smith 1994, 38–9). Within such a context no external catalyst is required to explain the development of the tower. In terms of structural development there already exists a preceding tradition of drystone roundhouse construction, while in a social context, architectural monumentality would have been well established and its meaning would have been understood by the indigenous community. Doubts have been expressed regarding the assumed contemporaneity of the ancillary buildings and the construction of the complex Atlantic roundhouses at the Orkney village sites of Gurness and Midhowe (MacKie 1994) and the Howe (Gilmour 2000). However, even if the external buildings are secondary at these particular sites the recovery of Iron Age dates from non-roundhouse cellular settlement at Kebister in Shetland demonstrates that some cellular forms are indeed contemporary with Atlantic roundhouses (Owen and Lowe 1999).

One thing is certain, the development of the complex roundhouse form cannot be entirely explained through its association with contemporary drystone structures as there are many examples of complex towers which developed in isolation. The most

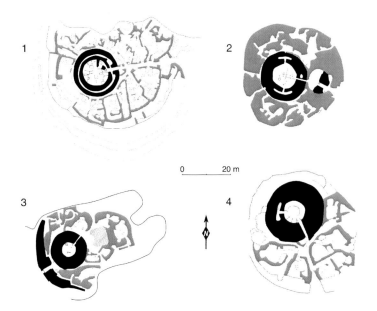

Figure 5.4 Complex Atlantic roundhouse villages: (1) Gurness, Orkney; (2) Keiss Road, Caithness; (3) Nybster, Caithness; (4) Howe, Orkney.

famous complex tower, Mousa on Shetland, developed without any surrounding settlement. Other well-known examples outwith the Northern Isles, such as Dun Carloway on Lewis, and Dun Troddan and Dun Telve, Inverness-shire, are isolated single structure settlements but also fully developed towers. In Shetland, although there are some indications of external buildings at sites such as Jarlshoff and Clickhimin, there is no evidence for planned village agglomerations similar to those seen on Orkney.

The construction of Atlantic roundhouses did not outlast the second century AD anywhere in Atlantic Scotland. Instead, smaller cellular forms were constructed from the third to the eighth centuries AD either in isolation as at Buckquoy on Orkney (Ritchie 1979), or within the shells of existing roundhouses as seen at Gurness and the Howe on Orkney and Old Scatness and Scalloway on Shetland (Hedges 1987; Ballin Smith 1994; Dockrill 1998; Sharples 1998). The layout of these forms can be paralleled with cellular Bronze Age settlement types and mark a return to non-monumental settlement construction in the area. Whatever their exact dating the population centres established at the roundhouse tower 'villages' in northern Atlantic Scotland outlast the *use* of the central roundhouse towers, suggesting that the meaning that complex roundhouses had as symbols was no longer relevant or at the very least had fundamentally changed by the third century AD (Heald and Jackson 2001).

Western Isles and Skye settlement sequence

Although the evidence from Coile a Ghasgain on Skye and Cladh Hallan on South Uist suggests there may be a significant Late Bronze Age/Early Iron Age stone-built hut circle component there are, as yet, no definite examples of simple thick-walled Atlantic roundhouses from the Western Isles comparable to those from Orkney. Every excavation that has taken place to date on sites previously classed as solid walled duns has uncovered evidence for intramural galleries or cells (Armit 1992). For example, both Beirgh and Dun Bharabhat on Lewis appeared as collapsed, featureless stony mounds, yet on excavation each revealed elements of complex architecture (Harding and Dixon 2000; Harding and Gilmour 2000). This apparent lack of evidence for a simple roundhouse horizon makes it difficult to support the traditional view that solid walled duns were the most common form of site in the Western Isles.

There is a lack of clear dating evidence for the construction of complex roundhouses in the Western Isles (Figure 5.5). A *terminus post quem* in the eighth century BC has been obtained for the construction of the complex roundhouse at Dun Bharabhat on Lewis while later secondary occupation provided a *terminus ante quem* around the first and second centuries BC (Harding and Armit 1990: 82). The construction of the complex roundhouse at Dun Vulan on South Uist is dated by the excavators to between the mid-first century BC and the second century AD (Parker Pearson and Sharples 1999: 39–40), although the dating samples used may have come from secondary contexts and an earlier construction date remains a possibility (Gilmour and Cook 1998; Armit 2000; Harding 2004, 129).

If the apparent lack of simple roundhouses in the Western Isles is a reality and the dating of complex forms is seen to be comparable to the northern examples then Atlantic roundhouses in the west began at the earliest *c.* 400 BC. More interestingly, the lack of simple prototypes could suggest that the monumental roundhouse form, complete with complex architectural devices, was adopted as a fully formed architectural package by Western Isles communities after it had developed elsewhere in Atlantic Scotland.

Unlike the northern examples there are no indications of complex cellular interiors in the Western Isles, or indeed elsewhere in Atlantic Scotland. Equally, although excavation of the outer area of sites in the Western Isles has not really taken place, it would appear from surface remains that there is no evidence of the kind of planned, nucleated settlement around roundhouses known in the north. Trenches placed outside Beirgh on Lewis have picked up external features (linear revetments, a cellular building and possible forecourt facade) related to the post-complex roundhouse cellular construction at the site (Harding and Gilmour 2000); while excavations at Dun Vulan, South Uist, have demonstrated the roundhouse featured secondary rectilinear external structures dating from the second to the seventh centuries AD (Parker Pearson *et al.* 1999). Dun Mor Vaul on Tiree and a number of sites on Skye have outworks which possibly contained extra-mural structures; however, these sites would appear to be the exception rather than the rule.

From the last few centuries BC and into the first century AD, contemporary with the use of complex Atlantic roundhouses, a new type of monumental settlement, the wheelhouse, is built. Wheelhouses are also circular drystone structures and occur most commonly revetted into sand in coastal machair environments, built into the interiors of existing Atlantic roundhouses or, more rarely, as free-standing buildings in their own right (Figure 5.6). These sites would have been unimposing when

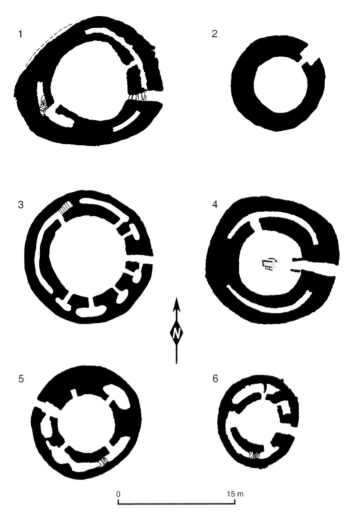

Figure 5.5 Complex Atlantic roundhouses in the Western Isles (after Parker Pearson *et al.* 1999): (1) Dun Vulan, South Uist; (2) Dun Mor, South Uist; (3) Beirgh, Lewis; (4) Dun Cuier, Barra; (5) Dun Carloway, Lewis; (6) Dun Bharabhat, Lewis.

viewed from the outside but their interiors featured a central open area often containing a lavish stone-built hearth surrounded by stone-built corbelled bays divided by regularly spaced, radial drystone piers which presumably supported a high roof of timber, turf and/or grass.[1] These interiors were clearly built to impress making wheelhouses part of the wider Atlantic monumental formula, albeit focused on internal rather than external display.

The wheelhouses at Jarlshof in Shetland are usually viewed as the type sites but by far the greatest numbers of sites occur in the Western Isles. In fact, examples are only known from Shetland and the Western Isles. There are no known examples from

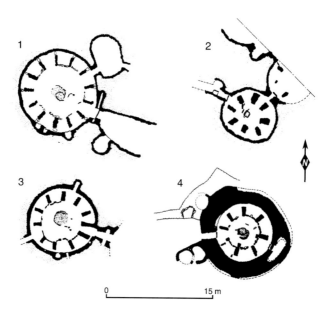

Figure 5.6 Excavated wheelhouses (after Armit 1996: fig. 8.1): (1) Sollas, North Uist; (2) Cnip, Lewis; (3) Kilpheder, South Uist; (4) Clettraval, North Uist.

Orkney, the north and west mainland or the Inner Isles. While the lack of wheelhouses in Orkney may seem strange it must be remembered that the interiors of many Orcadian roundhouses are divided radially using substantial slabs set around the walls, often leaving the central area free. The use of interior space therefore, including at least some of the social conventions that went with the space, had a wider currency throughout Atlantic Scotland, suggesting shared cultural traditions existed between communities even though the physical expression of these traditions were mediated and executed locally. The differential uptake of particular traditions like the wheelhouse form in some parts of the Atlantic Scottish zone but not others could be said to be indicative of the nature of Atlantic cultural similarities between areas throughout the Iron Age: close at some times, distinct at others, but still undeniably part of the same cultural milieu.

The dating of wheelhouses is somewhat problematic. Traditionally they were thought to be the settlements that directly replaced Atlantic roundhouses. The classic sequence at Jarlshof (Hamilton 1956) shows a wheelhouse replacing a complex Atlantic roundhouse while more recently the sequences at Old Scatness, Shetland (Dockrill 1998) and Eilean Maleit, North Uist, produced wheelhouses secondary to complex Atlantic roundhouses. In addition, wheelhouses were traditionally dated by metalwork and artefacts to the mid-first millennium AD. However, it has since been recognised that such datable finds are not always necessarily indicative of the primary occupations of these settlements (Armit 1992, 1996). The earliest absolute dating comes from Cnip where one of the two wheelhouses provided radiocarbon dates in the third century BC for bone deposited in the construction levels. By 100 AD both wheelhouses at Cnip were falling into disrepair. Possible earlier evidence for the origins of the wheelhouse form is suggested by the radiocarbon dates in the fifth and fourth centuries BC from a radially partitioned structure at Hornish Point, South Uist (Barber *et al.* 1989). Unfortunately, as the excavator notes these dates come from sea shell and may have been prejudiced by the marine reservoir effect. Dates from Sollas in North Uist suggest a span of occupation from the first to the third centuries AD (Campbell 1991: 139), but none were from demonstrably primary contexts (Armit 1996: 145). The wheelhouse at Kildonan III, South Uist, is considered to have been built and used in the first and second centuries AD (Gilmour 2000a: 160), while at the Udal on North Uist new structures were built over a wheelhouse in the first century AD (Crawford and Selkirk 1996).

Using the evidence available, the dating horizon for wheelhouses can roughly be regarded as the third century BC to the third century AD. Bearing in mind there is no unequivocal evidence for their actual construction after *c.* AD 100, the dates from Old Scatness, Shetland, suggest wheelhouses could have been occupied for long periods of time. Although the first wheelhouse at Old Scatness appears in the later first millennium BC, two wheelhouse structures on the site appear to have been occupied well into the second half of the first millennium AD (Dockrill 2003). Wheelhouses are best viewed, therefore, as a settlement form which run parallel with, and continue after, the later development of Atlantic roundhouses. Armit (1996: 158) claims wheelhouses represent a major change in the perception of the domestic sphere as monumentality is concentrated on the interior rather than the exterior. Although this lack of exterior monumentality may be important, it is worth making the point that wheelhouses do not represent any major break in domestic use as they continue the tradition of radially arranged interiors seen earlier and are stand-alone domestic settlements in many respects similar as a social unit to Atlantic roundhouses.

A widespread change in settlement forms occurs sometime in the second century AD with the end of the construction of monumental structures and moves towards the construction of smaller cellular buildings (Gilmour 2000a). Similar to northern Atlantic Scotland, cellular settlement forms are built across the Western Isles from the second to third centuries AD onwards: in open locations as at Bostadh (Neighbour and Burgess 1997); within complex Atlantic roundhouses as at Beirgh (Harding and Gilmour 2000); and replacing wheelhouse settlement as seen at Cnip (Armit 1992) and A'Cheardach Mhor, South Uist (Young and Richardson 1960).

Argyll and the Inner Isles

Despite representing a major part of Atlantic Scotland there has been remarkably little modern work carried out in Argyll, even though it contains a range of dry-stone sites which are clearly part of the same architectural traditions seen in the west and north. The evidence from Argyll has been slow to impact on discussions on Atlantic Scotland because work in the area has tended to adhere to the strict traditional classifications of *brochs* and *duns* (Maxwell 1969), meaning that the full

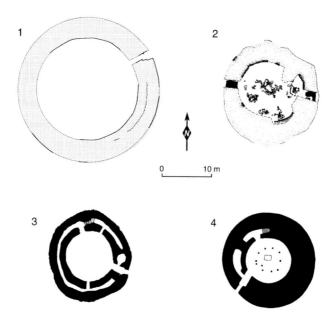

Figure 5.7 Atlantic roundhouses in the west: (1) Dun Glashan, Argyll; (2) Rahoy, Argyll; (3) Dun Mor Vaul, Tiree; (4) Dun Troddan, Inverness-shire.

diversity of structures in the area, particularly those displaying complex architec-ture, have not been fully considered or properly dated.

The chronology of the traditionally defined Argyll *brochs*, and therefore architec-tural complexity in the area, has relied very much on the evidence from Dun Mor Vaul, Tiree (MacKie 1974; Figure 5.7). Based on the recovered material assemblage and radiocarbon dates, MacKie placed the construction of the site in the first century BC or AD with occupation lasting until the mid-third century AD. However, the radiocarbon dates from the site have very wide margins of error, which greatly restricts their value while MacKie's interpretation of them has also been questioned (Lane 1990: 113; Harding 1997: 133–6). Earlier mid-first millennium BC dates were recovered from levels which the excavator interpreted as pre-*broch* but it is equally possible that they came from primary occupation levels at the site with subsequent levels and dates representing secondary occupation (Harding 2004: 130). Certainly, such a scenario would fit in with the dating and use of Atlantic roundhouses else-where in the Atlantic zone.

The hundreds of drystone sites in Argyll that do not possess the full range of archi-tectural devices required to qualify as *brochs*, and equally are too small to be consid-ered *forts,* are classed under the 'catch-all' term *dun,* regardless of their shape or individual features. Despite this very loose definition, *duns* have traditionally been regarded as a first millennium AD phenomenon, mainly due to the fact that eight out of the fourteen excavated examples have produced Early Historic material in the form of imported pottery, beads, and metalwork (Alcock and Alcock 1987; Neike 1984, 1990). However, to then apply a first millennium AD dating to all drystone *dun* sites, including roundhouse examples, is untenable. The majority of the sites that have been excavated to date such as Dùn Fhinn (Bigwood 1966), Kildonan Bay (Fairhurst 1939) and Eilean Righ 1 (RCAHMS 1988: 194) are of an irregular or rectilinear shape. The fact that these sites have produced first millennium AD dates should not be used as dating evidence for morphologically distinct circular examples better seen as belonging to the Atlantic roundhouses tradition. At those roundhouse sites that have been examined there has been in every documented case a failure to recognise that the dating evidence came from secondary or multiple occupations (Gilmour 1994: 59–87).

It is not denied that a large number of sites currently classed as *duns* date to the mid-first millennium AD, but rather that the strict use of traditional *broch* and *dun* terminology fails to recognise the existence of earlier roundhouse sites. Applying Armit's simple and complex roundhouse terminology removes this confusion and allows some separation of the earlier sites from the later first millennium AD examples, thus bringing the Argyll sequence in line with the Western Isles and northern sequences. Using Armit's terminology, Gilmour (1994) has demonstrated that three distinct types can be identified from the 306 sites previously classed as *duns* in Argyll: 95 rectilinear sites; 23 irregular sites; and 188 Atlantic roundhouses. Of these 188 drystone roundhouses, 23 were considered definitely complex sites and 144 as simple examples while 21 sites were classed as unknown due to presence of only median faces, or because old references to possible intra-mural features exist which are not visible today (op. cit. 17–29). The number of complex sites in the area is seen to dramatically increase as previously only seven *brochs* were recognised (Nieke 1984).

The sheer number of simple roundhouses would tend to imply that, unlike the Western Isles, sites without complex architecture are a reality in Argyll, and that their recognition is not simply a lack of architectural preservation (Gilmour 1994: 48–51). If simple sites are seen to be earlier than complex examples this may have an impact on the arguments for an origin of the simple type in the north. However, at this stage it cannot be ruled out that simple roundhouses may have been built and used alongside complex examples in Argyll. Equally, a number of the simple roundhouse examples might indeed belong to the mid-first millennium AD, alongside the rectilinear examples. Also, an analysis of the simple and complex roundhouses reveals that the complex sites generally have a greater wall-base percentage, perhaps indicating that these sites were built to a greater height (Gilmour 1994: 28). Another point of interest is that the average wall-base percentage is lower in Argyll than it is in the Western Isles which is in turn lower than roundhouses in northern Scotland (Armit 1992: 105). This may indicate a decreasing trend towards monumentality the further south one travels. It may be of some significance in this context that potential stone-built sites in Ireland dating to the Iron Age appear to be even less complex on the whole.[2]

Two simple roundhouses have been examined in Argyll and significantly each has provided early dating evidence (Figure 5.7). Rahoy, in Morven, which features a drystone wall some 3 m thick enclosing an internal area 12 m in diameter, was dated on account of its assemblage to the beginning of the Iron Age

(Childe and Thorneycroft 1938: 30). The recovery of a socketed and looped iron axe in a form which clearly imitated Late Bronze Age examples supports an early dating while a continentally inspired La Tène 1c brooch suggests occupation in the third or fourth centuries BC. The simple roundhouse at Dun Glashan is considerably larger and features a 5 m thick stone wall defining an internal area about 19 m in diameter. Small-scale excavations produced a coherent series of radiocarbon dates from deposits abutting the wall providing a *terminus post quem* of 400 to 90 BC for its construction (Gilmour and Henderson 2005).

Previously held assumptions about the dating of circular drystone sites in Argyll can therefore be challenged. Simple forms comparable to those in the north exist, while those that display evidence of complex architecture should now be viewed as a first millennium BC phenomenon in line with the dating of similar sites elsewhere in Atlantic Scotland. On present evidence only the rectilinear enclosures in Argyll can certainly be said to belong to the first millennium AD. The focus to date on those *dun* enclosures which belong to the first millennium AD offers close parallels to the study of ringfort enclosures in Ireland.

There has been no extensive research carried out into the existence of cellular settlement forms in Argyll and the Inner Isles, but there are some initial indications that there are types comparable with those seen elsewhere. Cellular forms could have formed elements of secondary occupation at Dun Mac Sniachan, Killdaloig, Dun Urgadul, An Caisteal and Dun Mhic Choigil (Fairhurst 1962; Bigwood 1964; RCAHMS 1975: 68–70, 1980: 95–6; Hedges and Hedges 1977), while early excavators may not have recognised the existence of later cellular structures constructed from edge-set slabs at Ardifuar, Dun Mor Vaul and Rahoy (Harding 2004: 272-3).

South-west Scotland

Sites of a potentially Atlantic character in south-west Scotland are not numerous and do not form a homogeneous group but they are sufficient to suggest that the coastal communities of the region were influenced by Atlantic cultural contacts (Figure 5.8). The oval stone walled fort at the Fell of Barhullion, Wigtownshire, consists of a massive but largely collapsed inner wall and a slighter outer wall, with separate groups of *chevaux-de-frise* in the southern, western and northern approaches to the site (Harbison 1971: 199). Two features are reminiscent of traits associated with Irish Western Stone Forts: one is the observation of a 'slight batter' to the massive inner wall, and the other is the reference to an intra-mural cell in the south-western portion of the inner wall 'which may have formed part of a gallery 1.30 m wide within the wall'. In the absence of excavation at the site little more can be said at this stage.

Seven sites in Galloway display elements of complex drystone architecture associated with the Atlantic roundhouse tradition (Cavers 2005: 175-82). Three of these – Stairhaven, Teroy and Doon Castle, Ardwell Point – would qualify as complex Atlantic roundhouses as they feature intra-mural cells and/or stairs. A fourth site, Crammag Head, certainly qualifies as a simple Atlantic roundhouse, but as it was largely destroyed by the construction of a lighthouse the possible existence of any

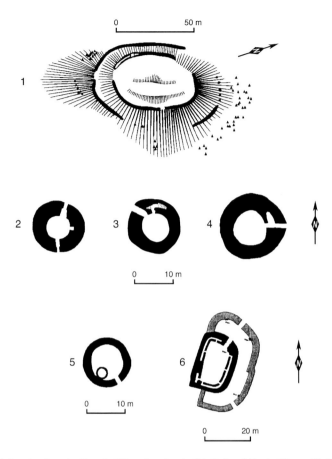

Figure 5.8 Atlantic sites in South-West Scotland: (1) Fell of Barhullion; (2) Doon Castle, Ardwell Point; (3) Stairhaven; (4) Teroy; (5) Crammag Head; (6) Castle Haven.

complex features cannot be ruled out. The final three – Castle Haven, Killantringan Bay and Craigoch, High Milton – are rectilinear in construction and have close parallels with similar forms in Argyll dated to the first millennium AD. Although these sites do not form a uniform group, they were undoubtedly influenced by architectural styles found further north in Atlantic Scotland. The circular examples are usually interpreted as later 'bastard forms' of the Atlantic roundhouse tradition (Cowley 2000: 174), built in response to the arrival of the Romans based on the dating evidence from the better known outlying sites of Buchlyvie, Leckie and Torwoodlee found in central and south-eastern Scotland (Armit 2003: 119-32). However, there seems little reason to date the Galloway examples to the same period, particularly given the lack of evidence for a strong Roman presence in this area, and it is more likely that they belong to the same dating horizon and cultural tradition as complex circular sites seen elsewhere in Atlantic Scotland. It is surely significant that all of these sites are found in coastal locations looking out to sea, while Doon Castle, Crammag Head and Teroy were all built within the fortifications of small promontory forts, perhaps reflecting a conscious decision by their builders to acknowledge and enhance their Atlantic identity and maritime cultural connections.

The most common settlement forms in the south-west are small fortified sites referred to as homesteads and like the *duns* of Argyll form a very loosely defined site grouping within which there is much diversity. The majority are oval or sub-circular enclosures where single earthen or stone ramparts, ranging from 2 to 8 m in thickness, enclose an internal area, some 17 to 24 m in diameter, containing one or more roundhouses. Like most later prehistoric sites, they could have feasibly been occupied anywhere within the later first millennium BC and the early to mid-first millennium AD. Significantly, those in the west tend to be smaller in diameter and are often located on rocky summits or promontories with commanding sea views. The western forms also feature more substantially built stone ramparts and many have their closest parallels with Irish ringforts and the *dun* enclosures of Argyll, perhaps further indicating the existence of Atlantic influences in the area.

It is not possible to suggest a sequence of development for the Atlantic sites of south-west Scotland due to a lack of modern excavation. Survey has only been partial throughout the region but enough has been done to demonstrate that the archaeology of the west differs from that of the east (RCAHMS 1997). Studies have tended to focus on the enclosed settlements of the area (hillforts, homesteads and palisaded enclosures) in an effort to relate them to the settlement records of Lothian and the Borders to the east and Northumbria to the south. These forms are mainly found in the east and there are many overlaps and parallels with adjacent regions as one might expect but the western coastal areas feature a suite of forms – promon-tory forts, complex roundhouses, stone forts, crannogs and sites within the home-stead class – which fit more comfortably within an Atlantic cultural context.

The Atlantic Scottish maritime continuum

The development being presented here then is the gradual appearance of monumen-tal stone-built roundhouse forms developing from indigenous Late Bronze Age tradi-tions of cellular and circular drystone settlement from the seventh century BC onwards (Figure 5.9). The earliest dated simple forms come from Orkney but undated exam-ples appear to occur in greater numbers in Argyll. The development of complex roundhouse forms begins in the fourth century BC but the construction of fully complex towers cannot be dated to before the second century BC. The wheelhouse form belongs to a broadly dated horizon from the third century BC to the third century AD (bearing in mind there is no evidence for the construction of these sites after AD 100). As such, the building and use of wheelhouses overlaps with the devel-opment of fully developed complex roundhouse towers. While the majority of wheel-houses are built in isolation, a number of wheelhouses appear to have been built within the shell of complex roundhouses. The end of the period of use of complex roundhouse sites seems to have resulted in two different conclusions: abandoning the

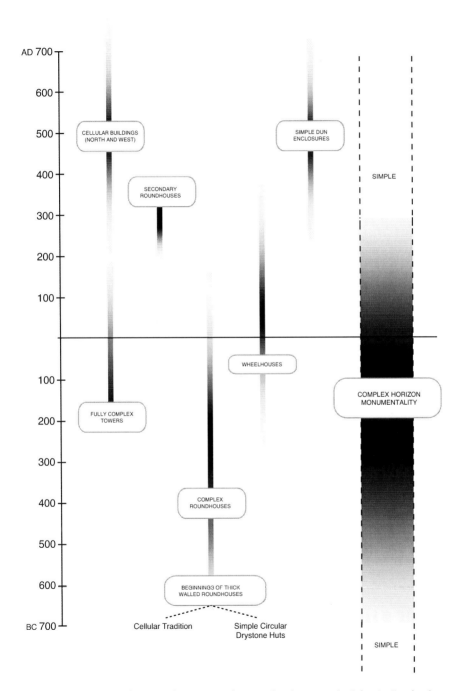

Figure 5.9 Later prehistoric drystone settlement development in Atlantic Scotland.

form and reverting to less monumental wheelhouse constructions and, conversely, constructing even more monumental complex towers. There is no evidence that complex monumental roundhouses were built after AD 200, suggesting that monumental construction had lost its significance to Atlantic societies, a development perhaps foreshadowed by the earlier appearance of the wheelhouse form. Significantly, at a number of sites, the immediately post-complex roundhouse occupation involves the construction of an inner skin of walling along interior side of the existing roundhouse wall to create a secondary roundhouse structure (Harding 2004: 262, fig. 10.5). It is difficult to interpret the construction of these secondary walls in purely functional terms as they are often more poorly built than the existing roundhouse walls and serve simply to reduce the available interior space. Their construction may represent a symbolic as well as physical break with the past, recognising the end of the use of the complex roundhouse and the meaning and power it originally conveyed. From the second to third centuries AD there was a widespread though not necessarily synchronous trend throughout Atlantic Scotland towards the construction of much less monumental cellular settlement forms. These cellular settlements continue to develop throughout the first millennium AD culminating in ventral figure-of-eight forms by the seventh to eighth centuries AD (Gilmour 2000a, 161-7; Figure 5.10).

The existence of maritime contacts in Atlantic Scotland are clearly demonstrated through the distinctive architecture of the Atlantic roundhouse tradition. However, further evidence of direct maritime contacts are more difficult to discern. Material assemblages throughout the period 600 BC to AD 100 are, similar to those from other Atlantic areas, predominantly utilitarian in nature and often not sufficiently diagnostic to demonstrate contact through the exchange of goods. For example, the decorated ceramic forms from Atlantic Scotland are one of the most distinctive aspects of the area because decorated pottery is unknown throughout the rest of Scotland. Ceramic forms from the three Atlantic areas, while not identical, are broadly related to each other, implying that a shared background and understanding of what forms and motifs were appropriate was in existence. Despite this shared tradition there is little evidence of trading contact in terms of actual exported pottery vessels between areas. Although we are far from well-dated pottery sequences for the Atlantic areas, initial studies would suggest that the Western Isles, the north, and Argyll and the Inner Isles followed rather separate paths (Lane 1990: 108): further evidence of similarity and divergence taking place within a related tradition, similar to the situation seen in the settlement sequences we have examined. Decorated pottery forms and motifs are most numerous in the Western Isles compared to the percentage of decorated forms in assemblages from the north. Argyll and the Inner Isles (except Coll, Tiree and Skye which can be seen to be part of the Western Isles/Hebridean tradition, cf. Lane 1990: 125, fig. 7.7) feature the lowest amount of decorated pottery, but this may be due to the lack of work carried out in the area.

Neutron Activation Analysis of Hebridean ceramics has suggested that pottery was produced and distributed locally (Topping 1987). There is no evidence for the exchange of forms or the imposition of ceramic styles and motifs accompanying the evidence of contact visible from the architectural trends. For example, the Shetland and Hebridean wheelhouse forms are very close in terms of spatial layout

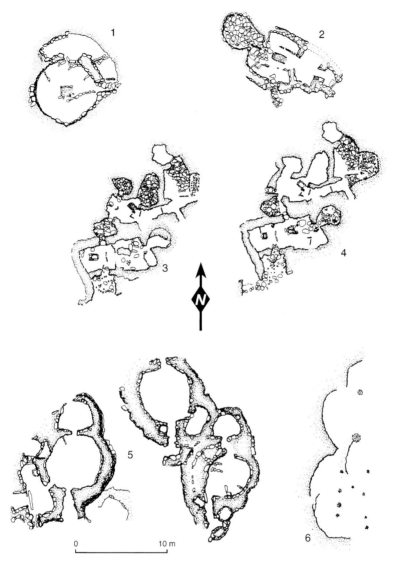

Figure 5.10 Cellular settlement forms (after Gilmour 2000: fig. 4): (1) Beirgh, Lewis;
(2) Buckquoy, Orkney; (3) Howe phase 8, Orkney; (4) Howe phase 8, Orkney; (5) Bostadh
Beach, Lewis; (6) Brough of Birsay, Orkney.

and construction implying close cultural contact, but this is not replicated in the
pottery evidence between the two areas where there is a paucity of decorated forms
in Shetland compared to the Hebrides.

Regionalism and local distinctiveness within an overall shared tradition is the
most instructive way to view the Atlantic province in the second half of the first

millennium BC. There is diversity in settlement characteristics, settlement types and pottery that largely follow regional trends broken up into the three areas we have examined. Even within these three areas themselves there is diversity as MacKie has noted in his discussions of small variations recognisable amongst local roundhouse forms (MacKie 1965: 105–10). Despite this diversity we cannot deny that these areas were in some form of contact resulting in development along similar lines and distinct as a group from developments in the rest of Scotland.

Contact between the Western Isles and the Shetlands is suggested by the wheel-house form; between the Shetlands and Orkney through the radially divided interiors of roundhouses; and between Argyll and the Western Isles which both lack nucleation around roundhouses and have apparently open interior areas within them (Figure 5.11). Local distinctiveness could be considered a characteristic element of communities throughout the Atlantic seaboard as the agricultural potential of most land was such that it did not allow the creation of large surpluses leading to the formation of large power groupings. This local distinctiveness is also a result of isolation – much of the settlement along the Atlantic province occurs within the coastal zone and is separated from the rest of Scotland by mountains. Communication is easier along the Atlantic coasts via the sea than overland to other parts of Scotland. As Cunliffe (1991: 310) comments on the area 'while the sea linked the far flung parts of the province together, it seems to have isolated it from the rest of the country'. Inevitably under such conditions, communities remain isolated from wider developments and in many cases are more likely to adhere to their own trends rather than respond to stimuli further afield. This was the case right up to the eighteenth century AD in Atlantic Scotland when much of the province was still relatively isolated from mainland developments, meaning there was often a time lag in Atlantic areas receiving new influences. Only 200 years ago the largest centres of population in Argyll were simple hamlets and external communication was mainly by boat (RCAHMS 1975: 3).

A point often overlooked when considering the evidence for Atlantic contact is that the very existence of a common Atlantic cultural milieu, where societies are at similar levels of development, may remove the impetus for the exchange of material forms between areas. The resource base, domestic assemblages, and ceramic forms (and presumably the contents) were already similar. Atlantic Iron Age assemblages, due to their very nature, are unlikely to help elucidate maritime routes of contact. Certainly the practice of plotting distributions of traded goods, the traditional method of defining contacts, may not be relevant in an Atlantic context and we should perhaps begin to examine more subtle expressions of contact.

At a very general level the trends in material assemblages seen in Atlantic Scotland tie in with the wider settlement trends of the area (Figure 5.12). While evidence from the Late Bronze Age is still sparse in Atlantic Scotland there are some indications that assemblages were more ornamental and indicative of long-distance contact during this period: along with a plethora of single, usually uncontexted, finds of bronze metalwork there is some evidence for comprehensive metalwork assemblages such as those from Jarlshoff on Shetland (Hamilton 1956),

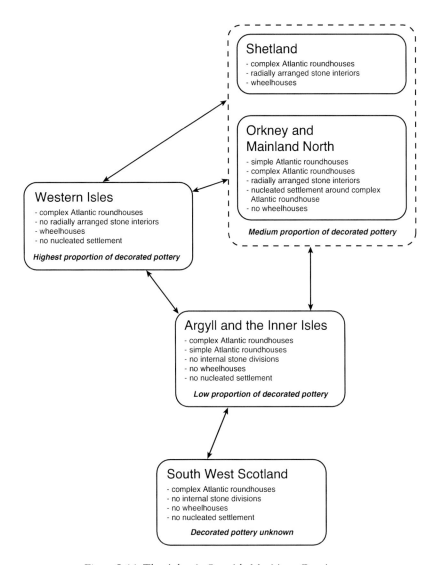

Figure 5.11 The Atlantic Scottish Maritime Continuum.

the Adabrock hoard from Lewis (Coles 1960: 50; Armit 1992: 101), and the considerable assemblage from Dunagoil on the Isle of Bute (Marshall 1964). A shift in the importance of long-distance contacts is implied during the Iron Age owing to the dominance of utilitarian assemblages as the sphere of cultural elaboration becomes more inward looking and moves to architectural monumentality. The beginning of undifferentiated, non-monumental cellular settlement from the third century AD coincides with an increase in ornamental artefacts (mostly portable

Late Bronze Age	Iron Age	AD 300 >
Open circular drystone huts Cellular settlement	Monumental architecture	Non-monumental settlement Cellular settlement
Plain Pottery Forms	Decorated Pottery Forms	Plain Pottery Forms
Prestige Metalwork	Utilitarian material culture	Prestige Metalwork (items of personal decoration)
LONG DISTANCE CONTACT	CONTACT WITHIN ATLANTIC SCOTLAND	LONG DISTANCE CONTACT
Outward looking society	Inward looking society	Outward looking society

Figure 5.12 General Atlantic Scottish developments.

objects of personal ornamentation) indicative of an opening up of long–distance contacts.

Long-distance contacts with areas such as Ireland are visible before 700 BC and after AD 300 through the exchange of ornamental artefacts. There is little evidence of such exchange in the intervening period but, as we have seen, maritime contacts within Atlantic Scotland are certain from the settlement record. If the lack of visible material contact within Atlantic Scotland does not necessarily mean that maritime contacts were not occurring within the area, it is worth examining whether there are similar cultural similarities with areas further along the Atlantic seaboard. The lack of traditional evidence for the exchange of exotica between abstract elite groupings should not be used as a reason to deny cultural contact between areas – cultural exchange could have been occurring in other ways, such as through the communication of fundamental beliefs, technology or ideas. Rather than simply looking for prestige trading contacts we should consider the evidence for shared cultural traditions between Atlantic areas, and the apparent long continuity of these shared elements. With this in mind we shall turn to the Irish settlement record, focusing on the western drystone forms, and examine whether we can recognise common cultural elements which may indicate the existence of some level of maritime contact with the Atlantic coasts of Scotland. In considering the Irish evidence it is worth recalling the nature of developments within Atlantic Scotland which displayed clear elements of a shared tradition at one level, along with regional diversity and local development at another.

Atlantic Ireland

There are a large number of stone-built sites in Ireland which, on initial observation, appear to have close parallels with drystone forms found elsewhere in Atlantic Europe. For example, it has long been recognised that sites such as Dún Aonghasa on the Aran Isles, or the Grianán of Aileach in Co. Kerry, are best paralleled with drystone sites dated to the Iron Age in Atlantic Scotland. Despite this, there have been major difficulties in dating the Irish sites to a similar chronological horizon owing to the combination of a lack of extensive excavation of those stone-built sites in the west which provide the closest parallels with other Atlantic sites, and the inconclusive dating evidence from those investigations which have taken place. There are currently no complex drystone sites in Ireland which have produced unequivocally Iron Age dating evidence. All too often, absolute dating methods have yielded Late Bronze Age dates at sites where Iron Age activity was expected, while, at other potential Iron Age candidates, material assemblages are taken to date occupation, and in turn construction to the second half of the first millennium AD.

The lack of a recognisable Iron Age settlement horizon remains an oddity of Irish archaeology. It has already been demonstrated (Chapter 4) that there was a tradition of circular/oval enclosure and circular domestic settlement in existence in the Irish Late Bronze Age that can be paralleled with contemporary sites elsewhere along the Atlantic seaboard. Traditional interpretations of the Irish Iron Age argue that after this there is a period of environmental and cultural decline with the majority of settlements occurring in as yet unrecognised open contexts. Settlements are not then supposedly recognisable until the second half of the first millennium AD with the development of the circular/oval enclosure form once again, but this time within an Early Christian cultural context. Such an interpretation is unsatisfying on a number of levels. There is no evidence that other Atlantic areas suffered so harshly from a significant climatic downturn at this time, and if anything, Ireland should have benefited from a more temperate maritime weather system through its geographical relationship with the Atlantic Ocean (Limbert 1996: 243–4). It would seem more likely that there was some degree of cultural continuity in the circular enclosure form from the Late Bronze Age into the Early Christian period.[3]

Irish Iron Age settlement: problems of classification

One of the major problems in the recognition of potentially Iron Age settlement forms in Ireland is the widespread use of the term 'ringfort' to describe all circular, or roughly circular,[4] enclosures – defined by either one or more earthen banks and ditches or by a stone wall. Ringforts are further subdivided into earthen examples (*raths*) and those built of stone (usually termed *cashels* or *cahers*).[5] Inevitably such a loose definition covers a wide diversity of stone and earthen structures; despite this the term is considered by the majority of archaeologists to have a distinct cultural and chronological significance. Ringforts are widely considered to belong exclusively to a narrow chronological horizon in the Early Christian period from the seventh to the ninth centuries AD (Lynn 1983; Edwards 1990: 10–11; Mytum 1992; Stout 1997; O'Sullivan 1998: 101; Waddell 1998).

While there can be little doubt that the majority of enclosures currently classed as ringforts do indeed date to the second half of the first millennium AD, it does not follow that all morphologically analogous enclosures must date to this period. There is little in the morphology and layout of ringfort enclosures to suggest that they are a new form of settlement whose genesis requires a specifically Early Christian cultural context. The basic form of oval enclosure is not novel and must have had prehistoric antecedents. In fact, the closest parallels to the earthen *rath* form of settlement outside of Ireland are the Iron Age enclosures of western Britain, while certain features of Irish drystone enclosures are most closely paralleled within an Iron Age context in Atlantic Scotland.

One problem with ringforts belonging to such a narrow chronological horizon is their sheer number. Ringforts are the most widespread and numerous type of site found in the Irish countryside, with their original numbers estimated at between 30,000 and 40,000 (O'Kelly 1970: 50). As modern survey and aerial photography programmes proceed, it is becoming apparent that even this great number may be too conservative, with estimates now placed at around the 60,000 mark (Stout 1997). Such numbers instantly raise suspicions over their classification as a homogeneous class and, as a result, their dating to such a restricted horizon.

The current view of ringforts being purely an Early Christian phenomenon is based on a very restricted and biased sample. Although it is claimed that around 200 ringforts have been excavated (Edwards 1990: 11), this still only represents 1 per cent of the current known resource and it has been argued that as only 5 per cent of the excavated number have been completely excavated, total excavation can only be said to have taken place at 0.05 per cent of the resource (Buckley and Sweetman 1991: 152; Limbert 1996: 253). The sample is biased in a number of ways: the vast majority of work has been done on sites in north-east Ireland; the sites in the north-east – and elsewhere – are selected by fieldworkers mainly interested in the Early Christian period and do not therefore usually include likely candidates for earlier occupation;[6] of these only a very small number have actually been reliably and closely dated; there have been very few excavations on drystone enclosures and as yet no fully published modern investigations; selection of sites has been driven by rescue concerns and therefore concentrates on areas around Dublin and Cork – as a result western Ireland and south-eastern Ireland are very much under-represented. Quite simply, the current view lumps together a vast and diverse range of enclosures as ringforts based on the evidence of a small and unrepresentative sample of excavated sites.

There is plenty of evidence to suggest that the tradition of building ringfort type enclosures began prior to the Early Christian period (Proudfoot 1970; Caulfield 1981; Warner 1983; Limbert 1996). Amongst the earthen rath evidence, Iron Age occupation is attested at the Rath of the Synods, Co. Meath (Ó Ríordáin 1971); Feerwore, Co. Galway (Raftery 1944); Lugg, Co. Dublin (Kilbride-Jones 1950); Lislackagh, Co. Mayo (Walsh 1995; Limbert 1996: 283–4) and less certainly at Cush, Co. Limerick (Ó Ríordáin 1940). The Late Bronze Age/Early Iron Age phase at Navan, Co. Antrim (Lynn 1992), can be interpreted as a phase of domestic occupation which is entirely analogous in terms of enclosed area and shape to ringforts (Raftery 1994: fig. 7; Limbert 1996: 250).

As for stone-built circular enclosures there are a range of examples demonstrating activity as early as the Neolithic and Early Bronze Age at Knockadoon, Lough Gur, Co. Limerick (Grogan and Eogan 1987); in the Bronze Age at Carrigillihy, Co. Cork (O'Kelly 1951, 1989: 221); while two stone enclosures from Aughinish Island, Co. Clare produced artefacts belonging to the Late Bronze Age/Early Iron Age transition (Kelly 1974: 21). Indications of Iron Age activity come from Carraig Aille 1 and 2, Co. Limerick (Ó Ríordáin 1949), Raheennamadra, Co. Limerick (Stenberger 1966), Cahercommaun, Co. Clare (Hencken 1938) and possibly at Kiltera, Co. Waterford (Macalister 1935). Iron Age dates for these sites have been firmly rejected in recent times but as all these excavations are rather old, the nature of the published evidence is such that it is impossible to firmly date these sites one way or the other. Arguments based on non-existent section plans or incomplete descriptions become circular and are quickly reduced to a matter of opinion (cf. Proudfoot 1970; Raftery, B. 1976; Caulfield 1981; Raftery, J. 1981; Lynn 1983). However, the existence of earlier elements at these sites does at least cast a further element of doubt on the supposedly exclusive Early Christian dating of ringforts.

Despite ample evidence for a prehistoric pedigree at a number of sites, there has been a marked reluctance to accept this activity as being relevant to the overall development of ringforts. Earlier activity is either dismissed as simply residual or relating to open settlement which pre-dates the enclosure phase. For example, Edwards (1990), following Lynn (1983), views the prehistoric material from Cush, Co. Limerick, Carraig Aille 1 and 2, Co. Limerick and Cahercommaun, Co. Clare as residual and prefers to date the sites to the Early Christian period owing to the greater number of Early Christian finds recovered. However, these assemblages cannot be confidently used to date construction because they could belong to a period of secondary occupation. In such cases we would not expect a large number of prehistoric finds as the sites would have been cleared out when the secondary occupation began. This is an argument particularly relevant to stone-built settlement. In Scotland, Ireland and to some extent south-west England, the dating of Atlantic stone-built settlements has been blurred by a lack of recognition in many cases that the latest, and therefore surviving, occupational evidence may not be chronologically indicative of construction and initial occupation. Monumental, stone-built structures, if regularly maintained, could have remained in use for hundreds of years or have been repeatedly reoccupied leaving in many cases minimal traces of their primary occupation. Evidence of such an episode of reoccupation is demonstrated at Carrigillihy, Co. Cork, where Early Christian occupation material is separated from Bronze Age evidence by only a thin sterile layer (O'Kelly 1951; Edwards 1990: 12). This is exactly the kind of relationship that could have been missed on earlier excavations. Given the proliferation of enclosure sites in the Early Christian period it seems unlikely that earlier circular enclosures would have escaped continued or secondary use and/or modification.

Evidence for activity preceding ringforts is quite common, with at least 22 examples known (Limbert 1996: 278), and is usually interpreted as a period of open settlement preceding the enclosure. It is this evidence that has been taken to support theories of pre-Christian transhumance as the dominant social form in the Iron Age.[7] However, this evidence is far from clear-cut and can equally be interpreted as further support for the prehistoric origins of Early Christian enclosures. The lack of enclosure evidence for earlier phases could of course be related to the Early Christian remodelling of sites – the re-cutting of a larger ditch on an earlier existing one would leave few traces of the original ditch's existence.[8] The evidence for ditch re-cutting is sparse (currently only three definite examples) but the presence of counterscarp banks is common. Limbert (1996: 252) claims that phases of ditch re-cutting at ringforts may be under-estimated because the majority of ditch sections are very narrow, meaning that remnants of old fill may remain unrecorded, especially if the original material consisted of primary silts which would appear as a sterile, natural layer. Equally, ditches are frequently waterlogged, providing a major obstacle to complete excavation (Edwards 1990: 20). More interestingly, some evidence of enclosure forms preceding Early Christian ringforts exists: palisade enclosures have been found underneath later earthen banks at Lisleagh 2, Cork; Oldcourt, Co. Cork; Clogher, Co. Tyrone; Coolcran and Lisdoo,[9] both Co. Fermanagh; while pre-Christian ditched enclosures have been recorded from Deer Park Farms, Co. Antrim and Millockstown, Co. Louth.

Despite this evidence, ringforts are still regarded as a solely Early Christian phenomenon by most archaeologists. For example, Stout rejects claims for the prehistoric origins of ringforts by simply stating that 'the stratigraphical approach to dating ringforts has proved unsatisfactory on many occasions' and goes on to warn against 'relying solely on stratigraphy as a dating device' (1997: 22–3). Instead, Stout argues that the absolute dating evidence and assemblages recovered from ringforts demonstrate that 'despite the extremes in date produced from a few excavations, it is still widely recognised that most ringforts date to the Early Christian period' (ibid.). This last quote reveals the problem in the current archaeological perception of these sites: ringforts date to the Early Christian period, so by definition earlier dates cannot relate to ringfort activity. There is no argument with the fact that the majority of ringforts do belong to the second half of the first millennium AD but we cannot rule out on present evidence that some enclosures may date to the Iron Age or earlier. Stout's suggestion that we should rely on recovered assemblages is part of the problem: recovered assemblages cannot always be used to confidently date construction. To make matters more difficult there are no finds in Ireland currently recognised as indicative of Iron Age activity (excepting La Tène metalwork which is rarely recovered in association with settlement) and it remains a possibility that earlier finds exist within the mass of more diagnostic types currently ascribed to the Early Christian period.

Stout (1997: 29, fig. 2) has produced a diagram of radiocarbon and dendrochronological dates which seems to suggest that ringforts date exclusively from AD 236 to AD 1387, with a clear concentration between AD 600 and AD 900. However, Stout's corpus of dates is not a representative sample. Only five stone *cashel* sites are included, all from Co. Sligo, whilst dates from the Atlantic-facing counties of Kerry, Galway, Clare, Mayo, Leitrim or Donegal are completely lacking; the vast majority of evidence comes from north-eastern Ireland – one-third from Co. Antrim alone. In addition, a number of earlier dates are not included because they are not interpreted as having come from 'true' ringfort sites. It is perhaps possible to omit early dates such as the uncalibrated date of *c.* 260 BC recovered from Big Glebe, Co. Derry, because it reportedly came from a charcoal spread beneath the enclosure phase and does not therefore meet the definition of a ringfort,[10] but it is completely unjustifiable to omit pre-Christian dates from enclosed levels at Deer Park Farms, Co. Antrim; Lisdoo, Co. Fermanagh; Lislackagh, Co. Mayo (Walsh 1995); and Dún Aonghasa, Aran Islands (Cottter 1993, 1995, 1996) as well as first millennium BC dates from sites such as Aughinish, Co. Limerick (Limbert 1996: 282).[11]

Drystone settlement in the Irish west

Doubts have been expressed over the significance of the western distribution of stone-built sites and the difference between stone *cashels* and earthen *raths* on the grounds that the division has more to do with local geology than cultural or functional affinities (Lacy 1983; Moore 1987; Buckley and Sweetman 1991; Cotter 1993: 1; Limbert 1996: 253–7). There is, rather unsurprisingly, a direct correlation between limestone areas and drystone site numbers (Limbert 1996: Illus. 9). However, high numbers are also found in other areas such as in Co. Roscommon, Co. Cavan and Co. Down, and although these could be partially explained through the occurrence of stone quarried from nearby mountain ranges, it does not fully explain the absence of sites in other mountainous areas, particularly the south-east of Ireland. To dismiss the distribution of drystone sites, some with complex architectural features echoed in areas beyond Ireland, on purely deterministic grounds ignores the role these sites may have had in expressing distinct cultural identities. The western distribution of drystone sites, determined by the availability of building stone or not, reflects the existence of a distinctive and highly visible form of architectural expression that must have held some level of cultural meaning to the communities that constructed them (Figure 5.13).

The earth and stone distinction has also been criticised as irrelevant on the grounds that many earthen ringforts were stone revetted. However, as the ringfort class includes a variety of diverse sites which need not be contemporaneous this is hardly surprising and need not call into question the possible cultural significance of drystone sites with wider Atlantic architectural affinities. Circular drystone sites do not seem to occur in areas dominated by earthen *raths* in the east (Buckley and Sweetman 1991), but earthen ringforts do occur in significant numbers alongside *cashels* in the west (Lacy 1983) – the implication being that these sites may date to different periods. In light of this, it is interesting to note that most of the early Iron Age settlement dating evidence comes from the west. This has a particular resonance with regard to the arguments presented in Chapter 4 that permanent settlement first becomes recognisable in many Atlantic areas by the Late Bronze Age, a phenomeno which may be related to the opening up of Atlantic contacts. It could be argued that the appearance of oval and circular forms of domestic enclosure in later prehistoric Ireland was an Atlantic western development – a view that would run contrary to the traditional idea that ringfort types of enclosure appeared for the first time in the east during the Early Christian period.

Figure 5.13 Drystone sites in Ireland discussed in the text.

The Western Stone Forts

The 'Western Stone Forts' are a group of sites spanning the traditional *cashel*, hill-fort and promontory fort classes that are lumped together simply because they display a range of complex architectural features which make them stand out from the otherwise homogeneous mass of featureless stone ringforts and hillforts. As such they are a poorly defined group and no full definition or comprehensive inventory has yet been compiled for them[12] although they usually include: the Grianán of Aileach and O'Boyles Fort, Co. Kerry; Inishmurray, Co. Sligo; Doonamo, Co. Mayo; the seven massive stone-built forts of the Aran Islands;[13] Ballykinvarga, Cahercommaun and Caherdooneerish, Co. Clare; Leacanabuaile, Staigue, Dunbeg, Cahergal and Loher, Co. Kerry (Rynne 1991; Cotter 1993: 3). These sites have been the subject of study of one of the Irish Discovery Programme projects, namely the Western Stone Fort Project, begun by C. Cotter in 1992 (Cotter 1993, 1995, 1996, 2000). Cotter (1993: 3) is the first to point out that these sites do not form a morphologically homogeneous group but, nevertheless, construct a 'broad' working definition of the Western Stone Forts based on the presence of a massive wall or walls; terracing; mural steps; narrow, often lintelled, entrances; intra-mural chambers/passageways and *chevaux de frise*.[14]

Excavations at the impressive drystone enclosure of Dún Aonghasa situated on the south-western edge of Inis Móre, the largest of the three Aran Islands, formed the main focus of the Western Stone Forts project. The site consists of an innermost *cashel*, nearly 50 m in diameter, surrounded by two other well-built stone ramparts enclosing an area of 5.7 ha (Figure 5.14). The inner *cashel* comprises a massive limestone wall (Wall 1), built in at least three stages, up to 5.8 m thick and rising to a restored height of 4.9 m.[15] Architectural elaboration of the wall includes a wall chamber along with two terraces on the inner face accessible via four flights of vertical steps and two sidelong flights. The wall is breached by one entrance passage and encloses a semi-oval area of 48.2 × 45.6 m (Cotter 1993: 5). The middle enclosure rampart (Wall 2) is 1.6 to 3.8 m thick and features a terrace, a set of sidelong steps,

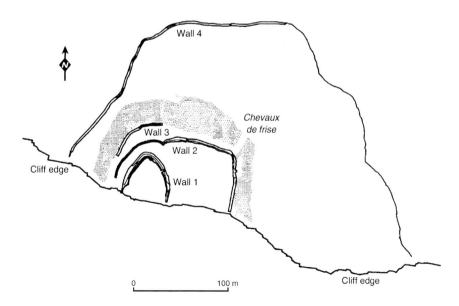

Figure 5.14 Dún Aonghasa plan (after Cotter 1993: fig. 3).

a blocked-up lintelled entrance and two faced openings. The outer enclosure rampart (Wall 4) also features a lintelled entrance and has traces of terracing. Between the two outer ramparts is a wide band of sharp edge slabs stuck into the ground interpreted as *chevaux-de-frise*.

Excavations have revealed Late Bronze Age occupation spanning at least 500 years, from *c.* 1300 BC to 800 BC, within the central *cashel* and the middle enclosure (Cotter 1993, 1995, 1996). Stratigraphically these Late Bronze Age deposits run under the inner and outer sections of Wall 1 (the main *cashel* wall[16]) providing a *terminus post quem* for these structures. However, this does not mean that Wall 1 was built in its entirety after the Late Bronze Age because excavations have not yet revealed whether the deposits run under the core 'middle' wall – this part of the wall could have been in existence before the outer and inner skins were added. The only other clear evidence of activity according to the excavator comes from the Early Christian period in the form of a late burial and a radiocarbon date of 658 to 851 cal. AD[17] (Cotter 1995: 10). Evidence for Early Christian activity 'is largely confined to the wall chamber in Wall 1, the entrance passage in Wall 2a and an artefact assemblage from cutting 1' (Cotter 1996: 14). However, stratigraphically these Early Christian deposits do provide a *terminus ante quem* for the drystone structure. If we accept that the *cashel* wall was built after the Late Bronze Age but before the Early Christian activity then an Iron Age date for the building of the main drystone enclosure cannot be ruled out – a period spanning *c.* 400 BC to AD 500 (Figure 5.15).

Cotter (1996: 14) states 'that there was no extensive occupation on the site during the period from *c.* 400 BC to 400 AD'. However, some Iron Age presence can be implied from the evidence. The stone trough in the interior (cutting 1) provides a date of 752 to 392 cal. BC indicating later activity than 800 BC as do two dates with the same range from the nearby Hut 2[18] (Cotter 1995: 11). A spread of burnt animal bone in the northern part of the inner enclosure, lying directly on bedrock and abutting a linear stone feature, provided a date which calibrates to between 750 and 150 cal. BC.[19] Significantly these dates, unlike many from the site, are associated with structural remains.

There are problems in trying to identify Iron Age activity at Dún Aonghasa. First, the archaeological deposits which overlay the Late Bronze Age occupation, where they survived, appeared to be mixed midden material and were quite thin (from 0.1–0.25 m thick). Cotter (1993: 11) notes that 'the recognition of discrete cultural layers is difficult (and often impossible). The assemblage from these deposits consists of Late Bronze Age artefacts, iron fragments and first millennium AD objects. This brings us to the next problem – crucial to the recognition of Irish Iron Age occupation – if there was Iron Age activity (as the radiocarbon dates suggest) how would we recognise it? Evidence of Iron Age occupation is poorly defined in Ireland and is often only recognised through the presence of La Tène metalwork. This is problematic in areas where La Tène metalwork is not prolific, as is the case with the Aran Isles and much of the western stone fort area in general, let alone the fact that La Tène metalwork is, in any case, rarely found on settlement sites (Caulfield 1981: 207). Unidentifiable iron artefacts, such as those at Aonghasa, are nearly always ascribed to the Early Christian period. Since it would appear that the midden deposits in the interior of

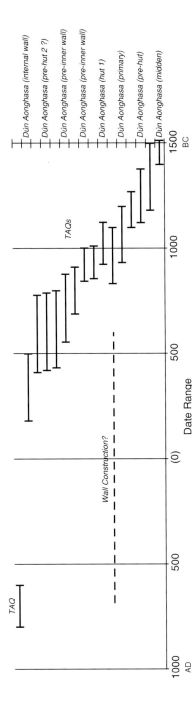

Figure 5.15 Range of dates recovered from Dún Aonghasa (after Limbert 1996: Illus.16).

Dún Aonghasa are a mix of items from the Late Bronze Age to the first millennium AD it is just conceivable that some of the iron artefacts may be dated earlier.

The predominance of Late Bronze Age artefacts and stratigraphy does not necessarily mean that this occupation was the most substantial at the site. Limbert (1996: 278) has pointed out that the survival of the Late Bronze Age material can be interpreted as 'an impact of enclosure rather than being indicative of its associated occupation; the thin stratigraphy is thickest adjacent and beneath the inner wall, which protected deposits from subsequent denudation'. Also, Cotter (1996: 3) states that the excavations 'revealed definite evidence for a secondary phase (or phases) of occupation at the site, possibly in the second half of the first millennium AD. This phase of activity may have resulted in considerable disturbance of the earlier occupation levels ...'. Such activity would account for the apparent mixing of the upper layers described above. Equally, as Cotter (1995: 10) points out, later structural evidence may have been destroyed when the nineteenth-century restoration work took place.

The excavation reports give the impression that Early Christian occupation is much more clearly attested to at the site. However, it must be kept in mind that the only evidence is a single radiocarbon date – obtained from under a clearly secondary feature – along with a series of unstratified artefacts. The survival of Early Christian deposits is largely due to their location in protected areas away from the elements: for example, in the wall chamber in Wall 1 and the entrance passage in Wall 2a. Any earlier activity in these areas is likely to have been swept out leaving only the latest and therefore surviving Early Christian activity. Also, it is worth noting that prior to the *Discovery* excavations the dating evidence for Dún Aonghasa came from a bronze fibula of Early Iron Age type found in the interior of one of the walls (O'Donovan 1839: 106). This find has since been discredited because its exact context was unrecorded at the time. Another indication of an Iron Age date comes from the associated *chevaux de frise*. Leaving the rather unconvincing evidence that these features indicate the existence of direct long-distance contacts with sites as far away as Iberia aside (Harbison 1971), they have elsewhere been consistently dated to the first millennium BC (Limbert 1996: 279, table 2).

As mentioned in Chapter 4, the trivallate drystone enclosure at Mooghaun South, Co. Clare, is thought to have been constructed sometime in the late tenth or early ninth centuries BC. Later evidence for activity stretching into the Medieval period comes from isolated deposits recovered from the inner enclosure, three circular stone-built huts and through the occurrence of two circular *cashels* built over the middle and outer ramparts respectively (Grogan 2005). Mooghaun is interesting when compared with Dún Aonghasa, not simply in terms of structural comparisons, but more particularly in the similar ways the evidence from both sites have been interpreted. Each site features evidence for initial Late Bronze Age occupation with later re-use spanning at least a millennium and a half. However, rather than describe the complete history of use of these sites, interpretations of both focus on occupation in either the Late Bronze Age or the mid-first millennium AD (Cotter 1996: 12–14; Grogan 1996: 56–7, 2005: 240–5). It can hardly be a coincidence that these are precisely the periods which are considered to be 'better understood' and which supposedly produce more diagnostic material.

Despite a lack of secure dating evidence the *cashels* and stone-built hut forms at Mooghaun were thought to represent exclusively early medieval activity. Excavations within the *cashel* overlying the middle enclosure failed to produce diagnostic material, but an early medieval dating was suggested on comparison with other Irish sites and recovery of three iron nails (Grogan 2005: 152–3). Two radiocarbon dates were recovered from excavations on the stone-built huts: one of the huts produced a range between cal. AD 723 to 974 while the other ranged between cal. AD 1275 to 1377.[20] The similarity between the huts and their proximity to each other led the excavators, despite the conflicting nature of the dates, to ascribe them to an early medieval construction horizon (Grogan 2005: 161-2). However, it remains a possibility that the recovered radiocarbon dates relate to secondary occupation: all three huts were oval, only *c.* 5 m in diameter, and were built using a double facing of orthostats filled with rubble, and can therefore be paralleled with a number of house forms dated to the Bronze Age in Ireland (Doody 2000). Most interestingly, they perhaps have their closest parallels with the partly kerbed house forms dated to the Late Bronze Age at Dún Aonghasa (Cotter 1995), which would make them contemporary with the drystone ramparts at Mooghaun.

Although the middle rampart is dated by *terminus post* and *ante quem* dates, the inner and outer ramparts are only dated from pre-rampart construction material. In the absence of radiocarbon dates from deposits abutting the inner and outer ramparts their dating must be considered insecure and a later dating remains a possibility. With this in mind it is interesting that a date recovered from an earth and stone bank built against the middle rampart provided a range between cal. 800 to 545 BC[21] and may therefore indicate some constructional activity during the Iron Age.

The interpretation of the finds recovered from the inner enclosure underline the problems of trying to recognise Iron Age activity at Irish sites in the absence of absolute dates. The only evidence within the enclosure consisted of a discontinuous spread of deposits that featured rotary quern fragments, evidence for bronze and iron metalworking, a bronze pin shank, portions of a bone comb, and burnt animal bone (Grogan 2005: 134). Although none of this material can be considered diagnostic – with the possible exception of the rotary querns which may represent a date sometime after the third century BC – the interim reports suggested a Bronze Age dating for the bronze working while the rest of the material was given a first millennium AD dating (Grogan 1996: 56–7). Significantly, after a radiocarbon date was recovered, indicating a range between cal. 47 BC and AD 113,[22] the deposits and the assemblage were re-interpreted as representing Iron Age activity (Grogan 2005: 244). In the absence of the radiocarbon date it is unlikely the interpretation would have changed. Despite the absence of intensive occupation and high status items such as those known from other – albeit eastern – Irish hillforts such as Haughey's Fort and Rathgall, the evidence for multivallation with simple entrances and associated industrial activity at Mooghaun is certainly comparable with Iron Age hillfort sites found elsewhere in western Europe.

At both Mooghaun and Dún Aonghasa the evidence for activity between the Late Bronze Age and Early Medieval horizons – which certainly exists – is treated as incidental and not particularly crucial to an overall understanding of either site. As a result, the significance of these sites to the understanding of the Irish Iron Age has been underestimated. For example, perhaps the closest parallels to Mooghaun and Dún Aonghasa in terms of rampart construction are stone-built hillfort forms dated to between 800 and 400 BC in Britain (Cunliffe 1991: 324–7; Osgood 1998: 55–75) while in overall layout they are comparable to the Iron Age multiple enclosure forts of south-western England and Wales (Fox 1961; Cunliffe 1991: 252–6).

The site of Cahercommaun, Co. Clare, consists of two outer concentric walls and an inner cashel, and is usually seen as the closest parallel to Dún Aonghasa as both sites share similar locations, layout and features, although Cahercommaun is built on the edge of an inland precipice (Figure 5.16). In this case the inner structure features a complete circuit of walling running up to the cliff edge and has an average diameter of 35 m. The inner wall, at up to 8.5 m thick, is more massive than Dún Aonghasa and still stands up to 4.3 m high. As at Dún Aonghasa, Cahercommaun's inner *cashel* wall features two terraces but the site differs in other respects, it has no *chevaux-de-frise*, no wall chambers and features evidence for five niches in the internal wall.[23]

Again, similar to Dún Aonghasa, the dating of the main structure remains problematic (Cotter 1999). Hencken (1938: 2–3) originally dated the site to the ninth and tenth centuries AD on the basis of a silver brooch dating to *c.* AD 800, a fragment of enamelled ornament, and a zoomorphic brooch. This dating was then quite rightly challenged (Raftery, B. 1972: 51) because the latter two artefacts were unstratified and could not, in any case, be ascribed a secure date on typological grounds, while the silver brooch – although more securely dated – was found in the fill of a souterrain and therefore could not be proven to be contemporary with the initial construction of the fort. Raftery (1972: 51–3) recognised a number of artefacts from the

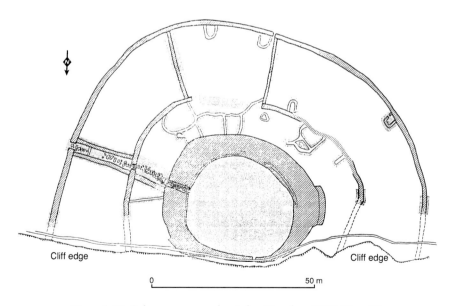

Figure 5.16 Cahercommaun plan (after Hencken 1938: Plate II).

Cahercommaun assemblage that pre-dated Hencken's dating, up to perhaps as much as half a millennium. Of particular interest, he notes that the blue glass beads, the iron and bone pins, the occurrence of stone axes and bone spearheads, and especially the blue glass bracelets, all have British Iron Age counterparts. Caulfield (1981: 210–11) went one step further and suggested a BC date for the construction and initial occupation of the site. He justified this dating through the occurrence of saddle querns and suggested that the small iron shears, 'lignite and glass bracelets and the iron penannular brooches and pins could well have such an early date' (1981: 211). Rynne (1982, 1992) agreed with an earlier dating for the site and further suggested that the skull, and iron hook found immediately underneath it, was indicative of Iron Age head-cult activity supporting a pre-Christian dating.[24]

There are a number of features of the occupation in the interior of the *cashel* that would suggest it is secondary to the initial use of the *cashel*. Excavation of the interior revealed thirteen fragmentary and irregular cellular structures built of poor masonry (Figure 5.17). This kind of cellular occupation is very similar in style to the secondary cellular re-use of drystone roundhouses known at a number of sites in Atlantic Scotland and dated to the first millennium AD. For example, at Beirgh on the Isle of Lewis several conjoined cells dating to between the early third and late sixth centuries AD were discovered built within an earlier first millennium BC complex Atlantic roundhouse shell (Harding and Gilmour 2000). The cellular buildings at Cahercommaun share a number of common features with their Scottish

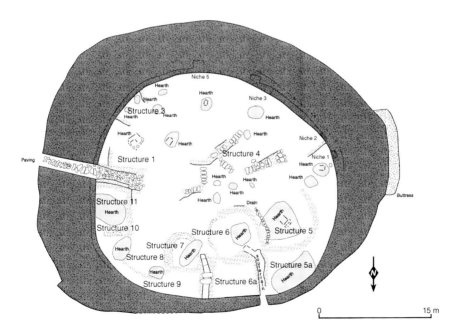

Figure 5.17 Cahercommaun: plan of inner *cashel* after excavation (after Hencken 1938: Plate VI).

counterparts: they are constructed of single-faced walls, apparently revetted into the 2 m deep stratigraphy of the site (Hencken 1938: Plate VII); the majority of associated hearths appear to be three-sided types demarcated by vertical slabbing; while the fill of the cellular buildings is reported as being composed mainly of rubble (op. cit.: 20) suggesting that they might have once been at least partially corbelled.

The stratigraphy of the site is described as 'generally consisting of stones and black earth mixed with animal bones and bits of charcoal' (Hencken 1938: 14) which in description sounds similar to the deposits encountered on Atlantic Scottish sites where small cellular settlement is built into earlier occupation and midden material. It seems likely that the standard of recording, though high for the time, would not have picked up the often poorly built, ephemeral remains of this secondary occupation. Indeed, recorded stratigraphical evidence is almost non-existent in the report and Hencken admits that the fill 'must have belonged to different periods' (Hencken 1938: 14). A glance at the sections from the site (Plate VII) reveals hearths occurring at different levels in the deposit, clearly reflecting multi-period use and, as such, they are unlikely to belong to the initial occupation of the site. It is possible, therefore, to envisage the small-scale irregular buildings as a secondary, cellular re-use of the central *cashel* at Cahercommaun, lasting – perhaps intermittently – over a number of centuries in the first millennium AD. This would go some way towards helping to explain the occurrence of finds of sub-Roman origin up to the silver brooch dated to ninth century AD.

If the occurrence of prehistoric finds is accorded significance and the first millennium AD occupation and assemblage is indeed secondary then the initial construction of Cahercommaun could be assigned to the same broad range as that suggested for Dún Aonghasa above (*contra* Cotter 1999). At both sites the evidence for Iron Age occupation would have been cleared out and almost completely removed prior to periods of secondary occupation in the Early Christian period.

The promontory site of Dunbeg, Co. Kerry (Barry 1981), is usually included in discussions of the Western Stone Forts on account of its thick drystone wall, which features three terraces and two intra-mural chambers either side of a low lintelled entrance (Figure 5.18). Excavation failed to reveal any diagnostic finds or occupation except that belonging to a drystone clochan dating to the tenth century AD. A sample of wood from the base of a ditch provided a *terminus ante quem* for the drystone rampart of AD 800 ± 75 (UB-2215) as this deposit abutted a retaining wall in the ditch constructed to cope with the weight and stress of the main rampart (Barry 1981: 308). A *terminus post quem* of 580 BC ± 35 (UB-2216), calibrated to the eighth century BC, came from a ditch partly overlain by the stone wall. Again the precise dating of the stone rampart is unclear and a wide date range, anywhere between 800 BC and AD 800, is possible. The *clochan* provides evidence for secondary use of the site. Owing to the unclear evidence Dunbeg is usually dated by structural comparisons with Iron Age Scottish sites, such as the blockhouse structures at Clickhimhin, Ness of Burghi, Loch of Huxter on Shetland and Crosskirk, Caithness (Lamb 1980; Figure 4.15).

The Western Stone Forts of the Grianán of Aileach, Co. Donegal, Staigue and Cahergal, Co. Kerry are morphologically similar to each other, and sufficiently

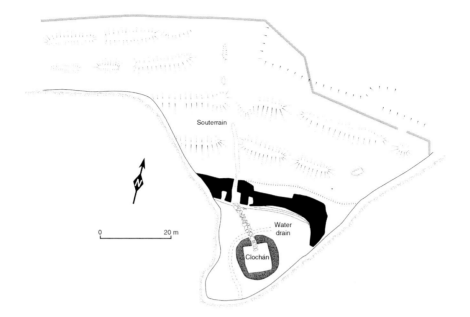

Souterrain

Water drain

Clochán

0   20 m

Figure 5.18 Dunbeg, Co. Kerry (after Barry 1981).

distinct from other stone fort sites that they can be considered together. Each site consists of a massive circular wall around 5 m thick and 30 m in diameter. The inner faces of the walls display terracing, two terraces at Staigue and Cahergal, and three at the Grianán of Aileach, featuring a distinctive series of interconnecting sidelong steps (Figure 5.19). All three sites also occupy prominent positions in the landscape providing commanding views and all are entered via a lintelled passage. Both Grianán and Staigue share further characteristics: each have two intra-mural chambers and external earthen defences. The *cashel* at Staigue is surrounded by a ditch with an external bank (often taken to have 'royal' or ritual connotations on earthen sites) while the Grianán of Aileach is surrounded by three earthen banks. Staigue features two wall chambers while the Grianán has two long intra-mural passages to the north-east and south-east running towards, but terminating before, the entrance passage.

Once again these sites cannot be dated with any degree of certainty. The three earthen banks at the Grianán have led many to suggest a Late Bronze Age/Early Iron Age date for the site but, of course, the drystone structure may have been built after the earthen enclosures. Lacy (1983: 112) states that the site 'clearly' belongs to the Early Christian period, but this has more to do with the fact that many writers have, without archaeological evidence, associated the site with Aileach, the ancient seat of the northern Uí Neill dynasty. It is harder to argue that the earthen defences and drystone structure at Staigue are not associated with each other because the ditch

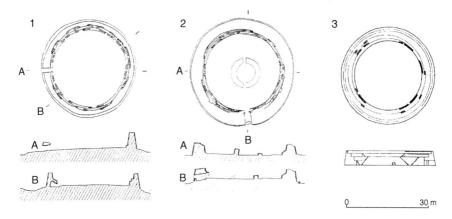

Figure 5.19 (1) Staigue Fort, Co. Kerry (after O'Sullivan and Sheehan 1996: fig. 126); (2) Cahergal, Co. Kerry (after O'Sullivan and Sheehan 1996: fig. 124); (3) the Grianán of Aileach, Co. Donegal (after Lacy 1983, 112: fig. 54).

and external bank follow the exact dimensions of the circular walls. Again no firm dating evidence is available apart from architectural comparisons, but it is worth mentioning that a gold dress-fastener of Bronze Age type was found between 1840 and 1860 'in or at the outer wall of Staigue Fort' (O'Sullivan and Sheehan 1996: 195). Some small-scale excavations have taken place at Cahergal (Manning 1987: 21, 1991: 37) but they were inconclusive in terms of dating. Artefacts found include sheet bronze, iron slag and *tuyére* fragments indicating metalworking at some stage at the site. There is nothing amongst the finds to indicate an Early Christian dating or rule out Later Prehistoric activity and all of the finds would sit comfortably within an Iron Age context.

Excavations at Leacanabuaile, Co. Kerry (Ó Ríordáin and Foy 1941) revealed a substantial *cashel*-type ringwall containing two wall chambers and a terraced inner face. Despite these wall features Leacanabuaile has never sat comfortably with sites such as Cahercommaun or Dún Aonghasa. The wall at Leacanabuaile seems, at 3.3 m, quite thin and very low, surviving only to 1.5 m in height, when compared to the more massive terraced examples. A glance at the site plan (Figure 5.20) shows the remains of six stone-built structures, three earlier circular *clochán* structures and three rectangular structures within the *cashel* walls. Owing to the association of a souterrain with one of the houses and a wall chamber, the *cashel* wall is seen as contemporary with the circular phase of building at the site (Ó Ríordáin and Foy 1941: 90–2). The finds from the site were chronologically unspecific but fall generally in the first millennium AD. The excavators dated the site to the ninth and tenth centuries AD, but the artefacts are not diagnostic enough to support a tight dating spanning just two centuries. Indeed, there seems nothing within the assemblage to justify such a late dating of the site. Both the bone combs and the iron knives are of a simple type,

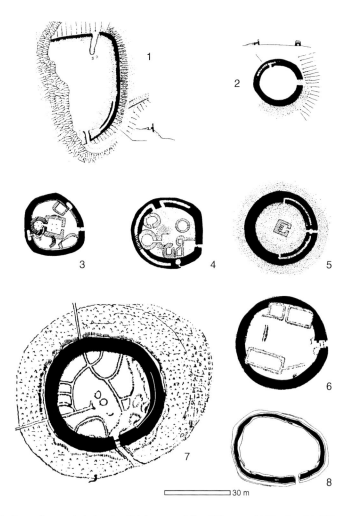

Figure 5.20 Complex *cashels* in the Irish west (after Warner 1983: fig. 81; Westropp 1897: fig. 7; Lacy 1983: fig. 71): (1) Sconce, Co. Derry; (2) Altagore, Co. Antrim; (3) Leacanabuaile, Co. Kerry; (4) Cahernamactirech, Co. Kerry; (5) Grianán of Aileach, Co. Donegal; (6) Cahermacnaughten, Co. Clare; (7) Ballykinvarga, Co. Clare; (8) O'Boyles Fort, Co. Donegal.

and an earlier dating around AD 500 seems more likely. Unlike Dún Aonghasa and Cahercommaun there is little evidence for prehistoric activity amongst the finds at this site, although it may be worth mentioning the bronze ring headed pin and a rusted iron fragment claimed to be an Iron Age fibula, which was apparently destroyed on cleaning (Ó Ríordáin and Foy 1941, 92–3). A mid-first millennium AD dating would place the site roughly within the transitory phase between the end of Iron Age and the beginning of Early Christian traditions. Such a dating could perhaps go some way in explaining the survival of wall chambers, and, less importantly, terraces, within what is otherwise a typical first millennium AD *cashel* site.

Excavations have also been carried out at Loher, Co. Kerry, a *cashel* which features a terraced inner face and mural steps. Like Leacanabuaile, Loher also features drystone houses of circular and rectangular *clochan* type. Significantly, however, summary accounts of the excavation describe a long stratigraphic sequence of occupation with early wooden circular structures being replaced by circular stone structures and finally by the *clochan* structures (O'Flaherty 1986: 26–7). This sequence would imply that there is almost certainly secondary re-use of the site after the building of the main *cashel* walls. Again it is this type of complex stratigraphic sequence that may have been missed during early excavations.

It can be seen, then, that the current excavated evidence suggests that Dún Aonghasa, Cahercommaun and possibly Dunbeg were constructed after the Late Bronze Age (ending around 700 BC), but before the second half of the first millennium AD. Equally, some activity in the Iron Age is certain at Moogahun South and highly probable at the Grianán of Aileach, Staigue and Cahergal. Only the construction of Leacanabuaile and Loher is likely to have occurred within an exclusively mid-first millennium AD context. As we shall see, such a dating for Leacanabuaile and Loher is perfectly acceptable because they are not massively built and are perhaps best viewed as a transitional form between monumental complex *cashels* and the later predominantly featureless (in terms of wall construction) examples more typical of the Early Christian period.

Complex drystone cashels in the Irish west

The Western Stone Forts are just one element of a range of complex drystone sites located along the western coasts of Ireland. At present there are only a handful of known complex drystone sites in the northern and Atlantic-facing counties of Ireland (Figure 5.20). These include sites such as Altagore, Co. Antrim, a small circular *cashel* featuring a clear intra-mural passage, and Sconce, Co. Derry, an irregular *cashel* which also features an intra-mural passage (Warner 1983: 178–81). O'Boyle's Fort, in Co. Donegal, is a well-preserved but partially reconstructed *cashel* built on an islet location similar to those used for island *duns* in Atlantic Scotland. The wall is some 4 m thick, survives up to 4.8 m high and, most significantly, contains two intra-mural passages. Lacy (1983: 136–7) describes a parapet running along the external side of the top of the wall which may on further examination provide evidence for median walling.

Amongst the hundreds of featureless simple *cashels* in Co. Clare there are at least twenty-six examples[25] (Henderson 2000: fig. 15) that display elements of complex architecture similar to those seen in the Western Stone Fort group, namely: terraces (of which one is the norm at any given complex site but there are examples with up to three); steps (vertical ladder like arrangements and sidelong varieties occur); median walls (usually two skins of walling but examples with three are seen); vertical joints in the stonework; all of which usually tend to occur along with massively constructed walls (greater than 3 m thick). Taken together these features could be considered as a diagnostic architectural package that conveyed monumentality within their specific indigenous cultural context. Certainly they make these sites stand out from the more numerous simple forms in the County which are also, on the whole, less massively built.

Of these complex sites the most impressive example in Co. Clare, after Cahercommaun, is Ballykinvarga (Figure 5.20). This site is often included in discussions of the Western Stone Fort group as it is completely surrounded by a wide circle of *chevaux-de-frise*, but it also features a number of architectural details seen on other *cashels* in Clare. It is an almost circular *cashel* with a maximum diameter of 51.5 m featuring a drystone rampart some 5 m thick, built up of three median wall skins, and surviving, in places, to a height of over 4.5 m. The wall has survived in better condition on its eastern side where the median walls suggest the existence of two terraces, which cannot be so clearly traced on the western side (Westropp 1897: 123; Harbison 1971: 203). It is possible that the occurrence of terraces is simply due to the differential collapse of the three median wall skins. The existence of vertical joints can clearly be seen in the stone work at Ballykinvarga and Westropp (1897) has suggested that these vertical joints may have been formed by the result of different construction teams working on separate parts of the wall coming together. Another interesting feature in the stonework, which may also be partly related to the creation of vertical joints, is construction using large limestone blocks stacked vertically, one on top of the other, rather than the more familiar technique of bonding the blocks together. Significantly, the occurrence of this vertical stacking technique and vertical jointing in stonework seems to be mainly restricted to *cashel* sites which also feature other complex architectural features (for example Staigue in Co. Kerry). On the whole, thin-walled featureless *cashels* do not exhibit the vertical stacking technique or vertical jointing.

There is still a considerable depth of deposit in the interior of the site making it an attractive and potentially very informative candidate for excavation. The uneven, grass grown rubble surface of the interior reveals the existence of inner enclosures arranged in a fairly regular radial pattern from the walls, perhaps best viewed as evidence for secondary occupation. While this may relate to relatively recent activity it is worth bearing in mind that these features are overlain by a decent grass sod layer and the lintel stone appears to be *in situ* (this would no doubt have been removed if the site had recently been re-used for keeping livestock). The arrangement of secondary internal structures against the *cashel* wall is also seen at other 'complex' sites in Co. Clare including Cahercloggaun, Caherbullog, Cahermore-Ballyallaban, and Caherblonick; similar secondary structures are also seen against the stone walls of the hillfort at Turlough Hill, Co. Clare and against the terraced stone rampart at the promontory site of Doonaunmore.

The idea that the architectural features found on complex sites are more likely to occur together is supported by the fact that one feature never occurs in isolation: there are always at least two or more complex features present at any one site. This comes perhaps as no surprise in the case of terracing, median walls and steps because the creation of a terrace often requires the construction of an additional skin of walling (a median wall) and it follows that if you had terraces you would need steps to get up to them.[26] However, the consistent occurrence of one or more of these features within *cashel* walls built in the vertical stacking style and displaying vertical joints is striking and may suggest that all of these sites were built during a period of similar drystone construction techniques. As mentioned above, the more common featureless *cashels* do not display vertical stacking but have their blocks bonded together in a manner more akin to modern drystone construction. Westropp (1893–1917) noted this difference on a number of occasions and considered the vertical stacking technique to be the earlier constructional form (Figure 5.21).

The group of twenty-seven complex *cashels* recognised in Co. Clare can be further subdivided into those sites that feature the median wall technique, or at least multiple wall-skins, and those that do not (Henderson 2000: fig. 15). Those sites that do not feature median or multiple walls are most probably later than those that do, and could perhaps belong to a transitional phase in the middle centuries of the first millennium AD between fully complex sites and featureless *cashels*. They may therefore be comparable in terms of date with sites such as Leacanabuaile and Loher in County Kerry. This view is, of course, impossible to prove at present because it is based entirely upon general observations on a group of unsurveyed and unexcavated sites. However, it does at least consider the diversity of the Clare sites rather than lumping them together, and reveals the desperate need for problem orientated survey and excavation programmes in the area. The identification of twenty-seven complex sites amongst the *cashels* of Co. Clare is a significant number considering that no modern survey work has yet taken place. The actual number of complex sites can be expected to increase because in the absence of excavation complex architectural features are only recognisable on well preserved sites. Leacanabuaile, for example, appeared as a featureless grass-grown stone mound until excavation took place. A similar problem existed in Atlantic Scotland until large-scale excavation and survey programmes revealed a greater number of complex sites in areas that were previously thought to contain predominantly simple forms (Armit 1992; Gilmour 1994). Problem orientated survey, freed from the restraints of ringfort terminology, coupled with the excavation of drystone sites in other areas of Ireland,

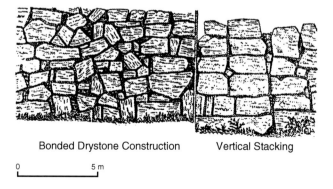

Bonded Drystone Construction   Vertical Stacking

0   5 m

Figure 5.21 Wall construction forms in Co. Clare as recognised by Westropp (1893–1917).

would be likely to significantly add to the corpus of sites with complex architectural features.

As in Co. Clare, the majority of *cashels* along the Dingle Peninsula, Co. Kerry, have featureless double-faced, rubble-filled walls and circular *clochan* structures inside, which one would fully expect date to the second half of the first millennium AD. However, a significant few feature complex architectural traits potentially surviving from earlier periods of occupation. For example, Cahermurphy, Glanfahan (Cuppage 1986: 202–4), has three small step-like terraces on the northern part of its internal wall along with internal evidence of occupation which could be secondary to the main wall (Figure 5.22). The five circular conjoined *clochans* form a courtyard by the entrance giving the whole site a similar layout to the courtyard-houses of western

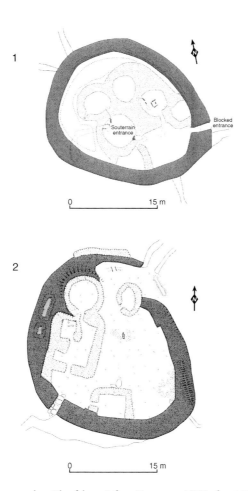

Figure 5.22 (1) Cahermurphy, Glanfahan (after Cuppage 1986: fig. 118); (2) Caherconner, Glanfahan (after Cuppage 1986: fig. 120).

Cornwall (Cunliffe 1991: 256, fig. 13.8). Caherconner, Glanfahan (Cuppage 1986: 206–8) has a sub-oval enclosing wall featuring a wall passage souterrain along with an interior that was heavily modified in the nineteenth century (Figure 5.22). The relationship between wall passages and the development of souterrains is an interesting one which has not yet received much attention. As Warner (1983: 181) states 'it is tempting to compare the idea of the intramural passage' to the development of the 'souterrain wholly, or partly, within the bank' of Irish earthen ringforts. Cahernamactirech, Co. Kerry, is a fine example of a *cashel* featuring intra-mural passages (Figure 5.20). The *clochans* in the interior of this galleried *cashel* are certainly secondary; one *clochan* built into the *cashel* wall cuts off what would have originally been a continuous passage. It is possible that the site is not completely circular because it has been rebuilt in the areas where the galleries abruptly end and because from here the walls become straighter. The 'watch-house' in the enclosing wall is therefore also likely to be secondary as it blocks the intra-mural gallery.

Cahersavane on the Inveragh Peninsula, Co. Kerry, is another interesting site because the *cashel* wall, although collapsed in many places, features four terraces (Figure 5.23). What is perhaps most significant, however, is, like Staigue also on the Inveragh Peninsula, Cahersavane is surrounded by the remains of an internal ditch and external bank, the occurrence of which on earthen sites is traditionally taken to indicate royal and/or ritual status. In terms of dating the site it is perhaps significant that two potentially early structural features (terracing and earthwork enclosures) occur together.

General Atlantic Irish settlement trends 700 BC–AD 200

Despite the evidence for complex architectural features amongst the circular dry-stone settlements of the western Atlantic coasts of Ireland direct comparisons with Atlantic Scottish roundhouses remain difficult. Irish ringforts have a typical internal

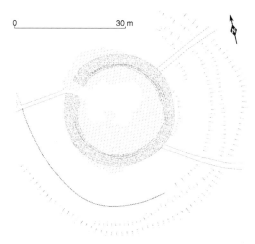

0 ————————— 30 m

Figure 5.23 Cahersavane, Co. Kerry (after O'Sullivan and Sheehan 1996: fig. 119).

diameter of *c.* 27–30 m (Stout 1997: 15) while Atlantic Scottish roundhouses average an external diameter of *c.* 20 m with internal diameters typically *c.* 12–14 m (Armit 2003). Such sizes reflect patently different types of settlement: the former being enclosures with internal domestic buildings, while the latter are best seen as elaborate domestic buildings in their own right. However, it must be remembered that the Irish figures are averages based on a vast sample of sites, which most probably belong to many different periods. Many studies of Irish ringforts rely on purely statistical information gleaned from surveys, but they tend to concentrate on the mean figures produced rather than the full range of diameters in existence. It stands to reason that if the original classification is too wide then the smaller and larger sites within the sample do not receive the attention they deserve. A glance at the recorded ranges of ringfort diameters in the available Irish county survey volumes is revealing. For example, in the south-west Midlands as a whole earthen enclosures measuring from 15.5 m to 75 m are all included within the ringfort class (Stout 1997: 15).

Interestingly, the diameters of drystone enclosures are consistently smaller than earthen examples and many fall within the range of Atlantic Scottish roundhouses. For example, the average diameter of circular stone enclosures in south Donegal is *c.* 20 m while in County Kerry it is 23 m (Stout 1997: 15). The site of Doon Glebe, Co. Donegal, has an overall diameter of 20 m and although heavily collapsed the stone wall still survives up to a height of 0.6 m (Lacy 1983: 134; Figure 5.24). An intra-mural passage roofed with flagstones, some of which are still *in situ*, can be traced for about 6 m. Although unexcavated, in description at least, this site sounds very much like a Scottish complex Atlantic roundhouse, and perhaps provides a hint of what large-scale excavation programmes of smaller *cashel* sites could reveal.

However, making such direct comparisons between Scottish and Irish sites is misleading. It is unreasonable to expect direct matches, and indeed none can be found on the ground – the architectural features used on Irish sites in order to display monumentality are on the whole completely different. For example, there are no Scottish examples of the characteristic V-shape arrangements of sidelong stairs seen at Cahergal, Staigue, and the Grianán. The occurrence of terracing is often compared with the scarcements seen on Scottish Atlantic roundhouse sites, but they are each of quite different construction. Irish terraces are usually formed by the building of an

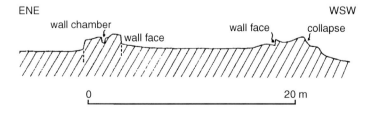

Figure 5.24 Doon Glebe, Co. Donegal (after Lacy 1983, 133: fig. 69).

extra skin of walling creating a platform wide enough to walk along and are often accessed by stairs, whereas Scottish scarcements are usually constructed from thin, tabular stones protruding from, and bonded into, internal roundhouse wall faces. Atlantic roundhouse scarcements are not wide enough to easily walk upon (usually *c.* 0.3 m wide) and are thought to have been used to support wooden floors or some form of timber arrangement. Median wall faces are known in Scotland, especially amongst the *duns* of Argyll, but no terraces have ever been recorded. The intra-mural passages at the Grianán and the corbelled wall chambers at Staigue do, however, have quite close Scottish parallels.

This lack of direct correlation between the Irish and Scottish sequences does not make the idea of shared traditions any less valid – indeed, we should expect the settlement sequences from each area to be different, partly conforming to local traditions while being immersed in the moves towards monumentality and display in the round seen elsewhere. The danger lies, of course, in how far one takes such architectural similarities as evidence of long-distance contact. The appearance of monumental drystone architecture in the first millennia BC and AD in Ireland and Scotland is best viewed as indigenous responses to local developments, as previous traditions of drystone construction exist in both areas. However, the similar, though by no means identical, appearances and architectural devices shared by the Irish and Scottish sites imply they were serving similar roles in Atlantic societies developing along related lines. The similarities between the sites are too close to claim they developed in total isolation, but equally they are not enough alike to suggest the introduction of monumental architectural techniques from one partic-ular area. It is most useful to view the development of Irish and Scottish drystone sites being mainly influenced by the local needs and traditions of their own communities, but at the same time being immersed in wider Atlantic trading and/or belief systems which encouraged the exchange of ideas leading to a form of parallel development. The concept of distinctive local developments within a wider, similar, Atlantic tradition was clearly demonstrated in the Atlantic areas of Scotland. Northern Scotland and the Orkney Islands, the Shetlands, the Western Isles, Argyll and south-west Scotland all share obviously physically related drystone architectural traditions, but the trajectory of development is distinctive within each area.

There are thousands of circular drystone settlements along the western Atlantic coasts of Ireland, which, taken as a whole, represent a diverse and varied group of structures. It can be argued that there was a similar, though as yet completely unrecognised, horizon of drystone architectural complexity within this range of sites roughly co-terminous with developments in Scotland and indeed wider Atlantic trends (Figure 5.25). The lack of utility of the very broad ringfort termi-nology, which, by definition, dates sites to the sixth century AD or later, and the fail-ure to recognise the existence of secondary occupations has meant this earlier horizon has remained undetected. The lack of work carried out in western Ireland makes it difficult at this stage to test the validity of an Irish Iron Age horizon of architectural complexity. All that can be said is that in light of present knowledge

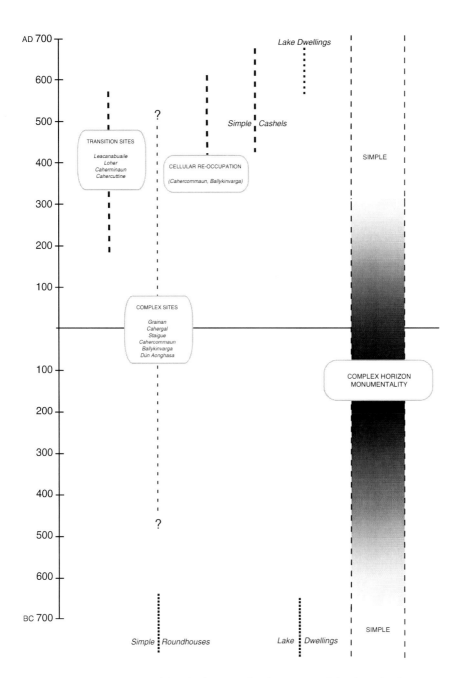

Figure 5.25 Later prehistoric drystone development in Atlantic Ireland.

the existence of such a horizon is at least possible. In the absence of anything approaching a regional sequence or localised examination of sites it is not yet possible to examine the relationship between distinct areas within Ireland as was done for Atlantic Scotland. Presumably, however, areas along the Atlantic coasts of Ireland could be related to each other in a similar way: distinct regional sequences within a wider Atlantic network of contacts and influences.

Material assemblages of Atlantic Scotland and Ireland

Atlantic Scottish and Irish Iron Age assemblages, in common with all Iron Age Atlantic assemblages, are viewed as rather restricted and ultimately utilitarian in nature. There is a popular perception that this cultural poverty is due to the peripheral and culturally isolated position of Atlantic communities (isolated from each other as well as the wider European world). However, Atlantic assemblages, while certainly not providing evidence of large-scale trading activity between areas, do demonstrate the existence of some level of contact and, more importantly, a shared way of life. Rather than examining Atlantic assemblages on their own merits, archaeologists have in the past tended to stress the lack of Hallstatt and La Tène objects, and used this absence as an example of cultural isolation. The lack of such objects has meant that Atlantic areas could not be tied into sequences in southern Britain or west-central Europe and this situation has helped foster views of Atlantic communities as backward or retarded.

There is of course no reason, except for the convenience of archaeologists constructing chronologies based on typology, why we should expect to find Hallstatt or La Tène objects in Atlantic areas. If the development of settlement and society in the west is viewed as a mainly Atlantic orientated phenomena beginning in the Late Bronze Age, the lack of occurrence of La Tène objects may be entirely irrelevant, and indeed such objects may have held little meaning for Atlantic Iron Age societies. For example, in Atlantic Scotland and Ireland, societies with monumental architecture may not have needed a more elaborate material culture – status may have been measured through other means, such as architectural display or livestock.

At present one of the major problems in recognising Iron Age activity in Ireland is that there are no diagnostic artefacts indicative of Iron Age occupation. La Tène objects are normally considered to be the only datable form, but even these can often only provide a very wide date range between 300 BC and AD 300. In any case they are very rarely encountered in settlement contexts and are therefore of little value as an indicator of Iron Age domestic occupation. The recognition of Iron Age activity is made even more difficult if, as is suspected at the majority of sites examined above, there was later Early Christian occupation: such occupation provides diagnostic artefacts which are then used to date the whole assemblage, resulting in an over-representation of Early Christian activity at the expense of any earlier Iron Age objects that may be present. An indication of the potential range of artefacts that could represent Iron Age activity can be gleaned by comparing recovered Irish assemblages with known Iron Age assemblages from other Atlantic sites.

The material culture of Atlantic Scotland

In the past considerations of Atlantic Scottish material culture have placed too much emphasis on the occurrence of rare 'exotic' artefacts such as Roman pottery, ring headed pins or spiral bronze rings, in attempts to link the poorly dated sequences of Atlantic Scotland with developments in southern Britain (cf. MacKie 1969). Clarke (1971) has demonstrated that such finds do not form a reliable basis for meaningful study, and that we should instead consider Atlantic Scottish assemblages and the life they represent on their own merits.

The utilitarian nature of Atlantic Scottish material assemblages make it impossible to make any chronological distinctions at this stage, but it is possible to define a typical range of items dating broadly from the sixth-century BC to around the second-century AD. Following Harding (2005a) we can distinguish utilitarian and more ornamental objects allowing the definition of Standard and Ornamental Atlantic Scottish Assemblages. By far the largest part of recovered assemblages consist of utilitarian artefacts, which, as a group, represent the existence of a distinctive and shared way of life between communities in Atlantic Scotland.

Standard Atlantic Scottish assemblage

- hammerstones
- whetstones
- polishing stones
- spindle whorls
- stone weights (loom, thatch and net)
- strike-a-lights
- simple (not composite) bone combs
- quernstones (saddle and rotary)
- crucibles
- pottery
- occasional stone lamp
- wooden utilitarian artefacts

The second and much rarer set are those ornamental artefacts that could indicate the existence of wider contacts. In fact, none of these objects can sustain a picture of contact on a large scale and the majority were most probably locally produced, but again they do provide evidence of an awareness of traditions occurring elsewhere.

Ornamental Atlantic Scottish assemblage

- ring headed pins
- bone dice
- spiral bronze rings
- pottery
- Samian ware

- yellow and blue glass beads
- amber beads
- spiral-ornamented beads
- dumb-bell shaped beads in glass or wood

These ornamental objects are the only artefacts that display evidence for contacts outwith the Atlantic Province itself, but their impact on the development of indigenous communities must have been minimal because they are, for the most part, rare and form a very small percentage of recovered assemblages.

Projecting ring headed pins have quite an exclusive Scottish distribution with a good number from the Atlantic regions (although this may simply be due to the greater amount of excavation carried out in this area). The pin is best viewed as a Scottish variant of the ring headed pin tradition and is most likely derived from Late Bronze Age sunflower forms or southern English involuted pins (Clarke 1971). The pins can be broadly classified and there are related types in southern Britain and Ireland. The occurrence of ring headed pins in Atlantic Scotland indicates an awareness and adherence to cultural practices seen elsewhere, which could only have been communicated through maritime contacts.

The significance of spiral bronze rings has been over-exaggerated by some authors but they do not form recognisable diagnostic types (they are after all simply lengths of bronze twisted into a spiral) and cannot be accurately dated because they were used over several periods from the Middle Bronze Age well into the first millennium AD (Clarke 1971: 26). Equally, they have a wide distribution throughout Britain and Ireland. This, coupled with the lack of chronological clarity, make the utility of distribution maps extremely limited.

Initial studies of decorated pottery forms imply that although motifs and general concepts were shared between areas, there is currently no evidence for the direct exchange of forms. There is a desperate need for further studies of assemblages to provide datable sequences. The significance of Roman pottery is similarly difficult to ascertain at present; certainly there is little evidence of the existence of links on any significant scale as finds are limited to just one or two sherds on a handful of sites. Even at these sites the Samian sherds occur in rather late, apparently mid-first millennium AD contexts.

Finds of purple and opaque yellow glass beads are relatively common at Atlantic Scottish sites. Most of the beads are poorly provenanced but can be seen, according to Guido's (1978) established glass bead chronology, to belong broadly to the period covering the first millennium BC and the first half of the first millennium AD. The occurrence of glass beads is often thought to indicate wider trading contacts, but the research that has been carried out to date suggests that most are probably of local (i.e. Scottish) manufacture.[27] For example, highly decorated multicoloured beads (Guido's class 14) are characteristic products of Iron Age Scotland and involve decoration executed in a style which cannot be paralleled in the rest of Europe, further supporting the idea that the beads were at least assembled locally. What is clear is that the technology in Scotland was not different from established pan-European traditions of glass technology. Henderson (1994: 236) has suggested that raw colourless or weakly tinted glass could have been imported and then the distinctive Scottish colourants added, but, equally, glass could have been locally manufactured – there is as yet no way to prove or disprove this. The occurrence of beads in Atlantic Scotland is at least indicative of contacts within the system but not on a large scale (there are only a few beads from each site).

The material found at Atlantic Scottish sites is not comparable to Iron Age assemblages found elsewhere in Europe. The closest parallels with such an assemblage are with some of the assemblages in Ireland. However, the discovery of a similar range of artefacts at an Irish site would not necessarily be used to date it to the Iron Age.

Material assemblages of the Irish Iron Age

Many Irish ringforts are dated to the Early Christian period purely on the typological associations of their assemblages. For example, Stout (1997: 23) has expressed a general mistrust of stratigraphical evidence and argues that we should instead concentrate on the 'clear' dating evidence provided by recovered assemblages. However, as argued above, this may result in a concentration on Early Christian finds to the detriment of possible earlier elements within an assemblage. While there are no artefacts considered diagnostic of Iron Age domestic occupation, the situation is further confused in that many of the objects widely believed to represent Early Christian activity are equally not closely dated. Much of the difficulty lies in the fact that the rich assemblage and sequence from Lagore crannog, Co. Meath (Hencken 1950), has become the type site for typological studies of Early Christian Ireland. However, Lagore itself does not have a secure sequence and even a cursory examination of the excavation report reveals uncertainties over the security of some of the stratigraphic relationships (Lynn 1983). There are a number of finds listed in the report that appear to be earlier than the mid-seventh century AD dating of the site. For example, a bronze dagger and looped spearhead of Bronze Age type; a leaf-shaped spearhead of La Tène type; horse bits of pre-Roman Iron Age form; spear ferrules and butts with La Tène and Roman parallels; a shouldered spearhead of post-Roman type; early ring headed pin forms; a millefiori pin of a type earlier than the seventh-century AD; and ceramics of possible prehistoric type such as a sherd of Neolithic A, Samian ware and Romano-British pottery. Stone tools such as flint scrapers and knives also suggest early dates, and a set of bone dice were discovered which, although they are shorter and wider than those of the British Iron Age and are generally regarded as Roman, are still earlier than the mid-seventh century AD. Hencken refers to these finds as 'pre-crannog' but often has little stratigraphical reason for doing so because the majority come from unsure or unstratified deposits. There are too many of these finds to have appeared by chance, or to have been brought in amongst the material used to build the crannog. The problems of the Lagore sequence are common to many Early Christian assemblages: there is certainly earlier material within the assemblage, but it is not considered significant and neither is the potential impact of the earlier finds on the close dating of assumed Early Christian types.

As was claimed for the Dún Aonghasa assemblage there are elements, such as the corroded iron fragments, which could represent Iron Age activity but are placed within the Early Christian period on the presumption that iron objects were not a feature of the Irish Iron Age. However, early occurrences of iron are known in Ireland dating to the seventh century BC due to associations with Hallstatt C forms. Iron objects are not datable again until the beginning of the first millennium AD by reference to other objects. Poor preservation and a lack of typological characteristics or associations may mean there is an unrecognised body of iron artefacts (Scott 1979: 195; Champion 1989: 293). Without a consideration of what actually could represent Iron Age activity it seems unlikely that any evidence will ever be found because objects are on the whole dated by association.

Elements of assemblages such as bone and antler tools or stone tools receive little attention in reports, but could offer close parallels to the Standard Atlantic Scottish Assemblage and reflect similar lifestyles. In many cases stone tools at Irish sites are considered to be residual artefacts, indicating the use of an area long before the construction of the site (Lynn 1983: 48). However, stone tools are a common find in Atlantic Scottish contexts dated to the Iron Age. The occurrence of ring headed pins, bone dice, spiral bronze rings and beads (all finds to rival the Ornamental Atlantic Scottish Assemblage) are common in Irish assemblages, but often ignored as attention concentrates on the more elaborate Early Christian artefacts. Equally, potential Iron Age artefacts are not attributed to the Iron Age due to the assumed Iron Age hiatus in material culture and because much of the material is very difficult to date. For example, amber, shale, lignite and jet artefacts are common on Irish sites but, with a date range from the second millennium BC to the first millennium AD, they are not chronologically specific. It seems probable that there is a range of unrecognised objects within Irish assemblages which could represent Iron Age activity – activity that could be paralleled on sites in Atlantic Scotland.

The lack of evidence for ceramics in the Irish Iron Age remains a problem. If there was a level of cultural contact with Atlantic Scotland should we not expect to find decorated pottery in Ireland? As we have seen, however, there is no evidence for the exchange of ceramic forms between the regional groupings of Atlantic Scotland itself, so it is perhaps unlikely that they would be traded further afield. Despite the lack of evidence for the exchange of material culture Atlantic Scotland can still be defined as a broad cultural zone and it is possible that a similar situation may exist in Ireland.

At present there is a perceived 1,000 year gap between the coarse flat rimmed wares of the Irish Late Bronze Age and the appearance of so-called Souterrain ware in north-east Ireland usually dated to the seventh or eighth centuries AD (Lynn 1983; Edwards 1990: 74). We are far from ceramic sequences for either Late Bronze Age or indigenous Early Christian forms since both flat rimmed ware and Souterrain ware were simple, coarse and relatively undiagnostic. It is possible the Iron Age gap is to some extent illusory because some ceramics within an Iron Age horizon have been recorded, such as the sherds associated with Roman imports at Freestone Hill, Co. Kilkenny (Raftery 1994: 208), or those associated with La Tène objects at Cush, Co. Limerick (O'Riordain 1940), and arguably from the early levels of the ringfort at

Dunsilly, Co. Antrim (McNeill 1992: 106; Limbert 1996: 263). However, the absence of ceramics from barrow burial contexts dated to the Iron Age is undoubtedly real, and further supports the concept of a largely aceramic Iron Age (Mount 1995).

It seems more likely that domestic containers were made from organic materials such as wood in the Irish Iron Age. There is a considerable amount of evidence for wooden vessels dating to the Early Christian period from bogs and crannog sites (Edwards 1990: 75–8) but, as with iron finds, some of the wooden objects commonly ascribed to the Early Christian period may belong to the Iron Age. Interestingly, the Early Christian period was also largely aceramic; despite evidence for external contacts and the existence of ceramic imports from the fourth century AD onwards there is no indigenous pottery until three or four centuries later. It seems the ceramic imports had little effect on indigenous traditions, further supporting the view that the use of wood and other organic forms may reflect a cultural tradition – a cultural choice – rather than an inability to produce ceramics.

The Irish material record has other features in common with Atlantic Scotland and wider trends. Both areas appear to take part in Late Bronze Age exchange networks up until the sixth century BC and then embark upon a more inward looking period, albeit with some evidence for similarities in their settlement and artefactual records. From the third century AD onwards it has been argued that there was once again an opening up of contacts in Atlantic Scotland and this coincides with similar evidence in Ireland.

Conclusions

Within the numerous and varied corpus of Irish drystone sites there potentially lies an unrecognised strata of Iron Age sites that could offer close parallels to sites in Atlantic Scotland. The Irish evidence remains controversial, and as such is open to a variety of interpretations which ultimately come down to a simple matter of opinion. In the absence of new excavations and problem orientated survey work taking place a more definite interpretation is impossible. However, there are a sufficient number of problems to seriously question traditional interpretations of the Irish Iron Age.

An acceptance of traditional interpretations of the Irish Iron Age requires an acceptance of the following points: enclosure forms almost identical to those seen in the Iron Age record of south-west England and Wales occurred at least 600 years later in Ireland; drystone architectural features present in an Iron Age context in Scotland occurred independently in Ireland at least half a millennium later; there is a period of, as yet undefined, Iron Age open settlement in Ireland that is not seen anywhere else in north-western Europe; features such as souterrains evolved independently in Ireland from the seventh century AD despite the fact their origins are placed within an Iron Age context elsewhere in Atlantic Europe; there are no Irish Iron Age assemblages despite the occurrence of a similar range of material on Irish sites to that seen at Scottish and other Atlantic Iron Age sites.

Put simply, this would mean that the Irish evidence does not in any way correlate with what is seen elsewhere in north-western Europe. Ireland would have to be

viewed as an area of considerable cultural decline from the middle of the first millennium BC until the first millennium AD, from which point a new range of settlements
appear displaying a number of archaic features present in other Atlantic areas around
six to seven hundred years earlier. Such a view is patently unsatisfying and becomes
less and less credible as settlement sequences in areas such as Atlantic Scotland and
south-west England are increasingly more clearly defined.

Ireland takes part in wider Atlantic and European traditions throughout the
prehistoric period up until the mid-first millennium BC, and then again from the first
few centuries of the first millennium AD. In the intervening Iron Age there is little
direct material evidence of the exchange of goods but features present in the Irish
settlement and artefactual record suggest that developments at this time had a close
affinity with areas such as Atlantic Scotland. It seems likely that complex drystone
Irish sites such as the Western Stone Forts were constructed around the same time as
complex forms in Atlantic Scotland, certainly the current dating evidence does not
preclude such a view. On saying this, the majority of the Irish Western Stone Fort
sites were also used in the Early Christian period and it remains a possibility that a
number of their architectural features do indeed belong to this period. However,
such features would be best viewed as being developments from traditions first established in an earlier Iron Age context rather than as completely separate inventions
within an Early Christian milieu. While contacts may have declined compared to
other periods, Atlantic ways of life initiated or developed during the Late Bronze Age
continued, and therefore societies evolved in related ways – visible at one level
through the traditions of drystone architectural monumentality. Such similarities
imply that Atlantic societies had an awareness of each other and developed along
similar though not identical lines. Individual communities had distinct regional characteristics and identities, but at a general level there is an Atlantic *directedness* in development created by the natural inclination for communities along the coast to remain
in contact at some level.

6 The western approaches
South-west England and Armorica
c. 750 BC–AD 200

Introduction

Together with south-eastern Ireland and south-west Wales, south-west England and Armorica form a group of projecting sea-girt promontories, between which maritime routes from the Atlantic, the English Channel, and the Irish Sea converge (McGrail 1990: fig. 4.5). Noting the importance of this area, Mackinder (1902: 19–20; Figure 1.4) dually referred to it as the 'Channel Entries' and the 'maritime antechamber of Britain', while modern day geologists and geographers still refer to the zone as the 'western approaches' (Embleton 1984). The nature of Iron Age maritime links between southern Britain and Armorica have been much better documented compared to those of more northern regions such as Atlantic Scotland and Ireland, largely due to the research interests of Professor Barry Cunliffe. Cunliffe's programmes of excavation and long-term research objectives, collectively known as the Atlantic Façade Programme, have included work at Hengistbury Head, Dorset (Cunliffe 1987), Mount Batten, Devon (Cunliffe 1988a), Le Câtel, Jersey (Cunliffe 1992) and, with Patrick Galliou of the University of Brest, at Le Yaudet, Brittany (Cunliffe and Galliou 1995, 2000, 2004, 2005). As a part of this work the evidence for visible material contacts between Armorica and south-west England have been reviewed over the past two decades (Cunliffe 1982, 1987, 1988b, 1990, 1991: 180–5; 2000, 2001), while a monograph, *Armorica and Britain: Cross Channel relationships in the late first millennium BC* (Cunliffe and de Jersey 1997), extensively discussed the evidence for imported material, mainly pottery and coins, manufactured in Brittany and found in Britain.

Cunliffe (1990, 1997, with de Jersey 1997: 38–40) has cited the similarities between western British bronze vessels and Armorican ceramic forms alongside the Iberian style brooches from Cornwall, Devon and Brittany, the distribution of Greek and Carthaginian coins, and the occurrence of 'Mediterranean' type bronze figurines in Ireland and western Britain, as evidence that Atlantic communities on both sides of the Channel were in some form of maritime contact leading to the dissemination of shared concepts and similar patterns of behaviour throughout the second half of the first millennium BC. The classical references to the 'tin-trade' provide a context for sustained cross-Channel contacts (Cunliffe 1982). In terms of the direct exchange of forms, the evidence is slight, though not insignificant, and similarities between areas, comparable to those examined in the previous chapter, are visible in terms of shared ideas and traditions.

Ceramic developments in south-west England and Armorica

Evidence for cultural similarities during the Iron Age between south-west England and Armorica are perhaps clearest through similarities in ceramic development. The ceramic sequences will be briefly reviewed below, not only to gain insight into the extent of contacts, but also as an essential precursor to the detailed consideration of the settlement sequences from each area carried out later. In the absence of more secure dating material, the occurrence of ceramic forms are regularly used to date phases of occupation on settlement sites in Armorica and especially south-west England.

South-west England

The development of ceramic forms in the south-western Iron Age is reasonably clear. Late Bronze Age/Early Iron Age forms consist of undecorated straight-sided, bucket-shaped vessels which evolved directly from indigenous Middle Bronze Age Trevisker types (Patchett 1944: 41–8). Their closest parallels are with the Deverel-Rimbury urn forms found further east (particularly those from Dorset). This connection with eastern English developments is perhaps one of the last reflections of the importance of the south-eastern part of England and its wider maritime connections during the Late Bronze Age.[1] In addition, simple indigenous forms, often impressed with thumb or stick, are found throughout the south-west at this time and are thought to span the transition into the Iron Age (Quinnell 1996: fig. 1).

From the fourth century BC until sometime in the first century BC a number of new and vigorously decorated pottery styles are produced throughout the peninsula, collectively termed South Western Decorated ware (Pearce 1981: 100–3, fig. 3.7; Quinnell 1986: 111; Todd 1987: 180–1, fig. 6.10; Cunliffe 1991: 84–5, 180–1, figs. A:20 and A:21). The term covers a diverse range of smoothly finished bowls and jars with boldly incised curvilinear patterns created through shallow tooling, stamping and, less frequently, with the roulette wheel (Cunliffe 1991: 180–1; Figure 6.1). Petrological study has demonstrated that forms, each with their own distinctive clay type, were produced at least six centres and distributed throughout Cornwall and Devon into Somerset and as far north as Mendip (Peacock 1969, 1979; Quinnell 1986: 113–14; Cunliffe 1982: Ill. 236; 1991: 462, fig. 17.17).

In the first century BC a new style of pottery known as Cordoned ware appears just as South Western Decorated wares begin to die out (Figure 6.2). The form comprises dark coloured bowls, necked-jars and large everted-rim jars, which are decorated with cordons or raised bands, and some of which at least appear to have been wheel-thrown (Pearce 1981: 103–4, fig. 3.8; Todd 1987: 180–2; Cunliffe 1991: 182, fig. A:34; Quinnell 2004: 109). Cunliffe (1991: 182) claims that stylistically Cordoned ware has much in common with developments in north-western France and central-southern Britain in

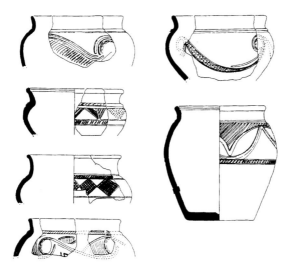

Figure 6.1 South Western Decorated ware (after Cunliffe 1991: fig. A:20).

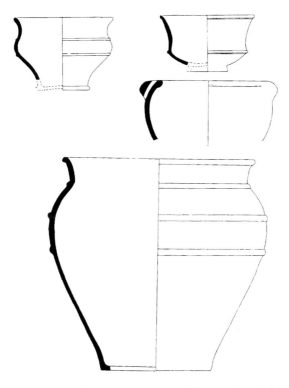

Figure 6.2 Cordoned ware (after Cunliffe 1991: fig. A:34).

the second half of the first century BC, and that 'they are best explained therefore as the result of local trading contacts between these areas in the post-Caesarian period' (ibid.). Although Cordoned ware forms are found in the centre-south of Britain (at Hengistbury Head and its surrounding hinterland) and the south-west peninsula, their distribution in the latter area is restricted to the west of the peninsula, extending only as far east as Mount Batten, suggesting that the Devonshire area was excluded from exchange networks at the time – here it is likely that South Western Decorated wares continued until the Roman conquest.

There was undoubtedly some fusion between South Western Decorated and Cordoned wares in the first century BC and it is sometimes not possible to separate them stratigraphically. At Killibury (Miles 1977) and Threemilestone (Schwieso 1976: 64), for example, cordons appear on South Western Decorated forms. At several sites, however, Cordoned ware can be clearly seen to directly follow South Western Decorated forms and it is now firmly established that the Cordoned ware tradition continued, with developments, well into the first half of the first millennium AD. Quinnell (2004: 108–27) has identified three main Cordoned ware phases, the first of which is entirely pre-Roman and the most original, featuring cordoned cup and bowls forms as well as the use of cordons on large storage jars and cooking pots. The second phase starts sometime in the Roman period, the indigenous cup and bowl forms all but disappear and cordons begin to be used on new styles copying Roman imports. The third phase is not particularly typologically distinct but simply refers to the continued use of cordons up until the fifth or sixth centuries AD. The later occurrences of cordons are largely restricted to larger vessels, as Cunliffe (1991: 182) has noted, making finds of cordons on smaller cups and bowls of indigenous form a good indicator of activity in the first centuries BC/AD.

Armorica

The general development of Iron Age ceramic styles in Armorica is also broadly known (Wheeler and Richardson 1957; Giot *et al.* 1968; Giot *et al.* 1971; Daire 1990; Giot 1995: 305–48; Cunliffe and de Jersey 1997: 37–47). Late Bronze Age/Early Iron Age forms dating from the sixth to the fourth centuries BC display clear west-central European influences with profiles and types similar to Hallstatt forms found further east. Indigenous Armorican situla type vessels develop wide-flaring rims and pedestal bases, while significantly, as was briefly mentioned in Chapter 4, their bodies are decorated with elaborate horizontal zones of stamped geometric patterning. Other vessels including bowls were similarly decorated. Vessels are often coated in graphite giving them a metallic appearance – an effect further enhanced by their general angularity (Giot 1995: 318). The inspiration for these decorative styles is widely considered to have been metal vessels and other types of decorated metalwork that were traded through Europe in the fifth century BC (Schwappach 1969; Cunliffe 1990; Cunliffe and de Jersey 1997: 38).

Ceramic styles with distinctive curvilinear decoration and softer profiles occur in Armorica from the Early La Tène period (*c.* 450–250 BC), mainly as the result of contacts with the Marne and Moselle regions to the east and continue in use throughout the Middle La Tène (*c.* 250–120 BC). The best examples of Armorican curvilinear decoration can be seen on the vase from Saint-Pol-de-Léon and the open bowl from Hénon, each of which have comparable designs to those seen on contemporary metalwork from the Marne region (Figure 6.3). Throughout the third and second centuries BC stamped and incised decoration continues but in increasingly less elaborate motifs of simple arcs or groupings of stamped circlets.

From the beginning of the Late La Tène (*c.* 120 BC) stamped and incised decoration virtually disappears and the technique of graphite coating is less widely employed. Fast wheel thrown pottery becomes popular and with it comes an array of new decorative techniques such as the application of finely tooled cordons and parallel rilling of the body, the former technique creating forms very close to the south-western Cordoned ware discussed above (Figure 6.4). From the Caesarian period and into the Roman period (56 BC onwards) there are a range of further changes to ceramic forms inspired from imported wares from the Roman world.

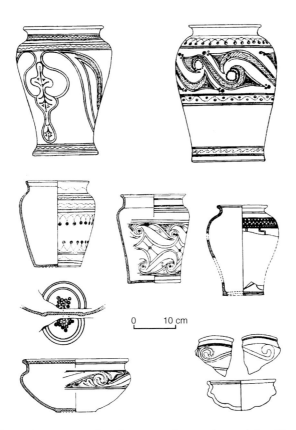

0   10 cm

Figure 6.3 Armorican pottery: fourth to second centuries BC (after Giot 1995: 328).

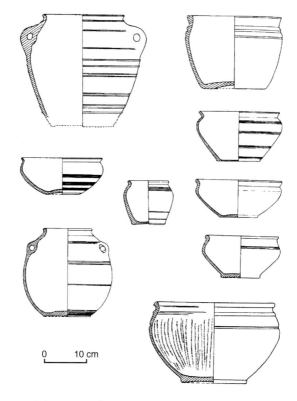

Figure 6.4 Armorican late La Tène pottery (after Giot 1995: 340).

Ceramic contacts

Cunliffe and de Jersey (1997: 57–67) have assembled a detailed gazetteer of all known occurrences of Iron Age pottery imported from Armorica to southern Britain. This gazetteer reveals that there are very few positively identified imports from the Early and Middle La Tène periods (*c.* 450–120 BC), and that by far the vast majority of sherds date to the Late La Tène (*c.* 120 to 56 BC), and of these more than 90 per cent come from Hengistbury Head in Dorset.

It is significant that the few early sherds that have been identified were found in the south-west. The most convincing of these is a single base sherd that pre-dates a Roman cemetery excavated at Poundbury, Dorset (Cunliffe and de Jersey 1997: Site 212), whose closest parallels, both in fabric and decoration, are with assemblages from Brittany and date the sherd to the middle of the third century BC (op. cit. 3). The examples of stamp decorated pottery from Cornwall are similar in many respects to Armorican stamped wares of the fifth to second centuries BC, but the stylistic characteristics of the vessels usually suggest indigenous production.[2] Two sherds from Carn Euny, however, have been tentatively identified as imports (Cunliffe and de Jersey 1997: 4; Christie 1978: fig. 53, nos 4 and 5). Cunliffe (1997: 4) has also singled-out a graphite-coated wheel-made bowl from Meare Village West (Bullied and Gray 1948: pl. XVI, no. P90), which features a high neck with a wide cordon and is very close to Armorican Middle La Tène forms of the second century BC.

There is a real paucity of imported Armorican Early to Middle La Tène ceramic forms, especially when one considers the volume of excavations that have been carried out in southern Britain. The evidence for British ceramics exported to Armorica[3] is even more sparse and currently consists of a single sherd of South Western Decorated ware made in Devon, found at the promontory site of Le Yaudet in Brittany (Cunliffe and de Jersey 1997: 1). The absence of imported ceramics, however, does not necessarily negate the existence of contacts between the two peninsulas. Exchanges may simply have been focused on other media including, as Cunliffe (1990; with de Jersey 1997: 38–40) has suggested, high quality metalwork. The general similarities in ceramic developments and, as will be examined below, the settlement evidence between south-west England and Armorica during the fifth to the second centuries BC suggest that, although there is little evidence for intense trading activity, communities on either side of the Channel were in contact.

Of the later Armorican imports in southern Britain very little material has been found in the south-west; instead the emphasis of exchange appears to switch to central-southern Britain concentrating at the Late Iron Age port of Hengistbury Head in Dorset. With sherds of over 550 separate Armorican vessels present at Hengistbury it was possible to create a type series based upon fabric and form (Cunliffe 1982a: 43–5; Cunliffe and Brown 1987: 303–21). Three basic wares were identified: Black Cordoned ware (252 examples), Rilled Micaceous ware (241 examples) and Graphite-coated ware (60 examples). Of these only Black Cordoned ware is found in the south-west – with the notable exception of the Graphite-coated bowl from Meare mentioned above[4] (Cunliffe and de Jersey 1997: figs. 30–2). More importantly it was undoubtedly Armorican Black Cordoned ware which initially stimulated, directly or indirectly via contacts with central-southern Britain, the development of Cordoned forms in the south-west peninsula – just as it stimulated the development of indigenous Hengistbury Class B derivatives in the centre-south (Cunliffe 1978: fig. 32).

Cross-channel networks of exchange in the first millennium BC

Cunliffe's research and excavation programmes have facilitated the identification of the main periods and probable nodes of contact between southern Britain and north-western France throughout the first millennium BC (Figure 6.5). In numerous publications Cunliffe (1987, 1988a, 1990; with de Jersey 1997) has argued for continuous contacts between Armorica and south-west England from the Late Bronze Age until the first century BC, supported by the evidence recovered from Mount Batten (Cunliffe 1988a). After this the main axes of trade appear to shift up-Channel to Hengistbury Head and the centre-south of England for a short period (*c.* 120–60 BC). After the Roman invasion of Gaul in 56 BC the main routes of cross-Channel trade

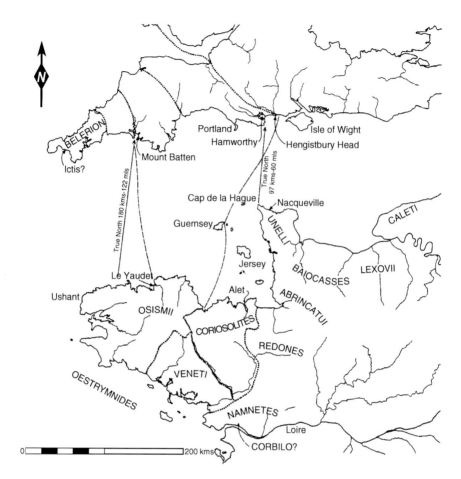

Figure 6.5 Trade routes and axes of contact suggested by Cunliffe (after Cunliffe 1997: fig. 35).

are pulled further east to Poole harbour and the Thames in south-east England due to the demands of the Roman Empire which was based on establishing efficient road networks and naturally favoured the shortest sea crossing possible.

Evidence for the existence of a port of trade in the south-west comes from the recovery of a range of imported artefacts, including a significant Late Bronze Age assemblage, two Iberian fibulae, and two Italo-Etruscan bronzes, from a rocky promontory at Mount Batten overlooking the Plymouth Sound (Cunliffe 1988a). Although structural and occupational evidence is lacking from the site, Cunliffe (1988a, 1990: 250) has argued that the assemblage is sufficient to assume the location had been linked to 'interregional systems of exchange from the late Bronze Age to the end of the middle La Tène period'. There was a noticeable drop in contacts by the first century BC, the only evidence coming from two small sherds of Black Cordoned ware made in northern Brittany and datable to the first half of the first century BC (Cunliffe 1988a: 40, 102, fig. 27). It seems most likely that these sherds arrived from local maritime trade with Hengistbury rather than direct contacts with France.

Conversely, evidence for contacts started *c.* 120 BC at Hengistbury Head. Late Iron Age occupation was traced along the northern shore in a zone some 750 m long and up to 100 m wide. Of this area only 4 per cent has been excavated, producing some 17,968 pot sherds. If the number of Armorican vessels recovered, estimated at 553 vessels, is in any way representative of the site as a whole, bearing in mind trenches were evenly spaced throughout the site, then Cunliffe suggests the total number of imported sherds could be as high as 6,300 Black Cordoned wares, 5,000 Rilled Micaceous wares and 1,500 Graphite coated vessels (Cunliffe and de Jersey 1997: 47). Add to this the evidence of over one thousand Dressel 1 amphorae and the importance of the site begins to be appreciated. In addition, the evidence for imported wine, glass and figs, and for metals, shale, corn and pottery being brought to the site from other parts of central and western Britain all strongly suggest that Hengistbury Head was a major port-of-trade articulating exchanges between southern Britain and Armorica throughout the Late Iron Age (Cunliffe 1978: Ill. 236; 1987: 339–43; with de Jersey 1997: 47–51). Alongside the two Black Cordoned ware sherds at Mount Batten, the existence of maritime coastal contacts with south-western communities is further implied through the occurrence of seventeen sherds of South Western Decorated ware at Hengistbury.

The existence of Iron Age ports-of-trade in north-western France have yet to be definitively identified, but initial investigations indicate at least some level of trading activity at Alet near Saint Malo, Ille-et-Vilaine, in the form of sixteen rims and bases of Black Cordoned ware (Cunliffe 1982; de Jersey 1993). At Nacqueville near Cherbourg there are Dressel 1b amphorae and possible armlets of imported Kimmeridge shale (Cunliffe and de Jersey 1997: 53), while a sherd of South Western Decorated ware has been recovered from Late Iron Age occupation levels at the promontory site of Le Yaudet on the north coast of Brittany (Cunliffe and Galliou 1995). It has also been argued that Guernsey was involved in maritime trade in the Late Iron Age and early Roman period, perhaps being used as a stopping-off point, with activity likely to have centred on the harbour at St Peter Port (Burns *et al.* 1996).

The six locations mentioned above only provide a very partial view of what was presumably a much more complex local and cross-Channel system with riverine and coastal routes undoubtedly playing a major role (Cunliffe and de Jersey 1997: 53–6). Clearly maritime trade from ships was taking place but we know very little about how it was organised or where the actual ports of arrival and departure actually were. Due mainly to the spectacular evidence recovered from Hengistbury Head, Dorset, research has concentrated on the end of the first millennium BC and the relationship between the centre-south of Britain and northern Brittany. To date there has been no detailed consideration of the settlement sequences from Armorica and south-west England and it is to this evidence that we shall now turn.

Iron Age settlement in south-west England and Armorica

The existence of shared traditions between south-west England and Armorica is most obvious in the settlement archaeology. Excavations over the past twenty years in Armorica have revealed that the domestic unit – the enclosed farmstead – is comparable in size and form to those of south-west England and south-west Wales (Cunliffe 1990). Cultural parallels between Armorica and south-west England are perhaps most widely known, however, from the restricted distributions of promontory forts and souterrains on both sides of the channel (Figure 6.6).

Early writers saw a clear link between the 'cliff-castles' of south-west England and the promontory forts of Armorica, particularly those on the coasts of Finistère and the Morbihan (Wheeler and Richardson 1957: 103–12; Cotton 1959; Thomas 1966: 78). A plausible historical context for the introduction of promontory fortifications from Armorica to south-west England appeared to come from Caesar's descriptions of the fortifications and commercial activities of the Veneti (*Bellum Gallicum* III 8; Cotton 1959: 116; Fox 1973: 141), backed up by the discovery of Armorican stamped wares from the promontory site at Gunard's Head (Gordon 1940: 110). Writers such as Hawkes (1966) argued that promontory forts, alongside souterrains and Cordoned wares, were introduced to south-west England by Armorican refugees fleeing the Roman advance of 56 BC.

Such views are no longer tenable because promontory forts and souterrains have since been shown to pre-date the Caesarean episode in both south-west England and Armorica (Quinnell 1986: 115; Cunliffe 1991: 182). Also, although souterrains in Brittany and Cornwall may have been performing similar roles they were quite different structurally. The use of promontory sites and souterrains are best viewed within the context of some level of cultural contact between the two areas, contact which ultimately facilitated the propagation and maintenance of similarities. The similarities are not close enough to require the existence of large-scale trading contacts or population movements to explain their occurrence, but are sufficiently alike to imply that respective communities had an awareness of what was happening across the Channel.

South-west England

Iron Age settlement

The south-west peninsula has a distinctive settlement sequence which maintains an identity throughout the first millennium BC separate from that of the rest of Britain (Cunliffe 1990, 1991). Although there have been many general reviews of the south-western English Iron Age (Fox 1964, 1973; Thomas 1966; Pearce 1981, 92–132; Quinnell 1986; Todd 1987: 151–89: Cunliffe 1991: 180–5, 247–61; Griffith and Quinnell 1999: 62–68; Rowe 2005), there are relatively few modern published excavations or surveys, meaning that most sites tend to be dated on the occurrence of ceramic forms, exotic imported items, single poorly defined radiocarbon dates, or from morphological characteristics. With reference to the settlement sequences of Atlantic Scotland and especially Ireland, using such raw criteria for dating tends to

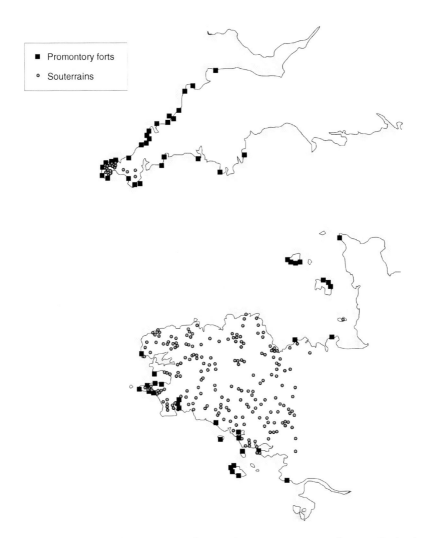

Figure 6.6 Distribution of promontory forts and souterrains in south-west England and Armorica (after Cunliffe 1991: fig. 9.2).

mask the existence of long periods of occupation, often ignores evidence for earlier activity, and can ultimately provide erroneously late construction dates.

The most striking feature of the Iron Age in the south-west is the appearance of a wide range of enclosed forms spanning several traditional monument classes, including circular enclosures (known locally as rounds), promontory forts (cliff-castles), souterrains (fogous), multiple enclosure forts, courtyard house settlements, and a handful of small hillforts (Figure 6.7). As in Atlantic Scotland and Ireland

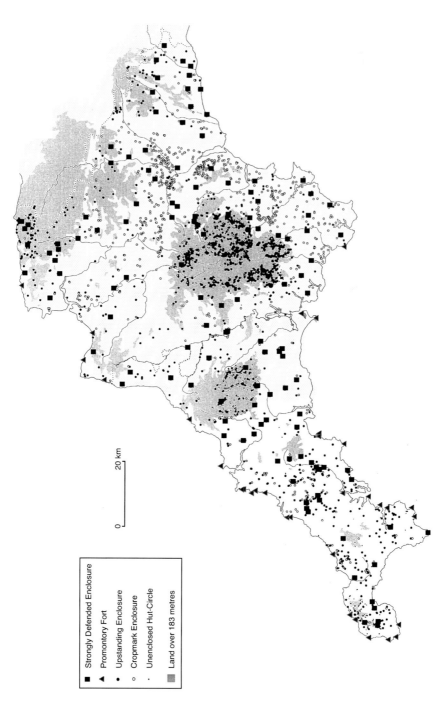

Figure 6.7 Distribution of enclosed settlements in south–west England dating from *c.* 2500 BC to AD 600 (after Griffith and Quinnell 1991: figs. 7.1 and 7.4).

periods of occupation on sites lasting hundreds of years can be identified and enclosure forms display strong continuity with their Late Bronze Age predecessors:

> In Cornwall ... the basic settlement enclosure – the round – showed little change between the late second millennium BC and the late first millennium AD, whereas in the south-east an urban system had evolved, matured and all but disappeared during that span.
>
> (Cunliffe 1994: 18)

In many respects the settlement sequences of the Iron Age in the south-west suggest a stable and conservative society. South-western communities develop in parallel with those in Armorica throughout the first millennium BC in a manner which suggests sustained contacts over a long period of time rather than short but intense periods of contact.

Iron Age enclosures *c*. 700–100 BC

Upland settlement

The beginning of the Iron Age in the south-west has traditionally been seen as a time of transition in settlement patterns from the high moorlands of Dartmoor, Exmoor, Bodmin and Penwith to lowland locations. It has been argued that this shift was caused by the worsening impact of cold and wet sub-Atlantic conditions taking hold in the mid-millennium BC on upland locations, coupled with the effects of continuous grazing (Simmons 1970; Pearce 1981; Bell 1984; Todd 1987; Cunliffe 1991). However, the widespread nature of this shift has perhaps been over-estimated as it is clear that settlement, although diminished, continued in a number of upland moors throughout the first millennium BC. Certainly peat growth on upland moors can be very localised, resulting in different sequences on different parts of the same moor (Caseldine and Hatton 1996).

It would appear then that there was a general shift to lower locations over a few centuries and that communities at lower altitudes, such as on Bodmin Moor, may have been less affected. It is unlikely that the climate caused noticeable periods of stress to family groups within their lifetimes. The worsening climatic conditions would therefore have been imperceptible, and adaptations in subsistence practice, and ultimately settlement locations, would occur gradually rather than in the form of a mass exodus from upland areas.

At the beginning of the Iron Age (*c*. 700 BC) similar settlements and economic strategies to those of the Late Bronze Age were carried out on the moors and higher ground, despite the postulated climatic deterioration. Stone-built sites such as Kestor and Foale's Arrishes on Dartmoor, Bodrifty in Cornwall, Garrow Tor on Bodmin, and Dainton in south Devon, were occupied or began in these areas in the mid-first millennium BC. These sites constitute groups of stone huts scattered amongst fields or paddocks with stone boundaries and are therefore very similar to, and a direct continuation of, Late Bronze Age forms.

Occupation at Bodrifty in Cornwall continued from the Late Bronze Age up until at least the first century BC in an apparently unbroken sequence in which stone roundhouses become enclosed alongside the appearance of South Western Decorated ware sometime in the fourth century BC (Dudley 1957; Figure 6.8). Five of the roundhouses are considerably larger than typical Late Bronze Age stone hut forms and appear to date to the second half of the first millennium BC. Early forms of pottery were found in all the excavated huts but decorated forms were found exclusively in the larger huts – labelled A, C and E on the plan – implying that they were occupied up until the first century BC while the others most probably went out of use some time before (Dudley 1957, 22). On the basis of the recovery of a jar sherd with handles, supported by the occurrence of a few stray late provincial Roman sherds, occupation at Hut C was thought to have continued into the first century AD (op. cit. 23–4). Perhaps significantly the doorways of the larger examples are orientated towards the south-east and those of the smaller huts to the south-west.[5] In being more massively built than the earlier Bronze Age hut circles on Dartmoor, these larger huts could have been following the wider British Iron Age trend of the construction of imposing large roundhouses. Certainly the internal ring of post-holes, thought to be roof supports, recorded at Huts A and E (Figure 6.9) are a common feature of timber roundhouses elsewhere in Iron Age Britain.

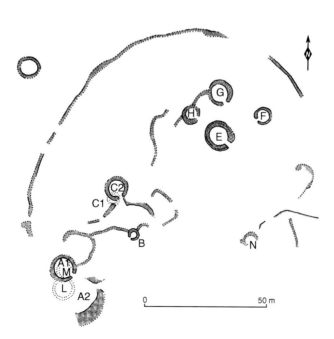

Figure 6.8 The settlement at Bodrifty, Cornwall (after Dudley 1957: fig. 2).

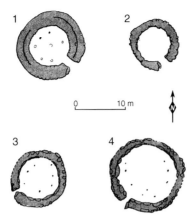

Figure 6.9 House plans from Bodrifty and Kestor (after Fox 1955; Dudley 1957).

The site of Kestor in north-eastern Dartmoor consists of twenty-seven circular stone roundhouses amidst a network of rectilinear field systems. Of these the largest enclosed roundhouse, known as the Round Pound, along with one of the smaller roundhouses and its adjoining paddock and field have been excavated (Fox 1955; Figure 6.10). The smaller roundhouse, about 10 m in diameter, is well constructed and comparable to those seen at Bodrifty. It features a circular setting of posts with a central post to support a roof, a paved area and a hearth (Figure 6.9). Of more interest is the larger oval stone enclosure, the Round Pound, which encloses a large single roundhouse, *c.* 11.3 m in diameter, to which it was attached by four radial walls. Within the roundhouse lay a small bowl furnace and a forging pit, apparently used for the production of iron.[6] Both roundhouses are dated to the sixth to fourth centuries BC on the basis of pottery and the fact that peat growth had already begun prior to their foundation (Fox 1955: 36, fig. 12; Silvester 1979). How long Kestor was occupied is a matter of conjecture but a third or second century BC abandonment seems likely as no South-West Decorated forms were recovered.

Similar stone roundhouses featuring comparable ceramics and built within enclosures are seen at Foales Arrishes (Silvester 1979), Shovel Down and the last structural phases at Shaugh Moor Enclosure 15[7] (Wainwright and Smith 1980; Quinnell 1996: 77). These sites, along with Bodrifty and Kestor, have all produced utilitarian assemblages consisting of a few spindle whorls, polished stones and querns, and in the absence of evidence of exotic items or wider trading contacts are best viewed as self-sufficient farmsteads.

The majority of sites on Dartmoor do not appear to have continued after the third or second centuries BC due to an absence of South Western Decorated ware. However, recent settlement evidence dating to the second half of the first millennium BC has been discovered at Gold Park, Shapley Common (Gibson 1992), situated on the north-east edge of the moor. A circular timber house, *c.* 8.5 m in diameter, and associated features provided radiocarbon dates ranging from 390 to 121 cal. BC. This phase provided a rim of South-West decorated ware associated with a hearth. A simple stone roundhouse, about 6 m across, replaced the timber structure and was dated between 197 cal. BC and AD 17 cal. More South-West decorated sherds were found in association with a number of small trenches and stone cairns nearby. This is the first evidence of a structure of late first millennium BC date from Dartmoor, previous evidence of activity consisted of a few stray sherds and published spindle whorls (Quinnell 1996: 78).

The general picture, is however, still one of decreasing activity on Dartmoor throughout the first millennium BC until the Roman and post-Roman periods, by which time there is virtually no evidence of use at all (Quinnell 1996). Sites such as Bodrifty on the less elevated Cornish moors continued longer because the local climatic effects were less pronounced. Ways of life in western Cornwall appear to have continued much as they had since the Late Bronze Age while communities in the centre and east of the peninsula had to adapt and move to lower land, not overnight but over a period of a few centuries. This difference is reflected in the distribution of multiple enclosure forts from the fourth century BC throughout Devon and areas of eastern Cornwall, but not in the west where only univallate *round* enclosures are found. This perhaps further illustrates deep set cultural traditions of continuity with Late Bronze Age ways of life in this area.

Univallate and multiple enclosure settlements

Evidence for the gradual shift of settlement to lower altitudes is seen from the middle of the first millennium BC when a range of enclosure forms – promontory forts, univallate enclosures and multiple enclosure sites – begin to be constructed throughout the valleys and coastal areas of south-west England. It is possible that a number of promontory forts were occupied even earlier (from the Late Bronze Age) given the ceramic evidence from Maen Castle and Trevelgue (Nowakowski 2004). Promontory enclosures remain an ill-defined type but it seems likely that they were in use throughout the second half of the first millennium BC. The dominant form during the Iron Age, however, appears to have been the small univallate homestead or 'round' (Thomas 1966).

Rounds

It is estimated that between 750 and 1,000 rounds originally existed in the south-west peninsula (op. cit. 88–90), reflecting a dense distribution directly comparable to that of Irish ringforts. Rounds are simple banked and ditched enclosures usually featuring one entrance with a few huts placed inside, typically placed close against the bank. The majority of examples are comparable in size – enclosing around one hectare – and are generally circular or oval in plan, but sub-rectangular and even triangular examples are known (Johnson and Rose 1982; Figure 6.11). Most are sited on, or near, good arable land and are best viewed as the farmsteads of family or extended family groupings. As will be examined below, there are some larger and

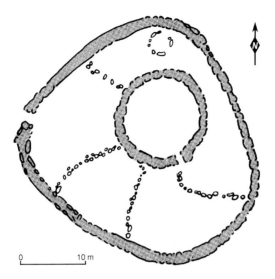

Figure 6.10 The Round Pound at Kestor, Devon (after Fox 1955).

more strongly defended examples included both within this and the multiple enclosure class, which appear to have been sites of more elevated status and which display evidence of being involved in wider trading networks.

Despite their very broad definition, rounds are considered in most general works to be a distinct type with occupation belonging to a clear dating horizon from the second century BC through to the fifth century AD – although none are actually thought to have been constructed after the third century AD (Pearce 1981: 107–9; Todd 1987: 222–7). Many authors make a point of stressing that the erection of defensive enclosures at round sites cannot be dated in the south-west prior to 200 BC and that their main period of use therefore lies in the first half of the first millennium AD (cf. Todd 1987: 168; Cunliffe 1991: 182). However, on closer examination many round enclosures can be seen to be very similar in layout and appearance to early Iron Age upland enclosures like Bodrifty and Kestor, particularly the Round Pound (Figure 6.10).

As argued for Irish *raths*, the fact that activity at south-western rounds, from the excavated evidence appears to belong predominantly to the first millennium AD does not necessarily date all the similar sites to this period of activity. Around twenty examples in the south-west have been excavated and between them they provide evidence of occupation on 'round' sites ranging from *c.* 500 BC to AD 500 (Quinnell 1986, 115–18; Figure 6.12).

Perhaps the best example of continuity in traditions of settlement passing from the Bronze Age into the Iron Age comes from Trevisker (ApSimon and Greenfield 1972). Here a small Bronze Age enclosure, consisting of two circular timber

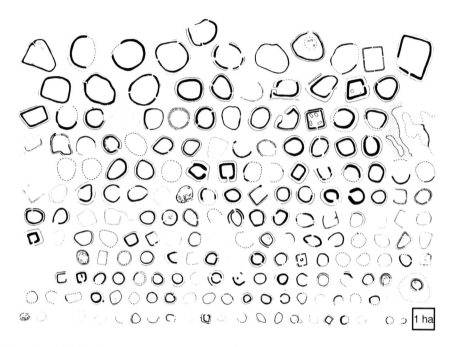

Figure 6.11 Univallate enclosures in Cornwall (after Johnson and Rose 1982: figs. 2 and 3).

roundhouses with ancillary structures and ditches was succeeded, after an apparently barren interval, by a larger Iron Age 'round' (*c.* 1.2 ha) traditionally radiocarbon dated to *c.* 200 BC (op. cit. 313–19, 367, 369; Figure 6.12). However, the radiocarbon date used to support this dating actually calibrates anywhere between 350 and 100 cal. BC.[8] The date was recovered from material on the floor of a timber roundhouse, about 13 m across, built within the smaller inner enclosure, and was associated with South Western Decorated ware. Therefore, an initial construction date sometime in the fourth century BC cannot at this stage be ruled out for this enclosure. Three Iron Age circular timber roundhouses with slab-lined drains were identified within an excavated internal area of *c.* 400 square m. The houses could be seen through their association with Cordoned ware and a limited quantity of Roman ceramics to continue up until the second century AD.

Threemilestone, near Truro, is the only published round currently considered by its excavator to have been occupied entirely within the first millennium BC (Dudley 1960; Schweiso 1976). It is also, perhaps significantly, one of the most fully excavated sites, with excavation of around three-quarters of its interior completed (Schweiso 1976: 53; Figure 6.13). At least nine roundhouse gullies were recognised, of which the excavator suggests only five could ever have been contemporary (op. cit. 65).

The site is dated to the pre-Roman period due to the occurrence of South Western Decorated ware and an absence of any Romano-British or later imported

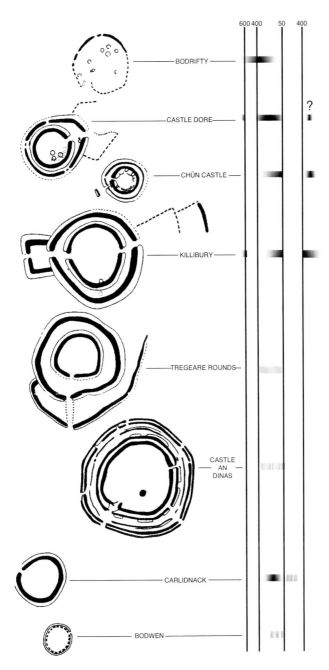

Figure 6.12 Excavated enclosures from Cornwall (after Johnson and Rose 1982: fig. 13).
(Continued)

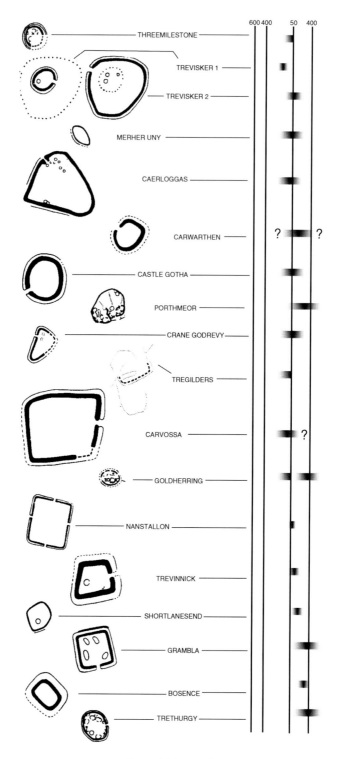

Figure 6.12 cont'd

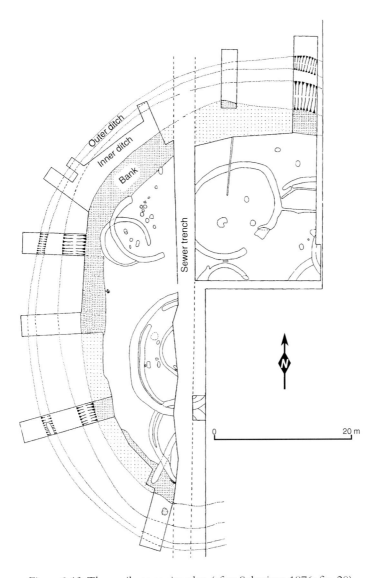

Figure 6.13 Threemilestone site plan (after Schwieso 1976: fig. 20).

Roman vessels. The majority of excavated rounds have provided at least some South Western Decorated sherds, further supporting a pre-second century BC origin for the form. Many of the South Western Decorated sherds from Threemilestone are similar to other examples found at the Rumps promontory fort (Brooks 1974) and at Bodrifty (Dudley 1957) and could therefore indicate an early dating for the site. However, Cordoned wares were also found and, significantly, no stratigraphical division between the two traditions could be discerned (Schwieso 1976: 64).

The occurrence of only a handful of Cordoned sherds, some of which mixed South Western curvilinear and applied cordon decoration, coupled with the use of the same gabbroic clay for both traditions, suggested that they were likely to be early occurrences of Cordoned ware. For this reason occupation at the site was dated up to *c.* 75–50 BC (ibid.).

Despite clear evidence for the pre-Roman Iron Age construction of univallate enclosures at Trevisker and Threemilestone there has been a general tendency to date the construction and use of round sites to the first millennium AD, either ignoring evidence for earlier activity or simply dismissing it as residual.

Occupation at the oval round of Castle Gotha, St Austell, which encloses several timber roundhouses and one stone-walled oval structure, occurred mainly 'in the first century AD, with an overlap into the centuries before and after' according to the excavators (Saunders and Harris 1982: 109, fig. 3). A closer examination of the ceramic evidence, however, suggests that the site was most probably established sometime in the third century BC and subsequently occupied over 500 years up until the end of the second century AD (op. cit. 132–43). The occurrence of South Western Decorated wares again suggest an early construction date, while the presence, in increasing numbers, of Cordoned wares, Roman traded vessels and Romano-Cornish pottery forms indicate the continuation of occupation into the first few centuries AD. The excavators state that since only small amounts of South Western Decorated ware were recovered, the main period of occupation belonged to the first century AD (op. cit. 149). Such a situation should, however, be entirely expected, the evidence of earlier occupation is usually less substantial than that of more recent activity, and should not result in dating the initial construction of the site itself to the first few centuries AD. There seems little doubt that the enclosure was first established sometime in the Iron Age from the evidence of the South Western Decorated and Cordoned wares. Hints of Bronze Age activity immediately underlying the enclosure further support this view (op. cit. 112–13). Bearing in mind the limited extent of the excavation of the interior, the house structures and their finds – including two bronze brooches, a small bronze head representation, evidence of bronze and iron metalworking, Samian ware and Roman flagon sherds – undoubtedly relate mainly to occupation in the first or second centuries AD (Schweiso 1976: 66), but this fact should not mask the evidence for earlier activity at the site.

A watching brief at Carlidnack Round, Mawnan (Harris and Johnson 1976), a nearly circular univallate earthwork with a diameter of some 90 to 100 m, produced around 70 sherds of pottery. These were all dated to the first or second centuries AD and were used to date the construction of the round (op. cit. 76). However, eight sherds with wave decoration (Jar 1, sherds 1–9) are almost certainly earlier and belong to the South Western Decorated class. They can be closely paralleled with examples from Bodrifty (Dudley 1957: 27; fig. 10, no. 1), Trevisker (ApSimon and Greenfield 1972: 335, fig. 20, no. 54), and Caerloggas (Thriepland 1957: 63, fig. 24, no. 72), and would therefore suggest that there had been pre-Roman Iron Age activity at the site.

Limited investigations at Bodwen Round just south of Bodmin Moor (Harris 1977, 51–6; fig. 19) unearthed seven South Western Decorated sherds (ibid. fig. 21, nos. 2–8) with internally grooved everted rims similar to forms known from the Rumps cliff-castle (Brooks 1974: fig. 22, no. 14; fig. 24, no. 2), Trevisker (ApSimon and Greenfield 1972: fig. 20, no. 1), Threemilestone (Schwieso 1976: fig. 24, no. 42), Caerloggas (Thriepland 1956) and Castle Dore (Radford 1951: figs. 14 and 16). The fact that these sherds were found in the ditch fill of the site, have parallels with early forms from Iron Age sites, and that no Cordoned ware was discovered, all suggest that this round must have been constructed before the first century BC.

The shape of the enclosure of Caerloggas, St Mawgan-in-Pydar (Thriepland 1956), although predominantly oval, has a rectilinear element in the form of an almost right-angled corner to the west, yet the site provides good evidence of pre-Roman Iron Age activity (Figure 6.12). Nine small oval huts with stone revetment walls were excavated, and there were partial remains of more. The presumably earliest, and incidentally most circular, huts were associated with South Western Decorated and Cordoned pottery forms alongside pre-invasion imported amphora sherds (op. cit. 53–69). As a result, the initial construction date of the site can be pushed back to at least the first century BC and not the first century AD as argued by the excavator (op. cit. 51). Further indications of an initial prehistoric Iron Age construction come from the form of the inturned and narrowed entrance passage, paralleled at a number of other Iron Age sites in north-western Europe, and the discovery of a bronze shield mount decorated in a La Tène Iron Age style best dated to the first century BC. Occupation continued into the second century AD evidenced by Samian ware sherds, imported wine flagons, and three second century AD brooches.

Similar to the *dun* enclosures of Argyll and, as will be examined later, enclosure forms in Armorica, there appears to have been a move towards the construction of more rectilinear forms from the beginning of the first millennium AD. The dating evidence from the south-west indicates that circular enclosure forms are more likely to provide evidence of prehistoric activity while rectilinear forms provide evidence dating to the first millennium AD (Figure 6.12). Evidence for construction in the first half of the first millennium AD has been obtained from rectilinear enclosures at Tregilders (Trudigan 1977); Trevinnick (Fox and Ravenhill 1969); Carvossa (Douch and Beard 1970); Grambla (Saunders 1972) and Shortlanesend (Harris 1980). However, although rectilinear sites are undoubtedly a form dating to the first half of the first millennium AD, excavations at Trethurgy (Miles and Miles 1973; Quinnell 2004) suggest that circular forms also continued to be built. Trethurgy is the most extensively excavated round to date, and with its drystone oval enclosure wall and oval internal stone buildings built close against it, gives the outward appearance of a prehistoric site similar in many respects to Threemilestone (Figure 6.14). However, on investigation it was found to belong exclusively to the late Roman period with occupation beginning in the second century AD and lasting up until the early sixth century AD (Quinnell 2004: 165–82). The dating of Trethurgy warns against simply using site morphology as a chronological indicator and indicates the long survival of round enclosure traditions in the area.

The excavations carried out so far suggest that univallate enclosures or rounds in the south-west have a date range spanning around one thousand years from the middle of the first millennium BC to the middle of the first millennium AD.[9]

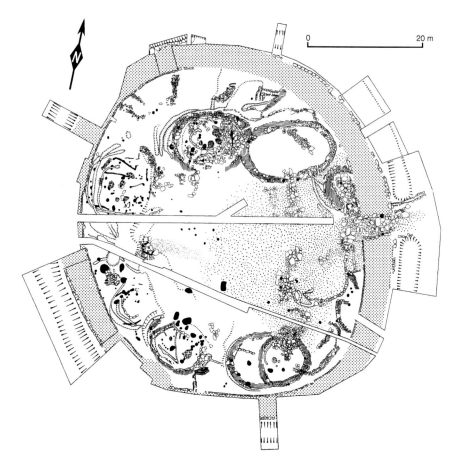

Figure 6.14 Trethurgy site plan (after Quinnell 2004: fig. 5).

Their conservative nature and appearance throughout this period make them – in the absence of intrusive investigation – impossible to date with any further clarity. However, the general trend, admittedly based on a rather restricted sample, seems to have been for the construction of curvilinear enclosures in the first millennium BC to more rectilinear types in the Romano-British period. A farmstead function seems certain, with perhaps a stronger emphasis on arable farming when compared with multiple enclosure sites in the south-west (see below), given the common association of rounds with field systems and finds of cereals, and saddle and rotary querns. Due to the problems of chronological clarity, despite a dense distribution in the landscape (from one per 2.1 km² to one per 4.5 km²) insights into social organisation remain difficult (Thomas 1966; Johnson and Rose 1982). Rounds are best interpreted as the homesteads of a non-nucleated population and, as such, are similar to enclosed homesteads found throughout western Britain. However, their closest parallels, as will be examined below, are with contemporary univallate enclosures in southern Wales, Armorica and potentially Ireland.

Multiple enclosure forts

Multiple enclosure sites are found throughout eastern Cornwall and Devon, with similar forms also known in south Wales (Fox 1953, 1961). Their typical morphology involves a central, roughly circular enclosure with an entrance, to which widely spaced outer concentric enclosures were added (Figure 6.15). With their widely spaced, and not particularly massively built ramparts, these sites are usually not viewed as primarily defensive enclosures. Instead it has been argued that they served a specifically pastoral enclosure function (cf. Fox 1953: 18–20; Thomas 1966; Silvester 1979; Pearce 1981: 104–7; Quinnell 1986: 114; Todd 1987: 166). Although such a function has not been proven beyond doubt, no other convincing alternative has yet been presented. The settlement itself was located in the inner enclosure, which was normally no bigger than 2 hectares in area and presumably accommodated a family or extended family unit. The outer enclosures are interpreted as areas for keeping stock.

Although examples with two or three enclosures are the norm there are a few more complex examples with a series of earthworks some covering up to 8 hectares or more such as Milber Down and the imposing site at Clovelly Dykes. Fox (1952, 1961) was quick to point out that there is considerable variety in the size, form and number of earthworks within this broadly defined class. Concentric circular enclosures with widespread ramparts such as Tregeare Rounds (Baring-Gould 1904), or Killibury (Miles 1977), are seen as the classic forms (Johnson and Rose 1982: 165–7, fig. 4), but enclosures with more varied attached annexes or outworks of differing sizes are actually the more numerous in the field (op. cit. 167–71, figs. 5, 6 and 7). Johnson and Rose (1982: 170–1) suggest that some of the larger and more complex, but unexamined, stone enclosures on the higher moorland, such as

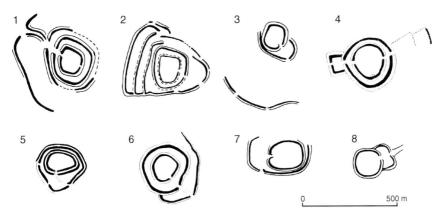

Figure 6.15 Multiple enclosure forts in south-west England (after Cunliffe 1991: fig. 13.4).

Roughtor or Stowe's Pound, may also have been performing roles similar to that of multiple enclosure forts on the lowlands in the Iron Age. If this turns out to be the case it would provide further evidence of continuity of lifestyles on the moorlands of the south-west, with circular stone forms that originated in the third or second millennium BC. The only excavated example of this type, Carn Brae, Redruth (Mercer 1981), was dated to the Neolithic, but evidence of later occupation and use was recovered in the form of Iron Age ceramics (op. cit. 185–7).

The most extensively excavated multiple enclosure fort is the bivallate example at Killibury, Cornwall (Miles 1977). Excavation of the inner enclosure revealed evidence of a dense domestic occupation between the fourth and first centuries BC, while a trench through the two outer enclosures indicated that activity in these areas was slight. Antiquarian investigations at the similar site of Tregeare Rounds (Baring-Gould 1904) also provided evidence of a pre-Roman Iron Age date range through the exclusive occurrence of South Western Decorated ware (op. cit. fig. 2, fig. 3), and nothing of Roman date or later (op. cit. 83).

Of the examples featuring more than three enclosures only one, Milber Down, has been excavated, and it revealed occupation no earlier than the first century BC continuing into first century AD. The dating of Milber Down suggests that although the other few, admittedly less complex, dated sites indicate beginnings in the fourth to third centuries BC, the use of multiple enclosure forts continued into the early Roman period. As such the date range of multiple enclosure settlements is the same as that suggested here for round enclosures.

The inner domestic enclosures at multiple enclosure settlements are directly comparable with round enclosures, so much so that it is possible to view these sites as essentially rounds that feature outer stock enclosures. Multiple enclosure settlements may represent farmstead units, contemporary with rounds, which had a stronger emphasis on pastoral activities. This specialisation appears to have occurred around the fourth century BC and may therefore be related to the abandonment of farmsteads situated in upland areas. The comparison with round enclosures has added significance in that it further supports a pre-Roman dating for these sites. It is possible that the conceptual separation of multiple enclosure settlements and rounds has encouraged the view of round settlements being a primarily first millennium AD phenomenon (cf. Todd 1987).

Similar to rounds, there is little evidence from recovered assemblages that multiple enclosure forts functioned as the residences of an elite.[10] However, given the imposing nature of these sites and their specialised pastoral function in a community which, like many pastoralists, presumably counted its wealth chiefly in terms of flocks and herds, they may have occupied a social niche above other farmsteads (Pearce 1981: 107).

Hilltop enclosures

The south-western settlement record, in common with other northern Atlantic areas, is defined by the ubiquity of small defended homestead enclosures, and sites approaching the dimensions of the hillfort enclosures seen further east are rare.

Most sites claimed as hillforts in the south-west do not fulfil the range of features normally required for the use of the term: most are very small (under 2 hectares), feature simple univallate ramparts, lie on hill-slopes of low ground and do not seem to have been built with defence in mind (Todd 1987: 157). In fact really only three sites in the south-west – Castle Canyke and Castle-an-Dinas in Cornwall and Hembury in Devon – stand out in terms of size and have constructional features directly comparable with other hillforts, but even these sites are not particularly huge in scale when compared to hilltop enclosures in Wessex and the Welsh Marches.

Castle Canyke (Weatherhill 1985a: 69) is an oval bivallate enclosure with diameters of 348 m and 308 m. Although the ramparts are much destroyed and no features are discernible, the site is generally comparable in size and layout to some of the earlier simple forms in Wessex (cf. Cunliffe 1991: 348–52, fig. 14.24). Castle-an-Dinas, St Columb Major (Wailes 1963, 1964, 1965), features three closely spaced ramparts and has a diameter of *c.* 220 m (Figure 6.17). Johnson and Rose (1982) argue that the site was initially a univallate enclosure – the outer rampart featuring no less than six entrances – which, at a later date, probably after it had been abandoned, had two concentric enclosures constructed within it. Whatever the case, in the later phases of use of the site all three ramparts certainly formed a functioning whole, creating an imposing and strongly defended location with the inner enclosure surviving to a height of 7.5 m today (Weatherhill 1985a: 114). Excavations carried out from 1962 to 1964 were of a very small scale and inconclusive in terms of dating construction, but some Iron Age occupation was found near the spring hollow in the interior of the fort, and near the inner entrance (Wailes 1963, 1964, 1965).

The most convincing example of a hillfort in the south-west is Hembury in Devon, excavated between 1930–35 and 1980–85, which produced a sequence and features comparable to hillforts known further east (Liddell 1930, 1931, 1932, 1935; Todd 1984, 1987: fig. 6.2). There appears to have been a classic early palisaded stage (Cunliffe 1974, 228, 1991: 313–14) followed by the construction of timber framed box rampart defences, broadly dated by Todd (1987: 158) to between 650 and 450 BC. The box rampart was then replaced by a dump rampart, revetted by a low stone wall, while two large ditches and a further rampart were also constructed around the site, with a third ditch and rampart protecting the north. Two large inturned gates were constructed in the west and north-eastern sides and are similar to those known from developed Wessex hillforts (Cunliffe 1991: 330–40, figs. 14.9 to 14.13). The later phases were dated from the fourth century BC to the first century BC (Todd 1984: 260–1). Areas excavated in the interior revealed no structural evidence or domestic occupation, and significantly, no trace of the storage pits or granary structures familiar at hillforts in the centre-south.

Some of the large stone-built enclosures in the upland areas of the south-west may also qualify as hillforts on account of their size, but they remain uninvestigated. The stone-built fort at Trencrom, Cornwall, for example, has been provisionally dated to the Iron Age on the basis of stray ceramic finds (Weatherhill 1981: 57–8). There is an interesting but very much understudied series of small hillforts on the eastern and southern fringes of Dartmoor suggesting continued use of the uplands, most likely for grazing, during the Iron Age (Todd 1987: 161–2). Many of these univallate enclosures are associated with reave-like boundaries suggesting the continuation of Late Bronze Age practices of land allotment and use.

Strongly defended enclosures

A number of other enclosures in the south-west stand out because they feature imposing closely spaced ramparts but, at less than two hectares in size, are too small to be considered as hillforts, yet equally do not sit comfortably within the multiple enclosure or round classes. In their seminal paper on Cornish enclosures, Johnson and Rose (1982: 163) noted this problem and remarked that a distinction between unimposing 'defended sites' and 'strongly defended sites' may prove to be a more useful division in the field than the traditional multiple enclosure, round, promontory fort and hillfort classes.

One such site is the circular drystone site of Chûn Castle on the West Penwith Moors. This intriguing site has in the past been used to provide evidence for Atlantic influences through its design (Leeds 1927, 1931; Hencken 1932). Leeds (1927: 223–40), for example, claimed that the site had been physically built by Iberian invaders due to its apparent similarities with the drystone 'castros' of north-western Iberia.[11] Such diffusionist views are now rightly discredited, but the site does display a number of features which can be broadly paralleled with other Atlantic stone-built sites, and which may therefore reflect something more than simply the use of the same building material.

Chûn Castle consists of two massive granite walls, with associated ditches, enclosing an area some 100 m across within which twelve oval and sub-rectangular structures have been built (Figure 6.16). The inner wall is around 4.5 m thick and while it survives to only *c.* 0.5 m today, in the nineteenth century it reportedly stood 4 m high (Leeds 1927: 212, 234–5; Todd 1987: 163). The outer wall is around 1 m thick today, but initially could have been as thick as the inner wall. Support for this view comes from the surviving piece of thick outer walling seen at the entrance and the fact that no rear coursing survives elsewhere on the wall, implying that it has been heavily robbed. A complex entrance arrangement survives in the form of a narrow funnelled passageway flanked by a curtain wall.

The interior of the site was partially excavated at the end of the 1920s by E. T. Leeds (1927, 1931). Alongside the examination of a furnace and a well, three of the oval structures next to the internal wall were dug into. The most coherent of these was a circular structure, about 5 m in diameter, interpreted as a house with a possible hearth and associated domestic pottery (Section 14 on Figure 6.16). Three hearths were found in a rather incomplete oval structure to the north of the entrance (Leeds 1931: 38–42), while half of an oval structure was examined in the south-eastern quarter of the site and found to be divided into two chambers by a 0.6 m thick interstitial wall (Section 18 on Figure 6.16). The pottery recovered from these structures – Cordoned sherds and, significantly, several sherds of Roman amphorae – indicate occupation between the first century BC to the first few centuries AD (Leeds 1927: 220). It has been suggested that the furnace and well features may belong to an

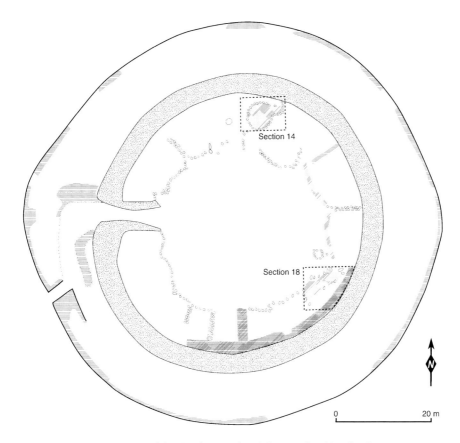

Figure 6.16 Chûn Castle site plan (after Leeds 1927: fig. 3).

even later post-Roman occupation reflecting re-use of a convenient drystone site (Thomas 1956).

There can be little doubt that these internal structures are secondary to the initial construction, and presumably occupation, of the heavily built walls at Chûn. As such these walls must be ascribed a pre-first century BC Iron Age dating. During his excavations, Leeds (1931: 35) came to a similar conclusion stating that 'it may be taken for granted that the blocks which form these visible divisions have nothing to do with the original disposition of the dwellings within the castle'. He points to the fact that the structures occur at different levels sunk into an 'upper layer' of deposit which is secondary to the internal wall, itself built directly on to the underlying bedrock. Also, crucially, he states that there was evidence for earlier structures underneath the present level of structures (op. cit. 36). The few sherds of South Western Decorated ware that were recovered along with the presumably indigenous coarse pottery with incised horizontal bands could all belong to this earlier phase (op. cit. 220–1).

The latter ware included a sherd with 'S' shaped incisions between the horizontal bands which, although it could have been produced locally, can be closely paralleled with Breton stamped wares dated to the third century BC (ibid.).

It is tempting to compare this secondary occupation with that examined at sites such as Cahercommaun in Ireland and Beirgh in Atlantic Scotland. As at these other sites, it is cellular in nature, employs the use of edge-set slabs alongside traditional coursing, and occurs at different levels amongst a mass of rubble and secondary deposit. The oval structure divided into two cells by interstitial walling can be directly paralleled with the cellular structures seen throughout Atlantic Scotland. In addition, walling to the south of the entrance gives the appearance of creating a passageway in some ways comparable to the intra-mural passageways seen in some Irish and Scottish drystone sites. It is unclear how far this walling would have continued to the south due to the effects of robbing and the resulting debris.

The ceramics recovered from Chûn suggest that the site was involved – at some level – in cross-Channel trading networks. Although the original report made no separation of the ceramics recovered, the assemblage can be split into three main groupings: an earlier group dating broadly from *c.* 300 to 100 BC, a larger group dating from *c.* 100 BC to AD 100, and a small group of Dark Age sherds reflecting later re-use of the site. The earlier assemblage consists of South Western Decorated sherds and a 'medium coarse ware' which included some incised sherds offering general parallels with Breton stamped wares although most likely produced locally. The later assemblage appears to be predominantly composed of Cordoned wares but provides more concrete evidence of contacts in the form of numerous finds of Dressel 1 Roman wine amphorae along with scraps of Roman pottery. The rest of the material recovered from the site was utilitarian and undiagnostic, but the existence of an iron nail and fragment, a circular mould for a 'tin-cake', a possible 'gaming piece', and a fragment of a shale bracelet is perhaps suggestive of some level of activity beyond that of a simple subsistence level farmstead. Iron slag, tin-dross and charcoal was recovered from at least one of the secondary buildings, attesting to some on-site metalworking activity. Unfortunately, as all of these finds were unstratified they cannot be confidently ascribed to a specific period of activity at the site. However, the assemblage of amphorae and other Roman ceramics are sufficient to suggest that Chûn was participating in long-distance trading networks in the last century BC and into the first few centuries AD. Taken together with the imposing appearance of the site and the indications of metalworking activity, it is possible to view Chûn as a site of elevated importance in the south-west.

Given the limitations of the early report and excavations at Chûn it is difficult to fully assess the significance of the site and it is often dismissed in general discussions as something of an aberration. However, the site can be compared with other strongly defended enclosures in Cornwall. A similar, but completely unstudied, stone-walled fort with a double fortification stands at Caer Brâne, Sancreed (Weatherhill 1981: 39–40; Todd 1987: 163) while a circular stone-built site of similar dimensions exists at Bartinnê Castle (Weatherhill 1981: 34).

The occurrence of bivallate concentric ramparts built within or alongside a slight outer rampart, so clearly seen at Chûn, is a layout that can be identified at a number of other sites in the south-west (Figure 6.17). Castle-an-Dinas, Ludgvan (Weatherhill 1981: 42–53), for example, features two concentric stone ramparts with an additional slight outer earthern and stone rampart and has a diameter of just over 100 m. The stone walls were, unfortunately, heavily robbed during the construction of a nineteenth-century folly on the site. Castle Pencaire, Cornwall (Weatherhill 1985a: 57–9), similarly features two concentric stone ramparts and has an overall diameter of about 120 m. Prideaux Castle, Cornwall (Weatherhill 1985a: 120), is of a similar scale and features two concentric ramparts within a third slighter rampart and other similar examples include Padderbury Top, Dingerein Castle, Carnsew, and Tokenbury (Johnson and Rose 1982; Weatherhill 1985a). Although a much larger site, the layout of Castle-an-Dinas, St Columb Major, is also broadly comparable to the examples discussed above.

Aside from Chûn, only one other strongly defended site, the earthen enclosure of Castle Dore (Radford 1951), has been excavated. This site consists of two closely spaced ramparts enclosing an area around 79 m across, within which circular domestic huts were built. The external rampart swings outwards to form an outer area in front of the entrance. Due to the existence of this outer enclosure the site is normally included within the multiple enclosure fort class, but given that the outer area created is relatively small, the concentric ramparts are closely spaced and massively constructed (surviving up to 5 m in height), it would seem more appropriate to compare this site with strongly defended, imposing sites like Chûn. In all probability the outer enclosure serves to strengthen and emphasise the approach to the main entrance – in the earliest phase (Period I) two ditched banks formed a passageway and linked the two ramparts together (Quinnell and Harris 1985: fig. 1).

The site was excavated in 1936 and 1937 and initally given a first millennium AD dating (Radford 1951). However, a reconsideration of this dating, based on the pottery recovered, demonstrated that all the structural phases of the site date from the fourth century BC to the first century AD (Quinnell and Harris 1985). Most significantly, along with the previously known rich finds of shale, glass and bronze armlets, sherds of Roman amphorae were identified during the reconsideration of the site.

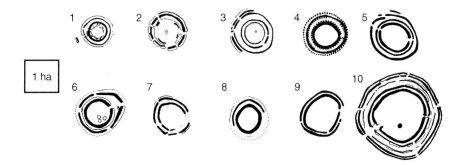

Figure 6.17 Strongly defended sites in Cornwall: (left to right) (1) Chûn Castle; (2) Caer Brâne; (3) Castle-an-Dinas, Ludgvan; (4) Castle Pencaire; (5) Prideaux Castle; (6) Castle Dore; (7) Dingerein Castle; (8) Carnsew; (9) Tokenbury; (10) Castle-an-Dinas, St. Columb Major.

A construction date in the fifth to fourth centuries BC is suggested by the fact that no South Western Decorated ware was recorded from levels relating to Period I (Quinnell and Harris 1985: 125). In this phase at least six circular huts were built against the inner rampart. In the following occupation, Period II, there was much evidence for domestic occupation through the overlaying of huts, dated to the Iron Age through the occurrence of South Western Decorated ware, but unfortunately a large number of post-holes could not be confidently ascribed to any period due to a lack of stratigraphic evidence. By Period III the gate was modified to form a 9 m long passage which narrowed the inner entrance to a width of around 2.5 m – creating an effect comparable to the funnelled entrance at Chûn. In Period IV the rampart was heightened and one oval stone-walled hut was constructed to the south of the entrance and another towards the outer gate. These are considered to be the latest structures in the sequence, and have been interpreted as part of a post-Roman re-occupation of the site that includes a projected re-organisation of the interior dating from the fifth to eighth centuries AD (Rahtz 1971). However, Quinnell and Harris (1985: 127–9) have demonstrated that there is a previously unrecognised Iron Age structural phase indicated by the occurrence of eight sherds of Cordoned ware and the fact that a large amount of the later structural evidence cannot be accounted for. This evidence includes arrangements of post-holes (Radford 1951: 65–6) that are more likely to be the remains of four-post and six-post post structures, rather than the Dark Age rectangular halls suggested by Rahtz (1971). The later occupational evidence comes only from two stone walled oval houses which cannot be stratigraphically linked to the interior post-holes.

The most significant aspect of Quinnell and Harris' re-interpretation is the re-dating of the finds. The glass beads can now be ascribed to the pre-Roman Iron Age along with the two Iron Age glass bracelets (Fitzpatrick 1985; Henderson 1985). The occurrence of 22 Dressel 1a sherds (datable from the mid-second century BC to the mid-second century AD) reveal a site with wide trading contacts, capable of obtaining high status goods. Other traded ceramics include three white body sherds which may be part of a first century AD flagon, and the most westerly find so far of a Spanish Dressel 1 – Pascual 1 sherd dating from the first century BC to the first century AD.

The finds from Castle Dore and the ceramics from Chûn suggest that both sites had access to long-distance exchange networks by the end of the first millennium BC.[12] It is possible, though not demonstrable in the absence of more excavation, that many of the other strongly defended sites identified above were also involved in wider trading activities. Evidence for Dressel 1 amphorae, alongside other exotic ceramic forms, also comes from the round enclosures of Castle Gotha (Saunders and Harris 1982) and Caerloggas (Thriepland 1956), the former also producing four sherds of Spanish type (Saunders and Harris 1982: no. 88). Dressel 1 amphorae has also been recovered from the courtyard house enclosure at Carn Euny (Christie 1978: 406).

Courtyard houses in western Cornwall and Scilly

While univallate enclosures continue to be the dominant settlement type through-out the south-west peninsula, a group of distinctive complex drystone settlements, referred to as courtyard houses, were built in western Cornwall and the Scilly Isles from the second century BC onwards. The courtyard house is a roughly circular earth and stone structure, *c.* 15 to 25 m in diameter, featuring a single paved entrance leading into a central 'courtyard', off which a series of circular and sub-rectilinear rooms are built into the thickness of the surrounding wall (Figure 6.18). The majority of surviving examples are found on high ground in the same general locations as rounds, and several are actually built within existing rounds, as can be seen at Carn Euny, Goldherring, and Porthmeor (Hirst 1936; Guthrie 1969; Christie 1978; Figure 6.19). However, the isolated courtyard house or small group, often with associated field systems, are the more numerous type in the landscape with some eighty-two examples known.

Courtyard houses are traditionally seen as an exclusively Roman period phenomenon and certainly the majority of sites, particularly the larger and more complex

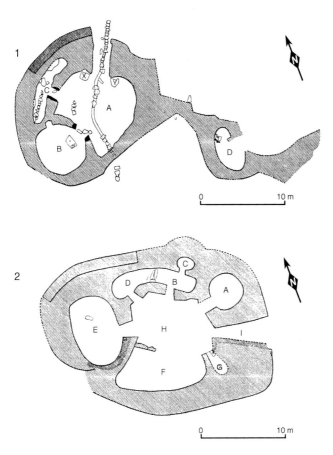

Figure 6.18 Typical courtyard house forms (after Hencken 1933: figs. 1 and 11): (1) House 5 at Chysauster; (2) House 6 at Chysauster.

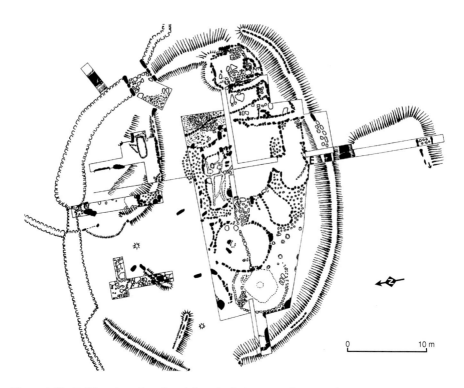

Figure 6.19 Goldherring site plan (after Guthrie 1969: fig. 1a). The enclosure and earliest occupation at this site are pre-Roman in date according to the ceramics (Schweiso 1976) with the enclosure being re-used for the construction of cellular courtyard-house forms from sometime in the third century AD (Guthrie 1969: 24). This re-use of an older enclosure for cellular forms is similar to the re-use of Atlantic roundhouses and *cashel* forms in Ireland and Atlantic Scotland discussed in Chapter 5.

examples, were constructed and occupied from the first to the fourth centuries AD (Quinnell 1986: 120). However, the occurrence of Cordoned ware and in some cases South Western Decorated ware at a number of sites suggests that the form may have begun as early as the second century BC, if not some time before. Certainly court-yard houses are best paralleled with sites assumed to date from this period elsewhere in the northern Atlantic zone (Hencken 1933: 278–83: fig. 12).

The layout of courtyard houses is directly comparable with the assumed hierar-chical organisation of internal space recognised at Atlantic roundhouses, wheel-house and related cellular forms in Scotland (Foster 1989a,b). Sites in both areas contain carefully demarcated areas of space, presumably used for clearly defined activities, set around a more open central area, entry to which is controlled by one entrance. Certain cells have better finished masonry or evidence of corbelling further distinguishing them from each other, while access to the largest and presum-ably dominant space is most usually located directly opposite the main entrance.

Further constructional similarities can be recognised. At Chysauster House 6, for example, in the northern intra-mural passage (marked as D and B on Figure 6.18), the remains of corbelling can be seen similar to the ground floor intra-mural chambers of complex Atlantic Scottish roundhouses. This same elongated chamber leads via a paved and stepped entrance to a further, circular, intra-mural cell which was also once corbelled (marked C on diagram). The basal courses in many intra-mural chambers at Chysauster are composed at least partly of large orthostats. In the 'head' room of Building 5 these increase in size from the sides to the centre opposite the entrance where a tall pointed slab is located – a feature paralleled in a number of cellular settlements in Scotland. In Building 6 the 'head' room also incorporates several box features in its floor.

Courtyard houses incorporate features seen in both complex Atlantic roundhouses and later cellular structures, implying that the organisation and experience of domestic life in both areas was similar. The similarities are, of course, not close enough to claim that they are the result of direct cultural contacts or the movement of populations between these zones. The existence of cellular drystone forms along the north Atlantic coastline could have developed independently, simply as a way of coping with exposed and, perhaps, increasingly harsh conditions at the turn of the millennium. Equally, the fact that a range of domestic functions was common to the majority of such settlements partially explains their parallel development.

However, the restricted western distribution of courtyard houses implies there was some level of maritime contact between west Cornwall and the Scilly Isles. The fact that examples in Scilly and western Cornwall are similar to each other without being identical is comparable to the occurrence of related though distinct drystone traditions within Atlantic Scotland; it is impossible to view the development of courtyard house forms on Scilly and western Cornwall as unrelated events, yet there is little evidence for material contacts between the areas.[13] It remains a fact that there is nothing comparable to the courtyard-house form known elsewhere in England; the only parallels are to be found along the Atlantic coasts amongst the mass of unstudied drystone sites in north-west Wales, the drystone settlements of Atlantic Scotland, and potentially the drystone *cashel* and *clochan* traditions of western Ireland. Cellular type structures dating to the end of the first millennium BC are also found in Armorica but these seem to be mainly, though not perhaps exclusively, associated with salt production.

There is a diverse array of drystone structures present in Scilly and western Cornwall but they remain largely unstudied and unrecorded. An impression of the potential significance of some of these structures can be gleaned from the excavations carried out at Nornour and Little Bay on the Scilly Isles. At Nornour, eleven drystone buildings were found eroding out of coastal sand dunes (Dudley 1967; Butcher 1970, 1978; Figure 6.20) and the conglomeration of buildings revealed evidence of more than a millennium of occupation and modification, radiocarbon dated from the middle of the second millennium BC up until the early Roman period (Butcher 1978). The dating of the construction of individual structures is difficult, but a number of elements, such as the occurrence of stone-lined pits and tanks, can be paralleled with drystone settlements similarly dating from the Bronze Age to the first millennium AD in Atlantic Scotland.

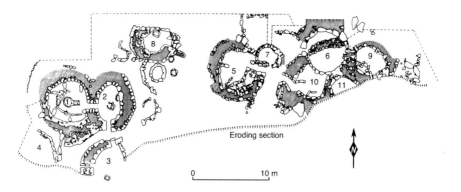

Figure 6.20 Nornour site plan, Isles of Scilly (after Butcher 1978: fig. 6).

In particular, the radial divisions in two houses (Houses 1 and 5) are reminiscent of wheelhouse settlements. When excavated both buildings provided evidence of Iron Age ceramics (op. cit. 71) while the chambers in House 1 produced a large quantity of exotic Roman metal objects and coins spanning the period AD 70 to AD 380. Roman objects were found exclusively within Houses 1 and 2 and included enamelled brooches, bracelets, finger rings, glass beads, coins, decorative studs, a bronze spoon and a chisel (Butcher 1978: 65). In the first report (Dudley 1967) it was suggested that the brooches and other bronze objects were made on the site, but Butcher has called to attention the absence of evidence for manufacturing (Butcher 1978: 54) and has instead produced a tantalising alternative explanation for the presence of so many trinkets: that they are offerings at a shrine visited by passing mariners of the early first millennium AD. The objects come from a diverse range of sources throughout England, Wales and the continent, leading Butcher to suggest 'that Nornour was visited over a period of at least 150 years (the date-range of the main groups of brooches being *c*. AD 70–220) by people bringing offerings made on the main sea-routes from the northern ports of Gaul to the west and north of Britain' (op. cit. 65). Butcher's explanation fits the evidence from the site better than the metalworking interpretation, particularly given the fact that Roman finds were wholly absent from the rest of the site.

A similar settlement featuring conjoined roundhouses, one of which had radial divisions and stone features closely paralleled in House 1 at Nornour, was excavated at Little Bay (Neal 1983). Unlike Nornour, however, no evidence for Iron Age or Roman occupation was recovered, finds consisted of indigenous gritty ceramics and stone objects, and, crucially, radiocarbon determinations taken from the lower and higher levels of the deposit suggested an occupation entirely within the second millennium BC. Extensive evidence of Bronze Age activity was also obtained from Nornour but was thought to pre-date the construction of the roundhouses. Bearing this in mind it seems likely that the evidence for later Iron Age and Roman activity at Nornour represented a major re-occupation and re-use of an essentially Bronze

Age site. Evidence for Bronze Age activity may have been lacking from internal fittings, such as the radial chambers in House 1, because they had been cleared out prior to re-use − although the occurrence of Iron Age ceramics in some units at Nornour confirm occupation continued into this period, and this occupation is likely to have included the construction of new elements at the settlement.

Whatever their exact dating, at the very least the layout and form of Nornour and Little Bay indicate a use and delimitation of social and domestic space similar to that seen on other later prehistoric drystone settlements in the northern Atlantic zone. The fact remains that the drystone settlements of the northern Atlantic seaboard represent indigenous traditions of settlement construction that are broadly similar to each other and have little to do with continental La Tène or later Roman architectural influences. However, the development of courtyard houses throughout the first few centuries AD, and the re-use of sites such as Nornour, may reflect the growing impact and importance of maritime contacts with the expanding Roman world, particularly given the very restricted western 'maritime' distribution of these sites and their close association with lodes of tin and gold. These maritime routes likely had a long pedigree but are more archaeologically visible in the Roman period due to the occurrence of exotic artefacts. For example, the Dressel 1 amphora base from Carn Euny (Christie 1978) may be a reflection of such contacts.

Atlantic Iron Age settlement in Wales

Before considering the evidence from Armorica, some mention should be made of developments in Wales. The natural barrier of the Cambrian mountain range divides the country into two main lowland zones, an Atlantic coastal zone on one side, and a zone of valleys, the Welsh Marches, on the eastern side. The existence of contrasting socio-economic systems in each zone throughout the Iron Age further emphasises this geographical division; in the hillfort dominated Marches zone the trend is towards large fortified (community) settlements, many over 6 hectares in size, while in the west, in common with other northern Atlantic areas, the landscape is dominated by small strongly defended homesteads, the vast majority of which are under 1.2 ha[14] (Figure 6.21).

The Iron Age settlement patterns of the south-western zone, from the Usk valley to Pembrokeshire, can be most closely paralleled with those of south-west England. A similar range of sites exists including promontory forts, multiple enclosure forms, and univallate enclosures (Williams and Mytum 1998). Several coastal promontory forts have been partially examined, mainly in early antiquarian cuttings, and although dating evidence from their limited material assemblages is lacking they would seem to be analogous in form and features to examples found elsewhere in the Atlantic zone (cf. Baring-Gould *et al.* 1899; Wainwright 1971a). The dominant settlement type throughout the second half of the first millennium BC is the univallate enclosure delimited by an earthen or stone rampart. Due to the fact that during the sixth to the fourth centuries BC settlement appears to occur mainly in defensible locations such as hilltops or inland promontories, sites of this earlier period are widely referred to as hillforts (Williams 1988; Davies 1995; Williams and Mytum 1998).

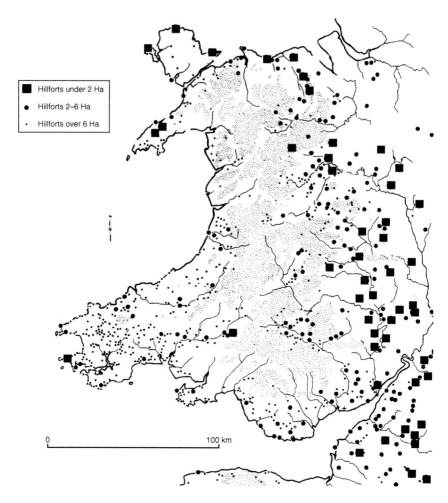

Figure 6.21 Distribution of Iron Age enclosures in Wales (after Davies 1995: fig. 35.1).

However, the majority of these sites, at under 2 hectares, are quite small and often only consist of a single enclosing rampart, making it perhaps more appropriate to refer to them simply as enclosed settlements (similar in many respects to enclosure forms found elsewhere in the Atlantic zone).

Castell Henllys in Pembrokeshire is one such site considered by its excavator to be a hillfort, but at just over 1 hectare in size, is perhaps better regarded as a defended enclosure (Mytum 1999). A long and complex sequence of occupation has been identified, beginning in the fifth century BC, which features a number of elements that can be paralleled with enclosure forms elsewhere in the Atlantic zone. At least twelve roundhouse structures have been excavated, though they were certainly not all contemporary, surrounded by an enclosure bank with an elaborate entrance passageway featuring two guard chambers and incorporating a massive stone wall which survived up to 1 m in height. In a later phase the entrance was extended out to connect to an outer bank creating an effect similar to that seen at other Atlantic drystone sites such as Chûn Castle in Cornwall, and Cahercommaun, Co. Clare, Ireland, as well as at a number of hillforts in the Welsh Borderlands and Marches (Cunliffe 1991: 337–9, fig. 14.15). The outer line of defences to the north of the enclosure consisted of a stone-built *chevaux-de-frise*, some eight to nine stones deep, which taken in combination with the elaborate entrance arrangements suggest that monumentality and display were important concerns for the builders of Castell Henllys. The finds from the site are indicative – in Atlantic terms – of some level of status consisting of some glass beads, part of a shale bracelet, a few iron pieces, bronze slag and a massive sling-shot hoard. Atlantic Wales is more or less aceramic, similar to Ireland, but a few stamped sherds were recovered from Castell Henllys that can be most closely paralleled with forms in south-west England. The site was abandoned sometime in the first century BC or AD and was later re-used as part of a Romano-British farm occupied up until the fourth century AD (Mytum 1999).

A general move to lower valley locations can be traced from the third century BC onwards, broadly contemporary with the settlement shift seen in south-west England, during which time a proliferation of small univallate enclosures, known locally as *raths*, were constructed.[15] Similar to the rounds of south-west England, a number of Welsh *raths* were occupied in the Roman period, but in contrast to the English enclosures, the Welsh examples have all provided clear evidence of construction prior to the Roman period. The most well known and most fully excavated example of the Welsh *rath* form is Walesland Rath in Pembrokeshire (Wainwright 1971), a univallate oval enclosure constructed sometime in the third century BC, if not earlier, and occupied up until the third century AD (Figure 6.22). The site is comparable in scale and appearance with examples in south-west England, particularly Threemilestone Round, Cornwall. At least six circular houses were identified, several of which were re-built many times, while alignments of post-holes located just behind the rampart were considered to be four and six-poster granary structures. Multiple enclosure sites comparable to those from eastern Cornwall and Devon also appear to have been common. Excavated examples include Harding's Down West Fort in Glamorganshire (Hogg 1974) which revealed evidence for occupation in the latter part of the pre-Roman Iron Age. The promontory site of The Knave, also Glamorganshire, is more likely to be a heavily eroded multiple enclosure fort (*contra* Williams 1939) and interestingly also produced pottery forms very similar to South Western Decorated wares. A well-dated sequence of enclosures at Llawhaden in south-west Dyfed provides some evidence of moves towards the construction of small but heavily defended sites from the second century BC (Williams 1988; Williams and Mytum 1998); the enclosures at Woodside, Dan-y-Coed, and Drim can be considered *raths* but they feature massively constructed enclosing ramparts ranging from 5 to almost 9 m in thickness (Figure 6.22).

Influences derived from both the Atlantic and the Welsh Marches area are evident in south-west Wales. The occurrence of four-poster granary structures on almost all

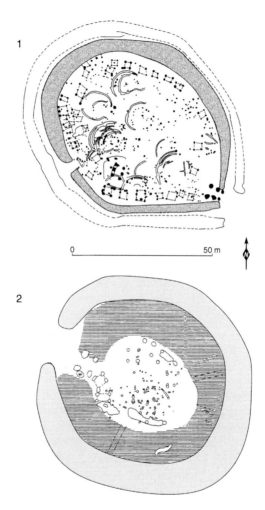

Figure 6.22 Welsh *raths*: (1) Walesland Rath (after Wainwright 1971; Cunliffe 1991: fig. 13.13); (2) Drim Camp (after Williams 1988: fig. 8).

the sites that have been excavated suggest the existence of economic practices similar to those seen further east, as does the occurrence of banjo type enclosures such as Pen y Coed in Carmarthenshire (Murphy 1985; Williams and Mytum 1998: 126–7, fig. 78). Exchange and production appears to have been on a local and regional basis but a range of finds suggest the influence of Atlantic routes. Finds from a site located in a sand dune at Merthyr Mawr Warren on the Ogmore estuary, Glamorganshire (Fox 1927) suggest the location may have had an importance in articulating maritime trade routes (Savory 1990). A unique 'Braubach' style sherd found here (Savory 1976a) is very similar to the stamp ornamented Armorican imports of the fifth century BC from Carn Euny, Cornwall (Christie 1978: fig. 34.4). The site has also produced three Early La Tène bronze brooches and Late La Tène Armorican coins (Davies 1995: 691). Savory (1990) has cited a pot from Bacon Hole, Glamorganshire (Savory 1974), a mould from Worm's Head, Glamorganshire, the La Tène I or II bracelets from Coygan Camp, along with the Clynnog collar, Caernarvonshire (Savory 1976a) as further evidence of Atlantic maritime contacts. As in the other Atlantic areas it appears that the direct importation of exotic objects was rare – they may have been of limited relevance to Atlantic societies – but there is at least some evidence to suggest that objects may have arrived via Atlantic routes.

Drystone hut-circle settlements of varying complexity, often with associated field systems, are found in considerable numbers in north-west Wales. The recognition of general settlement trends that can be compared with the rest of the northern Atlantic zone is difficult due to the complete lack of a reliable chronological framework (Smith C. A. 1974, 1977; Kelly 1988, 1991; Smith G. 1999). Diagnostic artefacts, especially those of pre-Roman Iron Age date, are extremely rare from this area. Smith (1977) has attempted a morphological classification of the enclosed stone hut sites[16] but there is a lot of blurring of distinctions between classess, and he is only partly successful in suggesting that his Class Ib sites represent stock stations[17] (due to the large amount of unroofed space) while all the others represent mixed farms of differing levels of wealth and status. Smith applies the highest status to sites that display 'nucleation' (Class IIc are seen as his richest type), but it could equally be argued that sites with only one stone-built roundhouse were households of the elite – the study of settlement plans is only one element of determining social status and cannot be considered in isolation. Smith (1997: 49–50) offers a very wide chronological range for these sites from the fourth millennium BC to the middle of the first millennium AD. He suggests that the round enclosures date from the fourth to the late first millennium BC, while the appearance of sub-rectangular buildings alongside round sites occurs from the late first millennium BC and continues throughout the Romano-British period. It is believed by many authors that the unenclosed, upland stone hut sites are of Bronze Age date while the enclosed forms belong to the Iron Age (Cunliffe 1991: 269–71; Kelly 1991; Davies 1995).

At a very general level, the projected development of drystone settlement in north-west Wales is similar to the sequences seen elsewhere in the northern Atlantic, and is perhaps most closely comparable with the drystone *cashels* of Ireland. In terms of simple comparison, Smith's Class IIa appear similar in plan to the *cashels* with associated *clochan* structures seen in Co. Kerry especially those along the Dingle Peninsula. A number of forms also have close parallels with the courtyard houses of south-west England.

There are other settlement types in north-west Wales which further complicate an already diverse and largely undated settlement record. Small multivallate enclosures are seen in Atlantic coastal areas such as Castell Odo in Caernarvonshire (Alcock 1960), which starts as several circular timber houses from the fifth to the fourth centuries BC and then develops in the fourth to third centuries BC into a complex, enclosed ringfort best compared to those seen in south-west Wales. Unusually, for western Britain, north-west Wales has some large hill-top settlements featuring *c.* 20 to 80 circular stone huts usually totally enclosed by stone ramparts such as Tre'r Ceiri, Garn Boduan and Conway Mountain, all in Caernarvonshire (Hogg 1960). Unfortunatley, these sites remain undated, but they most likely belong to the Iron Age and represent evidence of articulation with the communities of the hillfort dominated zone of the Welsh Borderlands.

Armorican Iron Age settlement *c.* 750–56 BC

Similar to the distinctive nature of the south-western English settlement record, the Iron Age sites of Armorica are widely perceived to represent a separate cultural tradition (Giot 1960a: 15; Duval 1990: 279). It is common in French publications, for example, to refer to Armorica as being only *superficiellement celtisé* or for a distinction to be specifically made between *peuples armoricain* and indigenous populations from the rest of France.[18] The western part of the peninsula, west of the river Rance, will be the focus here, although from time to time evidence from the rest of the Armorican peninsula will be considered.[19] This area is often referred to as Brittany, or more correctly perhaps, as Lesser Armorica (cf. Duval 1984, 1990), and includes the departments of Finistère, Côtes-d'Armor, Morbihan, and the western part of Ille-et-Vilaine. The area can be defined as a distinct unit archaeologically from the distributions of souterrains, stelae, decorated pottery, and promontory forts, which taken together form a cultural area more closely paralleled with south-western England than with any area of France. Although the separate identity of Armorica is most visible in the western part of the peninsula it is not restricted to this zone; similar cultural traits, particularly in the latter part of the Iron Age (*c.* 300–56 BC), define the whole peninsula extending east into lower Normandy and south-east into the departments of the Loire.

Enclosures

As in south-western England, the most common form of site ascribed to the Iron Age in Armorica are simple circular or rectilinear enclosures, interpreted, from the evidence of the excavations carried out to date, as stand-alone indigenous farmsteads (Le Bihan 1984; Menez 1994; Leroux *et al.* 1999). The average sizes of these farming enclosures, ranging from between 0.2 to 1 hectare (Giot 1995: 271), are comparable with western British enclosures, suggesting that there were corresponding levels of social organisation in existence on either side of the Channel and that the basic social unit was the family or extended family (Cunliffe 1990: 248). The actual recognition of domestic units as distinct from utilitarian structures within Armorican settlements is often very difficult. However, on excavation, the recognition of one to three domestic dwellings is most common although it is possible that in some cases there are several houses or domestic cells in existence (Le Bihan *et al.* 1990: 98).

The Armorican landscape appears to have been densely filled during the Iron Age due to the sheer amount of enclosures identified from aerial prospecting. The majority of the enclosures excavated date to the last few centuries BC creating the view that there was an expansion in settlement at this time, most probably accompanying an intensification in agriculture (Le Bihan 1984; Le Bihan *et al.* 1990; Giot 1995; Menez 1996). However, if we accept the convincing arguments that souterrains were always associated with settlements (Giot 1973, 1990, 1995: 286–295; Giot *et al.* 1976), then the dense distribution of over 300 souterrains in Brittany could reflect, given their dating, a densely filled but well-organised rural landscape during earlier periods of the Iron Age as well[20] (Figure 6.23).

The type of enclosure devices employed range across banks, ditches, walls and palisades in isolation or combined together. Univallate enclosures are the norm but double, split and, in some cases, multivallate examples have been recorded. The sequences and internal organisation of Armorican sites are difficult to assess due to a lack of datable material and often, more ominously, a lack of stratigraphy. Excavations and, in turn, site plans, appear as a mass of post-holes, pits, grooves and ditches which are often extremely difficult to disentangle and attribute to particular phases. The site that provides more than a confused plan of all periods is rare, and often all excavators can do is offer probable sequences, if indeed any are offered at all. This obviously

Figure 6.23 Iron Age farming enclosures and souterrains (after Le Bihan *et al.* 1990: fig. 1).

makes the recognition of changes in site morphology between sites over time all the more difficult to recognise.

There are a number of well-built stone structures in Armorica but it is not possible to define a tradition of stone architecture such as those known in Atlantic Scotland, Ireland, north Wales, and, to a lesser extent, south-west England. On saying this, the role of stone in the Armorican Iron Age has been very much under-estimated. In a recent study of all the currently available complete house plans from Armorican sites, 57 per cent of the sample included some element of stone walling (Menez *et al.* 1990: 122). The study also calculated that there are currently ten plans per 25,000 m^2 for sites with post-holes and wattle and daub construction compared to thirteen plans per 4,000 m^2 for buildings that feature at least some walls of stone (ibid.).

At a very broad level enclosed sites in Armorica can be said to fall into two categories: those with rectilinear plans and those with circular/curvilinear plans. There is as yet no systematic chronology for such sites, but it has long been a widely held assumption that sites with curvilinear enclosures tend to be prehistoric while rectilinear sites more often provide Gallo-Roman dates (Giot 1995: 271). Unfortunately, the distinction between these two types of site are rarely clear-cut on the ground and the excavated evidence, largely driven by rescue and commercial concerns, is sporadic to say the least, particularly regarding the investigation of circular and oval forms.

A recent overview of enclosure forms in western Armorica (Finistère) revealed there are a number of circular enclosures with diameters less than 60 m, which remain entirely unexamined (Maguer 1996: 103). This is surprising when one considers that it is Breton rounds that are most often stated to be comparable in size and shape to the rounds of south-west England (Cunliffe 1990). These circular enclosures exist alongside a range of more numerous quadrangular enclosures, the majority of which are around 1 hectare in size (Sanquer 1981; Reddé 1985). Significantly, Maguer (1996: 107) notes that the sizes and shapes of enclosures in Finistère are much closer to those found in western Britain and Ireland than anything from the continent.

Circular and oval enclosures also form a significant but largely unstudied group in northern Armorica (Haute Bretagne), where over 100 examples are known, the majority of which share the same basic dimensions between 0.5 and 1 hectare (Langouët 1990: Figure 6.24). Interestingly the finds recovered from rectilinear enclosures in this area tend to correspond to the Gallo-Roman period (*Terra sigilatta* ceramics, *tegulae* and Dressel 1a amphorae) while those from curvilinear examples are more likely to represent indigenous pre-Roman Iron Age activity (Arbousse-Bastide 1993: 95). In particular, the absence of Dressel 1a amphorae from curvilinear sites could be taken as a strong indication of their pre-first century BC origins.

Contrary to the north of Haute-Bretagne, where 51 per cent of enclosures are considered to be curvilinear (Langouët and Daire 1990), sites with quadrangular plans are thought to be the more dominant form in southern and eastern Armorica (Naas 1999: 54), perhaps reflecting this area's closer geographical and cultural relationship with west-central Europe. The curvilinear form is still relatively common, however, and there are a number of sites with relatively regular oval plans, again usually around 1 hectare in size (Figure 6.25). Significantly, Naas (1999: 56) makes a

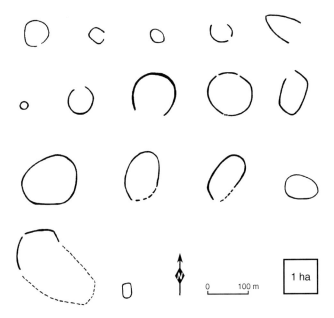

Figure 6.24 Curvilinear enclosures in la Haute Bretagne: Type A1 (after Arbousse-Bastide 1993: figs. 7 and 11).

distinction between sites with regular geometric rectilinear plans incorporating right-angles (Figure 6.26), and those with less regular quadrangular/rectilinear plans (Figure 6.27). On the evidence of excavated examples and surface collections to date, Naas claims that the former appear to date to the Gallo-Roman period while the latter commonly provide evidence of prehistoric La Tène occupation.

While the excavated evidence in the study area does not contradict such a view, the current data-set is rather restricted because excavation has occurred exclusively on quadrangular enclosures – no oval or curvilinear sites have yet been investigated. Nineteen quadrangular enclosures in the area have been examined, although of these none can be said to have been fully excavated (Mueret 1999: 35–42). Nonetheless, three-quarters of these enclosures provided evidence of occupation spanning the third century BC to the second century AD, and were significantly mainly of the irregular variety[21] (Mueret 1999: 35–42).

Those sites with more regular geometric plans produced Gallo-Roman dates, for example, Graibusson in Corps-Nuds, Ille-et-Vilaine (Meuret 1999: 38) and Champ d'Aviation in Plumeliau, Morbihan (Naas 1999: 56), were built in the second half of the first century BC and abandoned by the end of the first century AD. The majority, however, appear to have been established and occupied from the first century AD onwards, as at Reiters, Kerropert in Pluméliau, and Val en Availles-sur-Seiche (Meuret 1999: 35–40), alongside Phase 1 of La Dérmadais in Porcaro (Olivier Blin

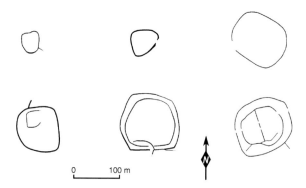

Figure 6.25 Curvilinear enclosures in southern and eastern Armorica (after Naas 1999: fig. 28).

in Fromentin-Simoni 1993), Saint-Hilaire in Plumeliau, Morbihan, and La Villejames in Guérande, Loire-Atlantique (unpub.).

Bearing in mind the considerable diversity of undated enclosure forms, the work carried out to date suggests that, at a broad level, irregular quadrangular and curvilinear enclosures are more likely to date to the prehistoric period, while enclosures with more regularly laid out geometric plans commonly correspond with first millennium AD Gallo-Roman occupational evidence (Maguer 1996: 111; Meuret 1999: 45; Naas 1999: 56). If this observation is true the general development of Armorican enclosures during could be said to broadly correspond with the settlement sequences seen in other northern Atlantic regions.

However, caution is necessary; while this observation may serve as a rule of thumb in the field, it is far from being a strict morphological classification because it does not cover the full range of enclosure forms encountered and exceptions to this general pattern of development occur. Gallo-Roman layers are extremely rare on

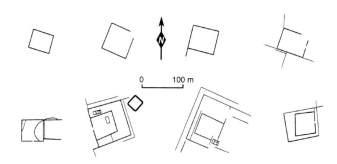

Figure 6.26 Enclosures with regular geometric rectilinear plans incorporating right-angles (after Naas 1999: fig. 32).

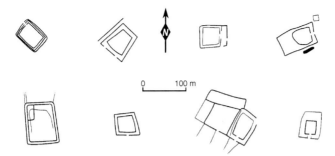

Figure 6.27 Enclosures with less regular quadrangular/rectilinear plans (after Naas 1999: fig. 33).

oval sites but do exist, while evidence of construction and occupation in the Late La Tène, from the second to the first centuries BC, comes from oval enclosures at Penvillers in Quimper, Finistère (Le Bihan 1997) and Jeusseries in Rétiers, Ille-et-Villaine (Meuret 1999: 35–6). In addition, there are a range of enclosures that incorporate both curvilinear and rectilinear elements which have so far escaped investigation (Leroux *et al.* 1999). Such sites are likely to reflect multi-period or long-term occupation, making general observations about their dating impossible in the absence of excavation.

The occurrence of a wide range of quadrangular enclosures, built from the third century BC onwards alongside oval forms, is perhaps indicative of Armorica's unique position directly between the west-central European area of influence and the Atlantic. Certainly, Armorica was primarily an Atlantic area in the Late Bronze Age, but one clearly open to west-central European influences. As we shall see, throughout the Iron Age these influences appear to increase as Armorica is drawn into the west-central European world, and particularly the influence of the advancing Roman Empire. It comes perhaps as no surprise that the closest parallels to other Atlantic areas come from the western Atlantic facing part of the peninsula. The frequency of quadrangular forms appears to increase the further east one travels along the peninsula. Indeed, enclosure forms larger than 1 hectare appear to be rare in the west (promontory locations excepted), with larger and more complex enclosure forms more common in the eastern part of the peninsula, closer to west-central European forms (Naas 1999: 54). For example, ten trapezoidal enclosures were identified in south-eastern Armorica of a type unknown in the west, but which can be closely paralleled with sites dated to the Late La Tène further east in northern Gaul (op. cit. 55–6: fig. 31).

Having briefly considered the general enclosure forms attention will now turn to the excavated evidence. The evidence from Armorica is piecemeal and fragmentary because it comes primarily from rescue excavations. Evidence from the end of the Hallstatt and the Early and Middle La Tène periods (*c.* 700–120 BC) is especially rare.

As such it is difficult to construct a meaningful overview of the settlement archaeology, and much of the study has to be done on a site-to-site basis.

Settlements of le Premier Age du Fer: 750–450 BC (Hallstatt C and D)

Similar to the situation for the Late Bronze Age, structural evidence for the beginning of the Iron Age (*c.* 750–450 BC) is lacking; however, large-scale excavations at Mez-Notariou on the Island of Ushant, have revealed an unexpectedly dense concentration of ten orthogonal post-hole structures, found within an excavated area of just 3,000 square m, that date to *c.* 650–450 BC (Le Bihan and Robic 1988, 1990, 1993; Le Bihan and Villard 2001). The site was dated from the massive ceramic assemblage recovered, which consisted of *c.* 50,000 sherds from the end of the Late Bronze Age to the beginning of the Early La Tène. Less than 1 per cent of this assemblage consisted of Late La Tène or Gallo-Roman forms. The buildngs at Mez-Notariou are also distinctive, and differ from buildings seen elsewhere in Armorica, or France for that matter. They are constructed from three to four concentric rings of post-holes and appear to have an average size of around 30 square m – as such they have more in common with circular house forms seen elsewhere in the Atlantic zone.

At present this site is unique and has no parallels, making it difficult to assess the wider social significance of the dense concentration of buildings discovered in the situation elsewhere in Armorica. It seems likely that this uniqueness owes much to the site's location at the most north-westerly point of the Armorican peninsula, marking the entrance to the English Channel. The island would have been an obligatory point of passage for ships using Atlantic sea routes and it is possible that this opened up the community at Mez-Notariou to a wide range of cultural contacts, though, as is common on Atlantic sites, evidence for such exchange is difficult to prove as no imported or exotic objects have yet been found. The evidence for a village-like habitation at Mez-Notariou represents earlier evidence for settlement nucleation in Brittany than was previously believed. Ultimately, the findings demonstrate the limited nature of the Armorican settlement record in that it takes only one site to completely challenge previously held assumptions.

Early and Middle La Tène settlement: 450–120 BC

There is very little occupational evidence that can be dated to the Early and Middle La Tène periods in Armorica, but some evidence comes from three stone-built farmsteads in Brittany: Kersigneau in Finistère, and Talhouët and Kerlande, both in the Morbihan.

Kersigneau is a stone-built oval enclosure, some 36 m in diameter, which contains at least four buildings and two rock-cut souterrains (Giot *et al.* 1989, 1991: Figure 6.28). It is clear that there were several phases of construction and re-organisation; for example, the enclosing wall appears to have been built in two phases which do not join neatly together (bearing in mind the north-west portion of the site has been disturbed). The western house structure was built at the end of the Early La Tène and was used throughout the Middle La Tène. Such a dating would

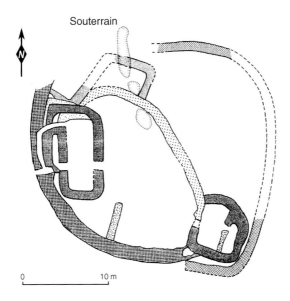

Souterrain

0   10 m

Figure 6.28 Kersigneau in Saint Jean en Plouhinec, Finistère (after Giot *et al.* 1989, 1991; Giot 1995: 268).

mean that the western part of the enclosing wall, at least, was constructed in the Early La Tène. More Early La Tène activity comes from the north-western quadrant where there are the remains of two stone-built sub-rectangular house forms associated with the two souterrains, both of which were out of use and filled in by the Middle La Tène. Most interestingly, the enclosing wall is 1.8 m thick and features a secondary intra-mural passage built into its western side which provides a protected entrance into a sub-rectangular house structure. This feature obviously invites comparisons with intra-mural passages seen at a number of Scottish and Irish drystone sites, and indeed the overall layout of the Kersigneau recalls that of an Irish *cashel* or Cornish round.

The massive stone-built oval enclosure at Talhouët also features internal buildings dated to the Middle La Tène on the basis of the recovered ceramic assemblage (Tanguy 1988). The centre of the enclosure consists of two stone-built dwellings, one circular and one rectangular, with an accompanying square yard (Figure 6.29). This unit is interpreted by the excavator as a farmstead with the surrounding empty space used to keep livestock (ibid. 79). Both the circular and rectangular buildings are interpreted as domestic dwellings due to the occurrence in each of stone-lined hearths. The buildings are built from solid stone walls consisting of outer coursed faces with a rubble fill, measuring *c.* 1.4 m thick and surviving up to 0.6 m. The interior areas of each, at 23 m² for the circular building and 28 m² for the rectangular one, are also comparable. These internal areas are less than the average size of domestic farmstead dwellings in the Late La Tène, and Tanguy (1998: 79) notes that they are as such closer in size to the Iron Age dwellings in Britain. He goes

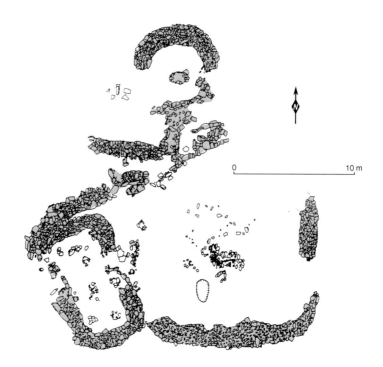

Figure 6.29 The central structures within the enclosure of Talhouët, Morbihan (after Le Bihan *et al.* 1990: fig. 11).

on to suggest that the similarity of the circular dwelling to house forms seen in Britain is striking. This may be true, particularly if one compares the structure with some of the stone-built examples in south-west England, but it would be difficult to attach any real cultural significance to this simple observation at this stage. In any case, the rectangular structure has little in common with British examples, and if anything its closest parallels lie with sites in the Paris Basin and west-central Europe.

Occupation at the double stone-built enclosure of Kerlande is thought to date to the Early La Tène period (Lecorner 1973: 70) and consists of a rectangular enclosure, measuring 45 by 31 m, partially attached on its eastern side to an oval enclosure measuring 40 by 32 m (Figure 6.30). The co-existence of these two forms at one site obviously warns against classifications based purely on morphology. However, it is unclear whether the enclosures were contemporary and excavation at their intersection was inconclusive due to disturbance. The excavator argued that the rectangular enclosure is the oldest due to its fragmentary state of repair, but it is equally possible that it was simply more heavily disturbed or served a different function (perhaps as a stock enclosure) and was not as massively built as the circular enclosure – with this in mind it is interesting to note that the only internal structural evidence came from the circular enclosure.

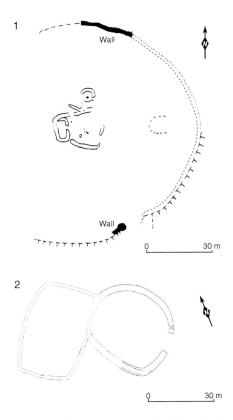

Figure 6.30 Early and Middle La Tène enclosures: (1) Talhouët, Morbihan (after Le Bihan *et al.* 1990: fig. 10); (2) Kerlande, Morbihan (after Lecornec 1973: fig. 1).

These three sites obviously represent an insufficient sample to argue for a related cultural tradition of stone architecture, but it is interesting to note that all three belong to a pre-Late La Tène horizon in the western part of Brittany. There are a number of similar unexcavated enclosures with ramparts composed entirely of stone such as at Bois d'Elliat, Eliant and Plogastel-Saint-Germain, both in Finistère (Maguer 1996: 108). Giot *et al* (1991: 104) suggest that stone-built sites must have been much more frequent than the current evidence suggests. They argue that stone-built sites on the Armorican peninsula may be more difficult to recognise compared to their wooden and earthen counterparts because the former have been subject to such extensive stone robbing since the Gallo-Roman period that they have become virtually undetectable. Such a view would run contrary to the assumed better survival rate and visibility of sites constructed of stone known in other Atlantic regions. However, Brittany differs from these regions in that it has become a region of intensive agricultural productivity. The same agricultural activity that has heavily disturbed the sites constructed of wood and earth in the region may have dictated the complete removal of stone-built forms – so while the truncated remains of the former are still visible from aerial prospection there would be little other than, at most, a slight spread of stones to highlight a stone-built site. There were apparently no foundation trenches dug for the stone walls at any of the three sites examined above: Kerlande and Talhouët were built directly on top of soil deposits, while Kersigneau appears to have been more stably constructed directly onto a natural rock sub-surface. Certainly all three sites were in an extremely poor state of repair on discovery, with stone walling barely surviving to two or three courses in height (only *c.* 0.3 m high and covered in vegetation; at Kersigneau and Kerlande there was little trace of the existence of the Early La Tène structures before excavation took place). It is also important that these three sites are situated on currently uncultivated moorland and yet are still in a poor state of repair – any such sites on modern productive cultivable land would surely have been dismantled long ago. The only other area where stone construction survives is amongst the predominantly Late La Tène sites of the coastal zones (discussed below) and this is presumably due to the excellent preservation provided in many cases by a protective covering of sand and, to a lesser extent, because there are few agricultural pressures on such a zone.

Earthen enclosures dating from the Late Bronze Age to the Middle La Tène are not well known in Armorica. However, a number of enclosures with extensive Late La Tène occupation have provided evidence for earlier occupation. These sites include Kerlaéron, Quimper (Le Bihan 1985); Polvern-Hennebont (Le Bihan 1990); Pouilladou-Prat (Bardel 1988; Le Goffic 1992); Bellevue-Augan (Hinguant *et al.* 1997; Fromentin-Simoni 1993); Paule (Arramond and Menez 1992); and Le Haut Chesney, Hede (Fromentin-Simoni 1993; Beguin 1995). Unfortunately, although earlier occupation has been identified from these sites, it is rarely associated with structural evidence. There can be little doubt, however, that the isolated farmstead enclosure was the main unit of settlement during the earlier part of the Iron Age. The lack of evidence may be simply due to the concentration of excavation on quadrangular enclosures, and it is perhaps significant in this respect that Kerlande, Talhouët and Kersigneau all have oval plans comparable to those Iron Age enclosures encountered elsewhere in the Atlantic west.

One site which has provided Early and Middle La Tène structural phases is Le Boisanne à Plouër-sur-Rance, Côtes-d'Armor (Menez 1996). It is the most fully excavated and published farmstead in western Armorica and can be considered a working type-site for the region. The site does not differ greatly from typical Iron Age farmsteads found elsewhere in continental north-western Europe but the existence of a <u>souterrain</u> and distinctive decorated Armorican pottery means it can be considered fully part of the western Armorican traditions (Duval 1990: 282). It is worth quickly considering the sequence recovered from this site because it provides a full impression of the nature of an Armorican farmstead and tracks the important transition into the Late La Tène period.

Le Boissane was established as a small enclosure sometime in the sixth to the beginning of the fifth century BC.[22] Two curvilinear ditches belong to this period and enclose a single post-built domestic structure which Menez (1996: fig. 158) reconstructed as a rectangular structure even though an oval form seems more likely from the layout of the six structural post-holes discovered. Two ditched enclosures on the eastern side are interpereted, on the absence of any structural evidence, as cultivated yards or livestock enclosures (Figure 6.31). The size of the entire establishment during this phase was *c.* 1,000 square m and is best interepreted as a small but well-organised farmstead catering for a family or extended family group (Menez 1996: 187). Occupation continued with periodic expansions and re-organisations, including the construction of a souterrain, by the beginning of the fourth century BC. The overall layout of the site takes on a more compartmentalised and quadrangular appearance from the third century BC, with well-defined activity areas separated into individual enclosures by ditches and/or palisades.

During the Late La Tène, from the middle of the second century to the end of the first century BC, the farmstead continues to expand, finally enclosing *c.* 6,000 square m, an area six times greater than its first construction. There are major expansions to the west interpreted as livestock/agricultural enclosures along with the construction of three new rectangular buildings. Ramparts and ditches are abandoned during this phase and the site is divided into areas by simple palisade fences. Significantly, fields are visible for the first time during this phase, located to the west of the site and delimited by small embankments.

Equally, the material culture of the Late La Tène phase of the site is richer than the preceding periods and provides evidence for the opening up of exchange networks and outside contacts, a phenomenon which can be paralleled at many other Armorican Late La Tène farmsteads. Le Boisanne does, however, have some quite early evidence. A fragment of a Greco-Italic amphora and a sherd of grey Ampurias ware, both mid-second century BC, are unusual in an Armorican context and provide some evidence of early articulation with long-distance exchange networks. The majority of sites on the Armorican peninsula do not provide amphorae datable to before the first century BC (Galliou 1990). Le Boisanne has also produced 79 fragments of Dressel 1a or b amphorae. However, as these finds are entirely from the fill of ditches it is difficult to assess the overall importance of amphorae on the site. Other rich finds from this phase include a glass bracelet, three lignite bracelets (the nearest source being Kimmeridge shale in Dorset), a large number of millstones (indicative of agricultural intensification), and decorated pottery, the clay for which can be sourced 35 kilometres away. The farmstead falls out of use by the end of the first century BC.

The Le Boissane sequence indicates that farmstead enclosures are a form which develop as indigenous types from the late Hallstatt into the La Tène up until the Roman conquest. The expansion of the site in the Late La Tène, accompanying evidence for the construction of fields, is indicative of the expansion in agriculture envisaged at this time (see below). There is also evidence for the site becoming involved in wider trading contacts from the second century BC onwards. By the end of the first century BC, however, the site was abandoned. This abandonment can again be paralleled at other Late La Tène sites and may, as Le Bihan (1990) argues, have been related to events surrounding the Roman invasion in 56 BC. As will be briefly examined below, this abandonment precedes a major re-organisation of the Armorican landscape, including the implementation and development of urban centres, from the Augustan period onwards.

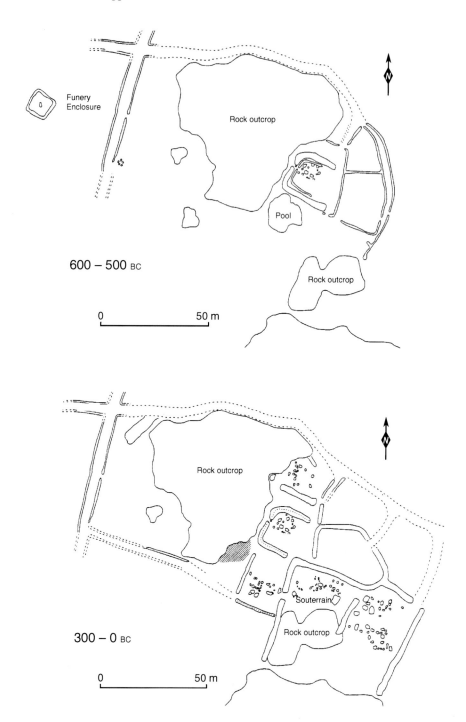

Figure 6.31 The farmstead at Le Boisanne: Phase 1 600–500 BC (top) and Phases 3 and 4 300–0 BC (bottom) (after Menez 1996: figs. 157–163).

Later La Tène settlement: expansion and complexity c. *200* BC*–56* BC

As the Le Boissane sequence indicates, there appears to have been economic expansion and diversification in the last few centuries BC (Menez 1996; Leroux *et al.* 1999). The vast majority of farmstead enclosures examined to date belong to this period: Braden I and II (Le Bihan 1984, 1987, 1988, 1990); Le Petit Coulebart; Les Champs Brunet (Menez 1994); Graibusson (Leroux 1992); Polevern-Hennebont (Le Bihan 1990); Ligne Anne, petit enciente (Meuret *et al.* 1992); l'Armorique en Plouret (Bardel, unpub); while a number of sites with evidence of earlier occupation are seen to expand in the Late La Tène: Le Boissane (Menez 1994); Pouilladou-Prat (Bardel 1988; Le Goffic 1992); and Paule (Arramond and Menez 1992).

This expansion in settlement numbers and sizes is often accompanied by evidence for the construction of organised field boundaries (Gautier *et al.* 1997). It seems likely that this phenomenon is related to the expansion of the Roman Empire in Gaul. Evidence for the intensification of agriculture and the diversification of the economy – seen through an upsurge in activities such as craft-working, metal-working, and salt production – may be a direct result of trading contacts with the advancing Roman world and its hinterland. The fact that later La Tène enclosures appear more quadrangular in plan, and are thus closer to their west-central European counterparts, supports the view of increased east-west influences and contacts at this time.

Agricultural intensification can be implied from the widespread use of four-poster granaries and silos, alongside the adoption of rotary quernstones, the latter dated in Brittany from the beginning of the second century BC when they are thought to replace saddle querns (Le Bihan *et al.* 1990: 110; Menez 1996). As we have already considered, the use of four-poster granaries and silos in the Late La Tène, reflecting a changing economy, may be a factor in the demise of the indigenous practice of using souterrains for storage. The relatively widespread occurrence of Dressel 1 amphorae and wheel turned pottery, alongside exotic items such as lignite bracelets and metalwork must be viewed within the context of long-distance contacts. Localised exchange between Armorican farmsteads also appears to increase, with finds of good quality ceramic forms, millstones, and 'salt briquetage troughs' providing clear evidence for localised exchange activity (Galliou 1990).

Further evidence for economic intensification and the increasing influence of the Roman world can be seen through the production, sometime in the first century BC, of indigenous coinages in Finistère, parts of the Côtes-d'Armor and Ille-et-Vilaine (de Jersey 1994: 76–121, fig. 63). Coins are produced according to the general conventions used elsewhere in Gaul and can be considered a graphic example of the incorporation of Armorica into Gaulish and Roman exchange networks. However, the occurrence of the distinctive *cheval androcéphale* motif exclusively on indigenous coins from Armorica demonstrates that the area retained a coherence and unity separate from the rest of Gaul (Duval 1984, 1990). The development of coinage in Armorica has been set out in detail by de Jersey (1994); the first coins are seen in lower Normandy and the lower Loire with the production of imitations of Greek and Punic imports in the late fourth to third centuries BC (op. cit. 40–53). By the middle of the second century BC indigenous forms were being produced in

Ille-et-Vilaine, Mayenne, Sarthe, and the lower Loire (op. cit. 54–73, fig. 34). Only by the first century BC, however, was production seen in western Armorica through a range of coins which have been attributed to the Osismii (op. cit. 91–2). Problems remain with the dating of issues in western Armorica, but it seems certain that production began a short time *before* the Gallic Wars (ibid.). The problems of chronology and lack of association of coins with Late La Tène settlements make comments about the wider role of coinage in western Armorican society difficult and they are best viewed here as further evidence of economic diversification in the area.

From the second century BC a number of farmsteads display evidence of craft-working areas producing a wide range of items, including ceramics, statuettes, millstones, and metal tools (Langouët 1990). The vast majority of Late La Tène farmsteads produce some evidence for the practice of metalworking usually in the form of iron slag (Le Bihan *et al.* 1990: 110). Evidence for forges comes from Kermoisan à Quimper (Le Bihan and Galliou 1974), while Braden I (Le Bihan 1990) has provided evidence for two restricted metalworking areas producing iron slag and a pair of blacksmith's clamps.

Distribution maps of Dressel 1a amphorae highlight the importance of Brittany and the re-invigoration (at least in terms of archaeological visibility) of contacts across the Channel with southern Britain (Figure 6.32). As we have seen, the major port appears to be at Hengistbury in the centre-south rather than a location in south-west England. As the evidence from Hengistbury indicates, the existence of this exchange system was relatively short-lived (Cunliffe and de Jersey 1997) because after the Caesarian conquest of Gaul a new system of trade emerges between northern France and south-east England.

The development of salt production in the Late La Tène provides further evidence of economic diversification. It would appear that salt extraction was practised from the Late Bronze Age up until the beginning of the La Tène period and then, after an apparent hiatus in the Early and Middle La Tène, production was again intense during the Late La Tène and Gallo-Roman periods (Gouletquer 1970; Tessier 1986; Gouletquer and Daire 1994: 12; Langouët *et al.* 1994: 107). The increase in salt production would have, through the preservation of foodstuffs, facilitated economic independence at individual farmsteads and increased the viability of stock raising. As a commodity salt must have been of major economic importance to Armorican Gaul, and it is tempting to tie the periods of intense salt extraction activity with the periods when east-west contacts are most evident in Armorica.[23] In support of this view many of the salt extraction sites during the Late La Tène have produced Dressel 1a amphorae.

Excavations in the coastal zone have revealed a series of stone-built oblong and sub-rectangular structures, which date to the Late La Tène and appear to be mainly, though not perhaps exclusively, involved in salt extraction.[24] Some small salt production sites are purely specialised manufacturing sites such as at Île d'Arc, Morbihan, where four simple rectangular cuttings were made into a beach; lined with clay, these functioned as furnaces and water basins for the drying of salt bricks from seawater (Daire and Langouët 1994: 22–7). Other sites are rather more substantial, consisting of one or two sub-rectangular drystone buildings, interpreted as workshops, revetted

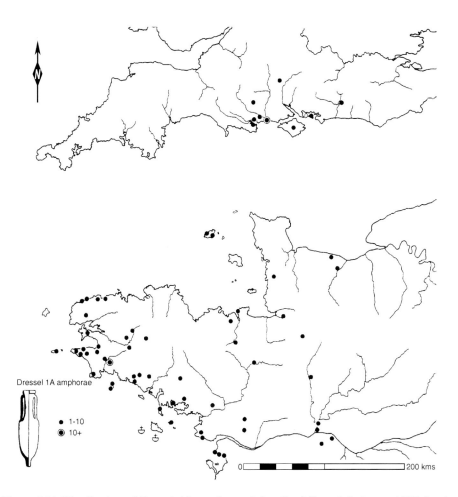

Figure 6.32 Distribution of Dressel 1A amphorae (after Cunliffe and de Jersey 1997: fig. 6; after Galliou 1982).

into coastal sand dunes as at Ilur on sud de l'île, Landrellec, the Île d'Arz, Morbihan and the Île d'Yoc'h in Landunvez, Finistère (op. cit. 15–31). Several others are altogether more complex and served as domestic dwellings as well as industrial workshops. Such sites are associated with a range of additional structures and cover much larger areas. The size of the structures varies between 35 m² to just 5 m² and they are usually visible as low walls (maximum height 1 m) around 1 to 1.5 m thick which, similar to many of the other walls we have examined, consist of two coursed faces with a rubble and/or earth fill. Buildings so delimited are interpreted as living spaces, storage areas or workshops through the presence or absence of hearths and the types of artefacts recovered. Some of these larger and more complex sites suggest the hierarchic arrangements of space but there has been too little excavation work to determine such relationships with any certainty.

A good example of the more complex form is the site of Ebihens, located on Saint-Jacut-de-la-Mer, a small island off the north coast of Brittany, which consists of several drystone structures located in two different zones referred to in the excavation report simply as Zone A and Zone B (Langouët 1989). Here buildings are delimited by low lines of stones with Zone A comprising a cluster of small sub-rectilinear structures, while about 100 m away Zone B incorporates a larger, isolated and more carefully constructed rectilinear building, termed the 'Habitat Isolé', on the neck of a nearby promontory (Figure 6.33). Almost identical sub-rectangular village arrangements, also dating to the Late La Tène, can be seen at Goulvars and Kerné, both on the Quiberon peninsula, Morbihan (Hyvert and Le Bihan 1990; Figure 6.34).

As cellular settlements located in coastal sand dunes, these sites could perhaps be compared with contemporary cellular forms found further north in the Atlantic zone. Although oblong and rectilinear plans are the norm, curvilinear structures do exist. One of the buildings at Goulvars, for example, features two co-joined corbelled cells (Menez *et al.* 1990: fig. 3.18). A number of sites also feature edge set slab hearths while wall niches have been recorded at Ebihens (Langouët 1988). However, the similarities are only very general and cannot be used to support models of cultural contacts or continuity. The Armorican sites grew out of an entirely different set of circumstances (contacts with west-central Europe) and are mainly concerned with salt production.

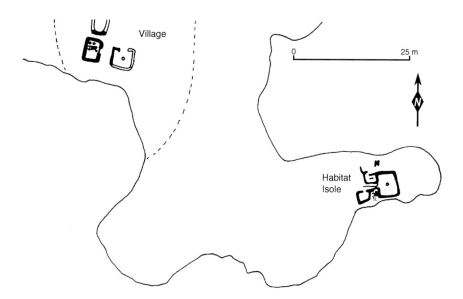

Figure 6.33 The village at Ebihens, Saint-Jacut-de-la-Mer (after Hyvert and Le Bihan 1990: fig. 2; after Langouët 1989).

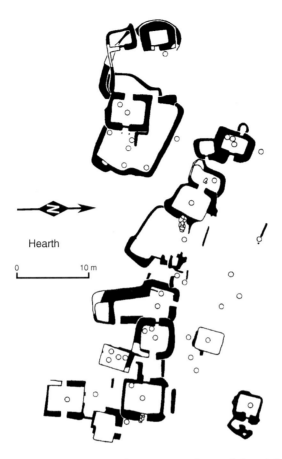

Figure 6.34 Plan of Goulvars on the Quiberon peninsula, Morbihan (after Cunliffe 1997: fig. 125; after Hyvert and Le Bihan 1990: fig. 7).

The articulation of Late La Tène contacts in Armorica

It is far from clear whether the increased west–east trading contacts apparent during the Late La Tène were articulated on a small scale at a farmstead to farmstead level or at more specialised sites where contacts could be initially implemented and, more importantly, controlled (cf. Galliou 1990; Giot 1995). Traditionally, hillforts and larger fortifications are thought to perform specialised trading and exchange functions. Coastal promontory enclosure sites such as Alet and Le Yaudet may have been involved in specialised trading activity at this time and we may therefore assume that some defended enclosures inland were performing a similar role. It would be surprising, given the evidence for the opening up of east–west contacts and economic intensification, if there were no moves towards centralisation beyond the activities recognised at individual farmsteads.

It is generally believed that the majority of Armorican hillforts belong to the Later Prehistoric period in line with developments seen from the Hallstatt C period onwards elsewhere in Europe. However, despite the fact that the majority of Armorica hillforts have produced Iron Age pottery, further precision in dating is difficult as many sites have also produced traces of activity from other periods ranging from the Neolithic (e.g. Toul-Goulic en Tremergat, Côtes-d'Armor) up until the Middle Ages (e.g. Péran en Plédran, Côtes-d'Armor) in addition to Iron Age occupation (Giot 1995: 273–4).

Similar to south-west England, hilltop enclosures are not a common type in Armorica:[25] the majority are quite small, rarely over a few hectares in total area, and are therefore difficult in many cases to distinguish from larger farming enclosures. There have been no modern excavations of hillfort enclosures in Armorica, work has instead focused on the rescue excavation of farmsteads in lower lying areas, with the result that our impressions of hilltop sites are still very much based on the limited excavation work carried out at the Camp d'Artus and Kercaradec, both in Finistère, and Le Petit Celland, Manche, by Wheeler in the late 1930s (Wheeler and Richardson 1957). Unfortunately, as Wheeler's excavations tended to concentrate on the defences, we know virtually nothing about the internal organisation of hilltop enclosures in Armorica.

There are some similarities with hilltop enclosures seen elsewhere in northern Atlantic areas. The unexcavated site of Castels-Finans en Saint-Aignan, Morbihan (Giot 1995: 274), for example, features a rampart of loose stones, similar to that of Mooghaun in Ireland, which encloses *c.* 4 hectares and has an elaborate inturned stone entrance arrangement. At Kercaradec, Finistère, three lines of defence enclose an area of 2.2 hectares (Wheeler and Richardson 1957: 54–61). Wheeler and Richardson suggest the space between the outer ramparts may have delimited an area in which to keep stock, similar to multiple enclosure forts in south-west England (op. cit. 55). In addition, the two external defences were simple dump ramparts but the main internal defence was found to be a well-finished stone-built stepped rampart, some 6 m wide (Wheeler and Richardson 1957, Plate XXVII), creating a terraced wall similar to those seen at a number of Irish western stone fort sites.[26] Le Bihan (1984) has identified some final Hallstatt sherds in the Kercaradec assemblage but the majority of sherds are characteristic of the first century BC, most notably sherds of graphite-coated wares featuring applied cordons and internally grooved rims (Daire 1992: 274; Maguer 1996: 119). No Roman ceramics were recovered, perhaps suggesting abandonment by the time of the Roman conquest; but it must be kept in mind that only a very small proportion of the site was excavated.

Although the appearance of hilltop enclosures in Armorica cannot be taken to indicate the existence of Atlantic cultural contacts, the general affinities and size of enclosures in the peninsula are closer to those found in western Britain and Ireland than to examples found in the rest of France. This has been ignored in French discussions, which have tended to concentrate on the recognition, definition and function of *oppidum* sites at the expense of all other forms (Duval 1984: 79; Maguer 1996: 103). The French obsession with these sites has meant that nearly all large Iron Age hillforts in France have, at some point, been referred to as *oppida* (Giot 1995: 283).

The larger hilltop enclosures in Armorica have not escaped such attention and claims have been made that a number of them represent sites of *oppidum* status.

However, under the current widely accepted archaeological usage of the term (cf. Collis 1975, 1984; Cunliffe and Rowley 1976) none of the Armorican enclosures display the range of features required to justify the label *oppidum*. *Oppida* are considered to be large nucleated fortified settlements which are distinguished from hillforts by the existence of a range of, for want of a better term, 'urbanised' features: they are residential, religious, industrial, market and administrative centres. In France this term is applicable to a number of sites in central and eastern Gaul in the Late La Tène (Nash 1976) but not to the large fortified enclosures of the Armorican peninsula.

In central Gaul, immediately to the north of the Roman Province, the formation of large political groupings, considered by some to represent 'archaic states', has been well documented (cf. Nash 1976, 1978, 1981; Haselgrove 1987; Cunliffe 1988b; de Jersey 1994). It is precisely in this area that large nucleated *oppida* appear. Armorica had a markedly different social structure subject to different influences than areas immediately to the east, such as central Gaul. *Oppida* grew out of a particular set of circumstances in areas adjacent to Roman territory and it is therefore wholly inappropriate to search for identical *oppida* sites within the unique social milieu of Armorica. Here urban centres did not develop from indigenous Iron Age centres but had to be created from scratch in the Augustan period (Galliou 1983: 32).

Further evidence that the settlement systems of central Gaul and Armorica are different comes from comparing Caesar's descriptions in *Bellum Gallicum* of his military activities in each region (de Jersey 1994: 23). When describing his campaigns in Armorica he states that the Veneti were able to regroup in a succession of strongholds (*Bellum Gallicum* III.14). This clearly contrasts with the descriptions of his actions in central Gaul where it would appear that Caesar was able to conquer the tribal areas through the destruction of their key *oppida*. Such evidence implies that power in central Gaul was much more centralised and focused at a small number of large sites in keeping with the 'archaic states' model. Conversely, in Armorica power appears to be much more decentralised and based around smaller and more numerous centres. The latter system would be far more difficult to conquer outright and may help to explain why there are reports of sporadic unrest in north and west France even after the decisive battle at Alesia (BG VIII.4–5, 7, 26).

It was Wheeler and Richardson (1957: 31) who first considered some of the Armorican enclosures to be *oppida* mainly on the grounds of size and the use of the *murus gallicus*[27] rampart construction technique. It must be kept in mind that Wheeler was heavily influenced by the writings of Caesar and was excavating sites in northwestern France with the ultimate aim of proving contemporaneity with Caesar and his campaigns in Gaul between 58 and 50 BC, often at the expense of other occupational information at the sites. In *Bellum Gallicum* (III.9–16), Caesar uses the word *oppidum* several times in reference to Venetic sites but, as Giot (1995: 283) has pointed out, Caesar's usage of the word certainly differs from that created by modern archaeologists, and he may have simply been referring to a 'centre' or a 'camp'.

Wheeler also considered the apparent association between *oppida* and *murus gallicus* ramparts to have an importance – as have a number of archaeologists since.

Many of the *oppida* of temperate Europe display *murus gallicus* rampart construction, but it is not a constructional form unique to *oppidum* sites and is now known from a number of much smaller and functionally more restricted sites in Armorica: the Camp d'Artus, Finistère; Huelgoat, Finistère; the promontory site of Le Yaudet, Côtes-d'Armor; Le Petit Celland, Manche; Saint-Jean-de-Savignie, Manche/Calvados; Moulay, Mayenne; while evidence of nails and timber is known from Beg-en-Aud, Finistère.

According to Wheeler and Richardson (1957: 31, 104), there are two Armorican enclosures large enough to be potential *oppida* while Giot (1995: 286) has since added a third candidate. The most well known of these sites, the Camp d'Artus in Finistère, is large enough, at over 30 hectares, to compare with the *oppida* of temperate Europe. However, despite revealing evidence for Late La Tène occupation there was little to suggest the site functioned as a major administrative centre.[28] Wheeler and Richardson (1957: 31) himself doubted that the site could have supported a large population for any length of time and predictably suggests it was built by the Osismes as a fortification against Caesar. Lescouët en Guégon, Morbihan, is, like the Camp d'Artus, around 30 hectares in size and features massive ramparts up to 9 m high, while Poulailler en Landéan, Ille-et-Vilaine, covers an area of around 20 hectares. Both of these sites are massive, but their defences are incomplete which is not generally indicative of sites with a central, administrative or urban function. Giot (1995: 286) has suggested that these sites may represent some form of collective shelter for tribal groups which were either unfinished or used intermittently. The latter usage may support some form of seasonal use, perhaps pastoral and/or ritual in character, while the former suggests rapid construction perhaps during a time of upheaval, and it is tempting to tie this in with the Roman presence in the Late La Tène.

As the above examples demonstrate, it is often the size of the larger Armorican enclosures when compared to the rest of the enclosures on the peninsula that earn them the title of *oppidum*.[29] However, size alone should not be considered as a defining factor in determining the extent to which a site has adopted a level of complexity indicative of a centralised function – particularly in the Atlantic zone. It is the range of activities present at the site that should be of central importance. There are indications of sites with a centralised and/or specialised trading function in the Armorican Late La Tène, but there are none which display the full combination of administrative, industrial and market centre elements that are crucial to the definition of what constitutes an *oppidum* elsewhere in Europe.

Paule, Saint-Symphorien in Côtes-d'Armor, for example, displays a number of the features associated with *oppida* but within a much smaller enclosure (Arramond and Le Poiter 1990; Arramond *et al.* 1990, 1992; Arramond and Menez 1992). The quadrangular defended enclosure covers only 1 hectare, but is delimited by two or possibly three ramparts and ditches (Figure 6.35). Occupation begins in the Early La Tène and the site goes through several phases of refurbishment until sometime in the second century BC when it takes on a monumental, strongly defended appearance with the construction of a large V-shaped ditch, up to 4.3 m deep, and a rampart thought to have orginally been *c.* 5 m high. From this period onwards

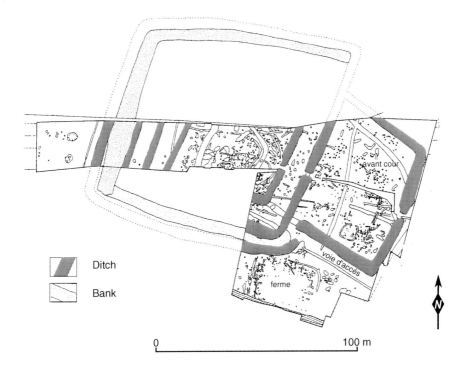

Figure 6.35 Paule, Saint-Symphorien site plan, Côtes-d'Armor (after Arramond and Menez 1992: fig. 1).

the site appears to have developed a role as a trading, craftworking and metal-working centre.

Evidence for metalworking comes from the east of the enclosure where an area of *c.* 3,000 square m, containing quantities of iron, bronze and gold-working slag and associated material such as crucibles, pits and a vitrified oven, is delimited by a rampart with a ditch. The sheer quantity of metalworking debris at Paule (iron slag is measured in terms of tens of kilograms) is without parallel in the rest of Brittany and indicates industrial levels of production far beyond the requirements of the site. The fact that this much metalworking material was allowed to enter the archaeolog-ical record at all and was not re-used, is in itself startling and suggests metal was not in short supply at the site. Additional evidence of specialised craftworking activity comes from the discovery of a number of small stone statuettes.

Paule has produced a vast number of Dressel 1a amphorae dating to the last quar-ter of the second century BC, indicating involvement in the articulation of long-distance trade (there are currently more amphorae recorded from Paule than from the rest of Brittany as a whole). Trade in wine was not a common practice in Brittany *c.* 120–100 BC, suggesting the inhabitants of Paule must have had a considerable degree of wealth to afford, and have access to, such a luxury. Significantly, part of an Italian wine patella with the head of a swan was also found that may indicate at least the partial adoption of Roman practices.[30] The repetitive character of the broken fragments suggests that the amphorae were buried a short time after the wine was consumed (Arramond and Menez 1992: 37).

The deep ditches of the site produced quantities of ceramics dating through to the second half of the first century BC, the date of the Roman campaigns in Armorica, after which the site appears to have been abandoned for a few decades until around 15/10 BC when there is some evidence of a much reduced Gallo-Roman presence at the site. The site is finally abandoned for good around the middle of the first century AD.

The layout of the site suggests a degree of organisation into clear activity zones consisting of a central occupation area, the metalworking forecourt to the east discussed above, and an area interpreted as a farming enclosure to the south. The central occupation zone forms around 3,000 square m of the site's area and consists of a mass of post-holes, pits, two large semi-subterranean storage pits and a souterrain. The souterrain is dated from the fifth to fourth centuries BC on the evidence of the ceramics recovered, after which it appears to have gone out of use. After the collapse of the souterrain a range of oval storage pits with wooden partitions are dug. Most striking, however, are the construction of two vast semi-subterranean storage pits dating to the Late La Tène (Arramond and Menez 1992: 16–20). The first of these pits is oblong and measures 7 m long, 1.1 m wide and two m deep. Three groups of post-holes and hollow impressions indicate a wood-lined structure with three partitions. The second pit is much larger, some 11 m long on its west-east axis, 2 m wide, 2.5 m deep, and is arranged in a T-shape which continues beyond the limits of the excavation to the south. Post-holes and impressions of wooden panelling indicate a structure similar to that of the previous pit. It is unclear whether these buildings were roofed or concealed at ground level (e.g. covered by clay and earth) or even sheltered by a building. Using just the surviving areas these structures offered storage volumes of 15 cubic m and 95 cubic m respectively which would easily lead one to consider whether the site performed some form of centralised storage function for the surrounding area. Further evidence of a centralised role comes from the remains of very large ovens from the Late La Tène levels (measuring 2 m by 0.7 m and up to 0.5 m deep), capable of feeding a much larger number of people than one would assume actually lived at the site.

The evidence provided by the massive rampart constructions, organised layout, extensive craftworking activities, large central storage pits and rich material culture suggests that the inhabitants of Paule possessed some degree of power. This power may have been the result of the site acting as a regional trading and production centre. It would have been well positioned for such a role because it sits near some of the richest tin deposits in Brittany along the route of an ancient thoroughfare partially marked in the landscape by tumuli[31] (Arramond and Menez 1992: 60–1). Paule fits the criteria of an elite residence controlling communications and exerting a hold on the surrounding land. The size of the series of ramparts and ditches could be seen to play a more defensive role than is seen at the usual Armorican enclosures. Interestingly, one metal fragment from the site has been interpreted as a possible piece of a sword scabbard and if accepted becomes, along with the ramparts, the only militaristic element of the site.

Moulay in Mayenne also displays some of the features associated with *oppida* and has been designated an *oppidum* by its excavator (Naveau 1974, 1976, 1986). Again it must be stressed that although this site displays some elements that perhaps differentiate it as a site of some importance there is little to support the view that it was an *oppidum*. The site covers 12 hectares and is defended by a massive bank (averaging 6 m high and 20 m wide) along with stretches of drystone rampart, surviving up to 3 m high, on the naturally defended sides, including a double stretch at one point. The use of stone alongside the already massive earthen defences is interesting as 'it seems that this may have been created as much from the desire to display a symbol of prestige as from a genuine defensive need' (de Jersey 1994: 26). Despite these defences, there was sparse occupational evidence from the small-scale excavations carried out in the interior, and certainly nothing to support the view that the site served as an administrative or market centre. Evidence for craftworking and exchange from the site came from a large number of Grand-Mesnil granite querns found in a ditch about 800 m north-east of the enclosure. These querns are known from a number of sites in Mayenne and beyond, and their discovery in bulk may indicate that Moulay was involved in their trade and production (Naveau 1974: 18–27).

The evidence from Paule and Moulay suggests that during the Late La Tène there were sites on the Armorican peninsula which developed more specialised trading and production roles, as a result of the conditions created by increasing contacts with the Roman world. Such sites may have been smaller versions of the sites involved in exchange found closer to west-central Europe such as les Allueds in Maine-et-Liore (de Jersey 1992). This 7 hectare site features alongside several rectangular buildings apparently divided into zones, over thirty wells and a range of Roman ceramics including a vast amount of Dressel 1a amphorae. The small yet strongly monumental nature of Paule and Moulay may be comparable – in terms of their role within Atlantic society – with the strongly defended sites involved in wider trading networks identified in south-west England. Due to a lack of excavated evidence it is not possible to assesss how many sites similar to Paule and Moulay there were in Armorica, but during a recent study of aerial photographic data from southern and eastern Armorica (Leroux *et al.* 1999) quadrangular enclosures with massive ditches (*c.* 3 to 6 m wide) and small domestic interiors (*c.* 2,000 square m or less), directly comparable to the Paule, were recognised as a distinct group (Meuret 1999: fig. 30). Surface finds from these sites suggest that they have a pre-Gallo-Roman dating centred on the Late La Tène (ibid.). Future investigations of these enclosures and indeed the full range of enclosure forms in the peninsula are essential to the future understanding of the Armorican Iron Age.

The same Roman influences which initially stimulated economic intensification and cross-Channel exchange ultimately bring it to an end. After the Roman conquest of Gaul in the middle of the first century BC, the focus of cross-Channel exchange switches to shorter routes between northern France and south-eastern England. The distribution of Dressel 1b amphorae in Gaul and Britain clearly display this shift, with exchange networks now focusing on the Seine as the prominent route of entry (Fitzpatrick 1985: 313–19). Evidence from Alet (Galliou 1984: 30; Bender and Caillaud 1986) and Le Yaudet (Cunliffe and Galliou 1995) suggests that cross-channel trade continues in Armorica but at a much diminished level in relation to the trade between northern Gaul and south-east Britain.

 There also appears to have been a co-terminus dislocation in settlement from the middle of the first century BC to the end of the first century AD during which a number of indigenous farmsteads go out of use. From the first century AD there is a marked expansion in settlement throughout the Armorican peninsula as new Gallo-Roman villa sites with associated Roman field systems are constructed.

Evidence from Braden I in the commune of Quimper, Finistère (Le Bihan 1984, 1988, 1990), provides further insights into the trends of the Late La Tène. The site displays a wide range of features including structural evidence, habitation, stock areas, graves, craftworking and evidence for periodic re-organisation. Braden I has been examined in sufficient detail to provide a firmly dated chronological sequence in the first century BC, which is broken down into four structural phases (Le Bihan 1988b, 1990; Figure 6.36).

The first enclosing palisade ditch, delimiting an area *c.* 6,000 square m, is dug in Phase I (120–80 BC) but defence does not appear to have been a major considera-tion because the entrance to the site is 12 m wide and there appear to be no associ-ated gate features. Four-poster granaries are identified against the inside of the northern enclosure ditch. In Phase II (80–40 BC) the previous ditch is filled and two new ditches are constructed. The internal area of the farmstead is made slightly smaller but overall the site now encloses *c.* 8,000 square m. Also at this time the entrance to the site is contracted and more controlled using parallel antennae palisades. There is also some post-hole evidence nearby indicative of a gate structure. It was impossible in most instances to clearly define the shapes of buildings from the mass of post-holes recovered and the most Le Bihan offers are 'zones of habitation' (Le Bihan 1990; figs. 5–8). However, a post-constructed circular building with a porch and a diameter of 4 to 5 m was defined in the north-east corner of the site, and is thought by the excavator to belong to Phase II although he does not rule out a Phase I date (Le Bihan 1988: 96).

In Phase III (40–10 BC) the site is re-organised again and the notion of enclosure becomes unclear. To the east are discontinuous lines of palisade, while the west and south appear undefended, although this may be due to the limits of the excavation trench. The northern part of the Phase II ditch is re-used as a rampart with a stone core. At the same time there is some evidence for stone walling being used in build-ings as the foundations to a *clayonnage* wall (before this at the site *clayonnage* struc-tures were simply built straight on to the soil). By Phase IV (10 BC–AD 60) the situation is even more unclear, with the only evidence of enclosure occurring to the east. Le Bihan argues that during each phase the area of habitation seems to reduce while the enclosure gets larger (there is evidence for at least two domestic areas in Phases I and II, only one in Phase III and no definite evidence at all for a domestic

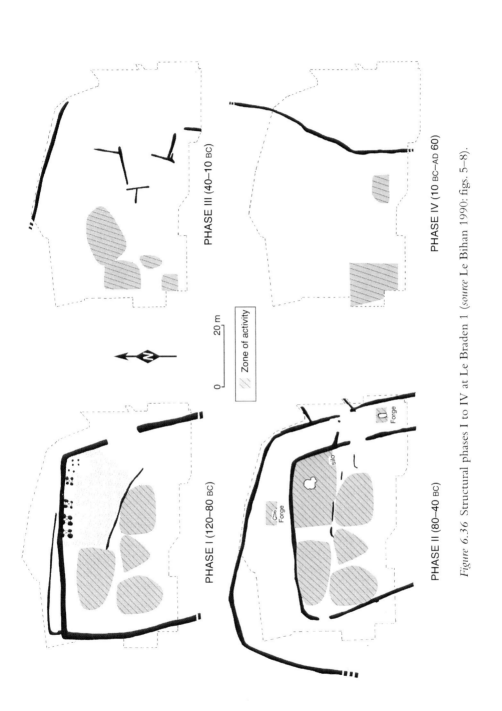

PHASE I (120–80 BC)

PHASE II (80–40 BC)

PHASE III (40–10 BC)

PHASE IV (10 BC–AD 60)

Forge

silo

Forge

Forge

N

0   20 m

Zone of activity

Figure 6.36 Structural phases I to IV at Le Braden 1 (*source* Le Bihan 1990: figs. 5–8).

structure in Phase IV). As each phase progresses, the amenities seem to become less numerous and Le Bihan suggests that this may be due to de-population related to the establishment of a Roman presence in Armorica. This may be true but it is equally possible that the fragmentary nature of Phases III and IV are largely due to erosion because they are the most recent.

For Le Bihan (1990) it is the changes that occurred around 40 BC, and specifically the use of stone at the site, that are the most significant. He feels these changes in site organisation and the materials used are the result of Roman influences taking a stronger hold on Armorican society a few decades after the Gallic War. As such he claims that similar changes should be recognised at other Armorican farming establishments at around the same time (Le Bihan 1990).

The La Tène sites in Quimper in the vicinity of Braden I are the closest thing we have to a regional sequence in Armorica. Nine Gallic sites have been discovered there since 1980 (three in the vicinity of Braden) in addition to the former discoveries of La Tourelle (Le Men), de Kermoisan (Le Bihan and Galliou 1974) and the hilltop site of Kercaradec (Wheeler and Richardson 1957). Of these sites, eight have dates in the Late La Tène: Braden I and II; Creach-Gwen (Le Bihan 1988a); Prat-ar-Rouz (Le Bihan 1985); Kermoisan; Kercaradec; Kernier (Menez 1988); and Lestonan (Le Bihan, unpublished). If nothing else the density of the sites in this area support the view that the farming population was very homogeneous and dense throughout the whole of Armorica and the high occurrence of Late La Tène sites supports the postulated agricultural expansion at this time.

Le Bihan's attempts to recognise similar changes as those seen at Braden I are only moderately successful. He points to Prat-ar-Rouz and Braden II as providing evidence of a change to ramparts with a stone core around the middle of the first century BC; of the other sites in Quimper he states it is not possible to comment due to a lack of excavated information. In looking for the change from a surrounding palisade ditch to a stone-based structure *c.* 40 BC throughout the rest of the peninsula, Le Bihan (1990: 267) points out that a similar move to stone-built structures in preference to wood is seen at around the same time at Hennebont-Polvern (Menez 1985, 1987), La Boissane (Menez 1988, 1996) and Plouaret-l'Armorique (Bardel unpub.). This is not a particularly impressive number of examples and de Jersey (1994: 28) is quick to point out that the significance of such changes may be over-emphasised due to the extremely limited Armorican database of excavated sites.

It is of interest that a number of sites display abandonment in the middle of the first century BC at the time of the Caesarian conquest (e.g. Le Braden II; Les Champs Brunet; le Petit Coulebart; Polvern-Hennebont; Pouilladou-Prat; Ligne Anne petit enciene; Le-Haut-Chesney; La Boissane; along with a period of temporary abandonment at Paule). While there is no doubt that the structural changes at Braden I were influenced to some degree by Roman traditions (after all it is certain from an examination of the recovered assemblages from Late La Tène farmsteads that Romanisation was having an impact), it remains unclear to what extent Roman influences were responsible and, if so, how widespread these changes were. Apart from a burnt house at Braden II there is little evidence of the violent destruction of these sites. It must be kept in mind that periodic re-organisations were a common feature of all Iron Age sites in Armorica.

Further evidence of a dislocation comes from survey work in eastern Brittany which suggests that the majority of Iron Age boundaries are replaced by smaller Roman divisions from the end of the first century BC (Astill and Davies 1997: 66), with a number of Iron Age settlements becoming Roman fields (op. cit. 65). There are some examples of continuity from a native farming establishment to a Gallo-Roman villa, such as at Saint-Evarzec/Le Cavardy (Finistère) (Le Bihan *et al.* 1982), but they remain rare. Also, it is evident that some of the larger enclosed sites, such as Le Yaudet (Cunliffe and Galliou 1996), Kercaradec (Wheeler and Richardson 1957), and Alet (Bender 1986: 51), carried on into the Roman period, perhaps due to their importance as trading centres.

56 BC and beyond: Roman conquest and re-organisation

The widespread abandonment of Armorican farmsteads at the end of the first century BC is likely to have been related to the disruption caused firstly by the Gallic Wars and then conquest in 56 BC. After the conquest there is much evidence to suggest that while under Roman control the Armorican landscape and economy was completely re-organised. Farming enclosures take on more direct influences from traditional Roman villas and become more regular and rectilinear in shape, such as the excavated example at Vallée de L'Yvel in Morbihan (Gautier 1996). The enclosures often surround laid out rectangular plan buildings where again direct Roman influence is suggested through the occurrence of tile fragments, flues and floors or hypocaust *pilae*, as found at Les Landes de la Ruée (Astill and Davies 1997: 71). These Gallo-Roman villas become the main farmstead type throughout Armorica, in many cases occupying areas previously exploited by indigenous farmsteads. Aerial photographic and excavation evidence suggests that while these settlements remained roughly equivalent in size and function to previous forms, there was a marked increase in their density. This increase in numbers occurs alongside evidence for the construction of Roman field boundaries and a network of roads.

Evidence for increasing social complexity can be gleaned from the aerial photographic enclosure data for the Pays de Rance, Côtes-d'Armor. In the pre-Roman Iron Age, there is little evidence of centralisation or organisation, and farmstead sites appear to be randomly spread out throughout the landscape (Figure 6.37). The only site that may have been serving a more central or specialised role is the promontory site of Alet (Langouët 1984), enclosing some 12 hectares and known to have been involved in trade with southern Britain (Cunliffe 1987). In the Gallo-Roman period there was a major re-organisation of the landscape; an increase in farming establishments implies agricultural intensification and an urban centre is founded at Corseul, linked to the farming hinterland by a network of Roman roads (Figure 6.38).

There is then a gradual intensification in the number of farming enclosures seen throughout the Iron Age. The first major increase is seen during the Late La Tène, a trend which continues, after a brief hiatus, into the first few centuries AD. These developments are best viewed in relation to the demands of the expanding

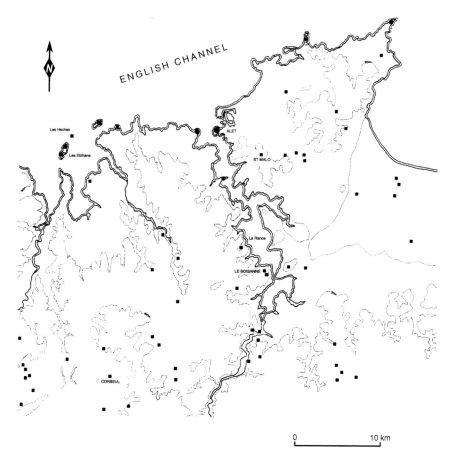

Figure 6.37 Iron Age sites in the Pays de Rance, Côtes-d'Armor (after Menez 1996: fig. 167).

Roman Empire. In the Late La Tène the increase in farming establishments, native field boundaries and coastal settlements implies an increasing emphasis on cereal and salt production, presumably at the expense of previous pastoralist practices (Astill and Davies 1997: 77). The common occurrence of Dressel 1 amphorae from these sites implies that there were contacts in existence to the east at this time. Amongst these settlements a few develop into more complex sites, such as at Paule and Moulay, apparently directly involved in the articulation of trade with the expanding Roman world.

After the conquest the agricultural productivity of the Armorican peninsula is intensified, alongside the development of larger trading networks and the establishment of new urban centres. In the Augustan period new urban centres are created by the Romans and new towns are founded throughout the peninsula such as at

Figure 6.38 Gallo-Roman sites in the Pays de Rance, Côtes-d'Armor (after Menez 1996: fig. 168).

Vannes (*Durioritim*), Brest, Carhaux, and Corseul (*Fanum Martis*) (Galliou 1983: 32). From this period influences via the Atlantic become completely superseded by trading links to the east. La Tène decoration on pottery disappears and indigenous ceramics take on a distinctively Roman character, including the production of fine tableware such as bowls and flagons, while imported material is typically Gaulish Samian or *Terra nigra* ware (Astill and Davies 1997: 272)

Conclusions

Similar to the nature of the evidence from Atlantic Scotland and Ireland, the existence of maritime contacts between Armorica and south-west England cannot be defined in the traditional archaeological manner of charting reciprocal distributions of traded objects. Instead, cultural contact can be inferred from the general settlement and ceramic similarities between the two peninsulas, and their shared distinctiveness compared to their respective mainland neighbours:

> Standing back from the detail the most striking fact to emerge is the stark cultural contrast between Brittany and the rest of France and between Cornwall and western Devon and the rest of England, and the very considerable cultural similarities which the two regions share with each other.
>
> (Cunliffe 1990: 247)

The ceramic and settlement evidence reviewed here suggests that the similarities between the two areas were closest between *c.* 600 and 200 BC. The construction and use of promontory forts and souterrains on either side of the Channel implies the existence of shared cultural traditions while the main domestic forms – single or small numbers of buildings within univallate enclosures – are also directly comparable and similar in layout and size to contemporary Welsh raths and Irish ringforts.

From the second century BC, and especially during the first century BC, the two areas begin to move apart as Armorica becomes more and more involved in contacts with west-central Europe and the developing Roman world. The expansion of Roman influences during this period – cemented by the creation of the Roman province of *Gallia Transalpina* in southern Gaul by 120 BC (Cunliffe 1988a: 53–8) – had a very strong influence on political and social developments in Gaul. As we have seen, the influence of the expanding Roman consumer markets, either directly or indirectly, permeated through to Armorica stimulating economic diversification, expansion in settlement, and agricultural intensification in the peninsula during the last two centuries BC, as well as initially invigorating cross-Channel contacts with central-southern England. The relationship between the Roman world and Gaul has been described by a number of authors in terms of a core/periphery relationship (Nash 1976; Haselgrove 1987; Cunliffe 1988a; de Jersey 1994: 23–4). At its simplest level, the Roman demand for resources had a knock-on effect throughout Gaul and intensified contacts between Late La Tène communities through exchange, trading, and most probably raiding.

Despite the evidence for stronger eastern influences in Armorica at this time, however, it must be stressed that the peninsula retained a distinctive identity in the centuries prior to invasion. The development of quadrangular settlement forms may have been stimulated by contacts with west-central Europe but they remain a distinctly indigenous form. The high proportion of small quadrangular sites, rarely exceeding 1 hectare in size, is a striking feature of the Armorican peninsula – elsewhere in France enclosures quite commonly exceed 30 hectares. Menez (1994: 260) has argued that the tradition of digging deep ditches in Armorica could also be considered a distinctive regional characteristic. In general, archaeologists have concentrated on the functional aspects of Iron Age enclosures in Armorica and have downplayed any potential monumental role, often dismissing large ramparts as simply being animal pens or providing protection from the elements. Deep ditches are a common occurrence on Late La Tène farmsteads – on average they survive to a depth of around 1 to 2.5 m – and clearly distinguish Late La Tène enclosures from later Gallo-Roman sites, suggesting the digging of deep ditches may have had a significance beyond the purely functional – perhaps in terms of expressing identity and status. This behaviour could mark a further point of convergence with Iron Age enclosures in the south-west which also tend to feature deep ditches, as well as reflecting the wider moves towards monumentality seen throughout the western Atlantic zone from *c.* 200 BC.

As we have seen, there is little evidence in Armorica for the growth of the centralised *oppida* seen elsewhere in Gaul. Instead, there is some evidence, from the excavations at Paule and Moulay, of the development of smaller strongly defended units involved in more centralised craft production and the articulation of Late La Tène contacts. These sites can perhaps be most closely paralleled with strongly defended enclosures in the south-west such as Castle Dore and Chûn, both of which also seem to have been involved in trading activity around the first centuries BC and AD.

Despite the fact that few settlements dating from the sixth to the third century BC have been excavated in Armorica, there are indications of a development from curvilinear forms earlier in the Iron Age to rectilinear forms by the close of the millennium. Those early sites that have been examined are curvilinear or feature circular elements in construction (e.g. Kerlande, Talhouët, Kersigneau and arguably the primary phase at Le Boisanne). Souterrains are most usually associated with curvilinear enclosures, such as Kermoysan en Plabennec, Finistère and Kerméno en Grand-Champ, Morbihan, which may have significance given that souterrains appear to date from the Early to Middle La Tène (Giot 1995: 269). Those aerial photographic surveys that have taken place (Langouët and Daire 1990; Arbousse-Bastide 1993; Maguer 1996; Leroux *et al.* 1999) reveal the existence of a range of curvilinear enclosures that have their closest parallels with settlements in south-west England but which remain totally unexamined because excavation in Armorica has concentrated almost exclusively on rectilinear forms. From sometime in the late third century BC farmsteads with irregular quadrangular enclosures with rounded edges begin to be constructed (corresponding with evidence for intensified contacts with west-central Europe) and become the dominant type throughout the peninsula by the second century BC. After a possible hiatus in construction in the second half of the first century BC (Le Bihan 1990) regularly laid out geometric rectilinear Gallo-Roman settlements are built throughout the first few centuries AD.

The south-west English settlement sequence is broadly comparable – in the sense that curvilinear and oval enclosure forms are the norm up until around the close of the first millennium BC after which point a range of rectilinear forms are constructed (Figure 6.12). However, there is far less evidence for Roman influences on indigenous settlement patterns, even after the Roman conquest of Britain in AD 43/44, and certainly nothing approaching the re-organisation of the landscape and establishment of new centres seen in Armorica in the Augustan period. Instead, indigenous ways of life continue relatively undisturbed. The round continues to be the main settlement form and a number were occupied from the Iron Age well into the Romano-British period, including Castle Gotha occupied from the third century BC into the late second century AD, and Trevisker from at least the second century BC to the second century AD. From the first century AD a number of rectilinear rounds are constructed including Trevinnick and Shortlanesend, while the construction of the oval site of Trethurgy sometime in the second century AD, and occupied up to the sixth century AD, indicates the continuation and survival of Iron Age curvilinear traditions.

There is some evidence for change in indigenous settlement practices: multiple enclosure forts and hillforts were out of use by the first century AD, while no new multivallate sites or promontory defences[32] appear to have been constructed (Johnson and Rose 1982: 156), but it remains unclear whether this can be considered a direct result of the Roman conquest. It has been suggested that the lack of such sites implies that only univallate enclosures would have been allowed to continue under Roman rule, tolerated because of their role in reflecting status in the indigenous social system (Quinnell 1986: 124). The building of new rounds, and in particular more Roman influenced rectilinear examples, from the beginning of the first millennium AD, many of which had access to exotic Roman goods, may reflect the continuation and re-contextualisation of indigenous traditions within a Roman context.

Ceramic developments are close enough throughout the Iron Age to suggest that some level of cultural exchange was taking place, while the rare occurrences of imported ceramics provide evidence of direct contacts. In common with the nature of Atlantic settlement similarities throughout the zone, ceramic forms are related without being identical, yet close enough to suggest the exchange of ideas and concepts. The existence of a shared repertoire of symbols and forms implies some ideological convergence between communities living on the two peninsulas. If one accepts the arguments that the use of souterrains and promontory forts may have had a ritual significance to Atlantic communities, then, as well as indicating similarities in social structure and behaviour, such sites may also reflect similarities in belief.

The occurrence of burials in stone lined cists, sometimes arranged in cemeteries, in south-west England and Brittany also suggest commonalties in ritual practice and belief (Cunliffe 1991: 505). Four substantial cemeteries are known in south-west England: at Mount Batten in Devon, and Harlyn Bay, Trelan Bahow and Trevone in Cornwall. However, the details of these cemeteries remain obscure because apart from a single cist excavated at Trevone (Dudley and Jope 1965) and the partial re-excavation of Harlyn Bay (Whimster 1977) none of the sites were ever adequately recorded. Uncontexted objects, including the Iberian style brooches from Harlyn Bay (Whimster 1977: 77–8) and Mount Batten (Boudet 1988), alongside finds of bronze and iron ring headed pins, bracelets of Kimmeridge shale, glass beads and indigenous polished slate artefacts, as well as two La Tène bracelets from Trevone (Dudley and Jope 1965), suggest a date range spanning the fourth century BC to the first century AD. Significantly there were no Roman objects. From Whimster's excavations (1977: 69) it seems likely that most burials did not contain grave goods but the occurrence of a range of prestige objects may indicate the existence of elites in south-west England who were involved at some level in controlling maritime trade routes. The coastal location of the majority of these burials, many in prominent positions overlooking the sea, may reflect a symbolic connection between the dead and the sea (Todd 1987: fig. 6.9). Further evidence of a maritime aspect to these burials comes from the occurrence of more roughly-built, but undeniably related, cist graves on the Isles of Scilly; the most well known being three at St Mary's at Porth Cressa and Poynter's Garden, which also produced brooches and glass beads (Ashbee 1974: 120–47), and the recent find of a sword and a mirror dating to the second century BC from a stone lined cist at Bryher (Thomas 2006).

The Breton cist graves also have a coastal aspect and were originally thought to have an exclusive Iron Age dating based on the results of early antiquarian diggings (Giot 1975), but more recent excavations at Saint-Urnel (Giot and Monnier 1977) have suggested that at least some of the burials at that site were of sub-Roman date (Cunliffe 1990: 248). This may not, of course, apply to all such cemeteries, but as a result all that can be said at present is that the possibility of similar Iron Age burial forms exists. There are other significant differences: the south-western English graves demonstrate partial continuity with other south British traditions, in that they feature crouched inhumations with the head aligned to the north (Whimster 1977), whereas in Brittany extended inhumation is the norm (Giot 1960); in addition there appears to be a correlation in Brittany between Iron Age cemeteries and the siting of stone stelae (Raftery 1994: 182; Daire and Villard 1996), the latter being a form completely absent in south-west England. It seems most likely, then, that the south-western burial practice reflects a blending of the traditions present in Brittany and southern Britain.

The restricted distribution of stone stelae in western Armorica is considered by many to be a further example of the uniqueness of the area in the Iron Age[33] (Duval 1990; Cunliffe 1990: Daire and Villard 1996). From the 600 examples known, Giot (1976) has defined two main types: low (*bassess*) and elevated (*hautes*) – the former usually hemispherical, spherical, ovoid or elliptical, and the latter more pillar-like and circular or polygonal in section. Most are carved from granite and are thought to date from the fifth to the fourth centuries BC (Daire and Villard 1996).

Some stelae are engraved: most notably the low stele from Kermania, Point l'Abbe, Finistère, and the elevated example from St Anne en Trégatel, Côtes d'Armor, which are carved with rectilinear and curvilinear designs using motifs common in Early and Middle La Tène art (Daire and Villard 1996). Similar decorated stones, also of suspected Iron Age date, are found in Ireland,[34] although none are thought to be in their original positions (Raftery 1994: 181–2; Waddell 1998: 362–5). It was once fashionable to compare the designs on the French stelae with those on the Irish stones, particularly the examples from Turoe and Castlestrange, in an effort to suggest the possibility of direct Atlantic cultural links between Brittany and Ireland (Henry 1933, 1940; Raftery 1944: 45; 1951: 213; Rynne 1961: 125; 1972: 79; Giot 1995: 271). However, it has since been argued that the designs on the Turoe stone represent a more advanced stage of La Tène art than that seen on the Breton stones and can, in any case, be more closely paralleled with designs on metalwork from Britain (Duignan 1976; Waddell 1982). Waddell (1982: 27; 1998: 365) has pointed out that the occurrence of La Tène decoration on stones may simply have been part of a

much wider western European phenomena which could well have included decoration on timber posts:

> It is unlikely that the intricate symbolism of La Tène art, where some motifs
> must have been charged with magical meaning, was only expressed in stone and
> bronze.
>
> (Waddell 1998: 365)

Whatever the case, the occurrence of decorated stelae in Ireland and Brittany
suggests, if not direct links, the existence of shared traditions between Irish and
Breton Iron Age communities.

The similarities in settlement and ceramic developments, taken together with the
evidence for material contacts between western Britain and the continent, are sufficient to suggest there were maritime contacts between Armorica and south-west
England during the Iron Age. Although evidence of actual traded forms is lacking,
there is ample evidence for the exchange of cultural ideas that must imply some
movement of people and goods from area to area. This is very much the nature of
Atlantic contact throughout the northern Atlantic zone: material assemblages are
largely utilitarian and display little evidence for the presence of exotic goods, let alone
the exchange of forms, but Atlantic communities are enough alike to suggest that they
developed within a shared awareness of each other – an awareness that could only
come about through the existence of cultural contacts.

Cunliffe (1990: 247) views the broad similarities in settlement and material culture
between south-west Britain and Armorica prior to *c.* 120 BC as a result of contacts
created from the continuous demand for metals during the Iron Age,[35] a need
emanating from west-central Europe and ultimately the Mediterranean:

> Two regions with such similar mineral resources are hardly likely to have devel-
> oped extensive trading relationships with each other unless external forces
> created a demand.
>
> (Cunliffe 1990: 250)

It is likely that the constant need for raw materials kept the two areas in contact
over a long period of time, with Armorica and the Loire route used by west-central
Europe as the gateway to Atlantic resources. The concentration of ceramic forms at
Hengistbury Head, and accompanying drop off of contacts at Mount Batten, suggest
that networks of contact shifted away from south-west England from the beginning
of the first century BC to a more central-southern English source, presumably
because it had access to a wider range of resources for export to the Roman
consumer markets. After the Roman invasion of Gaul in 56 BC cross-Channel routes
were established further to the east at the shortest possible sea crossing between
northern France and south-east England, allowing an easier link-up to established
Roman road networks which were always preferred over sea-routes by the Romans
for the movement of bulk goods.

With the establishment of Armorica as fully part of the Roman world by the first century AD, linked to the rest of the Empire through efficient road networks, and the creation of shorter Channel crossings to the east, the south-west, once conquered, was very much a peripheral part of the Roman world – Roman roads are unknown, and the area never developed its own coinage. Mineral resources such as tin were no doubt procured from elsewhere (probably mainly Iberia from the first century AD), meaning that the south-west had little role to play in the new Roman order and going some way to explaining the continuation of settlement forms and levels of social organisation in the south-west virtually unchanged from the Iron Age period. Not until the evidence of the migrations of Christians in the fifth and sixth centuries AD did the sea routes once again have a major impact on the communities of south-west England and Armorica (Bowen 1972: 70–91; 1977: fig. 4).

7 Atlantic communities and the sea

Introduction

Debates about the existence of prehistoric maritime contacts along the Atlantic seaboard tend to fall into two mutually exclusive arenas of discussion where one must either reject all suggestions of contact in favour of indigenous development or embrace visions of thousands of Childean argonauts clogging up the Atlantic sea-lanes from Cadiz to Shetland. Clearly, however, more subtle relationships took place between Atlantic communities during the Iron Age. There are difficulties in defining the kind of contacts that existed precisely because they do not appear to be visible through the movement of material culture on any large scale. Instead, our view of Iron Age communities is based almost exclusively on settlement evidence. In the absence of distinctive material assemblages it seems likely that the appearance of settlements played a role in the construction of Atlantic social groups and identities. The settlement evidence reveals a range of communities immersed in a common state of existence, an existence that was dominated by the sea. It is perhaps hard for us in the age of air travel to appreciate the major role the sea would have played in people's everyday lives in the past. At the beginning of the twentieth century it was commonplace in many Atlantic coastal areas to carry out everyday journeys such as a trip to the local shop by boat. It is not unreasonable to assume that Iron Age communities were in at least episodic contact by sea and viewed themselves as being part of a series of maritime peoples who lived on the very edge of the known world – the sea being a common point of access (both physical and conceptual) for all the peoples of the shore.

Despite the lack of regional settlement sequences and well dated stratified ceramic assemblages from the western Atlantic zone, it is clear from the evidence examined in the preceding chapters that Atlantic Scottish, Irish, south-western British, and Armorican communities developed along related but distinct lines. Radiocarbon dating has lengthened the late chronologies used prior to 1970 when Hawkes' ABC system was still in use in southern England (Hawkes 1959) but, despite this, the legacy of earlier chronologies and interpretations remain. This fact, coupled with the problems of dating sites on the basis of secondary occupations, has meant that a number of key Atlantic site types such as complex Atlantic Scottish roundhouses, south-western 'rounds', and Irish drystone forts and ringforts, are often still dated too late resulting in gaps in Atlantic settlement records between the Late Bronze Age and the last few centuries of the Iron Age. As we have seen, there is strong evidence for continuity in settlement forms and locations throughout the first millennium BC in most areas, with lengthy occupations and periods of secondary re-use a common occurrence.

Recognising such continuities does not imply that Atlantic communities were socially or culturally static. European Iron Age studies have for too long been dominated by interpretations based upon the study of the rapidly evolving Hallstatt and La Tène societies of west-central Europe. After a bright phase of contact and innovation in the Late Bronze Age, the Atlantic Iron Age is usually thought of as a period of withdrawal from wider European trade networks, and one where communities were stable but conservative and less dynamic. As a result, it has been all too easy to dismiss Atlantic communities as peripheral to events in Europe and view the zone as a cultural backwater where nothing much happened. However, the social world of the Atlantic Iron Age at the close of the first millennium BC was significantly different to that of the Late Bronze Age; important social and cultural transformations occurred, not least the development of monumental architecture, and these require interpretation and ultimately inclusion within wider European Iron Age narratives.

Atlantic Europe in the first millennium BC

1200–600 BC: contact and the establishment of shared maritime social practices

The most visible expression of shared Atlantic identity in the first millennium BC – the metalwork of the Atlantic Late Bronze Age – came at a time when there was evidence for wider cultural linkages and contacts throughout western Europe. The raw materials of the Atlantic zone were desired by metal consuming communities in west-central Europe and the Mediterranean, and it is likely that the resulting contacts with these areas, either directly or indirectly, encouraged Atlantic communities to express and define their own identities.

The communities of the Atlantic Late Bronze Age formed a wide framework of interacting local systems united through the exchange and production of similar metalwork forms. The acceptance and use of these distinctive metalwork types and their widespread deposition suggests the existence of commonalities in meaning and ritual practice between Atlantic communities (Needham and Burgess 1980; Bradley 1990). As a result Atlantic groups contrast with contemporary Urnfield communities in west-central Europe, characterised by organised cemeteries and more modest metal consumption. The deposition of high status metalwork within these two adjacent areas occurs at different degrees of intensity and within different cultural contexts. In Atlantic areas there are few formal burials and ritual deposition takes place within a watery context: in pits, rivers, bogs, lakes, and potentially the sea.[1] Whilst in west-central Europe throughout the first millennium BC high status metalwork is commonly found in burial contexts. Thus the deposition of distinctive metalwork types in Atlantic areas can be regarded as a visible element of ritual practices which contrast with those of Urnfield influenced areas and we can begin to talk in terms of the existence of two distinct cultural zones (Brun 1988), with different ideological outlooks.

Although our view of Late Bronze Age society is based almost entirely on metalwork, there can be little doubt that the increase in trade represented by such objects, and in turn the projected increase in maritime contacts, had a major impact on Atlantic societies. It was at this time that the hut-circle or simple stone roundhouse was established. Significantly, these Late Bronze Age forms mark the first appearance on any significant scale of permanent settlement – a phenomenon that is likely to be related to improvements in agricultural technology and practice being disseminated along the Atlantic sea routes alongside metalwork forms. The growing intensity of landscape use from this point onwards, and the construction of permanent settlements with their own territories and field systems, would have led to the need for groups to define individual claims to land and resources. The construction of enclosures around settlements, which were more about being seen than defence, would have been part of this process and in this we can perhaps trace the beginnings of concerns with settlement monumentality – a concern which of course was to develop so dramatically in the Iron Age. Undoubtedly, it must be within Late Bronze Age society that the importance of settlements as visible and long-lasting symbols in the landscape was established.

The contrast in the archaeological data from mobile bronze objects in the Late Bronze Age to static field monuments in the Iron Age has been one of the principal stumbling blocks to coherent synthesis. Equally, the widespread exchange of metalwork is thought to require the presence of elites in the Late Bronze Age who become archaeologically invisible by the Iron Age. Metalwork aside, there is little supporting evidence for the presence of elites in the Late Bronze Age. For example, there is even less evidence for the differentiation in the settlement record at this time compared to the succeeding Iron Age. The production and exchange of fine metalwork forms would have required craft specialists and organisation, but it does not automatically require the simplistic self-interest groupings assumed under the chiefdom model (*contra* Brun 1991, 1993, 1998; Gilman 1988). If the types produced were embedded with ritual meaning then their exchange may relate to shared beliefs and ritual practices (deposition) rather than simply the expression of status or wealth. The amount of material in circulation is usually taken to indicate mercantile trade rather than symbolic exchange but it may equally be a reflection of how important bronze, or more specifically its deposition, was to Atlantic ritual practices and how widespread these practices were. Exchanges involving quite large amount of material over time could have been taking place between otherwise autonomous and largely equal groups at the community or even individual household level. Of course, importance in the ritual sphere is another way of gaining status and power but this does not automatically imply the presence of entrepreneur elites; more complex yet unknown systems of symbolic prestige and ritual rivalry may have been in existence. Certainly, the concept of elites controlling Atlantic trade networks seems inadequate to fully explain the distributions of highly symbolic metalwork forms. Rather than elites disappearing by the Iron Age, therefore, it may have been that the medium of symbolic exchange had simply changed from bronze metalwork to the outward and inward appearance of settlements: dwellings became much more than simple domestic spaces and incorporated depositional, symbolic and ritual activities as essential parts of day-to-day life.

A number of the metalwork forms exchanged in the Atlantic zone have a long currency and types change less frequently than in the central European or Nordic zones leading some to view the area as a periphery (Burgess 1968: 13). Whilst some of the forms and techniques used in the west could be considered conservative, to view the area as a periphery at this time is untenable. Atlantic communities were taking part in an active and competitive metalwork exchange system and the area was the major source of copper and tin for west-central Europe during a period where such ores were prized above everything else. The apparent conservatism in forms is perhaps more a testament to the strength of indigenous ritual traditions, which would have been less malleable to change, making Atlantic communities very selective in what they accepted from the outside. The maintenance of archaic traditions is a feature of Atlantic societies in the first millennium BC and is also present in the development of settlement forms throughout the Iron Age.

The Atlantic Iron Age 600 BC–AD 200: shared concepts and traditions

With the transition to iron and its associated ideology in west-central Europe, Atlantic areas became less involved in, and more distinct from, mainstream European events. Atlantic groups clung to past ways of life and ritual belief, ultimately leading to the over-production, or at least massive deposition, of metalwork reflected most vividly in the thousands of non-functional Armorican axes produced and deposited at the end of the Late Bronze Age. This over-production is often talked about in terms of system collapse. Whilst it is true that prestige bronze objects appear to become less important to Atlantic societies, there is little evidence of a wider economic decline or collapse; in fact continuity and apparent stability in settlement patterns is common in most areas.

The isolation of the north-western Atlantic zone was exacerbated by the rise of hillfort dominated zones in central-southern Britain and eastern Scotland (Figure 7.1). As a result, from c. 600 BC there is a general decline in the intensity of contacts between Atlantic zones and west-central Europe. The outer fringes of the Atlantic zone, Atlantic Scotland and western Ireland, became most isolated from continental events and it is interesting that it is in these areas that the most developed indigenous traditions of monumental drystone settlement construction occur. Although distinct, these traditions were undeniably related and suggest the existence of cultural contacts between Atlantic Scotland and Ireland throughout the Iron Age.[2] At the same time, south-west England and Wales have their closest parallels not within the rest of Britain but with developments across the English Channel in Armorica, suggesting the existence of a second major zone of northern Atlantic interaction – an inner zone – which probably also included the coastal communities of south-eastern Ireland. Unlike the outer zone, communities in south-west Wales and south-west England, although retaining an Atlantic character, would have been more open to west-central European influences via their contacts with Armorica.

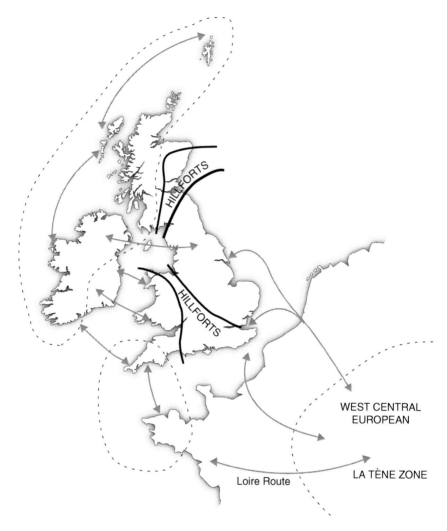

Figure 7.1 Spheres of interaction in the northern Atlantic zone 600–100 BC.

It is certainly true that, compared to the Late Bronze Age, trading links with Atlantic groups were less important to west-central European communities during the Iron Age. This does not mean, however, that contacts along the Atlantic seaboard ceased; indeed it seems highly unlikely that an area with a developed maritime tradition and technology would simply sever all other forms of contact after the apparent demise of the bronze exchange networks. Seamanship is, by its very nature, a skill that needs to be maintained through practice, ensuring that sea journeys would still have been taking place. Maritime contacts were perhaps not as frequent or intense as before, but they would have persisted through the Iron Age. Evidence for wider contacts is seen through the occurrence of the western British bronze vessels, Iberian style brooches, Greek and Carthaginian coins, and 'Mediterranean' type bronze figurines, but there is little evidence for the exchange of material goods on any significant scale between areas. Symbolic and ritual relationships, formed with other Atlantic communities through the exchange of prestige metalwork during the Late Bronze Age, may have continued into the Iron Age simply through face-to-face contacts and the exchange of ideas. Small-scale movements of people involved in economic, diplomatic, and religious transactions need not be more visible than the current evidence suggests.

Although west-central European groups became more focused on links with the Mediterranean during the Iron Age (Cunliffe 1988b), east–west links between the Atlantic world and continental Europe did not completely cease; there would have been a continuous demand for metal resources by west-central European and Mediterranean communities, albeit at a much diminished level compared to the Late Bronze Age. As was examined in Chapter 6, there is evidence to suggest that Armorica and the Loire route served as a gateway to Atlantic resources for west-central European groups throughout the Iron Age (Cunliffe 2000). Equally, from the third century BC La Tène objects and artistic influences were finding their way into northern and eastern parts of Ireland, most likely via groups in northern England.

As evidence of material contacts decline, there is a recognisable move from *c.* 600 BC towards more complex and distinctive forms of architecture and settlement in Atlantic areas. This is seen in Atlantic Scotland with the beginnings of the thick walled drystone roundhouse; in Ireland arguably with the beginnings of the drystone *cashel* tradition; and in south-west Wales and England through the construction of small univallate enclosures. The move towards enclosed settlement in the middle of the first millennium BC is very much a pan-European phenomenon (cf. Thomas 1997) but the resulting settlement types found throughout the northern Atlantic zone – mainly small, visually imposing homesteads – have much in common. The widespread occurrence of promontory forts and souterrains, coupled with the lack of hillfort type settlement or visible burial traditions throughout the Iron Age suggest the existence of further cultural similarities. From the fourth century BC sites become more complex and indicative of displaying status and identity within the zone with the start of complex Atlantic roundhouse architecture in Scotland and potentially related complex forms in Ireland; *rath* enclosure forms in south-west Wales; multiple enclosure forts and univallate 'rounds' in south-west England; and univallate enclosures and multiple enclosure farmsteads in Armorica.

The peak of complexity and display throughout the zone is seen from the second century BC onwards. In Scotland the development of the complex roundhouse tower becomes fully established alongside another monumental form, the wheelhouse, from the last centuries BC up until the second century AD. In Ireland chronological precision is lacking but drystone forts and *cashels* with complex elements of architecture comparable with those in Scotland exist. In south-west Wales, south-west England and Armorica the existence of a number of more strongly defended enclosures can be recognised amongst the mass of univallate sites and, in this case, may be related to the opening up of trading contacts with west-central Europe and ultimately Rome.

The increasing intensity of contacts with developing west-central European and Roman markets also seems to have had an effect on the layout of indigenous enclosures in Armorica and south-west England. From the third century BC quadrangular enclosures with rounded edges appear to be the dominant form in Armorica and by the turn of the millennium some south-western rounds begin to be built with decidedly rectilinear plans. Interestingly, the resulting types in each area are still indigenous forms and share more in common with each other, in terms of morphology and size, than with types in west-central Europe. While the Roman invasion of Armorica in 56 BC resulted in a major re-organisation of the agricultural landscape, the later invasion of Britain in AD 43/44 seems to have had a much lesser impact on south-western England and Wales where indigenous ways of life continued in many respects. Atlantic Scotland and Ireland remained largely unaffected by the Romans and it is only these areas that witness the final expressions of indigenous Atlantic monumental settlement traditions.

By the second to third centuries AD the construction of non-monumental sites is the norm throughout the northern Atlantic seaboard. In Armorica, south-west England and Wales unimposing Gallo-Roman farmsteads are the dominant type. In Atlantic Scotland monumental traditions of drystone roundhouse construction come to an end and are replaced by smaller cellular structures sometimes built within the walls of earlier Atlantic roundhouses. While the development of complex drystone fort forms may continue in western Ireland, cellular settlement is also represented in the form of stone-built *clochans*, many of which occur within *cashels* resembling the cellular re-use of Atlantic roundhouses in Scotland.[3]

Settlement trends in the first millennium BC

There is little indication of regional traditions in settlement types in the Late Bronze Age and the occurrence of simple, unimposing forms contrasts sharply with the widespread production and deposition of elaborate bronze metalwork. The move towards more complex and visually imposing settlement types from *c.* 600 BC coincides with a drop in the evidence for metalwork deposition. This change may indicate transformations in the way Atlantic groups negotiated and expressed their wider social identities, with the shift from portable artefacts to static field monuments reflecting in some measure the degree of mobility of the communities concerned, or at least the perceived importance of wider exotic contacts versus indigenous identities. Despite the occurrence of distinctive decorated pottery traditions in Atlantic Scotland, south-west England and Armorica, Iron Age material assemblages along the Atlantic seaboard remain largely utilitarian and are not diagnostic enough to express distinct social identities: certainly there is very little evidence for the exchange of objects between areas at this time. Whatever the case, Atlantic societies became more inward looking (within the Atlantic zone), and began to negotiate their identities and place in the landscape through the very visible local means of the elaborate and imposing appearance of their settlements. It is perhaps significant that the most visible forms of settlement elaboration – the drystone traditions of Atlantic Scotland and Ireland – occur precisely in those areas that are the most isolated. While these outer areas remain remote from continental influences there is some evidence of new networks of exchange established through Armorica, linking west-central Europe directly with the metal-rich Atlantic system.

The occurrence of less differentiated, non-monumental settlement forms from the beginning of the first millennium AD coincides with an increase in access to imported exotic artefacts. For example, settlement forms become less elaborate in Atlantic Scotland around the same time as there is evidence for an opening up of trading contacts around the third century AD through the exchange of items of personal decoration such as brooches and composite bone combs (Armit 1996). Equally, in south-west England, Wales, and Armorica, settlement elaboration becomes less pronounced after these areas gain access to a wider range of exotic goods through their involvement in wider Roman trade networks.

It is only just beginning to be appreciated in archaeology that widespread modes of cultural behaviour can be directly related whilst being deployed in specifically local ways. During the Iron Age the communities of the Atlantic seaboard can be seen to relate more closely to each other than to their immediate landward neighbours. There can be little doubt that throughout the prehistoric period and beyond, the sea facilitated contacts between these communities ensuring that the Atlantic area became a recognisable zone prone to stimulating itself, creating broad similarities over long distances. At one level it is possible to define an overall Atlantic identity for the western seaboard of Europe. At a closer level of scrutiny, diversity within the zone can be recognised as each regional sequence responds to its own internal dynamics and displays distinctive characteristics. The communities of Armorica have their closest parallels with those of south-west England, which in turn are close to those in south-west Wales. Many of the enclosures of southern and eastern parts of Ireland resemble those in south-west England and Wales while the drystone settlement record of western Ireland appears to be most closely paralleled in Atlantic Scotland. Interlocking networks of contact over a long period of time would easily promote such a broad level of similarity between areas. Within this broad Atlantic zone it is possible to define distinct cultural areas such as Atlantic Scotland, and at a further level of resolution, evidence of regional diversity within this area through the study of the Northern, Western Isles, Argyll and south-west Scottish sequences, all of which are undeniably related but equally locally distinctive.

Similarities, and therefore one must assume contacts, appear to be strongest between adjacent communities, implying that interlocking small-scale down-the-line contacts were more significant in the creation of apparent cultural similarities during the Iron Age than regular long distance contacts between widely disparate areas. The potential for communication offered by the sea, and perhaps a conscious history of previous contacts, ensured that communities developed with an awareness of each other, even if they were not in a direct and constant trading relationship. It is not unreasonable to assume then that Atlantic groups viewed themselves as being part of a series of maritime peoples who shared the sea as a common point of contact and as a result maintained cultural links. The recognition of the simple fact that the sea provided a medium of contact between Atlantic communities provides the opportunity for cultural interaction to take place, but it does not fully explain how such contacts created similarities over time.

Related diversity: the Iron Age communities of north-western Iberia

So far discussion has focused on the recognition of regional diversity occurring within a broader Atlantic tradition amongst the communities of the northern half of the Atlantic zone. In order to gain some appreciation of wider Atlantic contacts we will now take a moment to consider the effects of northern Atlantic influences in north western Iberia. As with other Atlantic societies, the Iron Age communities of north western Iberia formed a diverse group that were open to and influenced by maritime contacts which ensured they sustained identities distinct from their inland neighbours. Unlike other Atlantic regions, however, the communities of this area occupied a pivotal position between the Mediterranean world and the Atlantic and, as a result, they maintained contacts with communities from both areas throughout the first millennium BC (González-Ruibal 2004).

From the tenth to the end of the seventh centuries BC, Atlantic influences appear most dominant. The occurrence of metalwork forms derived from Atlantic models suggest not only the existence of maritime exchange networks but also that similar social practices were in place in north-western Iberia where these forms were accepted, interpreted and developed (Ruíz-Gálvez 1998: 204-8). Accompanying the evidence for wider maritime links, permanent settlements appear for the first time in the form of fortified hilltop enclosures, known locally as *castros*, which significantly feature stone-built roundhouses as the main household unit (Figure 7.2). There are also over twenty examples which feature stone *chevaux-de-frise* around them similar to those seen at stone forts in western-Ireland, Wales and Scotland (Harbison 1971). On saying this, there is no reason why *castros* should not be viewed as an indigenous development, although their initial construction in the Late Bronze Age may have been a direct result of social conditions created by intensified Atlantic contacts at the beginning of the first millennium BC (Ruíz-Gálvez 1991). In common with other Atlantic areas there is a lack of visible burial traditions from the Late Bronze Age until the appearance of Roman burials in the second century AD.

With the collapse of the Atlantic bronze networks in the seventh century BC, communities in north-western Iberia become more inward looking. There is some evidence for contact with ports to the south through the discovery of small amounts of Iberian, Greek and Punic items but this seems largely restricted to coastal communities as only glass beads tend to be found further inland (González-Ruibal 2004: fig. 8). Imported artefacts appear to have played less of a role in society and settlements produce largely utilitarian assemblages comparable to those from other Atlantic areas.[4] More elaborate objects made in gold such as bracelets, earrings and torcs are known, and highly decorated stamped and incised pottery forms also occur but these are very much indigenous elements and serve to underline the strong regional character of north western Iberian communities. The occurrence of massive warrior statues is another unique characteristic of the area and perhaps reflects the continuation of warrior values first established in the Late Bronze Age. Expressions of community power and identity are most visible through the construction of more visually imposing and complex defences at *castro* settlements. In the Late Bronze Age earthen ramparts and ditches were the norm but from the fifth century BC onwards the construction of stone wall enclosures becomes more widespread and sites featuring more than one enclosing rampart are common (Parcero and Cobas 2004: 25-32). Castro Montaz in Galicia, for example, features a monumental enclosing stone wall which is 4 m thick and has at least one step or median wall face that survives to over 2 m in height (Carballo 2002).

Perceptions of *castros* are distorted by the fact that investigations have focused on the large and impressive examples most of which enclose around 20 hectares such as Citânia de Briteiros, Citânia de Sanfins and Sabroso in northern Portugal and Monte Tecla in Galicia. Smaller sites enclosing less than 2 hectares are common, particularly in northern Galicia, but they have been far less studied. Some examples, such as Castro de Baroña on the Galician coast, were built in defended promontory loca-tions and therefore offer closer parallels with defended sites known in the northern

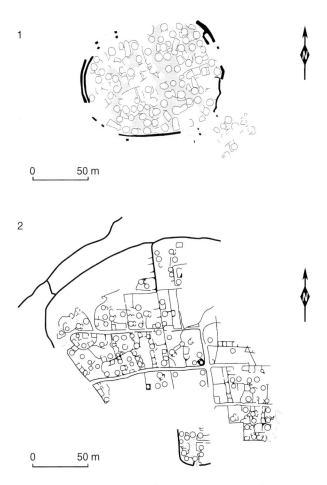

Figure 7.2 North western Iberian *castros* (after Quieroga 2003: fig. 13): (1) a pre-Roman example at Cividade de Terroso, Portugal and (2) the Roman influenced layout at Citânia de Sanfins, Portugal.

Atlantic zone. Equally, the fact that most *castros* were heavily occupied and re-organised in the Roman period, from the first century BC to the second century AD, has meant that studies have focused on this period of their use (Queiroga 2003). It is clear, however, that the monumental construction of *castro* sites was also taking place during the fifth to second centuries BC in line with the movements towards monumentality seen elsewhere along the Atlantic seaboard.

As in other Atlantic areas the construction of monumental settlement forms would have been a communal activity, where local groups came together and actively constructed visible elements of their social identity in the landscape. This activity, alongside the construction of promontory forts along the Galician coast, reflects the existence of shared ideas about settlement and its meaning in the landscape. Atlantic influences can therefore be recognised in a less direct or tangible sense through the occurrence of a similar symbolic syntax (monumental stone-built settlements, circular houses, enclosed promontories, utilitarian assemblages and a lack of burials) suggesting that ideas and ways of life were being exchanged along the Atlantic coasts rather than artefacts at this time (González-Ruibal 2004: 313).

Similar to the situation in western Armorica, from the end of the second century BC the influence of the expanding Roman world is seen through the occurrence of Dressel 1 amphorae and the construction of rectangular structures within settlements. Interestingly there is also some evidence for the local production of ceramics with burnished reticulated decoration and 'hanging medallion' designs which can be paralleled with contemporary forms in Brittany and southern England (González-Ruibal 2004: figs. 13 and 14). This apparent knowledge of northern ceramic forms may be an indication that north western Iberia was also participating, via Atlantic sea routes, in the trade in wine known to have taken place between Armorica and southern England between 120 and 40 BC (Cunliffe and de Jersey 1997).

The independent communities of north western Iberia were the last in Spain to be conquered by Rome and despite aggressive campaigns from the second century BC they did not completely capitulate until 19 BC under Augustus. Contacts with the Roman world stimulated the development of urban characteristics at the majority of *castro* sites such as regular planned layouts and open public spaces. Many of these sites, such as Citânia de Sanfins and Briteiros, are large enough, at around 20 hectares in size, to be considered urban capitals and feature regular street grids which are subdivided into smaller units for the individual households (Silva 1986). Significantly, however, the houses themselves remain circular in plan which is perhaps an indication of how deeply imbedded Atlantic social systems were in the area. As in southwest England and Armorica, the indigenous social systems were strong enough to retain a distinctive character even under Roman rule, with elements of Roman culture simply absorbed into indigenous traditions.

A common Atlantic language?

Similarities in language are often considered to be an important signifier in terms of identifying the existence of cultural contacts between areas (Coulmas 1992); certainly for the communication of shared beliefs and practices along the Atlantic seaboard to have taken place, some level of common language would have been vital. As was mentioned in Chapter 3, it has been argued by a number of authors that a common trade language or lingua franca developed along the Atlantic coasts in tandem with the widespread exchange of metalwork forms during the Late Bronze Age (Koch 1986, 1991; Piggott 1979, 1983; Sherratt and Sherratt 1988; Ruíz-Gálvez 1991; Waddell 1995; Cunliffe 2001).

Koch (1986) and Waddell (1995) have suggested that any such Atlantic trading language, or more likely languages, would probably have been a form of proto-Celtic.[5] There is much controversy about precisely when the Atlantic fringes of Europe, particularly Ireland and Galicia, became Celtic speaking (Mallory 1984; Waddell 1991a, 1991b, 1995). It is not beyond the realms of possibility, however, that a distinctive Atlantic trade language, a form of proto-Celtic, was established some-time during the Late Bronze Age (*c.* 1250 to 600 BC). It is impossible on current evidence to determine whether the languages used during the Atlantic Late Bronze Age were related to Celtic (Q Celtic or proto-Celtic) but it is significant to note that many Atlantic areas definitely were Celtic speaking by at least the middle of the first millennium BC. It is potentially even more significant that the Atlantic fringes of Ireland, north western Iberia,[6] and possibly Scotland, retained the more archaic Q Celtic form perhaps implying that we should be looking towards the Atlantic zone as the 'homeland'[7] of Celtic languages rather than central Europe. Communities in west-central Europe could also have been speaking a form of proto-Celtic at this time but, given the existence of significant cultural differences between the zones, it is likely to have been different, or at least to have evolved in a different way, from an Atlantic proto-Celtic lingua franca. In other words, while the languages between the two zones may have been broadly related throughout the prehistoric period, the development of differences over time is simply a reflection of the fact that Atlantic groups were in more regular contact with each other than with communities in west-central Europe. It is likely that these differences became more distinct during the Late Bronze Age when contacts between Atlantic areas appear to be at their most intense.

With the collapse of the Atlantic Late Bronze Age exchange networks *c.* 600 BC, the outer Atlantic areas of Atlantic Scotland, Ireland and Iberia became more isolated from developments in west-central Europe. Q-Celtic (usually accepted as the oldest form of Celtic known) persisted in these areas (Figure 7.3). The previous Atlantic lingua franca/proto-Celtic areas of Armorica, Wales and south-west England, however, may have become P-Celtic speaking around this time in common with developments in west-central Europe and invigorated by the spread of La Tène tradi-tions from the middle of the first millennium BC. These three areas form an inter-mediary zone between outer Atlantic communities completely removed from La Tène influences and the La Tène homelands of west-central Europe. They remain distinctively Atlantic in some respects (particularly in settlement and social organisa-tion) but also accept some La Tène influences such as P-Celtic (though they retain their distinctiveness and never become fully involved with La Tène exchange networks or trends). In Figures 7.4 and 7.5 it can be seen that the outer zone of

Figure 7.3 Atlantic Late Bronze Age 900–600 BC. Main concentrations of Atlantic traditions and possible extent of Atlantic lingua franca (proto-Celtic or Q-Celtic).

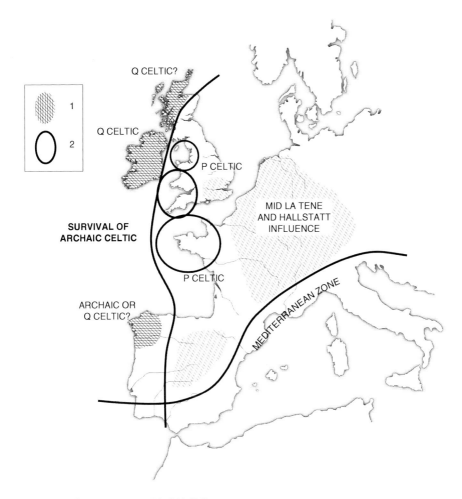

Figure 7.4 Atlantic Europe 600–300 BC.
1. *Outer Atlantic Zone* – Ireland and Scotland display more evidence of contacts with each other than elsewhere and may have retained or developed the more archaic Q-Celtic form. North western Iberia may also have retained an archaic form related to Q-Celtic and/or an Atlantic Late Bronze Age *lingua franca*.
2. *Inner Atlantic zone* – Armorica, south-west England and Wales display some evidence of contacts with the early La Tène world (from 450 BC) and may have become P-Celtic speaking at this time.

Iberia, Ireland and Scotland remain largely removed from continental developments which may go some way to explain the late survival of Q-Celtic in these areas into the first millennium AD.[8] At a very broad level, then, language similarities throughout the Atlantic zone may reflect another element of shared identity between communities, and certainly the linguistic evidence does not contradict the general areas of interaction suggested from the settlement evidence.

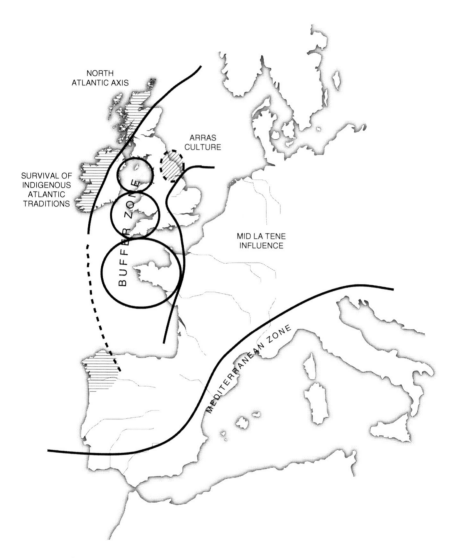

Figure 7.5 Atlantic Europe 300–100 BC.

1. *Outer Atlantic Zone* – North eastern half of Ireland receives a restricted range of La Tène metalwork (swords and style have strong Arras connections). Western and southern Ireland remains more Atlantic influenced and potentially has closest parallels with Atlantic Scotland (both areas virtually devoid of La Tène influence).

2. *Inner Atlantic zone* – Armorica used as a gateway to Atlantic resources by west central European groups (and later by the expanding Roman world).

Atlantic identities and the sea

Western Atlantic identity can be defined at a broad level archaeologically through the occurrence of architecturally imposing (usually stone-built) settlements, similar site forms such as souterrains and promontory forts, the lack of an elite material culture or evidence of traded prestige goods, the occurrence of locally produced but often highly decorated ceramics, the absence of burials, and the dominance of the household as the main social unit. Not all areas possessed the full range of these features and degrees of resemblance between areas varied in time and space. Large-scale homogeneity dissolving at smaller scales into regional or even local heterogeneity can be considered the leitmotif of the Atlantic Iron Age. In this sense the Atlantic seaboard is not a uniform block but is composed of a range of diverse communities which evolve at different rates and in different ways over the centuries. Crucially, however, from a diachronic perspective their evolution is related and, standing back from the detail, can be distinguished from developments occurring in the rest of Europe. As we have seen, regional innovation and expression is a major feature of Atlantic areas, but this expression is carried out within an existing framework of exchange and an existing set of social and material conventions. So while there is little support for a view of Atlantic communities forming a cohesive cultural complex there is a long-term, albeit perhaps largely unintentional, *directedness* to their development which ensured basic levels of cultural commonality.

The recognition of cultural similarities throughout the Atlantic zone begs the question whether Atlantic communities themselves viewed each other as a related group of maritime peoples. Spanning individual group identities it is possible that prolonged maritime contacts between coastal areas would have fostered a shared sense of coastal identity amongst Atlantic groups definable from groups based inland. Whether this identity was ever expressed in terms of a 'people of the sea' as opposed to a 'people of the land' is beyond our capacity to know but it is perhaps significant to note that the Celtic name *Armorican* literally translates as 'dwellers by or from the sea' while the placenames used for the peninsula make a clear distinction between the coastlands, or *Armor*, and the wooded interior, or *Argoat* (Sherratt 1998: 136). It is possible that survival of these names is a reflection of conceptual distinctions made by indigenous groups in the first millennium BC.

It is of course impossible to reconstruct with any degree of certainty how a community located on the Atlantic coast viewed themselves and the world around them. What is important, however, is to realise that they saw themselves as central to current events, as indeed they were in their own localised terms, and that their particular environment was the norm. They would not see themselves as 'peripheral' or 'marginal' societies in the way that many archaeologists are keen to label them today. A speculative but hugely enjoyable cosmological map of the Atlantic coasts, presented by Stuart Needham at a conference on the Atlantic Bronze Age in 1998 (Needham 1998), illustrates this point. The map was an attempt to see the world as a Late Bronze Age community might do, in this case one conveniently centred in the Vendée, western France, halfway along the Atlantic seaboard (Figure 7.6). The details of the map are unimportant (indeed the very process of constructing a map may have been alien

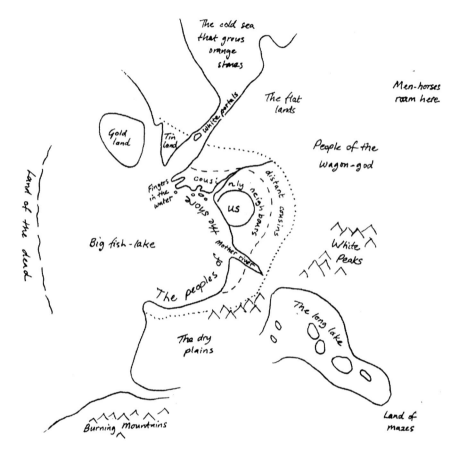

Figure 7.6 Stuart Needham's (1998) hypothetical world view of an Atlantic community centred on the Vendée, western France.

to such a community) but it does serve to confront the ways in which we arrange archaeological data in modern cartographic terms. As Needham admits, his map owes more to J. R. R. Tolkien and Herodotus than the community in question, but it does at least create an impression of how such a group may have seen the world and, more importantly, it alters our perception of how they may have viewed themselves.

An interesting feature of the map is the way it tries to reflect the difference between first-hand knowledge and the increasingly distorted accounts of regions further away passed on orally down-the-line by others. Seafarers would have possessed a wider cognitive geography than others and this may have resulted in coastal communities knowing more about distant coastal areas than closer but less regularly visited areas inland. Under such conditions it is possible to gain a glimpse into the mechanism of shared concepts between Atlantic coastal communities over large distances.

In mapping such a world view (in a cognitive or cartographic sense) it becomes obvious that for a community located on the Atlantic coasts, the sea takes up a significant proportion of the space and thus most likely had a major impact on their world view. In any other part of Europe communities would be surrounded by a variety of potential influences and would be aware of what lay beyond their immediate environs in each direction. However, communities living along the Atlantic existed in an entirely different spatial context, one roughly aligned along a north–south axis and in which influences from and information of other Atlantic communities arrived by sea. The communities living along the Mediterranean or North Sea certainly had a great awareness of the sea but their view of their place in the world was likely to have been much different. For example, the Mediterranean, as an enclosed sea, was surrounded by land and was small enough that its boundaries were known and could be fixed in the mind. It was a different matter, however, to stand on an Atlantic shore and look out; one would be forced to confront the unknown, an uncertainty of what lay beyond the horizon. The Atlantic Ocean was a source of awesome and unforgiving natural power, much more so than the tide-less Mediterranean, and it was a seemingly infinite expanse which extended into the uncharted west, where each night the sea swallowed the Sun.

There is now a wider appreciation of the importance of recognising the potential ideological significance of landscape features to pre-modern societies (Bradley 1993, 1998, 2000; Barrett 1994; Tilley 1994, 1996). The sea formed a major part of the Atlantic coastal landscape and it is likely that it would have been imbued with a strong ritual significance. It would have offered opportunities in the sense that prestige objects, people, and ideas arrived via the sea, and could be sought after by accessing it, but it would also have offered mystery, danger, and in some cases death – some mariners never came back – and was thus a natural force to be respected. It is with some significance, therefore, that the western limits of the Atlantic are marked as the 'land of the dead' on Needham's map (Figure 7.6).

As we saw in Chapter 3, from *c.* 1200 BC onwards there is evidence for a widespread Atlantic orientated belief system based upon the deposition of prestige metalwork in watery locations – it is not a major leap of imagination to assume that the sea would have had a role to play in this system and would have, alongside rivers, lakes, and bogs, been viewed as a natural entity of considerable ritual significance by Atlantic peoples. The sheer power of the seemingly 'infinite' Atlantic cannot have failed to have had an impact on those communities living beside it. It was certainly 'wild' in the sense that unlike other natural features in the landscape it could not have been altered or 'domesticated' through human control.[9] Religious attitudes to winds, tides, and the forces that control the sea may have been as important in Atlantic belief systems as seasonality was to agrarian centred societies.[10] The apparent lunar emphasis in megalithic ritual practice, for example, implies that tidal regimes may have been seen as important from an early date in Atlantic areas.

The Atlantic landscape would have been embedded with meaning and mythological narratives in the first millennium BC. Community identities, mythologies and ancestral histories would have been represented in spatial form by the landscape itself and actively created and renegotiated through specific actions within that landscape.

The construction of monumental sites is one visible aspect of this. It was suggested in Chapter 4, for example, that at least some promontory sites may have been visible symbols of the relationship between the sea and Atlantic communities, featuring ritual aspects dedicated to, or connected with, the sea. They were focal locations which structured the experiences and narratives embedded in the landscape and were places where groups could come together to express and restate their community identities. The ritual connotations of promontory locations have a long pedigree, from the siting of burial monuments in the late Neolithic through to the building of Christian churches and cemeteries in the first millennium AD.[11] Their re-use (or continued use) in the Iron Age and later periods might be seen as a conscious effort to be associated with a place of spiritual power, whether to draw strength by relation or by desecration, as well as highlighting the continuity of traditions in Atlantic areas.

The most visible elements of the Atlantic landscape, however, were the strongly defended settlements – the main social unit of Atlantic societies – which were 'built to be seen and impress' (Cunliffe 2001: 337). There is diversity in form across the Atlantic zone from the complex roundhouses and *cashels* of Atlantic Scotland and western Ireland to the 'round' enclosures of south-west Britain and western Armorica but as a group they have much in common. Most sites are relatively small in terms of overall area, even the enclosure forms rarely exceed 1 hectare in size, and they are usually interpreted as housing family or extended family units. Despite their apparently passive domestic use, the sites of the Atlantic zone commonly feature massively constructed walls or ramparts. Equally, they were built to stand alone, enhancing their visibility, and despite the fact that they often occur in densely packed landscapes, they almost always occur in isolation: there is little evidence for the occurrence of nucleated settlements or, the suggested communal role of promontory forts aside, of larger sites carrying out central roles. As a result, Atlantic groups are usually perceived as consisting of non-hierarchical, independent household communities. What makes the Atlantic sites stand out as a related group from settlements in neighbouring areas are their monumental appearance and their permanence in the landscape.

The outward appearance of settlements appears to have taken on an increasingly important symbolic role in Atlantic societies throughout the first millennium BC. The construction of visually imposing settlement forms in the Iron Age occurs at a time when there is little evidence for the exchange of objects between Atlantic groups. Indigenous material assemblages are largely undiagnostic and undifferentiated with groups instead expressing elements of their social identities through the appearance of their settlements. The physical appearance of settlements would have carried symbolic messages about the inhabitants which would have been understood by members of the local community. In this way, Atlantic settlements were key constituents in an Atlantic landscape that was socially constructed and experienced by Iron Age communities.

The occurrence of similarities in settlement form beyond local areas and across the western Atlantic zone implies that shared ways of reading the landscape existed between more distant groups linked by sea – that at a broad level the Atlantic landscape was constructed and used according to shared symbolic conventions. In this way it is possible to define the existence of some shared level of Atlantic identity during the Iron Age. Similar ways of inhabiting and constructing the landscape, most visible through similarities in the household form, may have allowed communities to perceive themselves as a group of related coastal peoples with a shared level of identity beyond that of the local community. This level of identity may not have been clearly defined, or even consciously expressed, and local identities likely remained the key identifier for individual households. Instead cultural continuities would have been created through the existence of maritime contacts between groups along the Atlantic seaboard, the overall geographic extent of which many groups may have remained unaware.

Continuities in the constructed appearance and residual meanings of the Atlantic landscape would have been accentuated through the occurrence of long occupations at settlement sites and their widespread re-use. The fact that many sites were constructed from stone obviously has significance in terms of their permanence in the landscape. It meant that sites could be inhabited for multiple generations and once abandoned were more likely to be re-used. The building of settlements in stone was largely governed by material conditions but what was done with the available stone in terms of creating distinctive architectural forms was culturally mediated and thus has a significance in defining Atlantic group identities. Building in stone meant that sites and, as a result, families were more likely to remain in one location ensuring that houses, as symbols of individual households or social groups, persisted in the mythology of the landscape. As a result, stone-built settlements were capable of communicating social meanings across generations, helping to create deeply ingrained continuities in the Atlantic landscape.

The Atlantic landscape was socialised through centuries of activities, a process that has a recognisable structure and *directedness* reflected through the archaeological monuments that survive today. The durability of stone-built structures ensured that they took on an increased importance in Atlantic societies as symbols of group identity and legitimacy. The Atlantic Iron Age landscape consisted of socially and symbolically meaningful localities where clear material evidence of past generations and their presence in the landscape survived. In such a context, connections with ancestors could be more easily expressed, with the result that the continued occupation, re-occupation and/or modification of sites can be interpreted as a culturally meaningful act that was meant to create a link to or, conversely, eradicate the past. The meaning and significance of structures would, of course, have changed over time but their very real presence in the landscape would also have fostered deep-set cultural similarities.

Ultimately, the similarities in the Atlantic archaeological record were created through the intended and unintended outcomes of actions of individuals and communities. These actions occurred within a context of culturally mediated forms of behaviour, of which the construction of monumental settlements is one aspect. At the synchronic scale individuals and communities acted according to their understanding of the world and intentionally referenced and re-worked local traditions and wider social values. From a diachronic perspective culturally informed community level and, to a lesser extent, individual actions created continuities both within and outside the range of human awareness creating an overall structure to similarities along the Atlantic seaboard. Material and environmental conditions clearly have a role to play in creating the opportunities for similarities to develop but they explain nothing in themselves – it is the cultural and social world of individual communities that take on a recognisable character allowing us to talk in terms of shared Atlantic traditions.

The recognition of unconscious, long-term continuities does not mean that Atlantic societies were simply passive victims of their group identity. Although societies were governed by commonly understood standards and acceptable behaviour creating broad cultural similarities, change could occur at any point through the actions of individuals or groups of individuals. Those individuals would of course act according to widely held beliefs and common ways of understanding the world, but they would be capable of original actions based on individual readings of given situations. This capability is usually referred to as agency and a realisation of its effects helps to explain regional and local divergence in the Atlantic record without necessarily having to cite external factors. The transformations that occurred in settlement forms in the Iron Age were more likely the result of the ways local groups constructed their collective identities in the short-term, but they would have undoubtedly been influenced by long-term continuities. Atlantic social identities evolved in a more permanent constructed environment than areas that constructed forms in wood – stone-built sites were symbols that endured through time and as a result their histories and associated mythologies were more likely to influence what future generations did, and how they experienced their lives. This does not of course mean that sites had a fixed meaning from generation to generation which was understood and accepted in the same way and at all times. Meanings of sites would have been constantly created and reproduced through the social practices that took place on or near them, but the very existence of stone sites as markers of previous communities, coupled with the existence of contacts between Atlantic groups, ensured a level of *directedness* in developments over time. The fact that meanings changed and that local communities could develop according to their own internal agendas is self-evident otherwise the Atlantic zone would be a homogeneous area of cultural uniformity. There are differences because settlements, objects and symbols get their meaning from their specific cultural contexts; however, the general similarities between areas imply that some of these meanings are shared, otherwise we would have a much more diverse archaeological record.

The interaction of wide-ranging maritime contacts and the role of specific cultural contexts were therefore not mutually exclusive but inter-dependent elements in the creation of broad levels of Atlantic identity. This identity was superimposed over a real variety of cultural contexts and it can only be fully elucidated through the analysis of local contexts and their wider articulation with each other. This book has attempted to do this from a diachronic perspective, but in doing so it becomes apparent that to fully understand the dynamics of Atlantic groups more work needs to be done on the differences between them at a synchronic scale. In other words, to fully examine the concept of Atlantic identity it is the diversity that is of interest: how did Atlantic groups distinguish themselves from each other? A number of interesting differences have been touched upon which demand further study, including: the social meaning of the diversity of site forms within the Atlantic

Scottish zone; the reasons behind the continued development of monumental dry-stone forms in western Ireland into the first millennium AD; the distinct identity claimed for Iron Age communities in south-west England versus their apparent close trading relationships with coastal communities in central-southern England; the unique role of Armorican communities in providing access to Atlantic resources for west-central European groups; and the re-contextualisation of Mediterranean and Atlantic orientated influences by the communities of north-west Iberia. There is a degree of difference and distinction throughout the zone that needs to be engaged with to create a more fully rounded view of Atlantic communities that will ultimately develop our understanding of the European Iron Age as a whole. It is time to bring Atlantic areas in from the periphery and fully consider their role in wider Iron Age developments: certainly there is more to the European Iron Age than notions of Celtic identity and the concerns of the elite Hallstatt and La Tène groups.

Notes

1 Atlantic Europe: the lands of the continuity of tradition

1 The Romans conquered Armorica in 56 BC and southern Britain in AD 43/44. Ireland and Atlantic Scotland were largely unaffected and Iron Age traditions continued here unhindered into the first millennium AD.

2 'Directedness' is a term coined by Richard Dawkins (1990) to describe the unconscious yet essentially non-random process of natural selection. Contacts and interaction along the Atlantic seaboard ensured general similarities throughout the prehistoric period but, similar to the process of natural selection, there was unlikely to have been any grand design or premeditated plan on the part of Atlantic communities to create zones of similarity. In many cases, the maintenance of socio-cultural similarities between separate communities through the episodic re-invigoration of natural routes of contact may have been an entirely unconscious process.

3 Although this is the most popular interpretation not everyone accepts that the poem refers to a journey as far as Britain. For example, Penhallurick (1986: 128) argues that the poem refers to a much shorter Atlantic coastline due to the skin-covered boats reportedly used and that therefore the *Oestrymnis* and reference to *Albiones* could refer to somewhere in south-western Iberia. Pliny described a people called the *Albiones* living on the Biscayan shore of Spain and Penhallurick argues that there is no reason why others of the same name could not have lived in southern Spain or Portugal. Although his interpretation is certainly possible Penhallurick fails to discount adequately or explain the reference to the island of *Hierni* normally taken to refer to Ireland. In his favour, however, Phoenician pottery has only ever been recorded as far north as the western coasts of Galicia (see Veleda Reimao Quieroga 1992: fig. 51).

4 The main source is thought to have been the lost text of the Stoic traveller Posidonius compiled around 90 BC (Tierney 1960; Cunliffe 1982a: 41).

5 As Todd (1987: 185) puts it: 'Classical sources repeating snatches about trade with barbarians on the fringes of the known world, or beyond it, are about as reliable as second-hand references to American Indians in the sixteenth century by historians who had never sailed the Atlantic.'

6 To many people the actual definition of what constitutes a Celt, other than some form of generic, indigenous and ancient ancestor, is unclear and largely unimportant to their usage of the term to describe themselves. In Scotland, Ireland and Wales notions of Celticness have more to do with stressing cultural boundaries and distinctiveness from the dominant cultural group of the British Isles, the English, than any archaeological or historical fact. Celtic identity is used in a similar way by the Bretons despite the fact that the rest of France would also consider themselves to be direct descendants of the Celtic Gauls. The Galicians of north-west Spain also use their deeply felt sense of Celtic identity to distinguish their cultural independence from the rest of Spain – where, once again, the actual definition remains unclear as Celts have also been incorporated into general Spanish nationalist histories and ideologies.

7 The Act of Union in 1707 created the concept and country of Great Britain in which many Scots felt culturally dominated by the English. In 1800 Ireland was forced into the United Kingdom. Celt was adopted as an ethnonym by the Irish, Scots and Welsh as a reaction against the concept of Britishness.

8 Wooding (1996: 3) refers to this group of archaeo-geographers as the 'western seaways theorists'.

9 One from Mount Batten, Plymouth and two from a grave at Harlyn Bay, Cornwall (these fibulae are discussed further in Chapter 4).

10 Fox's Highland Zone comprises the upland areas of Britain north and west of the Severn–Humber line including the south-west peninsula (for a full definition see Fox 1932: 29, 40–2).

11 Sherratt (1990) has demonstrated how complex such relationships can be in reference to the megalithic cultures of the Atlantic and Baltic. He describes the interaction between the two areas as an Atlantic coastal relationship and then considers the effects incoming farming groups from central Europe have on the trajectory of developments in the Atlantic maritime zone. A similar relationship can be identified in the Late Bronze Age when elements of central European prestige bronze economies are adopted by Atlantic communities but re-contextualised in the process. This would imply, as the earlier evidence suggests, that the Atlantic sphere of influence existed before it absorbed elements of central European practice.

2 Atlantic land and sea

1 Both south-west England and Armorica share a common 'lands-end' mythology. In Cornwall the peninsula at Land's End is seen as an important local and national landmark. Finistère literally means 'the end of the earth' whereas the Pointe du Raz in the ancient kingdom of Cornouaille (named after Cornwall in the mid-first millennium AD after the British population incursions) is also seen as an important landmark for being the 'lands-end' of Finistère and France.

2 The results from the C14 dated profile of Redbog suggest the decline occurred *c.* 800 BC (Weir 1995). However, the dating of many pollen profiles in Ireland is relative or insecure and it is therefore impossible to determine from the present data whether there was a synchronous decline across Ireland.

3 Evidence for marine transgressions in the first millennium BC are sometimes thought to have been important in terms of reflecting climatic deterioration and disrupting maritime contacts. Reconstructing sea-levels for the Atlantic coastal regions is extremely difficult as data from particular areas reflect very much localised conditions and it is difficult to know how far such evidence is applicable to other areas (Willis 1961; Evans 1969; Turner 1981: 261–4). For example, the effects of glacio-isostatic uplift in Scotland are such that although the north-western coasts are on the whole sinking, parts of them are rising, as are significant parts of the east coast. In general, however, as far as it is possible to determine, there appears to have been a rise in sea levels, in the range of about 1 m, throughout the Atlantic zone during the Late Bronze Age and beginnings of the Iron Age. There was then a steep fall in sea-level of at least 2 m – or at least considerable fluctuation within a 2 m range – from the fourth to the first century BC (de Jersey 1994: 6, fig. 4). From the beginning of the first millennium AD there was an increase of around 3 m reaching a level similar to – at the most no greater than 1 m below – current sea-level (cf. De Lumley *et al.* 1976: 6; Lamb 1982; Devoy 1990: 17). Such wide fluctuations over our period of study would likely have had a considerable effect on the current preservation and visibility of Iron Age coastal sites such as small harbours, boat nausts, salt extraction sites and other maritime related installations. However, the changes would have been slow and therefore largely irrelevant to Iron Age peoples during their lifetimes.

4 It is sobering to note that some of the islands of Atlantic Scotland, such as Tiree and Sanday, were already famous for their large-scale production of cereals by the time they enter the historic period. This was also reflected in their valuations by early historic authorities. For example, the Norse rates of land taxation for Sanday was many times higher than land taxes elsewhere in the Orcadian archipelago.

5 In contrast, the small bone assemblage from Caer Cadwgan, Dyfed (Austin 1984, 1985) revealed sheep were twice as numerous as cattle. This is similar to reports from Dinorben in north Wales and the apparent predominance of sheep-rearing in the mountainous central zone (Cunliffe 1991: 397–8).

6 Orographic clouds form over high ground and are visible on both sides of the English Channel from boats crossing north or south. It is interesting also that Ptolemy's map shows and names prominent headlands. Visible from up to 20 nautical miles out to sea, a knowledge of the landmarks allows course correction as the coast is approached.

7 Instead the Mediterranean has been the centre of ancient shipwreck discovery as it produces conditions beneficial to their survival: it is less stormy, tideless and has generally soft sandy seabed conditions. Wooden shipwrecks also survive well in the Baltic Sea as it is too cold for shipworm to survive and, like the Mediterranean, is an enclosed sea

3 The Atlantic Late Bronze Age (1200–600 BC)

1 Kristiansen (1998: 85–8) outlines further examples of such buffer zones in the Alps between Italy and the Central European Urnfields and between the Lausitz and Nordic zones. Each features strikingly similar characteristics to those in Brun's Atlantic/Urnfield buffer zone including the deposition of metalwork from both cultural traditions, different burial traditions on either side of the zone, and some evidence for fortified settlement but a rarity of domestic settlement and burial evidence within the zone.

2 Just as there is an array of evidence to demonstrate local interaction, there is also good evidence for direct long-haul contacts such as the assemblage of metalwork from Huelva in south-west Iberia. Thought to represent either a sunken cargo or a ritual deposit created over a period of time, it features spearheads cast in Ireland and brooches from Sicily alongside examples of the widespread Atlantic Carp's Tongue sword form (Ruíz-Gálvez 1995).

3 The leaf-bladed Irish Ballintober form swords are dominant in Britain and Ireland while straight-bladed sword forms are more common in the French Rosnoën phase (Burgess 1968: 5).

4 One of which was an early find and is now missing.

5 Lead-bronze is not taken up throughout all areas of Britain until 750–650 BC (Burgess *et al.* 1972: 226; Northover 1982; Champion 1999).

6 In south-east England this phase is also sometimes called the Bexley Heath tradition, after the hoard from Bexley Heath, Kent. However, the majority of hoards are representative of the Carp's Tongue Complex recorded in northern France and as such is the term preferred here (Burgess 1968: 17).

7 Burgess (1968: 19–26) considers local forms of socketed axes, along with the spear, as one of the best indicators of regional differences between the metalworking industries of Britain from 750 to 650 BC (see also Megaw 1979: 312–331, fig. 6.3). In Ireland during the Dowris phase bag shaped socketed axes were completely dominant (Eogan 1983); in Scotland, during the Duddingston phase (Coles 1960), there are extensive influences from Ireland and England but no indigenous socketed axe forms; in northern England, during the Heathery Burn phase (Burgess *et al.* 1972: 234), the 'Yorkshire' type of three-ribbed socketed axe is dominant (Fox, C. F. 1932: 158); in the south of England, the Broadward group centred on the Thames Valley area (Burgess *et al.* 1972) is most identified by the distinctive spearhead of the same name; axes of 'South Welsh' type are found in Wales and the south-west of England (which incidentally has a monopoly on the relevant moulds for the type).

8 The increase in deposition in the Dowris period can clearly be seen when compared to the numbers of hoards from previous periods: there are 5 hoards from the Middle Bronze Age and 25 from the Bishopsland phase; compared to 130 from the Dowris period (Cooney and Grogan 1994).

9 The concentrated deposition of Rosnoën swords at the mouth of the Loire in the region of Nantes (Briard 1995: 128) may mark the existence of a symbolic and physical boundary between areas of different metalworking tradition. In the St-Brieuc-des-Iffs phase eastern continental type swords have been found from or near the Loire but the resulting indigenous St-Brieuc-des-Iffs type swords that were produced in the area were distinctively Atlantic in execution (Briard 1995: 134). The origins of the range of finds from the famous Venat hoard (Figure 3.15) demonstrate the wealth and complexity of the exchange made possible by west-flowing rivers.

10 The majority of Urnfield types are small, poor quality pieces such as bracelets, rings and pendants. The hoards of St-Brieuc-des-Iffs and Theil á Billy, Lior-et-Cher have produced some higher status items: two small bronze rivets similar to those on continental helmets, one from each hoard, along with small bronze rings thought to be part of a heavy belt of continental type (Briard 1995: 130).

11 It is of particular interest that the trace element analysis of Wilburton phase bronzes and the Dover wreck cargo appear to be examples of metal raw materials going from the north Alpine area to the Atlantic zone rather than vice versa. At one level such a discovery supports the purely economic view that supplies of metal were unpredictable in Bronze Age Europe and the most readily available sources were used. However, there may be a more complex level of exchange taking place such as the existence of social and/or political relationships between south-east England and the continent or that there was a particular importance attached to sources from far away places.

12 Some have argued for the independent invention of leaf-shaped swords in Ireland but the chronology is not clear enough to support such a view (see Colquhoun and Burgess 1988: 19; Eogan 1965; Needham 1982; Waddell 1998: 205). Whatever the case, it is certain that the development of Atlantic swords throughout the Late Bronze Age was repeatedly inspired by forms and innovations from the continent.

13 Evidence for prestige feasting comes from the finds of cauldrons, buckets, spits and cups in hoards, as well as the assemblages of animal bones interpreted as the remains of feasting recovered from the ditch fills of a number of hilltop enclosures.

14 There are two classes of Atlantic cauldron: earlier Class A type (Gerloff 1987) and a later Class B (Leeds 1930). The Class A type is characterised by a spheriodal body with a corrugated neck and a rim which turns sharply inwards to produce a flat top. The Class B type are generally better made and do not feature a corrugated neck while the rim is usually everted with a rolled lip.

15 The U-notched Cloonlara wooden shield has been radiocarbon dated to the beginning of the Late Bronze Age (3150±90 BP, OxA–3228; Hedges *et al.* 1993), while the wooden V-notched Kilmahamogue mould from Co. Antrim (Jope 1951) produced a very early but not impossible date between 1950 and 1540 BC (3445±70 BP, OxA–2429; Hedges *et al.* 1991).

16 The earliest field systems are known from the mid-third millennium onwards in the Atlantic zone, with examples dating to the Late Neolithic in Ireland (Pilcher 1969; Caulfield 1978; Mitchell 1989; Cooney 1991; Jones and Gilmer 1999) and the Northern and Western Isles of Scotland (e.g. Barber 1997; Whittle *et al.* 1986). However, it would appear that the majority of field systems and boundaries in the Atlantic zone date to the mid-second and early first millennia BC (Johnston 2000). Examples are not known in continental Europe until the Late Bronze Age.

17 Although the dating evidence is inconclusive – skulls occur in the Thames dating to all periods while metalwork is also deposited from all periods – the apparent association of some remains with Late Bronze Age metalwork allows the possibility of a linked deposition (Bradley and Gordon 1988: 504–8).

18 The La Tène migrations into the Po Valley in the fifth and fourth centuries BC and central Asia Minor in the third-century BC do appear to have imposed a Gallo-Brittonic Celtic language. The Po Valley migrations occurred over a sustained period of time and cannot be considered a one-off event but the effects on language of the Asia Minor incursion are less easily explained.

19 It is perhaps for this reason that the hierarchies suggested for the Late Bronze Age are very similar to the traditional three-tier 'Celtic' model put forward for continental European Iron Age societies (Cunliffe 1997: 107–110). Equally, of course, the structure of society in the Iron Age may not have differed greatly from the Late Bronze Age. It is argued in this book that the foundations for the development of Atlantic Iron Age societies were laid in the Late Bronze Age, with strong evidence for continuity between the periods.

20 It is likely that the sailors were also men, so it is perhaps unsurprising that Atlantic contact items relate to male symbolism.

21 Although some are found in Carp's-Tongue sword hoards such as Ile Verte, Finistère (Briard 1961: 44–8) and Kerlouan, Finistère (Briard 1965: 212–13), indicating that the beginnings of their production overlaps with the end of the Carp's-Tongue phase.

22 A fragmentary Armorican axe was recovered from the Early Iron Age site of All Cannings Cross, Wiltshire (Cunnington 1923: 119, Pl.18:3) though it may have been a relic.

23 Prestige/symbolic La Tène metalwork was produced in bronze and gold – the media used in the Late Bronze Age. It seems that iron technology had little impact on the production of prestige goods and that bronze remained the preferred medium for ritual items.

24 Period 2 at Rathtinaun, for example, provided Dowris phase artefacts in association with radiocarbon determinations calibrating between 490 BC and AD 140 (Raftery 1994: 33–5). Ritual deposition of metal seems to decline after the Late Bronze Age but it is possible that it remained important in some areas, particularly in Ireland. Bronze metalwork is usually only dated typologically, meaning that the apparent Irish 'Dark Age' from *c.* 600 to *c.* 300 BC may be due to conservatism and the late survival of the earlier traditions of bronze-working and deposition perhaps due to isolation (unintended or intended) from the earlier La Tène developments seen in the rest of Europe. La Tène inspired bronzes are not seen in Ireland until the third century BC when a restricted range of types appear in the north-eastern half of the country – the result of secondhand flow of trade from Britain. There is no overlap between the Dowris material and La Tène material dating from the third century BC onwards, although they were presumably deposited in different contexts.

25 The Lisdrumturk cauldron from Co. Monaghan, for example, has iron rivets which may be replacements or repairs and are generally used to date the cauldron to around 600 BC (Lucas 1968: 117). Equally, of course, these repairs could have been made much later in which case the use of the cauldron would represent a survival of bronze forms and ways of life.

4 Atlantic settlement in the first millennium BC

1 Earlier periods in the northern Atlantic zone do of course provide evidence for domestic settlement but it tends to be sparse and rather ephemeral, with the majority of structural evidence coming from ritual monuments. The Late Bronze Age is the point at which domestic settlements become a visible and major part of the landscape.

2 Radiocarbon dates from Carrigillihy (O'Kelly 1989: 222): 3100±50 BP (1510–1220 BC, GrN–12916) and 2180±50 BP (1130–850 BC, GrN–12917).

3 GrN–20231, 3165±30 BP; GrN–20230, 3070±60 BP; GrN–20228, 2990±30 BP; GrN–20229, 2955±25 BP; GrN–20227, 2870±35 BP.

4 The situation is actually more complex than this: an examination of the top of Wall 1 demonstrated that the visible internal wall alignments bare little or no relation to earlier phases of wall construction (Cotter 1995: 4). A small trench across the southern end of Wall 1

revealed a series of foundation lines (op. cit. 5), but significantly these were found to bear little or no relation to the two clear wall faces in the north-western wall chamber (Cotter 1995: 10). These wall faces are shown to be some 2.5 m and 6 m into the wall (op. cit., fig. 6), while the innermost of the southern faces is only about 1 m in from the internal face (Cotter 1995: plate 2). It is probable therefore that these are secondary faces and therefore later than the original construction of the wall.

5　Some of these stone enclosures have been tentatively identified as corrals: for example those at Stannon Down, Bodmin (Mercer 1970, fig. 6).

6　Armorican and other socketed axe forms are known from Carn Brea (Borlase 1754) while others occur at Kenidjack Castle, Cornwall and Woodbury Castle, the Trendle, and Membury in Devon (Pearce 1976; Todd 1987: 157).

7　It may be that after the breakdown of Late Bronze Age trade routes that Mediterranean communities had to forge their own direct links with the Atlantic world. Evidence for a Mediterranean presence in the northern Atlantic is slight however and consists of a small range of exotic finds discussed below.

8　Iron has been found in a number of Late Bronze Age hoards: there is an iron socketed sickle dated to the late seventh century BC in the Llyn Fawr hoard, Wales (Savory 1976); of the 17 axes dated 650–600 BC at Sompting, Sussex, one featured a corroded mass of iron; iron socketed spears were found together with three bronze socketed spears and the blade of a dirk in the hoard at Melksham, Wilts. (Gingell 1979); Potterne, Wiltshire (Turnbull 1983); Lisdrumturk, Co. Monaghan, Ireland, Class B cauldron dated to 600 BC and repaired with iron rivets; an iron horse bit from occupation at Aughinish, Co. Limerick was discovered in association with a Dowris bronze tanged chisel and continental Hallstatt C copper, alloy pin; at Rathtinaun, Co. Sligo, level 2 included Dowris metalwork with some transitional iron pieces: a swan's neck pin, fleshook, shaft hole axe and bladed implement. A number of Late Bronze Age types were produced in iron: iron looped and socketed axeheads are found from Midlothian to Wiltshire and also in Ireland (i.e. at Lough Mourne and Toome, Co. Antrim). In south-west England few iron objects survive the acid soils and all date to after 400 BC. Smelting has been identified at Trevelgue, Cornwall and it has been argued that iron from the south-west peninsula was reaching Danebury hillfort in Hampshire in the sixth century BC (Salter and Ehrenreich 1984: 151–2). There was iron smelting at All Cannings Cross, Wiltshire in the seventh century BC.

9　The situation is similar in Iberia. The early introduction of iron technology is evidenced by iron slag found in crucibles from the Late Bronze Age settlements of Peña Negra (González Prats 1986, 1992) and Cerradinha (Tavares da Silva and Soares 1978), iron objects from the Ría de Huelva deposit (Ruíz-Gálvez 1995) and an iron skeuomorph chisel from Senhora da Guia, Baiões (Silva and Lopez 1984). Despite this early evidence there is then no recognisable tradition of iron working in Atlantic Iberia until after the Roman conquest.

10　Iron was at first very difficult to work because it required very high temperatures which were virtually impossible to reach in western European bowl furnaces. This may partly explain its slow uptake in such areas. It had to be repeatedly heated and hammered to remove impurities otherwise artefacts that were inferior to bronze were produced and it could not be cast which made it unsuitable for the production of typical Atlantic Bronze forms. Some of the early examples of iron objects in the west are simply copies of forms previously produced in bronze, such as the sword and sickle from the Llyn Fawr hoard in Glamorgan. These forms were in every way inferior to their bronze counterparts and the benefits of using iron may not have been immediately apparent to bronze societies.

11　Iron was also resisted by Nordic bronze societies as there is no evidence of Hallstatt iron objects in this zone until after 500 BC (Bukowski 1986).

12　Hallstatt C innovations in Britain and Ireland were also selectively adopted, and were largely confined to new sword types (produced in bronze) and the import of a limited range of horse gear and personal objects such as razors.

13 A fragment of a bronze oinochoe from Tronoën and a decorated scabbard from Kernavest-Quiberon.

14 As Cunliffe (1997: 164) points out, other hillfort zones may have been performing similar roles such as in the region between the Trier and the Rhineland which also sits between two different socio-economic systems.

15 The Cerrig-y-Drudion 'hanging bowl' is considered to be of British manufacture (Stead 1982), but as Cunliffe points out (1990: 249–50) this – along with other cases of indigenous manufacture – does not negate the argument that stylistic similarities existed between western Britain and Armorica. Such similarities may run deeper than common artistic traditions and could represent, for example, the existence of common ritual practices and beliefs.

16 Ruíz-Gálvez (1991) argues that sedentary settlement was established along the Iberian coastline between the tenth and seventh centuries BC largely as the result of Atlantic contacts, which also brought new technologies and linguistic changes. This permanent settlement is most visibly seen in the stone-built roundhouses of the Iberian *castros* or hilltop enclosure sites from the Late Bronze Age onwards.

17 Another popular generalisation is that it was the Romans that finally brought rectangular building styles to the British Isles, first through contacts from the first century BC and then through conquest from the first century AD onwards. It is perhaps significant in this context then that the full expression of complex monumental roundhouse forms is seen only in Scotland and Ireland, areas which were largely unaffected by the Roman presence in Britain.

18 It is difficult to carry out a survey of building forms in Armorica because of the lack of information from sites prior to the late La Tène or Gallo-Roman periods (cf. Menez *et al.* 1990). There is some evidence to suggest, however, that we might expect earlier examples to be round: Late Bronze Age forms are, as we have seen, predominantly round; timber roundhouses comparable to British forms are known from the early Iron Age site of Mez-Notariou on the l'île of Ouessant (Le Bihan and Robic 1988, 1990, 1993); a small circular stone-built building thought to date to the earlier part of the Iron Age was examined in the interior of the camp of Kervedan, Ile de Griox (Thriepland 1943; Wheeler and Richardson 1957; Menez *et al.* 1990: fig. 2); another circular stone roundhouse dating to the Early and Middle La Tène and featuring massively built walls up to 1.5 m thick and surviving to 1 m in height was excavated at Talhouët, Morbihan (Tanguy 1988); while circular post-houses dating to the first century BC co-existing with rectangular forms have been recorded at various Late La Tène sites including Braden 1 and Polvern in Hennebont (Menez *et al.* 1990: fig. 3). These sites are discussed further in Chapter 6.

19 Although rectangular forms are the dominant type throughout northern France, Belgium and Holland, there is some evidence for the construction of roundhouse forms, comparable to those in Britain, in a broad coastal band facing the southern English coastline from Brittany to the Netherlands (Harding 1972; Dechezlepretre *et al.* 1997). These sites often occur in association with rectangular structures, as at Nijnsel in the Netherlands (Harding 1972: fig. 8), but their comparable dimensions with timber forms in Britain, and the existence at some sites of entrance porches, may be a reflection of cross–Channel cultural contacts with communities in southern England in the first millennium BC.

20 Out of 51 sites listed in Wheeler and Richardson's gazetteer of north-western France 39 are univallate (Wheeler and Richardson 1957); univallate forms are dominant in Guernsey and Jersey (Bender and Cailland 1986: 49); univallate sites predominate in Ireland (Westropp 1910, 1911, 1912; Raftery 1994); in Argyll only 17 of the 66 known promontory sites are multivallate while most examples in the Western Isles and the north of Scotland are also univallate (Lamb 1980: 68).

21 Numerous sites are also found on the east coast, mainly north of the Forth but with some examples in Berwickshire (Lamb 1980, fig. 1). These sites, defended by one or more ramparts, range in date from the mid-first millennium BC to the historical Pictish period

(Ralston 1980). Some sites, such as the example at Cullykan in Banffshire, were in use for many centuries (Armit 1997: 59). The massive promontory fort of Burghead in Moray is believed to have been an important Pictish naval base and perhaps even a royal centre in the first millennium AD (ibid.; Henderson 1967: 22). If this is the case it is possible that other promontory forts may have played a similar naval role in the pre-Roman Iron Age.

22 550±100 BC (GIF–715) from the Catuélan ditch and 320±110 BC (GIF–1302) from the Pleinne-Garrene ditch.

23 The meaning of this term and its application to sites in Armorica is discussed further in Chapter 6.

24 Several promontory forts in Finistère are associated with natural harbours: Kermovan au Conquet; Primel Tregastel à Plougasnou; Kastell Ac'h à Plougerneau; and l'Aber en Crozon (Maguer 1996: 105). The bivallate site at the Pointe de Lostmarc'h, Finistère, seems a likely trading candidate – it is located at the entrance to the Bay of Douarnez and sits adjacent to an easily navigable sandy beach; Iron Age ceramics have been discovered within its defences (Maguer 1996: 116). A number of Cornish sites, such as Hillsborough and Wind Hill, also lie immediately adjacent to good natural harbours, as do many unival-late examples in western Ireland and Scotland.

25 There has been a lack of examination of coastal sites but what little has been done suggests that more intensive campaigns of excavation in coastal locations could prove informative. Waddell (1992: 39) points to the coastal sites at Dalkey Island, Co. Dublin (Liversage 1968), White Park Bay, Co. Antrim (Collins 1970) and Brean Down on the southern shore of the Bristol Channel (Bell 1990) that have all provided evidence for the existence of contacts across the Irish Sea; the Irish sites had clay moulds for Late Bronze Age metalwork while the English site produced two gold bracelets of Welsh or Irish derivation. The examination of unimposing coastal locations may provide the links in the exchange system that ultimately helped to maintain broad cultural similarities throughout the Atlantic zone. For example, finds of Late Bronze Age metalwork are relatively common in the sandy beaches of western Scotland (Coles and Livens 1958) while an inter-tidal wooden jetty structure discovered in the Shannon estuary was found to date to 793–553 BC (O'Sullivan 1996). Exotic finds from Mount Batten (Cunliffe 1988a) and the Welsh coastal site of Mehyr Mawr, Glamorganshire (Savory 1976) suggest some level of maritime contact existed into the Iron Age period.

26 Dunagoil would be classed as a coastal hillfort rather than a promontory fort *sensu stricto*, but the site shares many similarities with promontory forts. It is located directly on the shoreline in a clear relationship with the sea and at least three rock-cut boat nausts have been located in its environs (Harding pers. comm.).

27 Despite their western distribution, early interpretations of souterrains, unlike those of promontory forts, have not been widely used to support ideas of population movement or form part of a wider Atlantic culture – but see Hawkes (1966) and also Thomas (1972: 75) who has remarked upon the similarities of the predominantly coastal distribution of souterrains from western Brittany to north-east Scotland and the pattern of the much earlier tradition of megalithic tombs.

28 The majority of excavated souterrains, and significantly all of those excavated in the last few decades, have been associated with above ground structures of some type, and those without invariably have unexcavated ground surfaces, or were early excavations carried out without knowledge of the possibility of, often ephemeral, associated ground level evidence.

29 The distribution of souterrains is often described in publications as relating to the terri-tories of the Osismii and the western parts of the Veneti and the Coriosolitae. However, as these relate to suggested tribal groupings of the late La Tène while souterrains date from the end of the Late Bronze Age until the end of the Middle La Tène; such an orien-tation is problematic and avoided here.

30 A storage interpretation is supported from the evidence from Kermoisan and Bellevue, both Finistère (Giot 1995: 293–5); 2,000 sherds were recovered from the former and 3,630 from the latter, many of which formed complete vessels and were found to be

standing on their base as if they had been being used for storage. Trewardreva fogou in Cornwall contained ash pits (Polwhele 1793–1806: II, 129) which Todd (1987: 175) has interpreted were used for the preservation of gulls eggs!

31 Tanguy (1973) has highlighted the close similarities in Cornwall, in terms of construction and use, between souterrains and later subterranean storage areas known as hulls. Hulls were used from the medieval period until the beginning of the twentieth century as dairies, storing butter, milk, cream and eggs intended for market (op cit. 38, fig. 1). Tanguy (1973: 40) suggests 'that hulls might therefore appear to be, in conception and use, a direct ethnic survival of the fogou tradition'.

5 The *Ultima Thule:* Atlantic Scotland and Ireland 700 BC–AD 200

1 Some authors make the distinction between aisled wheelhouses, where the piers are separated by a small aisle, and those where the piers are bonded into the wall. This distinction is seen as unnecessary because the architecture of wheelhouses seems to be identical in every other respect (Armit 1990). Aisled wheelhouses may be slightly earlier as they are seen as the more unstable form – there is some evidence of efforts to block up the aisles recorded at Cnip, in an attempt to make the structure more stable.

2 Not true of a range of Irish sites collectively known as the Western Stone Fort group which are much more massively built than anything in Scotland. However, simple enclosures may be the norm in Ireland (see later discussion).

3 Like Atlantic Scotland, the potential of continuity of prehistoric settlement forms into the first millennium AD is high in Ireland due to the absence of Romanisation.

4 Rectangular and D-shaped variations occur, although whether these sites should be termed 'ring' fort is a matter of debate. It would also be expected that such sites can be confidently ascribed to a later date than circular examples.

5 This subdivision is not always clear in the field as some *raths* feature erratic stonework or stone-faced banks.

6 For example, the houses in many of the north-eastern sites tend to be rectangular and therefore one would fully expect a late date. There has been a similar bias towards the selection of late-looking *dun* sites for excavation in Argyll.

7 Limbert (1996: 278) points out that the evidence for open settlement must be viewed within the north-eastern bias of excavations. Open settlement may have been a reality in this area but this model cannot be confidently applied to the whole country.

8 Excavations at Lisleagh 1, Co. Cork (Monk 1995) revealed the complete removal of the original rampart and infilling of original ditches to double the habitation space with new ramparts. Long periods of occupation at earthen sites, similar to that suggested for stone-built settlement, would seem to be quite common – presumably with periods of major clearing and modification (e.g. Cush: Mytum 1992: fig. 4.2).

9 At Lisdoo, Fermanagh, the palisade has a *terminus antequem* of 340 cal. BC–AD 250 cal. (UB–2202).

10 Stout also omits an early date of 1840 ± 110 BP from Raheenamadra, Co. Limerick (Stenberger 1966), because it was not positively demonstrated to relate to a period of enclosure at the site and contrasted with the other four dates which fell between 606 and 975 BC. Caulfield (1981: 208) may be justified in believing that the interpretation of the context as pre-enclosure may have been 'strongly influenced by the early radiocarbon evidence'.

11 Just as there is great difficulty in distinguishing unexcavated Early Christian ringfort enclosures from potential Later Prehistoric ones, there are also difficulties at the later end of the traditional Early Christian chronological horizon. At present only excavation can distinguish between Early Christian enclosures and later Anglo-Norman ringworks and mottes. For example, excavations at Pollardstown (Edwards 1990: 19) produced twelfth to fourteenth century AD artefacts despite being considered a purely Early Christian site prior to excavation.

12 An inventory of sites is currently being compiled as part of the Discovery Programme Western Stone Fort Project (Cotter 1993, 1995, 1996, 2000).

13 Dún Fearbhaí, Dún Formna, Dún Eoghanachta, Dún Aonghasa, Dún Eochla, Dún Chonchuir and Dúcathair. It seems unlikely that all seven Aran sites date to the same period. For example, Dún Fearbhaí and Dún Formna are rectilinear and certainly very different in appearance to the other five sites.

14 *Chevaux-de-frise* only occur at four sites (Doonamo, Co. Mayo; Ballykinvarga, Co. Clare; Dún Aonghasa and Dúcathair, Aran Is.) and therefore do not form part of a useful definition.

15 Grianán of Aileach, O'Boyles Fort, Cahercommaun, Leacanabuaile, Staigue, Cahergal, Dunbeg and the seven Aran Islands forts were all 'restored' in the nineteenth century by their excavators or, more usually, the Office of Public Works. Unfortunately, records of restoration work is either non-existent or extremely vague. However, Cotter (1993, 8–9) provides a photograph of the walls at Dún Aonghasa dated to 1875 which provides clear evidence of the existence of terracing at the site prior to restoration. Also some early anti-quarian descriptions (dating to 1839 and 1859) exist for some of these sites which describe the existence of features such as terracing, stairs and wall chambers before restoration work took place (Limbert 1996: 253).

16 The central *cashel* wall at Dún Aonghasa is composed of three distinct walls built up against each other (Cotter 1993: 8–9). This median wall technique is paralleled at a number of other Irish and Scottish sites.

17 GrN-20236, 1285±40 BP.

18 Stone trough (cutting 1): UB-3645, 2374±36 BP; Hut 2 dates: GrN-20238, 2435±45 BP and GrN-20234, 2470±35 BP.

19 AA-10274, 2295±60 BP.

20 UB-4282: 672±22 BP and UB-4316: 1171±44 BP.

21 UB-4277: 2534± BP.

22 UB-4314: 1963±35 BP.

23 Although not seen at Dún Aonghasa, niches are present at Ballykinvarga, Cahermoyle and Cahermullach, Co. Clare.

24 A recent reassessment of the site rejected the evidence of prehistoric activity as residual and, although adding an earlier fifth to eighth century AD phase (based on typological dates suggested for the zoomorphic brooch, enamelled ornament and two looped iron pins), reiterated Hencken's original ninth-century AD dating for the main construction of the site (Cotter 1999: 80–2).

25 Ballykinvarga, Cahercommaun, Caherahoagh, Caherdoula, Cahermullach, Cahermore-Ballyallaban, Cahermore-Glenquin, Caherbullog, Cahernaspekee, Caherscribben, Moheraroon, Caher-Moheraroon, Caherdoon, Poulgorm, Caherfeenagh, Caherduff, Doonaunmore, Poulacarran, Cashlaun Gar, Cahergrillaun, Caherdooneerish, Cahermoyle, Cahercuttine, Caherminaun, Cahercloggaun, Caherblonick.

26 It is assumed that wooden ladders or steps are used on sites that do not feature stone steps. Westropp (1913: 252) states that the two recesses in the internal *cashel* wall at Cahermullach may have been gaps for wooden ladders.

27 XRF analyses (Henderson 1982) of Scottish glass beads, along with electron-probe analy-sis on the examples from the Howe on Orkney (Henderson 1994), indicate that they were most probably manufactured in Scotland. In general, the chemical composition of purple and yellow beads suggest a Scottish origin for the colourants used (Henderson 1994: 234–6).

6 The western approaches: south-west England and Armorica *c.* 750 BC–AD 200

1 Although the ceramic evidence comes mainly from grave contexts, it is worth noting there were never any Urnfields as far west as Devon or Cornwall (Petersen 1981; White 1982).

2 The single occurrence of a stamped sherd at Porthmoer (Hirst 1936: fig. 6, VII, 1), and examples from Trevelgue and Halligye (both unpublished), have all previously been considered as French imports (Todd 1987: 180). However, although these sherds can be closely paralleled with forms in Finistère and the Côtes d'Armor, closer inspection of the fabrics used indicate that they were produced locally (Cunliffe pers. comm.).

3 Cunliffe and de Jersey (1997: 1) list the evidence of British material exported to Armorica other than ceramics as consisting only of some armlets found at Nacqueville, Alet and Le Yaudet which *may* possibly be made from Kimmeridge shale, and a single Durotrigian coin from Jort in Calvados. This represents a very small amount of material indeed and one can only assume that more evidence will come to light as more excavation is carried out on Iron Age sites in Brittany and Normandy.

4 Cunliffe (1997: 4) suggests that it is possible that the Meare Village West vessel arrived sometime in the second century BC before Hengistbury began importing a large number of Armorican vessels from 120 BC. The site also has two possible Black Cordoned sherds leading Cunliffe to suggest it may have served as an important regional foci for exchange (ibid. 31).

5 The majority of Iron Age roundhouse entrances in Britain are set towards the east or south-east. It has been suggested that this may have a cosmological significance and was done so that doorways would face the rising sun (particularly at equinox and mid-winter solstice) which may have been identified with birth and renewal (Oswald 1997).

6 Silvester (1979: 178–9) argues that metalworking within a stone and timber house is improbable, and the evidence may therefore be of a more recent date than the Iron Age and he suggests a medieval intrusion. However, the apparent improbability of iron-working within a settlement structure is countered by the evidence from sites in North Wales such as Crawcwellt and Bryn-y-Castell (Crew 1990), where iron production is closely associated with Iron Age settlement.

7 Evidence for activity in the later first millennium BC comes from the final phase finds of a rotary quern (Wainwright and Smith 1980: fig. 21) and a sherd of stamped decorated pottery (ibid. 98, fig. 18). Rotary querns are an Iron Age phenomenon and have been dated to the fifth century BC at the earliest at Danebury (Cunliffe and Pool 1991: 396), while the stamped decorated sherd is of gabbroic fabric and is similar to those in Cornwall dated to the fifth/fourth centuries BC (Quinnell 1986: 111; 1996: 78). Taken together they suggest final phase activity at Shaugh Moor spanning the Late Bronze Age and Early Iron Age.

8 NPL-135, 2135 ± 90 BP.

9 Although use of rounds continues into the sixth century AD, there is no evidence for the construction of new sites after the third century AD.

10 The find of an iron dagger handle from Milber Down is the only potentially high status find yet recovered from a multiple enclosure site, although it must be remembered that very few have been excavated.

11 While Iberian *castros* undoubtedly share some basic concepts with Chûn (and other Atlantic sites) there are significant differences that undermine the direct diffusionist construction view. *Castros* were built on a much larger scale with large numbers of circular houses, often organised into streets and enclosed within an area of, on average, around 3 hectares, but in some cases as much as 15 hectares (e.g. Citânia de Sanfins, Paços de Ferreire, Portugal). Equally, there are a number of features at these sites, such as the fine sculptured posts and lintels and saunas from the *castros* of Sabrosso or Briteiros, which have no parallels in the northern Atlantic zone.

12 Interestingly, in comparison to evidence for tin working at Chûn, it has been reported that an uncontexted tin ingot was recovered from Castle Dore, but unfortunately this find remains unpublished (Quinnell 1986: 121).

13 The possible existence of a souterrain on Scilly may offer another cultural link (Ashbee 1990, 49–51).

14 Cunliffe (1991: 262) states that it is 'estimated that of the 580 hillforts in Wales about 230 enclose less than 0.4 ha, and of these three-quarters lie in the south west'.

15 The removal of the 'hillfort' label from earlier sites suggests that univallate enclosure forms, similar in many ways to *rath* type enclosures, were being built from the middle of the first millennium BC.

16 There are over 285 such sites in north-west Wales but Smith's classification considers only those for which site plans were available amounting to only 83 sites.

17 A number of these sites can be compared with sites of a similar layout seen in Co. Clare (especially the eastern half) and Co. Limerick. Many also appear as stone-built equivalents of the multiple enclosure forts seen in south-west England and associated parts of south-east Wales.

18 Similar to the distinctions made by Caesar in *Bellum Gallicum*: crucially he considers the north-western French tribes as something apart from the rest and uses the term *armoricus* or *armoricanus* to distinguish them. He also mentions their 'naval' situation and the maritime associations of the Veneti (II 34; III 8; V 53; VII 75). As his knowledge of Gaul increases, he uses terms like *armoricus* (adjective) and *amoricanus* (noun) in a similar way as *belgicus* (V 53; VII 75; VIII 31).

19 The western limits of Armorica are defined by the ocean but, archaeologically, the eastern and south-eastern limits are far less clear. Armorica is most often associated with Brittany (the departments of Finistère, Morbihan, Côtes-d'Armor and Ille-et-Vilaine), but similar cultural traits can be seen to cover a much larger area extending east into lower Normandy, and south-east into the departments of the Loire. The definition of Armorica used here follows de Jersey (1994: 1–2) and includes the four Breton departments along with the departments of Manche, Calvados and Orne (lower Normandy), and Loire-Atlantique, Maine-et-Loire, Mayenne and Sarthe, in the pays de la Loire.

20 It should be kept in mind that souterrains began to be used during *le Premier Age du Fer*, from 700 BC onwards, with the main *floruit* through the Early and Middle La Tène and then fell out of use after 100 BC (Giot 1995: 295). At the very least the distribution of souterrains represents a dense human presence in the area.

21 Les Jeusseries in Retiers; Saint-Malo-de-Phily; Verger in Availles-sur-Seiche; La Rouaudiére in Domalain; Beaumont in Gennes-sur-Seiche; Grand Vendon en Athée; Grand-Fournea in Availles-sur-Seiche.

22 Unlike other Armorican sites the enclosures at *Le Boissane* seem unusual as they are incomplete and appear open to the west, north-west and south. Investigations at the site revealed that it was originally protected in these areas by two natural granite outcrops which were incorporated into the site layout but were then quarried away after the site was abandoned (Menez 1996, 174–6).

23 Gouletquer (1970) claims that development of salt production in the Late La Tène is closely linked to the development of iron technology during this period in Armorica because the technology stimulated the development of *briquetage*. The only other period where metalworking is detectable in Armorica is during the Late Bronze Age – the only other prehistoric period which has evidence of significant salt production.

24 The production of salt is recognised through the remains of *briquetage* (salt 'bricks'), rectangular or cylindrical clay containers in which the salt was produced, clay pillars on which racks of drying bricks were placed above a furnace, and the existence of burnt chocking stones.

25 In Finistère, for example, only the Camp d'Artus, enclosing around 30 hectares, is comparable in size to hillfort sites known elsewhere. The only other two hillfort candidates in the region, Castel-Don and Kercaradec, are barely over 2 hectares in size (Maguer 1996: 108, fig. 5).

26 There was a long-held belief that terraced ramparts were a characteristic of the Atlantic seaboard and that their construction provided evidence of seaborne contacts (Lamb 1980: 59). Along with the example at Kercaradec, they had been found at Portadoona and Carrigillihy, Co. Cork (O'Kelly 1951), and the promontory site at Gurnards Head, Cornwall (Gordon 1940).

27 The term *murus gallicus* was first used by Julius Caesar in *Bellum Gallicum* (VII 23) to describe the defences of the *oppidum* of Avaricum (Bourges). The term refers to a timer-laced

rampart, with heavy wooden beams in the front face tied to similar beams in the rear face by cross-members and held in place by iron nails. The spaces between the beams were filled by regular courses of stone walling.

28 Admittedly, the excavations in the interior of the site were quite restricted and, typically for the period, resources were concentrated almost exclusively on defining the nature of the defences. In 1987 extreme storm conditions uprooted a number of trees throughout the inside of the site, but significantly no cultural material was recovered from the soil unearthed by the fallen trees (Cunliffe pers. comm.). Larger scale excavations in the future may, however, reveal more positive results.

29 In his definition of an *oppidum*, Collis (1984: 8) states that 20–25 hectares is the dividing line between hillforts and *oppida*. Apart from the Camp d'Artus and Lescouët there are no sites in Armorica that would qualify as *oppida* under this criteria. The size requirements appear to have been relaxed when applied to sites in Armorica: Duval (1984: 280) states that an *oppidum* must be at least 10 hectares while Langouët (1980, 1987: 47) goes even further and claims a number of sites in the territory of the Coriosolitae as *oppida* even though some are only 1 or 2 hectares in size.

30 This is the only definite find of such a patella yet known from a settlement site in Brittany although Arramond and Menez (1992: 66) also point to a similar fragment from the cremation site of Stang à Plonéour-Lanvern (Finistère).

31 Two brown earth tumuli, thought to date to the Bronze Age, exist 100 m to the west of the site. Arramond and Menez (1992: 60) put forward the tantalising suggestion that these mounds could contain the elite graves of Paule and fulfil another element of comparison with Central European *oppida*.

32 Some promontory locations may have continued to be used: at Trevelgue cliff castle later re-occupation was restricted to the inner earthwork, while the discovery of a few Roman sherds indicated some activity at Gurnard's Head (Gordon 1940).

33 Greater Armorica, east of the River Rance, for the most part lacks souterrains and stelae although there is an outlying group of stelae reported in northern Mayenne (Naveau *et al.* 1987).

34 These are Killycluggin, Co. Cavan; Castlestrange, Co. Roscommon; Mullaghmast, Co. Kildare; Derrykeighan, Co. Antrim; and Turoe, Co. Galway. A further stone is claimed from the island of Cape Clear, Co. Cork (O'Leary and Shee Twohig 1993) which would seem to add weight to the idea of a western Atlantic decorated stone tradition but, as Waddell (1998: 372) points out, the decoration on the stone, and therefore the dating of it, remains extremely unclear meaning that its significance must remain uncertain.

35 Cunliffe (1990) also points to the survival of classical references to the tin trade as further evidence of its existence from at least the sixth to the second centuries BC.

7 Atlantic communities and the sea

1 The deposition of high status metalwork in the Late Bronze Age is often interpreted as a pattern of votive, non-funerary deposits complementary to burials (Cooney and Grogan 1994). Eogan (1964: 285) refers to such deposits as 'graveless grave goods'. Bradley (1990: 110–11) recognises the prominence of weaponry in rivers in western Europe and views it as a transfer of weaponry from burial in the Early Bronze Age to rivers by the Late Bronze Age.

2 The similar, though by no means identical, architectural devices and appearances shared by Irish and Scottish drystone sites in the Iron Age is very similar to the level of correlation seen between chambered tombs such as Newgrange, Co. Meath, and Maeshowe, Orkney, in the third millennium BC. This suggests that the maintenance of ideological and socio-cultural similarities between separate Atlantic communities through the episodic re-invigoration of natural routes of contact is likely to have had a deep continuity stretching over thousands of years.

3 Elements of cellular construction are found throughout the northern Atlantic zone. Although undated, cellular structures are also known in Wales at sites such as Tre'r Ceiri, Castell Odo and Garn Boudan in Caernarvonshire and within the numerous but undated stone-built roundhouse settlements in north-West Wales. In Cornwall vertically slab built structures are found inside rounds such as at Chûn Castle (Leeds 1927: 209) and the cellular-like courtyard traditions of sites such as Chysauster, Porthmeor and Carn Euny. Cellular structures have also been identified in the coastal sand dune areas of Brittany, at sites such as Goulvars and Les Ebihens, but here seem to be related to salt extraction (Hyvert and Le Bihan 1990).

4 Some evidence of similarities comes from the hillforts of A Lanzada and Montealegre, both of which produced decorated bone combs whose closest parallels are with types in Britain and Ireland (González-Ruibal 2004: 303, fig. 11). Also, it is worth recalling the occurrence of north-western Iberian style fibulae in south-west England, Brittany and Aquitania (Cunliffe 1990: 247).

5 The term 'Celtic' is used here in its linguistic context: in 1707 Edward Lhuyd recognised that the indigenous languages of Scotland, Ireland, the Isle of Man, Wales, Cornwall and Brittany were part of a related language group which he decided to term 'Celtic'. Prior to Lhuyd's work no one in Britain or Ireland had ever considered themselves a Celt or Celtic (James 1999: 16–25). It would have led to much less disagreement amongst later academics if he had instead chosen a different term that did not come with the baggage of the historical Celts recorded by classical writers. Most crucially the use of this term does not necessarily mean that the languages spoken in the Atlantic regions were the same as those of the historical Celts living north of the Alps. Cunliffe (2001: 296) has proposed that 'Atlantic Celtic' might be a better term for the Atlantic languages to express this difference.

6 It is a matter of debate whether the first millennium BC language of Galicia was Q Celtic or not but there is evidence from the tribal and place names of the area that it retained a very archaic form of Celtic (Tovar 1961: 76–90; de Hoz 1992: 379–81).

7 Kristiansen (1994: 12) does 'not consider it justified to derive either Celtic culture or language from the larger central European Urnfield and Hallstatt traditions. Any such identifications should be restricted to the western groups, which rather points towards western Europe and the Atlantic regions as the original homeland of Celtic languages.' However, there is unlikely to be any single 'homeland' for Celtic languages. The Celtic languages we know from the mid-first millennium onwards will have developed through a complex series of interaction between individual areas. Renfrew (1987: Chapter 9) suggests that Celtic grew out of a common Indo-European tradition leading to a parallel development of Celtic languages in different areas which served to influence each other through peer polity interaction leading to the forms recognisable in the mid-first millennium BC. No single homeland is needed for such a scenario (it must first be accepted, however, that Indo-European is a Neolithic or Early Bronze Age phenomenon and that it is closely related to Celtic – the latter point especially cannot be proven at present). If Renfrew's assertion is true it does not necessarily invalidate the Atlantic Late Bronze Age lingua franca argument as languages would still have to have developed in parallel, implying a level of contact between Atlantic areas, and dialects could still have become more homogeneous as a result of the wider contacts seen in the Late Bronze Age.

8 It is unclear what version of Celtic (if any) was spoken in Scotland prior to the introduction of Q-Celtic form in the fourth century as a result of the Dalriada incursions from Ireland.

9 Being a sailor may have been an important way of gaining status in Atlantic society – at the very least it would have led to a degree of specialism within society; sailing was a practice which required its own skill set and expertise (knowledge of which may have been restricted). As well as owning a powerful means of transport, ship owners would also need to be able to support a crew for periods of time, perhaps seasonally. The very act of taking to the sea may have been a way of enhancing social and ritual standing for all involved; travel itself can add exotic value to objects and people alike (Helms 1988). If it

can be assumed that men were the sailors then this may have been one way that male orientated warrior values were communicated throughout the zone in the Late Bronze Age (Coombs 1998).

10 It is impossible to gauge how far the sea was used for the ritual deposition of metalwork because metal is very unlikely to survive in a harsh maritime environment, especially if the items were deposited in the coastal zone. Metalwork finds from the sea do occasionally crop up, however, such as the Late Bronze Age metalwork dredged from the Minch (Armit 1996: 101) and the numerous metalwork finds that are found in beach deposits along the coasts of the northern Atlantic zone.

11 The ritual importance of promontory forts may have been largely due to their, often quite dramatic, locations at the interface between land and sea. Small islands surrounded by sea may have had a ritual significance for similar reasons. Certain islands seem to have been regarded as sacred: Anglesey, according to Tacitus, was a Druid preserve at the time of the Roman invasion, while Plutarch related the story of a traveller, Demetrius of Tarsus, who had visited other holy islands, possibly in the Hebrides, during Agricola's campaigns (Armit 1997: 90). The use of remote islands and promontories by later Celtic Christian monks may be a reflection of these much earlier traditions.

Abbreviations

AA	*Archaeologia Atlantica*
AC	*Archaeologia Cambrensis*
AI	*Archaeology Ireland*
AJ	*Antiquaries Journal*
ArchJ	*Archaeological Journal*
BAR	*British Archaeological Reports*
CA	*Cornish Archaeology*
CurrA	*Current Archaeology*
CBA	*Council for British Archaeology*
IJNA	*IJNA*
JEA	*Journal of European Archaeology*
JIA	*Journal of Irish Archaeology*
JRSAI	*Journal of the Royal Society of Antiquaries of Ireland*
OJA	*Oxford Journal of Archaeology*
PDAS	*Proceedings of the Devonshire Archaeological Society*
PDAES	*Proceedings of the Devon Archaeological Exploration Society*
PPS	*Proceedings of the Prehistoric Society*
PRIA	*Proceedings of the Royal Irish Academy*
PSAS	*Proceedings of the Society of Antiquaries of Scotland*
RAO	*Revue Archeologique de l'Ouest*
RCAHMS	*Royal Commission on the Ancient and Historical Monuments of Scotland*
SAR	*Scottish Archaeological Review*
UJA	*Ulster Journal of Archaeology*
WA	*World Archaeology*

Bibliography

Aalen, F. H. A. (1978) *Man and the Landscape in Ireland*, Academic Press: London.

Alcock, L. (1960) Castell Odo: An embanked settlement on Mynydd Ystum, near Aberdaron, Caernarvonshire, *AC*, 109: 78–135.

Alcock, L. (1963) Celtic Archaeology and Art, in Davies, E. (ed.), *Celtic Studies in Wales. A Survey*, pp. 3–46, University of Wales Press: Cardiff.

Alcock, L. and Alcock, E. A. (1987) Reconnaissance excavations on early historic fortifications and other royal sites in Scotland, 1974–84: 2, Excavations at Dunollie Castle, Oban, Argyll, 1978, *PSAS*, 117: 119–47.

Almagro Basch, M. (1940) 'El hallazgo de la Ría de Huelva y el final de la Edad del Bronce en el Occidente de Europa', *Ampurias*, 2: 85–143.

Almagro Basch, M. (1952) 'España Protohistórica', in Menéndez Pidal, R. (ed.) *História de España*, vol. 1, pp. 141–240, Espasa-Calpe: Madrid.

Almagro Basch, M. (1962) *Inventaria Archaeologica España*, fasc. 6, E7-10, Madrid.

Almagro Basch, M. (1963) 'Estela sepulcral grabada de la Granja de Céspedes en Badajoz', *Memorias de los Museos Arquelógicos Provinciales (1958–1961)*, 11: 19–20.

Almagro Basch, M. (1966) 'Les Estelas Decoradas del Suroeste Peninsular', *Bibliotheca Praehistorica Hispana* 8, Consejo Superior de Investigaciones Científicas: Madrid.

Almagro Basch, M. (1974) 'Nuevas estelas decoradas de la Península Ibérica', *Miscelánea Arqueológica*, 1: 5–39.

Almagro Basch, M. (1952) 'España Protohistórica', in Menéndez Pidal, R. (ed.) *História de España* vol. 1, pp. 141–240, Espasa-Calpe: Madrid.

Almagro-Gorbea, M. (1977) 'El Bronze final y el Período Orientalizante en Extremadura', *Bibliotheca Praehistorica Hispana* 14, Consejo Superior de Investigaciones Científicas: Madrid

Almagro-Gorbea, M. (1986) 'Bronze Final y edad del hierro', in *Historia de Espana*, *Prehistoria*, Madrid.

Almagro-Gorbea, M. (1988) 'Representaciones de barcos en el arte rupestre de la Península Ibérica. Aportacíon a la navegacíon precolonial desde el Mediterráneo Oriental', *Congreso Internacional sobre el Estrecho de Gibraltar*, 1: 389–98.

Alvar, J. (1981) *La Navegacíon Prerromana en la Península Ibérica: Colonizadores e Indigenas*, Universidad Complutense de Madrid: Madrid.

Anderson, A. O. and Anderson, M. (eds. and trans.) (1961) *Adomnán's Life of Columba*, Oxford Medieval Texts, Oxford University Press: Oxford.

ApSimon, A. M. and Greenfield, E. (1972) 'The Excavation of the Bronze Age and Iron Age Settlement at Trevisker Round, St Eval, Cornwall', *PPS*, 38: 301–81.

Arbousse-Bastide, T. (1993) 'Une nouvelle approche des enclos fossoyés du nord de la Haute-Bretagne', *Dossiers du Centre Régional d'Archéologie d'Alet*, 21: 67–100.

Armit, I. (ed.) (1990) *Beyond the Brochs: Changing Perspectives on the Scottish Iron Age*, Edinburgh University Press: Edinburgh.

Armit, I. (1990a) 'Epilogue: the Scottish Atlantic Iron Age', in Armit, I. (ed.): 194–210.

Armit, I. (1992) *The Later Prehistory of the Western Isles of Scotland*, BAR, Brit. Ser. 221, Archaeopress: Oxford.

Armit, I. (1996) *The Archaeology of Skye and the Western Isles*, Edinburgh University Press: Edinburgh.

Armit, I. (1997) 'Architecture and the household: a response to Sharples and Parker Pearson', in A. Gwilt and C. Haselgrove (eds) *Reconstructing Iron Age Societies*, Oxbow Monograph 71, pp. 266–9, Oxbow: Oxford.

Armit, I. (2003) *Towers in the North: The Brochs of Scotland,* Tempus: Stroud.

Armit, I. (2000) Review of M. Parker-Pearson, N. Sharples with J. Mulville, *Between Land and Sea: Excavations at Dun Vulan, South Uist, Sheffield*, 1999, *Antiquity*, 74: 244–5.

Arnold, B. (1985) 'Navigation et construction navale sur les lacs suisses au Bronze final', *Helvetia Archäol*, 16: 91–117.

Arramond, J. C. and Le Poiter, C. (1990) 'Paule, Saint-Symphorien: habitat de l'Age du Fer', in *Les Gaulois d'Armorique* (Actes du XII colloque AFEAF, Quimper 1988), (RAO suppl. 3): 153–5.

Arramond, J.-C. and Menez, Y. (1992) 'Le Camp du Saint-Symphorien à Paule dans les Côtes-d'Armor', *Musée d'Histoire de Saint-Brieuc*: Saint-Brieuc.

Arramond, J.-C., Menez, Y. and Le Poiter, C. (1990) 'Paule, pierre de mémorie', *Musée d'Histoire de Saint-Brieuc*: Saint-Brieuc.

Arramond, J.-C., Menez, Y. and Le Poiter, C. (1992) *Archéologie et travaux routiers départementaux: Le camp du Saint-Symphorien à Paule dans les Côtes-d'Armor*: Saint-Brieuc.

Ashbee, P (1974) *Ancient Scilly. From the First Farmers to the Early Christians*, David and Charles: London.

Ashbee, P. (1990) 'A souterrain on Scilly?', *CA*, 29: 49–51.

Ashbee, P. (1999) 'Halangy Down, St Mary's, Isles of Scilly, Excavations 1964–1977', *CA*, 35.

Astill, G. and Davies, W. (1997) *A Breton Landscape,* University College London Press: London.

Austin, D. (1984) *The Caer Cadwgan Project: interim report 1984*, St David's University College: Lampeter.

Austin, D. (1985) *The Caer Cadwgan Project: interim report 1985*, St David's University College: Lampeter.

Balaam, N. D., Smith, K. and Wainwright, G. K. (1982) 'The Shaugh Moor project: Fourth report – environment, context and conclusions', *PPS*, 48: 203–78.

Ballantyne, C. K. and Dawson, D. A. (1997) 'Geomorphology and Landscape Change', in Edwards, K. J. and Ralston, I. B. M. (eds) *Scotland: Environment and Archaeology, 8000 BC–AD 1000,* pp. 23–44, John Wiley and Sons: Chichester.

Ballin Smith, B. (ed.) (1994) *Howe: Four Millennia of Orkney Prehistory*, Society of Antiquaries of Scotland Monograph Series No. 9: Edinburgh.

Ballin Smith, B. and Banks, I. (eds) (2002) *In the Shadow of the Brochs. The Iron Age in Scotland*, Tempus: Gloucestershire.

Barber, J. (ed.) (1997) *The Archaeological Investigation of a Prehistoric Landscape: excavations on Arran 1978–1981*, Scottish Trust for Archaeological Research: Edinburgh.

Barber, J. (1985) *Innsegall: The Western Isles*, John Donald: Edinburgh.

Barber, J., Halstead, P., James, H. and Lee, F. (1989) 'An unusual Iron Age burial at Hornish Point, South Uist', *Antiquity*, 63: 773–8.

Barceló, J. (1989) 'Las estelas decoradas del sudoeste de la Península Ibérica' in Aubet, M (ed.) *Tartessos. Arqueología Protohistórica del Bajo Guadalquivir*, pp.189–208, Ausa: Sabadell.

Barclay, G. J. (1981) 'Newmill and the Souterrains of Southern Pictland', *PSAS*, 110: 200–8.

Barclay, G. J. (1985) 'Excavations at Upper Suisguill, Sutherland', *PSAS*, 115: 159–98.

Bardel, J.-P. (1988) 'Prat/Pouilladou, établissement de l'âge du Fer', *Bulletin d'information archéologique de la circonscription des Antiquités de Bretagne*: 18–20.

Baring-Gould, S. (1904) 'An Exploration of Tregear Rounds', *Journal of the Royal Institute of Cornwall*, 16: 73–83.

Baring-Gould, S., Burnard, R., and Anderson, I. K. (1899) 'Exploration of the stone camp on St. Davids Head', *AC*, 16: 105–31.

Barrett, J. C. (1981) 'Aspects of the Iron Age in Atlantic Scotland: a case study in the problems of archaeological interpretation', *PSAS*, 111: 205–19.

Barrett, J. C. (1997) 'Different perceptions of organising life', *Archaeological Dialogues*, 4: 49–52.

Barrett, J. C. (1994) *Fragments from Antiquity: an archaeology of social life, 2900–1200 BC,* Blackwell: Oxford.

Barrett, J. C. (2001) 'Agency, the Duality of Structure, and the Problem of the Archaeological Record', in Hodder, I. (ed.) (2001) *Archaeological Theory Today*, pp. 141–64, Polity Press: Cambridge.

Barrett, J. C. and Bradley, R. (1980) *Settlement and Society in the British Later Bronze Age,* BAR Brit. Ser. 83, Archaeopress: Oxford.

Barrett, J. C. and Foster, S. M. (1990) 'Passing the Time in Iron Age Scotland', in Hanson, W. S. and Slater, E. A. (eds), *Scottish Archaeology: New Perceptions,* pp. 44–56, Aberdeen University Press: Aberdeen.

Barrett, J. C., Bradley, R. and Green, M. (1991) *Landscape, Monuments and Society: the prehistory of Cranborne Chase*, Cambridge University Press: Cambridge.

Barrett, J. H., Nicholson, R. A. and Ceron Carrasco, R. (1999) 'Archaeoichthyological evidence for long-term socio-economic trends in Northern Scotland: 3500 BC to AD 1500', *Journal of Archaeological Science,* 26: 353–88.

Barry, T. B. (1981) 'Archaeological excavations at Dunbeg promontory fort, Co. Kerry', *PRIA*, 81C: 295–329.

Beguin, F. with Lebouteiller, P. (1995) 'La céramique d'un enclos du second Age du Fer à Hédé (35), au lieu-dit 'La Bas-Chesnay', *RAO*, 12: 111–16.

Bell, M. (1984) 'Environmental archaeology in South West England', in H. C. M. Keeley (ed.), *Environmental Archaeology: A Regional Review*, pp. 42–54, Directorate of Ancient Monuments and Historic Buildings Occasional Paper No. 6: London.

Bell, M. (1990) *Brean Down Excavations 1983–1987*, English Heritage Archaeological Report No. 15: London.

Bell, M, (1995) 'People and Nature in the Celtic World', in Green, M. J. (ed.), *The Celtic World*, pp. 145–58, Routledge: London.

Bell, M. (1996) 'Environment in the First Millennium BC', in Champion, T. C. and Collis, J. R. (eds), *The Iron Age in Britain and Ireland: recent trends*, pp. 5–16, John Collis Publications: Sheffield.

Bendala Gálan, M. (1977) 'Notas sobre las estelas decoradas del Suroeste y los orígenes de Tartessos', *Habis*, 8: 177–205.

Bendala Gálan, M. (1987) 'Reflexiones sobre los escudos de la estelas tartésicas', *Boletín de la Asociación Española de Amigos de Arqueología*, 27: 12–17.

Bender, B. and Cailland, R. (1986) *The Archaeology of Brittany, Normandy and the Channel Islands: an introduction and guide,* Faber & Faber: London.

Bennet, I. and Grogan, E. (1993) 'Excavations at Mooghaun South, Co. Clare. Interim report 1', *Discovery Programme Reports*, 1: 39–43.

Bigwood, W. (1964) 'Dun at Glenramskill, Campbletown', *Discovery and Excavation in Scotland*, 1964: 18–19.

Bigwood, W. (1966) 'Dun Fhinn', *Discovery and Excavation in Scotland*, 1966: 98–9.

Bond, D. (1988) 'Excavation at the North Ring, Mucking, Essex: a Late Bronze Age enclosure', *East Anglian Archaeological Reports* 43.

Bond, J. M. (2002) 'Pictish pigs and Celtic cowboys: food and farming in the Atlantic Iron Age', in Ballin Smith, B. and Banks, I. (eds) (2002): 177–84.

Bond, J. M., Nicholson, R. A. and Simpson, I. (2005) 'Living off the land; farming and fishing at Old Scatness', in Turner *et al.* (eds) (2005): 211–20.

Borlase, Revd W. (1754) *Antiquities historical and monumental of Cornwall*, EP Publishing (reprint): Truro

Borlase, W. C. (1868) 'Excavations in subterranean chambers at Chapel Euny, Sancreed, Cornwall', *Proceedings of the Society of Antiquaries*, 5: 161–70.

Boudet, R. (1988) 'Iberian type brooches', in Cunliffe, B. W. (1998): 64–5.

Bowen, E. G. (1957) *Wales: a Physical, Historical and Regional Geography*, Methuen: London.

Bowen, E. G. (1968) 'The Irish Sea province', *CurrA*, 8: 203–4.

Bowen, E. G. (1969) *Saints, Seaways and Settlements in the Celtic Lands*, Univ. of Wales Press: Cardiff.

Bowen, E. G. (1970) 'Britain and the British Seas', in Moore, D. (ed.) (1970): 13–28.

Bowen, E. G. (1972) *Britain and the Western Seaways*, Thames & Hudson: London.

Bowen, E. G. (1977) *Saints, Seaways and Settlement*, University of Wales Press: London.

Boyd, W. E. (1988) 'Cereals in Scottish antiquity', *Circaea*, 5: 101–10.

Bradley, R. (1971) 'Stock raising and the origins of the hill-fort on the South Downs', *AJ*, 51: 8–29.

Bradley, R. (1978) *The Prehistoric Settlement of Britain*, Henley and Boston: London.

Bradley, R. (1981) 'Economic growth and social change: two examples from Bronze Age Europe', in Sheridan A. and Bailey G. (eds), *Economic Archaeology*, pp. 231–7, BAR, Internat. Ser. 96, Oxford.

Bradley, R. (1984) *The Social Foundations of Prehistoric Britain: Themes and Variations in the Archaeology of Power*, Longman: London.

Bradley, R. (1988) 'Hoarding, recycling and the consumption of prehistoric metalwork: technological change in western Europe', *WA*, 20(2): 249–60.

Bradley, R. (1990) *The Passage of Arms*, Cambridge University Press: Cambridge.

Bradley, R. (1993) *Altering the earth. The origins of monuments in Britan and continental Europe*, Society of Antiquaries of Scotland Monograph Series, 8: Edinburgh.

Bradley, R. (1997) *Rock Art and the Prehistory of Atlantic Europe: Signing the Land*, Routledge: London.

Bradley, R. (1998) *The Passage of Arms. An Archaeological Analysis of Prehistoric Hoards and Votive Deposits*, 2nd edn, Oxbow Books: Oxford.

Bradley, R. (2000) *An Archaeology of Natural Places*, Routledge: London.

Bradley, R. (2005) *Ritual and Domestic Life in Prehistoric Europe*, Routledge: London.

Bradley, R. and Gordon, K. (1988) 'Human skulls from the River Thames, their dating and significance', *Antiquity*, 62: 503–9.

Bradley, R., Entwhistle, R. and Raymond, F. (1994) *Prehistoric Land Divisions on Salisbury Plain: The Work of the Linear Ditches Project*, English Heritage: London.

Braudel, F. (1972) *The Mediterranean and the Mediterranean World in the Age of Philip II*, 2 vols (vol. 2 published 1973), Collins: London and New York.

Briard, J. (1961) *Dépôts de l'Age du Bronze*, Travaux du Laboratoire d'Anthropologie Préhistorique de la Faculté de Rennes, Université de Rennes: Rennes.

Briard, J. (1965) *Les dèpôts bretons et l'âge du bronze atlantique*, Editions Ouest-France: Rennes.

Briard, J. (1974) 'Bronze Age Cultures: 1800–600 BC', in Piggott *et al.* (eds) Piggott, S., Daniel, G. and McBurney, C. (eds), *France before the Romans,* pp. 131–56, Thames & Hudson: London.

Briard, J. (1979) *The Bronze Age in Barbarian Europe: From the Megaliths to the Celts*, Routledge and Kegan Paul, Bridgford: London.

Briard, J. (1995) 'L'Âge du Bronze', in Giot, P. R., Briard, J. and Pape, L. (eds), *Protohistoire de la Bretagne*, pp. 25–198, Editions Ouest-France: Rennes.

Briard, J. and Nicolardot, J.-P. (1985) 'Un habitat de hauter côtier de l'Age du Bronze en Bretagne', *Up and Settlement in Brittany*, BAR, 143: 365–83.

Briard, J., Nicolardot, J.-P. and Robino, P. (1988) 'Le Vivier (Quiberon) et Grosse Roche (Saint-Jacut)', *Dossiers de Protohistoire no.2: Architectures des Ages des Métaux, fouilles récentes*, Paris, Errances: 9–18.

Briggs, C. S. (1987) 'Buckets and Cauldrons in the Late Bronze Age of North-west Europe: a review', in Blanchet J. C. (ed.), *Les Relations entre le Continent et les Illes Britanniques à l'Age du Bronze*, pp. 161–87, Amiens.

Brooks, R. T. (1974) 'The excavation of the Rumps Cliff Castle, St. Minver, Cornwall', *CA*, 13: 5–50.

Brown, N. (1988) 'A Late Bronze Age enclosure at Lofts Farm, Heybridge', *PPS*, 54: 249–302.

Brun, P. (1988) 'L'entité "Rhin-Suisse-France orientale": nature et evolution', in Brun, P. and Mordant, C. (eds), *Le groupe Rhin-Suisse-France orientale et la notion de civilisation des Champs d'Urnes*, 1, Mémoirs du Musée de Préhistoire d'Ile-de-France: Nemoirs.

Brun, P. (1991) 'Le Bronze Atlantique et ses subdivisions culturelles: essai de définition', in Chevillot, C. and Coffyn, A. (eds) (1991): 11–24.

Brun, P. (1993) 'East-West relations in the Paris Basin during the Late Bronze Age', in Scarre C. and Healy F. (eds), *Trade and Exchange in Prehistoric Europe*, p. 33, Oxbow Monographs: Oxford.

Brun, P. (1998) 'Le complexe culturel atlantique: entre le cristal et la fumée', in Jorge, S.O. (ed.): 40–51.

Buchsenschutz, O. (1994) 'Introduction', in Buchsenschutz, O. and Méniel, P. (eds), *Les Installations Agricoles de L'Age du Fer en Ile-de-France: actes du colloque de Paris, 1993*, Etudes d'histoire et d'archeologie vol. IV, pp. 9–24, Presses de l'école normale superieure: Paris.

Buckley, D. G. and Hedges, J. D. (1987) *The Bronze Age and Saxon Settlements at Springfield Lyons, Essex: an interim report*, Essex County Council Occasional Papers 5: Norwich.

Buckley, V. M. and Sweetman, P. D. (1991) *Archaeological Survey of County Louth*, The Office of Public Works: Dublin.

Bukowski, Z. (1986) 'Bemerkumgen zur Problamatik des Frühen Eisens in Mittel- und Nord-europa. Inga Serning in Memoriam', in Ambrosiani, B. (ed.), *Die Bronzezeit im Osteegebiet*, Stockholm.

Bullied, A. and Gray, H. St. G. (1917) *The Glastonbury Lake Village*, Vols. I and II, Glastonbury Antiq. Soc: Glastonbury.

Bullied, A. and Gray, H. St. G. (1948) *The Meare Lake Village, Volume I*, Taunton Castle, Taunton.

Burgess, C. (1968) 'The later Bronze Age in the British Isles and north-western France', *ArchJ*, 125: 1–45.

Burgess, C. (1974) 'The Bronze Age', in C. Renfrew (ed.), *British Prehistory: a new outline*, pp. 165–232, Duckworth: London.

Burgess, C. (1979) 'A find from Boyton, Suffolk, and the end of the Bronze Age in Britain and Ireland', in Burgess, C. and Coombs, D. (eds), *Bronze Age Hoards: Some Finds Old and New*, p. 67, BAR, Brit. Ser.: Oxford.

Burgess, C. (1980) *The Age of Stonehenge*, Phoenix Press: London.

Burgess, C. (1985) 'Population, climate and upland settlement', in Spratt, D. and Burgess, C. (eds), *Upland Settlement in Britain*, pp. 195–230, BAR Brit. Ser, 143: Oxford.

Burgess, C. (1989) 'Volcanoes, catastrophe and the global crisis of the late second millennium BC', *CurrA*, 117: 325–9.

Burgess, C. (1991) 'The East and the West: Mediterranean influence in the Atlantic world in the Later Bronze Age, ca. 1500–700 BC', in Chevillot, C. and Coffyn, A. (eds), *L'Age du Bronze Atlantique*, pp. 25–45, Actes du premier Colloque du Parc Archéologique de Beynac, Association des Musées du Sardlais: Beynac.

Burgess, C., Coombs, D. and Davies, D. G. (1972) 'The Broadward complex and barbed spearheads', in Lynch, F. and Burgess, C. (eds), *Prehistoric Man in Wales and the West: Essays in honour of Lily F. Chitty*, pp. 167–81, Adams & Dart: Bath.

Burgess, C., Henderson, J. and Rees, T. (1994) 'Garenin', *Discovery and Excavation in Scotland, 1994*: 96.

Burgess, C., Church, M. and Jackson, A. (1995) 'Garenin', *Discovery and Excavation in Scotland 1995*: 87.

Burgess, C. M. G. (1999) 'Promontory enclosures on the Isle of Lewis, the Western Isles of Scotland', in Frodsham, P., Topping, P. and Cowley, D. (eds.), *We are always chasing time. Papers presented to Keith Blood*, Northern Archaeology 17/18, Northern Archaeology Group: Newcastle upon Tyne.

Burns, B., Cunliffe, B. and Sebire, H. (1996) *Guernsey: an Island Community of the Atlantic Iron Age*, Oxford University Committee for Archaeology Monograph 43: Oxford.

Bury, J. B. (1905) *The Life of St. Patrick and his Place in History*, The Macmillan and Co. Limited: London.

Butcher, S. A. (1970) 'Excavations at Nornour, Scilly, 1969–70: Interim Report', *CA*, 9: 77–80.

Butcher, S. A. (1978) 'Excavations at Nornour, Isles of Scilly, 1969–73: the Pre-Roman Settlement', *CA*, 17: 29–113.

Campbell, E. (1991) 'Excavation of a wheelhouse and other Iron Age structures at Sollas, North Uist, by R. J. Atkinson in 1957', *PSAS*, 121: 117–73.

Campbell, H. F. (1920) *Caithness and Sutherland*, Cambridge University Press: Cambridge.

Carballo, A (2002) *A Cultura castrexa na comarca de Deza*, Seminario de Estudios de Deza: Lalin.

Caseldine, C. J. and Hatton, J. M. (1996) 'Into the Mists? Thoughts on the Prehistoric and Historic Environmental History of Dartmoor', *PDAS*, 52: 21–47.

Caulfield, S. (1978) 'Neolithic fields: the Irish evidence', in Bowen, H. C. and Fowler, P. J. (eds). *Early Land Allotment in the British Isles: a survey of recent work*, pp. 137–43, BAR, Brit. Ser., 48: Archaeopress: Oxford.

Caulfield, S. (1981) 'Celtic Problems in the Irish Iron Age', in Corráin, D. Ó. (ed.), *Irish Antiquity. Essays and Studies presented to Professor M. J. O' Kelly*, pp. 205–15, Four Courts Press: Dublin.

Cavers, M. G. (2005) *Crannogs and later prehistoric settlement in Western Scotland with particular reference to Dumfries and Galloway and Argyll and Bute*, unpub. Ph.D. thesis, University of Nottingham.

Celestino Pérez, S. (1990) 'Las estelas decoradas del suroeste peninsular', *Cuadernos Emeritenses* 2 (La cultura Tartésica y Extremadura), Mérida: 45–62.

Cerón-Carrasco, R., Church, M. and Thoms, J. (2005) 'Towards an economic landscape of the Bhaltos peninsula, Lewis, during the Mid to Late Iron Age', in Turner *et al.* (eds) (2005): 221–34.

Champion, T. C. (1979) 'The Iron Age in southern Britain and Ireland', in Megaw, J.V. S. and Simpson, D. D. A. (1979) *Introduction to British Prehistory from the Arrival of Homo sapiens to the Claudian Invasion*, pp. 344–45, Leicester University Press: Leicester.

Champion, T. C. (1989) 'From Bronze Age to Iron Age in Ireland', in Stig-Sørenson, M. L. and Thomas, R. (eds), *The Bronze Age–Iron Age Transition in Europe*, pp. 287–303, *BAR Internat. Ser.* 483, vol. 2, Archaeopress: Oxford.

Champion, T. C. (1999) 'The Later Bronze Age', in Hunter, J. and Ralston, I. B. M. (eds), *The Archaeology of Britain*, pp. 95–112, Routledge: London.

Chapman, M. (1992) *The Celts: The Construction of a Myth*, Macmillan: London.

Chevillot, C. and Coffyn, A. (eds) (1991) *L'age du Bronze Atlantique. Ses facies, de l'ecosse a l'Andalousie et luers relations avec le Bronze Continental et la Méditerranée*, Actes du 1er Colloque du Parc Archéologique de Beynac, Publications de l'association de musées du Sarladais: Beynac.

Childe, V. G. (1935) *The Prehistory of Scotland*, Kegan Paul: London.

Childe, V. G. (1946) *Scotland before the Scots*, Methuen: London.

Childe, V. G. and Thorneycroft, W. (1938) 'The Vitrified Fort at Rahoy, Morven, Argyll', *PSAS*, 72: 23–43.

Childe, V. G. (1954) *What happened in history*, Penguin: Harmondsworth.

Chitty, L. F. (1965) 'Irish Bronze Axes assigned to the Guilsfield Hoard, Montgomeryshire', *AC*, 114: 120–9.

Christie, P. M. (1978) 'The excavation of an Iron Age souterrain and settlement at Carn Euny, Sancreed, Cornwall', *PPS*, 44: 309–434.

Christie, P. M. (1979) 'Cornish souterrains in the light of recent research', *Bulletin of the London Institute of Archaeology*, 16: 187–213.

Christie, P. M. (1986) 'Cornwall in the Bronze Age', *CA*, 25: 81–111.

Church, M. (2002) 'The archaeological and archaeobotanical implications of a destruction layer at Dun Bharabhat, Lewis', in Ballin Smith, B. and Banks, I. (eds) (2002): 67–75.

Clark, E. (1961) *Cornish Fogous*, London.

Clark, P. (ed.) (2004) *The Dover Bronze Age Boat in Context: Society and Water Transport in Prehistoric Europe*, Oxbow: Oxford.

Clarke, D. V. (1971) 'Small finds of the Atlantic Province: Problems of approach', *Scottish Archaeological Forum*, 3: 22–54.

Cleary, R. M., Hurley, M. F., and Twohig, E. A. (eds), (1987) *Archaeological Excavations on the Cork-Dublin Gas Pipeline (1981–82)*, Cork Archaelogical Studies: Cork.

Clinton, M. (2001) *The Souterrains of Ireland*, Wordwell: Wicklow.

Coffyn, A. (1983) 'La fin de l'Age du Bronze dans le centre-Portugal', *O Arqueólogo Português* 1 (series IV): 169–96.

Coffyn, A. (1985) *Le Bronze Final Atlantique dans la Peninsula Iberique*, Publication du Centre Pierre Paris II: Paris.

Coffyn, A. and Sion, H. (1993) 'Les relations atlantiques méditerranéennes. Eléments pour une révision chronologique du Bronze final atlántique', *Mediterrâneo*, 2: 285–310.

Coffyn, A., Gomez, J. and Mohen, J.-P. (1981) *L'apogee du bronze atlantique. L'age du bronze en France I*, Picard: Paris.

Coles, B. and Coles, J. M. (1986) *Sweet Track to Glastonbury*, Thames & Hudson: London.

Coles, J. M. (1960) 'Scottish Late Bronze Age metalwork: typology, distributions and chronology', *PSAS*, 93: 16–134

Coles, J. M. (1962) 'European Bronze Age Shields', *PPS*, 21: 16–134.

Coles, J. M. and Harding, A. F. (1979) *The Bronze Age in Europe: an introduction to the prehistory of Europe c. 2000–700 B.C.*, Methuen: London.

Coles, J. M. and Livens, R. G. (1957–8) 'A Bronze Sword from Douglas, Lanarkshire', *PSAS*, 91: 182–6.

Colley, S. (1987) 'The marine faunal remains', in Hedges, J. W. (1987): 126–34.

Collins, A. E. P. (1970) 'Bronze Age moulds in Ulster', *UJA*, 33: 23–36.

Collis, J. (1975) *Defended sites of the late La Tène in Central and Western Europe*, BAR, Supplementary Series 2: Oxford.

Collis, J. (1984) *The European Iron Age*, Batsford: London.

Collis, J. (1994) 'The Iron Age', in Vyner, B. (ed.), *Building on the past: a celebration of 150 years of the Royal Archaeological Institute*, pp. 123–48, Royal Archaeological Institute: London.

Collis, J. (1996) 'Celtes, culture, contacts: confrontation et confusion', in Boudet, R. (ed.), *l'Age du Fer en Europe sud-occidentale*, Aquitania 12: 447–56.

Collis, J. (1997) 'Celtic Myths', *Antiquity*, 71: 195–201.

Colquhoun, I. and Burgess, C. (1988) *The Swords of Britain*, Prahistorische Bronzefunde: Munich.

Cooke, I. M. (1993) *Mother and Sun, the Cornish Fogou*, Men-an-Tol Studio, Penzance: Cornwall.

Coombs, D. G. (1971) 'Late Bronze Age metalwork in the south of England', unpub. Ph.D. thesis, University of Cambridge.

Coombs, D. (1975) 'The Dover harbour find – a Bronze Age wreck?', *AA* 1: 193–5.

Coombs, D. (1989) 'The Wilberton complex and Bronze Final II in Atlantic Europe', in Brun, P. and Mordant, C. (ed.) *Le Groupe Rhin-Suisse-France Orientale at la Notion de Civilsation des Champs d'Urnes*, pp. 571–582, Memoirs du Musée de Préhistoire d'Ille de France, No. 1.

Coombs, (1998) '"Hello Sailor" – Some reflections on the Atlantic Bronze Age', in Jorge, S. O. (ed.) (1998): 150–6.

Cooney, G. (1991) 'Irish Neolithic landscapes and land use systems: the implications of field systems', *Rural History* 2.2: 123–9.

Cooney, G. and Grogan, E. (1991) 'An Archaeological Solution to the "Irish" Problem?', *Emania* 9: 33–43.

Cooney, G. and Grogan, E. (1994) *Irish Prehistory: A Social Perspective*, Wordwell: Dublin.

Cotter, C. (1993) 'Western Stone Fort Project. Interim Report', *Discovery Programme Reports*, 1: 1–19.

Cotter, C. (1995) 'Western Stone Fort Project. Interim Report', *Discovery Programme Reports*, 2: 1–11.

Cotter, C. (1996) 'Western Stone Fort Project. Interim Report', *Discovery Programme Reports*, 4: 1–14.

Cotter, C. (1999) 'Western Stone Fort Project. Cahercommaun Fort, Co. Clare: a reassessment of its cultural context', *Discovery Programme Reports*, 5: 41–96.

Cotter, C. (2000) 'The Chronology and Affinities of the Stone Forts along the Atlantic Coast of Ireland', in Henderson, J. C. (ed.) (2000): 117–54.

Cotter, C. H. (1974) *The Atlantic Ocean*, Glasgow.

Cotton, M. A. (1959) 'Cornish cliff castles', *Proceedings of the West Cornwall Field Club*, 2: 113–21.

Cotton, M. A. (1961) 'Observations of the classification of hillforts in southern England', in Frere, S. S. (ed.), *The Problems of the Iron Age in Southern Britain*, pp. 61–8, Institute of Archaeology, Occasional Paper 11: London.

Coulmas, F. (1992) *Language and Economy*, Blackwell: Oxford.

Cowen, J. D. (1951) 'The earliest bronze swords in Britain and their origins on the continent', *PPS*, 17: 195–213.

Cowen, J. D. (1967) 'The Hallstatt sword of bronze: on the Continent and in Britain', *PPS*, 33: 377–454.

Cowley, D. (2000) 'Site morphology and regional variation in the later prehistoric settlement of south west Scotland', in Harding, J. and Johnston, R. (eds), *Northern Pasts: Interpretations of the Later Prehistory of Northern England and Southern Scotland*, BAR, Brit. Ser. 302, pp. 167–76, Archaeopress: Oxford.

Crabtree, P. (1990) 'Subsistence and Ritual: the faunal remains from Dún Ailinne, Co. Kildare, Ireland', *Emania*, 7: 22–5.

Crane, P. (1999) 'Iron Age promontory fort to medieval castle? Excavations at Great Castle Head, Dale, Pembrokeshire', *AC*, 148: 86–145.

Crawford, I. (1974) 'Scot (?), Norseman and Gael', *Scottish Archaeological Forum*, 6: 1–16.

Crawford, I. and Selkirk, A. (1996) 'The Udal', *CurrA*, 147: 84–94.

Crawford, O. G. S. (1912) 'The distribution of Early Bronze Age settlements in Britain', *Geographical Journal*, 40: 184–203.

Crawford, O. G. S. (1936) 'Western Seaways', in Buxton, L. H. D. (ed.), *Custom is King: Studies in Honour or R. R. Marett*, pp. 181–200, Hutchinson's scientific and technical publications: London.

Crew, P. (1990) 'Excavations at Crawcwellt, 1986–89: A Late Prehistoric Upland Iron-Working Settlement', *Archaeology in Wales*, 29: 11–16.

Crofts, Rev. C. B. (1955) 'Maen Castle, Sennen; the Excavation of an Early Iron Age Promontory Fort', *Proceedings of the West Cornwall Field Club*, 1.3: 98–115.

Cunliffe, B. W. (1972) 'The Late Iron Age metalwork from Bulbury, Dorset', *A J*, 52: 293–308.

Cunliffe, B. W. (1978) *Hengistbury Head*, Paul Elek: London.

Cunliffe, B. W. (1982a) 'Britain, the Veneti and beyond', *OJA*, 1: 39–68.

Cunliffe, B. W. (1982b) Settlement hierarchy and social change in southern Britain in the Iron Age. *Analecta Praehistorica Leidensia* 15.

Cunliffe, B. W. (1983) 'Ictis: is it here?', *OJA*, 2: 123–6.

Cunliffe, B. W. (1984) 'Relationships between Britain and Gaul in the first century B.C.', in Macready, S. and Thompson, F. H. (eds) (1984) *Cross-Channel Trade Between Gaul and Britain in the pre-Roman Iron Age,* pp. 3–23, Society of Antiquaries Occasional Paper IV, New Series: London.

Cunliffe, B. W. (1987) *Hengistbury Head, Dorset. Volume 1: The prehistoric and Roman settlement, 3500 BC-AD 500*, Oxford University Committee for Archaeology, Monograph 13.

Cunliffe, B. W. (1988a) *Mount Batten, Plymouth. A Prehistoric and Roman Port*, Oxford University Committee for Archaeology Monograph 26: Oxford.

Cunliffe, B. W. (1988b) *Greeks, Romans and Barbarians*, Batsford: London.

Cunliffe, B. W. (1990) 'Social and economic contacts between western France and Britain', in the Early and Middle La Tène Period', in J. L'Helgouach (ed.) (1990), *La Bretagne et l' Europe Prehistoriques,* pp. 245–51, *RAO,* Supplement no 2, Rennes.

Cunliffe, B. W. (1991) *Iron Age Communities in Britain*, 3rd edn, Routledge: London.

Cunliffe, B. W. (1992) 'Le Câtel de Rozel, Jersey: the excavations of 1988–90', *AJ*, 72: 18–53.

Cunliffe, B. W. (1994) 'After Hillforts', *OJA*, 13: 71–84.

Cunliffe, B. W. (1995a) *Iron Age Britain*, Batsford: London.

Cunliffe, B. W. (1995b) 'Diversity in the Landscape: the Geographical Background to Urbanism in Iberia', in Cunliffe, B. W. and Keay, S. (eds), *Social Complexity and the Development of Towns in Iberia. From the Copper Age to the Second Century AD*, Proceedings of the British Academy, 86: 5–28.

Cunliffe, B. W. (1997) *The Ancient Celts*, Oxford University Press: Oxford.

Cunliffe, B. W. (2000) 'Brittany and the Atlantic Rim in the Later First Millennium BC', *OJA*, 19: 367–86.

Cunliffe, B. W. (2001) *Facing the Ocean: The Atlantic and its Peoples, 8000 BC–AD 1500*, Oxford University Press: Oxford.

Cunliffe, B. W. (2002) *The Extraordinary Voyage of Pytheas the Greek*, Penguin Books: London.

Cunliffe, B. W. and Brown, L. (1987) 'The Later Prehistoric and Roman pottery', in Cunliffe, B. W. (1987): 205–321.

Cunliffe, B. W. and de Jersey, P. (1997) *Armorica and Britain. Cross Channel Relationships in the Late First Millennium BC*, Studies in Celtic Coinage, Number 3, Oxford University Committee for Archaeology, Monograph 45: Oxford.

Cunliffe, B. W. and Galliou, P. (1995) 'Le Yaudet, Ploulec'h, Côtes d'Armor, Brittany. An interim report on the excavations of 1991–4', *AJ*, 75: 43–70.

Cunliffe, B. W. and Galliou, P. (2000) 'Britons and Bretons: some new evidence from Le Yaudet', *ArchJ*, 157: 200–28.

Cunliffe, B. W. and Galliou, P. (2004) *Les fouilles du Yaudet en Ploulec'h, Cotes-d'Armor*, Oxford University School of Archaeology Monograph 58: Oxford.

Cunliffe, B. W. and Galliou, P. (2005) *Les fouilles du Yaudet en Ploulec'h, Cotes-d'Armor, volume 2: Le site: de la Préhistoire à la fin de l'Empire gaulois*, Oxford University School of Archaeology Monograph 63: Oxford.

Cunliffe, B. W. and Poole, C. (1991) *Danebury: An Iron Age Hillfort in Hampshire. Volume 4. The excavations 1979–1988: the site*, CBA Research Report 73.

Cunliffe, B. W. and Rowley, T. (eds) (1976) *Oppida: the Beginnings of Urbanisation in Barbarian Europe*, BAR, Supplemental Series 2: Oxford.

Cunnington, M. E. (1923) *The Early Iron Age Inhabited Site of All Cannings Cross*, George Simpson & Co: Devizes.

Cuppage, J. (1986) *Archaeological Survey of the Dingle Peninsula*, Oidhreacht Chorca Dhuibhne: Ballyferriter.

Curwen, E. C. (1938) 'The Hebrides: a cultural backwater', *Antiquity*, 12: 261–89.

Daire, M.-Y. (1990) 'Archeologie Insulaire en Bretagne: Un point de vue sur les sites de l'age du fer', in J. L'Helgouach (ed.) (1990), *La Bretagne et l' Europe Prehistoriques*, pp. 269–78, *RAO*, Supplement no 2, Rennes.

Daire, M.-Y. (1992) *Les céramiques armoricaines de la fin de l'Age du Fer*, Travaux du Laboratoire d'Anthropologie de l'Université de Rennes I, 39.

Daire, M.-Y. and Langouët, L. (1994) Des Ateliers de Bouilleur de Sel', in Daire, M.-Y. (ed.), *Le Sel Gauloise: Bouilleurs de sel et ateliers de briquetages armoricains à l'Âge Fer*, pp. 15–57, Centre Régional d'Archéologie d'Alet, Saint-Malo.

Daire, M.-Y. and Villard, A. (1996) 'Les steles de l'Age du Fer à décors géométriques et curvilignes. Etat de la question dans l'Ouest aroricain', *RAO*, 13: 123–56.

Daniel, G. E. (1941) 'The dual nature of the Megalithic colonisation of prehistoric Europe', *PPS*, 7: 1–49.

Davidson, D. A. and Carter, S. P. (1997) 'Soils and their evolution', in Edwards, K. J. and Ralston, I. B. M. (eds), *Scotland: Environment and Archaeology, 8000 BC–AD 1000*, pp. 45–62, John Wiley and Sons: Chichester.

Davies, J. L. (1995) 'The Early Celts in Wales', in Green, M. (ed.), *The Celtic World*, pp. 671–702, Routledge: London.

Davies, M. (1946) 'The diffusion and distribution pattern of the Megalithic monuments of the Irish Sea and North Channel coastlands', *AJ*, 26: 40–6.

Dawkins, R. (1990) *The Blind Watchmaker*, Penguin Books: London.

de Hoz, J. (1992) 'Testimonios lingüísticos relativos al problema céltico en la Península Ibérica', in Almagro-Gorbea, M. and Ruiz Zapatero, G. (eds), *Los Celtas: Hispania y Europa*, pp. 357–401, Actas del Escorial: Madrid.

de Jersey, P. (1992) *La Tène and early Gallo-Roman north-west France*, unpub. D.Phil. thesis, University of Oxford.

de Jersey, P. (1993) 'The early chronology of Alet, and its implications for Hengistbury Head and cross-Channel trade in the late Iron Age', *OJA*, 12: 321–35.

de Jersey, P. (1994) *Coinage in Iron Age Armorica*, Studies in Celtic Coinage, Number 2, Oxford University Committee for Archaeology, Monograph 39: Oxford.

De Lumley, H., Renault-Miskovsky, J., Miskovsky, J.-C. and Guilaine, J. (1976) 'Le cadre chronologique et paléoclimatique du Postglaciaire', in Guilaine, J. (ed.), *La préhistoire française 2: les civilisations néolithiques et protohistoriques de France*, pp. 3–16, CNRS: Paris.

De Valera, R. (1951) 'A group of "horned cairns" near Ballycastle, Co. Mayo', *JRSAI*, 81: 161–97.

Dechezlepretre, T., Billard, C., Blancquaert, G., Fournier, P. and Langlois, Y. (1997) 'Les constructions à plan circulaire de Haute Normandie', *RAO*, 14: 49–56.

Denford, G. T. (1975) 'Economy and location of Bronze Age "arable" settlements on Dartmoor', *Bull. Inst. Archaeol. Univ. London*, 12: 175–96.

Dent, J. S. (1982) 'Cemeteries and settlement patterns of the Iron Age on the Yorkshire Wolds', *PPS*, 48: 437–57.

Dent, J. S. (1985) 'Three cart burials from Wetwang, Yorkshire', *Antiquity*, 59: 85–92.

Devoy, R. J. N. (1990) 'Controls on coastal and sea-level changes and the application of archaeological-historical records to understanding recent patterns of sea-level movement', in McGrail, S. (ed.), *Maritime Celts, Frisians and Saxons*, CBA Research Report, 71: 17–26.

Dickson, C. A. (1994) 'Plant Remains', in Ballin Smith', B. (ed.) *Howe: Four Millennia of Orkney Prehistory*, pp. 125–39, Society of Antiquaries of Scotland Monograph No. 9: Edinburgh.

Dickson, C. A. and Dickson, J. H. (1984) 'The Botany of the Crosskirk Broch Site', in Fairhurst, H., *Excavations at Crosskirk Broch, Caithness*, pp. 147–55, Society of Antiquaries Monograph No. 3: Edinburgh.

Dickson, C. and Dickson, J. H. (2000) *Plants and People in Ancient Scotland*, Tempus: Stroud.

Dion, R. (1968) 'Transport de l'étain des Îles britaniques à Marseille à travers de la Gaule', *Actes du 93, Congrès national des Sociétés Savantes, Tours 1968: Archéologie*: 423–38.

Dockrill, S. J. (1998) 'Northern Exposure: Phase 1 of the Old Scatness Excavations, 1995–8', in Nicholson, R. A. and Dockrill, S. J. (eds) *Old Scatness Broch, Shetland: Retrospect and Prospect*, pp. 59–80, Bradford Archaeological Sciences Research 5, NABO Monograph No. 2.

Dockrill, S. J. (2003) 'Broch, wheelhouse and cell: redefining the Iron Age in Scotland', in Downes, J. and Ritchie, A. (eds) (2003): 82–94.

Dockrill, S. J., Bond, J. M. and Batt, C. M. (2005) 'Old Scatness: The First Millennium AD Broch, Scotland', in Turner *et al.* (eds) (2005): 52–65.

Doody, M. G. (1987a) 'Ballyveelish, Co. Tipperary', in Cleary, R. M., Hurley, M. F., and Twohig, E. A. (eds) (1987) *Archaeological Excavations on the Cork-Dublin Gas Pipeline (1981-82)*, pp. 8–35, Cork Archaeological Studies: Cork.

Doody, M. G. (1987b) 'Late Bronze Age Huts at Curraghatoor, Co. Tipperary', in Cleary, R. M., Hurley, M. F., and Twohig, E. A. (eds) (1987a), pp. 36–42, Cork Archaeological Studies No. 1, University College Cork: Cork.

Doody, M. (2000), Bronze Age Houses in Ireland, in Desmond, A., Johnson, G., McCarthy, M., Sheehan, J. and Shee Twohig, E. (eds), *New agendas in Irish Prehistory*, pp. 135–60, Wordwell Bray: Co. Wicklow.

Douch, H. L. and Beard, S. W. (1970) 'Excavations at Carvossa, Probus, 1968–1970: Preliminary Report', *CA*, 9: 93–8.

Downes, J. and Ritchie, A. (eds) (2003) *Sea Change: Orkney and Northern Europe in the later Iron Age AD 300–800*, Pinkfoot Press: Balgavies.

Drewett, P. (1982) 'Later Bronze Age downland economy and excavations at Black Patch, East Sussex', *PPS*, 48: 321–400.

Du Chatellier, P. (1890) 'Oppidum de Castel-Meur en Cleden (Finistère)', *L'Anthropologie*, I: 401–12.

Dudley, D. (1957) 'An excavation at Bodrifty, Mulfra, near Penzance', *ArchJ*, 113: 1–32.

Dudley, D. (1960) 'Pendeen Earthwork, Threemilestone, Truro, Cornwall', *Royal Institute of Cornwall Supplement*: 3–13.

Dudley, D. and Jope, E. M. (1965) 'An Iron Age Cist-Burial with Two Brooches from Trevone, North Cornwall', *CA*, 4: 24–43.

Dudley, D. (1967) 'Excavations on Nornour in the Isles of Scilly, 1962–6', *ArchJ*, 124: 1–64.

Duignan, M. (1976) 'The Turoe Stone: its place in insular La Tène art', in Duval, P-M. and Hawkes, C. (eds), *Celtic Art in Prehistoric Europe: Five Protohistoric Centuries. Proceedings of the colloquy held in 1972 at the Oxford Maison FrançÁaise*, pp. 201–17, Seminar Press: London.

Duval, A. (1984) 'Regional groups in Western France', in Macready, S. and Thompson, F. H. (eds) *Cross-Channel trade between Gaul and Britain in the pre-Roman Iron Age*, Society of Antiquaries Occasional Paper (New Series) IV: 78–91.

Duval, A. (1990) 'L'Armorique vue du "continent"', in L'Helgouach, J. (ed.) (1990), *La Bretagne et l' Europe Prehistoriques*, pp. 279–86, *RAO*, Supplement no 2, Rennes.

Duval, A. (1990a) 'Quelques aspects du mobilier métallique en fer anciennement recueilli à Tronoën, en Saint-Jean-Trolimon (Finistère)', *Les Gaulois d'Armorique*, Actes du XII colloque AFEAF, Quimper 1988, *RAO* suppl. 3: 23–45.

Edmonds, E. A., McKeown, M. C. and Williams, M. (1975) *British Regional Geology. South West England*, 4th edn, HMSO: London.

Edwards, H. J. (1917) *Caesar, Bellum Gallicum*, Loeb Classical Library: London.

Edwards, K. J. and Whittington, G. (1997) 'Human activity and landscape change in Scotland during the Holocene', in Gordon, J. E. (ed.) *Reflections on the Ice Age in Scotland: an update on Quaternary studies*, pp. 130–6, Scottish Natural Heritage: Edinburgh.

Edwards, N. (1990) *The Archaeology of Early Medieval Ireland*, University of Pennsylvania Press: Philadelphia.

Ellison, A. (1980) 'Settlements and Regional Exchange: a case study', in Barrett, J. C. and Bradley, R. J. (eds), *Settlement and Society in the British Later Bronze Age*, pp. 127–40, BAR. Brit. Ser. 83, Archaeopress: Oxford.

Elsdon, S. M. (1978) 'The Pottery' in Christie P. M., The excavation of an Iron Age souterrain and settlement at Carn Euny, Sancreed, Cornwall, *PPS*, 44: 396–424.

Embleton, C. (1984) 'Caledonian Highlands', in Embleton, C. (ed.), *Geomorphology of Europe*, pp. 92–131, Macmillan: London.

Eogan, G. (1964) 'The Later Bronze Age in Ireland in the light of recent research', *PPS*, 30: 268–351.

Eogan, G. (1965) *Catalogue of Irish Bronze Swords,* Stationery Office: Dublin.

Eogan, G. (1974) 'Regionale Gruppierungen in der Spätbronzezeit Irlands', *Archäol Korrespondenzbl*, 4: 319–27.

Eogan, G. (1983) *Hoards of the Irish Later Bronze Age*, Dublin University: Dublin.

Eogan, G. (1994) *The Accomplished Art. Gold and Gold-Working in Britain and Ireland during the Bronze Age (c. 2300–650 BC)*, Oxbow: Oxford.

Eogan, G. (1995) 'Ideas, people and things: Ireland and the external world during the Later Bronze Age', in Waddell, J. and Shee Twohig, E. (eds), *Ireland in the Bronze Age: Proceedings of the Dublin Conference, April 1995*, pp. 128–35, The Stationery Office: Dublin.

Evans, J. G. (1969) 'The exploitation of molluscs', in Ucko, P. J. and Dimbleby, G. W. (eds), *The Domestication and Exploitation of Plants and Animals*, pp. 477–84, Gerald Duckworth: London.

Exley, C. S. and Stone, M. (1966) 'The grannitic rocks of South West England', in Hosking, K. F. G. and Shrimpton, G. J. (eds), *Present Views of Some Aspects of the Geology of Cornwall and Devon*, pp. 131–84, Royal Geological Society of Cornwall: Penzance.

Fairhurst, H. (1939) 'The Galleried Dun at Kildonan Bay, Kintyre', *PSAS*, 73: 185–228.

Fairhurst, H. (1962) 'An Caisteal: An Iron Age fortification in Mull', *PSAS*, 95: 199–207.

Fairhurst, H. (1971) 'Kilphedir and hut-circle sites in Northern Scotland', *SAF*, 3: 1–10.

Fairhurst, H. (1984) *Excavations at Crosskirk Broch, Caithness*, Society of Antiquaries of Scotland Monograph Series 3: Edinburgh.

Farrell, A. W. and Penney, S. (1975) 'The Broighter Boat: a reassessment', *Irish Archaeological Research Forum*, 2: 15–28.

Fernández-Castro, M. (1995) *Iberia in Prehistory*, Blackwell: Oxford.

Fitzpatrick, A. (1985) 'The Iron Age glass bracelets from Castle Dore', *CA*, 24: 133–40.

Fitzpatrick, A. (1994) 'Outside in: the structure of an Early Iron Age house at Dunston Park, Thatcham, Berkshire', in Fitzpatrick, A. and Morris, E. (eds), *The Iron Age in Wessex: Recent Work*, pp. 68–72, Trust for Wessex Archaeology and AFEAF: Salisbury.

Fleming, A. (1978) 'The prehistoric landscape of Dartmoor, Part 1, South Dartmoor', *PPS*, 44: 97–124.

Fleming, A. (1983) 'The prehistoric landscape of Dartmoor, Part 2: north and east Dartmoor', *PPS*, 49: 195–241.

Fleming, A. (1984) 'The prehistoric landscape of Dartmoor: wider implications', *Landscape History*, 6: 5–19.

Fleming, A. (1985) 'Land tenure, productivity, and field systems' in Baker, G. and Gamble, C. (eds), *Beyond Domestication in Prehistoric Europe: Investigations in Subsistence Archaeology and Social Complexity*, pp. 129–46, Academic Press: London.

Fluere, H. J. and Roberts, J. E. (1915) 'Archaeological Problems of the West Coast of Britain', *AC*, 70: 405–20.

Forde, C. D. (1930) 'The Early Cultures of Atlantic Europe', *Archaeologia Aeliana*, 32: New York.

Foster, S. M. (1989a) 'Analysis of spatial patterns in buildings (access analysis) as an insight into social structure: examples from the Scottish Atlantic Iron Age', *Antiquity*, 63: 40–50.

Foster, S. M. (1989b) 'Transformations in social space: Iron Age Orkney and Caithness', *SAR*, 6: 34–55.

Foster, S. (1990) 'Pins, combs and the chronology of Later Atlantic Iron Age settlement', in Armit, I. (ed.): 143–74.

Fox, A. (1953) 'Hill-slope forts and related earthworks in south-west England and South Wales', *ArchJ*, 109 (1952): 1–22.

Fox, A. (1955) 'Excavations at Kestor, an early Iron Age settlement near Chagford, Devon', *Transactions of the Devonshire Association*, 86: 21–62.

Fox, A. (1957) 'Excavations on Dean Moor, 1954–6', *Transactions of the Devonshire Association*, 89: 18–77.

Fox, A. (1961) 'South western hillforts', in Frere, S. S. (ed.), *The Problems of the Iron Age in Southern Britain*, pp. 35–60, Institute of Archaeology: London, Occasional Paper 11.

Fox, A. (1964) *South West England*, Thames & Hudson: London.

Fox, A. (1973) *South West England 3500 BC–AD 600*, 2nd edn, David & Charles: Newton Abbot.

Fox, A. and Ravenhill, W. L. D. (1969) 'Excavation of a rectilinear earthwork at Trevinnick, St. Kew, 1968', *CA*, 8: 89–96.

Fox, A., Radford, C. A. R., Rogers, E. H., and Shorter, A. H. (1950) 'Report on the Excavations at Milber Down, 1937–8', *PDAES*, 4: 27–66.

Fox, C. F. (1927) 'A settlement of the Early Iron Age on Merthyr Mawr Warren, Glamorgan', *AC*, 82: 44–6.

Fox, C. F. (1932) *The Personality of Britain*, National Museum of Wales: Cardiff.

Fox, C. F. (1947) *The Personality of Britain*, National Museum of Wales: Cardiff (Fourth Edition).

Frankenstein, S. (1979) 'The Phoenicians in the Far West: a function of Neo-Assyrian imperialism', in Larsen, M. (ed.) *Power and Propaganda*, pp. 263–94, Mesopotamia 7: Copenhagen.

Frankenstein, S. (1994) 'Regional development in the first millennium BC the Phoenicians in Iberia', in Kristiansen, K. and Jensen, J. (eds), Europe in the First Millennium BC, pp. 41–4, Sheffield Archaeological Monographs 6: Sheffield.

Frankenstein, S. and Rowlands, M. (1978) 'The internal structure and regional context of Early Iron Age society in south-western Germany', *Bulletin of the Institute of Archaeology*, 15: 73–112.

Fries, J. C. (1995) *Vor- und Fr̦hgeschtliche Agrartechnik auf den Britishen Inseln dem Kontinent: eine vergleichende studie*, Verlag Maria Hopfii: Espelkamp.

Fromentin-Simoni, F. (1993) *Archéologie et grands travaux routiers, Rennes-Saint-Malo, Rennes-Lorient*.

Fulford, M. G. (1989) 'Byzantium and Britain: a Mediterranean perspective on post-Roman Mediterranean imports in western Britain and Ireland', *Medieval Archaeology*, 33: 1–6.

Gaiffe, O., Laporte, L., Rouzeau, M-H., Rouzeau, M. with Bodeur, Y., Gruet, Y., Maggy, Ch. and Pirault, L. (1995) 'Le camp protohistorique de Penchâteau au Pouliguen (Loire-Atlantique)', *RAO*, 12: 117–38.

Gálan Domingo, E. (1993) *Estelas, Paisaje y Territorio en el Bronce Final del Suroeste de la Península Ibérica*, Editorial Complutense: Madrid.

Galliou, P. (1982) *Corpus des amphores découvertes dans l'ouest de la France. I, les amphores tardo-républicaines*, Archéologie en Bretagne supplement 4.

Galliou, P. (1983) *L'armorique romaine*, Les Bibliophiles de Bretagne: Braspars.

Galliou, P. (1984) 'Days of wine and roses? Early Armorica and the Atlantic wine trade', in Macready, S. and Thompson, F. H. (eds) (1984): 24–36.

Galliou, P. (1990) 'Commerce et Societe en Armorique à l'Age du Fer', *Les Gaulois d'Armorique*, Actes du XII colloque AFEAF, Quimper 1988, *RAO* suppl. 3: 47–52.

Gautier, M. (1996) 'Les parcellaires antiques du Porhoët et de la vallée de l'Yvel (Morbihan)', in Chouquer, G. (ed.), *Les formes du paysage, Tome 1: Etudes sur les parcellaires*, pp. 49–56, Errance.

Gautier, M., Naas, P. and Leroux, G. (1997) 'Archéologie des Paysages Agraires Armoricains. Éléments pour une nouvelle approche', in Chouquer, G. (ed.) *Les Formes du Paysage*, pp. 45–56, Archéologie aujour-dui, editions Errance: Paris.

Gearey, B. R. (1992) *Pollen Taphonomy in a Bleak Climate*, unpub. dissertation, Sheffield University Department of Archaeology and Prehistory: Sheffield.

Gearey, B. and Charman, D. (1996) 'Rough Tor, Bodmin Moor: Testing some archaeological hypotheses with landscape palaeoecology', in Charman, D. J., Newnham, R. M. and Croot, D. G. (eds), *Devon and East Cornwall: Field Guide*, pp. 101–19, Quaternary Research Association.

Geikie, A. (1901) *The Scenery of Scotland: Viewed in Connection with its Physical Geology*, 3rd edn, Macmillan & Co: London.

Gent, H. (1983) 'Centralized storage in later prehistoric Britain', *PPS*, 49: 243-67.

Gerloff, S. (1987) 'Bronze Age Class A cauldrons: Typology, origins and chronology', *JRSAI*, 116: 84–115.

Gerritsen, F. (2003) *Local Identities. Landscapes and Community in the Later Prehistoric Meuse-Demer-Scheldt Region*, Amsterdam University Press: Amsterdam.

Geselowitz, M. (1988) 'Technology and social change: ironworking in the rise of social complexity in Iron Age Europe', in Gibson, B. and Geselowitz, M. (eds), *Tribe and Polity in Late Prehistoric Europe. Demography, Production, and Exchange in the Evolution of Complex Social Systems*, Plenum Press.

Gibson, A. (1992) 'The excavation of an Iron Age settlement at Gold Park, Dartmoor', *PDAS*, 50: 19–47.

Gibson, C. (2000) 'Plain Sailing? Later Bronze Age Western Iberia at the cross-roads of the Atlantic and Mediterranean', in Henderson, J. C. (ed.) (2000): 73–98.

Gillies, W. and Harding, D. W. (eds) (2005) *Celtic Connections Volume 2: Archaeology, Numismatics and Historical Linguistics*, University of Edinburgh Archaeology Monograph Series, 2: Edinburgh.

Gilman, A. (1998) 'Stratification and coercion in late prehistoric Europe', *Trabalhos de Arqueologia da EAM*, 3/4: 263–7.

Gilmour, S. (1994) *Iron Age Drystone Structures in Argyll*, Unpub. M. A. thesis, University of Edinburgh.

Gilmour, S. (2000a) 'First millennia settlement development in the Atlantic West', in Henderson, J. C. (ed.) (2000): 155–170.

Gilmour, S. (2000b) *Later Prehistoric and Early Historic Settlement Archaeology of the Western Seaways: A Study of the Western Settlement Record from Shetland to Brittany in the First Millennia BC and AD*, unpub. Ph.D. thesis, University of Edinburgh.

Gilmour, S. (2002) 'Mid-first millennium BC settlement in the Atlantic West?', in Ballin Smith, B. and Banks, I. (eds) (2002): 55–66.

Gilmour, S. and Cook, M. (1998) 'Excavations at Dun Vulan: a reinterpretation of the reappraised Iron Age', *Antiquity*, 72: 327–37.

Gilmour, S. and Henderson, J. C. (2005) *Excavations at Dun Glashan, Argyll, Final Report*, unpub. report submitted to Historic Scotland.

Gingell, C. (1979) 'The Bronze and Iron hoard from Melksham and another Wiltshire find', in Burgess, C. and Coombs, D. (eds), *Bronze Age hoards: some finds old and new*, pp. 245–52, BAR, Brit. Ser., 67: Oxford.

Giot, P. R. (1958) 'A propos des affinités hispano-armoricaines à l'Age du Fer', *Annales de Bretagne*, 65: 15–26.

Giot, P. R. (1960a) *Brittany*, Thames & Hudson: London.

Giot, P. R. (1960b) 'Les souterrains Armoricains de l'Age du Fer', *Annales de Bretagne*, 67: 45–65.

Giot, P. R. (1963) 'Les civilisations atlantiques du néolithique a l'age du fer', *Colloque Atlantique Brest 11 September 1961*, Travaux du laboratoire d'athropologie et prehistoire de la faculté des Sciences: Rennes.

Giot, P. R. (1964) 'Les lingots de fer bipyramidaux en Bretagne', *Annales de Bretagne*, 71: 51–60.

Giot, P. R. (1973) 'Les souterrains armoricains de l'Age du Fer', *Document Archéologia*, 2: 48–58.

Giot, P. R. (1975) 'Habitats et sépultures à l'Age du Fer en Armorique', in Duval, P. M. and Kruta, V. (eds), *L'habitat et la nécropole à l'Age du Fer en Europe occidentale et centrale*, pp. 55–60, Paris.

Giot, P. R. (1976) 'Les civilisations de l'Age du Fer en Armorique', *La Préhistoire Francaise, II – Civilisations néolithiques et protohistoriques*: 781–8.

Giot, P. R. (1990) 'Souterrains et habitats à l'Age du Fer en Armorique', *Les Gaulois d'Armorique*, Actes du XII colloque AFEAF, Quimper 1988, RAO suppl. 3: 53–61.

Giot, P. R. (1995) 'L'Âge du Fer', in Giot, P. R., Briard, J. and Pape, L. (eds), *Protohistoire de la Bretagne*, 2nd edn, pp. 203–366, Editions Ouest-France: Rennes.

Giot, P. R. and Monnier, J. L. (1977) 'Le cimitière des anciens Bretons de Saint-Urnel ou Saint-Saturnin en Plomeur (Finistère)', *Gallia*, 35: 141–71.

Giot, P. R., Daire, M. Y. and Querre, G. (1986) 'Un habitat protohistorique, le Moulin de la Rive en Locquirec (Finistère)', *Travaux du Laboratoire d'Anthropologie*, 36, Rennes.

Giot, P. R., Lecerf, Y. and Onnée, Y. (1971) *Céramique Armoricaine de l'Age du Fer 2*, Rennes.

Giot, P. R., Le Roux, C. T., Onnée, Y. (1968) *Céramique Armoricaine de l'Age du Fer*, Rennes.

Giot, P. R., Briard, J. and Pape, L. (1995) *Protohistoire de la Bretagne*, 2nd edn, Editions Ouest-France: Rennes.

Giot, P. R., Guigon, P. and Merdrignac, B. (2005) *The British Settlement of Brittany. The First Britons in Brittany*, Tempus: Stroud.

Giot, P. R., Lecref, Y., Lecornec, J. and Leroux, C.-T. (1976) 'Souterrains armoricains de l'âge du Fer', *Travaux du Laboratoire d'Anthropologie*: Rennes.

Giot, P. R., Morzadec, H., Onnée, Y. and Marguerie, D. (1989) 'Un enclos ceinturé du second âge du fer: Kersigneau Saint-Jean en Plouhinec (Finistère). La partie occidentale', *Bulletin de la Société Archéologique du Finistère*, 118: 85–113.

Giot, P. R., Morzadec, H., Onnée, Y. and Marguerie, D. (1991) 'Un enclos ceinturé du second âge du fer: Kersigneau Saint-Jean en Plouhinec (Finistère). La partie orientale', *Bulletin de la Société Archéologique du Finistère* 120: 93–104.

González Prats, A. (1986) 'Peña Negra', *Arqueología en Alicante*: 126–8.

González Prats, A. (1992) 'Una Vivienda Metalúrgica en la Peña Negra (Crevillente, Alicante)', *Trabajos de Prehistoria*, 49: 243–57.

González-Ruibal, A. (2004): *Facing Two Seas: Mediterranean and Atlantic Contacts in the North-West of Iberia in the First Millennium BC*, OJA, 23: 287–317.

Gordon, A. S. R. (1940) 'The excavation of Gunard's Head, an Iron Age cliff castle in Western Cornwall', *ArchJ*, 97: 96–111.

Gosden, C. (1994) *Social Being and Time*, Blackwell: Oxford.

Gouletquer, P. L. (1970) *Les briquetages armoricains: technologie du sel en Armorique*, Travaux Laboratoire d'Anthropologie-Préhistoire.

Gouletquer, P. and Daire, M.-Y. (1994) 'Le Sel de la Prehistoire et de la Protohistoire', in Daire, M.-Y. (ed.), *Le Sel Gauloise: Bouilleurs de sel et ateliers de briquetages armoricains à l'Âge Fer*, pp. 5–13, Centre Régional d'Archéologie d'Alet: Saint-Malo.

Grant, A. (1988) 'Bone deposition and animal husbandry: the animal bone remains', in Cunliffe, B., *Mount Batten, Plymouth. A Prehistoric and Roman Port*, Oxford University Committee for Archaeology, Monograph 26: 28–34.

Green, M. (1986) *The Gods of the Celts*, Sutton Publishing Limited: Gloucester and New Jersey.

Green, M. (ed.) (1995) *The Celtic World*, Routledge: London.

Griffith, F. and Quinnell, H. (1999) 'Settlement *c*. 2500 BC to *c*. AD 600', in Kain, R. and Ravenhill, W. (eds) (1999) *Historical Atlas of South-West England*, pp. 62–8, University of Exeter Press: Exeter.

Grinsell, L. V. (1958) *The Archaeology of Wessex*, Methuen: London.

Grogan, E. (1995) 'Excavations at Mooghaun South, 1993. Interim report', *Discovery Programme Reports*, 2: 57–61.

Grogan, E. (1996) 'Excavations at Mooghaun South, 1994. Interim report', *Discovery Programme Reports*, 4: 47–57.

Grogan, E. and Eogan, G. (1987) 'Lough Gur Excavations by Seán P. O' Ríordáin: Further Neolithic and Beaker Habitations on Knockadoon', *PRIA*, 87C: 299–506.

Grogan, E. (2005) *The North Munster Project, Volume 1: The later prehistoric landscape of south-east Clare*, Discovery Programme Monographe No. 6, Wordwell: Dublin.

Guido, M. (1978) *The Glass Beads of the Prehistoric and Roman Periods in Britain and Ireland*, Society of Antiquaries: London.

Guilbert, G. (1973) 'Moel y Gaer, Rhose Mor. A progress report', *CA*, 37: 38–44.

Guilbert, G. (1975) 'Moel y Gaer, 1973: an area excavation on the defences', *Antiquity*, 49: 109–17.

Guthrie, A. (1969) 'Excavation of a settlement at Goldherring, Sancreed, 1958–1961', *CA*, 8: 5–40.

Halbout, P., Pilet, C. and Vaudour, C. (eds) (1987) *Corpus des objets domestiques et des armes en fer de Normandie*, Cahier des Annales de Normandie 20.

Hambleton, E. (1999) *Animal Husbandry Regimes in Iron Age Britain*, BAR, Brit. Ser. 282: Oxford.

Hamilton, J. R. C. (1956) *Excavations at Jarlshof*, HMSO, Ministry of Works Archaeological Report 1: Edinburgh.

Hamilton, J. R. C. (1968) *Excavations at Clickhimin,* HMSO: Edinburgh.

Hamlin, A. and Lynn, C. E. D. (1988) *Pieces of the Past: Archaeological Excavations by the Dept of the Environment for Northern Ireland 1970–86*, HMSO: Belfast.

Harbison, P. (1971) 'Wooden and stone *Chevaux-de-frise* in Central and Western Europe', *PPS*, 37: 195–225.

Harbison, P. (1975) 'The coming of the Indo-Europeans to Ireland: an archaeological view-point', *Journal of Indo-European Studies*, 3: 101–19.

Harbison, P. (1979) 'Celtic migrations in western Europe', in Tovar, A. (ed.), *Salamanca in Actas del 2 coloquio sobre lenguas y culturas prerromanas de la peninsula iberica*, (Tübingen, 17-19 junio 1976), pp. 225–35, Ediciones Universidad: Salamanca.

Harding, A. (1984) *The Myceneans and Europe,* Academic Press: London.

Harding, A. (1990) 'The Wessex connection: Developments and perspectives', *Römlsch Germanisches Zentralmuseum Mitteilungen* 15, Orientalisch-Ägäische Einflüsse in der Europäischen Bronzezeit: 139–54.

Harding, A. F. (1984) 'Aspects of social evolution in the Bronze Age', in Bintliff, J. (ed.), *European Social Evolution. Archaeological Perspectives*, pp. 135–46, Bradford University Press: Bradford.

Harding, D. W. (1972) 'Round and rectangular: Iron Age houses, British and Foreign', in C. and S. Hawkes (eds), *Greeks, Celts and Romans*, pp. 43–60, Dent & Sons: London.

Harding, D. W. (1984) 'The function and classification of brochs and duns', in Miket, R. and Burgess, C. (eds), *Between and Beyond the Walls, Essays on the Prehistory and History of Northern Britain in Honour of George Jobey*, pp. 206–20. John Donald: Edinburgh.

Harding, D. W. (1997) 'Forts, duns, brochs and crannogs: Iron Age settlements in Argyll', in Ritchie, G. (ed.), *The Archaeology of Argyll*, pp. 118–40, Edinburgh University Press: Edinburgh.

Harding, D. W. (2004) *The Iron Age in Northern Britain. Celts and Romans, Natives and Invaders*, Routledge: Oxford.

Harding, D. W. (2005a) 'The Iron Age in Atlantic Scotland and the western seaways', in Gillies, W. and Harding, D. W. (eds) (2005): 166–180.

Harding, D. W. (2005b) 'The Atlantic Scottish Iron Age: External Relations Reviewed' in Turner *et al.* (eds) (2005): 32–51.

Harding, D. W. and Armit, I. (1990) 'Survey and excavation in West Lewis', in I. Armit (ed.) (1990): 71–107.

Harding, D. W. and Dixon, T. N. (2000) *Dun Bharabhat, Cnip: An Iron Age Settlement in West Lewis, Vol. 1. Structures and Material Culture*, Calanais Research Series 2, University of Edinburgh: Edinburgh.

Harding, D. W. and Gillies, W. (2005) 'Introduction: Archaeology and Celticity', in Gillies, W. and Harding, D. W. (eds) (2005): 1–14.

Harding, D. W. and Gilmour, S. (2000) 'The Iron Age settlement at Beirgh, Riof, Isle of Lewis: Excavations, 1985–95', *Vol. 1, The Structures and Stratigraphy*, Calanais Research Series 1, University of Edinburgh: Edinburgh.

Härke, H. (1979) *Settlement Types and Settlement Patterns in the West Hallstatt Province*, BAR, Internat. Ser., 57: Oxford.

Härke, H. (1989) 'Transformation or collapse? Bronze Age to Iron Age settlement in west central Europe', in Sorenson, M. L. and Thomas, R. (eds), *The Bronze Age – Iron Age Transition in Europe. Aspects of Continuity and Change in European Societies c. 1200 to 500 B.C.*, BAR, Internat. Ser. 483, pp. 184–203, Archaeopress: Oxford.

Harris, D. (1977) 'Bowden, Lanlivery: a multi-period occupation', *CA*, 16: 43–59.

Harris, D. (1980) 'Excavation of a Romano-British Round at Shortlanesend, Kenwyn, Truro', *CA*, 19: 63–76.

Harris, D. and Johnson, N. (1976) 'Carlidnack Round, Mawnan', *CA*, 15: 73–6.

Harrison, R. J. (2004) *Symbols and Warriors: Images of the European Bronze Age*, David Brown Book Co.: Bristol.

Haselgrove, C. (1987) 'Culture process on the periphery: Belgic Gaul and Rome during the late Republic and early Empire', in Rowlands, M., Larsen, M. and Kristiansen, K. (eds), *Centre and Periphery in the Ancient World*, pp. 104–24, Cambridge University Press: Cambridge.

Haselgrove, C. (1989) 'The later Iron Age in southern Britain and beyond', in Todd, M. (ed.) *Research on Roman Britain 1960–1989*, Britannia Monograph 11, London: 1–18.

Haselgrove, C. (1999) 'The Iron Age', in Hunter, J. R. and Ralston, I. B. M. (eds.), *The Archaeology of Britain an introduction from the Upper Palaeolithic to the Industrial Revolution.* Routledge, London: 113–34.

Hawkes, C. F. C. (1931) 'Hill-forts. A retrospect', *Antiquity*, 5: 60–97.

Hawkes, C. F. C. (1940) *The Prehistoric Foundations of Europe to the Mycenaean Age*, Methuen: London.

Hawkes, C. F. C. (1956) 'The British Iron Age: cultures, chronology and peoples', *Congress Internationale Pré- et Protohistoriques, Actes de la IV Session*, Madrid: 729–37.

Hawkes, C. F. C. (1959) 'The ABC of the British Iron Age', *Antiquity*, 33: 170–82.

Hawkes, C. F. C. (1966) 'British prehistory: the invasion hypothesis', *Antiquity*, 40: 297–8.

Hawkes, C. F. C. (1977) *Pytheas: Europe and the Greek Explorers*, Blackwell: Oxford.

Hawkes, C. F. C. (1984) 'Ictis disentangled, and the British tin trade', *OJA*, 3: 211–33.

Hawkes, C. F. C. and Smith, M. A. (1957) 'On some buckets and cauldrons of the Bronze and Early Iron Ages: The Nannau, Whigsborough and Heathery Burn Bronze Buckets and the Colchester and London Cauldrons', *AJ*, 37(3-4): 131–98.

Hawkes, J. (1938) 'The significance of channelled ware in neolithic western Europe', *ArchJ*, 95: 126–73.

Heald, A. and Jackson, A. (2001) 'Towards a new understanding of Iron Age Caithness', *PSAS*, 131: 129–48.

Hedges, J. W. (1987) *Bu, Gurness and the Brochs of Orkney* (Vols. 1-3), BAR, Brit. Ser. 163–5: Oxford.

Hedges, J. W. (1990) 'Surveying the foundations: Life after "Brochs"', in Armit, I. (ed.): 17–31.

Hedges, J. W. and Bell, B. (1980) 'That tower of Scottish prehistory – the broch', *Antiquity*, 54: 87–94.

Hedges, J. W. and Hedges, M. E. (1977) 'Excavations at Dun Mhic Choigil, Kintyre', *PSAS*, 108: 376–7.

Hedges, R. E. M., Housley, R. A., Bronk, C. R. and van Klinken, G. J. (1991) ' Radiocarbon dates from the Oxford AMS system: Archaeometry datelist 12', *Archaeometry*, 33: 121–34.

Hedges, R. E. M., Housley, R. A., Bronk, C. R. and van Klinken, G. J. (1993) 'Radiocarbon dates from the Oxford AMS system: Archaeometry datelist 17', *Archaeometry*, 35: 305–26.

Helms, M. (1988) *Ulysees' Sail - An Ethnographic Odyssey of Power, Knowledge and Geographical Distance*, Princeton University Press: Princeton.

Hencken, H. O'N. (1932) *The Archaeology of Cornwall and Scilly*, Methuen and Co. Ltd: London.

Hencken, H. O'N. (1933) 'Excavations at Chysauster, 1931', *Archaeologia*, 83: 237–84.

Hencken, H. O'N. (1938) *Cahercommaun: A Stone Fort in County Clare*, John Falconer for the Royal Sociey of Antiquaries of Ireland: Dublin.

Hencken, H. O' N. (1950) 'Lagore Crannog: an Irish royal residence of the 7th to 10th centuries AD', *PRIA*, 53: 1–247.

Hencken, H. O'N. (1942) 'Ballinderry Crannog No. 2', *PRIA*, 47: 1–76.

Henderson, I. (1967) *The Picts*, Thames & Hudson: London.

Henderson, J. (1982) *X-ray Fluorescence of Iron Age glass*, Unpublished Ph.D. thesis, University of Bradford.

Henderson, J. (1985) 'The glass from Castle Dore: Archaeological and chemical significance', *CA*, 24: 141–8.

Henderson, J. (1994) 'Glass', in Ballin-Smith, B. (ed.), *Howe: Four Millennia of Orkney Prehistory*, Society of Antiquaries of Scotland Monograph Series No. 9, Edinburgh: 234–5.

Henderson, J. C. (1998) 'Islets through time: the definition, dating and distribution of Scottish crannogs', *OJA*, 17.2: 227–44.

Henderson, J. C. (2000) 'Shared traditions? The drystone settlement records of Atlantic Scotland and Ireland 700 BC–AD 200' in Henderson, J. C. (ed.) (2000): 117–54.

Henderson, J. C. (ed.) (2000) *The Prehistory and Early History of Atlantic Europe, Papers from a session held at the European Association of Archaeologists Fourth Annual Meeting in Göteborg 1998*, BAR, Internat. Ser. 861, Archaeopress: Oxford.

Henig, M. (1988) 'Cast figurines', in Cunliffe, B. W., (ed.) *Mount Batten: A Prehistoric and Roman Port*: 70–2.

Henry, F. (1933) *La Sculpture Irlandaise pendant les douze premiers siecles de l'ère chrétienne*, Paris.

Henry, F. (1940) *Irish Art and the Early Christian Period*, Methuen: London.

Herity, M. and Eogan, G. (1977) *Ireland in Prehistory*, Routledge: London.

Herity, M. (1981) 'A Bronze Age farmstead at Glencree, Co. Mayo', *Popular Archaeology*, 2: 258–65.

Herring, P. (1994) 'The cliff castles and hillforts of West Penwith in the light of recent work at Maen Castle and Treryn Dinas', *CA*, 33: 40–56.

Hill, J. D. (1989) 'Re-thinking the Iron Age', *SAR*, 6: 16–23.

Hillgarth, J. N. (1961) 'The East, Visigothic Spain and the Irish', *Studia Patristica*, 4: 442–56.

Hillgarth, J. N. (1984) 'Ireland and Spain in the Seventh Century', *Peritia*, 3: 1–16.

Hingh, A. de (1998) 'The archaeology of the agricultural landscape: land-use and access to land in later prehistoric society in north-west Europe', in Haring, B. and Maaijer, R. de (eds), *Landless and Hungry? Access to Land in Early and Traditional Societies*, pp. 1–18, CNWS, Leiden.

Hingley, R. (1990) 'Public and private space: Domestic organisation and gender relations amongst Iron Age and Romano-British households', in Samson, R. (ed.), *The Social Archaeology of Houses*, pp. 123–62, Edinburgh University Press: Edinburgh.

Hingley, R. (1992) 'Society in Scotland from 700 BC to AD 200', *PSAS*, 122: 7–53.

Hingley, R. (1995) 'The Iron Age in Atlantic Scotland: Searching for the meaning of the substantial house', in Hill, J. D. and Cumberpatch, C. (eds), *Different Iron Ages: Studies in the Iron Age of Temperate Europe*: pp. 185–94, BAR, Internat. Ser. 602, Oxford.

Hinguant, S., Le Goff, E., Jean, S. and Marguerie, D. (1997) 'Le site gaulois de Bellevue à Augan (Morbihan): un établissement rural en limite de deux influences armoricaines', *RAO*, 14: 57–80.

Hirons, K. R. (1983) 'Percentage and accumulation rate pollen diagrams from east Co. Tyrone', in Reeves-Smyth, T. and Hamond, F. E. D. (eds), *Landscape archaeology in Ireland*, pp. 95–117, BAR, Brit. Ser. 116, Oxford.

Hirst, F. C. (1936) 'Excavations at Porthmeor, Cornwall', *Journal of the Royal Institution of Cornwall*, 24: 1–81.

Hodson, F. R. (1964) 'Cultural groupings within the pre-Roman Iron Age', *PPS*, 30: 99–110.

Hogg, A. H. A. (1960) 'Garn Boduan and Tre'r Ceiri, Excavations at two Caernarvonshire Hillforts', *ArchJ*, 117: 1–39.

Hogg, A. H. A. (1972) 'Hillforts in the coastal area of Wales', in Thomas, C. (ed.), *The Iron Age in the Irish Sea Province*, pp. 11–23, CBA Res. Rpt., 9: London.

Hogg, A. H. A. (1974) 'Excavations at Harding's Down West Fort, Gower, Glamorgan', *AC*, 122: 55–68.

Hornell, J. (1946) 'The role of birds in early navigation', *Antiquity*, 20: 142–9.

Housley, R. A. and Coles, G. (eds) (2004) *Atlantic Connections and Adaptations. Economies, Environments and Subsistence in Lands Bordering the North Atlantic*, Symposia of the Association for Environmental Archaeology 21, Oxbow: Oxford.

Huth, C. and Stäuble, H. (1998) *Ländliche Siedlungen der Bonzezeit und älteren Eisenzeit: ein Zwischenbericht aus Zwenkau*, in Küster, H., Lang, A. and Schauer, P. (eds). Archäologische Forschungen in urgeschichtlichen Siedlungslandschaften, pp. 185–230, Universitätsverlag Regensburg: Regensburg.

Hyvert, J. and Le Bihan, J. P. (1990) 'Les habitats côtiers armoricain à l'Age du Fer', in *Les Gaulois d'Armorique*, Actes du XII colloque AFEAF, Quimper 1988, *RAO* suppl. 3: 71–84.

Jacobsthal, J. (1938) 'An Iberian Bronze found at Sligo', *JRSAI*, 68: 51–4.

Jahier, Y. (1997) 'Les sites de Cahagnes et de Courseulles-sur-Mer (Calvados), deux gisements protohistoriques à édifices circulaires', in *Les Installations Agricoles á l'age du fer en France septrionale, Résumés des Communications*, Colloque du Programme Collectif de recherche 29 and 30, November 1977 (unpublished).

James, S. (1997) 'The Celts: discovery or invention?', *British Museum Magazine*, Summer 1997: 18–22.

James, S. (1999) *The Atlantic Celts. Ancient People or Modern Invention?*, British Museum Press: London.

James, H. and Williams, G. (1982) 'Rural settlement in Roman Dyfed', in Miles, D. (ed.), *Rural Settlement in Roman Britain*, pp. 289–312, BAR, Brit. Ser. 103, Oxford.

Jarrett, M. G. and Wrathmell, S. (1981) *Whitton: An Iron Age and Roman Farmstead in South Glamorgan*, University of Wales Press: Cardiff.

Jeffries, J. S. (1974) 'An excavation on the coastal promontory fort at Embury Beacon, Devon', *PPS*, 40: 136–56.

Jobey, G. (1980) 'Settlement potential in Northern Britain in the later second millennium BC', in Barrett, J. and Bradley, R. (eds), *Settlement and Society in the British Later Bronze Age*, pp. 371–6, BAR, Brit. Ser. 83, Oxford.

Johnson, D. S. (1977) *Phantom islands of the Atlantic: The Legends of Seven Lands that Never Were*, Walker: New York.

Johnson, N. and Rose, P. (1982) 'Defended settlement in Cornwall – An illustrated discussion', in Miles, D. (ed.), *The Romano-British Countryside. Studies in Rural Settlement and Economy*, pp. 151–209, BAR, Brit. Ser. 103: Oxford.

Johnson, N. and Rose, P. (1994) *Bodmin Moor. An Archaeological Survey. Volume 1: The Human Landscape to c.1800*, English Heritage Archaeological Report No. 24.

Johnston, R. (2000) 'Field systems and the Atlantic Bronze Age: thoughts on a regional perspective', in Henderson, J. C. (ed.) (2000): 47–56.

Joly, F. and Embleton, C. (1984) 'Armorican Massif', in Embleton, C. (ed.), *Geomorphology of Europe*, pp. 178–81, Macmillan: London.

Jones, C. and Gilmer, A. (1999) 'Roughan Hill, a final Neolithic/Early Bronze Age landscape revealed', *AI* 13, 1: 30–2.

Jope, E. M. (1951) 'A Late Bronze Age shield mount of wood from Co. Antrim', *UJA*, 14: 62–5.

Jope, E. M. (1954) 'The Keshcarrigan Bowl and a bronze mirror-handle from Ballymoney', *UJA*, 17: 92–6.

Jorge, S. O. (1996) 'Regional Diversity in the Iberian Bronze Age: On the visibility andopacity of the Archaeological Record', *Trabalhos de Antropologia e Etnologia*, 36: 193–214.

Jorge, S. O. (ed.) (1998) *Existe uma Idade do Bronze Atlântico?*, Trabalhos de Arqueologia 10, Instituto Portugués de Arqueologia: Lisbon.

Kalb, P. (1980) 'Zur Atlantischen Bronzezeit in Portugal', *Germania*, 58: 25–59.

Kelly, E. P. (1974) 'Aughinish Island', in Delaney, T. G. (ed.), *Excavations, 1974*: 20–1.

Kelly, F. (1997) *Early Irish Farming*, Early Irish Law Series IV, Dundalgan Press.

Kelly, R. S. (1988) 'Two late prehistoric circular enclosures near Harlech, Gwynedd', *PPS*, 54: 101–51.

Kelly, R. S. (1991) 'Recent research on the hut group settlements of north-west Wales', in Burnham, B. C. and Davies, J. L. (ed.), *Conquest, Co-existence and Change*: 102–11.

Kenney, J. F. (1929) *The Sources for the Early History of Ireland: Ecclesiastical*, Octagon Books: New York.

Kilbride-Jones, H. E. (1950) 'The excavation of a composite Early Iron Age monument with 'henge' features at Lugg, Co. Dublin', *PRIA*, 53 (C5): 311–32.

Kimmig, W. (1983) *Die Hueneburg an der oberen Donau*. Völlig neubearbeitete Auflage, Führer zu archäologischen Denkmälrn in Baden-Württemberg, Konrad Theiss Verlag.

Koch, J. T. (1986) 'New Thoughts on Albion, Ierné, and the Pretanic Isles', *Proceedings of the Harvard Celtic Colloquium*, 6: 1–28.

Koch, J. T. (1991) 'Eriu, Alba, and Letha: When was a language ancestral to Gaelic first spoken in Ireland?', *Emania*, 9: 5–16.

Kossack, G. (1959) *Südbayern während der Hallstattzeit*, Römisch-Germanische Forschungen, Band 24: Berlin.

Kristiansen, K. (1984) 'Ideology and material culture: an archaeological perspective', in Spriggs, M. (ed.), *Marxist Perspectives in Archaeology*, pp. 72–100, Cambridge University Press: Cambridge.

Kristiansen, K. (1987) 'From stone to bronze: the evolution of social complexity in Northern Europe, 2300–1200 BC', in Brumfield, M. and Earle, T. K. (eds), *Specialization, Exchange and Complex Societies*, pp. 30–51, Cambridge University Press: Cambridge.

Kristiansen, K. (1994) 'The emergence of the European World System in the Bronze Age: Divergence, convergence and social evolution during the first and second millennia BC in Europe', in Kristiansen, K. and Jensen, J. (eds), Europe in the First Millennium BC, pp. 7–30, Sheffield Archaeological Monographs 6: Sheffield.

Kristiansen, K. (1998) *Europe before History*, Cambridge University Press: Cambridge.

Kristiansen, K. (2004) 'Sea faring voyages and rock art ships', in Clark, P. (ed.) (2004): 111–21.

Krusch, B. (ed.) (1885) 'De Virtutibus Sancti Martini', in *Monumenta Germaniae Historica*, Vol. 1.2, pp. 238–328, Hannover.

Lacy, B. (1983) *Archaeological Survey of County Donegal*, Donegal County Council: Lifford.

Lamb, H. H. (1981) 'Climate from 1000 BC to 1000 AD', in Jones, M. K. (ed.), *The Environment of Man: The Iron Age to the Anglo-Saxon Period*, pp. 53–65, BAR, Brit. Ser., 87: Oxford.

Lamb, H. H. (1982) *Climate, History and the Modern World*, Macmillan: London.

Lamb, H. H. (1997) *Climate, ii*, Methuen: London.

Lamb, R. G. (1980) *Iron-Age Promontory Forts in the Northern Isles*, BAR, Brit. Ser., 79: Oxford.

Lambot, B. (1990) 'Les Sanctuaires funéraires de Champagne', in Brunaux, J.-L. (ed.), *Les Sanctuaires Celtiques et leurs rapports avec la Monde méditerranean: actes du colloque d'Amiens-en-Saint-Riquier*: 8–11.

Lane, A. (1990) 'Hebridean pottery: Problems of definition and chronology, presence and absence', in Armit, I. (ed.): 108–30.

Langouët, L. (1980) 'Les oppida pré-romains des Coriosolites', *105ème Congrès national des Societés Savantes, Caen, 1980, Archèologie*: 255–66.

Langouët, L. (1984) 'Alet and cross-channel trade', in Macready, S. and Thompson, F. H. (eds): 67–77.

Langouët, L. (1987) *La prospection archéologique en Haute-Bretagne*, Dossiers de Centre Regional d'Archeologic d'Alet.

Langouët, L. (1988) 'Un des habitats de La Tène Finale sur l'île des Ebihens en Saint-Jacut-de-la Mer (Côtes-du-Nord)', *Dossiers de Protohistoire no.2: Architectures des Ages des Métaux, fouilles récente*, Errances, Paris: 81–6.

Langouët, L. (ed.) (1990) 'Le passé vu d'avion dans le nord de la Haute-Bretagne, apports de la prospection aérienne et la sécheresse de 1989', *Dossiers du Centre régional d'archéologie d'Alet (suppl. M)*, Saint Malo.

Langouët, L. and Daire, M.-Y. (1989) *La Civitas Gallo-Romaine des Coriosolites: Le Milieu Rural*, Institut Culturel de Bretagne, Centre Regional d'Archeologic d'Alet.

Langouët, L. and Daire, M.-Y. (1990) *Le passé vu d'avion dans le nord de la Haute-Bretagne. Apports de la prospection aérienne et la sécheresse de 1989*, Les Dossiers du Centre Regional d'Archeologic d'Alet.

Langouët, L., Gouletquer, P. and Bizien-Jaglin, C. (1994) 'Chronologie et Technologie: methodes d'etude', in Daire, M.-Y. (ed.), *Le Sel Gauloise: Bouilleurs de sel et ateliers de briquetages armoricains à l'Âge Fer*, pp. 105–22, Centre Régional d'Archéologie d'Alet, Saint-Malo.

Le Bihan, J. P. (1984) *Villages gaulois et parcellaires antiques au Braden en Quimper, Cahiers de Quimper Antique n°1*, Quimper.

Le Bihan, J. P. (1985) 'Le Braden I, Kerlaéron, Prat-ar-Rouz', *Bulletin de la Société Archéologique du Finistère*, T. 114: 57–68.

Le Bihan, J. P. (1987) 'Le Braden I', in Galliou, P. and Le Bihan, J. P. (eds), Chroniques d'archéologie antiques et médiévales (années 1988 et 1987*), Bulletin de la Société Archéologique du Finistère*: 39–43.

Le Bihan, J. P. (1988a) 'Créach-Gwen en Quimper', *Bulletin de la Société Archéologique du Finistère*, T. 117.

Le Bihan, J. P. (1988b) 'Structures d'habitat dans un hameau de La Tène finale: Le Braden I en Quimper', *Dossiers de Protohistoire no. 2: Architectures des Ages des Métaux, fouilles recentes*, Errances, Paris: 87–102.

Le Bihan, J. P. (1990) 'Les mutations sur les sites ruraux de la Tène finale à Quimper (Finistère)', *Les Gaulois d'Armorique*, Actes du XII colloque AFEAF, Quimper 1988, *RAO* suppl. 3: 261–70.

Le Bihan, J. P. (1997) 'Quimper - Les hautes de Penvillers', *DRAC: Bilan Scientifique 1996*, Rennes: 42–4.

Le Bihan, J. P. and Galliou, P. (1974) 'Un groupe de bas-fourneaux antiques découverts près de Quimper (Finistère)', *Bulletin de la Société Archéologique du Finistère*, 118: 17–30.

Le Bihan, J. P. and Robic, J.Y. (1988) 'Le village de l'Age du Fer de Mez-Notariou à Ouessant', *Journée préhistorique et protohistorique de Bretagne, Rennes, 15 octobre 1988*: 26–9.

Le Bihan, J. P. and Robic, J.Y. (1990) 'Le village du premier Age du Fer de Mez-Notariou, Ile d'Ouessant (Finistère)', *Les Gaulois d'Armorique*, Actes du XII colloque AFEAF, Quimper 1988, *RAO* suppl. 3: 157–62.

Le Bihan, J. P. and Robic, J.Y. (1993) 'Un village de transition Bronze-Fer, Mez-Notariou à Ouessant', *L'habitat et l'occupation du sol à l'Age du Bronze en Europe*, colloque Ed. C.T.H.S., Paris: 103–16.

Le Bihan, J-P. and Villard, J-F. 2001: *Archéologie d'une île à la point de l'Europe: Ouessant. Tome 1 – Le site archéologique de Mez-Notariou et le village du premier âge du fer.* Centre de Recherche Archéologique du Finistère. *RAO:* Rennes.

Le Bihan, J.-P., Galliou, P. and Carrie, P. (1982) 'La villa gallo-romaine du Carvady à Saint-Evarzec', *Bulletin de la Société Archéologique du Finistère*, 110: 85–112.

Le Bihan, J. P., Bardel, J. P., Menez, Y. and Tanguy, D. (1990) 'Les etablissements ruraux du second âge du fer en Armorique', *Les Gaulois d'Armorique*, Actes du XII colloque AFEAF, Quimper 1988, RAO suppl. 3: 97–113.

Le Goffic, M. (1992) 'Le site de l'Age du Fer de Rubiou en Spézet (Finistère) *RAO, Supplement no. 9*: 89–110.

Lecornec, J. (1973) 'Le site à enclos de Kerlande à Brandivy (Morbihan)', *Annales de Bretagne*, 80: 61–70.

Leeds, E.T. (1927) 'Excavations at Chûn Castle in Penwith, Cornwall', *Archaeologia*, 76: 205–40.

Leeds, E. T. (1930) 'A bronze cauldron from the River Cherwell, Oxfordshire, with notes on cauldrons and other bronze vessels of allied types', *Archaeologia*, 80: 1–36.

Leeds, E. T. (1931) 'Excavations at Chûn Castle in Penwith, Cornwall (Second Report)', *Archaeologia*, 81: 33–42.

Leroux, G. (1992) Corps-Nuds Graibusson. *Bulletin Scientifique*, SRA Bretagne.

Leroux, G., Gautier, M., Meuret, J-C. and Naas, P. (1999) *Enclos Gaulois et Gallo-Romains en Armorique. De la prospection aérienne à la fouille entre Blavet et Mayenne*, Documents archéologiques de l'Ouest: Rennes.

Lethbridge, T. C. (1952) 'Excavations at Kilphaeder, South Uist and the problem of the brochs and wheelhouses', *PSAS*, 18: 176–93.

Lewis, A. R. (1958) *The Northern Seas*, Princeton University Press: Princeton.

Lhuyd, E. (1707) *Archaeologica Britannica, giving some account Additional to what has been hitherto Publish'd, of the Languages, Histories and Customs of the Original Inhabitants of Great Britain: From Collections and Observations in Travels through Wales, Cornwall [sic], Bas-Bretagne, Ireland and Scotland. Vol. 1. Glossograph*, Oxford.

Liddell, D. M. (1930) 'Report on the excavations at Hembury Fort, Devon', *PDAES*, 1: 1–24.

Liddell, D. M. (1931) 'Report on the excavations at Hembury Fort, Devon', *PDAES*, 1: 90–120.

Liddell, D. M. (1932) 'Report on the excavations at Hembury Fort, Devon', *PDAES*, 1: 162–90.

Liddell, D. M. (1935) 'Report on the excavations at Hembury Fort, Devon', *PDAES*, 2: 135–75.

Limbert, D. (1996) 'Irish Ringforts: a Review of their Origins', *ArchJ*, 153: 243–89.

Lindsay, W. M. (ed.) (1911) *Isidore, Etymologiarum Siue Originum*, Clarendon Press: Oxford.

Liversage, G. D. (1968) 'Excavations of prehistoric and Early Christian sites at Dalkey Island, Co. Dublin, 1956–9', *PRIA,* 66C2: 53–233.

Lo Schiavo, F. (1991) 'La Sardaigne et ses relations avec le Bronze Final Atlantique', in Chevillot, C. and A. Coffyn (eds), *L'Age du Bronze Atlantique*, pp. 213–26, Actes de Premier Colloque du Parc Archéologique de Beynac, Association des Musées du Sardlais, Beynac.

Lodewijckx, M. and Bakels, C. (2000) 'The Interaction between Early Farmers (Linearbandkeramik) and Indigenous People in Central Belgium', in Henderson, J. C. (ed.) (2000): 33–46.

Longouët, L. (1989), *Un Village Coriosolite sur l'Ile des Ebihens (Saint-Jacut-de-la Mer)*, Centre Régional d'Archéologie d'Alet: Saint Malo.

Lowe, C. (1998) *Coastal Erosion and the Archaeological Assessment of an Eroding Shoreline at St Boniface Church, Papa Westray, Orkney*, Sutton Publishing/Historic Scotland.

Lucas, A. T. (1968) 'National Museum of Ireland: Archaeological Acquisitions in the Year 1965', *JRSAI*, 98: 93–159.

Lynch, A. (1981) *Man and Environment in South West Ireland, 4000BC–AD800: A Study of Man's Impact on the Development of Soil and Vegetation*, BAR, Brit. Ser., 85: 253–67.

Lynn, C. J. (1983) 'Some 'early ring-forts and crannogs', *JIA*, 1: 47–58.

Lynn, C. J. (1986) 'Navan Fort: a draft summary of D. M. Waterman's excavations', *Emania*, 1: 11–19.

Lynn, C. J. (1992) 'The Iron Age mound in Navan Fort: a physical realisation of Celtic religious beliefs?', *Emania*, 10: 33–57.

Lyons, J. (1982) *Geography of Western Europe*, Tallaght.

Macalister, R. A. S. (1935) 'The excavation of Kiltera, Dromore, Co. Waterford', *PRIA*, C 43: 1–16.

Macauley, D. (ed.) (1992) *The Celtic Languages*, Cambridge University Press: Cambridge.

MacEoin, G. (1986) 'The Celticity of Celtic Ireland', in Schmidt, K. H. (ed.), *Geschichte und Kultur der Kelten*, pp. 161–174, Hiedelberg.

Macinnes, L. (1984) 'Brochs and the Roman occupation of Lowland Scotland', *PSAS*, 114: 235–50.

MacKie, E. W. (1965) 'The origin and development of the broch and wheelhouse building cultures of the Scottish Iron Age', *PPS*, 31: 93–146.

MacKie, E. W. (1969) 'The historical context of the origin of the brochs', *Scottish Archaeological Forum*, 1: 53–9.

MacKie, E. W. (1974) *Dun Mor Vaul – An Iron Age Broch on Tiree*, University Press: Glasgow

MacKie, E. W. (1991) 'The Iron Age semi brochs of Atlantic Scotland: A case study in the problems of deductive reasoning', *ArchJ*, 148: 149–81.

MacKie, E. W. (1994) 'Midhowe and Gurness brochs in Orkney; some problems of misinterpretation', *ArchJ*, 151: 98–157.

MacKie, E. W. (1995) 'The early Celts in Scotland', in Green, M. J. (ed.), *The Celtic World*, pp. 654–70, Routledge.

MacKie, E. W. (1997) 'Dun Mor Vaul revisited: Fact and theory in the reappraisal of the Scottish Atlantic Iron Age', in Ritchie, G. (ed.), *The Archaeology of Argyll*, pp. 141–80, Edinburgh University Press: Edinburgh.

MacKie, E. W. (1998) 'Continuity over three thousand years of Northern prehistory: the 'Tel' at Howe, Orkney', *AJ*, 78: 1–42.

MacKie, E. W. (2000) 'The Scottish Atlantic Iron Age: Indigenous and isolated or part of a wider European world?', in Henderson, J. C. (ed.) (2000): 99–116.

MacKie, E. W. (2002) *The Roundhouses, Brochs and Wheelhouses of Atlantic Scotland c.700 BC – AD 500. Architecture and material culture. Part 1: The Orkney and Shetland Isles*, BAR, Brit. Ser. 342: Oxford.

Mackinder, H. (1902) *Britain and the British Seas*, Heinemann: London.

Maclean, R. (1992) 'The Fogou: an investigation of function', *CA*, 31: 41–64.

Macready, S. and Thompson, F. H. (eds) (1984) *Cross-Channel Trade Between Gaul and Britain in the pre-Roman Iron Age*, Society of Antiquaries Occasional Paper IV, New Series: London.

MacWhite, E. (1951) *Estudios sobre las relaciones atlánticos de la Península Hispánica en la Edad del Bronze*, Seminario de Historia Primitiva del Hombre, Madrid.

Maguer, P. (1996) 'Les encientes fortifiees de l'age du fer dans le Finistère', *RAO, Supp. 13*, 103–21.

Maguire, D. J., Ralph, N., and Fleming, A. (1983) 'Early Land Use in Dartmoor – Palaeobotanical and Palynological Investigations on Holne Moor', in Jones, M. (ed.), *Integrating the Subsistence Economy*, BAR, Internat. Ser., 181: 57–105.

Mallory, J. P. (1984) 'The origins of the Irish', *JIA*, 2: 65–9.

Mallory, J. P. (1995) 'Haughey's Fort and the Navan Complex in the Late Bronze Age', in Waddell, J. and Shee Twohig, E. (eds) *Ireland in the Bronze Age*. Stationery Office, Dublin: 73–86.

Manning, C. (1987) 'Cahergal, Kimego West', in Cotter, C. (ed.), *Excavations 1986*, Dublin: 21.

Manning, C. (1991) 'Cahergal, Kimego West', in Bennett, I. (ed.), *Excavations 1990*, Dublin: 37.

Marcus, G. J. (1980) *The Conquest of the North Atlantic*, Woodbridge: Suffolk.

Marguerie, D. (1990) 'L'environnement a l'Âge du Fer en Armorique', in Duval, A., Le Bihan, J-P. and Menez, Y. (eds), *Les Gauloise d'Armorique: La Fin de l'Âge du Fer en Europe Temperée – actes du XIIe colloque AFEAF, Quimper, Mai 1988,* Revue Archéologique de l'Ouest, Supplement No. 3: 115–20.

Marsden, P. (2003) *Sealed by Time, The Loss and Recovery of the Mary Rose, The Archaeology of the Mary Rose, Vol. 1*, Cromwell Press: Trowbridge.

Marshall, D. N. (1964) 'Report on Excavations at Little Dunagoil', *Transactions of the Buteshire Natural History Society*, 16: 30–69.

Martín de la Cruz, J. C. (1987) *El Llanete de los Moros, Montoro, Córdoba*, Excavaciones Arqueológicas en España 151, Madrid.

Massy, J.-L., Mangel, E., Meniel, P., and Rapin, A. (1986) 'La nécropole de Tartingy (Oise)', *Revue archéologique de Picardie*, 314: 13–81.

Maxwell, G. (1969) 'Duns and Forts - A Note on Some Iron Age Monuments of the Atlantic Province', *Scottish Archaeological Forum*, 1: 41–6.

Maxwell, I. S. (1972) 'The location of Ictis', *Journal of the Royal Institute of Cornwall* 6: 293–319.

McCormick, F. (1991) 'The mammal bones from Cnip Wheelhouse, Lewis', Typescript.

McCormick, F. (1992) 'Early faunal evidence for dairying', *OJA*, 11: 201–9.

McCullagh, R. P. J. and Tipping, R. (eds) (1998) *The Lairg Project 1988–1996: the evolution of an archaeological landscape in northern Scotland*, Monograph 3, Scottish Trust for Archaeological Research, Edinburgh.

McGrail, S. (1981) *The Ship: Rafts, Boats, and Ships from Prehistoric Times to the Medieval Era*, HMSO: London.

McGrail, S. (1983) 'Cross-Channel seamanship and navigation in the late-first millennium BC', *OJA*, 2: 299–337.

McGrail, S. (1987) *Ancient Boats in North-west Europe*, Longman: Harlow.

McGrail, S. (1990) 'Boats and boatmanship in the late-prehistoric southern North Sea and Channel region', in McGrail, S. (ed.), *Maritime Celts, Frisians and Saxons: papers presented to a conference at Oxford in November 1988*, CBA Research Report 71, London 71: 32–48.

McGrail, S. (1993) 'Prehistoric seafaring in the channel', in Scarre, C. and Healy, F. (eds), *Trade and Exchange in Prehistoric Europe*, pp. 199–210, Oxbow: Oxford.

McGrail, S. (1995) 'Celtic Seafaring and Transport', in Green, M. J. (ed.), *The Celtic World*, pp. 254–84, Routledge: London.

McGrail, S. (1998) *Ancient Boats in North-West Europe*, 2nd edn, Longman: London.

McGrail, S. (2001) *Boats of the World from the Stone Age to Medieval times*, Oxford University Press, Oxford.

McGrail, S. (2004) 'North-west European seagoing boats before AD 400', in Clark, P. (ed.) (2004): 51–66.

McGrail, S. (2006) *Ancient Boats and Ships*, 2nd edn, Shire Archaeology: Malta.

McIntyre, A. (1999) 'Survey and excavation at Kilearnan Hill, Sutherland, 1982-3', *PPS*, 128: 167–202.

McNeill, T. E. (1992) 'Excavations at Dunsilly, Co. Antrim', *UJA*, 54–5: 78–112.

McOmish, D. (1996) 'East Chisenbury: Ritual and rubbish at the British Bronze Age-Iron Age transition', *Antiquity*, 70: 68–76.

Mederos Martín, A. (1996) 'La Conexión Levantino-Chipriota. Indicios de Comercio Atlántico con el Mediterráneo Oriental durante el Bronce Final (1150–950 BC)', *Trabajos de Prehistoria*, 53.2: 95–115.

Megaw, J. V. S. (1979) 'The later bronze age (1,400 B.C.- 500 B.C.)', in Megaw, J. V. S. and Simpson D. D. A. (eds), *Introduction to British Prehistory*, pp. 242–343, Leicester University Press: Leicester.

Megaw, J. V. S. and Megaw, M. R. (1996) 'Ancient Celts and modern ethnicity', *Antiquity*, 70: 175–81.

Megaw, J. V. S. and Megaw, M. R. (1998) 'The mechanism of (Celtic) dreams?: a partial response to our critics', *Antiquity*, 72: 432–5.

Menez, Y. (1986) *Hennebont: rapport de fouilles, juillet 1986.*

Menez, Y. (1988) 'Pluguffan-Kernier (Finistère). Sondage sur un habitat datable de la transition La Tène finale – Gallo-romain précoce', *Dossiers de Protohistoire no.2: Architectures des Ages des Métaux, fouilles récentes*, Errances, Paris: 111–20.

Menez, Y. (1994) 'Les enclos de type "ferme indigène" en Bretagne: quelques réflexions issues de treize ans de fouilles', in Buchsenschutz, O. and Méniel, P. (eds) *Les Installations Agricoles de l'âge de fer en Ile-de-France, Actes du Colloque de Paris, 1993. Etudes d'Histoire et d'Archeologie Vol. IV*, pp. 255–76, Presses de L'Ecole Normale Supérieure.

Menez, Y. (1996) *Une ferme de l'Armorique gaulois: Le Boisanne à Plouer-sur-Rance (Côtes-d'Armor)*, Documents d'Archéologie Française: 58, Paris.

Menez, Y., Hyvert, J., Langouët, L., Le Bihan, J. P. and Tanguy, D. (1990) 'Les bâtiments du second Age du Fer en Armorique', *Les Gaulois d'Armorique*, Actes du XII colloque AFEAF, Quimper 1988, *RAO* suppl. 3: 121–37.

Mercer, R. J. (1970) 'The Excavation of a Bronze Age Hut-Circle Settlement, Stannon Down', *CA*, 9: 17–46.

Mercer, R. J. (1980) *Archaeological Field Survey in Northern Scotland volume I, 1976–79*, University of Edinburgh Department of Archaeology Occasional Paper 4, Edinburgh.

Mercer, R. J. (1981) *Archaeological Field Survey in Northern Scotland volume II, 1980–1*, University of Edinburgh Department of Archaeology Occasional Paper 7, Edinburgh.

Mercer, R. J. (1985) *Archaeological Field Survey in Northern Scotland volume III, 1982–3*, University of Edinburgh Department of Archaeology Occasional Paper 11, Edinburgh.

Mercer, R. J. (1996) 'The excavation of a succession of prehistoric roundhouses at Cnoc Stanger, Reay, Caithness, Highland, 1981–2', *PSAS*, 126: 157–90.

Meuret, J.-C., Gruel, K. and Villard, A. (1992) 'Ranée, Ligne Anne', *Bilan scientifique de la région Bretagne*: 58–9.

Meuret, J.–C. (1999) 'De l'avion à la fouille, Une impérieuse nécessité', in Leroux *et al.* (1999): 35–50.

Meyer, K. (ed.) (1909) *Tecosca Cormaic*, Todd Lecture Series Vol. 15, Dublin.

Miles, H. (1977) 'Excavations at Killibury Hillfort, Egloshayle 1975–6', *CA*, 16: 89–121.

Miles, H. and Miles, T. J. (1973) 'Excavations at Trethurgy, St. Austell: Interim Report', *CurrA*, 12: 25–9.

Minshull, G. N. (1984) *Western Europe*, Hodder & Stoughton: Hong Kong.

Mitchell, F. (1976) *The Irish landscape*, Collins: London.

Mitchell, F. and Ryan, M. (1997) *Reading the Irish Landscape*, Revised edition, Townhouse: Dublin.

Mitchell, G. F. (1989) *Man and Environment on Valencia Island*, Royal Irish Academy: Dublin.

Mohen, J-P. (1980) *L'âge du fer en Aquitaine du 8e au 3e siècle*, CNRS: Paris.

Moloney, A. (1993) *Excavations at Clofinlough, Co. Offaly*, Irish Wetlands Unit Transactions 2, Dublin.

Monk, M. (1995) 'A tale of two ringforts: Lisleagh I and II', *Journal of the Cork Historical and Archaeological Society*, 100: 105–16.

Monkhouse, F. J. (1974) *A Regional Geography of Western Europe*, 4th edn, Longman: London.

Monteagudo, L. (1977) *Die Beile auf der Iberischen Halbinsel*, Prähistorische Bronzefunde IX, 6, Munich.

Moore, D. (ed.) (1970) *The Irish Sea Province in Archaeology and History*, Cambrian Archaeological Society: Cardiff.

Moore, M. J. (1987) *Archaeological Inventory of County Meath*, Stationery Office: Dublin.

Moore, M. J. (1996) *Archaeological Inventory of County Wexford*, Stationery Office: Dublin.

Mount, C. (1995) 'Excavations at Rathdooney Beg, Co. Sligo, 1994', *Emania*, 13: 15–22.

Muckleroy, K. (1980) 'Two Bronze Age cargoes in British waters', *Antiquity*, 54: 100–9.

Muckleroy, K. (1981) 'Middle Bronze Age trade between Britain and Europe: a maritime perspective', *PPS*, 47: 275–97.

Muckleroy, K., Haselgrove, C. and Nash, D. (1978) 'A pre-Roman coin from Canterbury and the ship represented on it', *PPS*, 44: 439–44.

Müller Wille, M. (1965) *Eisenzeitliche Fluren in den festlandischen Nordseegebeiten*, Geographischen Kommission für Westfalen, Münster.

Mulville, J. (1997) 'Animal Bones', in Sharples, N., (ed.) *The Iron Age and Norse settlement at Bornish, South Uist: an interim report on the 1997 excavations*, School of History and Archaeology, University of Wales, Cardiff, Cardiff Studies in Archaeology, Specialist Report 4.

Mulville, J. and Thoms, J. (2005) 'Animals and Ambiguity in the Iron Age of the Western Isles', in Turner *et al.* (eds) (2005): 235–45.

Murphy, K. (1985) 'Excavations at Pen-y-coed, Llangynog, Dyfed 1983', *Carmarthenshire Antiquary*, 21: 75–112.

Murray, J. (1991) 'Megaliths again – a view from the Solway', *SAR*, 8: 26–32.

Musset, R. (1937) *La Bretagne*, A. Colin: Paris.

Musset, R. (1952) 'Le Bretagne péninsulaire', in *La France: géographie et tourisme* 12: 141.

Musson, C. R. with Britnell, W. J. and Smith, A. G. (1991) 'The Breiddin hillfort: a later prehistoric settlement in the Welsh Marches', CBA Res. Rep. 76: London.

Mytum, H. (1992) *The Origins of Early Christian Ireland*, Routledge: London.

Mytum, H. (1999) 'Castell Henllys', *CA*, 161: 164–72.

Naas, P. (1999) 'Les enlcos: essai de typologie et organization des réseaux de clôture', in Leroux *et al.* (1999): 51–62.

Nash, D. (1976) 'The growth of urban society in France', in Cunliffe, B. W. and Rowley, T. (eds), *Oppida: The Beginnings of Urbanism in Barbarian Europe, Papers presented to a conference at Oxford, October 1975*, pp. 95–133, BAR Internat. Ser. S11, Oxford.

Nash, D. (1978) 'Territory and state formation in central Gaul', in Green, D., Haselgrove, C. and Spriggs, M. (eds), *Social Organisation and Settlement: Contributions from Anthropology, Archaeology and Geography*, pp. 455–75, BAR Internat. Ser. S47.

Nash, D. (1981) 'Coinage and state development in central Gaul', in Cunliffe, B. W. (ed.), *Coinage and Society in Britain and Gaul: Some Current Problems*, pp. 10–17, CBA Research Report 38.

Naveau, J. (1973) 'L'oppidum de Moulay (fouilles de l'année 1973)', *Bulletin de la Commission, Historique et Archéologique de la Mayenne* 244: 5–17.

Naveau, J. (1974) 'L'oppidum de Moulay (fouilles de l'année 1974)', *Bulletin de la Commission, Historique et Archéologique de la Mayenne* 245: 3–35.

Naveau, J. (1976) 'L'oppidum de Moulay (fouilles de l'année 1975)', *Bulletin de la Commission, Historique et Archéologique de la Mayenne* 246: 61–98.

Naveau, J. (1986) 'Le camp gaulois de Moulay', *Dossiers Histoire et Archéologie* 106: 16–17.

Naveau, J., Jardin, F. and Mare, E. (1987) 'Les stèles présumées de l'Age du Fer en pays Diablinte', *La Mayenne, archéologie et histoire* 10: 3–19.

Neal, D. S. (1983) 'Excavations on a settlement at Little Bay, Isles of Scilly', *CA*, 22: 47–80.

Needham, S. (1982) *The Ambleside Hoard. A discovery in the Royal Collections*, London: British Museum Occasional Paper 39: London.

Needham, S. (1990) *The Petters Late Bronze Age Metalwork: An Analytical Study of the Thames Valley Metalworking in its Settlement Context*, British Museum, London.

Needham, S. (1996) 'Chronology and periodisation in the British Bronze Age', *Acta Archaeologica*, 67: 121–40.

Needham, S. (1998) 'Mapping a Bronze Age world view: commentary on figure in the introduction', in Jorge, S. O. (ed.) (1998): 2–8.

Needham, S. and Burgess, C. (1980) 'The Later Bronze Age in the lower Thames valley: the metalwork evidence', in Barrett, J. and Bradley, R. (eds), *Settlement and Society in the British Later Bronze Age*, BAR, Brit. Ser. 83, pp. 437–69, Archaeopress: Oxford.

Needham, S., Ramsey, C. B., Coombs, D., Cartwright, C. and Pettit, P. (1997) 'An independent chronology for the British Bronze Age Metalwork: The results of the Oxford Radiocarbon Accelerator Programme', *Arch J* 154: 55–107.

Neighbour, T. and Burgess, C. (1997) 'Traigh Bostadh, Lewis', *Discovery and Excavation in Scotland 1996*: 113–14.

Neihardt, J. G. (1974) *Black Elk Speaks: Being the Life Story of a Holy Man of the Oglala Sioux*, Abacus: London.

Nicholson, R. A. (2004) 'Iron Age fishing in the Northern isles: the evolution of a stored product?', in Housley, R. A. and Coles, G. (eds) (2004): 155–62.

Nicholson, R. A. and Dockrill, S. J. (eds) (1998) *Old Scatness Broch, Shetland. Retrospect and Prospect*, Bradford Arch. Sc. Res. 5, NABO Mon. 2: Bradford.

Nieke, M. R. (1984): *Settlement Patterns in the Atlantic Province of Scotland in the first Millennium AD: A Study of Argyll*, (3 vols.) unpub. Ph.D. thesis, University of Glasgow.

Nieke, M. R. (1990) 'Fortifications in Argyll: Retrospect and future prospect', in Armit, I (ed.): 131–42.

Nisbet, H. (1994) 'Excavation of a vitrified dun at Langwell, Strath Oikel, Sutherland', *Glasgow Archaeological Journal*, 19: 51–74.

Northover, J. P. (1982) 'The exploration of long-distance movement of bronze in Bronze and Early Iron Age Europe', *Bulletin of the Institute of Archaeology, University of London* 19: 45–72.

Northover, P. (1982) 'The metallurgy of the Wilburton Hoards', *OJA,* 1: 69–109.

Nowakowski, J. (1986) *National Trust Archaeological Survey of Gunard's Head*, CA Unit: Truro.

Nowakowski, J. (2004) 'Revisiting Trevelgue Head – sixty years on', *CA*, 39–40: 190–191.

O'Connell, G. (1973) *The Burren: a Guide*, Mid-Western Regional Tourism Organisation.

O'Connor, B. (1980) *Cross-Channel Relations in the Late Bronze Age*, BAR, Internat. Ser. 91: Oxford.

Ó Donnabháin, B. (2000) 'An appalling vista? The Celts and the archaeology of later prehistoric Ireland', in Desmond, A., Johnson, G., McCarthy, M., Sheehan, J. and Shee Twohig, E. (eds) *New Agendas in Irish Prehistory. Papers in commemoration of Liz Anderson*, pp. 189–96, Wordwell Bray: Co. Wicklow.

O'Donovan, J. (1839) *Ordnance Survey Letters, County Galway*.

O'Flaherty, (1986) 'Loher', in Cotter, C. (ed.), *Excavations 1985*, Dublin: 26–7.

O'Kelly, M. J. (1951) 'An Early Bronze Age ringfort at Carrigillihy, Co. Cork', *Journal of the Cork Historical and Archaeological Society*, 56: 69–86.

O'Kelly, M. J. (1970) 'Problems of Irish ring-forts', in D. Moore (ed.) (1970): 50–4.

O'Kelly, M. J. (1989) *Early Ireland. An Introduction to Irish Prehistory*, Cambridge University Press: Cambridge.

O'Leary, P. and Twohig, E. (1993) 'A possible Iron Age pillarstone on Cape Clear, Co. Cork', *Journal of the Cork Historical and Archaeological Society*, 98: 133–40.

Olwyn Owen, O. and Lowe, C. (1999) *Kebister: The one-thousand year old story of one Shetland township*, Society of Antiquaries of Scotland Monograph Series No. 14: Edinburgh.

Ó Ríordáin, S. P. (1940) 'Excavations at Cush, Co. Limerick', *PRIA,* 45C: 83–181.

Ó Ríordáin, S. P. (1949) 'Lough Gur Excavations: Carraig Aile and "The Spectacles"', *PRIA,* C 52: 39–111.

Ó Ríordáin, S. P. (1971) *Tara, the Monuments on the Hill*, Dundalgan Press: Dundalk.

Ó Ríordáin, S. P. and Foy, J.B. (1941) 'The excavation of Leacanabuaile stone fort, Co. Kerry', *Journal of the Cork Historical and Archaeological Society* 46: 85–99.

O'Sullivan, A. (1996) 'Later Bronze Age intertidal discoveries on North Munster estuaries', *Discovery Programme Reports*, 4: 63–71.

O'Sullivan, A. (1998) *The Archaeology of Lake Settlement in Ireland*, Discovery Programme Monograph 4, Royal Irish Academy: Dublin.

O' Sullivan, A. and Sheehan, J. (1996) *The Iveragh Peninsula: An Archaeological Survey of South Kerry*, Cork University Press: Cork.

Osgood, R. (1998) *Warfare in the Late Bronze Age of North Europe,* BAR Internat. Ser. 694, Archaeopress:Oxford.

Oswald, A. (1997) 'A doorway on the past: Practical and mystic concerns in the orientation of roundhouse doorways', in Gwilt, A. and Haselgrove, C. (eds), *Reconstructing Iron Age Societies: New Approaches to the British Iron Age*, pp. 87–95, Oxbow: Oxford.

Parcero Obiñña, C. and Cobas Fernandez, I. (2004) 'Iron Age Archaeology of the Northwestern Iberian Peninsula', *e-Keltoi Journal of Interdiciplinary Celtic Studies*, 6: 1–72.

Parker Pearson, M. (1996) 'Food, fertility and front doors in the first millennium BC', in Champion, T. C. and Collis, J. R. (eds), *The Iron Age in Britain and Ireland: Recent Trends*, pp. 117–32, Sheffield Academic Press: Sheffield.

Parker Pearson, M. and Richards, C. (1994a) 'Ordering the world: Perceptions of architecture, space and time', in Parker Pearson, M. and Richards, C. (eds), *Architecture and Order: Approaches to Social Space*, pp. 1–37, Routledge: London.

Parker Pearson, M. and Richards, C. (1994b) 'Architecture and order: Spatial representation and archaeology', in Parker Pearson, M. and Richards, C. (eds), *Architecture and Order: Approaches to Social Space*, pp. 38–72, Routledge: London.

Parker Pearson, M. and Sharples, N. with Mulville, J. and Smith, H. (1999) *Between Land and Sea: Excavations at Dun Vulan, South Uist*, Sheffield Academic Press: Sheffield.

Parker Pearson, M., Sharples, N. and Mulville, J. (1996) 'Brochs and Iron Age society: A reappraisal', *Antiquity*, 70: 57–67.

Parker Pearson, M., Marshall, P., Mulville, J., Smith, H. and Ingrem, C. (2000) *Cladh Hallan: Excavation of a Late Bronze Age to Early Iron Age Settlement, August–September 2000*, unpub. Report: University of Sheffield.

Patchett, F. M. (1944) 'Cornish Bronze Age pottery', *ArchJ*, 101: 17–19.

Patchett. F. M. (1951) 'Cornish Bronze Age pottery', *ArchJ*, 108: 44–65.

Pattison, P. and Fletcher, M. (1996) 'Grimspound, One Hundred Years On', *PDAS*, 52 (1994): 21–34.

Peacock, D. P. S. (1969) 'A contribution to the study of Glastonbury ware from South-Western Britain', *AJ*, 49: 41–61.

Peacock, D. P. S. (1979) 'Glastonbury Ware: an alternative view', in Burnham, B. C. and Kingsbury, J. (eds), *Space, Hierarchy and Society*, pp. 113–18, BAR, Internat. Ser. 59: Oxford.

Pearce, S. M. (1976) 'An axe-head from Penolva, Paul', *CA*, 15: 114.

Pearce, S. M. (1979) 'The distribution and production of Bronze Age metalwork', *Devon Archaeological Society*, 37: 136–46.

Pearce, S. M. (1981) *The Archaeology of South West Britain*, Collins: London.

Pearce, S. M. (1983) *The Bronze Age Metalwork of South-Western Britain*, BAR, Internat. Ser. 120: Oxford.

Peña Santos, A. and Rey, M. (2001) *Petroglifos de Galicia*, A Coruña.

Penhallurick, R. D. (1986) *Tin in Antiquity: Its Mining and Trade Throughout the Ancient World with Particular Reference to Cornwall*, Institute of Metals: London.

Petersen, F. F. (1981) *The Excavation of a Bronze Age Cemetery on Knighton Heath, Dorset*, BAR, Brit. Ser. 98: Oxford.

Piggott, S. (1958) 'Native economies and the Roman occupation of North Britain', in Richmond, I. A. (ed.) (1958) *Roman and Native in North Britain*, pp. 1–27, Thomas Nelson and Sons: Edinburgh.

Piggott, S. (1966) 'A scheme for the Scottish Iron Age', in Rivet, A. L. F. (ed.) (1966), The Iron Age in Northern Britain, pp. 1–16, Edinburgh University Press: Edinburgh.

Piggott, S. (1974) *The Druids*, Penguin: Hamondsworth.

Piggott, S. (1979) 'South-West England – North-West Europe: Contrasts and Contacts in Prehistory', *Devon Archaeological Society*, 37: 10–21.

Piggott, S. (1983) 'The Coming of the Celts. The Archaeological Argument', in MacEoin, G. (ed.), *Proceedings of the Sixth Internatinal Congress of Celtic Studies, Galway 1979*, pp. 138–48, Dublin.

Pilcher, J. R. (1969) 'Archaeology, palaeoecology and C-14 dating of the Beaghmore stone circle site', *UJA*, 32: 73–90.

Pleiner, R. (1980) 'Early iron metallurgy in Europe', in Wertime, T. and Muhly (eds), *The Coming of the Age of Iron*, pp. 375–415, Yale University Press: New Haven.

Pleiner, R. (1981) 'Die Wege des Eisen nach Europa', in Pleiner, R. (ed.), *Frühes Eisen in Europa*: 115–28.

Plummer, C. and Earle, J. (eds) (1892) *Two of the Saxon Chronicles Parallel*, Clarendon Press: Oxford.

Polwhele, R. (1793) *The History of Devonshire, Volume 1*, London and Exeter.

Powell, T. G. E. (1972) 'The problem of Iberian affinities in prehistoric archaeology around the Irish Sea', in F. Lynch and C. Burgess (eds), *Prehistoric Man in Wales and the West. Essays in honour of Lily F. Chitty*, pp. 93–106, Adams & Dart: Bath.

Proudfoot, V. B. (1970) 'Irish raths and cashels: some notes on origin, chronology and survival', *UJA*, 33: 37–48.

Queiroga, F. M. V. R. (1992) *War and castros: New approaches to the Northwestern Portuguese Iron Age*, unpub. D.Phil. thesis, University of Oxford.

Queiroga, F. M. V. R. (2003) *War and the Castros: New Approaches to the Northwestern Portuguese Iron Age*, BAR, Internat. Ser. 198, Archaeopress: Oxford.

Quinnell, H. (1986) 'Cornwall during the Iron Age and the Roman period', *CA*, 25: 111–35.

Quinnell, H. (1996) 'Becoming marginal? Dartmoor in later prehistory', *PDAS*, 52 (1994): 75–83.

Quinnell, H. and Harris, D. (1985) 'Castle Dore: The chronology reconsidered', *CA*, 24: 123–32.

Quinnell, H. (2004) *Trethurgy. Excavations at Trethurgy Round, St Austell: Community and Status in Roman and Post-Roman Cornwall*, Cornwall County Council: Turo.

Radford, C. A. R. (1951) 'Report on the excavations at Castle Dore', *Journal of the Royal Institution of Cornwall*, Series I: 1–119.

Radford, C. A. R. (1956) 'Imported pottery found at Tintagel, Cornwall', in D. B. Harden (ed.), *Dark Age Britain*, pp. 59–70, Methuen: London.

Radford, C. A. R. (1966) 'Cultural relationships of the Early Celtic World', *Proceedings of the 2nd International Congress of Celtic Studies*, Cardiff: 3–27.

Raftery, B. (1972) 'Irish hill-forts', in C. Thomas (ed.) (1972): 37–58.

Raftery, B. (1976) 'Rathgall and Irish hillfort problems', in D. W. Harding (ed.), *Hillforts - Later Prehistoric Earthworks in Britain and Ireland*: 339–57.

Raftery, B. (1984) *La Tène in Ireland: problems of origin and chronology*, B&M Raftery: Marburg.

Raftery, B. (1990) *Trackways Through Time: Archaeological Investigations on Irish Bog Roads, 1985–1989*, Headline Publishing: Dublin.

Raftery, B. (1991a) 'The Celtic Iron Age in Ireland: Problems of Origin', *Emania* 9: 28–32.

Raftery, B. (1991b) 'Zur Frage irisch-iberischer Beziehungen während der Eisenzeit', in *Festschrift für Wilelm Schüle*, Veroffentlichung des Vorgeschichtlichen Seminars Marburg, Sonderbrand 6, Internationale Archäologie 1: 259–67.

Raftery, B. (1992) 'Celtas, cultura y colonización: reflexiones sobre la Edad del Hierro en Irlanda', in M. Almagro-Gorbea (ed.), *Los Celtas: Hispania y Europa*, pp. 91–120, Madrid.

Raftery, B. (1994) *Pagan Celtic Ireland*, Thames & Hudson: London.

Raftery, B. (2005) 'Ireland and Scotland in the Iron Age', in Gillies, W. and Harding, D. W. (eds) (2005): 181–9.

Raftery, J. (1944) 'The Turoe Stone and the Rath of Feerwore', *JRSAI*, 74: 23–52.

Raftery, J. (1951) *Prehistoric Ireland*, Batsford: London.

Raftery, J. (1972) 'Iron Age and Irish Sea Province: some problems for research', in Thomas, C. (ed.) (1972): 1–10.

Raftery, J. (1981) 'Concerning chronology', in Ó Corráin, D. (ed.), *Irish Antiquity: Essays and Studies Presented to Professor M. J. O'Kelly*, pp. 82–92, Tower Books: Cork.

Rahtz, P. (1971) 'Castle Dore – A reappraisal of the Post-Roman structures', *CA*, 10: 49–54.

Ralston, I. B. M. (1980) 'The Green Castle and the promontory forts of north-east Scotland', *Scottish Archaeological Forum*, 10: 27–40.

RCAHMS (Royal Commission on the Ancient and Historical Monuments of Scotland) (1911) *Report 3 - County of Caithness*, HMSO: Edinburgh.

RCAHMS (1928) *Outer Hebrides, Skye and the Small Isles*, HMSO: Edinburgh.

RCAHMS (1971) *Argyll. An Inventory of the Ancient Monuments 1 – Kintyre*, HMSO: Edinburgh.

RCAHMS (1975) *Argyll. An Inventory of the Ancient Monuments 2 – Lorn*, HMSO: Edinburgh

RCAHMS (1980) *Argyll. An Inventory of the Ancient Monuments 3 – Mull, Tiree, Coll and Northern Argyll*, HMSO: Edinburgh.

RCAHMS (1981) *Argyll. An Inventory of the Ancient Monuments 4 – Iona*, HMSO: Edinburgh.

RCAHMS (1984) *Argyll. An Inventory of the Ancient Monuments 5 – Islay, Jura, Colonsay and Oronsay*, HMSO: Edinburgh.

RCAHMS (1988) *Argyll. An Inventory of the Ancient Monuments 6 – Mid-Argyll and Cowal*, HMSO: Edinburgh.

RCAHMS (1997) *Eastern Dunfriesshire: an archaeological landscape*, HMSO: Edinburgh.

Read, R. C. (1970) *Cornish Middle Bronze Age Pottery*, unpub. Ph.D., thesis, University of London.

Reddé, M. (1985) 'Vraies et fausses encientes militaires d'epoque romaine', *Les viereckschanzen et les enceintes quadrilatérales en Europe celtique*, Actes du 9éme colloque de l'AFEAF, Châteaudun, 16-19 mai 1985, Colloques Archéologie Aujourd'hui, éd Errance: 21–6.

Redmond, M. (1995) 'A survey of the promontory forts of the Kerry Peninsulas', *Journal of the Kerry Archaeological and Historical Society*, 28: 5–63.

Renfrew, A. C. (1968) 'Wessex without Mycenae', *Annual of the British School at Athens*, 63: 277–85.

Renfrew, A. C. (1973) *Before Civilisation: The Radiocarbon Revolution and Prehistoric Europe*, Jonathan Cape: London.

Renfrew, A. C. (1979) *Investigations in Orkney*, Society of Antiquaries of London Research Report No. 38: London.

Renfrew, A. C. (1987) *Archaeology and Language: The Puzzle of Indo-European Origins*, Pimlico: London.

Ried, M. L. (1989) 'A room with a view: An examination of round-houses, with particular reference to northern Britain', *OJA*, 8: 1–39.

Ritchie, A. (1979) 'Excavation of Pictish and Viking-age farmsteads at Buckquoy, Orkney', *PSAS*, 108: 174–227.

Ritchie, J. N. G. and Ritchie, A. (1991) *Scotland: Archaeology and Early History* (revised edition), Edinburgh University Press: Edinburgh.

Robinson, D. E. (ed.) (1990) *Experimentation and Reconstruction in Environmental Archaeology*, Oxbow: Oxford.

Rowe, T-M. (2005) *Cornwall in Prehistory*, Tempus: Stroud.

Rowlands, M. J. (1971) 'The archaeological interpretation of prehistoric metalworking', *WA*, 3: 210–14.

Rowlands, M. J. (1976) *The Production and Distribution of Metalwork in the Middle Bronze Age in South Britain*, BAR, Brit. Ser., 31: Oxford.

Rowlands, M. J. (1980) 'Kinship, alliance and exchange in the European Bronze Age', in Barrett, J. and Bradley, R. (ed.), *Settlement and Society in the British Later Bronze Age*, pp. 15–55, BAR Brit. Ser. 83, Archaeopress: Oxford.

Ruíz-Gálvez, M. (1984) *La Península Ibérica y sus relaciones con el círculo cultural atlántico*, Universidad Complutense: Madrid (2 vol.).

Ruíz-Gálvez, M. (1986) 'Navegacion y comercio entre el atlantico y el Mediterreaneo a fines de edad del bronce', *Trabajos de Prehistoria*, 43: 9–41.

Ruíz-Gálvez, M. (1987) 'Bronce Atlántique y "cultura" del Bronce Atlántico en la Península Ibérica', *Trabajos de Prehistoria*, 44: 251–264.

Ruíz-Gálvez, M. (1989a) *La Europa atlántica en la Edad del Bronce*, Cátedra: Barcelona.

Ruíz-Gálvez, M. (1989b) 'La orfebrería del Bronce Final: el poder y su ostentación', *Revista de Arqueología Extra*, 4: 46–57.

Ruíz-Gálvez, M. (1991) 'Songs of a Wayfaring Lad. Late Bronze Age Atlantic exchange and the building of the regional identity in the west Iberian Peninsula', *OJA*, 10:3: 277–303.

Ruíz-Gálvez, M. (1992) 'La Nova Vendida: Orfebrería, herencia y agricultura en la Protohistoria de la Península Ibérica', *Spal*, 1: 219–251.

Ruíz-Gálvez, M. (1995) *Ritos de paso y puntos de paso. La Ria de Huelva en el mundo del Bronce Final Europa*, Servico de publicaciones Universidad Complutense: Madrid.

Ruíz-Gálvez, M. (1997) 'The West of Iberia: The meeting point between the Mediterranean and the Atlantic at the end of the Bronze Age', in Balmuth, M., Gilman, A. and Prados-Torreira, L. (eds) *Encounters and Transformations: The Archaeology of Iberia in Transition*, pp. 95–120, Sheffield Academic Press: Sheffield.

Ruiz-Gálvez, M. and Galán Domingo, E. (1991) 'Las Estelas del Suroeste como Hito de Vías Ganaderas y Rutas de Comercío', *Trabajos de Prehistoria*, 48: 257–73.

Rutten, M. G. (1969) *The Geology of Western Europe*, Elsevier Pub. Co.: Amsterdam and New York.

Rynne, E. (1961) 'The introduction of the La Tène into Ireland', *Bericht über den V. Internationalen Kongress für Vor - und Frühgeschichte, Hamburg 1958*, Berlin: 705–9.

Rynne, E. (1972) 'Celtic stone idols in Ireland', in Thomas, C. (ed) (1972): 79–98.

Rynne, E. (1982) 'The Early Iron Age in County Clare', *North Munster Antiquarian Journal*, 24: 4–18.

Rynne, E. (1989) 'The Grianán of Aileach, Co. Donegal', *Donegal Annual*, 41: 54–56.

Rynne, E. (1991) 'Dún Aengusa – Daingean nó Teampall?', *AI*, 5: 19–21.

Rynne, E. (1992) 'Dûn Aengus and some similar Celtic ceremonial centres', in Bernelle, A. (ed.) *Decantations: A Tribute to Maurice Craig*, pp. 196–207, Dufour Editions: Dublin.

Salter, C. and Ehrenreich, R. (1984) 'Iron Age iron metallurgy in Central Southern Britain', in Cunliffe, B. W. and Miles, D. (eds), *Aspects of the Iron Age in Central Southern Britain*, pp. 146–161, Oxford University Committee for Archaeology Monograph 2, Oxford.

San Juan, G., Ghesquiere, E. and Meniel, P. (1996) 'Un site d'habitat protohistorique avec un cercle de trous de poteaux à Cagny (Calvados)', *RAO*, 13: 89–102.

Sanders, N. K. (1957) *Bronze Age Cultures in France*, Cambridge University Press: Cambridge.

Sanquer, R. (1981) 'Les encientes quadrangulaires dans le Finistère', *B.S.A.F.*, 110: 83–95.

Santa Olalla, J. M. (1938–1941) *Esquema paletnológico de la Península Hispánica*, Seminario de Historia Primitiva del Hombre: Madrid.

Saunders, C. (1972) 'The Excavations at Grambla, Wendron 1972: Interim Report', *CA*, 11: 50–2.

Saunders, A. D. and Harris, D. (1982) 'Excavation at Castle Gotha, St Austell', *CA*, 21: 109–53.

Savory, H. N. (1948) 'The "Sword-bearers." A Reinterpretation', *PPS*, 14: 155–76.

Savory, H. N. (1949) 'The Atlantic Bronze Age in South West Europe', *PPS*, 15: 134–41.

Savory, H. N. (1954) 'The excavation of an Early Iron Age fortified settlement on Mynydd Bychan, Llysworney (Glam.), 1949–50 Part I', *AC*, 103: 85–108.

Savory, H. N. (1956) 'The excavation of an Early Iron Age fortified settlement on Mynydd Bychan, Llysworney (Glam.), 1949–50. Part II', *AC*, 104: 14–51.

Savory, H. N. (1968) *Spain and Portugal*, Thames & Hudson: London.

Savory, H. N. (1971a) *Excavations at Dinorben 1965–9*, National Museum of Wales: Cardiff.

Savory, H. N. (1971b) 'A Welsh Bronze Age hillfort', *Antiquity*, 45: 251–61.

Savory, H. N. (1974) 'An Early Iron Age metalworker's mould from Worms Head', *AC*, 123: 170–4.

Savory, H. N. (1976) 'Some Welsh Late Bronze Age hoards - old and new', *AA*, 1.2: 111–25.

Savory, H. N. (1976a) *Guide Catalogue of the Early Iron Age Collections, National Museum of Wales*: Cardiff.

Savory, H. N. (1978) Some Iberian influences on the Copper Age pottery of the Irish Channel area, *Bol Seminario Estudio Arte Arqueologico*, 44: 5–13.

Savory, H. N. (1990) 'Review of Cunliffe 1988: Greeks, Romans and Barbarians', *AC*, 139: 82–3.

Sayers, W. (2004) 'Sails in the North: Further Linguistic Considerations', *IJNA*, 33: 348–50.

Schauer, P. (1972) 'Zur Herkunft der bronzenen Hallstatt Schwerter', *Archäologisches Korrespondenzblatt*, 2: 261–70.

Scott, B. G. (1979) 'The introduction of non-ferrous and ferrous metal technologies to Ireland: motive and mechanisms', in Ryan, M. (ed.), *The Origins of Metallurgy in Atlantic Europe*, pp. 189-204, Stationery Office: Dublin.

Schweiso, J. (1976) 'Excavations at Threemilestone Round, Kenwyn, Truro', *CA*, 23: 180.

Sharpe, A. (1992) 'Treryn Dinas: Cliff Castles Reconsidered', *CA*, 31: 65–68.

Sharples (1984) 'Excavations at Pierowall Quarry, Westray, Orkney', *PSAS*, 114: 75–125.

Sharples, N. (1998) *Scalloway: A Broch, Late Iron Age Settlement and Medieval Cemetery in Shetland*, Oxbow: Oxford.

Sharples, N. and Parker Pearson, M. (1997) 'Why were brochs built? Recent studies in the Iron Age of Atlantic Scotland', in Gwilt, A. and Haselgrove, C. (eds), *Reconstructing Iron Age Societies*, pp. 254–65, Oxbow Monograph, 71: Oxford.

Shee Twohig, E. (1993) 'Megalithic tombs and megalithic art in Atlantic Europe', in Scarre, C. and Healy, F. (eds), *Trade and Exchange in Prehistoric Europe*, pp. 87–100, Oxbow: Oxford.

Shennan, S. (1993) 'Commodities, transactions and growth in the central European Early Bronze Age', *JEA*, 1(2): 68–92.

Shepherd, R. (1993) *Ancient Mining*, Institution of Mining and Metallurgy: London.

Sherratt, A. G. (1990) 'The genesis of megaliths, monumentality, ethnicity and social complexity in Neolithic north-west Europe', *WA*, 22(2): 147–67.

Sherratt, A. G. (1993a) 'What would a Bronze-Age world system look like? Relations between temperate Europe and the Mediterranean in later prehistory', *JEA*, 1.2: 1–58.

Sherratt, A. G. (1993b) 'Who are you calling peripheral? Dependence and independence in European prehistory', in Scarre, C. and Healy, F. (eds), *Trade and Exchange in Prehistoric Europe*, pp. 245–55, Oxbow: Oxford.

Sherratt, A. G. (1994a) 'Core, periphery and margin: perspectives on the Bronze Age', in Mathers, C. and Stoddart, S. (eds), *Development and Decline in the Mediterranean Bronze Age*, pp. 335–45, John Collis Publications: Sheffield.

Sherratt, A. G. (1994b) 'The emergence of elites: Earlier Bronze Age Europe, 2500–1300 BC', in Cunliffe, B. (ed.), *Prehistoric Europe. An Illustrated History*, pp. 245–76, Oxford University Press: Oxford.

Sherratt, A. G. (1995) 'Reviving the Grand Narrative: Archaeology and Long-term Change', *JEA*, 3: 1–32.

Sherratt, A. G. (1996) 'Settlement patterns' or 'landscape studies'? Reconciling Reason and Romance. *Archaeological Dialogues*, 3.2: 140–59.

Sherratt, A. G. (1998) 'Points of exchange: the Later Neolithic monuments of the Morbihan', in Gibson, A. and Simpson, D. (eds), *Prehistoric Ritual and Religion*, pp. 119–38, Sutton Publishing: London.

Sherratt, A. G. and Sherratt, S. (1988) 'The Archaeology of Indo-European: an alternative view', *Antiquity*, 62: 584–95.

Silva, A. C. F. and A. Lopes (1984) 'Depósito de fundidor do final da Idade do Bronze do Castro da Senhora da Guia (Baiões, S. Pedro do Sul, Viseu)', *Lucerna – Homenagen a D. Domingo Pinho Brandão*, Porto: 73–110.

Silva, A. C. F. (1986) *A Culture Castreja no Noroeste de Portugal*, Pacos de Ferreira: Lisbon.

Silvester, R. J. (1979) 'The relationship of first millennium settlement to the upland areas of the south west', *PDAS*, 37: 176–91.

Sims-Williams, P. (1998) 'Celtomania and Celtoscepticism', *Cambrian Medieval Celtic Studies*, 36: 1–36.

Simmons, I. G. (1970) 'Environment and Early Man on Dartmoor', *PPS*, 35: 203–19.

Small, A. (1966) 'Excavations at Underhoull, Unst, Shetland', *PSAS*, 98: 225–48.

Smith, C. A. (1974) 'A morphological analysis of late prehistoric and Romano-British settlements in north-west Wales', *PPS*, 40: 157–69.

Smith, C. A. (1977) 'Later prehistoric and Romano-British enclosed homesteads in north west Wales: an interpretation of their morphology', *AC*, 126: 38–52.

Smith, G. (1984) 'Penhale coastal promontory fort, Perranzabuloe', *CA*, 23: 180.

Smith, G. (1999) 'Survey of prehistoric and Romano-British settlement in north-west Wales', *AC*, 148: 22–53.

Smith, H. (1999) 'The Plant Remains', in Parker Pearson, M. and Sharples, N. with Mulville, J. and Smith, H., *Between Land and Sea: Excavations at Dun Vulan, South Uist*. Sheffield. Environmental and Archaeological Research Campaign in the Hebrides, Volume 3, pp. 297–336, Sheffield Academic Press: Sheffield.

Smith, H. and Mulville, J. (2004) 'Resource Management in the Outer Hebrides: an assessment of the faunal and floral evidence from archaeological investigations', in Housley, R. A. and Coles, G. (eds) (2004): 48–64.

Smith, R. A. (1905) *Guide to the Antiquities of the Early Iron Age*, British Museum: London.

Smith, R. A. (1926) 'Two Early British bronze bowls', *AJ*, 6: 276–83.

Sørensen, M. L. (1987) 'Material order and cultural classification: the role of bronze objects in the transition from bronze age to iron age in Scandanavia', in Hodder, I. (ed.), *The Archaeology of Contextual Meanings*, pp. 90–101, Cambridge University Press: Cambridge.

Sørensen, M. L. (1989) 'Period VI reconsidered: continuity and change at the transition from Bronze to Iron Age in Scandinavia', in Sorenson, M. L. and Thomas, R. (eds), *The Bronze Age - Iron Age Transition in Europe. Aspects of Continuity and Change in European Societies c.1200 to 500 BC* BAR, Internat. Ser. 483: Oxford.

Staelens, Yvette J. E. (1983) 'The Birdlip cemetery', *Trans Bristol Gloucestershire Archaeol Soc*, 100, 1982 (1983): 19–31.

Startin, W. (1982) 'Halligye Fogou: Excavations in 1981', *CA*, 21: 185–86.

Stead, I. M. (1972) 'The Cerrig-y-Drudion "hanging bowl"', *AJ*, 62: 221–34.

Stead, I. M. (1982) 'The Cerrig-y-Drudion "hanging bowl"', *AJ*, 62: 22–34.

Stenberger, M. (1966) 'A ringfort at Raheennamadra, Knocklong, Co. Limerick', *PRIA*, C 65: 37–54.

Stout, M. (1997) *The Irish Ringfort*, Irish Settlement Studies 5, Four Courts Press: Dublin.

Stuvier, M. and Pearson, G. W. (1993) 'High-precision bidecadal calibration of the radiocarbon time scale, AD 1950-500 BC and 2500-6000 BC', *Radiocarbon*, 35(1): 1.

Sutherland, D. G. (1997) 'The Environment of Argyll', in Ritchie, G. (ed.) *The Archaeology of Argyll*, RCAHMS, pp. 22–36, Edinburgh University Press: Edinburgh.

Schwappach, F. (1969) 'Stempelverziete Keramik von Armorica', *Fundberichte aus Hessen*, 1: 313–87.

Switsur, V. R. and Wright, E. V. (1989) 'Radiocarbon ages and calibrated dates for the boats from North Ferriby, Humberside – a reappraisal', *ArchJ*, 146: 58–67.

Synge, J. M. 1907: *The Aran Islands*. London.

Tanguy, D. (1988) 'L'habitat du Second Age du Fer de Pluvinger (Morbihan)', *Dossiers de Protohistoire no.2: Architectures des Ages des Métaux, fouilles récentes*, Paris, Errances: 71–80.

Tangye, M. (1973) '"Hulls" in Cornwall: a survey and discussion', *CA*, 12: 31–52.

Tanner, M. (2004) *The Last of the Celts*, Yale University Press: Newhaven and London.

Tavares da Silva, C. and Soares, J. (1978) 'Uma jazida do Bronze Final na Cerradinha (Lagoa de Santé André, Santiago do Cacém)', *Sétubal Arqueología*, 4: 71–97.

Taylor, J. J. (1980) *Bronze Age goldwork of the British Isles*, Cambridge University Press: Cambridge.

Taylor, R. (1982) 'The hoard from West Buckland, Somerset', *Antiquities Journal* 62: 13–17.

Taylor, R. (1993) *Hoards of the Bronze Age in Southern Britain*, BAR, Brit. Ser., 228: Oxford.

Taylor, T. (1996) 'Boleigh, Cornwall', in *Time Team 96: the site reports*, Channel Four Television, London: 5–9.

Tessier, M. (1986) 'L'âge du fer en pays de Retz', *Actes du VIIIe colloque sur les âges du fer*, Aquitania supplément, 1: 187–90.

Theuws, F. and Roymans, N. (eds) (1999) *Land and Ancestors: cultural dynamics in the Urnfield period and the Middle Ages in Southern Netherlands*, Amsterdam University Press: Amsterdam.

Thier, K. (2003) 'Sails in the North – New Perspectives on an Old Problem', *IJNA*, 32: 182–90.

Thomas, C. (1956) 'Evidence for post-Roman occupation of Chûn Castle, Cornwall', *AJ*, 36: 75–8.

Thomas, C. (1958) *Gwithian Ten Years' Work*, West Cornwall Field Club: Camborne.

Thomas, C. (1959) 'Imported pottery in Dark Age Western Britain', *Medieval Archaeology*, 3: 89–111.

Thomas, C. (1963) 'Trial excavations at Mulfra Vean, 1954', *CA*, 2: 23–8.

Thomas, C. (1966) 'The character and origins of Roman Dumnonia', in Thomas, C. (ed.), *Rural Settlement in Roman Britain*: pp. 74–98, CBA Research Report 7, London.

Thomas, C. (ed.) (1972) *The Iron Age in the Irish Sea Province*, CBA Res. Rpt., 9: London.

Thomas, C. (1972a) 'The Irish settlements in Post-Roman Western Britain: a survey of the evidence', *Journal of the Royal Institution of Cornwall* 6: 251–74.

Thomas, C. (2006) 'An Iron Age sword and mirror cist burial from Bryher, Isles of Scilly', *CA*, 41 & 42: 8–86.

Thomas, R. (1989) 'The Bronze-Iron transition in Southern England', in Thomas, R. and Sørensen, M. L. (eds), *The Bronze Age-Iron Age Transition in Europe: Aspects of continuity and change in European Societies c. 1200 to 500 BC*, pp. 263–86, BAR, Inter. Ser., 483, Archaeopress: Oxford.

Thomas, R. (1997) 'Land, kinship relations and the rise of enclosed settlement in first millennium BC Britain', *OJA*, 16: 211–18.

Thrane, H. (1988) 'Import, affluence and cult – interdependent aspects?', in Hardh, B. (ed.), *Trade and Exchange in Prehistory: Studies in Honour of Berta Stjernquist*, pp. 187–96, Acta Archaeologica Lundensia: Lund.

Thrane, H. (1995) 'Penultima Thule: the Bronze Age in the western Baltic region as an analogy to the Irish Bronze Age', in Waddell, J. and Shee Twohig, E. (eds) *Ireland in the Bronze Age*, pp. 149–57, Stationery Office: Dublin.

Thriepland, L. M. (1945) 'Excavations in Brittany, Spring 1939', *ArchJ*, C: 128–49.

Thriepland, L. M. (1956) 'An excavation at St. Mawgan-in-Pydar, North Cornwall', *ArchJ*, 113: 33–81.

Tierney, J. J. (1960) 'The Celtic ethnography of Posidonius', *PRIA*, 60: 189–275.

Tilley, C. (1994) *A Phenomenology of Landscape. Places, paths and monuments*, Explorations in Archaeology: Oxford.

Tilley, C. (1996) 'The power of rocks: topography and monument construction on Bodmin Moor', *World Archaeology*, 28: 161–176.

Tipping, R. (1994) 'The form and fate of Scotland's woodlands', *PSAS*, 124: 1–54.

Tooley, M. J. (1990) 'Sea-level and coastline changes during the last 5,000 years', in McGrail, S. (ed.), *Maritime Celts, Frisians and Saxons*, CBA Research Report 71, pp. 1–16, London.

Todd, M. (1984) 'Excavations at Hembury, Devon, 1980-3: a summary report', *AJ*, 64: 251–68.

Todd, M. (1987) *The South West to AD 1000*, Routledge: London.

Topping, P. G. (1987) 'Neutron activation analysis of later prehistoric pottery from the Western Isles of Scotland', *PSAS*, 52: 105–29.

Törbrugge, W. (1971) 'Vor– und frügeschichtliche Flussfunde', *Bericht der Römisch-Germanischen Kommission* 51–52: 1–146.

Tovar, A. (1961) *The Ancient Languages of Spain and Portugal*, S. F. Vanni: New York.

Treherne, P. (1995) 'The warrior's beauty: the masculine body and self-identity in Bronze Age Europe', *JEA*, 3.1: 105–44.

Trudigan, P. (1977) 'Excavations at Tregilders, St Kew, 1975-6', *CA*, 16: 122–8.

Turnbull, A. (1983) 'Bronze Age and Hallstatt finds from Rangebourne, Potterne (metalwork)', *Wiltshire Archaeology and Natural History Magazine*, 77: 45–8.

Turner, J. (1964) 'The anthropogenic factor in vegetational history I, Tregaron on Whixall Mosses', *New Phytologist*, 63: 73–90.

Turner, J. (1981) 'The Iron Age', in Simmons, I. and Tooley, M. (eds), *The Environment in British Prehistory*, Duckworth: 250–81.

Turner, V., Nicholson, R. A., Dockrill, S. J. and Bond, J. M. (eds) (2005) *Tall Stories? Two Millennia of Brochs*, Shetland Litho: Lerwick.

Tylecote, R. (1987) *The Early History of Metallurgy in Europe*, Longman: Harlow.

Ulriksen, J. (1994) 'Danish sites and settlements with a maritime context, AD 200–1200', *Antiquity*, 68: 797–811.

Varela Gomes, M. and Pinho Monteiro, J. (1977) 'Las estelas decoradas do Pomar (Beja, Portugal). Estudio comparado', *Trabajos de Prehistoria*, 34: 165–214.

Vendryes, J. (1920) 'Les Vins de la Gaule in Irlande et l'Expression Fín Aicneta', *Revue Celtique*, 38: 19–24.

Waddell, J. (1982) 'From Kermaria to Turoe?', in Scott, B. G. (ed.), *Studies on Early Ireland: Essays in Honour of M. V. Duignan*, pp. 21–8, Association of Young Irish Archaeologists: Belfast.

Waddell, J. (1991a) 'The Celticization of the West: an Irish Perspective', in Chevillot, C. and Coffyn, A. (eds) (1991): 349–66.

Waddell, J. (1991b) 'The question of the Celticization of Ireland', *Emania*, 9: 5–16.

Waddell, J. (1992) 'The Irish Sea in prehistory', *JIA*, 6: 29–40.

Waddell, J. (1995) 'Celts, Celticisation and the Irish Bronze Age', in Waddell, J. and Shee Thwohig, E. (eds) *Ireland in the Bronze Age*, pp. 158–69, Proceedings of the Dublin Conference, April 1995, Dublin.

Waddell, J. (1998) *The Prehistoric Archaeology of Ireland*, Galway University Press: Galway.

Waddell, J. and Shee Twohig, E. (1995) *Ireland in the Bronze Age: Proceedings of the Dublin Conference, April 1995*, Dublin.

Wailes, B. (1963) 'Excavations at Castle-an-Dinas, St Columb Major: interim report', *CA*, 2: 51–5.

Wailes, B. (1964) 'Excavations at Castle-an-Dinas, St Columb Major: interim report', *CA*, 3: 85.

Wailes, B. (1965) 'Excavations at Castle-an-Dinas, St Columb Major: interim report', *CA*, 4: 65.

Wailes, B. (1990) 'Dún Ailinne: A Summary Excavation Report', *Emania*, 7: 10–21.

Wainwright, F. T. (1953) 'Souterrains in Scotland', *Antiquity*, 27, 219–32.

Wainwright, F. T. (1963) *The Souterrains of Southern Pictland*, Warner: London.

Wainwright, G. J. (1967) *Coygan Camp: A Prehistoric, Romano-British and Dark Age Settlement in Carmarthenshire*, Cambrian Archaeological Association: Cardiff.

Wainwright, G. J. (1971) 'The excavation of a fortified settlement at Walesland Rath, Pembrokeshire', *Britannia*, 2: 48–108.

Wainwright, G. J. (1971a) 'Excavations at Tower Point, St Brides, Pembrokeshire', *AC*, 120: 84–90.

Wainwright, G. J. and Smith, K. (1980) 'The Shaugh Moor Project: Second Report – the Enclosure', *PPS*, 46: 65–122.

Wainwright, G. J., Fleming, A, and Smith, K. (1979) 'The Shaugh Moor Project: First Report', *PPS*, 45: 1–35.

Wallerstein, I. (1974) *The Modern World System. Capitalist Agriculture and the Origins of the European World-Economy in the Sixteenth Century*, Academic Press: New York.

Walsh, G. (1995) 'Iron Age settlement in Co. Mayo', *AI*, 32: 7–8.

Walton, K. (1974) 'A geographer's view of the sea', *Scottish Geographical Magazine*, 90: 4–13.

Warner, R. (1979) 'The Irish souterrains and their background', in Crawford, H. (ed.), *Subterranean Britain*, pp. 100–44, John Baker: London.

Warner, R. (1980) 'Irish souterrains: Later Iron Age refuges', *AA*, 3: 81–99.

Warner, R. (1981) 'Fortification: Observations on the beginnings of fortification in Later Iron-Age Ireland', *Bulletin of the Ulster Place Name Society* (2nd series), 3: 45–52.

Warner, R. (1983) 'Ireland, Ulster and Scotland in the Earlier Iron Age', in O'Conner, A. and Clarke, D. V. (eds), *From the Stone Age to the 'Forty-Five'*, pp. 160–87, J. Donald: Edinburgh.

Waterbolk, H. T. (1995) 'Patterns of the peasant landscape', *PPS*, 61: 1–36.

Watkins, T. (1976) 'Wessex without Cyprus: 'Cypriot daggers' in Europe', in Megaw, J. V. S. (ed.) *To Illustrate the Monuments. Essays on Archaeology presented to Stuart Piggott*, pp. 135–43, Thames & Hudson: London.

Watkins, T. (1981) 'Excavation of a settlement and souterrain at Newmill, near Bankfoot, Perthshire', *PSAS*, 110: 165–208.

Weatherhill, C. (1981) *Belerion. Ancient sites of Land's End*, Alison Hodge: Cornwall.

Weatherhill, C. (1985a) *Cornovia. Ancient sites of Cornwall and Scilly*, Alison Hodge: Cornwall.

Weatherhill, C. (1985b) 'The ships of the Veneti: a fresh look at the Iron Age tin ships', *CA*, 24: 163–9.

Webster, J. (1995) 'Sanctuaries and sacred places', in Green, M. (ed.) (1995) *The Celtic World*, pp. 445–64, Routledge: London.

Weir, D. (1995) 'A palynological study of landscape and agricultural development in County Louth from the second millennium BC to the first millennium AD. Final report', *Discovery Programme Reports* 2, Dublin: 77–126.

Wells, P. (1984) *Farms, Villages and Cities. Commerce and Urban Origins in Late Prehistoric Europe*, Cornell University Press: Ithaca and London.

Westropp, T. J. (1893) 'Prehistoric stone forts of central Clare', *JRSAI*, 23: 281–91.

Westropp, T. J. (1896) 'Prehistoric stone forts of northern Clare', *JRSAI*, 26: 142–57: 363–69.

Westropp, T. J. (1897) 'Prehistoric stone forts of northern Clare (Part III)', *JRSAI*, 27: 116–27.

Westropp, T. J. (1898a) 'Forts near Loop Head, Co. Clare', *JRSAI*, 28: 409–12.

Westropp, T. J. (1898b) 'Prehistoric Remains in the Burren, Co. Clare (Carran and Kilcorney)', *JRSAI*, 28: 353–66.

Westropp, T. J. (1899) 'Prehistoric remains in the Burren, Co. Clare (Part II – Kilcorney and the Eastern Valleys)', *JRSAI*, 29: 367–84.

Westropp, T. J. (1901) 'Prehistoric remains in north-western Clare', *JRSAI*, 31: 1–17: 273–91.

Westropp, T. J. (1905) 'Prehistoric remains (forts and dolmens) along the borders of the Burren in the County of Clare', *JRSAI*, 35: 205–29: 342–61.

Westropp, T. J. (1908) 'Types of the ring-forts and similar structures remaining in eastern Clare (The Newmarket group)', *PRIA*, 27C: 217–34.

Westropp, T. J. (1909) 'Types of the Ring-forts and similar structures remaining in eastern Clare (Quin, Tulla and Bodyke)', *PRIA* 27C: 371–400.

Westropp, T. J. (1910) 'A study of the early forts and stone huts in Inishmore, Aran Isles, Galway Bay', *PRIA*, 28C: 174–221.

Westropp, T. J. (1910) 'A study of the fort at Dun Aongusa, in Inishmore, Aran Isles, Galway Bay: its plan, growth and records', *PRIA*, 28C: 1–46.

Westropp, T. J. (1915) 'Prehistoric remains (forts and dolmens) in Burren and its south western border, Co. Clare', *JRSAI*, 45: 45-62: 249–74.

Westropp, T. J. (1911a) 'Prehistoric remains (forts and dolmens) in the Burren, Co. Clare', *JRSAI*, 41: 343–67.

Westropp, T. J. (1911b) 'Types of the ring-forts remaining in eastern Clare (Killaloe, its Royal Forts and their History)', *PRIA*, 29C: 186–212.

Westropp, T. J. (1913) 'Prehistoric Remains (Forts and Dolmens) in the Corofin District, Co. Clare', *JRSAI*, 43: 232–260.

Westropp, T. J. (1914) Types of the ring-forts remaining in eastern County Clare (Clonlara, Broadford, Cullaun, and Clooney), PRIA, 32C: 58–77.

Westropp, T. J. (1916) 'Notes on certain primitive remains (forts and dolmens) in Inagh and Killeimer, Co. Clare', *JRSAI*, 46: 97–120.

Westropp, T. J. (1917) 'Notes on the primitive remains (forts and dolmens) in central Co. Clare', *JRSAI*, 47: 1–20.

Westropp, T. J. (1917) 'Prehistoric remains in north western and central Co. Clare', *JRSAI*, 47: 67–74.

Wheeler, R. E. M. (1943) *Maiden Castle, Dorset*, Oxford, Society of Antiquaries Research Reports: 12.

Wheeler, R. E. M. and Richardson, K. M. (1957) *Hillforts of Northern France*, Oxford.

Wheeler, R. E. M. Archive: Notebooks relating to Wheeler's field survey of the earthworks of Brittany. Institute of Archaeology: Oxford, 1938.

Whimster, R. (1977) 'Harlyn Bay reconsidered: the excavations of 1900-1905 in the light of recent work', *CA*, 16: 61–88.

Whimster, R. (1989) *The Emerging Past: Air Photography and the Buried Landscape*, RCHME: London.

White, D. A. (1982) *The Bronze Age Cremation Cemeteries at Simons Ground, Dorset*, Dorset Nat. Hist. & Archaeol. Soc: Dorchester.

Whittle, A., Keith-Lucas, M., Milles, A., Noddle, B., Rees, S. and Romans, J. C. C. (1986) *Scord of Brouster: An Early Agricultural Settlement in Shetland, Excavations 1977–1979*, Oxford University Committee for Archaeology: Oxford.

Wildgoose, M., Burney, C. and Miket, R. (1993) *Coile a Ghasgain, by Ord Sleat, interim report*, Skye.

Wilkins, D. A. (1984) 'The Flandrian woods of Lewis', *Journal of Ecology*, 72: 251–8.

Williams, B. B. (1978) 'Excavations at Lough Eskragh, County Tyrone', *UJA*, 41: 37–48.

Williams, A. (1939) 'Excavations at the Knave promontory fort Rhossili, Glamorgan', *AC*, 94: 210–19.

Williams, G. (1981) 'Survey and excavation on Pembrey Mountain', *Carmarthenshire Antiquaries Society*, 17: 3–33.

Williams, G. (1988) 'Recent work on rural settlement in Later Prehistoric and Early Historic Dyfed', *AJ*, 68: 30–54.

Williams, G. and Mytum, H. (1998) *Llawhaden, Dyfed. Excavations on a Group of Small Defended Enclosures, 1980–4*, BAR, Brit. Ser., 275, Archaeopress: Oxford.

Willis, E. H. (1961) 'Marine transgression sequences in the English Fenlands', *Annals of the New York Academy of Science*, 95: 368–76.

Wooding, J. M. (1996) *Communication and Commerce along the Western Sealanes AD 400–800*, BAR, Internat. Ser. 654, Archaeopress: Oxford.

Wright, E. (1990) *The Ferriby boats. Seacraft of the Bronze Age*, Routledge: New York.

Wright, E. V., Hedges, R. E. M., Bayliss, A. and Van de Noort, R. (2001): 'New AMS radiocarbon dates for the North Ferriby Boats', *Antiquity*, 75: 726–34.

Young, A. and Richardson, K. M. (1960) 'A Cheardach Mhor, Drimore, South Uist', *PSAS*, 93: 135–173.

Young, A. (2001) 'Time Team at Boleigh fogou, St Buryan', *CA*, 39 & 40 (2000–1): 138–39.

Zimmer, H. (1901) Keltische Kirche in Brittanien und Irland. *Realencyklopädie für Protestantische Theologie und Kirche*, Liepzig; trans. A. Meyer (1902) *The Celtic Church in Britain and Ireland*, Nutt: London.

Zimmer, H. (1902) *Pelagius in Irland*. Berlin.

Zimmer, H. (1909–10) Über direkte Handelsverbindungen Westgalliens mit Irland im Alterum und frühen Mittelater, *Sitzungsberichte der königlich preussischen Akademie der Wissenschaften*.

Index

Printed in the USA/Agawam, MA
December 16, 2011

563020.025